T4-AKL-374

Kabir

Mystics of the East Series

Kabir

THE WEAVER
OF GOD'S NAME

V.K. SETHI

RADHA SOAMI SATSANG BEAS
PUNJAB, INDIA

Published by
S.L. Sondhi, Secretary
Radha Soami Satsang Beas
P.O. Dera Baba Jaimal Singh
Dist. Amritsar 143 204
Punjab, India

First Edition   1984   11,000 copies

Printed by letterpress at Indraprastha Press (CBT), Nehru House,
4 Bahadur Shah Zafar Marg, New Delhi-110 002 (India)

Lord, I weave the cloth of Thy Name.
   The fruitless toil
   Of weaving for the world
   Has come to an end;
   I have attained
   The dazzling state of bliss—
   Free from fear, free from pain,
I am the weaver, O Lord, of Thy Name;
   I weave and reap the profit
   Of inner rapport with Thee.
I am the weaver of the Lord's Name

—KABIR

Contents

Preface 15

LIFE 1

TEACHINGS 43

SELECTED POEMS 189

Kabir's Prayer 191
The Weaver of God's Name 192
The Propitious Moment 195
Who Drinks Elixir 197
Light the Lamp 199
Pious Liars 200
The Slumbering Wife 201
The Color of Nam 203
The Strength of Cravings 204
Without the Master 206
A Bride Yearning 208
Only While Living 210
Holy Baths 213
Many a Home 215
Tethered to Prejudice 217
The Blind See 219
The Ship of Nam 221
Indeed Mad 223
Shabd, the Word 225
Castles of Sand 228
Plaything 229

The Untold Tale 230
Kabir's Homeland 231
Who Dwell in Nam 234
The Created Gods 235
The City of the Dead 238
The Shameless Queen 240
The Treasure Map 242
Forgive Thy Child 243
Slaves of Mind 244
Within the Home 246
From the Same Light 248
Mystery of Mind 250
The Bird That Sings Within 253
Fear of God 255
The State of Sahaj 257
The Weaver of Banaras 259
Only Through Fear 261
The Oilman's Bullock 263
The Storm 265
The Depraved Priests 267
The Promised Day 269

The Find   271
When Realization Comes   273
A Lover's Thirst   274
Simran   275
Lost in the Wilderness   278
From One Color   279
The Only Succor   281
Particle of God   282
Assailed by Doubts   284
Pure as Gold   286
The Limits of Intellect   288
The One in the Many   289
Empty Within   291
Who Dies While Living   292
Deluded Pundits   294
The Swan   296
House of Clay   298
House at War   300
All Life Inviolable   301
Ways of Worship   303
Loaded with Stones   306
The Secret of Nam   308
Blind Man's Mirror   309
The Enlightened   310
The Avid Cat   311
The Bride's Agony   313
The Ruthless Autocrat   315
The Boat of Nam   318
The Malady of Ego   319
The Final Accomplishment   321
The Debt   322
The Diamond   324
The True Benefactor   326
Between the Eyes   327
The Hunt   329
The Loveless Wife   331
Sham Devotees   333

Son Begets the Father   334
Even Gods Crave   336
The Palanquin   339
An Inverted Well   341
Dwell in the Lord   342
Tale of Torment   344
To Meet the Most High   346
Behind the Mole   347
He Is Not Far   349
Upward Flows the River   350
Water Mixed with Water   352
Slanderer, Well-Wisher   353
The Tree of Karmas   354
The Wandering Bride   355
The Garden   357
Master Shows the Way   359
The True Devotee   361
Single Though Wedded   362
Home Within the Home   364
The Screen   365
Pure and Supreme   366
The Wealth of Nam   368
To Love the Master   371
A Lamp in Every Home   373
The Great Weaver   375
The Indifferent Wife   377
Shake Off Your Slumber   379
The Yarn of Love   380
Tax-free Wealth   382
The Thugs of Banaras   383
The Thirsty Swan   385
The Fortress   386
The Unloved One   388
The Divine Hue   390
Distilling Bliss   391
The Hour of Tryst   393
Thirst for the Lord   394

CONTENTS   xi

The Thief   395
Mad Neighbor   396
A Devotee's Yearning   398
The Bestower of Bliss   402
The Net   404
Free from Fear   405
The World's Lures   407
Not the Way   409
The Lord's Sheriff   411
The Knot   413
The Rare Wealth   414
The Flame of Longing   415
Sad Lotus   416
The One I Longed For   417
The Bumblebee   418
One Cardinal Truth   419
Web of Learning   420
The Day That Counts   421
This Precious Chance   422
A Lover's Stratagem   423
The Erudite   425
The Lord's Slave   427
The Empty Game   428
A Rare Devotee   429
Pain of Separation   431
No Terror   432
The Lord's Reflection   433
Worship the True Worshipper   435
The Wine of Love   436
The Land of No Return   437
Truants from Devotion   439
Key to Ecstasy   441
The Haze of Confusion   442
The Jewel of Love   444
Everlasting Companion   445
Danced Enough   446
No More Weaving   447

The True Worship   449
The Music of Nam   450
The Beloved Comes Home   451
I Am Thine   453
Lord, End This Misery   454
Divine Water   455
Where, O Pundit?   457
The Days of the Week   458
The Steed of Mind   462
A Saint's Inner State   463
The Soul's Homecoming   465
Heaven   467
The Spinning Wheel   468
Worship Only the Supreme   469
Living in God's Will   472
The Rope Broken   473
Merging in His Order   474
To Attain Truth   476
Under the Sway of Nam   479
Fish Climbs to the Peaks   480
Futile Pursuits   482
The Disciple's Yearning   484
Why Adornments?   485
Multiplicity   487
Lonely Nights   488
Remove the Veil   490
Bliss of Sahaj   492
A Warning   495
Influence of Company   499
What Is Truth?   502
The Talons of Delusion   505
The Lamp of Nam   508
The Ocean, a Hoofprint   510
Which Is Greater?   513
Soothing Company of Saints   514
The Master's Gift   516
The Necklace   518

Without Seeing   521
How Long, O Lord?   523
No Credit to Kasi   524
No Place Is Unholy   525

I Will Not Die   528
I Am Not   529
The Wedding   530

SELECTED COUPLETS   533

Prayer   535
He Fills Every Vessel   539
He Is What He Is   542
Where Dwells the Lord   545
The Subtle Path   548
The Fire of Longing   553
Importance of the Master   556
Idol Worship   561
The Learned   567
The Gyani   571
True Beauty   574
The Faithful Wife   576
Absorption in Love   579
Depth of Love   583
The Intoxication of Love   585
Faith   588
In Praise of Fear   592
Merged into the One   594
Pride   595
Humility   596
Ways of the Mind   597
Controlling the Mind   602
The Rosary of the Mind   605
Absorption in Simran   609
The Glory of Simran   611
Dying While Living   615
The Creeper   618
On Slander   621
Intoxicants   625

Who Eat Meat   627
Company of the Evil   632
Company of the True   635
The Hawk of Death   638
The Herb of Immortality   642
Meeting the Master   644
Guru Is God   648
Master, the Perfect Craftsman   651
Master, the True Warrior   654
The Shabd of the Saints   657
The One Word   662
The Fruits of Nam   664
The One Absorbed in Nam   666
The Glory of Nam   668
A Sword's Edge   672
The Seed of Devotion   675
The Man of Valor   678
The Five Passions   685
    The Poison of Lust   686
    The Fire of Anger   689
    The Witch of Avarice   691
    The Bonds of Attachment   693
    The Malady of I   695
    The Satguru's Torch of Grace 699
Karmas   702
Longing, the Royal Path   705
Longing for Union   708
Longing, the Tormentor   713
The Price of Love   716

Not the Time to Sleep   718   The Drop and the Ocean   726
Kabir's Lord   721   The Color of Love   728
A Saint's True Home   724   Love's Fulfillment   729

                    Appendix   733
                    Glossary   743
              Selected Bibliography   753
                 Local Addresses   757
              Books on This Science   761

PREFACE

IT GIVES US GREAT PLEASURE to present *Kabir, the Weaver of God's Name,* another book in our series on the life and teachings of the mystics of the East. Kabir, the fifteenth-century Saint of Banaras, was a low-caste weaver with no formal education; his humble origin did not prevent him, however, from becoming renowned in his own lifetime as a great Saint, and his compositions were recited, as they are now, all over the country. Of all the mystics of India, Kabir is perhaps the most well known worldwide, and the popularity and spiritual depth of his writings have encouraged us to publish a more extensive translation of his poems and couplets than has been available till now.

The primary aim of the translations has been to bring out the spiritual meaning that is the essence of Kabir's compositions; they are therefore not a rigidly literal rendering of the original, nor are they poetic for the sake of being poetic. The complex imagery that abounds in Kabir's terse poetry has been deciphered and pieced together, analyzed and explained, and its esoteric meaning has been conveyed in language that is vigorous and vivid.

In "Life of Kabir," no attempt has been made to discuss the scholarly theories and controversies connected with Kabir's life story, as this is not the object of the present monograph. The author has, however, tried to utilize some of the incidents that are mentioned by medieval poets and Saints, in order to highlight the personality and spiritual character of the great Saint, which are also reflected in Kabir's writings. "Teachings of Kabir" is a complete comparative study revealing the unity of the message that all Saints bring, whether they are from one religious tradition or another, from recent times or ancient. Parallel expressions from the writings of various Saints illustrate that the path of the Saints, as propounded by mystics of East and West, is a living path that has been taught by all Saints at all times.

We are deeply beholden to Virendra Kumar Sethi for carrying out this work on Kabir after his exhaustive research on Mira. We are also grateful to the various people who have helped in the production of the book: Anthea Guinness, for typing the entire manuscript, preparing the press copy and giving many valuable suggestions; and Wayne and Miriam Caravella, for design and layout and seeing the book through the press under the overall supervision of Louise Hilger. Above all, it has been Maharaj Ji's keen interest, practical guidance and grace that have inspired the project from start to finish.

S. L. Sondhi
Secretary

Radha Soami Satsang Beas
September 1983

Life

ADORED BY DEVOTEES, decried by the orthodox and eulogized by his successors, Kabir is one of the most popular and well-known Saints of medieval India. But despite his popularity, contemporary poets and historians have shown an inexplicable unconcern about the chronology of his life. The story of Kabir, coming through oral traditions, has grown into a legend with the passage of time—though a legend with its own "poetical beauty."[1] These accounts are sometimes inspiring, with their instinctive sensitivity in portraying the personality of this remarkable Saint; and sometimes mystifying, with their exalted anecdotes overdrawn with miracles.

In the absence of contemporary records, Kabir's modern biographers have found his life history a riddle that continues to elude a solution. When and where Kabir was born, who his parents were, what his caste was, who his Guru was, whether he was married or single, whether he had offspring or was issueless, where and when he died, are some of the questions that still puzzle his biographers, and their deductions and conclusions are as diverse as their approach to the study of Kabir.

While examining the available sources, one finds that Kabir's early admirers have been eloquent in their praise of the Saint, but reticent about details of his life. The earliest account of Kabir comes from Nabhadas, a devotee who wrote about Saints and holy men in a poetic work called *Bhaktamal* ('a garland of devotees'), completed in 1585 A.D. Although silent about dates, parentage, caste and other particulars, he gives an excellent and impartial estimate of Kabir's character and approach, which is amply substantiated by even a casual perusal of his works. There is only one stanza on Kabir in the entire volume of *Bhaktamal,* but it throws light on the impact of Kabir's personality on the succeeding generation:

---

1. G.H. Westcott, *Kabir and the Kabir Panth*, p.18.

Never did Kabir accept
The distinctions of caste
Or the four stages of life,[1]
Nor did he revere
The six philosophies.[2]
'Religion devoid of love
Is heresy,' he declared.
'Yoga and penance,
Fasting and alms-giving
Are, without meditation,
Empty,' he affirmed.
Ramaini, sabdi and sakhi[3]
He employed to impart his message—
To Hindus and Turks[4] alike.
Without preference,
Without prejudice,
He said only what was
Beneficial to all.
Subduing the world,[5]
He uttered not words
To please or flatter others.
Such was Kabir,
Who refused to accept
The bias of the caste system
Or the supremacy
Of the six philosophies.[6]

But within the next three centuries, poets and Kabir's sectarian followers, known as Kabir-panthis, created a halo around him that gradually acquired variegated hues, obliterating his

---

1. Hindu scriptures enjoin on the pious Hindu to divide his life into four stages: celibacy and learning (*brahmcharya*); family life (*grihasta*); retirement while living in society (*vanprast*); complete renunciation (*sannyas*).
2. The six schools of Indian philosophy.
3. Three of the stanzaic forms commonly used by Kabir in his writings.
4. In medieval India, the Muslims were called 'Turks' because some of the early Muslim conquerors were of Turkish origin.
5. Literally, 'sitting astride the world', controlling the world as a rider controls his horse.
6. Nabhadas, *Bhaktamal, Chhappaya* 60.

4

LIFE

original luster. The Kabir-panthis, in the absence of an adept spiritual guide, became more Vaishnavite in outlook and tried to bring their preceptor into the Brahmanic fold.

By the advent of the eighteenth century, new themes had been added to the life of Kabir, including an immaculate conception and a miraculous birth. Thus, according to some, Kabir was the son of a Brahmin woman whom Ramanand, the famous sage of Banaras, not realizing that she was a widow, had blessed with the words, "May you have a son." The sage's words being irrevocable, she had an immaculate conception and gave birth to a child whom, out of fear of disgrace, she abandoned on the banks of the Lahartala Tank at Banaras.

The account was further amplified by Kabir-panthi poets, who claimed that the child was born, not as an ordinary human being is, but out of a large blister on its mother's palm.[1] The sectarian leaders soon superimposed a new variation on the miracle of his birth: Kabir descended from the heavens in the form of a column of brilliant light on the lotus leaves in the Lahar Tank and took the shape of a child.

It is almost impossible to determine the time when these legends came into circulation. Anantdas in his *Parichai* (c. 1595),[2] Priyadas in his commentary on *Bhaktamal* (1645)[3] and Mukund Kavi in his life of Kabir (1651)[4] do not mention anything about Kabir's birth and parentage. They describe him as a *julaha* or Muslim weaver who lived in Kashi.[5] A few Muslim scholars have mentioned the story of an immaculate conception, without any comment, while some modern authors have concluded that Kabir was the illegitimate son of a Brahmin widow.[6] Recent scholars reject both the theories as a clumsy

---

1. Maharaj Raghuraj Singh, *Ramrasikavali*.
2. *Kabir ki Parichai*, i.e., an introduction to Kabir, was written by Anantdas between 1588 and 1595. Some scholars give the year as 1610.
3. Known as *Rasbodhini Tika*, the commentary—actually an addition of many incidents about the life of devotees—was completed in 1645.
4. *Kabir Charit* by Mukund Gugli of Gujarat was written in 1651.
5. In medieval days, and even now, the term *julaha* is used only for a Muslim weaver; for Hindu weavers different terms were used in different provinces.
6. Dr. F.E. Keay, *Kabir and His Followers*, p.28; Dr. Ahmed Shah, *Bijak of Kabir* (1917), pp.4-5; Ayodhya Singh Upadhyaya 'Harioudh', *Kabir Vachnavali* (1916), pp.7-8; Shyam Sundar Das, *Kabir Granthavali* (1928), p.16 of introduction.

effort to bring Kabir into the Hindu fold and affirm that Kabir was the natural son of a Muslim weaver couple. Saint Ravidas, a contemporary of Kabir, says:

> He whose ancestors slaughtered cows on Id and Bakar-Id and revered sheikhs, martyrs and divines —and such too were the deeds of his father—he, Kabir, the son, attained such heights that he is revered in all the three worlds.[1]

Guru Amar Das calls Kabir a *julaha,* and Rajjab says, "From the womb of a Muslim weaver-mother was born Kabir, the great Saint."[2]

A poem attributed to Dharam Das, one of Kabir's main disciples, says, "Mother a Turk, father a Muslim weaver, the son became a great devotee."[3]

There seem to be two different motives behind the accounts of the miraculous birth of Kabir. One is to connect him with a Brahmanic or Hindu origin—a natural tendency on the part of the orthodox sections of society in succeeding generations, when they found it difficult to deny the greatness of a Saint born in a low caste. Similar attempts have been made to claim Saint Dadu, a Muslim carder, as a Brahmin; and Saint Ravidas, a cobbler, as a Brahmin in a previous life.

The second motive comes from the desire to project the Saint as an extraordinary person, not necessarily by virtue of his spiritual attainment but by miraculous tales of his incarnation into this world. Those who advance the theory of divine light taking the form of the child Kabir appear to be prompted by the idea that a great Saint like Kabir cannot come to the world through flesh and blood like ordinary mortals.

Most scholars agree with the Kabir-panthis that Niru, a

---

1. Adi Granth, *Malar,* Ravidasji, p.1293. For definitions of terms, see Glossary.
2. Guru Amar Das (1479-1574), the third Guru in the line of Guru Nanak; Rajjab, the chief disciple of Saint Dadu, lived in the sixteenth and early seventeenth century.
3. As quoted in *Kabir Kasauti,* p.14, a sectarian biography of Kabir by Lahna Singh, based on an earlier manuscript.

poor weaver, and his wife Nima found the infant Kabir on the leaves of a lotus plant in Lahar Tank in Banaras. Those who reject the theory of an immaculate conception say that he was the son of Niru and Nima. It is nevertheless interesting to note that early writings on Kabir do not give the names of his parents, although they clearly mention that he was the son of a Muslim weaver. The names of his parents seem to have emerged a century after Kabir's death, or perhaps even later.

The object of this note on Kabir is not to enter into the various controversies associated with his life history, but to present a profile of the life, personality and teachings of this eminent Saint of the fifteenth century. The birth, caste and social status of a Saint have little bearing on his greatness. Saints have neither a caste nor a nationality; they do not recognize such man-made distinctions. Kabir himself used to declare: "I am neither a Hindu nor a Musalman."[1]

Kabir was born in 1398 A.D.,[2] the son of a Muslim weaver Niru and his wife Nima, who lived on the outskirts of the holy city of Banaras. He was given the name Kabir, an Arabic word meaning 'the Most High' and used as an epithet for God. G.H. Westcott points out that there is no taboo on giving it as a name to a human being.[3] But one wonders how such a name, neither common nor known to the poor and illiterate Muslims of those days, was given to the son of a weaver who had no pretensions to the Arabic language.[4]

According to the religious custom, Niru went to the qazi, the Muslim priest, to receive divine injunction from the Koran and find a name for his son. The qazi opened the holy book and found the name Kabir. Reluctant to confer such a lofty name on a petty weaver's child, the qazi tried to find another name, but again the book opened to an epithet for God. He

1. *Kabir Sakhi-Sangrah*, p.75:4; hereafter cited as *K.S.S.*
2. See Appendix for discussion of the dates of Kabir.
3. Westcott, *Kabir*, pp.15-17.
4. Muslims of the poor class used to speak the local dialects of their areas. The story of naming the child, though unacceptable to some scholars, seems to be the only rational explanation of this extraordinary name.

wanted to try a third time, but Niru, happy with what was indicated by the Koran, started calling his son Kabir.

Kabir showed signs of a religious inclination from an early age. There was little scope for education among the poor and low-caste sections of the society: Muslim texts, written in Arabic and Persian, were beyond the comprehension of the masses; and Hindu scriptures, well guarded by the priestly hierarchy, could not be touched by a *mlechha*—an uncouth alien. Though deprived of formal instruction on account of his poverty and low caste, Kabir had, as is evident from his compositions, a keen intellect, a discerning mind and a capacity for understanding and analysis far beyond the ordinary.

From an early age Kabir started to assist his parents in small jobs connected with their profession. Gradually learning the techniques of his family trade, he became an adept weaver and proved an asset to his parents. At the same time his interest in matters other than the mundane continued to grow, taking the shape of a spiritual hunger for truth. During his adolescence, the quest for spiritual knowledge at times kept Kabir away from family work and his long periods of introspection irritated his parents; yet he continued to be the cynosure of the family and the neighborhood because of his affectionate nature, mild manners and kind disposition.

Sensitive and compassionate from an early age, Kabir could not bear to see anyone suffering. It is said that once, while he was still a child, his father wanted to sacrifice an animal on the occasion of a religious festival. Kabir was so upset at the idea of causing torment to the beast that his father had to yield to his earnest remonstrations and tearful entreaties and release the animal.

One winter morning, on his way to the market, Kabir met an old recluse shivering in the cold. Moved by his plight, young Kabir, whom Niru had lately given the duty of selling the finished cloth in the weekly market, offered the man a few yards from the cloth to protect him from the cold. When the poor old man begged for the entire piece of cloth, Kabir could not say no and gave it away. Returning home, he told what

8

had happened and patiently bore the scolding he received from his parents.[1]

It is generally accepted that Ramanand was Kabir's Guru. Nabhadas, Anantdas, Priyadas, Mukund Kavi, Mohsin Fani, Kabir-panthi literature and most modern scholars confirm that Kabir was Ramanand's disciple; but Westcott, Ramprasad Tripathi and a few others maintain that he was the disciple of Sheikh Taqi. They seem to base their views mainly on *Khazinat-ul-Asifia* by Ghulam Sarvar, written in 1868, wherein Sheikh Taqi is described as Kabir's Guru.

From Kabir's poems it appears that he visited a number of places and met many holy men, presumably in his search for a true path to God. From his own observations he had realized the hollowness of the rituals and modes of worship of both the Hindus and the Muslims. His quest was for something higher and more real than what the make-believe worship prevalent in Banaras could offer.

Kabir later taught a path based on the practice of Shabd, which aimed at God-realization while living—a path not of outward pursuits, but of going 'within'. Who initiated him into this path, a path as old as the creation and followed by earlier Saints like Jaidev, Namdev, Hazrat Nizamuddin, Khwaja Muinuddin and others? Was it some Sheikh Taqi—'Taqi' being a title that could be applied to any realized soul[2]—or was it some other Saint whose name Kabir may have thought proper not to reveal?

A formal initiation from Ramanand is, however, a traditionally accepted fact, conceded by almost all modern scholars and confirmed by most of the available records. Ramanand was not a *Shabd-margi* Saint.[3] He belonged to the Shri Sam-

---

1. Some poets and most Kabir-panthi writers end this episode on a happy note. They say that Kabir, unable to face his parents, stayed away from home the whole day. But, moved to mercy, the Lord took the form of a merchant and brought a large supply of groceries to the family. Kabir, on returning from his seclusion, learned of the incident and realized that God had come as the merchant, and in gratitude he distributed most of the bounty to the poor.
2. *Taqi* could mean one who has attained a state of complete surrender to God, called *taqavval*.
3. *Shabd-marg:* path of God-realization through the inner practice of the divine Shabd or Word.

9

pradaya, a religious tradition that worshipped Lord Vishnu of the Hindu trinity and his consort Lakshmi. Ramanand changed it to the worship of Ram and Sita, the incarnations of Vishnu and Lakshmi. He also preached reverence for all other Hindu deities. Dr. Bhuwaneshwar Nath Mishra, in his treatise on the Vaishnava school of practice, says: "Although some of his followers were the worshippers of the formless Ram, it will be wrong to say that Ramanand was an advocate of the *nirgun* school of devotion.... It is clear that [Ramanand] was purely a devotee of the Vaishnava school, and not the *yoga-margis* who seek the Deity within the body."[1]

It is therefore likely that Kabir was initiated into *Shabd-marg,* or the path of God-realization through the Word, by some saint whose identity is not established. But when he began to preach what he had learned, he found that the people resented him. The Muslims dubbed him an infidel; the Hindus asked him where he had learned his new theories, and who his Guru was. They sneered at him as a *nigura*—someone without a Guru, held in disdain by the Hindus in general.

From their ridicule and hostility, Kabir must have realized that in Banaras, an age-old citadel of formalism, idol worship and caste distinctions, he would neither be given a hearing nor be allowed to live in peace. He needed the protection of a person who had an unquestioned hold over the people of Banaras and whose disciple no one would dare to touch.

Such a person was Ramanand, a religious leader held in great esteem, almost awe, by the priestly class, the theologians and the people. But Kabir knew that Ramanand would never accept him as a disciple; even to approach him was not easy for he never looked at the face of untouchables and heterodox aliens.[2]

---

1. B.N. Mishra, *Vaishnava Sadhana aur Siddhant,* pp.178-179. The author supports his conclusions by quoting the views of eminent scholars like Acharya Ramchandra Shukla, Acharya Baldev Upadhyaya, Rajdev Singh and Lakshmi Shankar Varshneya. *Nirgun:* literally, 'without attributes'; devotion to the One Formless God who is beyond all attributes or qualities has been termed the *nirgun* school of devotion. *Yoga-margis:* literally, those following the path of yoga; B.N. Mishra equates Sant Mat with a type of yoga.
2. Priyadas, himself a disciple in the line of Ramanand, says in his commentary on the *Bhaktamal* that it was the practice of Ramanand not to look at the face of a low-caste Hindu or a Muslim. Traditions also confirm this account.

Kabir had to use a stratagem to gain his object. He discovered that the great sage used to go to the banks of the Ganges every day in the early hours of the morning for a bath. Kabir lay down on the steps of the ghat leading to the river. In the pre-dawn twilight Ramanand did not see Kabir and his foot hit Kabir on the head. Startled, Ramanand exclaimed, "Ram, Ram!" Kabir quietly got up and went away. He now declared that he was the disciple of Ramanand.

Some orthodox Brahmins and disciples of Ramanand, much perturbed, asked the sage, "Sir, was there a dearth of high-caste Hindus in the city that you chose to admit a Muslim weaver to the fold of your disciples?"[1] When Ramanand refuted their allegation, Kabir was brought before him.

Ramanand, to avoid looking at the face of a low caste, spoke to Kabir from behind a curtain and asked why Kabir was making a false claim. Kabir respectfully replied, "Sir, I was initiated by you on the steps of the ghat. You touched my forehead with your foot and gave me the mantra 'Ram Ram'." Ramanand, a noble and truthful soul, could not deny it and accepted Kabir as his disciple.

The relationship between Kabir and Ramanand had its own contradictions. Kabir was opposed to all external rites and rituals, most of which Ramanand revered. Though an upholder of the traditions of Hindu metaphysics and rigid formalism, Ramanand was also liberal enough to let his disciple follow his own method of worship. Thus the intellectual catholicity of Ramanand allowed the recusant dynamism of Kabir to thrive under his protection.

Though he always respected his Guru, Kabir never subscribed to Ramanand's traditional beliefs. It is said that Kabir's association gradually effected a change in his Guru's outlook. Every day Ramanand used to perform *mansi* or mental worship of his deity, Ram. He would form a mental picture of the idol, bathe it, decorate it with fineries and offer delicacies to it.

1. B.N. Mishra says: "Although Ramanand was liberal in his approach to devotion, it does not mean, as some believe, that he was opposed to the caste system" (*Vaishnava Sadhana*, p.179).

One day he was sitting inside his house engaged in worship, while Kabir was waiting outside the entrance to convey his respects to the Guru through the curtain.

Ramanand made a slip in his worship: He forgot to put the garland of flowers around the deity's neck before placing the crown on its head. He was perplexed because the circumference of the garland in his mental picture was not large enough to go round the crown, and it was an act of disrespect to remove the headpiece. Kabir called to him from outside, "Gurudev, untie the knot of the garland and then tie it around the idol's neck."

Ramanand was startled. How could Kabir know of his predicament? Apparently this low-caste disciple was no ordinary person. The venerable sage called out to one of his disciples, "Remove the curtain, for what can one hide from Kabir?" Ushered into his presence, Kabir respectfully bowed to his Master, but Ramanand stood up and embraced him.

The barrier between the Master and his disciple was thus removed, and Ramanand became more receptive to Kabir's teachings. Kabir began to give hints of the inner path to his Guru. At times he would shake his Master with strong remarks. It is said that once, on the death anniversary of Ramanand's ancestors, preparations were being made to make an offering of rice to the departed souls. Kabir said to his Guru, "Sir, this lowly Kabir is perplexed: The crows eat up the rice, how can it reach your ancestors?"

Ramanand gradually began to perceive the truth of what his young disciple would say. Ahmed Shah, in his impartial introduction to the *Bijak,* remarks: "There is every reason to suppose that Ramanand was largely influenced by Kabir."[1] The induction of low-caste devotees like Ravidas, Dhanna, Sadna and others into the fold of Ramanand's disciples was perhaps a direct outcome of his association with Kabir.

The Sanskrit treatises of Ramanand do not give the slightest hint of the change in him. The Ramavats, or followers of Ramanand, continued with formalism in dress, *tilak* or mark-

---

1. Ahmed Shah, *Bijak,* p.32.

ings on the forehead, rosary and rituals. However, a poem by Ramanand included in the Adi Granth,[1] confirms the oral tradition that Ramanand was initiated into the practice of Shabd by Kabir.[2] Describing it as a "brilliant poem," R.D. Ranade says that "this song of Ramanand has more Kabirism in it than Tulsism."[3]

Ramanand's tacit acquiescence to Kabir in allowing him to practice and preach a spiritual path diametrically opposed to his own implies that Ramanand had a feeling of respect for what Kabir taught, and its natural culmination was the acceptance of the path of Kabir, though perhaps very late in his life.

In this context, it should be kept in mind that in the Adi Granth—a unique collection of spiritual and devotional compositions which corroborate that the teachings of all Saints are identical—shabds or hymns of only those Saints and devotees are included who had faith in the One Formless God and who believed in the path of Nam or Shabd. The inclusion of Ramanand's hymn is significant, for it confirms that he had, at some time in his life, accepted the path of the Saints.

There is no contemporary evidence available to indicate whether Kabir was married or single. Priyadas is perhaps the first to say (in 1645) that Kabir was married. Dr. Triloki Narayan Dixit, in his analysis of the *Parichai* of Anantdas (1595), says that some lines of Anantdas clearly suggest that Kabir had

---

1. The Adi Granth is a compilation of devotional poems by Saints and devotees, compiled in 1604 by Guru Arjan Dev, the fifth Guru in Guru Nanak's line.

2. See also Appendix for note on Ramanand. The poem by Ramanand in the Adi Granth under *Rag Basant*, p.1195, is as follows:

Where need I go, for within my home I have been dyed in the divine hue. My mind has ceased from its wandering—it has become lame.

One day my mind was overcome with a longing to meet the Lord; I prepared sandalwood paste and perfumes from saffron, musk and many a fragrant herb, and proceeded to the temple to worship the Lord.

But that Lord my Guru revealed to me within my heart. Wherever I go, I find water and stone, while Thou, O Lord, fillest each particle of the creation.

I delved into Vedas and Puranas, and I searched; only go there if God is not here.

O Satguru, I sacrifice my all to you, you who have cut the chains of my confusion, my delusion. The Lord pervades all, says Ramanand, and the Guru's Shabd eradicates a million karmas.

3. R.D. Ranade, *Pathway to God in Hindi Literature*, p.101. Ranade suggests that Ramanand's poem is nearer to the teachings of Kabir than to the traditional worship of incarnations. Goswami Tulsi Das, a devotee of Ram, the incarnation of Vishnu, was a traditional Vaishnavite.

a family of his own.[1] Oral traditions give the name of his wife
as Loi. Mukund Kavi in his biography of Kabir (1651) gives
the name as Rupa. Raghodas in his *Bhaktamal* (1660)[2] mentions that Kabir had a son named Kamal. Most scholars, in
view of the strong oral tradition and the evidence of sixteenth
and seventeenth century poets, concur with the view that Kabir
was married and had a son Kamal, and a daughter Kamali.

Kabir-panthis, taking it as a slight to his noble personality,
vehemently deny that Kabir was a householder. Their writings
do not date earlier than the eighteenth and nineteenth centuries
and reflect a view that Saints do not 'debase' themselves to the
level of ordinary men by leading a family life. In support of
their contention, they cite Kabir's poems extolling the virtues
of continence. However, in one of his own couplets Kabir says
that he too was married, but when he realized that indulgence
in sex was a hindrance in spiritual progress, he kept aloof from
his wife.[3]

Kabir, like all Saints, recommended a family life rather
than forced celibacy and renunciation. He preached contentment, not rigid austerity; desirelessness, not compulsive abne-
gation. The continence of Kabir is a result not of suppression
but of the sublimation that is a natural sequel to the bliss of
inner spiritual experience.

A few poems of Kabir, included in the Adi Granth, depict
his wife's vexation over his hospitality to holy men. Always
kind and generous, Kabir would suffer himself and the family
to sleep on the floor in order to provide cots for his guests; he
would offer them bread and gladly go without his meals, and
let his wife and children allay their hunger with a handful of
roasted gram.[4]

---

1. Triloki Narayan Dixit, *Parichai Sahitya,* p.108.
2. *Bhaktamal Raghodas Krit,* ed. Agarchand Nahta. The year of this composition is
believed to be 1660 A.D. The poet, while writing about the successors of Guru Nanak,
mentions the line only up to Guru Har Krishan, the eighth Guru (p.176:348), which
indicates that the book was completed before Guru Teg Bahadur was discovered and
hailed as the ninth Guru in 1664.
3. *K.S.S.,* p.158:40. Kabir-panthis say that Loï was not his wife, but a disciple who,
being an orphan, was given shelter by Kabir. They also insist that Kamāl and Kamāli were
not his children, but a dead boy and girl whom Kabir had brought back to life.
4. The chick pea; the cheapest food available then, regarded as the food of paupers.

He regularly worked on his loom and sold the cloth in the weekly market. Living on his own honest earnings was a practice he followed till the end of his life. A light, portable loom was a part of his baggage whenever he went on his travels. Happy with what he earned, living from day to day, he never desired for more. In one of his songs he prays to the Lord not for wealth and luxuries, nor for the comforts of life, nor even for provision for a rainy day; he begs simply for daily bread for himself and his family.[1] His income was meager and poverty was the accepted way of his life, contentment being his most cherished treasure.

Once during the rainy season a few holy men unexpectedly arrived at Kabir's hut. Due to the rains, Kabir had not been able to sell his cloth in the market and there was not enough food in the house for the guests. He asked his wife, Loi, if some grocer could be persuaded to give a little flour and lentils on credit, which could be paid for on the next market day. But what grocer would agree to give things on credit to a poor low-caste weaver with an uncertain income!

Loi went to several grocers, but they all insisted on cash payment. One grocer, however, agreed to give provisions on credit, on the condition that she spend the night with him. Shocked, she smiled at his ridiculous demand, which the grocer took as her consent and obliged her with the required groceries.

That evening, when the guests had left, Loi informed Kabir about her conversation with the grocer. Kabir, deciding to use this as an opportunity to enlighten the grocer and make him aware of his folly, ordered Loi to get ready to go to the grocer's house.

It was a rainy day and still drizzling. Kabir told Loi to cover herself with a blanket as protection from the rain; then he lifted her onto his shoulder and carried her through the streets.

The grocer was surprised to note that neither was Loi's dress wet from the rain, nor were her feet muddy from the

---

1. Adi Granth, *Sorath*, Kabirji, p.656.

streets. He asked her how she had managed to keep her feet clean, and she replied, "My husband covered me with a blanket and carried me on his shoulder to your house."

The young grocer was astounded. Though the purity on Loi's face, marked with a touch of sadness, moved him deeply, he still looked at her in disbelief. But when she added that Kabir was waiting outside to take her back, the grocer realized the state of his own degradation and the greatness of Kabir. Falling on his knees, he begged her to forgive him and to take him to Kabir immediately. Kabir forgave the repentant grocer who, coming into closer association with the Saint, later became his disciple. Saints have their own ways to draw souls into their fold.

Kabir had a lofty ideal of righteousness, and as far as he or his family was concerned he would never compromise with his principles. His approach to daily life was marked by an innate simplicity, sincerity and truthfulness, and his ways would at times leave the worldly perplexed.

In the early days of his youth, once he went to the market to sell cloth. The price he asked was five *takas*,[1] but his customers would offer him only three, which he did not accept. It was almost evening. A broker, noticing Kabir's problem, offered to help him. Realizing that it was a well-woven piece of cloth, the broker, fully conversant with human psychology, started shouting, "Excellent cloth! Going very cheap—only twelve *takas!*" Within a few minutes customers were flocking round him, and the broker struck the bargain at eleven *takas*.

Keeping two *takas* as his commission, he placed the balance of nine in Kabir's hands. But the young weaver refused to accept more than five *takas*—the price he had originally asked and which he thought reasonable. It was a novel experience for Kabir, and he commented:

> If I tell the truth
> I am accused of falsehood;

---

1. A small unit of Indian currency during the medieval period.

> But lies, the world believes.
> A cloth worth takas five
> Through falsehood fetches
> Eleven as the price.

Though not conversant with the ways of the world, Kabir had thoroughly appraised the religious proclivities of the masses. Living in a city steeped in ritualism and dogma, ranging from practices sincere but deluded to venal and deceitful, Kabir knew that he had to wake the people from their spiritual complacence. He took recourse to strong language and drastic methods in order to shake the foundations of ritualism, a rickety edifice propped up by hypocrisy and superstition.

To some Brahmins who were extolling the holiness and virtues of Ganges water, saying that it could wash off the sins of even the worst criminals, Kabir offered from his bowl a drink of water from the Ganges. Aghast at what they thought a presumptuous act on the part of a low-caste weaver—offering water to noble Brahmins in his 'polluted' bowl—they were vociferous in their indignation. Kabir said, "My learned friends, if this water could not purify my wooden bowl, how can it ever wash away the sins and the layers of dross from the minds of criminals?"

Kabir's small family, consisting of himself, his wife, a son and a daughter, lived in an atmosphere of devotion and spiritual practice, inspired by Kabir's personal example. Loi had also been initiated by Kabir, and traditions give accounts of Loi as a dutiful wife and a devoted disciple who had completely surrendered her ego and will at the feet of her Master, Kabir.

Kamali, his daughter, was also his disciple. It is said that one day while she was drawing water from the well, a thirsty Brahmin, who was a stranger to the city, asked for some water. After quenching his thirst, the young Brahmin asked Kamali who she was. Learning that she was the daughter of a low-caste weaver, he was much annoyed. "Has your father not taught you to reveal your caste before offering water to a Brahmin? You have ruined my caste and put a blot on my purity."

Perplexed by the young man's anger, Kamali asked him to talk to her father.

The Brahmin accompanied Kamali to Kabir's cottage. Listening patiently to his complaints, Kabir said, "My friend, think well before you drink water. In the water frogs, fish, tortoise and crocodiles live, procreate and die. If the water is not contaminated by their blood, dead bodies and refuse, how can it be made impure by the mere touch of a human being? God has created all human beings from the same five elements; each body is filled with blood, flesh and bones and is equally pure or dirty. Those who read the Vedas call themselves pundits, those who read the Koran call themselves maulana; they give themselves different names, these pots made out of the same clay. They are all lost in their own delusions, not one of them knows the Lord."[1]

The Brahmin youth was much impressed and continued to visit Kabir for some time. He ultimately asked for initiation. It is said that Kabir also gave the hand of Kamali in marriage to him, and the couple later settled in Multan.[2] Some of Kamali's poems are found in the Multan area, reflecting the teachings of Kabir and bearing her stamp in the last lines: "Says Kamali, the daughter of Kabir."

As for Kamal, one couplet about him in the Adi Granth suggests that he brought wealth into the house by accepting gifts from Kabir's disciples, and Kabir was much upset with his son.[3] However, later writers have included Kamal's name in the list of Kabir's successors.[4] Some scholars believe that after some time Kabir forgave his renegade son and sent him to Gujarat to give satsangs.[5] H.H. Wilson holds that Saint Dadu was initiated by Sheikh Buddhan who, according to Wilson, was in the line of Kamal's successors.[6] There is hardly any evi-

---

1. Selections from *Bijak*, *Shabd* 47 and 30.
2. Dr. Chandrakant Bali, *Panjabi Prantiya Hindi Sahitya ka Itihas*, p.90.
3. Adi Granth, *Salok*, Kabirji, p.1370:115.
4. Raghodas, *Bhaktamal*, p.178.
5. This is claimed by Kabir-panthi literature. See *Bodh Sagar*, p.1515. Dr. Kanti Kumar Bhatt gives some details of Kamal's visit to Gujarat and also the names of some of his disciples in *Sant Kabir aur Kabir Sampradaya*, p.76.
6. H.H. Wilson, *Religious Sects of the Hindus*, p.57.

dence available in confirmation of this view, and although some poems of Kamal are extant, not much is known about him.

Kabir's disciples came from all castes and all levels of society. King Vir Singh Baghela, the ruler of a neighboring state, was among his devoted disciples. It is said that Vir Singh had a new palace constructed for himself. Elated with its beauty and grandeur, he invited all citizens to see it. Kabir, who happened to be in the town, was also urged by the crowd to go in. While he was coming out, Kabir met the king, who casually inquired, "Did you like my new palace?"

Kabir replied, "Yes, it is good except for two blemishes." "And what are they?" asked the king. Kabir said, "The first is that this palace will crumble and fall; the second, the one who has got it built will have to leave it."

The king was annoyed, but suppressing his feelings, he asked, "You seem to be a holy man, why do you utter such ominous words, and that too at such an auspicious hour when I am moving into my new palace?"

Kabir's reply was brief and firm: "O King, the law of this world is such that the sun that rises must set, the day that comes must go; whatever is created has to crumble, and whoever is born has to die." With these words, Kabir mingled with the crowd and walked away.

But Kabir's words, and even more so his dazzling personality, kept haunting the king's mind. He made inquiries about this unusual sage, came to him and became an ardent disciple.

There are no contemporary records available to give an idea of Kabir's physical appearance. Anantdas says that he was of fair complexion, with a slight tan; he was impressive, handsome and attractive. The few paintings preserved at some of the Kabir-panthi centers are not earlier than the nineteenth century and fail to convince scholars of their authenticity. A painting believed to be of the late eighteenth century in Mughal style, kept in the British Museum, shows Kabir as a man of medium height sitting on a weaving loom.

Some paintings of Kabir plying a loom are seen in India also, a few of them of the early eighteenth century. They seem to be a copy of an earlier painting. The features of the Saint in most of these paintings are almost the same: a thin, fair-complexioned man with a soft, kind expression, medium height, dressed in a loincloth and an upper garment of Muslim style, with a round cap on his head. His age in some of them appears to be seventy or even more.

Whatever his physical features were, from all available accounts scholars deduce that Kabir's was an exceptionally impressive personality with great magnetism and physical beauty. His living on his own honest earnings, his simplicity and purity, had a powerful impact on those who came in contact with him. His spiritual insight and personal charm kept even his opponents spellbound at times. Endowed with great spiritual power, attracting the rich and the poor, the learned and the simple to the circle of his disciples, he was yet humble and unassuming.

It is said that a great scholar of the Vedas and scriptures, a high-caste Brahmin called Sarvanand, had defeated many learned men in debate on subjects connected with theology, metaphysics and the six systems of philosophy. He had changed his name from Sarvanand to Sarvajit, that is, 'the conqueror of all'. His mother, in one of her pilgrimages to holy Banaras, had come in contact with Kabir and was initiated by him. Seeing her son's pride and knowing the futility of such erudition, she one day said to him that she would accept him as 'the victor of all' only when he defeated Kabir in debate.

The mother's remark pinched Sarvajit's pride. What is Kabir, he thought—only an ordinary weaver; it is hardly necessary for a scholar of my repute to engage myself in debate with such a man. Yet, his mother's remark appeared to be tinged with irony. Anxious to prove his merit and convince her, he proceeded to Banaras.

With books loaded on a bullock, Sarvajit arrived at Kabir's hut and called out, "Is this the home of Kabir?" The Saint had gone out for a short while, and hearing the call, Kabir's daughter Kamali came out. Seeing the learned man and the bullock loaded with books, she was amused and said: "Kabir's home is on a peak, the path is slippery and hard. Where even an ant's foot finds no hold, the pundits want to reach there with bullock carts of books!"[1]

Baffled by Kamali's reply, Sarvajit did not know what to say. Meanwhile, Kabir returned and Sarvajit challenged the Saint to hold a debate with him on any aspect of philosophy and the meaning of scriptures. Kabir humbly replied, "I am grateful that you have given me the honor of talking to a great scholar. I am only an illiterate weaver who has never before even seen such a large number of books."

But Sarvajit insisted. When Kabir asked him why he was keen to argue with a person like him, ignorant of what was written in the great scriptures, Sarvajit told him about his mother's challenge. Kabir said, "My friend, why do you bother to argue with me? I know I cannot overcome you in debate, so I admit my defeat." But Sarvajit felt that his mother would doubt his word and asked Kabir to give it in writing. Kabir replied that all the writing he knew was just to sign his name and would gladly put his signature to whatever Sarvajit wrote. He wrote, "Sarvajit has defeated Kabir" and brought the document, with Kabir's attestation, to his mother.

But when Sarvajit produced the proof of his triumph, instead of confirming his victory, it read, "Kabir has defeated Sarvajit." Much perturbed at the slip in writing Kabir's confession, he again went to the Saint. With a fresh note, duly signed by Kabir, Sarvajit returned to his mother. The note, however, again announced, "Kabir has defeated Sarvajit." Another trip to Banaras and another note had the same fate.

Sarvajit, greatly perplexed and upset, said, "Mother, this Kabir seems to be a magician. He does something and the words change."

Sarvajit's mother was aware of Kabir's greatness. She replied, "Son, he is a Saint, a man of God, not a magician. In his presence impurities of mind are thrown aside and truth pre-

---

1. *K.S.S.*, p.54:18. This couplet is included in many collections of Kabir's poems; tradition maintains, however, that it was an unpremeditated exclamation on Kamali's part when she saw the pundit and his load of books.

vails. You were overwhelmed by his personality and each time you unwittingly wrote the same thing. In order to argue about what the scriptures say, you had to study them thoroughly. In the same way, to draw Kabir into a debate you should first learn from him what his message is."

Seeing her son quiet, she added, "See how humble he is, not ashamed to admit his own ignorance. To defeat Kabir, you have to be humble with him, for arrogance can never vanquish humility."

Sarvajit went to Kabir again, but this time without the bullock loaded with books. A few days' association with the Saint opened his eyes; he returned a different person. He bowed to his mother and thanked her for urging him to go to Kabir. "Mother," he said, "Kabir is truly great. I fell at his feet and owned my defeat. He initiated me and took me into his fold." Sarvajit's mother was overjoyed: "Yes, my son, you have now found the path to real knowledge. One who owns defeat at the Saints' feet is the real victor—he wins their heart."

Most early scholars held the view that Kabir lived all his life in Banaras. But now there is enough evidence to confirm that during his long life he traveled a great deal and undertook many extended journeys. Uttar Pradesh, Bihar, Orissa, Rajasthan, Madhya Pradesh, and parts of Punjab are some of the provinces he often visited. Some scholars of the history of Maharashtra maintain that he visited Pandharpur, a religious city in South Maharashtra. There are relics associated with Kabir in all these provinces.

In his poems Kabir has used words from many languages and dialects: Braj, Avadhi, Bhojpuri, Maithili, Rajasthani, Bundelkhandi, Punjabi, Marathi and Gujarati. He has even employed words from Sanskrit, Persian and Arabic with equal facility. Evidently, like all Saints, he traveled widely in order to give his message to the masses. *Kabir Mansur,* a Kabirpanthi work, claims that he visited Balakh, Bokhara, Baghdad and other places in the Middle East. A few couplets of Kabir seem to suggest that he also went to Mecca. But there is no historical evidence to confirm his travels to the Middle East.

Recent research has revealed that Kabir visited Gujarat a number of times. In a thesis based on information gleaned from old manuscripts and other sources in Gujarat, Dr. K.K. Bhatt says that Kabir began his long tours at the age of thirty-five and went to Gujarat several times.[1] At Dwarka he initiated Chatur Singh, the prince of Jaisalmer, who later became a Guru in Kabir's line and came to be known as Gyaniji. Deen Dervish, a Gujarati poet-devotee who flourished in the eighteenth century, says that Kabir visited Patan, where he initiated King Jagjivan; and Palanpur, where he initiated Prince Ali Sher Khan, who later became the nawab of Palanpur. At Dwarka he initiated Shobhan Seth, a prominent merchant, and Chaube Radhumal, a Brahmin high priest; and while at Girnar, near Junagadh, he met a famous yogi, Gaibinath. There are over a hundred relics in Gujarat associated with Kabir.[2]

Tatwa and Jiwa, two brothers who lived on the banks of the river Narbada near Baroach, were keen seekers of truth. A small banyan tree on an island in the river just opposite their house started to wither. The two brothers tried to revive it, but the tree became dry. They decided to wash the feet of holy men coming to the nearby place of pilgrimage, Shukla Tirth, and sprinkle the 'sanctified' water on the roots of the dry tree. For years they followed this practice, but the result in each case was a disappointment. They began to wonder whether there was any God-realized Saint in the world and whether they would have to live and die without a true Guru.

During one of Kabir's visits to Gujarat, Tatwa and Jiwa heard about him, but they also learned that Kabir would not allow anyone to wash his feet. They invited Kabir to visit their home, and before entering the house Kabir washed his feet, as was the prevalent custom.[3] One of the brothers quickly collected a few drops of the water from the stone flags of their courtyard.

---

1. K.K.C. Bhatt, *Sant Kabir*.
2. Ibid.
3. In medieval times when people commonly walked from place to place, it was the custom to remove one's shoes outside the house and wash one's feet before entering.

23

Both Tatwa and Jiwa were greatly impressed by Kabir, but would not accept him as a Master till they had received a positive verdict from the banyan tree. Soon after Kabir had left the house, they hurried to the tree and sprinkled the water on its roots. It is said, within a few days they noticed that the tree was growing new leaves; another few days and it turned green. The brothers went straight to Kabir, who was still in Gujarat, and begged for initiation.[1]

This account is first given by Priyadas (1645). Nabhadas mentions the names of Tatwa and Jiwa as two great devotees, but not the miracle of the banyan tree.[2] In an island in the Narbada river near Shukla Tirth, about twelve miles east of the city of Baroach, there stands to this day a huge banyan tree which is called 'Kabir Vat',[3] spreading over an area of about four acres. A stone inscription records that Kabir visited the place in 1408 A.D. If this is correct, then Kabir must have been born much earlier than the generally accepted date of 1398. Dr. K.K. Bhatt, however, says that the inscription does not appear to be older than a hundred years.[4]

Another small incident connected with the two brothers, Tatwa and Jiwa, throws light on Kabir's strong common sense and his deep understanding of human nature. It is said that when the Brahmins came to know that two members of their community had accepted a Muslim as their Guru, they declared them outcasts and decreed that no one should have any dealings or association with them. The two brothers, thus ostracized, were much disturbed, for one had a daughter of marriageable age and the other, a son. As a result of the decree, they could not find suitable matches for them. When their

---

1. It appears that both the brothers, Tatwa and Jiwa, continued to impart Kabir's teachings in Gujarat, for a line of their successors is still extant there.
2. Nabhadas, *Bhaktamal, Chhappaya* 69.
3. This is the biggest of the three largest banyan trees in India, the other two being in Adayar, Madras and in the Botanical Gardens, Calcutta. The age of the tree could easily be over 500 years.
4. It is difficult to ascertain when the huge tree came to be named after Kabir—while it was still a small tree or much later. A locality of the Baroach city on the Kabir Vat side is also named after the Saint, 'Kabir Pura'. These confirm Kabir's association with Gujarat and his impact on the people there.

prayers and pleas fell on deaf ears,[1] they went to their Master, Kabir.

Kabir told them not to plead with the Brahmins nor to offer apologies, for they had not committed any crime. "Go back to your town," he advised them, "and announce that you are going to arrange the marriage between your daughter and your son, and everything will be all right."

When the Brahmins heard of the proposed marriage between two first cousins, they were shocked. They tried to persuade the two brothers to desist from committing this sin, but both Tatwa and Jiwa, in obedience to their Master's advice, held their ground. They said that since the Brahmins did not allow them to marry their children within the community, they were left with no alternative. As Kabir had visualized, the Brahmins called a meeting of the elders, the ban was unconditionally withdrawn, and the two brothers found suitable matches for their children.

During one of his tours, Kabir is said to have met a holy man who claimed that whenever he closed his eyes and remembered Lord Krishna, he saw his deity dancing with the *gopis,* the milkmaids of Vrindavan. Kabir asked the sadhu to sit and do so in his presence. The holy man closed his eyes and as he began to enjoy the dance, Kabir said, "When Krishna happens to come near you during the dance, catch hold of his hand and don't let it go."

The man at the first opportunity caught hold of the hand of Lord Krishna, who tried to release himself from the devotee's grip. In the struggle, the sadhu's eyes opened and he was amazed to see that he had firmly grasped his own hand. Bewildered and upset, the man looked at Kabir inquiringly.

Kabir said, "My good friend, do not be upset. What you have been seeing is a projection of your own mind. It is good that the illusion has broken." The holy man wanted to know more, and finding him in a receptive mood, Kabir explained to

---

1. Men thus turned out of the community were sometimes taken back on their asking for forgiveness from the high priests of their community and paying a fine as a token of repentance.

25

him further: "Mind is a powerful entity. Within moments it can cover distances far and wide. It can project the picture of whatever object or person one thinks of. More than the waves in the ocean are the waves of the mind. But if you make it still, you can fetch precious gems of devotion from its depths."[1]

Kabir continued: "If the one whom you saw was real, he would have talked with you, answered your questions and taken you to higher spiritual regions. You cannot visualize what you have never seen. If you try to and even succeed in seeing the object of your worship, it will only be the reflection of a mental image you have formed, not a reality. It will not respond to your actual spiritual needs."

He went on to explain that the true path to God lies in vacating the nine portals of the body, going within and journeying through the inner spiritual regions. The veil of ignorance disappears and the mystery of past, present and future is solved as soon as the soul crosses the region of mind, Maya and Kal. This is a high state of experience, not a vision produced by the mind. Here, under the guidance and protection of a perfect Master, one actually travels through the inner worlds, realizes what his true self is and obtains true knowledge—a knowledge that is beyond words and that cannot be contained within any books in the world.

Kabir paused, and seeing the man in a pensive mood, he added: This is not a state of momentary elation. It is a state of exaltation, of bliss that is lasting, because it is a result of experience. This experience is a reality, not a mental picture; it leads to the union of the soul-bride with her husband, the Lord. One who drinks the ambrosia of this bliss is cured of the malady of birth and death:

> Thus has Kabir drunk
> The nectar of God's love:
> Not an iota of thirst remains;
> Like the potter's well-baked vessel

---

1. *K.S.S.*, p.147:13.

He will not be put
On the wheel again.[1]

Before leaving, the holy man expressed his gratitude to Kabir for making him aware of true devotion.

Kabir had his own way of dealing with people. He would shock them in order to wake them from their stupor of religious superstition. A few accounts illustrate the radical ways that he would adopt to jolt those he chose to give enlightenment to. Jahan Gasht Shah, a Muslim dervish, had visited a number of places in India and met many holy men. Having heard of Kabir as a great devotee, he came to Banaras to meet him. Learning of the fakir's arrival, Kabir said to one of his disciples that this man, though a noble soul and a true seeker of God, had not freed himself from certain deep-rooted prejudices which had become a hindrance in his spiritual progress. He asked the disciple to bring a pig and tie it near the door of his hut.[2]

When Jahan Gasht came, he was scandalized to see a pig tied in front of Kabir's hut.[3] Incensed, he turned back. Kabir, seeing him go, came out and called, "O Dervish, why do you go without seeing me?" Jahan Gasht stopped. "Kabir, I had heard that you were a pious man, but I find that you have kept an impure being at your door. I expected you to know the tenets better—your conduct befits only a *kafir*."

Kabir walked over to Jahan Gasht, greeted him with a salaam and said, "Friend, I have kept the impure one outside my house; you have given it shelter within your heart. Did not your eyes flash with anger and hatred for me? Are anger and hatred pure and within the tenets of religion?"

At Kabir's words, the dervish stood nonplused. Kabir took him by the hand and led him into the house. He explained to the fakir that in God's creation no being should be despised.

---

1. *Kabir Granthavali*, ed. Shyam Sundar Das, p.13:6:1; hereafter cited as *K.G.*
2. Some scholars, like Kshitimohan Sen, hold that the pig was not tied there at Kabir's instructions, but just happened to come and sit there.
3. Among the Muslims, the pig is looked upon as an impure animal, and it is a sin to touch or even go near a pig.

How could one love God, if he had room for disdain and ha
tred in his heart? In the eyes of the Lord, no being is filthy, for
He has created each one of them to fulfill His own design.
There is no such thing as a *kafir* and a *momin*[1]—and if at all
there is, then a cruel and heartless man who injures God's
creatures is a *kafir,* and one who loves the Lord and sees Him
in all his creation is a true *momin,* whatever the caste or clime
in which one may be born. Jahan Gasht was deeply impressed
and spent a few happy days in Kabir's elevating company.

The way Kabir brought Dharam Das to the path also illustrates his unorthodox methods. Dharam Das was a businessman, wealthy and prosperous. He had a religious bent of mind,
but was deeply involved with rituals and idol worship. Once
while he was engaged in worship on the bank of the Ganges,
Kabir passed by that way. He stopped, looked at the small and
large idols Dharam Das was worshipping, and asked, "The
large stones that you have placed before you must be for weigh-
ing two seers,[2] and the smaller ones, for a quarter?"

Dharam Das, annoyed at such disrespect shown to his
deity, looked up in anger. Kabir said, "Tell me, have they ever
spoken to you, have they ever responded to your prayers?" But
before Dharam Das could give vent to his wrath, Kabir quietly
walked away. Later, Kabir's words kept ringing in the merchant's mind. Yes, he thought, all these years they have never
responded to my devotion.

Months passed. One day Dharam Das and his wife Amna
were performing a *havan*—a religious rite in which clarified
butter, incense and similar items are put into a fire to the
chanting of mantras. Kabir suddenly came and said, "Dharam
Das, you seem to be a great sinner." Dharam Das was startled
and Amna, who could not take this slur on her husband, re-
acted sharply, "How can my husband be a sinner? It is you
who are one!"

Kabir replied, "Look at the wood you are putting into the

---

1. A *kāfir* or 'infidel' is a non-Muslim, a non-believer in the tenets of Islam, while *momin*,
'the faithful', is a believer in the Prophet and in Islam.
2. A *seer* is equal to 2.2 lbs. or 1 kilo.

fire. It is full of insects and worms. How many innocent lives you are taking, and for what!" They examined a few pieces of the firewood. Many insects had made their home in the crevices and under the bark of the wood.

Full of remorse, they looked up, but Kabir had meanwhile gone away. Dharam Das recollected that this was the same person who had met him on an earlier occasion. He was disconsolate, the holy man had again disappeared, and he had lost the chance of talking with him. He blamed his wife: After a long time the sage had come and she had driven him away with her rude remarks.

The radiant face of Kabir kept hovering before the eyes of Dharam Das; he was seized with a burning desire to meet him again. Amna, unable to admit her fault, said, "Why not hold a large *yajna* ceremony and invite all sadhus for free meals?[1] I am sure he will come, for flies always swarm around sugar."

Dharam Das performed a number of *yajnas* in Banaras and other holy places. Hundreds of sadhus came to partake of the free meals, but not Kabir. The last *yajna* he performed on a large scale at Mathura, on the banks of the river Jamuna, but the Saint did not come. Dharam Das was in despair. All his toil was a waste. He had spent a fortune on the *yajnas,* his business had suffered and he had almost become a pauper. Life appeared meaningless and, in a fit of remorse, he decided to end it. As he was walking towards a desolate part of the river to drown himself, he saw a familiar figure.

It was the same radiant face, the same kindly smile. Dharam Das fell at Kabir's feet and said, "Day after day, for months I have searched for you, from place to place. I performed dozens of *yajnas* and I've lost all my wealth...."

Kabir said, "It had to be so. Your wife said, 'Flies always swarm around sugar'. Had I come earlier, you would always have thought devotees can be won over by wealth." He affectionately raised Dharam Das, saying, "Arise, Dharam Das, and remember that those who run after wealth, like hungry

1. A ritual ceremonial oblation accompanied by offering free food to Brahmins, holy men and the poor. Performing *yajnas* is regarded as an act of great merit by the Hindus.

dogs after a piece of bread, are not true devotees. A perfect Master covets nothing from his disciples. He accepts no payment for the knowledge he imparts. If he does, do not accept him as your spiritual guide. Satguru is a giver, not a beggar. Material wealth is like the shadow of a tree—it never stays in the same place. Do not worry, I will give you the wealth of Nam, a wealth before which the riches of the three worlds put together are trivial."

Dharam Das and his wife Amna were initiated by Kabir. Dharam Das eventually became Kabir's successor and settled at his home town Bandhogarh, now in the Vindhya Pradesh division of Madhya Pradesh.

For over seventy years Kabir had taught the path of God-realization, raising the voice of truth despite slander and criticism. Many Muslims, and Hindus of all castes, had joined the fold of his disciples. His simple exposition of spiritual truth in the language of the masses, his analysis of the existing norms of worship, his message emphasizing self-realization while living, and above all, his personal magnetism drew true seekers to his door. But the orthodox could not tolerate being deprived of their hold on the people. Their coin, embossed with orthodoxy on the one side and formalism on the other, had been declared counterfeit by Kabir, a coin that would never gain entry into the Lord's Treasury.

The qazis dubbed him a kafir, the Brahmins an apostate. Their attempts to cow him with threats had no effect. All these years Kabir had faced their harassment with undaunted courage, and their warped aspersions with casual indifference. Their attempts to vanquish him with arguments proved ineffective against the strong common sense and ruthless directness of Kabir:

"If you say God dwells only in the mosque or He dwells only in an idol, then who dwells in the rest of the world? You say, in the south is the home of Hari, or in the west is the abode of Allah, but not one of you has found the truth. Search for Him in your heart, search for Him deep within your self—this is the place where He lives, this is his true abode. The Brahmins

keep twenty-four fasts on each eleventh day;[1] the qazis fast in
the month of Ramazan, putting aside the eleven other months
as if only one month contains the treasure of God. Of what
avail are baths in Orissa,[2] what use bowing your head in the
mosques, when with deception you say your prayers? What use
pilgrimages to holy spots, with deceit in your heart? All the
men and women that be, are Thine own image, O Lord. Kabir
is the child of Ram and Allah, and he reveres all Saints and
holy men. O men and women, listen: Take refuge in the One,
repeat his Name; only then will you cross the ocean."[3]

Emphasizing that all beings have emanated from the same
Light, all are equal, Kabir says:

> In the beginning God projected Light,
> From that Light came into being all men;
> From the same Light emanated the entire universe,
> Whom then shall I call good, whom bad?[4]

Kabir would not spare those who claimed superiority by
virtue of birth in a particular caste or community. His remarks,
sometimes almost scathing, drew strong reactions and resentment from the orthodox:

> In the womb the soul has neither caste nor clan. All
> souls have sprung from the seed of Brahm,[5]

> No one is high, no one low; all are nurtured by Him
> who has given the form. O Brahmin, if you are
> special and superior to others, why did you not
> come to the world by a different road? O Turk, if
> you are born of a Muslim mother and if you are
> superior to others by virtue of circumcision, then

---

1. Fasting on *ekadashi* or the eleventh day before and after the full moon, that is, twice
a month or twenty-four times a year, is considered a pious act by the Hindus.
2. Refers to Jagannath Puri, a pilgrim place of the Hindus in Orissa.
3. Adi Granth, *Bibhas Prabhati*, Kabirji, p.1349.
4. Ibid.
5. Adi Granth, *Gauri*, Kabirji, p.324.

why were you not born circumcised from the
womb? Says Kabir, only he is low whose heart is
averse to God's Name.[1]

It is not difficult to imagine the wrath these outspoken
utterances must have produced in the orthodox circles of both
Hindus and Muslims. Even some scholars of the early twentieth century have shown their resentment over these poems of
Kabir by describing them as "debased and indecent."

With unerring precision, Kabir directed his assault on idol
worship, pilgrimages, fasting, penances and ritual baths, which
for ages had stood like a citadel bearing the distinctive insignia
of piety: ochre, yellow, red, blue, green or white garments,
various markings on the forehead and the body, and rosaries
of different types of beads. "They have made God into a plaything,"[2] he declared. He pointed out that Hindu and Muslim
high priests who practiced and preached such external observances were themselves spiritually blind; they tried to show light
to others, but themselves lived in the dark shadows of delusion.
Their guidance of others was like the blind leading the blind.

If it was only a scathing attack on their rituals, the pundits
and mullahs would not have been disturbed, for refutation
alone will seldom destroy entrenched traditions. But to criticism, Kabir added the positive force of a dynamic path, a living
faith, which rocked the superstructure of their hallowed dogmas. He exposed their sham holiness and posed sanctity. He
pointed out that they were promising heaven and salvation
through meaningless practices; they were selling religion and
filling their pockets in the name of God. They misguided the
innocent and thrived on their ignorance. Cruel at heart, they
professed to be kind; secretly craving worldly possessions, they
claimed to be detached. Fraud was their religion and mammon
their god. Kabir warned the people not to look upon them as
holy men—"They are the thugs of Banaras,"[3] he said.

1. *K.G.*, p.79:41.
2. Adi Granth, *Bhairau*, Kabirji, p.1158.
3. Adi Granth, *Asa*, Kabirji, p.475.

As opposed to this, Kabir offered the path of God-realization while living. A path not of empty promises, but of actual practice and experience. A path in which God's Name was not a matter of repetition on a rosary, but an inner revelation; where divine love was not an intellectual speculation, nor a one-sided emotion, but a positive awareness accompanied by a divine response. For Kabir's God was not an image confined to a temple or mosque, but the Supreme Spirit, whom the devotee could perceive and with whom he could converse by going within. Naturally, true seekers gathered around Kabir like moths to a flame, without bothering whether the lamp that emitted the Light belonged to a Brahmin, a mullah or a lowly weaver.

If Kabir used trenchant language to convey his thoughts, it was because he knew that soft words would not penetrate hearts closed by fanaticism; moonlight cannot melt glaciers. Traditional opponents, the Hindu priests and Muslim maulvis joined hands to counter Kabir's influence. But they had no answer to the path of truth that Kabir preached. They could not face him on the basis of their beliefs, nor of their learning, nor of their rituals, the origin and meaning of which they hardly knew. The only recourse left to them was to elicit the support of the state.

But the king of Banaras was himself an admirer of Kabir and, it is believed, was one of his devoted disciples. In the last decade of the fifteenth century, Sultan Sikander Lodi was also in Banaras. He readily fell a prey to the schemes of the religious dignitaries and ordered that Kabir be produced in the royal court.

Brought before the sultan, Kabir nodded a greeting to him as one does to an ordinary man. When asked by the qazi why he did not bow to the great king, he replied that he knew only one King and bowed only to Him. There was no answer to this, for it is an accepted axiom of Islam that the faithful should pay obeisance only to God.

The qazi charged him with heresy and called him a kafir. The Brahmins argued that Kabir belonged to a low caste and

33

had no right to criticize their holy modes of worship and way of life. Kabir replied that only he is a kafir who dwells in lies and delusion. "He is the true Brahmin who realizes Brahm; he is the true mullah who fights with his mind and subdues it; he is the real pundit, the real learned one, who realizes his primal state."[1]

In reply to the accusation that he called the God of Hindus and Muslims one, Kabir said, "Realize, O ignorant men, the One who speaks and dwells in the body is neither a Hindu nor a Turk. The imperceptible Allah is present within every vessel; seek within your heart and know it. Says Kabir: Within the Hindu and the Turk dwells the same One Lord."[2]

Sikander Lodi, though reputed to be a ruthless despot, was greatly impressed by Kabir's personality and straightforward-ness. He felt that it was no ordinary person who stood before him, but a true lover of the Lord. It is said that he dismissed the plaint against Kabir.

But the frustrated high priests would not give up and resort-ed to intrigue. They won over the favor of some of the close associates of the sultan, and the qazis particularly tried to prej-udice the king against Kabir through backbiting. The pundits and maulvis planned their campaign systematically. Witnesses were kept ready and the accusations against Kabir were enu-merated in a joint petition. Kabir was again summoned to the sultan's court.

Kabir surveyed the court, looked at the Hindus and Mus-lims standing together to accuse him, and smiled. Asked by the sultan what amused him, Kabir replied, "All my life I have tried to impress upon the Hindus and Muslims that God is one, the Father of both. I pleaded with them to forget their differ-ences and join hands in worshipping the One, the Lord of all. But they rejected my plea, ignored my appeals; because how could a Brahmin 'demean' himself by joining hands with a low-caste weaver? How could a maulvi 'degrade' himself by allying with a kafir? They could never bear to stand together in

1. *K.G.*, p.104:157:4; Adi Granth, *Bhairau*, Kabirji, p.1159; *K.G.*, p.105:159:1.
2. *K.G.*, p.82:56:4 and other selections.

the court of the King of kings, but today it amuses me to see them standing united in the court of a worldly king, a mortal like all others."

Though disconcerted by Kabir's reply to the sultan, the qazis and pundits presented their joint petition. The lowly Kabir has flouted all the glorious traditions of Islam and the noble conventions of the Hindus. He maligns the Vedas and the great pilgrim places; he rejects the deities and defames the great Brahmins of Kashi. He denounces pilgrimage to the holy Ka'aba, the forty days' fasting during Ramazan and preaches against the tenets of Islam. He ridicules the Hindu scriptures as well as the holy book of Islam. He is an infidel, a non-believer in God; he is a heretic and a kafir.

This time their invective had the desired effect. Convinced that the holy man who stood before him was guilty of blasphemy, Sikander Lodi was enraged—in the words of Anantdas, "as if ghee had been poured onto fire, as if somebody had twisted the tail of a deadly cobra, someone had plucked the whiskers of a sleeping lion."[1]

Kabir's answers to the king and the accusers were crisp and lucid. He had neither malice nor rancor towards his persecutors, nor did he fear the consequences. He refused to apologize, for it was no sin to preach devotion for the Lord.

His words could not enter the prejudiced heart of the king. The compassion of a bigot is short-lived; the fanatic's only argument is the sword. The sultan ordered that Kabir be drowned in the river. Kabir said, "Lord, I live and have always lived under Thy shelter. The world looks upon Thy lovers as its enemies. In life and in death, dear Lord, Thou alone art my support, my succor."[2]

His hands and feet bound with heavy chains, Kabir was thrown into the river. But the waves broke the chains and Kabir was seen floating on the water. The qazis and pundits commented, "O great Sultan, this is all a trick, because he is a magician." But Kabir said in ecstasy, "O Kabir, no one is mine

---

1. Anantdas, *Parichai*, as quoted by Dr. T.N. Dixit in *Parichai Sahitya*, p.44.
2. Ibid, p.45.

in this world; in the water and on the earth, my savior is the Lord."[1]

He was next tied and placed at the feet of an elephant. But the elephant would not move. The mahout goaded the beast, but again it refused to move. It would not step on the Saint for, in the words of Kabir, "in its heart too dwelt the Lord."[2] Kabir was then thrown into fire, but emerged, says Priyadas, "emitting a divine radiance."[3]

Sikander Lodi looked at the pundits and qazis, but they stood speechless. An awestruck silence prevailed among the people who had gathered as spectators to witness the sultan's 'justice'. The sultan rose, ordered Kabir's chains to be removed, and slowly walked up to him.

The two looked at each other—Kabir with compassion, the king with remorse and guilt. At length Sikander Lodi managed to say, "I did not realize your greatness. You are a man of God, a great dervish. . . . Please forgive me." With eyes downcast and head lowered, the king stood before Kabir, like an accused prisoner awaiting judgment.

With a gracious smile, Kabir said, "You are not at fault. Such was the will of God. He does what He deems fit. Look up, O Sultan, don't feel sad, forget what has happened. The Lord is all love and mercy; in His court, true repentance never goes unrewarded. Don't worry, the Lord will forgive you."

Sikander Lodi was amazed. There was not a tinge of resentment in Kabir's words. The Saint bore no grudge even towards his worst tormentor. It is no wonder that Kabir forgave the sultan. By nature he was loving and compassionate, as all Saints are, and to quote his own words: "Forgiveness is a game that only the Saints play."[4]

It is said that the disconsolate sultan then offered gifts of money and land, which Kabir gently declined to accept.

Some scholars express reservations regarding this episode

---

1. Adi Granth, *Bhairau*, Kabirji, p.1162.
2. Adi Granth, *Gond*, Kabirji, p.871.
3. Priyadas, *Bhaktamal Satik*, p.494, *Kavitt* 278.
4. *K.S.S.*, p.122:72.

and the miraculous escapes of Kabir. Saints, however, have often faced persecution from religious fanatics, who look upon God as their personal possession, His worship as their monopoly, and the interpretation of scriptures and the teachings of past spiritual adepts as their birthright. It would not be surprising if Kabir, like many other Saints, had to suffer at their hands.

Anantdas, Priyadas, Mukund Kavi, Raghodas and many later poets have mentioned the Sikander Lodi episode in their writings. Two poems in the Adi Granth, and with slight variations, in the *Kabir Granthavali,* mention the qazi's wrath, the attempts to annihilate Kabir, and his miraculous escapes. But in both collections the name of Kabir's tormentor is not given. He is simply referred to as a qazi, a Muslim religious head who in those days also enjoyed judicial powers. Some scholars accept that Kabir was persecuted by Sikander Lodi, because there were other instances of similar deeds perpetrated by the king, a few even being mentioned by the medieval historian Firishta.[1]

There is a difference of opinion among scholars whether Kabir was a contemporary of Sikander Lodi or not. P.D. Barthwal and others, on the basis of two short references to Kabir in the *Ain-e-Akbari,*[2] deny that Kabir was living during the time of Sikander Lodi, who reigned from 1489 to 1520 A.D.[3] However, these authors have based their conclusions on the English translation of *Ain-e-Akbari* by Jarrett, where he has somehow omitted the line "he [Kabir] lived during the period of Sikander Lodi"—*"dar zamane Sikandar Lodi bood."*

Westcott, Macauliffe, Briggs, Keay, Wilson, Garcin de Tassy and Grierson are among the Western scholars who accept Kabir as a contemporary of Sikander Lodi. S.S. Das,

---

1. A Brahmin named Bodhan (Lodhan, according to Elliot and Dawson) was sentenced by Sikander Lodi to be flayed alive and stuffed with husk, for declaring the God of Hindus and Muslims to be the same. Firishta mentions this in his *Tarikh-i-Firishta*; also mentioned by S.S.A. Rizvi in *A History of Sufism in India,* I:382. In medieval days, such punishments were common in India, the Middle East and also in Europe.
2. Written by Abu'l Fazl Allami in about 1598; he was a contemporary of Akbar, the Moghul emperor.
3. According to some scholars, he reigned from 1489 to 1526.

Mishrabandhu, H.P. Dwivedi, R.C. Shukla, R.C. Tiwari, G. Trigunayat[1] and many other scholars maintain that Kabir lived till 1518 A.D. and was thus a contemporary of the Lodi king. Vakhna and Rajjab, disciples of Dadu, and Swami Haridas, who was most probably a contemporary of Kabir,[2] have also mentioned the Sikander Lodi episode.

Kabir was now over a hundred years old, and though his mind was alert, his will indomitable and his spirit as vibrant as ever, the physical body was showing signs of age. He knew that the time to depart from this world was coming. He decided to leave Banaras and proceed to Magahar[3] to spend his last days there.

Some scholars infer that Sikander Lodi, though impressed with Kabir's spiritual attainment, had decided to banish him from the holy city in the interests of peace. There is no historical or traditional evidence available to support this view, but such a step on Sikander Lodi's part does not seem unlikely. Taking advantage of the initial harsh attitude of the authorities, the orthodox faction might have tried to persecute and harass Kabir's followers also. Even if not banished by the sultan, Kabir might have thought it proper to leave Banaras for the sake of his disciples. It is also likely that the Sikander Lodi episode brought additional fame to Kabir as a man of miracles, and he may have decided to leave Banaras to avoid the crowds coming to him for worldly boons.

Whatever the situation may have been, Kabir also wanted to give a last jolt to the people of Banaras, who had a deep faith in the sanctity of the city, kept inviolate by legends and superstitions: a person who dies within the precincts of the

---

1. See Bibliography for titles.
2. Acharya Parashuram Chaturvedi gives the probable dates of Swami Haridas as 1455 to 1538 A.D. (*Uttari Bharat ki Sant Parampara*, p.344; *Kabir Sahitya ki Parakh*, p.267). If these dates are correct, then Swami Haridas was a contemporary of Kabir. Some of his poems are included in the collection of compositions of Saints compiled by Rajjab at the instance of Saint Dadu. He is different from the Vaishnavite devotee Swami Haridas who was a contemporary of Akbar (1542–1605) and is believed to have taught music to the renowned musician Tansen.
3. Magahar, situated about 175 miles north-east of Banaras in the Basti District of Uttar Pradesh, 13 miles from Gorakhpur, was a small town in the time of Kabir and had a large population of Muslims, predominantly weavers.

holy city invariably goes to heaven. At the same time, tradition had put a stigma on Magahar, that one who dies in Magahar is born again, and that too as a donkey.

The news of Kabir's decision to spend his last days in the unholy city of Magahar spread through Banaras. Some pundits and orthodox men came to him and pleaded, "People from great distances come to the holy city to die here and thereby attain liberation. Do not leave Banaras for the condemned town of Magahar. O Kabir, all your life you have sinned against our gods, our ancient and noble ways of worship, our sacred tenets and traditions. A death in Banaras is your only chance to escape perdition."

Kabir's reply was bold and clear: "A hardened sinner will not escape the fires of hell even if he dies in Banaras; but a Saint of God, even if he dies in Magahar, emancipates the entire fold of his disciples."[1]

"And what is hell," he added, "what is wretched heaven? Saints have rejected both. By the grace of my Satguru, I neither care for the one, nor fear the other. I have ascended the divine throne and met the Lord. God and Kabir have become one: no one can distinguish who is who."[2]

A few of Kabir's own disciples had not been able to shake off the deep-rooted idea of the holiness of Banaras and the impurity of Magahar. They were shocked and unhappy. But their humble entreaties could not make Kabir waver from his resolve. He told them:

Brothers, you are simple and credulous:
If in Kasi,[3] Kabir leaves the body,
Then what credit to his Lord's grace?

What I was once,
I am not now.
I have reaped the benefit
Of my precious human birth;

1. Adi Granth, *Asa*, Kabirji, p.484.
2. Adi Granth, *Ramkali*, Kabirji, p.969.
3. Kasi is another name for Banaras.

As water once mixed in water
Can never be taken apart,
So has this weaver flowed
And merged into the Lord.

One who is always absorbed
In God's love and devotion,
What is there to wonder at
When he attains this high state?
Through the blessings of his Master,
Through the company of the Saints,
This weaver marches onwards,
He has conquered Kal's domains.

Says Kabir: Listen, friends,
Let no doubts remain:
He who has true faith in the Lord,
For him, holy Kasi and barren Magahar
Are the same.[1]

Kabir left Banaras for Magahar, a distance of about 175 miles. A few disciples accompanied him. The journey was slow, marked by a few long stops. He gave satsangs on the way, met old disciples and initiated new seekers. Some of his disciples tried to join him in his journey, but Kabir, always averse to moving in crowds and processions, did not permit them to do so. There are no records available to give an idea of this last journey of Kabir, painful for many of his disciples who knew they were seeing their Satguru for the last time. The love he had generated in their hearts was now turning into the agony of forthcoming separation, separation from the physical presence of their Satguru whom they deeply loved and adored.

Consoling them, encouraging them to attend to meditation and urging them to be steadfast in a life of honest earning, purity and dedication, Kabir moved on and reached Magahar

---

1. *K.G.*, p.167:402.

after a journey that must have taken at least two months.

Magahar was an ill-fated and barren town: besides the blot of unholiness attached to it, there was an acute shortage of water. Ami, the only river running nearby, used to remain dry except for one or two months of the rainy season. Magahar received two blessings from the Saint's visit: It is said that on Kabir's arrival the river began to flow and continued to run throughout the year; and second, the stigma on Magahar was removed.

One morning after giving darshan to his disciples, Kabir retired to his hut with instructions that he should not be disturbed. When he did not come out by noon, a few disciples, worried, went inside the hut. Kabir was lying on the floor, covered with a white sheet. His face radiated peace and bliss, but the body exhibited no signs of life. The wave that rose from the mighty Ocean had merged back into it.

The disciples were stunned. Though over a hundred years old, Kabir had always glowed with spiritual splendor and looked ageless. He had been active all his life, working at his loom, and at the same time devoting himself to the care and service of his flock of disciples. Always alert and untiring, he drew power from his inner repository of Shabd. Age and frail health could not fetter his indefatigable will nor affect his unflinching dedication to his divine mission.

Although Kabir all his life had denounced the empty formalism of both Hindus and Muslims with equal vehemence, and although he had often declared that he was neither a Hindu nor a Muslim,[1] his disciples entered into a dispute about the last rites. The Hindus wanted to cremate the body, the Muslims to bury it, according to their respective customs. With King Vir Singh Baghela voicing the Hindu view and Nawab Bijli Khan that of the Muslims, the difference of opinion soon turned into strong arguments and hot exchanges.[2]

---

1. "If you call me a Hindu, I am not; if you call me a Musalman, that too I am not" (*K.S.S.*, p.75:4).
2. Some scholars have wondered at the unusual coincidence of the two rulers, King Vir Singh and Nawab Bijli Khan, both being there at the same time. But it is not unlikely, as they must have heard of Kabir's departure for Magahar and of his failing health and, as disciples, they must have wanted to go to Magahar to see Kabir again before he left the world.

It is said that someone drew the attention of the disputants towards the Saint's body. The disciples entered the hut and found a large heap of fresh flowers lying in place of the body. Silenced, the two groups divided the flowers between them; the Hindus cremated their share and the Muslims buried theirs. The dispute that arose in a moment of emotional stress was forgotten. The haze of ritualism, which for a while had blurred their vision, lifted, and the disciples felt ashamed, realizing that even in his death Kabir had vindicated the futility of such formal beliefs.

It was a fitting finale to the epic life of a great Saint who, like the Saints of all times, belonged to no caste, and never allowed himself to be confined to the man-made ambits of caste, creed and country.[1]

---

1. What actually happened—whether it was really a miracle, or was contrived by a saner group of disciples—is shrouded in mystery. Knowing the difference of opinion that might arise among his followers, had Kabir asked some of his close disciples to slip away with the body? No satisfactory answer is available. Almost all early poet-biographers like Anantdas, Priyadas, Mukund and Raghodas, and Saints like Ravidas, Dadu, Rajjab, Vakhna, Malukdas, Garibdas, and Kabir's successor Dharam Das, besides many others, have mentioned the miracle of the disappearance of Kabir's body. And with the passage of time, failing to find a clue to what actually happened, the scholars of today with their scientific and analytical bent of mind are unable either to accept or to reject the account.

Teachings

HAILED AS A GREAT DEVOTEE AND SAINT by medieval poets, Kabir, in the context of twentieth-century thinking, is regarded by many scholars as a powerful social reformer. But Kabir was not a reformer, either by volition or by inclination. His mission was essentially spiritual, not social. But the presence of Saints has a mellowing influence on their surroundings. The divine fragrance of love and tolerance emanating from Kabir could not fail to inspire, elevate and 'reform' those who came in contact with him.

Kabir's role was not that of a reformer giving a new social order in place of the old; it was rather that of a transformer. He tried to transform hate into love, recrimination into tolerance, doubt into faith born of experience, and outward search for God into inner union with Him. He was neither an altruist nor a philosopher, neither a scholar nor a theologian. He was a man of God, a lover of the Lord. Having attained the highest form of spiritual experience—God-realization—he was an adept fully competent to guide others on the path, a perfect Master for whom spirituality was not an exposition of intricate scriptural truths, but a way of life.

A few lines of Saint Pipa, a contemporary of Kabir, illustrate the impact of Kabir and his teachings on those who came in contact with him:

> Had not Kabir come
> In this Iron Age,
> The scriptures and Kaliyuga
> In collusion would have driven
> Devotion to perdition....
> What would have been the fate
> Of sinners like me?
> Whose succor could I have sought?
> In whom could I have reposed my faith?

Listening to others
And doing what they did,
I too would have gone their way. . . .
The Merciful One vouchsafed
That Kabir should come
And resound the glory of Nam;
To maintain the eminence of true devotion
The Lord himself sent him.
When Kabir revealed
The resplendence of the true Name,
Then did Pipa obtain this treasure.[1]

Muslim authors like Mohsin Fani and Abu'l Fazl have described Kabir as a *muwahhid,* a believer in One God. Sheikh Sadullah (died 1522), another contemporary of Kabir, in reply to his son's query whether the celebrated Kabir was a Muslim or a kafir, said that he was a *muwahhid.* Asked whether a *muwahhid* differed from both the Muslim and the kafir, the Sheikh replied that the truth would be difficult to understand and such knowledge could only be acquired gradually.

In order to explain the true meaning of this word, Saiyid A.A. Rizvi quotes Khwaja Yaqub, a son of Sheikh Farid:

The muwahhid is he whose main concern is good action. Whatever he does aims at seeking divine grace. Water does not drown him and fire does not burn him. Absorbed in Tawhid (Wahdat al-Wujud) he is in a state of self-effacement. A sufi or a lover belonging to this category is concerned with nothing. If he makes a quest for himself, he finds God; if he seeks God, he finds himself. When the lover is completely absorbed in the Beloved, the attributes of the lover and Beloved become identical.[2]

---

1. Pipa, quoted by Dr. Ram Kumar Varma in *Sant Kabir,* p.51, from an old manuscript, "Sarab Gotika"; also quoted by many other scholars. For explanations of terms, see Glossary.
2. Khwaja Yaqub, *Ma'ariju'l-Wilayat,* quoted by S.A.A. Rizvi in *A History of Sufism in India,* I:373.

This complete absorption of the lover in the Beloved, the merging of the soul in the Lord or the flame into the Flame, is the ultimate goal of all Saints. Kabir says:

> Kabir, I have made Him
>> My companion
> Who is beyond pleasure and pain;
>> I will revel with Him,
> I will merge with Him
>> And never be parted again.[1]

In a couplet paying homage to Kabir, Saint Dadu in a subtle manner confirms the unity of the teachings of the Saints:

> He who was the Husband of Kabir,
>> Him will I woo and wed;
> With my body, mind and soul,
>> None else will I espouse.[2]

The 'Husband' of Kabir

Kabir has often described himself as the 'bride of God', the 'wife of Ram'. In his poems of longing, he pines for the Lord, identifying himself with a bride parted from her husband; in the songs of union, he declares that Ram, the long-awaited bridegroom, has come to wed the bride—Kabir—and take her to his divine abode.

At the same time, he emphatically states that Ram is not a Hindu deity, an incarnation or a personal god. He addresses the Lord with numerous names that are prevalent even today: Ram, Krishna, Govind, Madhav, Murari, Keshav, Madhusudan, Jagannath, Vitthal, Saringpani, taken from the Hindu tradition; and Allah, Khuda, Rabb, Rahim, Rahman, Karim, Sahib, Khalik, Khasam, from the Muslim. He uses these appellations for the One Almighty God, the Supreme Being—his Beloved, his Husband.

---

1. *Kabir Granthavali,* ed. Dr. Shyam Sundar Das, p.68:1 (hereafter cited as *K.G.*).
2. *Dadudayal,* ed. Parashuram Chaturvedi, p.217:9.

Kabir declares in clear terms that the object of his love and devotion is not any of the various incarnations, gods and deities:

> Attach yourself to that Lord whose devotion will
> end all pleasures, all pains; who will redeem you
> from your state of orphanhood. He did not incar-
> nate in the house of Dasrath, nor did he chastise the
> King of Lanka, nor was he born from the womb of
> Devki, nor played in the lap of Jasoda.[1]

Enumerating the various incarnations of the Hindu gods, he adds: "From his own knowledge speaks Kabir, worship of such deities is worship of the false. The One who is beyond them all prevails through the entire world....He has neither a mother, nor a father. No one begot Him, He begets none. What He is, He alone knows....He who descends into the womb is imperfect; he is imperfect who can be given a name. ...He neither comes nor departs. He has no father, mother or brother....Says Kabir, let no one go searching for Him afar. Still your mind, meditate on Him, for He, Ram, fills each particle of the creation."[2]

The Ram of Kabir is immutable, permanent and perfect. He says: "That which is permanent and changeless is True; what is born and dies is false."[3] Guru Nanak confirms the same idea when he says that originally only God was; He was at the beginning of the creation; He is and He shall ever be.[4]

He is as He is

The limitations of the material world, that of language and thought, make it impossible to describe the Supreme Being, the

---

1. *K.G., Barahpadi Ramaini*, stanza 9. Ram, the incarnation of Lord Vishnu, was the son of King Dashrath; he destroyed Ravan and his kingdom of Lanka (not the present Sri Lanka). Lord Krishna, another incarnation of Vishnu, was the son of Vasudev and Devki and was brought up by Jasoda.
2. Portions from *Barahpadi Ramaini, K.G.*, pp.183-185. Guru Ravidas also calls the Lord 'Ram', but says that his Ram is not the son of King Dashrath (*Ravidas Darshan*, p.1:1).
3. *K.G., Ashtpadi Ramaini*, stanza 7.
4. Adi Granth, *Japji*, M.1., p.1 (hereafter cited as A.G.).

Limitless One. Mind itself is formed from matter and even its most acute perception and subtle imagination can neither fully comprehend the Divine, nor aptly describe whatever little it may come to know of Him through intuition and introspection.

Philosophies such as monotheism, pantheism, deism and dualism, with their various branches, are the outcome of attempts to realize God through mental acumen and analysis and to put intellectual deductions into words.

Although Saints say that God is one, complete in himself, with no co-sharer in his supremacy and unassociated with anyone else in his monarchy, they always emphasize that He is beyond the comprehension of body, senses and mind. In the terms of language, He is indescribable and ineffable; yet in the terms of realization, He can be perceived and known by the soul on a high level of consciousness. In reply to a question whether God is one, two or many, Kabir says: "If I call Him one, that He is not; if I say He is two, it is a lie. The Lord is what He is. This is the only way Kabir can describe Him."[1]

In the Old Testament, in reply to a question from Moses, God says: "I am that I am."[2] Saint Ravidas says: "Lord, you are what you are; there is nothing I can compare you with."[3] Guru Ram Das states the same thing: "Thou art the Supreme Being, great, imperceptible; we search and search, but cannot fathom Thy depth. Thou art beyond—beyond all limits; Lord, Thou alone knowest what Thou art....Thy ineffable tale, Thou and only Thou knowest; by meditating on Thee I am blessed, blessed, blessed, my Lord."[4]

Beyond physical reach

Kabir's description of God as absolute, indefinable and "He is as He is" was significant in the context of the contemporary philosophical trends. Besides the ritualistic phase of the prevalent religions, their metaphysical aspects were also given great

---

1. *Bijak, Sakhi* 120.
2. Exod. 3:14. All Biblical quotations are from the Authorized King James Version, except where otherwise indicated.
3. A.G., *Bilawal,* Ravidasji, p.856.
4. A.G., *Kanra,* M.4, p.1296.

importance by the learned of his time. Many intellectual schools
of ancient Hindu philosophy were current and their various
interpretations were in vogue. Banaras was also a center of
scholars who relished debates with one another on their respective philosophies and dogmas and their interpretations.
Kabir, in his simple but subtle manner, pointed out that the
divergent views on God, creation, soul, maya, and their inter-
relationship are irrelevant without a direct experience of the
Absolute Truth; and once the seeker attains this experience,
they are redundant.

God cannot be described in the vocabulary of this world,
for where He is, there is no language. Kabir expresses this in
his own way: "If I say He is outside, it will bring disgrace to
my Master (who has enabled me to realize Him within); if I
say He is only within, it is a lie, for within and without I see
Him at all times through my Master's power and grace. These
eyes cannot see Him, hands cannot grasp Him; boundless and
imperceptible, He cannot be written in books. Only they know
Him who realize Him, for through words no one will understand or believe what He is."[1]

Saint Shiv Dayal Singh, known as Swamiji Maharaj, says:
"The Supreme Being is unfathomable, boundless and eternal.
All mystics who have reached Him became silent at that point,
for they could not describe Him; and here, I too am silent."[2]

Shams-i-Tabriz says: *"Dalil-i-tauhid, radd-i-tauhid ast"*[3]—
that one who tries through arguments to prove that God is
one, is rejecting the very idea of his oneness.

Yet Saints, who come to show the path of God-realization,
have to describe Him, and they do so by adopting the idiom
and parlance of the physical world.

Saints say God is Truth. He is the True Being—Sat Purush.
The 'truth' of Saints is that which is imperishable, immutable
and everlasting, which has neither a past nor a future. Beyond

1. H.P. Dwivedi, *Kabir*, p.134.
2. Swami Ji Maharaj, *Sar Bachan Radhaswami* (*Chhand Band*), *Hidayatnama*, p.177
(hereafter cited as *S.B.*).
3. All Persian quotations have been taken from Maharaj Sawan Singh, *Gurmat Siddhant*,
two vols.

the limits of time and space, it is ever present.

The Lord cannot be attained through intellect, and his presence cannot be demonstrated through arguments. All pondering on God, all polemics about what He is and where He is are futile. Kabir says: "Neither day reaches there nor night, nor can one reach there in one's dreams. There stays Kabir where there is neither sun nor shade."[1] In other words, God is beyond the duality of good and evil, pleasure and pain, heaven and hell; He cannot be conceived of through mental speculation or understood through imagination. Saints stay in that realm beyond duality, they abide in God. Those who realize Him do not indulge in arguments about his existence. According to Kabir, "Those who see Him do not speak; those who speak have not seen Him."[2]

Guru Nanak also says that the Lord cannot be understood by the process of thought:

> Thinking avails not, howso hard one thinks;
> Nor silence avails, howsoever one shrinks
> Into oneself; nor hunger goes
> With the pleasure-loads of the worlds.
> Of a myriad clevernesses, not one works.[3]

Saints say that the six philosophies (*shat darshan*) and their various branches, with all their intellectual analysis, have no knowledge of God. Swamiji declares: "The six philosophies and the scriptures have not reached where dwells my Beloved Lord, Radha Soami."[4] Kabir says:

> God is higher than the earth and the sky, He is
> boundless; the six philosophies are lingering in
> doubt, and so too the eighty-four 'attained sages'.[5]

---

1. *K.G.*, p.42:4.
2. *Kabir Sakhi-Sangrah*, p.113:4 (hereafter cited as *K.S.S.*).
3. *A.G.*, *Japji*, M.1, p.1, trans. Dr. Gopal Singh.
4. *S.B.*, p.12:89.
5. *K.G.*, p.42:11. Old yogic traditions claim that there have been eighty-four accomplished yogis or *siddhas* (perfected ones) who attained 'perfect success' or 'realization' through their yogic practices.

In other words, He is beyond the materialistic ('earth') and the esoteric ('sky') interpretations of the philosophies.

In the chamber of the heart

Though God pervades every particle of creation, He remains invisible, at best a concept which most people accept as a belief. Their 'knowledge' that God is omnipresent is gleaned from books; it is something they have read, heard and learned to believe, not something they have themselves realized. Books and scriptures give the hypothesis of God's omnipresence, but do not give the method and steps by which the seeker can prove it for himself.

Saints say that the Lord is present everywhere, but the devotee cannot see Him in the creation unless he realizes Him within his own self. When once we see a person closely, we will recognize him if we see him again at any other place. If once a devotee manifests the Lord within himself, he will be able to recognize his presence everywhere else. Saints say that only when the seeker sees Him within his own body will he be able to see the Lord in each particle of the creation.

Kabir says: "Having recognized the Lord within, my thoughts rest only in Him. Now wherever I cast my eyes, I see none else but Him.... Since realization came, here, there, everywhere the Lord alone I see."[1]

In other words, for the true seeker the Lord is within his own body. He is not living in some isolated forest, desolate cave or snow-covered peak; nor does He reside in man-made temples, mosques and churches; nor is He confined within hand-crafted symbols and idols of stone, metal, ivory or wood. The human body is the living temple of God. Kabir says: "Within the body plays the unfathomable Formless One."[2]

Guru Amar Das confirms that the human body is the Lord's temple, within which becomes manifest the jewel of realization.[3] Guru Nanak calls "the body's fortress" the "temple

1. *K.G.*, p.102:149.
2. A.G., *Thinthi*, Kabirji, p.343.
3. A.G., *Bibhas Prabhati*, M.3, p.1346:2.

of God."[1] And St. Paul also says, in the New Testament: "Know ye not that ye are the temple of God, and that the Spirit of God dwelleth in you?"[2] "Ye are the temple of the living God."[3]

Maulana Rum says: "Your heart is the true mosque; within your body is the place to offer your salutations to the Lord." Guru Ravidas asks the seeker, "Why do you wander outside searching for Him? The Lord is within your own body."[4] And Saint Pipa echoes the same thought when he describes the human body as "the embodiment of God, the temple of God."[5]

Kabir expresses surprise that when the Bodiless One resides within the human body, no one seeks Him there; people do not try to realize the One who is so close to them.[6] Christ explains that the kingdom of God is not anywhere outside, it is within the human body.[7] The same truth is expressed by Dadu when he says that within his own body he found the Lord of all lords.[8] "O Dadu," he adds, "I have found the Beloved within, found Him who fills all the three worlds. On each couch rests my Lord, but men say He is far."[9]

Kabir says that the Lord is neither less 'here', nor more 'there'; to the brim He fills each pot.[10] The Beloved is within, do not go elsewhere looking for Him.[11]

In his well-known acrostic, *Bawan Akhari,* Kabir says: "He who is near, within your own body, why forsake Him and run far and wide? For whom the world wanders about, Him I found close to my heart."[12] He adds that he searched for Him in all directions, even on the peaks of lofty mountains, but

1. A.G., *Ramkali ki Var, Salok,* M.1, p.952.
2. 1 Cor. 3:16.
3. 2 Cor. 6:16.
4. *Sant Guru Ravidas Vani,* ed. B.P. Sharma, p.158.
5. A.G., *Dhanasari,* Pipa, p.695.
6. *K.G.,* p.14:9:2.
7. "Neither shall they say, Lo here! or, lo there! for, behold, the kingdom of God is within you" (Luke 17:21).
8. *Dadudayal,* p.44:12.
9. *Dadudayal,* p.43:3.
10. *K.G.,* p.64:5.
11. *K.S.S.,* p.106:4.
12. A.G., *Gauri, Bawan Akhari,* Kabirji, p.341:16.

failed to find Him. When he looked within, he "found the One who raised the citadel,[1] within the citadel itself."[2]

The gateway of liberation

Many religious texts accept that the Lord is within the human body, but very few indicate how and where one can find Him in the body. It is generally said that God resides in the heart of every human being. Though the Saints agree that He is within the heart, by 'heart' they do not mean the physical heart, nor that aspect of mind which feels and generates various human emotions. The Saints are explicit about where within our body the Lord is, and at the same time they tell us the way to find Him. The heart, in the terminology of the Saints, is a point between the two eyes, called the eye center.

The seat of mind and soul is behind the eyes, between the eyebrows, from where the consciousness spreads throughout the body. This point has been called by early Indian sages 'the third eye' and 'the divine eye', and by Muslim adepts 'the dark mole'. In the Adi Granth it has been described as 'the door of the home', 'the tenth', 'the tenth door', 'the road home', 'the gateway of liberation'. Guru Nanak says that with the five elements the Creator has made the fortress of the human body and has fixed nine doors to it; but within the tenth lives He, the Imperceptible, the Boundless One.[3]

Tulsi Sahib has described the eye center as 'the tenth door', 'the focal point of a telescope', and 'a point as minute as a poppy seed'. Swamiji, while adopting some of the above expressions, also calls it 'the gateway to the spiritual sky' and 'the tenth window'. "O soul, you are a prisoner within the nine doors, you do not find peace even for a single breath. Open the tenth window, go within and revel in ineffable bliss."[4]

Guru Nanak compares the human body to a city within which is situated a fortress at the tenth door. The township in

1. The human body.
2. A.G., *Gauri, Bawan Akhari*, Kabirji, p.341:20.
3. A.G., *Maru*, M.1, p.1036.
4. *S.B.*, p.145:6:7-8.

54

the firmament is God's true abode. The gates of the fortress are closed by doors hard as granite, which can only be opened by the Guru's Shabd. Taking the simile further, he says that within the fortress is the inner cave, our real home. The nine doors of the city are positioned by the Lord's will. Within the tenth dwells the Infinite, the Unfathomable Lord, and here of himself He reveals himself.[1]

Kabir also adopts the imagery of a fort and explains that one can conquer this formidable fort of the body only through the Master's grace and the power of divine love. This fort is equipped with strong walls, an intractable gate and the stubborn defenders of the senses and desires, and it is ruled by the redoubtable overlord, the mind.[2]

He also describes the eye center as 'the door to the west', 'east' being the world visible to the physical eyes. By 'west' Kabir refers to the regions opposite to the physical world, which are behind the eyes: "Above the western gate stands a heavy rock; in that rock is a window and above the window is the tenth door. O Kabir, endless and boundless is what one sees there."[3]

All Saints have referred to this point in one way or another. Saint Beni says: "At the boundless tenth door is the narrow lane leading to the Supreme Being. Above it is a shop, within the shop a niche and within the niche is the treasure kept in trust for you."[4]

Besides describing the eye center as 'the tenth door', Kabir also calls it 'the mole', 'the mole within the mole' and 'the star between the two moles':

> Between the two eyes is the Master,
> The messenger of the Lord.

---

1. A.G., *Maru, Dakhni*, M.1, p.1033.
2. A.G., *Bhairau*, Kabirji, p.1161.
3. Ibid, p.1159.
4. A.G., *Ramkali*, Beniji, p.974. The words *ghāti* and *thati* have been interpreted by scholars to mean 'residence' and 'window' respectively. These words from old Hindi actually mean 'a difficult path or narrow lane' and 'any money or precious article kept on trust for someone'; they are still used in modern Hindi in this sense.

Between the black and the white moles
Is the shining star,
And within the star dwells
The unknown and unseen Lord.[1]

In another poem Kabir says that he has described a rare and priceless pearl.[2] Men describe it differently—some say it is light, others declare it is heavy; both are under a delusion. The various deities, gods and goddesses, the ascetics and the learned have sung its praises, have read and written much, but none of them could find this precious pearl. It is within the mole of the mole; a rare devotee alone finds it.[3]

The third eye, the inner eye or eye center, has no connection with the physical eyes. Guru Arjan Dev asserts: "Those eyes are different, O Nanak, with which my Beloved is seen."[4] The function of the physical eyes is confined to the physical world:

Within your own body resides your Lord,
Why open the outer eyes to look for Him?
Says Kabir: Listen, O friends,
I found the Lord behind the mole.[5]

The eye center, according to the Saints, is the point from where the soul has diverged into the nine portals of the body; and it is also the point where the soul must converge in order to start on its homeward journey. But this starting point of the inner journey is narrow and fine. Dadu says that the palace within is minute, it is neither a city nor a town, nor does it have a name or an address.[6]

Jesus Christ asks his disciples to enter the inner worlds through the eye center, which he describes as 'a strait gate': "Enter ye in at the strait gate: . . . because strait is the gate, and

---

1. *Kabir Sahib ki Shabdavali*, I:64 (hereafter cited as *K.S.*).
2. Ultimate realization.
3. *K.S.*, II:52.
4. A.G., *Maru Var*, M.5, p.1100.
5. *K.S.*, I:7.
6. *Dadudayal*, p.47:36.

narrow is the way, which leadeth unto life, and few there be that find it."[1]

The path of the Saints, then, is an inward path; it starts from the eye center, runs through the inner spiritual regions and ends at the doorstep of the Lord. God is within, the path is within, the search for Him has to be made within the body; the seeker therefore has to go within and actually travel on the inner path. Though Kabir has described the eye center as "the narrow door of salvation—a tenth of a mustard seed," the soul has to withdraw to this point and go through this narrow gate in order to enter the regions of pure spirit, realms which are beyond the reach of matter, of disease and death.

The tenth door, the eye center, is not a metaphorical or poetic expression coined by the Saints, as some scholars and intellectuals claim. Nor is it an imaginary point. This point is real and the inner worlds are as palpable to the soul as the outer one is to the senses. The physical eyes, the eyes of the body, open onto the outer world of matter; the inner eye, the eye of the soul, opens onto the vast inner regions of spirit. All that the outer eyes see is subject to change, decay and death. The inner eye is equipped with the capacity to see the Supreme Being and the everlasting abode of Truth.[2] Kabir says, "That which is visible is perishable; contemplate on Him who is invisible. When you turn the key to the tenth door, then you will have the darshan of the Merciful One."[3]

To open the inner gate is not easy. Mind and soul are fully engrossed in the outer world. The soul, tied to the mind, is a captive in the cage of the physical body. It is unaware of its origin, its home, and the abiding bliss that awaits it within. Kabir says that the wife—soul—is involved in the nine houses of the external world and therefore cannot reach her Husband's abode, which is the tenth house within.[4]

---

1. Matt. 7:13-14.
2. Prophet Isaiah in the Old Testament also says: "And I will bring the blind by a way that they know not; I will lead them in paths that they have not known: I will make darkness light before them, and crooked things straight. These things will I do unto them, and not forsake them" (Isa. 42:16).
3. A.G., *Gauri, Bawan Akhari*, Kabirji, p.341.
4. A.G., *Gauri*, Kabirji, p.339.

When the inner eye opens, the devotee enters a world of light and spiritual beauty unequalled by anything belonging to the outer world of matter. Christ refers to the opening of the inner eye when he says: "If therefore thine eye be single, thy whole body shall be full of light."[1] Opening the single eye, the third eye or the door at the eye center is the first step on the path of self-realization. The true form of the soul is pure light; thus when the soul vacates the nine portals of the body and comes to the eye center, it will be in its own form or 'body'— "full of light."

The most important step in spiritual practice, then, is to control the mind and consciousness, which are running through the nine portals into the outer world. Kabir says: "On the ninth day[2] control the nine doors, put a dam across the flowing currents of the mind, become oblivious to all objects of attachment and avarice; thus live beyond ages and eons and taste the fruit of immortality."[3]

Guru Amar Das, referring to the eye center, says: "Stop the mind from running out through the nine portals, open the tenth which will lead you to your true home. There the divine melody rings day and night, and it is through the instruction of a Master that you can hear it."[4]

The Name of the Nameless One

Although Kabir has declared in unambiguous terms that his Lord, his Ram, is not an incarnation, some later commentators of his works and some modern scholars at times maintain that Kabir was a devotee of the well-known mythological figure, Ramchandra, the incarnation of Lord Vishnu. Vishwanath Singh, King of Rewa, 1813–1854, in his annotation of the *Bijak,* at places suggests that Kabir's Ram is not the formless Supreme Power, but the incarnation Ram. Similarly, when Kabir talks of Nam, Ram Nam or the Lord's Name, it is inter-

1. Matt. 6:22.
2. The poem is based on the days of the fortnight, each stanza for a different day.
3. A.G., *Thinti*, Kabirji, p.343.
4. A.G., *Majh*, M.3, p.124.

preted either as the name of King Ramchandra, or as one of the many names which people repeat orally or with a rosary. A sect of sadhus, claiming to be direct spiritual descendants of Kabir, even imprint the word *Ram* on their dress and often on their face and body.

Namdev, Beni, Kabir, Ravidas, Guru Nanak and his brilliant successors, as well as Dadu, Dariya, Paltu and other Saints have addressed God with many names, mostly adopting the names then prevalent among the devotees of the different orders. Not aligning themselves with any particular faith or mythology, they have used the various appellations of God to convey the idea of the One Supreme Being. Guru Nanak says, "I adore all Thy names."[1]

Guru Gobind Singh, in *Jap Sahib,* addresses God with over a thousand names, indicating that devotees, out of their love, worship Him with many names. Yet he clearly says that the Lord has no name: "I bow to the Nameless One."[2] And Guru Nanak explains that the Name the Saints talk of is beyond the reach of mind and the senses: "Invisible and imperceptible is the boundless Name."[3]

Kabir has described Nam or Ram Nam as a thing beyond the comprehension of mind and the reach of senses. Nam cannot be conveyed in words and yet it can be seen and realized:

> Is there anyone who can tell me of the Lord's Name, anyone who can bring to my view that unique thing which is invisible? All talk endlessly about his Name, but no one knows its profound secret. Outward talk and show is meaningless; he alone can give me joy and peace who himself sees, experiences and then reveals the Name. The true Name, O Kabir, cannot be conveyed through spoken words. Without himself realizing the Name, who can ever know its secret?[4]

1. Literally, 'I sacrifice myself to all the names you have'. A.G., *Basant,* M.1, p.1168.
2. Dassam Granth, *Jap,* p.1:4.
3. A.G., *Maru,* M.1, pp.1041-1042.
4. *K.G.,* p.120:218.

Persian mystics also say that Nam is not a thing of this material world, it is spiritual and divine; in fact, it is not different from the Lord himself: "Between the Name and the Named One, there is no difference."[1] "If you long to see the True One, dwell in his Name, for realizing the Name is realizing God."[2]

Saint Paltu says that one who wants to obtain the Name should remember that God has no name. His Name cannot be written or spoken; it cannot be reduced to any alphabet. If the seeker inquires about its form, it is formless; like wind it has no shape or outline. Yet the Saints see that Nam with their inner eye.[3]

As against the various names which can be written and spoken, which change with time and language, Kabir refers to the Nam that cannot be written and spoken as Sat Nam, 'the true Name'. The true Name that Saints extol is imperishable and changeless, not bound by the laws of time and space. Kabir says: "This is the Satguru's message: Sat Nam is the real essence of His being, it is the bearer of the tidings of your liberation.[4] Friends, listen to this Name with true devotion."[5]

This Nam is the primal Name, the original Name, the supreme power of the Lord himself. The various names that are prevalent in the world will not lead the soul to its home; it is only the practice of this primal Name that can do so. In the words of Kabir: There are a million names in the world, but not one of them leads to freedom;[6] the mystic primordial Name, few know how to repeat.[7]

It is only the inner practice of Nam that leads to salvation. Guru Ravidas confirms this when referring to Kabir: "Through

---

1. Hazrat Muinuddin Chishti.
2. Maulana Rum.
3. *Paltu Sahib ki Bani*, II:60, *Arill* 2 (hereafter cited as *Paltu Sahib*).
4. The Bible says that the Lord's chosen one—the one authorized to preach and convey His message—comes with 'the good tidings' of Nam, which brings liberation from bondage to the world: "The Spirit of the Lord God is upon me; because the Lord hath anointed me to preach good tidings unto the meek; he hath sent me ... to proclaim liberty to the captives, and the opening of the prison to them that are bound" (Isa. 61:1).
5. *K.S.S.*, p.87:47.
6. "Neither is there salvation in any other: for there is none other name under heaven given among men, whereby we must be saved" (Acts 4:12).
7. *K.S.S.*, p.84:5.

God's Name Kabir became renowned and tore to shreds the records of past lives."[1] All Saints have praised and advocated the practice of this primal Name; their message has always been the message of Nam. Guru Arjan Dev says: "In the house of Nanak, there is only Nam."[2]

The path of the Saints is the path of Nam; they cherish Nam, they relish Nam and they long to be one with Nam: "Parched earth longs for water, devotion craves an abode in the devotee's heart; Kabir has lost all cravings for the world, he longs only for Nam."[3]

Saints have described Nam as the creative power of the Lord. The idea of *adi nam*—the primordial Name—of Kabir, Guru Nanak and other Saints, implies that before the creation, Nam originally existed with God; in other words, Nam was with God, Nam was and is God. Guru Nanak says: "Whatever has been created has been created by Thy Name; there is no place empty of Thy Name."[4]

Guru Amar Das, referring to the creative power of Nam, says: "From Nam everything came into being, but without Satguru Nam cannot be realized."[5] Thus Nam has created the entire perceptible world, the world of matter, the astral and the causal worlds. Having created it, Nam also sustains and supports the entire creation. Guru Arjan Dev expresses the sustaining force of Nam in one of his most beautiful and popular compositions, the *Sukhmani*:

> Nam is the support of all beings,
> Nam is the support of all realms, high and low,
> Nam is the support of the skies and the underworlds,
> Nam is the support of all forms,
> Nam is the support of all continents and worlds;
> By listening to Nam one attains liberation.[6]

---

1. A.G., *Asa*, Ravidasji, p.487.
2. A.G., *Bhairau*, M.5, p.1136.
3. *K.S.S.*, p.23:29.
4. A.G., *Japji*, M.1, p.4:19.
5. A.G., *Suhi*, M.3, p.753.
6. A.G., *Gauri Sukhmani*, M.5, p.284.

A Persian mystic says: "Had the Nameless One not turned himself toward manifestation, the sound of Nam would not have emanated and the creation would not have come into being."

Saints and mystics do not altogether reject the written or spoken names of God. On the physical level, these spoken names have their importance insofar as they help in the initial stages of concentration and withdrawal of mind and soul from the physical body, as will be discussed later. But the Name that leads to salvation is not a written or spoken word, nor can it be seen and felt by the physical senses.

Nam, according to Saints, is of two types—one that can be written, spoken and read; the other, unwritten and unspoken. The written names can be in different languages and scripts, and attempt to describe one or more qualities of the Named One. But the unwritten Name neither belongs to any language nor can it be reproduced by any physical means.

In one of his poems, Swamiji explains the difference between the two types of 'name':

> I now explain the details of Nam, O brother, and its two aspects. I praise them as the alphabetic (*varnatmak*) name and the sonorous (*dhunatmak*) Name. What can be spoken and written is alphabetic or lettered; it is called Varnatmak Nam. This spoken name is the indicator of the Sound or Dhunatmak Nam, but without a Guru it is not fruitful. If you come in contact with a Master who is adept in the practice of Sound, then your soul through the Sound will merge into the source of Sound. . . . All spoken names are within the Varnatmak, but through their practice the Named One—the Dhunatmak—is met."[1]

Kabir also distinguishes between the lettered and unlettered names: "The fifty-two letters will perish. The true letter (Nam)

---

1. *S.B.*, p.95.

is not among them. Where there is speech, there will letters and words be; but where there is no speech and thought, there even the mind does not exist."[1]

Commenting on the holy scriptures, Kabir again emphasizes that the true Name, the unwritten letter, cannot be contained in any scripture: "The qazi expounds the holy Koran; the pundit, the Vedas and the Puranas. But that letter cannot be seen in them, for it has neither shape nor form."[2]

Some philosophies regard *akshar*, 'letter', as indestructible, for in some form or the other the spoken word has and will always be in the world. But Saints say that the alphabets which are called imperishable are not actually so; their form and their phonetic sound change from time to time. The true Nam is eternal as well as constant, it never undergoes a change and there is no agency in the entire creation that can effect a change in it. Describing Nam, Kabir says: "Beyond all words (*kshar*) and beyond all letters (*akshar*) is the Nam I speak of. I have brought with me the original Word (*shabd*) in this transient world."[3]

Kabir describes the Name of God as indivisible, permanent and indestructible; except Nam, everything is perishable—all heavens and astral worlds, all continents—and even the domain of Brahm (Brahmand) is subject to destruction.[4]

The Name of the Lord referred to by the Jewish mystics is not a written or spoken word; it is an everlasting power: "Thy word is true from the beginning: and every one of thy righteous judgments endureth for ever."[5] "His name shall endure for ever."[6] "Thy name, O Lord, endureth for ever; and thy memorial, O Lord, throughout all generations."[7] The Prophet Isaiah declares: "The grass withereth, the flower fadeth: but the word of our God shall stand for ever."[8] St. Peter echoes

---

1. A.G., *Gauri, Bawan Akhari*, Kabirji, p.340.
2. *K.S.*, I:72:29.
3. *K.S.*, II:60:25.
4. *K.S.*, II:89:2.
5. Ps. 119:160.
6. Ps. 72:17.
7. Ps. 135:13.
8. Isa. 40:8.

the same thought when he says: "The grass withereth, and the flower thereof falleth away: But the word of the Lord endureth for ever."[1]

Nam is the only truth in the world; all else—whether it be speaking, listening, acting, thinking or analyzing—is false, for it is bound to perish.[2] All scriptures, religious formalities, rituals and all external practices have been changing with time and are under the almost imperceptible influence of social, political, economic and physical conditions. The present formalism and ways of worship of all religions have gone through a process of evolution and will continue this trend of gradual change. But the method of practice on the path of Nam has always been the same, for it is an inner process, a spiritual experience, which at all times will be the same for whoever goes within and joins his consciousness with that power.

Whatever is subject to change, to decay and death, whatever is subject to the laws of time and space has been described by Saints as imperfect. In the words of Kabir, those who hold onto the imperfect names will come to the world again and again; those who merge into the perfect Name will attain the state of perfection. Never again will they come and go who realize the secret of the true Name.[3]

Guru Arjan Dev describes the practice of Nam as the highest form of worship: "Men study Vedas and scriptures in order to swim across the ocean of existence, they undertake many acts of piety, many rituals; but the practice of Nam is above them all."[4]

Shabd, the melody of Nam

Saints have identified Nam with Shabd, the divine word or melody. In the Adi Granth, where the entire creation is described as having come into being through Nam and that all that is created, has been created by Nam, it is also clearly stated that Shabd created the entire universe: "Through Shabd

1. 1 Pet. 1:24-25.
2. *K.S.*, II:107.
3. *K.S.*, II:108.
4. A.G., *Asa*, M.5, p.405.

emanates the creation, through Shabd it ends in dissolution, and through Shabd again it comes into being."[1] Shams-i-Tabriz says: "From the Sound (Word) the entire creation came into being, all light emanated from it."

In the Bible the Word is described as the creative power of God and, at the same time, it is identified with God: "In the beginning was the Word, and the Word was with God, and the Word was God. The same was in the beginning with God. All things were made by him; and without him was not any thing made that was made."[2]

Dariya Sahib of Bihar expresses the idea of Shabd as the creative power thus: "From Shabd came earth, from Shabd the firmament; through devotion to Shabd the light of divine love descends into the heart. Shabd created the entire world, Shabd has bound together diverse and vast regions."[3]

In some of his poems Swamiji declares that Shabd created the three worlds: Shabd created the physical, astral and causal regions; from Shabd came forth the regions of Sat Lok; Shabd resounds in every vessel (body), nothing is empty of Shabd.[4]

In one of his poems Kabir says that Shabd is the Creator or Lord of all: "Says Kabir, realize the Shabd, O brother, for Shabd is the Creator himself."[5]

Swamiji further adds: "When the Shabd was hidden, it was the Nameless One; when it became manifest, it became the Name.... Shabd is the cause of all, Shabd is the effect too.... Shabd is deathless, Shabd is everlasting; Shabd is changeless, Shabd is eternal. The Master is Shabd; so too is the disciple. Without Shabd all hopes of liberation are false hopes."[6]

Like the Lord, Nam or Shabd permeates every being. Kabir says that the invaluable diamond of Nam abides in each and

---

1. Guru Amar Das, A.G., *Majh*, M.3, p.117.
2. John 1:1-3. King Solomon in his prayer to the Lord says: "God of my fathers, Lord of mercy, you who have made all things by your word" (Wisd. 9:1; the New American Bible). The Bible further says: "By the word of the Lord were the heavens made" (Ps. 33:6); "The worlds were framed by the word of God, so that things which are seen were not made of things which do appear" (Heb. 11:3).
3. *Dariya Sagar*, p.50.
4. *S.B.*, p.88:2.
5. *Gyan Gudri aur Rekhta*, p.24:53.
6. *S.B.*, p.88:3.

every vessel.[1] At the same time he points out the 'sound' aspect
of Nam when he says: "When the soul listens to Nam with its
inner ear, only then does it become a pure swan and attain
liberation."[2]

Shabd and Nam, both synonyms for the same Truth, are
the most important and yet the most misunderstood aspects of
Sant Mat. Being a power that can only be grasped or comprehended through actual inner realization, Shabd or Nam can
neither be fully explained in any spoken language nor understood on the mental or intellectual level.

Shabd or Nam is the all-pervading energy or power of the
Supreme Being, which is contacted by the devotee in the form
of a divine melody. It is the *kalam, kalma* (word) or *kun* (order)
of the Koran; the Word, Name, logos, holy ghost, holy spirit
or living water of the Bible; the sonorous light of the Bud-
dhists; the *sarosh* (sound) of the Zoroastrians; the *akashvani*
(voice or music of the sky) or *dev vani* (celestial voice) of the
Hindu scriptures; the *divya dhwani* (divine sound) of the Jains;
and the *shabd* (word, sound), *nad* (melody), *anhat nad* (unstruck melody), *anhad nad* (limitless melody), *bani* (voice) and
hukam (order, divine command) of the Saints. Muslim mystics
have called it *nida-i-asmani* (call of the firmament), *nida-i-
sultani* (call of the Emperor), *bang-i-asmani* (sound of the skies)
and *kalam-i-ilahi* (word of God). Kabir and some Saints have
also described Shabd or Nam as the invisible string along
which the soul can climb back to the Lord.

All Saints and perfect Masters have taught the method of
Shabd practice as the way to God-realization. Swamiji, ex-
plaining that the path of Shabd is as old as the creation and not
a new philosophy laid down by any particular mystic of recent
times, says:

> Every Saint has propounded the practice of Shabd
> as the essence of all spiritual efforts. Without Shabd
> there is no release from the bondage of birth and

---

1. *K.S.*, II:106:22:1.
2. *K.S.*, II:108.

death. Shabd is profound and unfathomable; without Shabd one cannot obtain the state of everlasting bliss. Without Shabd no one can become perfect; without Shabd all means of realization are futile. . . . Kabir, the perfect mystic, sang the praises of Shabd. Nanak, the great Saint, expounded the practice of Shabd, and the resolute Tulsi also showed the path of Shabd.[1]

Though an all-pervading force, Shabd or Nam cannot be contacted by a seeker without the help and guidance, in fact, initiation by a perfect Master. The key to Shabd has been handed over to the Saints by the Lord himself; only they can open the lock to the inner gate of Shabd. But scholars and intellectuals, without trying to find a Master, have endeavored to understand Shabd or Nam on the mental level of erudition, research and analysis. The conclusions they have arrived at are invariably limited to the physical plane.

Thus, scholars have taken Nam to be the written words, and Shabd to be the music or melody produced by various instruments. But, as the Saints have repeatedly declared, Shabd or Nam created the entire universe, the inner worlds, the region of Brahm and even the realms beyond the reach of Brahm. Evidently, the power which created and which is sustaining the entire creation cannot be a name confined to any language, nor can it be a sound produced by a musical instrument.

Shabd or Nam has also been called *anhat shabd* and *anhad shabd* by the Saints. 'Anhat Shabd' is the unstruck sound or that sound which is not the outcome of an impact or collision of two objects. It is not produced by any physical action, nor is it the effect of any material cause. 'Anhad Shabd' or the unlimited sound is the sound which has no limits and which comes from beyond the limits of matter, mind and maya. As against the Varnatmak Nam or the lettered name, Shabd is the Dhunatmak Nam or sound current, the unlettered Name.

---

1. *S.B.*, p.89:3.

67

Guru Ravidas says that all dissertations, scriptures and the injunctions of the Vedas are within the thirty-four letters of the alphabet; sages like Vyas, after deep thought, declared that the highest truth is nothing but the Name of God.[1] In another poem Guru Ravidas says: "O Lord of all gods, Thy Saints adore Thee by sitting within their own heart and they speak to Thee without tongue."[2]

Kabir also declares that the Shabd or Word that the Saints speak of is not a written or spoken word: "Beyond words is the Word (Shabd), that Word of ours. O Kabir, when one eliminates his I-ness under the Master's guidance, only the Word remains."[3]

Saints worship the Lord through Shabd or Nam and teach the method of this worship to their disciples. They warn seekers that the various forms of worship undertaken according to one's own mind neither lead to the Lord nor are acceptable to Him. Shabd comes from the Lord; it is a direct link between Him and the soul, the royal road leading to the abode of eternal beatitude. Through the practice of Shabd, mind becomes pure, and the soul, divested of all coverings, merges into the divine melody of Shabd which leads the soul to its source—God. Saints say that the practice of Shabd is the worship acceptable to the Lord. They who attach themselves to the Shabd within become pure, spotless and true; they are then fit to become one with the Supreme Being.

Guru Amar Das says that except for the practice of Nam or Shabd, there is no other worship of the Lord; people trying to worship Him (through other means) are only wandering in delusion. The *gurumukh* realizes his true self by absorbing himself in the Lord's Name. The Immaculate One himself makes us worship Him through the Shabd imparted by the Guru, and this worship is acceptable to Him. Men worship Him but know not the true way of worship; they only accumulate dirt and stains by involving themselves in diverse practices. But the

---

1. A.G., *Sorath*, Ravidasji, p.658.
2. *Raidasji ki Bani*, p.36:83.
3. *K.S.*, I:59.

68

gurumukh knows how to worship God and he worships Him with a spirit of complete surrender in his heart.[1]

Christ makes it clear that the true worship of the Lord is the worship of the Word, which he describes as the Spirit; but, he says, men worship God according to their own beliefs and do not realize what they are worshipping: "Ye worship ye know not what: we know what we worship.... But the hour cometh, and now is, when the true worshippers shall worship the Father in spirit and in truth.... God is a Spirit: and they that worship him must worship him in spirit and in truth."[2]

Kabir also says that the world tries to worship the Lord but knows not the way of that worship which leads to Him: "The worship that the Lord approves not, in that worship the world is entangled. The worship that is dear to his heart, these worshippers know not."[3]

Shabd or Nam is contacted by the soul, not by the senses or the intellect. It is visible and audible only to the eye and to the ear of the soul. In the physical world the soul is dependent on the senses of action and perception for feeling and experiencing the world of matter. On the spiritual plane, soul is not bound by the senses, it is equipped with its own power of perception. The soul has the faculty to hear and to see; the former is called by Saints *surat* and the latter, *nirat*.

Saints have clearly explained that the inner experience of Shabd or Nam is not associated with the physical world, nor is it subject to the laws that govern it. Kabir says that the state he talks of can be fully understood only by a realized soul, not by the ignorant ones of the world. It is a realm one reaches without feet and where one acts without hands, where one eats without mouth—enjoys inner bliss without the senses—and moves freely without feet, and without tongue sings God's praises. Though firmly seated at one place, the devotee is free to roam in all directions and then return to the body. Without rhyme and voice he sings, without drum he produces resound-

---

1. A.G., *Ramkali*, M.3, p.910.
2. John 4:22-24.
3. *K.G.*, p.136:275.

ing beats. In that region, without tone and sound the unstruck melody reverberates, and there the Divine Being revels in bliss. There the devotee dances without steps and without a dancing attire; and though alone, he is always in company.[1] Kabir, the Lord's slave, submits that he has seen and experienced this state of bliss which only a true devotee will realize.[2]

Guru Angad also points out that Nam or Shabd is a subject beyond the material world. It cannot be seen by the physical eyes or heard by the physical ears, nor can one reach the abode of Nam by the aid of the physical feet and hands:

> See without eyes, hear without ears,
> Walk without feet, work without hands,
> Speak without tongue—
> Thus while living, die
> And realize the Order, O Nanak:
> Then alone the Beloved you'll meet.[3]

Dadu echoes the same thought when he declares:

> Without ears I hear everything,
> Without eyes I see one and all,
> Without mouth and tongue I speak;
> Such is the wonder that Dadu sees.[4]

And Maulana Rum's observations are similar to those of the Indian mystics:

> I fly without wings,
> I journey without feet,
> Without mouth or teeth I eat sugar,[5]
> With eyes closed I behold the inner worlds.

---

1. Though sitting alone in meditation, the devotee is in the company of the Divine Being within.
2. *K.G.*, p.105:159.
3. A.G., *Majh ki Var*, M.2, p.139. Guru Nanak and many Saints have identified *hukam* (command, order or cosmic law) with Shabd. See Kabir's poem, "Merging in His Order."
4. *Dadudayal*, p.66:199.
5. Nectar of divine bliss.

The light of Shabd

Thus the Nam of the Saints is an unspoken word, its sound a soundless melody; yet on the level of spiritual experience it is as much a reality as any word or sound of the physical world. As stated above, Shabd or Nam, according to the Saints, is seen without the physical eyes and heard without the physical ears. Almost all mystics have emphasized that Shabd or Nam has both sound and light in it. Kabir says that the soul can see only through the light of Shabd, without Shabd it is blind: "Without Shabd the soul is blind, it knows not where to go; till it reaches the door of Shabd, it wanders endlessly."[1]

Guru Amar Das says that without Shabd there is darkness within, neither can one find the Article (God) nor be rid of the rounds (of birth and death).[2] Guru Nanak also refers to the light of Shabd:

> My mind is detached, it is absorbed in a state of
> desirelessness, for it is pierced by Shabd. Within is
> the light and therein the Voice; (through it) I am
> attuned to the true Lord.[3]

In one of his poems Kabir, calling upon the soul to proceed to the inner region of Truth, says: "The firmament where He abides is flooded with the light of Shabd; there the Shabd blooms in its white resplendence and there the pure souls revel in bliss."[4] The same idea is further elucidated by him thus:

> Where the Shabd reverberates in resounding melo-
> dy, there I contacted its light and met my Master.[5]
> ...Says Kabir: One who churns his body finds the
> light of Shabd, O friend.[6]

---

1. *K.S.S.*, p.93:15.
2. A.G., *Majh*, M.3, p.124.
3. A.G., *Sorath*, M.1, p.634.
4. *K.S.*, II:13:28.
5. *K.S.*, I:83:15.
6. *Gyan Gudri, Jhulna* 8.

Other Saints also confirm that Nam or Shabd has both sound and light. Namdev says: "Where the effulgent light is seen, there rings the boundless Shabd. . . . The unstruck melody has the brilliance of the sun."[1] In another poem, also included in the Adi Granth, Saint Ravidas says:

> Thy Name is the lamp, Thy Name the wick,
> Thy Name is the oil which I pour therein.
> Of Thy Name I have kindled the light,
> With its illumination my entire home is bright.[2]

The Word is a guide to the soul on the spiritual journey; it lights the soul's inner path: "Thy word is a lamp unto my feet, and a light unto my path."[3]

Dariya Sahib of Marwar[4] says: Dariya met the perfect Master who revealed the refulgence of Nam.[5] Dariya, the sound is emitting light; its beauty I have no words to describe; all praise to the devotees who stay absorbed in it.[6] Dariya, where the melody is emitting brilliant light, there I have made my permanent home; there I have met the supreme power; there this slave sees the Lord.[7]

Swamiji, describing the significance of Shabd on the spiritual path, says that the entire world without Shabd is blind; Shabd is the sun and the moon in the inner regions; Shabd illuminates the inner worlds.[8] They whose inner being is illuminated by Shabd, they who have adopted Shabd as their succor, deserve all praise.[9]

The five melodies

Shabd, Nam or divine melody, the spiritual current emanating from the Supreme Being, coming down through all the spiri-

1. A.G., *Sorath*, Namdevji, p.657.
2. A.G., *Dhanasari*, Ravidasji, p.694, trans. Dr. K.N. Upadhyaya in *Guru Ravidas*.
3. Ps. 119:105.
4. Marwar is the name of part of Rajasthan.
5. *Dariya Sahib Marwarwale ki Bani*, p.2:20.
6. Ibid., p.13:17.
7. Ibid., p.13:19.
8. *S.B.*, p.91:5.
9. *S.B.*, p.90:4.

tual worlds and pervading the entire creation, is one. Yet, in its descent from the highest region of divine purity and perfection, it responds to the characteristics of the different realms it passes through, and is heard by the disciple as a different melody at different levels of consciousness. Just as the inner regions are five, Shabd—though essentially the same—is heard as five different sounds. In view of this aspect of Shabd, Saints have described the unstruck sound as *panch shabd* or 'the five melodies'.

Hafiz, the Persian mystic, referring to the five melodies of Shabd, says: "Be silent and listen to the five melodies that are emanating from the sky." He also makes it clear that the sky he speaks of is a very high spiritual region: "That sky is beyond the six (*chakras* of the body) and the seven skies."[1]

Saint Beni says that the way to the five melodies is through the center of the forehead, where the creator of the three worlds can also be met:

> In the forehead, surrounded by many jewels, is the
> lotus, within which is the lord of the three worlds.
> Here resound the five pure melodies of Shabd. Here
> undulates the divine whisk and reverberates the
> sound of conch with great resonance. With the
> knowledge given by the *gurumukh*, Beni smothers
> and annihilates the demons (passions and desires),
> and craves only for Thy Name.[2]

Guru Nanak also refers to the five melodies of the Anhad or boundless Shabd when describing the union of the soul with the True One: "My union is everlasting; my mind is now at rest; my home, the true temple, is adorned with bliss. The five melodies of Anhad Shabd resound: my Beloved has arrived at my home."[3]

Kabir, describing a true warrior, says that when the devotee conquers the five firmaments,[4] then only should he be looked

---

1. In Persian mythology the heavens or inner worlds are divided into seven skies.
2. A.G., *Ramkali*, Beniji, p.974.
3. A.G., *Suhi*, M.1, p.764.
4. Five inner regions.

on as a warrior who has fought the battle well. He gives his head (ego) and thus saves his head (soul); he reaches the presence of God and pays homage to Him.[1] And referring to the five melodies of the five regions, he says: "The five boundless Shabds ring in the company of the Supreme Being. O Thou pure, formless and absolute One, Kabir with devotion worships Thee."[2]

Guru Amar Das says: "Through the Guru's grace I am entranced by his love; with the sound of the five Shabds I will meet the Merciful One."[3] Guru Nanak says that the pure and unconnected ringing of the five Shabds is produced by the Lord himself and it is He who enables one to hear it.[4] Shams-i-Tabriz calls the five melodies 'the music in praise of the Lord' that rings day and night at His door; beyond the seventh sky resound the five melodies: if the seeker will leave his camp (body) within the six (chakras), he will hear it.

In a long poem urging the devotee to go within the mansion of his own body and see the Beloved, Kabir gives hints about the five inner regions, their respective lights and the five melodies of Shabd.[5] The melodies are ineffable; they can be experienced, but can be neither reproduced nor described. Saints have tried to give analogies for the inner melodies by describing them in terms of sounds produced by physical means in the world of matter. Kabir describes them as the melodies of the gong and conch, the drum and thunder, the *kingri* or *sarangi*—common stringed instruments—the flute and the bagpipe. Namdev, Beni, Guru Nanak, Dadu, Dariya, Paltu, Tulsi Sahib, Swamiji and many other Saints have also used these analogies in their works.

Although Shabd is within the body, it cannot be contacted in the world of matter. It is a divine power, a spiritual current emanating from the Supreme Father, and can be realized only by the soul. It can be experienced not within the nine portals of

---

1. *K.S.S.*, p.26:64.
2. A.G., *Bibhas Prabhati*, Kabirji, p.1350.
3. A.G., *Bhairau*, M.3, p.1128.
4. A.G., *Maru*, M.1, p.1040.
5. *K.S.*, I:65:22.

the body, but at the focal point of the soul, the gateway to the spiritual realms, called the eye center. In the words of Guru Amar Das, the devotee has to conduct a search within the city of his body through Shabd; only then will he obtain Nam, the bestower of all gifts.[1]

The search for Nam or Shabd cannot be undertaken by the seeker on his own. The method for going within, for contacting Shabd and for traveling on the inner path to God-realization is known only to the Saints. They hold the key to the gateway of salvation, and only they can connect the seeker's soul to the divine melody within.

He who holds the key

The key to the inner door is only with the spiritual adept, the perfect Master or Satguru, who has himself traveled through the inner regions and become one with the Absolute. Guru Amar Das says that the key is in the hands of the Satguru, the door cannot be unlocked by anyone else; through great good fortune one meets such a perfect Master.[2]

When Christ reveals his decision to appoint St. Peter as his successor, he declares: "And I will give unto thee the keys of the kingdom of heaven: and whatsoever thou shalt bind on earth shall be bound in heaven."[3]

'The key' is the method of meditation, of spiritual practice, which enables the seeker to go within, die while living—that is, vacate the physical body and withdraw his consciousness to the eye center—and enter the inner regions of divine bliss. Guru Angad Dev says that the Master himself is the key, and without him the door cannot be opened:

> Guru is the key; the cell of mind, covered over by the roof of the body, is secured with a heavy padlock. O Nanak, without the Master the mind's door cannot be opened, for none else has the key.[4]

1. A.G., *Ramkali*, M.3, p.910.
2. A.G., *Majh*, M.3, p.124.
3. Matt. 16:19.
4. A.G., *Sarang ki Var*, M.2, p.1237.

The Saints have called this point 'the granite gate', because
it is hard to open. But a seeker initiated by a perfect Master
learns to withdraw his attention or consciousness to the eye
center through spiritual practice and open 'the granite gate'.
Kabir says: "I sacrifice my entire being at the feet of my true
Master, who has applied the key and opened the lock within."[1]
And again:

> My Master has given me
> The key to the unyielding lock;
> Whenever I like, I open the door:
> Dressed in the dancing costume of love,
> I enter the town whenever I please,
> And I dance and dance in ecstasy.
> Says Kabir, Listen friends,
> I'll not come to this city again.[2]

Man tries to gain spiritual knowledge in the external world,
while the treasure lies within the body. Kabir says: The treasure is within, but man goes in its quest elsewhere and fails to
obtain the precious jewel. If he will seek in the company of an
adept who knows the secret, the treasure will become his.[3] He
adds: When he took the Master with him—the possessor of the
secret—the jewel was revealed, and with the Master's grace,
within moments he covered a path that was a million lives
long.[4]

Coming in contact with a perfect Master is, in fact, arriving
at the door to salvation. Guru Nanak says that the guru is himself the gate of liberation.[5] Saints have described the Master as
the key, the door and the way to the Lord, because only
through the Master can a seeker realize God. Christ also declares: "I am the way, the truth, and the life: no man cometh
unto the Father, but by me."[6] "I am the door: by me if any

1. *K.S.S.*, II:19.
2. *Town:* the inner regions; *city:* the physical world. *K.S.*, II:74:36
3. *K.S.S.*, p.5:59.
4. *K.S.S.*, p.5:60.
5. *A.G., Siri Rag,* M.1, p.62.
6. John 14:6.

man enter in, he shall be saved, and shall go in and out, and find pasture."[1]

Swamiji also calls the perfect Master the bearer of the key to inner mansions, and also 'the key': Open the door of Word by holding onto Guru, the key.[2]... Hold on, O friend, to Guru the key.[3]...I met Satguru, the merciful one, he applied the key and opened the door of the mole within.[4]...Satguru gave the key and the lock opened.[5]

Even in worldly matters, one needs a teacher or a guide in order to acquire proficiency in any skill. From birth onwards, man goes on learning from others. He learns many things, first from his parents and relations, and then from friends, teachers and professors. The mother teaches him to eat, sit and walk, and he learns to speak from his parents. If a child is born deaf, he also remains dumb—he cannot learn by himself to reproduce and modulate sounds to form words because he cannot hear others; his channel for learning how to speak is blocked by deafness. In other words, the physical link of parents or others who speak is necessary if a child is to develop his powers of speech.

Spirituality is a complex science, a method of practice in which a teacher is indispensable. It is an intricate path going through the maze of innumerable inner worlds, and an adept guide is needed at every step. Guru Amar Das says that the whole world wanders in delusion, and men following the dictates of their own mind come to grief.[6] Kabir says:

> Many study, ponder and labor to the point of death;
> many undertake varied practices, such as yoga,
> yajna and penances—all in vain. O Kabir, without
> a perfect Master they cannot obtain the Lord,
> though a million ways they adopt.[7]

---

1. John 10:9. Christ refers to his disciples as 'sheep' who can find pasture only by going within through him, the shepherd or Master.
2. S.B., p.151:16:13.
3. S.B., p.169:28:7.
4. S.B., p.298:11:7.
5. S.B., p.313:6:2.
6. A.G., Asa, M.3, p.425.
7. K.S.S., p.11:124.

Persian mystics like Rumi, Shams-i-Tabriz and Hafiz repeatedly warn the seeker against entering the inner realms without a perfect guide. Rumi says: "Seek a perfect Master, for without the Master this journey abounds with perils, lures, and pitfalls.....If you are without the protecting hand of the Master over your head, you will be bewildered and led astray by the voice of Satan." Hafiz echoes the same thought: "Never, never undertake this hazardous journey without the guidance of a perfect Master, for without such a guide you will be lost in the perilous darkness of the way."

Guru Angad Dev emphatically states that without a Master the inner darkness cannot dissolve, not even if the light of countless moons and suns were to shine simultaneously: "If a hundred moons were to rise and a thousand suns to shine, despite their dazzling light there would be utter darkness without the Guru."[1] Kabir says that if eight million, four hundred thousand moons were to shine to dispel the darkness of the night, even then the one without a Master would not be able to see.[2]

The perfect Master removes the darkness of ignorance, of maya and worldliness. It is only through him that the seeker realizes the omnipresence of God. Guru Nanak says: "On meeting the Satguru, darkness is dispelled and wherever one looks one sees the Lord permeating all."[3]

The state of highest attainment, God-realization, is obtained only through a perfect Master. Whoever has realized Him, has done so through the guidance of a spiritual adept. Guru Amar Das says: "Nama the calico printer[4] and Kabir the weaver attained the supreme state only through a perfect Master."[5]

Maulana Rum, referring to his Master, Shams-i-Tabriz, says the same thing: "This ordinary *maulvi* could never have become Maulana Rum had he not become a slave of Shams-i-Tabriz." And Kabir says that all spiritual accomplishment of

---

1. A.G., *Asa*, M.2, p.463.
2. *K.S.S.*, p.16:10.
3. A.G., *Ramkali*, M.1, p.877.
4. Saint Namdev, who was a calico printer by profession.
5. A.G., *Siri Rag*, M.3, p.67.

the devotee is the result of his Satguru's grace: "I have neither achieved nor could have achieved anything, nor had I the power to do so. Whatever is done, is done by my Master and that is how poor Kabir has become *kabir*."[1]

He who walks on the razor's edge

People tend to look on any holy man, mendicant, hermit, recluse or sadhu as a person competent to initiate a seeker into the path of spiritual realization. Such 'holy men' are mostly religious high priests, learned men, family priests or yogis and ascetics of different orders. They adopt outer garbs of holiness, such as a yellow, ochre, green, blue, white or black dress, wear beads of different types around the neck and wrists, carry rosaries, keep matted hair, smear ash over their body and put different marks on their forehead, arms and chest. Some go naked and eat from their hands; some wear a loincloth. Some carry a begging bowl, some a musical instrument, and some a spear, trident or mace.

Saints have always been critical of such ostentatious piety. The truly God-intoxicated soul, the realized one, prefers to live and dress like an ordinary person. Kabir says that there is a vast difference between a true Saint and the ordinary sadhus; the Saint is like a mango tree that bears ambrosial fruits, the sadhus are like the babool tree, each branch laden with piercing thorns.[2]

Referring to such pretenders to devotion, Kabir says: By wearing beads, putting holy marks on the forehead and shaving the head, no one becomes a devotee; such men go the way of the world and waste their human birth.[3] If by shaving the head one could obtain the Lord, let everyone get his head shaved; but alas, says Kabir, by repeated shearing, the sheep does not reach heaven.[4] The sheep that wears the skin of a lion will still walk with a sheep's gait; its voice will be woeful like that

1. *K.S.S.*, p.103:4. *Kabir* literally means 'the great'; here *kabir* at the end of the line has been used as an adjective.
2. *K.S.S.*, p.122:64.
3. *K.S.S.*, p.127:6.
4. *K.S.S.*, p.127:8.

of a jackal, and in the end it will become a prey to wild dogs.[1]

Guru Amar Das also says: "He who does not realize his true self and pretends to be holy, through his hypocrisy and pretension he will not be spared by Yama; he will be seized and put to shame."[2]

Kabir says that a blind man cannot guide a seeker through the intricate and thorny paths of a jungle; contact with filth cannot make one fragrant; a counterfeit coin cannot be exchanged for goods of immaculate quality; an inept swimmer cannot save others from drowning; a wolf cannot protect a fold of sheep; so also an imperfect guru, the so-called adept, who is devoid of inner realization and craves for worldly pleasures, prestige and gains, cannot lead the disciple on the inner path of salvation. He adds:

> He whose guru craves for worldliness,
> That disciple would also hunger for the world.
> Kabir, how can stains be removed
> If you wash the cloth with mud?[3]

As against this, says Kabir, a perfect Master, a Satguru, is one whose inner vision is open and who can open the disciple's eye, enabling him to see the Lord; he is the soap that removes the dirt accumulated for ages on the disciple's mind; he bestows the real coin of Nam, which can be exchanged in the highest Treasury for the precious jewel of divine love; he has himself crossed the turbulent ocean of the world and has the power to carry across a million sinners in his arms; he is the finest sandalwood tree, whose company makes ordinary trees—disciples—fragrant; though living in the world, he is above it—all the wealth of the world, all the pageantry of maya, lies at his feet, but he longs only for the Lord. He gives his disciples the nectar of inner joy before which the world and its pleasures appear as trivial as dross.

1. K.S.S., p.128:19.
2. A.G., Ramkali, M.3, p.910. Yama: The lord of death, who takes charge of souls at the time of death.
3. K.S.S., p.14:19.

According to Kabir, it is easy for a man to call himself a Saint, but to become a Saint is to walk on a sword's sharp blade: one unsteady step and he is bound to fall.[1] The real Saint, always steady and composed, walks with ease and grace and reaches the opposite shore. The gait of the worldly is not the gait of the Saint; do not call those pretenders 'Saints' whose affected gait is just a ruse to cover their worldliness. The true Saint is not an erudite scholar, for his knowledge is not that of books; nor is he proud of his spiritual attainment. He is selfless and truthful; he has regard for all and loves all beings.[2] Kabir sums up the qualities of the Saints thus:

> He has ill will for none;
> He has overcome all desires;
> Only the Lord does he love;
> He is far above the reach
> Of pleasures and passions;
> Such, O Kabir, are the traits
> Of a true Saint.[3]

Seeing him is seeing the Lord

In Sant Mat the Master or Satguru is that perfect Saint who comes from the Lord or who has reached Him and become one with Him. Only that spiritual adept can take others to the Lord, who has himself reached the highest state of consciousness, the highest spiritual region. In the realm of Truth—an immutable and everlasting state—only God exists, and the soul that reaches there invariably becomes one with God. Saints have described such a perfect Master as the doorway to God, the path to God, and God in human form.

Kabir says: Brother, he alone is the Saint or Satguru who enables others to see with their own eyes the Invisible One.[4] That Master I cherish, O friend, who fills the cup of true Name,

---

1. Indian Saints use the analogy of walking on the sharp edge of a sword to describe the difficult path of devotion that enables one to cross the abyss of this world of phenomena.
2. K.S.S., pp.117-124.
3. K.G., p.39:1.
4. K.S., I:3:5.

who himself drinks it and enables me to drink with joy...
who removes the veil from my eyes...and seeing whom, is seeing the Lord.[1] Christ conveys the same idea when he says:
"And he that seeth me seeth him that sent me."[2] "...he that
hath seen me hath seen the Father."[3]

Speaking about the perfect Master, Maulana Rum says:
"His hand is the hand of God, his eyes are radiant with God's
love." Kabir expresses the same thought in one of his couplets:
"When I met my Master, I met the Lord, for there is no differ-
ence between the two. In their thoughts, speech and actions,
Saints and the Lord are one."[4]

Guru Nanak states in the Adi Granth: "He whom the True
One likes, to him He grants all power and glory, and who is
there to interfere in His decision; God and Guru's form act as
one, and God loves the Guru, O Nanak."[5]

Saints say that worship of the perfect Master is worship of
God, to love the Satguru is to love the Lord, because the perfect Master and the Lord are one. Kabir says: The mirror of
the Formless One is the physical form of the Saints; if you long
to see the Invisible, see Him in the Saints.[6] They are the form
of the Formless himself, serve them with devotion and love. If
you want to see God in a form, look at a living Saint.[7]

In the face of a hostile crowd, Christ boldly declares: "I
and my Father are one."[8] The unity of God and the Master is
also one of the most important aspects of the teachings of the
Persian mystics. They are clear and emphatic in declaring that
the *murshid* (Master) and God are one. Maulana Rum says:
"If you accept the Master, then know that you have accepted
both God and the Prophet. Never look upon the Master as
separate from God, nor ever say that they are two. Realize that
God dwells in the Master; if you look at the Master as some-

---

1. *K.S.S.*, II:18:2.
2. John 12:45.
3. John 14:9.
4. *K.S.S.*, p.120:41.
5. A.G., *Maru*, M.1, p.1043.
6. *K.S.S.*, p.119:31.
7. *K.S.S.*, p.124:96.
8. John 10:30. Christ further says: "The Father is in me, and I in him" (John 10:38).

one different from the Lord, you will lose yourself and also the essence of spirituality. He who looks on the Master as different from the Lord is not a disciple, he is dead like a corpse."

Guru Nanak says that Satguru, like the Creator, is carefree; he has no fear of Yama, nor is he dependent on man. Whoever adores him becomes imperishable, and Kal cannot torment him. In the Guru the Lord has placed himself; Guru emancipates countless millions.[1] Swamiji also says: "Do not take the Master to be a man; he is the essence of the true Lord."[2] And he further explains that the living Master is as great as Kabir or any of the past spiritual adepts:

> He is Kabir, he is the true Name personified, recognize in him all the Saints. Your object will be achieved only through him; do not be led astray by delusion and pride.[3]

In the words of Maulana Rum: "The Master is Truth; like the Lord, he too is beyond the reach of senses. He instructs his disciples without opening his mouth." Guru Ravidas puts it in his simple and direct language: "He is the truly wise person who realizes that there is no difference between the Saint and the Eternal One."[4]

An anecdote connected with Kabir, and also included in *Anurag Sagar*,[5] brings out the oneness of the perfect Master and the Lord. When Rani Indramati, a disciple of Kabir, reached the Lord's abode, she was amazed to find Kabir presiding over that region of supreme bliss. She said, "Beloved Master, why did you keep yourself disguised in the physical world, and how did you manage to conceal your beauty and brilliance? Had you told me there that you are none other than

---

1. A.G., *Maru*, M.1, p.1024.
2. *S.B.*, p.140:12:3.
3. *S.B.*, p.140:12:8,9.
4. A.G., *Asa*, Ravidasji, p.486.
5. *Anurag Sagar*, believed to be written by Kabir, is a book of verse in the form of a dialogue between Kabir and his disciple Dharam Das. Modern scholars maintain that this book was written by Dharam Das and not Kabir, and can at best be described as the sayings of Kabir according to Dharam Das. There is a wide divergence of opinion among scholars with regard to the authenticity of some of the portions of *Anurag Sagar*.

the True Lord, I would have adored you as God; I would never have entertained the thought that you are a man and not God." Kabir replied that the physical world has not the power to bear even a millionth part of the brilliance of Sat Purush. And he added, "My child, had I revealed my true identity there, you would not have believed me. Now that you have realized the truth, your faith cannot be shaken by any power in all the three worlds."

Devotion to the Master, according to the mystics, is devotion to the Lord, for there is no difference between the two. Swamiji asks the disciple to always adore the Satguru because there is no deity or god equal to the perfect Master.[1] Radha Soami, the Supreme Being, adopts the human form of a perfect Master in order to awaken and emancipate souls.[2]

Guru Ram Das says: "I churned the sea of my body and discovered a unique truth—that Guru is God and God is Guru; says Nanak: There is no difference between the two."[3] And Kabir declares: "The Master and God are one; all else, O Kabir, is a reflection."[4]

The storehouse of radiance

The Master, necessary for the seeker in the physical world, is indispensable at every step of the disciple's inner journey. In the physical world he initiates the seeker into the path of spiritual practice, connects his soul to the Shabd or divine melody within and inspires love and devotion in his heart. Through his own personal example, careful guidance and spiritual power and magnetism, the Master helps the disciple to remain steadfast on the path, to attend to meditation and to face the tribulations of the world and the lures of the senses with courage and firmness.

In the inner spiritual worlds the Master's role is of great significance. He is constantly with the disciple in his Shabd form and leads him through the intricate maze of numerous

---

1. *S.B.*, p.133:2:1.
2. *S.B.*, p.6:2:1.
3. A.G., *Asa*, M.4, p.442.
4. *K.S.S.*, p.3:29.

paths, protecting him from the pitfalls placed at almost every step by the negative forces of mind and maya.

In his physical form the Master is the manifestation of Shabd, he is "the Word made flesh"[1]; in the inner spiritual regions his form is Shabd itself. The entire physical creation is perishable, and the physical body of the disciple, as also that of the Master, is subject to this law of the physical world. Although the physical body is not everlasting, the souls of both the disciple and the Master are eternal. The soul goes through the process of death, but itself never dies.

When the disciple vacates the nine portals of the body, he enters the inner regions in his real or spiritual form—the soul. The Master, who comes from Shabd, who has merged himself into Shabd, manifests in the inner realms in the form of Shabd. Guru Nanak says that the Master is Shabd and the disciple is the soul: "Shabd is the Guru, soul is the disciple of the melody (of Shabd)."[2]

Kabir refers to the Shabd form of the Master in some of his poems and declares that the Guru is Shabd and Shabd is the Guru. He describes the Satguru as the ship of Shabd, but adds that only a rare devotee realizes this secret.[3] "Adopt that Guru who is himself Shabd; all other gurus are false."[4] "The form of Shabd is Satguru—without origin and end; he is at the peak[5] of the body, have no doubts, O friend."[6]

Swamiji is a little more explicit when: "The Satguru's form is Shabd, he stays in the inner sky; your form, O disciple, is also spirit—in this form stay with the Guru within."[7] Identifying the perfect Master with Shabd, Kabir declares:

> Shabd is mine, I am of Shabd,
> Realize that Shabd if you crave salvation—
> Don't let this chance slip by.[8]

---

1. "And the Word was made flesh, and dwelt among us" (John 1:14).
2. A.G., *Ramkali*, M.1, p.943
3. K.S.S., p 10:118.
4. K.S.S., p.93:11.
5. The eye center.
6. *Akhrawati*, p.1.
7. S.B., p.42:9:10.
8. K.S.S., p.93:12.

This inner Shabd form of the Master, ever present with the disciple from the time of his initiation, is a form of pure spirit, of Word or Shabd, endowed with ineffable beauty and resplendence. Describing it, Kabir says: "Kabir caught a glimpse of his Master and has no words to praise his splendor. I contacted him, the storehouse of radiance; now he always stays within my eye."[1]

When the disciple's soul withdraws from the physical body and comes to the eye center—a point within the forehead behind the two eyes—it enters the sphere of the inner Master's radiance. On contacting the Master's Shabd form within, the disciple realizes that the Master is always with him, inside as well as in the outer world. Guru Arjan Dev says: "The gratifying form of my Master is on my forehead; now wherever I look, I see him always with me. His lotus feet are my life, my support."[2] And in the Bible it says: "And they shall see his face; and his name shall be in their foreheads."[3]

Dadu refers to the inner or radiant form of the Master when he says: Where the supreme Guru abides, there absorb your attention; turn your eyes inwards and you will see the wonder of wonders.[4] Retrace your attention, take the soul inwards, there merge in the radiant Master; he who does so, O Dadu, is the truly wise one.[5]

When the disciple reaches the radiant form of the Master, the curtain of ignorance is removed. Maulana Rum says: "If the Master will appear within your heart, you will know everything about the beginning and the end of the creation."

But Hafiz says that one cannot obtain a glimpse of the radiant form of the Master merely by closing one's eyes. The devotee has to purify his mind and open the inner eye to see this form of the Master: "To see him you must have a pure heart; he can be seen only by a pure eye; every eye is not a fit receptacle for the manifestation of his unique splendor."

---

1. *K.G.*, p.12:38. *Eye:* eye center or third eye.
2. *A.G., Devgandhari*, M.5, p.535.
3. Rev. 22:4.
4. *Dadudayal*, p.93:17.
5. *Dadudayal*, p.93:20.

Hazrat Muinuddin Chishti gives an indication of the inner form of the Master when he says: "O Master, if only one ray of your brilliantly illumined face were to shine in the sky, the sun would turn pale with shame."

Swamiji calls upon the soul to see the form of the Master by taking its seat at the eye center.[1] In another poem Swamiji portrays the anxiety of the devotee to go within and see the Master's radiant form: "My Master, pray reveal to me your real form. I know you have taken this physical form in order to guide and emancipate souls. But your true form is imperceptible and beyond my reach; pray reveal that one to me. . . . I love your physical form also; through this form please show me your inner form. . . . Your true form is the Shabd form; pray lead my soul to that form."[2]

In reply the Satguru assures the disciple: "Dear child, my true form is different and unique. It cannot be seen till I give the support of my power. . . . Attend to your meditation, control the mind and ascend to the inner sky to see that form."[3]

Kabir says that the Master is in the firmament—the inner sky of the astral world—where the disciple, on going within 'the heart' or eye center, meets the radiant or Shabd form of the Master: "My Master is in the firmament, the disciple in his heart. When the soul merges in Shabd, it is never parted from the Master."[4] But this union of the soul with the Master's Shabd form is only possible through the grace, help and guidance of the physical Master. Kabir says:

> The Master who reveals the truth of the entire creation has become manifest within me. The Master whom these physical eyes could never see was made visible to me by my (physical) Master.[5]. . .Knowledge, inner union, love, devotion, bliss, faith and, above all, an abode at the Satguru's feet within—

1. *S.B.*, p.41:8:1.
2. *S.B.*, p.274:15.
3. *S.B.*, p.275:16.
4. *K.S.S.*, p.5:58.
5. *K.S.S.*, p.1:2.

obtain them all through service and adoration of the
Master.[1]

When Christ took three of his disciples to "a high mountain," he appeared before them in his radiant form, "And was
transfigured before them: and his face did shine as the sun,
and his raiment was white as the light."[2] This experience was
granted to the disciples by the physical Master—Jesus Christ—
for it was he who took them to the inner spiritual region,
termed in the Biblical language of parables "a high mountain
apart."[3] Christ himself describes it as an inner experience—
"a vision"—when he asks them not to reveal it to anyone:
"And as they came down from the mountain, Jesus charged
them, saying, Tell the vision to no man."[4]

The real glory and spiritual power of the physical Master is
only realized on seeing him in his radiant form within. Kabir
says that he used to sing the praises of his Master so long as he
did not see him inside; since the moment he saw the Master in
his radiant form, he has nothing to say, for the radiance and
beauty of that form are beyond words.[5]

As a result of this experience, mind becomes quiet and absorbed within, and the fires of passions, desires and cravings
are extinguished: "I became pure, bliss alighted, my entire being was filled with love, and all my blemishes disappeared when
I met my Master who is ever present within. By going within
the body, my mind became quiet and affable; outside it was
ever restless. The fire has turned into water, Kabir, the scorching flames are dead."[6]

Meeting the radiant form of the Master is not an imaginary
experience when the disciple emotionally and mentally feels
himself very close to his spiritual preceptor. It is a deep and
elevating spiritual experience, which every disciple of a perfect
Master has when he goes within. On the spiritual plane the

1. *K.S.S.*, p.3:30.
2. Matt. 17:2.
3. Matt. 17:1.
4. Matt. 17:9.
5. *K.S.S.*, p.110:37.
6. *K.S.S.*, p.111:53-54.

radiant form of the Master is as real as his physical form is in the outer world. The Master is actually present at all times and on all levels of consciousness. On the physical plane he is Word personified; on the spiritual plane he is Word or Shabd; and on the level of the highest spiritual consciousness he is the source of Shabd, the Lord. On the physical plane the disciple comes in contact with the physical form of the Master; in the inner spiritual realms he meets the Master in the Shabd form; and on attaining the peak of spiritual development he finds that the Master and God are one.

Dying while living

The process of spiritual development begins when the disciple withdraws his consciousness to the eye center, or in other words, vacates the nine portals of the physical body and enters the inner spiritual world. In this manner he actually steps out of the body and the world of phenomena and steps into the realm of spirit or Shabd, becoming, for the moment, dead to his physical existence but alive to his spiritual identity.

In the practice of Nam, the direction of mind and soul is reversed; they are withdrawn from the nine portals of the body and concentrated at the eye center. Through this process of concentration, the consciousness vacates the body and comes to the eye center. In this state the body becomes senseless and the attention or consciousness, which functions on the physical level, is withdrawn from the body. This is the first step in the devotee's spiritual practice—a step that takes one from the outer world of gross matter to the subtle inner world of higher consciousness.

This process of withdrawing the soul and mind to the eye center has been termed 'dying while living' by the Saints.

The terms 'dying while living', 'dying before death' and 'dying to live again', used by Kabir, Guru Nanak and most of the Saints, have been interpreted by scholars, however, as metaphorical expressions. They maintain that the state of 'dying while living' implies becoming 'dead' or impervious to the world and its attractions; that is, adopting a mental attitude of complete detachment from all physical comforts and needs. Unaware of the actual spiritual process of dying while living, some scholars have confused it with a state of *vairag* or renunciation and have interpreted the term as 'living death'.

At the time of death, mind and soul, which permeate the entire body, withdraw from the hands, feet, arms, legs and trunk and come to the eye center. From this point they vacate the body, which becomes lifeless. In the spiritual practice, the devotee goes through the same process consciously and at will. His soul and mind, just as in the course of death, are withdrawn to the eye center, and the devotee is oblivious or dead to the outer world. But he is fully conscious of the inner regions through which he now travels at his own volition. During death the soul is helpless and, whether willing or unwilling, it has to leave the body permanently. But in the spiritual state of death —dying while living—the soul is in full command of itself and maintains an invisible link with the body, returning to it at the end of the period of meditation. During this temporary withdrawal of consciousness, the body becomes numb or senseless, but the functions of heart, lungs and other physical organs continue involuntarily, though at a slightly reduced rate.

Thus, physically unconscious, the devotee is in a state of superconsciousness, experiencing and enjoying the bliss of inner spiritual regions. He is fully aware of his true self and the divine worlds within, and on returning to the body he remembers his inner experiences in every detail.

Kabir says that one who attains this spiritual death will be released from the rounds of birth and death:

> He who dies while living,
> And lives again after dying,
> Will not be born again.
> Says Kabir: He who merges in the Name,
> His attention remains absorbed
> In the pure state of Sunn.[1]

---

1. A.G., *Maru*, Kabirji, p.1103.

The state of dying while living is attained by merging into Nam or Shabd, obtained from a perfect Master. Guru Nanak conveys the same idea thus: "They who die through the Guru's Shabd and come to life again, reach the threshold of salvation."[1] Such a devotee will not be required to face death again: "He who dies in Shabd will not die again."[2] This is the true *yoga* or union of soul with the Lord. Rejecting various yogic practices and garbs as futile, Guru Nanak says: "O Nanak, die while living; attain such a 'yoga'."[3]

Saint Namdev says: "Through the Word uttered by my Guru I have realized my true self, and while still living I have learned how to die. . . . Visoba Khechar[4] says: Death we transcend, O Namdev, when we experience it while living."[5]

Persian mystics have also referred to dying while living as an essential step to God-realization. Maulana Rum says: "My friend, die before death if you long for everlasting life." And: "O noble man, die before death, hand over your life to the Supreme Life, go beyond your body. If you do not die while living, you will not gain the fruit of bliss."

Hafiz says: "So long as you do not vacate the body, you cannot enter the lane of spiritual bliss." And Kabir declares: "Tall is the tree, the fruits are high in the sky; only he tastes the fruit who while living dies."[6]

All have to pass through the gates of death, there is no escape, for one who is born has to die one day. The fear of the unknown and the terror of death assail every being. But the devotee has no fear of death; he conquers death, for he daily crosses its threshold at will. In the words of St. Paul, he dies daily.[7] The process of dying is no more a mystery to the devotee, for he knows it through his own experience. Kabir says that the entire world has a dread of death, but the devotee looks at death with joy,[8] because he experiences it during

---

1. A.G., *Ramkali*, M.1, pp.941-942.
2. A.G., *Siri Rag*, M.1, p.58.
3. A.G., *Suhi*, M.1, p.730.
4. Saint Namdev's Master.
5. *Shri Namdev Gatha*, poem 1365.
6. *K.S.S.*, p.115:11.
7. "I die daily" (1 Cor. 15:31).
8. *K.S.S.*, p.116:21.

spiritual practice and, being connected with Shabd, knows that the regions of Shabd and ineffable bliss await him. He adds:

> If one dies while living,
> For him death is sweet;
> Death is sweet for him
> Who has experienced it
> Through the Master's grace. . . .
> Those who while living die
> By merging into the Lord
> Become immortal, O Kabir.[1]

Dying while living is the method of releasing the soul from the bondage of matter. True self-realization comes only when the devotee vacates his body and enters the spiritual worlds. When he learns to remove the garment of his body at will and steps into the inner regions in his spirit form, then he realizes that his true self is not the physical body, but the soul. He is now fit to contemplate on the Lord's qualities and become one with Him:

> Kabir, rare are they
> Who while living die;
> Free from all fear they merge
> In the Lord's qualities,
> And wherever they look
> Only Him they see.[2]

There are hints in the Bible about dying while living. As long as a disciple is confined to the limits of the body, he is tied to the physical world and is away from the Lord. When he vacates the body or is "absent from the body," he comes in the proximity of the Divine Being: "Whilst we are at home in the body, we are absent from the Lord. . . . We are confident, I say,

---

1. *K.G.*, p.80:46.
2. *A.G.*, *Salok*, Kabirji, p.1364:5.

and willing rather to be absent from the body, and to be present with the Lord."[1]

Saint Paltu says: "One by one all die, but few know how to die. O Paltu, one who dies while living crosses the ocean with ease."[2] Tulsi Sahib also says: "He alone can reach the abode of my inaccessible Beloved, who dies while living and again lives after such a death. He drinks divine nectar to his fill."[3]

Some collections of Kabir's poems have a whole section on dying while living. It is one of the most important and necessary parts of a devotee's spiritual exercise. Dadu has also written many couplets on the subject:

> The king and the pauper, all will die, none lives forever. O Dadu, he truly lives who while living dies.[4] Dadu, only then will you meet your Beloved when you die while living.[5] Dadu, know that the path of the Saints is arduous; only he will travel on it who, absorbed in the Lord's Name, dies while living.[6] O Dadu, hard is the path, none can step upon it alive; only he can tread on it who while living dies.[7]

Vacating the physical body and entering the inner spiritual regions is the way to obtain release from the chain of birth and death. The path to God-realization lies in dying while living. Kabir says that one who learns the art of dying while living enjoys the bliss of the five spiritual regions. Such a devotee obtains the treasure, he merges in the Lord and loses his own identity.[8]

Guru Angad Dev describes the way to achieve the state of dying while living and thereby realize the Lord:

---

1. St. Paul in 2 Cor. 5:6,8.
2. *Paltu Sahib*, III:76:99.
3. *Tulsi Sahib ki Shabdavali*, II:1:6.
4. *Dadudayal*, p.232:10.
5. *Dadudayal*, p.232:14.
6. *Dadudayal*, p.233:21.
7. *Dadudayal*, p.233:22.
8. *K.G.*, p.137:282.

> See without eyes, hear without ears,
> Walk without feet, work without hands,
> Speak without tongue—
> Thus while living, die
> And realize the Order, O Nanak;
> Then alone the Beloved you'll meet.[1]

Guru Amar Das tells us that one can recognize the Order or Shabd of God only by dying while living under the Master's guidance: "He who through the Guru's grace dies while living, recognizes the cosmic law. O Nanak, one who dies such a death attains everlasting life."[2]

Guru Nanak also confirms that the state of dying while living can only be attained through the Guru's grace: "The way through the world's ocean is hard and tempestuous; become detached in the midst of hope; through the Master's grace realize your self and thus die while living."[3]

While the physical body is inactive and 'dead' during the spiritual practice, the soul is fully alive and capable of traveling and moving in the inner regions. Describing this state, Kabir says that he enjoys the true bliss where one sings the Lord's praises in ecstasy without the tongue, where one walks without feet, plays musical instruments without hands, and sees without eyes; without actually dying, one becomes dead, and without being cremated one becomes ash.[4]

This state is attained only through the grace of a perfect Master. Kabir says that he has become deaf, dumb and lame, he has become insane—that is, oblivious of the world—such is the arrow of Shabd his Satguru has hit him with.[5] And again:

> The shaft pierced my heart,
> I am enthralled with joy—
> I am not dead, nor alive;

---

1. A.G., *Majh ki Var*, M.2, p.139. *Hukam* or 'order': Cosmic law, the Word.
2. A.G., *Bihagare ki Var*, M.3, p.555.
3. A.G., *Ramkali*, M.1, p.935.
4. *K.S.*, II:83:19.
5. *K.S.S.*, p.8:89.

Kabir, they become immortal
Who thus while living die.[1]

No-grief Land

The state of being 'within' that the Saints refer to does not imply mental introspection, nor is it a symbolic or figurative expression. Although many scholars have tried to interpret this term as a mental concept, it is neither theoretical nor metaphorical. By 'within' the Saints refer to the inner spiritual worlds, which though beyond the grasp of the physical senses are as real as any of the tangible things of the outer world.

On going within, or crossing the eye center, the devotee enters the vast domain of the spiritual regions. Saints have given only hints of these realms of bliss, for they defy description. In the world of matter one cannot find lasting happiness or pleasure unalloyed with grief and pain. Sorrow, disease and death are as much a part of this world as are the transient days of youth, health and life. As against this, it is hard to find misery and gloom in the inner spiritual worlds. As the disciple goes higher and higher, he experiences an ever-increasing joy. At the highest region of pure bliss there is nothing but divine love—love which is everlasting bliss; love which is God.

Kabir calls this region Be-gam-pur, 'the city of no gloom' or 'no-grief land':

> To kings and paupers,
> To emperors and fakirs,
> To one and all I give the call:
> If you long for eternal bliss
> Come and dwell in my home—
> No-grief Land is my abode, O friend.[2]

Guru Ravidas also calls this inner realm of bliss Be-gampur: "No-grief Land is the name of my town. Pain and fear do not exist here. There is no anguish of tax payment, nor are

---

1. *K.S.S.*, p.8:87.
2. *K.S.*, I:60:8.

there any goods to be taxed. There is neither fear, nor fault; neither dread, nor decline. Now I have attained my wondrous homeland, O brother, where safety and calm ever prevail. Everlasting and changeless is this domain of my Emperor. There is neither a second nor a third, here abides only the One. It is renowned as Abadan, the city of peace and plenty.[1] Here reside only the rich at heart, the contented. They revel as and where they wish; they know all the secrets of the Mansion and no one stops them from moving freely. Ravidas, a mere cobbler, declares: One who is my co-dweller in this town is my true friend."[2]

As mentioned earlier, the way to the inner spiritual world is within the human body, the eye center being the gateway. The spiritual regions described by the Saints, with their vast continents and islands, are also within the body. In order to reach them the devotee has to go within, pass through the eye center and enter into a new dimension of spiritual consciousness. Guru Amar Das describes the human body as a cave which is the repository of inexhaustible treasures and within which also resides God—the Boundless and Unseeable.[3] Within the body resides He himself, the Unfathomable One who cannot be seen. Within the body are numerous regions, continents, heavens and underworlds.[4]

Generally, in their compositions the Saints have given only vague hints about the color, sound and light of the various regions. A few poems of Kabir, though providing only a cursory account of the inner worlds, were meant exclusively for his disciples as part of their spiritual instructions. At the beginning of the twentieth century, some of these hymns came to the notice of scholars, and a few have been published.[5] These poems provided a guideline to the disciple, they did not undertake to furnish a detailed account of the inner realms, which according to

---

1. Guru Ravidas uses the word *Abadan* to convey the idea of prosperity. Abadan, a city in the Middle East, in those days was known as a center of learning, spiritual inclination and great prosperity.
2. A.G., *Gauri*, Ravidasji, p.345.
3. A.G., *Majh*, M.3, p.124.
4. A.G., *Suhi*, M.3, p.754.
5. e.g., *K.S.*, I:65:22.

the Saints cannot be depicted in the limited vocabulary of the material world.

Guru Nanak and the galaxy of Saints succeeding him, and Ravidas, Dadu, Paltu, Dariya, Garibdas, Charandas and almost all Saints of the medieval period preferred to give only vague indications of the spiritual regions. It was later Saints like Tulsi Sahib (1764-1845) and Swamiji (1818-1878) who tried to provide greater details of the inner worlds. Kabir, however, has generally described the inner regions through parables or unusual images:

> In the cave of the firmament ceaselessly rains ambrosia. Here without an instrument arise melodies, but one can realize this only in meditation. Without a lake, bloom lotus flowers over which swans hover in bliss. Without a moon there is moonlight, and wherever one looks one finds pure souls (swans) floating in joy. . . . Says Kabir, Listen, O friend, he who arrives here becomes immortal; he will never face death again.[1]

The inner spiritual region of supreme bliss is the home of the Saints. Kabir says that one cannot comprehend its beauty and bliss through erudition, analysis or intellectual speculation; nor can one reach this land through adherence to the caste system, ritual prayers and ceremonies. Canonic laws and dogmas do not reach there, and religious texts are ignorant of that land of pure bliss. He further adds:

> Where lightning flashes without clouds,
> Where dazzling light shines without a sun,
> Where pearls of radiant sheen
> Form without mother-of-pearl,
> Where the sweet music
> Of the divine voice resounds
> Without a speaker, without rhythm or tone;
> Such is my homeland, O friend.[2]

---

1. *K.S.*, I:64:19.
2. *K.S.*, I:59:7.

Dadu conveys his experience in similar terms:

> Where there are no suns, I saw a sun;
> Where there are no moons, I saw a moon;
> Where exist no stars, there I saw them twinkle;
> Dadu saw, and boundless was his joy.[1]

Saint Namdev has the same inner experience to share with his disciples: Without the leather covering, the drum beats, without monsoon there is thunder, without clouds it rains—if one could just grasp the essence.[2]

Describing the brilliance of the inner light, Guru Nanak says: As one sees lightning on a dark night, thus day and night see the divine light deep within yourself. The Lord is the embodiment of bliss, of ineffable beauty—He is seen through a perfect Master.[3] Referring to this light, the Prophet Isaiah says: "The sun shall be no more thy light by day; neither for brightness shall the moon give light unto thee: but the Lord shall be unto thee an everlasting light, and thy God thy glory. Thy sun shall no more go down; neither shall thy moon withdraw itself: for the Lord shall be thine everlasting light, and the days of thy mourning shall be ended."[4]

Saints, giving hints of the spiritual regions, say that the light of the first region in the soul's journey is like that of a thousand lamps of extraordinary brilliance; the light of the second stage is like that of the rising sun. Crossing these two realms, when the devotee enters the third region he finds a light dazzlingly bright but cool like that of a full moon. Guru Nanak gives hints of these regions when he says: "When you meet the Satguru, the Lord himself will ferry you across, and after the sky of the lamp and that of the sun, you will reach the home of the moon."[5]

All spiritual adepts who have gone within, crossed the inner

---

1. *Dadudayal*, p.51:81.
2. A.G., *Sorath*, Namdevji, p.657.
3. A.G., *Maru*, M.1, p.1041.
4. Isa. 60:19-20. *Mourning* refers to the misery of birth and death.
5. A.G., *Maru*, M.1, p.1041.

regions and attained God-realization, refer to the same experiences. Persian mystics like Maulana Rum also give hints of the inner worlds: "If you are among those who see the sun in its full brilliance at midnight, then try to converse with me. Remember, only the pure souls see that sun, and once they see it there is no difference between day and night for them." That is, the inner light always shines within them and they are constantly in touch with that region of brilliant light.

Maulana Rum adds: "In the inner regions there are countless oceans, rivers, forests and mountains; but man is ignorant of them, he cannot even imagine their majesty and expanse. In comparison with that inner world, this entire (physical) world is like a piece of string in a vast ocean." And Christ also remarks that "in my Father's house are many mansions."[1]

Another Persian mystic, Sanai, says that in this foreign land there are many skies (i.e., regions), and many are they who govern and rule them; in the path of the soul, there are great steeps and slopes, mighty mountains and vast oceans.

In these inner regions of light and spirit, the devotee meets the radiant form or Shabd form of the Master who has initiated him. Maulana Rum refers to this form and gives further hints of the soul's spiritual journey: "If you desire to see that magnificent form, then travel towards your true home. Pass through the sky and the great star; take courage and cross also the inner sun and moon, then will you be able to reach and place your head at the doorstep of the Lord's court."

The entire physical, astral and causal world has been called by the Saints the region of Brahm or Brahmand; and the regions beyond Brahm—the domain of pure spirit—are called Parbrahm, that is, 'the realm beyond Brahm'. This is a broad division of the entire outer and inner creation. Some Saints have divided the creation into four regions, calling the physical or material world 'Pind'; the astral 'And'; the causal 'Brahmand'; and the realms beyond Brahm, 'Sach Khand'.

Kabir, while describing Pind, gives some idea of the lower

---

1. John 14:2.

chakras or centers of the human body and the methods usually adopted by yogis to reach them. All these centers are within Pind or the physical world. Kabir rejects the practice of going into the *chakras* below the eye center. Saints have never entertained the idea of breath control and yoga and the austerities prescribed for undertaking these practices. In the conscious state, the seat of soul and mind is between the two eyebrows, and the devotee can and should start his inner journey from this point instead of descending to the lower centers of the body. Kabir says that the path to the inner spiritual regions will begin when the seeker goes to a perfect Master, adopts the practice of Nam and withdraws his consciousness to the eye center.

The names Kabir has given to these regions may have come down from earlier Saints. The first region is Sahansdal Kamal, 'the land of a thousand lamps'; the second is Trikuti, 'the confluence of the three'; the third is Daswan Dwar, 'the tenth door' or doorway to the realm of pure spirit; the fourth, Mahasunn or Bhanwar Gupha, has been divided into the region of 'the great darkness' and that of 'I am that'; the fifth region, Sach Khand, 'the region of eternal truth', has been further divided into three realms: the realms of Alakh or the Imperceptible One, Agam or the Inaccessible One, and Anami or the Nameless One.

Many Saints have given hints about these regions and used the same names. Nevertheless, it appears that the details of these regions were kept a well-guarded secret by most of the Saints, who shared it only with their initiates.

Guru Nanak has called these regions Dharam Khand, Gyan Khand, Saram Khand, Karam Khand and Sach Khand.[1] Dharam Khand is the region of action. It is the physical world or Pind; subject to seasons, dates and days, it is enveloped by wind, water, fire and earth. It is ruled by the law of cause and effect, and the soul is judged according to its actions here. Beings of various forms, shapes and kinds live here;

---

1. The description that follows is based on Guru Nanak's well-known work, the *Japji*, A.G., pp.7-8:34-37.

they bear diverse and endless names. Here the soul is unripe or imperfect, but can become perfect through devotion and God's grace.

Gyan Khand, the region of intellect or knowledge, is the astral region, beyond the eye center, also called And. Guru Nanak describes it as a vast region with many continents, worlds and underworlds, with numerous suns, moons and stars. It is inhabited by angels, gods, goddesses and deities.

The regions of Brahm, the region of universal mind, has been called by Guru Nanak, Saram Khand or the domain of bliss.[1] The sound of this region is full of beauty and attraction. This is a land of indescribable beauty and splendor. Mind, intellect and reason originate from here.

Parbrahm or the region beyond Brahm has been called by Guru Nanak, Karam Khand—the region of grace. The precincts of mind and maya end at the region of Brahm, and the land of pure spirit, love and God's grace starts when the soul goes beyond Brahm. The sound of Karam Khand, in the words of Guru Nanak, is full of power and force. Here the sense of duality ends and the soul realizes that it is a particle of the Supreme Being. Only brave and courageous souls reach here, that is, those devotees who have vanquished the forces of mind and maya. Here their thoughts dwell only on the Lord and they enjoy unmitigated bliss.

The final region is Sach Khand, 'the land of eternal Truth', the soul's true home. Guru Nanak says that here the Formless Lord resides. Here He presides, He surveys, and his will or order reigns supreme. The glory of this realm of supreme bliss is ineffable, and Guru Nanak says that "to describe it is as hard as steel."[2]

The description of the inner spiritual regions, as given by Guru Nanak, conforms with that of Kabir. While Kabir has dwelt more on the light and sound of these regions and has tried to provide more details of the inner journey, Guru

---

1. The word *saram* has been variously interpreted by scholars; Bhai Vir Singh has called Saram Khand 'the domain of bliss', which conforms with the general description of the region of Brahm given by other Saints.
2. A.G., *Japji*, M.1, p.8:37.

Nanak's description is both subtle and succinct, suggestive rather than explicit.

In the hymns of the Adi Granth, one also finds references to the eye center; the region of brilliant lights; Trikuti; Daswan Dwar, the tenth gate; Sunn and Mahasunn, the land of great darkness; and Sach Khand. The devotee has to withdraw his mind and soul from the physical body and enter the astral world through the eye center in order to become free from the physical bonds of the Pind region or Dharam Khand. In the same way the soul has to reach Trikuti, the realm of the universal mind, the top of Brahmand or Saram Khand; and has to go beyond this to still higher regions in order to be rid of the bonds of the causal world. While leaving Trikuti, the soul sheds the astral and causal coverings and transcends the bonds of cause and effect, mind and maya. Then, in the form of pure spirit the devotee enters the regions of spirit—Parbrahm—and proceeds further to arrive at his true home, Sach Khand.

According to the Saints, shedding the physical, astral and casual veils is a precondition to admittance into the court of the True One. Kabir says: In this town with nine doors (the body), stop the mind that keeps running about. When you go beyond Trikuti and open the Tenth Gate (Daswan Dwar), your mind will be intoxicated with ecstasy.[1]

Guru Amar Das confirms what Kabir says: "Even if a person subdues his body and undertakes intricate yogic postures, he will not be rid of the bane of his ego. Even if he adopts various spiritual practices, he will not obtain Nam. If through the Guru's Shabd he dies while living, the Lord's Name will come and dwell within his mind. O my mind, take the Satguru's refuge and adore him. Only through the Guru's grace will you get release and swim across the world's ocean of poison. The entire world of the three *gunas* is dross, it leads the mind into the evils of duality. The pundit reads, but remains tied by the chains of attachment; he fails to discern the truth because of his love for sense pleasures. When you meet the Satguru, you

---

1. A.G., *Kedara,* Kabirji, p.1123.

will go beyond Trikuti and enter the fourth stage—the gateway to freedom."[1]

Swamiji gives the same names to denote these regions as Kabir does, and his description tallies with that of Kabir. More details of the inner worlds and their important distinguishing features, such as light and sound, are given by Saints to their disciples at the time of initiation.

Dadu clearly points out the unity of Kabir's message with that of other Saints when he says, under the chapter on "Truth": "Poor Kabir kept saying the same thing all his life, he explained in many a way; but, Dadu, the world seems to be crazy, for it refuses to accept what he said. Those who cross the intricate vales within and reach that realm of Truth will say the same thing. But, O Dadu, why should they try to speak who still wander midway?"[2]

The thief without a head

Although the Lord is within the human body and the path is within, and the Master is ever present to guide and help the devotee, it is not easy to attain the goal. There are obstacles in the way: lures and attractions in the outer as well as the inner worlds entice the devotee and prevent him from progressing on the spiritual path. The biggest obstacle, perhaps the only obstacle, is the mind. Kabir calls it a thief because it steals the spiritual wealth of the devotee through its mighty companions —lust, anger, attachment, greed, avarice, jealousy, hate, and above all ego—who prevail upon man to dissipate the precious opportunity of human birth in vain pursuits. Kabir says:

> Throughout the three worlds the thief steals
> With great cunning and stealth
> And deprives devotees
> Of all their wealth.
> No one, O Kabir, recognizes the thief,
> For he goes about without a head.[3]

1. A.G., *Siri Rag*, M.3, p.33.
2. *Dadudayal*, p.167:156-157.
3. *K.S.S.*, p.147:10.

There is no physical foe in the world that man has not been able to subdue. He has tamed lions, elephants and tigers, conquered forts, kingdoms and nations, but he has not been able to vanquish his own mind. Kabir calls the mind a wild beast which has no horns, fangs, beak or body. It is an enemy hard to identify for it has neither head nor form nor shape.[1]

For ages men have adopted various means to tame the mind —austerities, penances, fasts, renunciation, intricate yoga practices, denying the body food, water and comforts—and have resorted to numerous ways to bully the mind into submission. But denying necessities and comforts to the body, torturing it in heat and cold, or subjecting it to a secluded life in a forest or cave cannot overcome the mind. Kabir says that by beating a snake-hole one cannot kill the snake.[2] These practices affect only the body, not the mind. If the body is locked in a dark cell, only the body will be incarcerated, not the mind. The body may be at one place, but the mind can roam about in all directions. Says Kabir, "Mind is like a monkey, not a moment does it stay still."[3]

In order to control the mind, it is necessary for the seeker to know what mind is and what its characteristics are. Saints say that mind is matter; it is not spirit or soul. Its origin or source is Brahm, in the region of universal mind, while that of soul is the Lord, in the region of everlasting bliss.

Itself inert, mind draws power from the soul. An electric bulb has no light; it emits light through the energy or electric current it receives from the powerhouse. In the case of mind, its connection with the soul has been made since the day of creation. Just as mind is dependent on the soul, so also the soul can act and function in the physical world only through the mind.

Kabir says that the devotee can only be free of the bondage of mind on reaching the state of *unmani* or the region of the universal mind, the realm of Brahm: "When the devotee grasps

---

1. *K.G.*, p.119:212.
2. *K.S.S.*, p.127:13.
3. *K.S.S.*, p.151:64.

104

the original source (of mind), the mind becomes still. He who knows this secret will know what mind is. Let no one's mind delude and hinder him from realizing the truth, for only he who is attuned to the Lord will obtain true peace. One has to take the help of the mind, for only on controlling the mind will one attain perfection. Through mind the mind can be controlled; there is none other like the mind.[1] This mind is energy, this mind is power, this mind is made of the five elements. He who takes his mind and fixes it in the region of Brahm, to him the mysteries of the three worlds are revealed."[2]

Guru Nanak makes the same observations about the mind: "This mind performs actions, this mind undertakes religious rituals; this mind is born of the five elements. This mind is evil, covetous and foolish; but when it practices Nam through the *gurumukh,* it becomes beautiful."[3]

Although the mind is born of matter, imbibes the qualities of the causal, astral and physical regions and derives its energy from the soul, still it is a powerful entity. Involvement in the external world, love of pleasure, fondness for variety and an insatiable hunger for the world and its objects are some of its main characteristics. Lust, anger, attachment, craving for sensual gratification, ego and ceaseless wandering from place to place and object to object are some of its basic tendencies. Soul, a particle of the Supreme Being, immaculate and divine in its primal state, is a complete slave to the mind and its designs.

In the physical world mind also is not free; urged on by its fondness for sense pleasures, it has become a slave of the senses. In the words of Kabir, mind does not leave sense pleasures, and sense pleasures do not leave mind. Such is the nature and tendency of both; thus both mind and senses have eclipsed the soul.[4]

Guru Ravidas says: "What can I really know, O Lord? I am sold at the hands of mind and maya. The fugitive mind runs in the four directions, and the five senses remain not

1. The mind is a great help in spiritual progress when it comes under the soul's control.
2. A.G., *Gauri Purbi,* Kabirji, p.342:31-33.
3. A.G., *Asa,* M.1, p.415.
4. *K.G.,* p.44:33:9.

steady. These senses together have spoiled my mind, and day after day they have erected barriers between me and the Lord Divine."[1]

Mind is always changing. Sometimes it is inclined towards devotion, sometimes towards sense pleasures; sometimes it is calm and restrained, sometimes angry and agitated. Kabir says that mind becomes thick and heavy, mind becomes thin and fine; mind becomes cool as water, mind becomes a blazing fire; whatever impulse arises in the mind, the same form it adopts.[2] In a moment mind becomes a benevolent giver, in a moment a covetous miser; one moment it acts like a king, the next like a miserable wretch. But if the mind submits to the Master, it will without doubt receive the Master's grace.[3]

Mind clings to the soul like a parasitic vine. With each birth the soul adopts a body and at death leaves it, but the mind, unaffected by death, remains clinging to the soul. "Mind never died, nor did maya, but the body died, and died a million times. Alas, mind's cravings and expectations did not die, O Kabir."[4]

Because of its desires and cravings for the world and its objects, the mind comes into the world again and again; and the soul, tied to the mind, has to keep incarnating along with the mind. Mind was originally a means for the soul to move and act in the world, to associate and reciprocate with others and to know and experience the vicissitudes of its physical surroundings. But the soul, submitting to mind's desires and cravings for pleasures, has become its slave. To take an example from Kabir, a farmer bought a sheep to meet his requirement for wool, but he neglected to keep an eye on it and the sheep quietly ate up all the cotton fruit and ruined his cotton crop.[5] For eons the soul has had no control over the mind and has been allowing it to ruin the soul's wealth—its original brilliance.

Mind's appetite for pleasure is boundless. In the words of

---

1. *Sant Guru Ravidas Vani* 107, trans. K.N. Upadhyaya in *Guru Ravidas*.
2. *K.S.S.*, p.148:27.
3. *K.S.S.*, p.148:28.
4. *K.G.*, p.26:11.
5. *K.G.*, p.27:3.

Tulsi Sahib, mind's hunger is voracious, like that of a demon.[1] Saints have described mind as uncontrollable like a mad elephant, restive like an untrained horse, restless like a wild deer, fickle like the waves and always changing like the colors of a chameleon.

Mind's habit of running after pleasures brings misery and unhappiness. Ignoring the real purpose of human birth, namely, God-realization, mind wastes this precious opportunity in vain pursuits. Kabir says: "Time is draining away like water held in the palms of your hands, but mind takes no heed. Like a moth it flies into the flame of passions and in the end is burned. O mind, why do you rejoice at the sight of pleasures? Don't you see the fire that will consume you? You are hugging the serpent of sense pleasures and squandering the wealth of human birth. Says Kabir, mind is vile and capricious; one learns this through the knowledge given by the Master. Mind, without devotion, will keep burning wherever it goes."[2]

The object of spiritual practice as taught by the Saints is to vacate the body, arrive at the eye center and journey into the higher spiritual realms. The Master initiates the seeker into the practice of Nam or Shabd, through which the devotee can bring his soul and mind to the eye center. But mind is fond of running about in the external world. It refuses to become still and come back to the eye center.

Referring to mind's habit of constantly wandering outside, Guru Ram Das says: "From moment to moment the mind wanders in the manifold delusions of the world; it does not settle in its home, the eye center."[3] Kabir refers to the problem of mind's restlessness, identifying himself with the struggling devotee: "My mind does not stay still within my own house. It has ruined many homes by its wayward habits."[4]

The devotee has to fight resolutely with his mind, vanquish it and make it still. If he succeeds in doing so, the battle is won and all obstacles to inner progress are removed. Kabir says:

1. *Ratan Sagar*, p.9.
2. *K.G.*, p.159:368.
3. *A.G.*, *Basant Hindol*, M.4, p.1179.
4. *K.G.*, p.88:79.

"What use keeping long matted hair, what use applying ash over the body, what use living in caves? If you conquer the mind, you will conquer the world and will become indifferent to sense pleasures."[1]

Guru Amar Das also says: "If mind dies, all wandering will cease; without subduing the mind, how can one attain the Lord? Only a rare one knows the potion that benumbs the mind. Through Shabd mind dies; this a true devotee knows."[2] Swamiji says that only they are true warriors who have killed their mind.[3]

Soul is originally pure and divine, and its natural tendency is inwards and upwards. But it is enveloped by mind, which has become impure in the company of the senses and through its deep-rooted attachment to the gross world of matter. The soul, tied to the mind, has to withdraw to the eye center in the company of the mind. The mind, then, has to be made pure; the dross of desires and passions that has accumulated over it, has to be removed before it becomes fit to reach the eye center.

Kabir says that as long as mind is smeared with the filth of passions and cravings, one cannot become free from the bondage of the world. When mind becomes pure, the soul will merge into the Pure One.[4]

Guru Nanak says: "By 'killing' the mind you will please the Lord, the practice of Shabd will be fruitful and mind will recognize the lord of the three worlds. Mind will give up its weaving and wavering, and you will realize your beloved Lord."[5]

Mind will 'die' or become still through the practice of Nam or Shabd under the guidance of a perfect Master. Listening to the Shabd, mind will gradually become pure and will become an ally of soul on its path of devotion. Kabir expresses this in some of his poems: Unless put under the shackles of the true Name, mind will run about wherever it pleases.[6] Mind is stub-

1. A.G., *Maru*, Kabirji, p.1103.
2. A.G., *Dhanasari*, M.3, p.665.
3. *S.B.*, p.143:2:7.
4. *K.G.*, p.133:263.
5. A.G., *Bilawal*, M.1, p.844.
6. *K.S.S.*, p.151:64.

born and mighty like a mountain, but the moment the crowbar of Shabd strikes it, it yields a mine of pure gold.[1] Explore the Shabd, O Kabir, and through it control your mind; this is the easy way to union.[2] By listening to the divine melody, mind will be absorbed within, it will merge into Gagan[3] and will then cease to come and go; in the region of Sunn it will gain its original state.[4]

Dadu expresses the same idea when he says that men adopt a million ways to control the mind, they try and try, but fail, and the mind continues to run in all directions. It can only be chained by the Lord's Name, there is no other way.[5] The fickle and restless one runs in all the four directions; chain it with the Guru's Word.[6]

Guru Nanak also declares in no uncertain terms that mind can only be controlled by the practice of Shabd imparted by the Master: Without the Master's Word, mind cannot become still.[7] This mind bewitched by maya is released by the practice of Shabd.[8]

Swamiji says that mind comes under control when it listens to the melody of Shabd: "Adopt a million ways, but the mind will pay no heed; when it listens to the melody of Shabd it will come under control."[9] "Except through Shabd this slumbering mind will not arise, though countless devices one may try."[10]

Guru Ram Das says that mind will be rid of its lust for roving outside by coming in contact with the Saints: "By meeting the Saints my mind has come to life. . . . Mind is vagrant, roving endlessly in many directions; through the Saints it has been captured and made still, just as a fisherman casts his net and captures the fish."[11]

---

1. *K.S.S.*, p.147:18.
2. *K.S.S.*, p.95:40.
3. Trikuti or the region of Brahm.
4. *K.S.S.*, p.96:47.
5. *Dadudayal*, p.118:69.
6. *Dadudayal*, p.118:66.
7. *A.G.*, *Asa*, M.1, p.415.
8. *A.G.*, *Ramkali Dakhni*, M.1, p.908.
9. *S.B.*, p.93:9:1.
10. *S.B.*, p.125:19:10.
11. *A.G.*, *Kanra*, M.4, p.1294.

Saints know that craving for pleasure is mind's innate nature, and all its behavior is motivated by its habit of pleasure-seeking. Its lust for sense pleasures will not be satisfied by allowing it to fulfill its desires, for mind's cravings have no end. Even when the body is unable to indulge in the senses, mind's craving for them continues unabated. It may change phases by moving from one form of fulfillment to another, but will not give up its desires. To satisfy the cravings of mind is to add fuel to the fire—the more one gives to the mind, the more it wants. Kabir says that the sapling of mind's cravings will not dry up by watering it, it will grow all the more.

Nor can the devotee bridle his mind by forced abstinence from worldly pleasures. It cannot be coerced into submission by renunciation, austerities, fasts, penances and self-denial. Chanting, singing hymns and indulging in religious ceremonies might keep it temporarily engrossed, but cannot change its restive nature. So great is mind's power of resilience that no amount of self-mortification can crush it.

Mind never sticks to one form of pleasure. It delights in variety and gives up one pleasure the moment it tastes something better. The Saints say that if mind once experiences the inner spiritual pleasure, the joy of the inner regions and the bliss of the sound and light, it will give up the outer pleasures.

Kabir says that the mind, which once relished the filthy pleasures of the world, on going within and enjoying the inner bliss begins to abhor them. Formerly it was like a crow pecking at dross; now it becomes a pure swan and savors only divine pearls.[1]

Dadu says the same thing differently: "When mind is absorbed in the Lord's devotion, where else can it go? Dadu, as salt dissolves in water, so stays the mind lost in inner bliss."[2] Guru Nanak says that when the Lord's Name has pierced the mind, what else can it dwell upon?...Mind is pierced by the Name of God; the Guru has bestowed the true gift.[3]

---

1. *K.S.S.*, p.147:17.
2. *Dadudayal*, p.112:22.
3. A.G., *Siri Rag*, M.1, p.62.

When the devotee's attention is turned within, the world's pleasures become tasteless for him. He then gives up his liking for sense pleasures and enjoys the bliss of inner worlds. Kabir says: 'He gives up these pleasures, and experiences that joy. When he partakes of that ambrosia within, he loses all taste for these (worldly) pleasures.'[1]

The weapons of the foe

The citadel of the body is guarded by mind with its powerful forces of lust, anger, attachment, avarice and ego. The devotee has to vanquish them, open the gateway of the fort—the door within—storm the fortress and capture mind, its overlord.[2]

The five passions keep the devotee tied down to the world and to the physical body of nine doors. Lust pulls the mind downwards, anger spreads it outwards, attachment keeps it chained to the world, avarice fans its desire for material possessions, and ego hinders and prevents it from turning towards the Lord. Envy, jealousy, spitefulness, pride, selfishness, haughtiness, enmity and many allied evils are the offshoots of these five passions. Kabir says:

> So long as the body's storehouse
> Abounds with the hoard
> Of lust and anger,
> Of ego and greed,
> Kabir, the learned and the lout
> Are no doubt the same.[3]

The battle against these enemies is to be fought with the weapons of Nam, of devotion, love and surrender to the Master. The path of the Saints is not that of suppression, it is a path of sublimation. It is transplanting the roots of mind from the physical world to the inner regions of bliss. The diversion of mind's currents from sense pleasures to the beatitude of the

---

1. A.G., *Gauri, Bawan Akhari*, Kabirji, p.342:35.
2. A.G., *Bhairau*, Kabirji, p.1161.
3. K.S.S., p.131:19.

spiritual world is not a forced exercise. It is a subtle process, an automatic result of spiritual practice.

The world and its objects and the pleasures available here are all transitory. They are unreal like a dream, and one should become awake to the everlasting spiritual bliss that awaits the soul within. Kabir says: Those who look upon this dream as real do not realize the suffering and misery of this world. The ignorant ones do not open their eyes, they continue in their state of slumber. Alarmed by the deadly serpent of the passions, I stay awake. The ruthless hunter's bow is always loaded with an arrow. He shoots arrows envenomed with the bane of passions. Thus hunts Kal, the deadly predator, day and night. The world is his hunting ground, men and women are the rabbits—his heedless prey. The huntsman has set the forest ablaze with the fires of maya and attachment; the strong winds of avarice further fan the fire, and the minions of Kal—passions and evil tendencies—surround the prey and force them into his range.

Kabir further says that, though hounded by peril and misery, men do not worship the Lord, they run after the mirage of sense pleasures. They forget death and look upon pain as pleasure. Alas, the luckless ones do not try to recognize the source of true health and happiness, they allow the pestilence of misery to infest their being. As the insect of the neem tree loves its bitter pulp, so the world devours the poison of sense pleasures as nectar. Men do not discern between this poison and the nectar of Nam; but they who do, attain true happiness.[1]

Such is the design of the creation that all the passions are provided with materials to excite and sustain them. In the words of Guru Nanak, "Physical beauty and lust are friends, taste of palate is tied to hunger; greed is involved with riches, and sleep relishes even a flimsy bed. Anger barks in vile wrath, blindly it shouts in vain. It is better to be silent, O Nanak, for without Nam whatever one utters is dirt. Power, wealth, beauty, high caste and youth are five formidable thugs. These

---

1. *K.G., Badi Ashtpadi Ramaini*, p.175:5.

thugs have duped the entire world, no one can protect his honor from them. But those who take the shelter of the Guru's feet hoodwink these thugs. Those who are without this good fortune continue to be deceived by them."[1]

Kabir advises disciples to contemplate on the virtues and try to inculcate them. Thus modesty, purity and chastity should replace lust; and gentleness, affection, tolerance and forgiveness should take the place of anger. One should dwell on the transient nature of the world when assailed by attachment, love the entire creation instead of a chosen few, and attain detachment through devotion to the Lord. The devotee should overcome greed with contentment, cruelty with kindness, and ego with humility.

Rishis and munis, ascetics and hermits adopted numerous means to vanquish the passions. Aware of the shortcomings of their practices, Indian mythology abounds with tales of their failures and falls despite their many decades of austere practices. Asceticism, escaping to forests, living in caves and seeking complete seclusion will not eliminate the passions from one's mind. The devotee must live in the world, fulfill his obligations towards his family, earn his livelihood and at the same time attend to his meditation.

Saints say that once the devotee goes within and begins to relish the inner spiritual joy, his attention will automatically withdraw from the passions and pleasures. Kabir says: "In one sentence I tell the essence, ponder over it: O friend, adore the Name of the Formless and be rid of the dross of passions."[2] The way to conquer the passions is the practice of Nam or Shabd, the association of Saints and the grace of a perfect Master.

Swamiji says: "Without the Master's grace and help you cannot gain release from the grip of passions; therefore practice the Nam that the Guru gives."[3] It is not through suppression but diversion of attention towards tastes higher and more

---

1. A.G., *Malar*, M.1, p.1288.
2. *K.S.S.*, p.143:5.
3. *S.B.*, p.119:9:8.

attractive than those of the senses that one can overcome the onslaught of the passions. Here the Master's help, grace and blessings are of prime importance, for it is he who puts the seeker on the inward path of spiritual bliss, guides him and stays with him at every step of the journey. In other words, the disciple conquers lust, anger, attachment, ego and other negative forces of mind only in the company of the Saints. Kabir says:

> O friend, you are afflicted with the thirst of cravings and hunger for the illusions of the world, and you never reflected on the truth. Intoxicated with pride, your mind is deluded; you never tried to imbibe the Master's Word within yourself. Lured by your taste for pleasures, prevailed upon by the senses, you are drinking the wine of base pleasures. With God's grace and good fortune I have been ferried across the ocean in the company of the Saints, like iron in the company of wood.[1]

God's grace, a new spiritual birth or initiation given by the Satguru, and the power of repeating the Lord's Name destroy the malady of the five passions. Kabir says: "I sacrifice myself at the feet of that father—the Master—who has given me a new spiritual birth, who has rid me of the evil company of the five, with whose help I have vanquished the five foes and crushed them under my feet, and with whose grace my mind has been submerged in the bliss of the *simran* of the Lord's Name."[2]

Canoes of stone

It is an inherent urge in man to search for God and meet Him. It is the natural pull of soul towards its source—the Lord. But not knowing where and how to find Him, people try to seek God in idols, scriptures and places of pilgrimage, in holy rivers and pools, in mountains and caves, and in temples and mos-

---

1. A.G., *Gauri*, Kabirji, p.335.
2. A.G., *Asa*, Kabirji, p.476.

ques. They adopt various means to attain Him: They resort to worship of stones and other man-made symbols; they renounce the world and retire to forests, put on various garbs and take to fasts and other forms of self-mortification; they tell beads and recite and read holy scriptures, give alms and perform deeds of charity; they undertake oblations, adopt celibacy and resort to numerous forms of external worship.

Doing all this, men feel happy and satisfied that they are pleasing the Lord. But they are only deluding themselves. Undertaking all these practices they think that they have attained spiritual heights; they boast of their so-called spirituality and seek to guide and teach others. Themselves deluded, they also delude others. According to Dadu, they are like a drug addict intoxicated with hemp and heroin who, though his purse is empty, claims that he is the treasurer of the king.[1] In spite of their elation, true spirituality eludes them.

Kabir, as mentioned earlier, strongly rejected all external observances and worship and had to pay the price for asserting the truth, by suffering persecution at the hands of the priestly class. Shams-i-Tabriz, Mansur-al-Hallaj and Sarmad among the Persian Mystics, and Namdev, Kabir, Ravidas, Guru Nanak, Guru Arjan Dev, Guru Hargobind, Guru Teg Bahadur, Guru Gobind Singh, Dadu, Mira, Paltu and others among the Indian Saints had to suffer insults, persecution, torture and even death for their outspoken condemnation of rituals and formal practices.

Idol worship is one of the most common forms of devotion prevalent in almost every religion in the world. Whether it is the worship of a statue, a painting, a symbol, a monument, a grave, or that of the sandals, clothes and furniture of a holy person who is no more in the world, they are all forms of idol worship. Saints say that God—the Supreme Spirit, the ocean of ultimate consciousness and the source of all sentience—can neither be enclosed in an idol nor represented by any material symbol. Rajjab, a seventeenth-century Saint, says: Man, the

---

1. *Dadudayal*, p.159:99.

sentient being, makes a god out of inert matter and thought-lessly worships and serves it. Even this much does not dawn on him—how can dead stone be turned into God? Man adores the handcrafted, he pays homage to what he buys from the market. Alas, O Rajjab, man is unaware of the One who cannot be fabricated, whose value cannot be ascertained.[1]

All types of external observances involve the devotee in outward pursuits and the adoration of dead matter; whereas the path to true realization is an inward journey, and true wor-ship is the adoration of God or of the Master who has merged into Him. Kabir says: All beings I see, I see them as idols of God. But the Saint is the living God himself; I have no concern with stones.[2] Love and devotion is the ship and Master its cap-tain. When you realize it, this vast ocean will become as tiny for you as the water-filled hoofprint of a cow.[3]

Worship of matter, of stone, is regarded by Saints as the lowest form of devotion. Love of matter or things fashioned from matter will always keep the soul tied to the material world. Kabir says that if by worshipping stone God could be met, then he would have gladly adored a mountain.[4]

Inert matter cannot reciprocate the devotee's love. It can-not lead his soul inside, nor guide it through the intricate phases of the spiritual journey. Kabir says that the worship of idols and of holy waters will all go to waste and bear no fruit.[5] A devotee may worship stones all his life, he will never obtain an answer to his prayers. The ignorant man who in vain hopes for a response will only lose his spiritual luster.[6] Of stone is the temple, of stone is the deity—only the deluded and the blind adore them.[7] Kabir says that such people are trying to cross the ocean in canoes of stone.[8] Their devotion is misplaced; it is as frail as a paper boat and they burden it with the heavy load of

1. *Sant Sudha Sar*, ed. Viyogi Hari, p.531.
2. *K.G.*, p.34:5.
3. *K.G., Ashtpadi Ramaini*, p.177:8.
4. *K.S.S.*, p.165:5.
5. *K.S.S.*, p.165:8.
6. *K.G.*, p.34:3.
7. *K.S.S.*, p.165:7.
8. *K.S.*, I:55:90:3.

idol worship and rituals. Says Kabir, they are sure to sink into the world's deadly sea.[1]

Dadu has almost the same thing to say: "If a crystal piece is carved into the shape of the sun, it will not remove darkness; darkness will be dispelled only when the real sun rises.[2] If a wife installs an idol of her husband who has gone abroad, it will not respond to her love.[3] In the same way, an idol of God cannot serve the object of the devotee.[4]

Guru Nanak says: "Blind and dumb, men dwell in darkness; they worship stones which are also inert and sightless. The stones themselves sink, how can they ferry you across?"[5] Saint Paltu denounces both Muslims and Hindus for their external worship. The former run to Ka'aba, the latter to Puri; Muslims run to the West, Hindus to the East; both are fools, they are groping in a heap of ash. One bows to tombs, the other to stones; both wander in delusion and vex their heads.[6]

Idol worship is also strongly denounced in the Bible: "Ye shall make you no idols nor graven image, neither rear you up a standing image, neither shall ye set up any image of stone in your land, to bow down unto it: for I am the Lord your God."[7] "Whom therefore ye ignorantly worship, him declare I unto you. God that made the world and all things therein, seeing that he is Lord of heaven and earth, dwelleth not in temples made with hands."[8] The Bible describes how a craftsman fashions an idol out of wood and in order to put it against the wall he fastens it with a nail: "And puts it on the wall, fastening it with it nail. Thus lest it fall down he provides for it, knowing that it cannot help itself; for, truly, it is an image and needs help."[9]

Visits to places of pilgrimage and baths in rivers and pools considered to be holy are equally fruitless. No amount of bath-

1. *K.S.S.*, p.165:10.
2. *Dadudayal*, p.143:142.
3. *Dadudayal*, p.144:144.
4. *Dadudayal*, p.144:143.
5. A.G., *Bihagare ki Var*, M.1, p.556.
6. *Paltu Sahib*, II *Rekhta* 99.
7. Lev. 26:1.
8. Acts 17:23-24.
9. Wisd. 13:15-16 (New American Bible).

ing and washing in them can remove the dross of karmas and evil tendencies accumulated over the mind. In the words of Kabir, what use is it to scrub the body when the dirt is within? The bitter gourd may 'bathe' in all the sixty-eight holy spots, but its bitterness will not depart.[1]

Vakhna, a seventeenth-century mystic, also says: "You may wash in sixty-eight waters, you may bathe at all the sixty-eight holy places; yet, O Vakhna, the stink of mind, the fish, will not go."[2]

Guru Nanak expresses the same idea thus: Man goes to bathe at the holy places with the evil mind and the body harboring a thief (the passions); while one part (the physical body) is bathed, the other part (the mind) acquires more filth. The bitter gourd washed from the outside still has nothing but bitterness within. The Saint is pure without such ablutions, while the thief after bathing is still a thief.[3]

The priestly class propagate countless ritualistic practices for their own selfish ends. Commentaries on scriptures and holy lore advanced by the pundits and priests keep men involved in a variety of formalities. Kabir describes such books as dungeons of ignorance and delusion; the formalities taught by the priests as its doors leading into the cell's darkness; and the priestly class as robbers who, having obstructed the path with boulders (idols), rob the innocent travelers:

> The pundits have made
> A cell out of soot,[4]
> And from the ink of rituals
> Its dismal doors;

---

1. A.G., *Sorath*, Kabirji, p.656. The *tumbi* is a gourd with an extremely hard shell and bitter pulp. Kabir suggests that any amount of washing of the shell will not remove its inner bitterness.
2. *Bakhnaji ki Vani*, ed. Swami Mangal Das, p.15:15.
3. A.G., *Suhi*, M.1, p.789. Christ also lays stress on inner cleanliness and purity: "Woe unto you, scribes and Pharisees, hypocrites! for ye make clean the outside of the cup and of the platter, but within they are full of extortion and excess. Thou blind Pharisee, cleanse first that which is within the cup and platter, that the outside of them may be clean also.... Ye are like unto whited sepulchres, which indeed appear beautiful outward, but are within full of dead men's bones, and of all uncleanness. Even so ye also outwardly appear righteous unto men, but within ye are full of hypocrisy and iniquity" (Matt. 23:25-28).
4. In some editions it reads 'a cell out of paper'.

> They have planted stones
>> In the earth
> And lie in ambush
>> To rob the world.[1]

Dadu is equally forthright in his views about scriptures when he asks: How can men earn release with the help of paper and ink? Without the Lord's Name, says Dadu, the bane of delusion cannot be dispelled.[2] Dadu has studied and searched for Him in the Vedas and the Koran, but the land where one can meet the Pure One is far from their reach.[3]

Saints repeatedly tell us that the path to God lies within the human body and all efforts to find Him outside are futile. Although they are kind and tolerant in their dealings with everybody, they are uncompromising in the matter of outward practices. A Saint's mission is to awaken men to the inner reality, not to acquiesce in their delusions. His denunciation is aimed not at any person, but at the organized systems, at the orthodox customs and conventions, and at those who profit by keeping seekers deluded in them.

In the words of Kabir: "Without true devotion the entire world is blinded by a haze of delusion, and Yama hovers over their head ready to hurl his deadly net. The Hindus kill themselves adoring idols and worshipping many deities, the Muslims undertaking holy journeys; jogis die raising and tending tufts of matted hair all their lives. None of them ever finds the Lord. Poets pass away weaving mythology in verse, and recluses and hermits in visiting all the holy places. Fasting ascetics waste their life in acts of self-mortification, plucking out their hair. But none of them ever finds the Lord. . . . The pundits die reading and reciting scriptures. But they who know the real method of spiritual practice and devotion search for God within their own body; says Kabir the weaver, they will surely meet the Lord.[4]

---

1. *K.G.*, p.34:2.
2. *Dadudayal*, p.158:90.
3. *Dadudayal*, p.158:88.
4. *K.G.*, p.146:317.

119

Equally emphatic is Guru Nanak's rejection of such external observances. Talking about pundits and orthodox ritualists, he says: "They read holy books, perform ritual prayers at dawn and sunset and engage in religious debates. They worship stones and pretend to deep meditation like the stork (that stands motionless on one leg, watching for fish). In their mouth is falsehood; they project the spurious as genuine, and they recite the three-line mantra[1] three times a day. They wear rosaries around their neck and a sacred mark on their forehead, a loincloth around their waist and a cloth wrapped around their head. If they knew the acts that please the Lord, they would have realized that their rituals are acts of bogus piety. Says Nanak: Dwell upon the True One; but without the Satguru, they know not the way."[2]

Swamiji also describes these external forms of worship and rituals as bogus piety, and indulging in them as churning water instead of milk.[3] Kabir calls these practices counterfeit and says that butter cannot be obtained from water. Guru Arjan Dev expresses the same idea: "The true Deity is within the house (the body), but men fail to see Him. They hang stones around their neck. Such wicked and worldly men wander in delusion; they churn water and waste their efforts."[4]

Saint Ravidas says: "What use repeating Krishna, Karim, Ram, Hari and Raghav if you have not realized the One? Vedas, scriptures, Koran and Puranas—not one of them has known the state of Sahaj. The manifold forms of worship that men resort to are counterfeit; the Truth is obtained only through the practice of Sahaj. Says Ravidas: I worship Him who belongs to no place and who has no name."[5]

Living in the city of Banaras, for centuries a stronghold of ritualism, Kabir had seen the hollowness of the forms of worship propagated by the priestly class. He knew that they were exploiting the credulous people by deluding them into under-

---

1. Gayatri mantra, which has only three lines, instead of the customary four, is recited by pious Hindus morning, noon and evening.
2. A.G., *Salok Sahaskriti*, M.1, p.1353:1.
3. *S.B.*, p.114:12:10-11.
4. A.G., *Suhi*, M.5, pp.738-739.
5. *Raidasji ki Bani*, p.3:4.

taking a variety of rituals and ceremonies. The gainers from these practices were always the priests and pundits who controlled the temples and religious institutions and presided over the ceremonies. Kabir had no hesitation in denouncing them:

> Delicacies, sweet and salty, are offered in abundance (to the idols) by the devotees; but after worship the priests walk away with the offerings, throwing dust on the deity's dry face.... Not one, not two, the entire world is deluded by them. One who is not deluded is Kabir the slave, who has taken the Lord's shelter.[1]

Diving for jewels

Saints' ruthless criticism of formalism is not without a purpose. Their approach is always constructive. If they try to shake us from traditional ways of worship, it is because they want to inculcate the true way of devotion in the seeker's heart. If they are iconoclastic, it is because they want men to turn from outer symbols of God to the reality within. They denounce man-made temples and mosques because they know that the true house of God is the human body. If they ask men to give up the pennies of outer rituals, they offer them the real gold of inner realization. But in the words of Kabir, men keep roaming on the shores and picking up empty shells; they do not dive into the sea where priceless jewels await them.

The treasure Saints offer is God-realization; the way to dive into the inner ocean of divine bliss is the spiritual practice which, step by step, takes the devotee back to his destination. Saints initiate seekers into a technique of meditation which consists of *simran* or repetition, *dhyan* or contemplation, and *bhajan* or listening to the melody of Shabd.

Controlling the mind or making it still is a prerequisite for withdrawing the consciousness from the nine portals of the body to the eye center. The Saints' method of spiritual practice is based on the nature of the mind. They note that mind has

---

1. *K.G.*, p.116:198.

three basic traits that stand in the way of the soul's inward journey. The first is its habit of constantly remembering and thinking about the world and its objects. Ever on the move, even during sleep it is not at rest and is dreaming about endless objects and faces.

The second basic trait of the mind, closely allied to its tendency to keep thinking about different worldly objects, is its habit of creating images. Mind's thinking habit is so intense that it visualizes the objects and faces it dwells on. Every thought of the mind is accompanied by its mental picture, and no mental picture is without a thought.

The third characteristic of the mind is that it craves pleasure. Its innate urge for pleasures keeps it brooding over them and seeking opportunities to gratify them. Saints explain that physical limitations of the body are no barrier to the mind's flights. Restrictions placed on the body cannot restrict the mind from thinking about and visualizing material things. And physical denial of pleasures does not preclude the mind from dwelling on them.

When a diver dives for pearls, he has to plunge deep into the sea; he cannot keep a part of his body on dry land.[1] In the same way, all the three qualities of the mind have to be turned inwards if the mind is to withdraw from the body and come to the eye center.

To control the mind's habit of constantly running outside and thinking of the world and its objects, Saints prescribe the technique of repetition. As a substitute for its habit of visualizing material things, they give the method of contemplation. And in place of worldly pleasures, they provide the mind with the ineffable joy of the divine melody, before which all other pleasures fade into insignificance.

Simran: Repetition

Simran, as taught by the Saints, is not an oral repetition. It has to be done by the mind, and not by the tongue, nor with the

1. "Pearls grow in oyster shells, and oyster shells are in the depth of the sea; he who dives and dies while living will acquire them, not he who stays 'alive' " (Kabir, *K.S.S.*, p.115:8).

help of beads, rosaries, prayer wheels or any such external devices. Kabir gives many examples to explain that simran should be done by the mind with full attention and concentration. The mind should be so attuned to simran that it goes on automatically even while the devotee is engaged in fulfilling his worldly obligations: The cow goes to the pasture for grazing, but its attention is constantly with the newborn calf left behind; the miser thinks always of his wealth; the lustful dwell upon the objects of their lust; so should the devotee keep his attention in simran. Only through such intense simran will the outer doors be closed—that is, the mind will retract from the physical body —and the inner spiritual door will be opened.[1]

The Persian Mystics have laid great stress on repetition, and like the Indian Saints insist that it should be done by the mind, not by the tongue. Rumi says that the repetition of the Lord's Name has to be done without tongue and palate. Such repetition brings the soul to the eye center, opens the tenth door and reveals the beauty and splendor of the inner realms.

Again he says: "That repetition is correct which opens the (inner) path; and that path is right on which the banker[2] is met; and the true banker is he who is not rich by virtue of money and jewels, but who is rich within himself."

Saint Ravidas says that when the devotee repeats the Lord's Name and dwells in it, from duality he will merge into non-duality.[3] Guru Arjan Dev has composed many hymns in praise of simran. He says: "He who lives absorbed in simran for even a moment, lives eternally in bliss."[4] In other words, absorption in simran will lead the devotee into the inner worlds of ever-lasting bliss and he will not be required to come back to the circle of birth and death.

Guru Teg Bahadur also says: "Know him as liberated in whose heart dwells simran. Between him and God there is no difference; O Nanak, know this to be true."[5]

---

1. *K.S.S.*, p.88:6,8,9,14.
2. The Master in his radiant form.
3. *Raidasji ki Bani*, p.7:14.
4. A.G., *Gauri*, M.5, p.239.
5. A.G., *Salok*, M.9, p.1428:43.

Repetition is the first step in the spiritual discipline of a devotee initiated by a perfect Master. When the practice is complete, that is, when the disciple attains perfection in repetition,
then the process becomes automatic or involuntary, rather than
a deliberate exercise. The devotee's mind then gives up its habit
of wandering outside, because it begins to relish simran; its attention turns inwards and it becomes fit to experience inner
spiritual bliss.

In a long poem in praise of simran, Kabir says that simran
leads the devotee to the door of salvation, turning his attention
from the physical world to the inner realms. The devotee who
attains proficiency in repetition becomes free from the load that
keeps him bound to the world and releases him from the chain
of coming and going.[1]

Guru Nanak says: "The Lord's Name is divine food,
absorb it to your heart's content. Obtain all boons through
simran—it is the real profit."[2] Guru Gobind Singh also praises
the benefits of simran: "Those who practice the Name with
full concentration, even for a moment, never return to the
snare of Kal."[3]

The agents of Kal, the negative power, often assail the devotee in the inner regions. They try to frighten him, tempt him,
mislead and deceive him by various means. But Saints say that
the moment the devotee repeats the names, all the forces of the
negative power take flight. In a poem about the inner worlds,
Kabir refers to these forces: They adopt evil forms, create
frightening spectacles and harrowing noises; the minions of
Dharam Rai (Kal) shout and try to intimidate the devotee. But
they all take to their heels the moment the names given by the
perfect Master are repeated.[4]

Guru Arjan Dev also says that no obstacles bother the devotee who repeats the Name. Hearing the Name, Yama runs
away to a distance. By repeating the Lord's Name no evil eye
can assail the devotee. By repeating the Lord's Name, neither

1. A.G., *Ramkali*, Kabirji, p.971.
2. A.G., *Bihagara*, M.1, p.556.
3. Dassam Granth, *Akal Ustat*, p.11:1:10.
4. *K.S.*, I:66.

demons nor deities can approach him.[1] Praising the power of simran, Kabir declares: "In the seven islands and nine worlds, such is the power of my Nam that Yama and all evil forces shudder in fear and my victorious drum resounds in the entire Brahmand."[2]

But all Saints emphasize that simran must be obtained from a perfect Master. Simran given by family priests, pundits and monks will be of no use spiritually. The words to be repeated and the exact technique of repetition are given to the disciple at the time of initiation by a perfect Master. Coming from a spiritual adept, the names are not ordinary words, but are charged with the Master's spiritual power. These words may be available in books, but not the spiritual energy of the Master, which alone gives them their force. Kabir says: "Repeat, repeat in your mind the Lord's Name; obtain this simran from a true Master."[3]

An arrow needs the propelling force of the bow to travel a long distance and hit the target; a bullet cannot hit the mark unless it passes through the barrel of a gun. In the same way Nam must come through the medium of a Satguru.

The treasure of simran can only be obtained from a spiritual adept. Guru Arjan Dev says that the Satguru blesses the disciple with the wealth of Nam; the disciple of a perfect Master is indeed fortunate.[4] And again: "The Master's word abides in the soul, it is indestructible—water cannot drown it, thieves cannot steal it, fire cannot consume it."[5] Christ refers to the treasure of meditation in similar terms when he says: "But lay up for yourselves treasures in heaven, where neither moth nor rust doth corrupt, and where thieves do not break through nor steal."[6]

Guru Arjan Dev enjoins upon the disciple to sacrifice his

1. A.G., *Bhairau*, M.5, p.1150.
2. *K.S.S.*, p.84:14. Christ also gives hints that the evil forces of the negative power are dispelled by the Spirit of God, that is, the Word: "But if I cast out devils by the Spirit of God, then the kingdom of God is come unto you" (Matt. 12:28).
3. A.G., *Ramkali*, Kabirji, p.971.
4. A.G., *Gauri*, M.5, p.286.
5. A.G., *Dhanasari*, M.5, p.679.
6. Matt. 6:20.

entire being at the feet of the Master who has given the method of repetition: "Be ever a sacrifice to that Master by whom you have been blessed with the simran of God's Name."[1]

The Master's personal spiritual power imbues the words of simran with a dynamic force. They pull the soul upwards, protect the devotee against pitfalls and endow him with great powers of will and concentration. Words taken from holy books or from any source other than a perfect Master are ineffective and inert. Saint Dariya of Marwar says: "The true words given by the true Guru and the long tusks of a mighty elephant are alike: The latter break open the gates of a fort, the former shatter the barriers of a million karmas. But the tusks without the elephant, O Dariya, cannot break the gates, they can only make bangles for delicate wrists and toys for children."[2]

Kabir repeatedly tries to impress upon the seeker the importance of initiation by a perfect Master into the method of simran: "Only that Name is true, only that Name is your own, which the Master bestows upon you. All other names are false —why run after them?"[3]

Dhyan: Contemplation

When the devotee, with the aid of simran, vacates the physical body and comes to the eye center, his attention slips down again and again, for it finds no object to hold it at the focus. To enable the attention to stay within, Saints give the technique of contemplation. Dhyan or contemplation turns the mind's attention from the world and its objects to the divine form it is taught to contemplate upon.

Mind is in the habit of constantly forming images, it is never blank. The screen of the mind is never without one picture or another. Saints utilize the mind's habit of thinking by applying it to repetition; they utilize its habit of visualizing by applying it to inner contemplation.

1. A.G., *Prabhati*, M.5, p.1338.
2. *Dariya Sahib Marwarwale ki Bani*, p.21:3-4.
3. *K.S.S.*, p.11:129.

126

Almost all religions enjoin on their votaries to contemplate on some idol, picture or symbol of their deity. Such external contemplation of material objects becomes a chain binding the devotee to the object contemplated upon. In fact, it is thus that the mind creates bonds with the physical world—by contemplating or dwelling constantly on the objects of the world.

Birth after birth these links become stronger and keep the mind and soul captive within the confines of matter. Contemplation of inert matter—whether it be the idol of a great prophet or Saint, or the temple of a powerful deity or a symbolic representation of a popular spiritual teacher—will not liberate the seeker from the shackles of birth and death. Kabir says that wherever one's attachments are, there he will go. Through mind, speech and actions, whatever a man dwells on, after death there will his abode be.[1]

Contemplation on trees, reptiles, birds and animals will take the soul to the level of those beings—all inferior to man. Man is the top of the creation, a perfect combination of all the five elements that form the basis of life in this creation. Other creatures, not fully endowed with the five elements and devoid of the finer qualities of mind, such as discrimination, understanding and analysis, are much lower on the ladder of life. Attachment to them will pull the soul down to their level.

Kabir says that having obtained the precious human birth, man should utilize it in that form of devotion which will enable him to escape from the vicious circle of birth and death:

> Adopt such a Master
> That a Master again you do not need to seek;
> Dwell in such a state
> That a dwelling again you do not have to make;
> Undertake such a contemplation
> That contemplation again
> You do not have to undertake.[2]

It is not the contemplation of a material form that Kabir

---

1. *Anurag Sagar*, p.41.
2. A.G., *Gauri*, Kabirji, p.327.

here advises the seeker to adopt, nor is it an external practice. Saints do not ask their disciples to undertake any type of outward contemplation. Saint Dharni Das, speaking of the inner contemplation, says: "I do not store my wealth in treasure chests nor bury it in the earth, nor do I keep it tied securely to my scarf. I hold that wealth, morning and evening, day and night, behind my eyes, softly veiled by the eyelids.... This wealth Dharni found through the grace of his Satguru.[1]

When the devotee has not seen the Lord, and man-made idols and the lower species of life are unfit for his contemplation, on whom should he contemplate? Mystics prescribe contemplation on the form of the perfect Master. The true Master is one who has realized God and become one with Him. In the words of Kabir, seeing such a Master is seeing the Lord himself.[2] And Christ also says: "He that hath seen me hath seen the Father."[3]

The Satguru's physical form is on the level of man, but within, his soul is one with the Supreme Being. To contemplate on him is to contemplate on God. Kabir says: "The Saints' physical form is the mirror of the Formless One. If you long to see the Invisible, see Him in the Saint."[4]

Guru Arjan Dev says: "The Saints are the form of the Eternal Being; they are the proper object to contemplate upon."[5] "By pleasing the Satguru I attained bliss; by contemplating on him I attained all boons."[6]

Persian mystics have also advocated contemplation on the Master's form. Hafiz describes the devotee's experience when contemplation becomes perfect: "When the Master's form was fixed in my heart,[7] the account of the beginning and the end was revealed to me.... O beloved, when in meditation I fixed your form within, then the arch resounded with your call."[8]

---

1. *Dharnidasji ki Bani*, p.18:9.
2. *K.S.*, II:18:2.
3. John 14:9.
4. *K.S.S.*, p.119:31.
5. A.G., *Sarang*, M.5, p.1208.
6. A.G., *Bhairau*, M.5, p.1141.
7. Saints often refer to the eye center as 'the heart'.
8. Mystics refer to the forehead as 'the arch' of the true mosque; at this point the devotee comes in contact with the sound current, here referred to as 'the call' by Hafiz.

Swamiji repeatedly tells the devotee, "Contemplate on the form of the Master, for without this practice you cannot obtain release from the ocean of phenomena."[1] "Contemplate on the form of your Master in the heart (eye center) and every moment repeat his Name."[2]

The only boon that a true seeker desires is God-realization, and contemplation is an important step to it. Guru Nanak says that one who enshrines the form of the Satguru in his heart obtains whatever boons he longs for.[3] Guru Amar Das is all praise for those who contemplate on the form of a perfect Master: "If I should get the dust of the feet of those who contemplate on the perfect Master, I will apply it to my forehead."[4]

True worship of the Lord is the practice of Nam given by the Master, true contemplation is that of the Master's form, and devotion to the Master is true devotion to the Lord. Kabir says: "The prime dhyan, the essence of true contemplation, is that of the Master's form; real worship is the worship of his holy feet; true Name is that which the Master gives; true love is the ultimate Truth."[5]

Bhajan: Listening to the Sound

The third aspect of the spiritual practice prescribed by the Saints is bhajan or listening to the melody of Shabd. When the mind and soul are withdrawn to the eye center with the help of repetition and held there with the aid of contemplation, the devotee comes in contact with Shabd. The divine melody of Word or Shabd is constantly resounding at the eye center of every human being. But one is not aware of its presence until one arrives at this point. When the devotee reaches the door behind the eyes, he hears the Shabd in its enchanting melody and is gradually absorbed in it. Once he comes in direct contact with the sound current, it draws him towards itself and takes him

---

1. *S.B.*, p.143:2:1.
2. *S.B.*, p.134:3:1.
3. A.G., *Dhanasari*, M.1, p.661.
4. A.G., *Bhairau*, M.3, p.1131.
5. *K.S.S.*, p.4:43.

upwards into the higher spiritual regions, ultimately to his real home.

Although this melody, in its full force and splendor, can be experienced only on going within, the Saints teach the method of listening to it even while the devotee is within the nine portals of the body. The perfect Master connects the disciple's soul to the Shabd at the time of initiation, and after a little practice the disciple starts hearing the Shabd during the period of his meditation.

The perfect Master is an adept in the spiritual practice, having himself become one with that power of the Supreme Being —the all-pervading and all-sustaining Shabd. Merged in Shabd, the Master is the personification of Shabd; he is the manifestation of the ultimate power on the physical level. He alone has the competence and power to put others on the path to the realization of Shabd.

The threefold technique of repetition, contemplation and listening to the sound current is taught to the seeker at the time of initiation. Initiation by a perfect Master is thus the first step on the spiritual path. Saints say that the Master is the gateway to salvation, the Master himself is the path to God. Saint Rajab says that without the Guru one cannot reach the destination, one cannot even know about it; without the path—the Master—how can the traveler even step into that foreign land?[1] Guru Arjan Dev says: "Without initiation from the Master, how can one acquire true knowledge; without seeing, how can one contemplate?"[2]

Kabir says that he realized the Truth only when the Master showed him the path; within the body he found the arduous route and through the arduous route, his destination.[3] Through instructions given by the Master, the difficult way becomes easy, the inaccessible inner regions attainable, and spiritual bliss—the dream of yogis, ascetics and pundits—a reality. Kabir says: The Satguru took mercy on me, he blessed me with

1. *Sant Sudha Sar*, p.524:6.
2. A.G., *Bhairau*, M.5, p.1140.
3. *K.G.*, p.10:9.

the eternal Word; its shade is cool, its fruit easy of access; the swan (soul) now revels in waves of bliss.[1] I will not leave the practice of the true Name which the Master has taught. Through it I have touched the Imperishable One, and I too have become imperishable.[2]

Guru Arjan Dev says in his acrostic: "O mind, take the shelter of the Saint, discard your cleverness, your crafty ways. He in whose mind dwell the Master's instructions is the truly fortunate one."[3] Saint Bhikha praises the Master's gift of initiation: "My Master has given me the alms of sound and light, which I see and hear without eyes and ears."[4]

The object of meditation is to merge the soul into Shabd. Success in the spiritual practice prescribed by the perfect Masters leads the soul to God-realization. Kabir describes the outcome of successful meditation thus: "When the body is motionless and the mind is still and *surat* and *nirat* are still too; O Kabir, the glory of such a moment not a billion years' happiness in the heavens can equal."[5] The crowning point of meditation is attained when the conscious repetition of names, the involuntary repetition by the mind, and even the unstruck music cease to exist, for the soul merging in Shabd itself becomes Shabd, the drop becomes the Ocean. Kabir continues: "The repeated will die, the unrepeated will die, even the Unstruck will be no more; the soul will merge into Shabd and transcend the bounds of Kal."[6]

The practice of Shabd or Nam purifies the mind and turns it inwards. Meditation removes all obstacles in the disciple's inner journey and destroys the store of karmas which bring the soul to the world again and again. Kabir says that the effects of a million sins are wiped out by practicing the Nam that the Satguru gives.[7] Faith and absorption in the true Name dispel all delusions and eliminate all karmas; and the Master fulfills

1. *K.S.S.*, p.10:111.
2. *K.S.S.*, p.8:97.
3. A.G., *Gauri, Bawan Akhari*, M.5, p.260.
4. *Bhikha Sahib ki Bani*, p.55:31:3.
5. *K.S.S.*, p.89:26.
6. *K.S.S.*, p.89:27.
7. *K.S.S.*, p.86:40.

the devotee's desires, for the devotee gives up all hopes, in a world alive with hope.[1]

As one sows

In the physical, astral and causal worlds nothing can happen without a cause. In the region of mind and maya every action has a motive force or cause behind it and, in turn, every action becomes the cause of further effects. This sequence of cause and effect, which keeps the soul confined within the perimeter of the worlds of mind and matter, is known as the law of karma.

The chain of cause and effect is long, complex and almost impossible to trace. For example, air travel is possible today because of a number of factors leading to the invention of the first airplane at the beginning of the century. This in turn was the result of the discoveries leading to the utilization of power; and prior to that, about two hundred years ago, the day a scientist observed the lid of his kettle jumping to the force of steam; and the chain of causes leading to this can take us back to the day man first learned to use fire. If one traces the chain of cause and effect, it will be found to be endless, almost eternal. From the moment of creation, the law of cause and effect has been a dominant and driving force.

In the scheme of creation, according to the law of karma, a soul's birth in the world, the environment in which it is born, the happiness and suffering it undergoes here are all the result of some earlier cause. And although it is impossible to solve the riddle whether the seed came first or the tree, there is no disputing the fact that there can be no seed without a tree, nor any tree without a seed. There is not an event or action in life without a cause, and every action, in turn, becomes the cause of some future effect.

Kabir says: "As are one's actions, so will be the life he lives."[2] Guru Nanak confirms it, saying: "As one sows, so does he reap; as one earns, so does he eat."[3] And again, "As one

1. *K.S.S.*, p.87:51.
2. *K.S.S.*, p.80:30.
3. A.G., *Suhi*, M.1, p.730.

does, so does he receive; what a man himself sows, he himself has to eat."[1] Kabir says that such is the law of this creation that "whatever one puts into a kettle, the same will pour out of the spout."[2]

Guru Arjan Dev describes the world as a field of karmas or actions. In his well-known hymns on the twelve months of the year, he declares that "what one sows, that he reaps"; according to his actions a man's fate is determined and he undergoes that which is "written on his forehead."[3]

Almost the same terminology has been used in the Bible to convey the idea of cause and effect, of every good and bad action leading to a corresponding result: "Whatsoever a man soweth, that shall he also reap. For he that soweth to his flesh shall of the flesh reap corruption; but he that soweth to the Spirit shall of the Spirit reap life everlasting."[4]

In the Old Testament also there are references to what Saints have described as the law of karma: "They that plow iniquity, and sow wickedness, reap the same.[5] For they have sown the wind, and they shall reap the whirlwind. . . . Sow to yourselves in righteousness, reap in mercy."[6]

A man's actions, whether good or bad, keep him bound to the world of mind and maya. Every action is a bond, a chain which keeps growing longer as a result of new actions, each act forging additional links. Kabir expresses it through the imagery of a rope, which is twisted together from thin strings to form a strong cord: "Man himself entwines the rope of karmas, which becomes a noose around his own neck."[7]

The motive force behind all karmas is the mind, and body is the instrument that executes the mind's dictates. As a result of these actions, the mind comes back to the world again and again in different bodies and surroundings. The soul, knotted together with the mind, has to follow. Kabir says that the soul,

---

1. A.G., *Dhanasari*, M.1, p.662.
2. *Bijak, Shabd* 21.
3. A.G., *Majh, Barah Maha*, M.5, p.134.
4. Gal. 6:7-8.
5. Job 4:8.
6. Hos. 8:7; 10:12.
7. *K.S.*, II:7:14:2.

tied by the chain of karmas, day and night comes and goes. Even after obtaining the human birth, it forgets devotion to God and repents at death.[1] Guru Nanak says: "Through karmas one gets the garment (of the body); through (God's) grace, salvation."[2]

Happiness and pain in this world are the results of past actions. Saints say that when a person has only good karmas to his credit, he is sent to the heavens to enjoy their fruit. Yet attaining paradise is not a release from the chain of cause and effect. After the fruits of those particular acts of merit have been enjoyed, the soul has to return to the physical world. Predominantly bad actions lead the soul to regions of suffering called hell. In both cases the soul eventually comes back to this world of matter.

The vast number of actions that a person performs in one birth is so great that he cannot atone for them in a single succeeding birth. The karmas not accounted for in the next birth are stored for a future birth. With each birth the store of karmas—called accumulated or *sanchit* karmas—keeps on growing, and even if a person could avoid doing any karma in a certain birth, he would still be given another birth because of his store of karmas.

A soul does not always come as a human being. As a result of its actions, cravings and desires, it goes into lower species of life—animals, birds, fish, reptiles, insects and even plants. Kabir says that through actions men are born again and again, and this chain never breaks.[3] Thus the soul continues to be born in various species over and again:

> In the immobile and the mobile,
> Among the worms and the moths
> Many births I had,
> In many forms I revelled.
> Since the day Thou subjected me, Lord,

1. *K.G.*, p.173, *Saptpadi Ramaini* 5.
2. A.G., *Japji*, M.1, p.2:4.
3. A.G., *Ramkali*, Kabirji, p.971.

To visitations to the womb,
In many a home have I made my sojourn.[1]

Guru Arjan Dev also says: "Many lives have you had as insects and worms, many lives as elephants, fish and deer; in many lives were you born a snake or a bird, and countless times you lived as a tree. After eons you have obtained the glory of human birth, now it's your chance—meet the Lord!"[2]

Persian Saints also endorse the theory of transmigration of the soul. Shams-i-Tabriz says: "A hundred forms we adopt in this world, sometimes one, sometimes another....A hundred thousand times we have come and gone from this world, for this world is a place of coming and going." Maulana Rum says that he has been born and has grown like grass in this world innumerable times, and has experienced eighty-four aspects of life. "If I were to reveal the account of my existence, then I have seen seven hundred and seventy[3] bodies, and endless times I have grown as vegetables."

The world is full of misery. Even if a soul is born in the human form and in rich surroundings with all the coveted physical comforts, it has to live under the shadows of disease and old age. And it has to go through the gates of death, only to be sent back to the world to undergo pleasure and pain according to its deeds. Luxury and comfort in the world is not freedom; a bird in a golden cage is yet a bird in captivity.

Good deeds cannot liberate the soul from the chain of birth and death, for such is the inexorable law of cause and effect that in order to enjoy the reward of good actions, the soul has to come back to this world. Kabir describes the effect of karmas with a vivid analogy: In the bower of the body is laid the flowerbed of karmas—such is the garden the Creator has designed. The spark of the Immortal—the soul—enters it and helps the creepers of karmas to spread and spread.[4]

---

1. A.G., *Gauri*, Kabirji, p.325.
2. A.G., *Gauri*, M.5, p.176.
3. Some scholars believe that *haft sad haftad* (700+70) should actually read *haft do haftad* (14+70), that is, 'eighty-four', a reference to the 84 hundred thousand species that constitute the cycle of transmigration.
4. *K.S.*, IV:21:ka.

Saint Bhikha also says: "Good and evil deeds are the ever-thriving dual plants, they bear the fruits of birth and death. The soul rambles from leaf to leaf and branch to branch and loses its name of 'the immortal one',"[1] for it takes birth and dies again and again.

Soul can obtain release from the bondage of cause and effect only in the human form. Thus, angels, deities, gods and goddesses all thirst for a human birth. Kabir says that even gods long for the human form; man has obtained such a precious body, now he should keep himself engaged in devotion; this is his opportunity, his only chance to contemplate and realize God within his own body.[2]

The priceless treasure of human birth is a gift from the Lord. Although Saints clearly state that all karmas, both good and bad, are shackles that keep the soul bound to the plane of matter, they advocate good deeds as against evil ones. To be kind, helpful, gentle, tolerant and non-violent is better than to be cruel, hateful and violent; to try to realize God, even through external practices, is better than to remain completely engrossed in worldly pursuits. For it is only as a result of good actions that the soul obtains the human birth—a chance to realize God and be released from the chains of mind, matter and maya.

The bonds of karma have been described as a threefold chain. Even if one were to succeed in breaking one or two of the strands, the third one is enough to keep the soul tied to the world. The three strands are the three types of karmas, called *prarabdh, kriyaman* and *sanchit.*

The fate karmas, with which a person is born in the world and which he has to undergo during his present life, are called *prarabdh* karmas. The actions or karmas that he does while living in the world are *kriyaman* or 'karmas being performed'. *Sanchit* or store karmas are those karmas that are accumulated life after life and have yet to be accounted for.

A soul is born into the world in a particular family and

1. *Bhikha Sahib ki Bani,* p.21:12:2.
2. A.G., *Bhairau,* Kabirji, p.1159.

environment <u>not by its choice</u> but according to its *prarabdh* or fate karmas. Life in the world runs along a predestined line of fate or destiny. And the world is so conceived that no one can exist without doing any action. The very process of life here involves action. All actions, voluntary or involuntary, in turn become the cause of a future effect. To live in the world, to support himself, a man has to act. Simple actions like walking, talking and even breathing involve him in the chain of cause and effect.

The actions in one human birth alone are so numerous that their effect cannot be gone through in the next life. The karmas that are not accounted for, which may be described as seeds not yet germinated, form a vast store. Thus the debit balance of the soul's karmic account keeps on increasing with each birth.

Such then is the design of the creation and the law governing it that a soul is born under the influence of karmas, lives and dies in karma, and even after death has to face the waiting store of *sanchit* karmas. Having once become a slave, it is a slave for all time.

Kabir says that man in this world is surrounded by the fire of karmas; whether he goes left or right—follows one way or another—he is always in the midst of that invisible fire. He lives and acts under the dictates of the law of cause and effect. He has a huge store of karmas to be accounted for behind him —his unrequited debt—and the future also is not free from this rigid bondage:

> There is fire on the left,
>> Fire on the right,
> In fire all move and act;
>> Behind and in front
> Deadly fires burn;
>> One's only refuge
> Is the Almighty One.[1]

---

1. *K.G.*, p.48:7.

To escape the fire

The seeker who realizes that the cause of his agony of repeated births and deaths is the ever-raging fire of karmas wonders if at all there is a way to escape. If the Saints try to make the seeker aware of his misery, they also show the path of release. They suggest three ways to overcome the force of the threefold affliction of karma; namely, acceptance, surrender and Shabd practice.

The devotee should realize that fate karma or his destiny has to be undergone. He is born with his destiny and there is no escape from it. The feelings of elation or resentment that accompany the process of going through one's destiny lead to further karmic bonds. Attachment and hate, friendship and enmity, pride and resentment are strong feelings that gradually form grooves on the mind and in the course of time become the cause of further effects.

Saints, therefore, suggest that the devotee should accept his destiny, the happy as also the unhappy events of his life, with a relaxed and detached attitude of mind. Whatever he is going through in this birth is the result of his own past actions, and he has to endure it. The ups and downs of life are a part of the design of this world of duality, of happiness and misery, of pleasure and pain, of prosperity and penury, of life and death. If such is the world's pattern and if there is no escape from the result of previous actions, Saints say why not try to accept things gracefully as they come. All the three regions of cause and effect are created with the consent and will of the Supreme Father. The devotee should, therefore, accept all events and circumstances in life as the Lord's will.

Kabir compares the human body to a pot made by the Great Potter. The pots are entirely at the potter's mercy—he can put them in the open to face the sun and rain or store them carefully within his house. He has molded them, he protects them from damage if he wants to and breaks them if he so desires. The pots have no say. Kabir says that in the same way the Creator has fashioned the human body; He can protect it and destroy it at his will. Realizing this, the devotee should try to live as and how the Potter keeps him.[1]

Living in God's will also includes doing one's duty in the world without getting involved in it and without bothering about the result of one's efforts. The devotee accepts all that comes in life as the Lord's will and attends to his worldly obligations as a task allotted by Him. This attitude strengthens his devotion and enables him to escape from the bondage of *kriyaman* karmas, from the fruits of his day-to-day actions.

To attain patience and courage for accepting the hardships and affluence of life with equanimity is difficult. Even more so is to act in the world without feeling oneself to be the doer, that is, to eliminate I-ness from all actions. But this is the only way to live in the world of karmas and yet be 'karma-free'—to act and be immune to the fruit of actions.

Saints do not prescribe the impossible. The devotee can achieve this state of detachment through the practice of Shabd or Nam and the grace of a perfect Master. Kabir says that the happy and unhappy results of previous good and bad karmas will not decrease or increase even by a grain. Why should the devotee worry or become anxious? Asking him to serve the Saints and live according to their directions, Kabir says that this will release him from a million maladies in the future; in this way alone will a soul be ferried across the ocean with ease.[2]

The practice of Shabd gives spiritual courage and strength to the disciple for going through his destiny with composure. Thus he goes through his *prarabdh* or fate karmas cheerfully and pays off the debt without incurring new commitments in the process. And he escapes the danger of acquiring new karmas by acting without involvement and attachment. Thus fate karmas are accounted for by going through them; and creating new karmas is avoided through detachment and elimination of ego. Yet the *sanchit* or accumulated karmas still remain to be accounted for.

Saints agree that the soul cannot become free unless all karmas are eliminated; even the seed of karma must lose its power

---

1. *K.G.*, p.77:34.
2. *K.S.*, II:1:1:1,5.

of germination. Kabir tells the devotee to give up pride of high caste and lineage, give up unnecessary involvements, and look for the state of true freedom; for only when the seed and its power of germination are destroyed, will the soul obtain an abode in 'the bodiless realm'—the region of pure spirit.[1]

Saints tell the devotee that the way to destroy the vast store of accumulated karmas is the practice of Nam or Shabd. This is the only way to annihilate them. Ramanand declares: "The Guru's Shabd eradicates a million karmas."[2] Guru Arjan Dev says that a million karmas are destroyed by repetition of the Lord's Name.[3] Asking the disciple to undertake the practice of Shabd, Swamiji says: "By the might of Shabd vanquish the negative power. . . . Shabd will wipe out the groove of karmas; Shabd will carry you and merge you with the source of Shabd."[4]

One obtains the human birth only after numerous incarnations in the circle of eighty-four hundred thousand species. It is, therefore, a precious and rare chance to meet the Lord. But such is the design of this world that the moment a soul is born, it forgets its past miseries; and as a person grows up, the soul's natural inclination towards God is completely overshadowed by his attraction for worldly objects. Saints try to remind man of his misery and urge him to be rid of the bondage of karmas, which is keeping him tied to the world.

Kabir says: "When you descended from the womb and landed in the world, with the first breath you forgot the Lord. O friend, now sing the praises of God. . . . You wandered through the intricate forests of the eighty-four lakh species before coming into the human frame. If you lose this chance, you will find neither shade nor shelter. Says Kabir: Adore the Lord, adore Him who is never seen to come, nor known to depart."[5]

The practice of Shabd is the only means of burning the huge 'haystack' of accumulated karmas. All Saints have repeatedly

---

1. *K.G.*, p.182, *Ashtpadi Ramaini, Doha* 5.
2. A.G., *Basant Hindol*, Ramanandji, p.1195.
3. A.G., *Gauri Sukhmani*, M.5, p.264.
4. *S.B.*, p.91:5:11,13.
5. A.G., *Gauri*, Kabirji, p.337.

implored man to give his entire attention to Nam and meditation. Rajjab, a Saint from Rajasthan, says: "According to your
own good and bad deeds you were born here. What you sowed,
the same is given you to reap. Why complain now? Why did
you not adore the Lord earlier?...Just as the shadow of a well
never comes out of the well, so now, O Rajjab, keep your attention within—absorbed in the Lord."[1]

Kabir puts it in his direct way: "Realize the one and only
Name and erase the stain of karmas. Then will the soul become
immaculate, then will it be free from fear and pain."[2] Is there
no other way to erase this stain, no other practice to destroy
the store of karmas and become pure? Kabir says: "Place your
hope only in the one Name; discard all other hopes and expectations. Depending on other things will destroy you like a pawn
on the chausar board."[3]

Saints say that except for the practice of Nam, whatever
practices one undertakes, further tighten the noose of karmas.
Guru Arjan Dev is emphatic on this point: "A myriad practices you undertook, but whatever you did became heavy
shackles on your feet."[4] "Even through a million means one
cannot be released; all cleverness, all ruses only make the load
heavier. Serve the Lord with purity and love and arrive with
honor in His court."[5]

Attachment to the world brings the soul back to the world;
attachment to Shabd takes it back to the source of Shabd. All
Saints point out the futility of worldly pursuits, of love for the
world and its objects and faces. Kabir describes the world as a
large tree where birds come together to spend the hours of the
night and go their way at sunrise; as a weekly market where
people go to buy and sell their goods—to pay off the debts of
past karmas and incur new ones—and return at sunset; as the
sea where the waves of karmas bring boats together and, after

1. *Sant Sudha Sar*, p.529:47, 51.
2. *K.S.S.*, p.84:17.
3. *K.S.S.*, p.85:25. *Chausar* or *chaupar*, an Indian game played with dice, in which the player tries to 'kill' the opponent's pawn by moving his own pawn onto the square occupied by his opponent's.
4. A.G., *Maru*, M.5, p.1075.
5. A.G., *Gauri*, M.5, p.178.

a while, disperse them again; as a stage where the soul is given a part according to its past deeds and, after playing the allotted role, makes its exit.

Rajjab says: "One actor has performed his role and left; another, dressed up for his part, enters the stage; and yet another, O Rajjab, is on his way. Such is the Creator's play."[1] Vakhna, an advanced devotee of Saint Dadu, like Kabir and other Saints, says that the way to obtain release from the chain of karmas is the Master's grace and the disciple's devotion: "Wandering endlessly through the maze of eighty-four, I have at last arrived at your door. It is you who pointed out that God is the succor of the fallen and forlorn. If one is tied by man-made laws, one can pay the price and be released; but those bound by the shackles of karmas can only be set free by you, my Master, the beloved of the Lord."[2]

Kabir says that a million karmas are destroyed in a moment when the devotee takes the Master's shelter.[3] Using the analogy of a blacksmith, Kabir shows the way to erase the record of *sanchit* or 'store' karmas: "On the anvil of meditation, with your *surat* and *nirat* as the pair of tongs, hit forcefully with the hammer of Nam and eradicate the groove of karmas."[4]

Who kill, will be killed

All spiritual paths have a code of ethics; so does the path of the Saints. It does not consist of external observances like fasts, eating a special diet on particular days of the month, or ritual charities to priests and other selected people. While the general principles of truthfulness, honesty, tolerance, kindness and righteous conduct are some of the qualities coveted by the disciples of the Saints, the devotee is also required to desist from partaking of non-vegetarian food, alcohol, drugs; in fact, all types of intoxicants and anything containing them. He should lead an honest and morally pure life and give regular time to spiritual practice.

---

1. *Sant Sudha Sar*, p.531:65.
2. *Bakhnaji ki Vani*, p.173:162.
3. *K.S.S.*, p.10:115.
4. *K.S.*, II:101:5:3.

Kindness, mercy and love for all creatures is an essential part of spiritual practice. Cruelty, hatred and killing for food or pleasure have no place on the path of the Saints. Kabir asks the devotee to be merciful and kind to all, because from the tiny ant to the mighty elephant all beings belong to God.[1] Guru Nanak says: "He who dies while living realizes everything[2] and develops inner compassion for all. O Nanak, he obtains true glory who recognizes the Lord in all creatures."[3]

The devotee who recognizes the Lord in the entire creation can never think of hurting or harming any living being, let alone killing one. Sheikh Sadi says that the man devoid of feelings of mercy and kindness towards God's creatures is dead like a portrait on a wall. Hafiz also declares that if a person longs for a permanent abode in the heavens, he should be kind and compassionate to all God's beings.

In the words of Guru Nanak, in all beings, of the water, earth or sky, here, there, everywhere resides the Lord.[4] Guru Arjan Dev asks the devotee to practice truth, contentment and compassion—the essence of all pious deeds.[5]

The rays of divine love will not enter a hard and cruel heart. A person who harms others, kills God's creatures and devours them cannot go within and merge with Shabd. Guru Arjan Dev points out that humility and mercy are essential if the devotee is to go back to his original home and become one with God: "Become the dust of everyone's feet and merge in the Lord; do not cause pain to any creature, go back to your Home with honor."[6] Guru Nanak, in his hymn on the days of the fortnight, advises devotees to enthrone the One in their hearts and give up killing, selfishness and attachment.[7]

Kabir strongly criticizes the priests and mullahs, who advocate killing and meat-eating and even prescribe it on religious

---

1. *K.S.S.*, p.141:6:2.
2. "Realize everything" implies realization of the ultimate Reality.
3. A.G., *Ramkali*, M.1, p.940. The last line could also be interpreted as 'who sees himself in all creatures', that is, who realizes that all creatures have a soul like him and are therefore equally important in the creation.
4. A.G., *Bhairau*, M.1, p.1127.
5. A.G., *Siri Rag*, M.5, p.51.
6. A.G., *Gauri ki Var*, M.5, p.322.
7. A.G., *Bilawal, Thinti*, M.1, p.840. *Thinti* is a traditional poem cycle in which each stanza is based on a day of the lunar fortnight.

grounds. To the pundits and Hindu priests, he says: "O Pande, what evil ways you have adopted. . . . You kill living creatures and call it piety; then tell me, what will you term impiety? You call one another holy men; what then will you call the butcher?"[1] To the mullahs, Kabir says: "You violently slaughter innocent animals and claim it is *halal*—in keeping with the canons of the creed. But when God puts before you the record of these cruel deeds, imagine what your fate will be."[2]

Guru Ravidas is also clearly against killing and eating meat: "Do not kill any creature; in all beings dwells the Lord. O Ravidas, the sin of killing will not be atoned for, even if one were to give a million cows in charity."[3]

Dadu, another Muslim mystic like Kabir, expresses the same idea when he says: O Dadu, every being is a temple of God, where dwells the Eternal One. Why demolish that which bears the Lord's mark?[4] Says Dadu, you slaughter the helpless goat, you cut its throat while repeating the *kalma;* even if you perform *namaz* five times a day, you are deluded in your faith.[5] Dadu, he is ruthless, deluded and callous who eats meat; he is heartless, vile and depraved who deprives a living being of its life.[6]

Tulsi Sahib of Hathras refers to Kabir, Guru Nanak and other Saints while advocating a vegetarian diet: "The fowler catches birds to eat; in the same way will Yama catch and torment him. All who eat fish and meat will be seized by Kal, the ruthless butcher. They who eat meat are of no worth. If you don't believe me, read the words of Nanak and Kabir, of Dadu and Dariya and of all other Saints. . . . Nanak, among the Saints, is truly great; whatever he said is true. . . . Through the Shabd practice he reached the supreme abode and himself became the Boundless and Supreme. Tulsi bows to him and

---

1. A.G., *Maru*, Kabirji, p.1103.
2. A.G., *Salok*, Kabirji, p.1375:199.
3. *Ravidas Darshan*, ed. Prithvi Singh Azad, p.184:85.
4. *Dadudayal*, p.274:28.
5. *Dadudayal*, p.148:10. Orthodox Muslims slaughter an animal while repeating the *kalma*, a short eulogy of God and Prophet Mohammed. The meat is thus considered to become fit for eating, according to the canon of the creed.
6. *Dadudayal*, p.276:40.

declares: Nanak Sahib was extremely kind and compassionate, he never preached killing God's creatures. O Tulsi, all meat-eating is the result of men's craving for taste and of their selfishness; for the sake of their palate and lust of tongue men advocate eating meat. I tell you again, in his writings Nanak does not ordain eating meat."[1]

The Saints' insistence on a vegetarian diet is based on the law of karma. According to the Saints, those who kill will in turn be killed; who make the living their food, will one day become food for others. Such is the process of cause and effect that every debt has to be paid, the account of every deed has to be cleared. In the court of retribution there is neither any mercy nor any appeal. Vajid, a Muslim mystic of Rajasthan, says:

> In the Lord's court, petitioned the goat:
> 'The qazi seized me and dragged me,
> He severed my head;
> In return, O Lord,
> Let his head be cut off.'
> Justice, O Vajid, will indeed be rendered,
> Both to the strong
> And to the weak.[2]

Kabir also says that those who take hemp, fish and wine will go to hell in spite of all their fasts, pilgrimages and numerous pious deeds.[3] Dariya Sahib of Bihar expresses the same thought when he declares: He who desists from killing, even from hurting other creatures, that devotee is dear to Allah. He who kills living beings and who eats meat hastens towards the gates of hell.[4] Like your own life, is life dear to every being; do not kill, do not take intoxicants; discard your ego, your claims to superiority.[5]

Kabir is severe in his denunciation of the meat-eater, whom

1. *Ghat Ramayan*, II:124, 149, 152.
2. *Panchamrit*, ed. Swami Mangal Das, p.95:3. Vajid is also known as Vajind in Rajasthan.
3. A.G., *Salok*, Kabirji, p.1377:233.
4. *Dariya Granthavali, Brahm Prakash, Chaupai* 466-468.
5. Ibid., *Gyan Sarode, Chaupai* 25-26.

he calls a demon in human form.[1] Those who kill will in turn be killed, whether they kill for food or for sport.[2] Meat is the food of dogs, not his who is blessed with a human form.[3] Advising people to eat grains and vegetables, Kabir says:

> Who eats grain is a man,
> Who eats meat, a dog;
> Who renders the living being dead
> Is a devil incarnate.[4]

Saint Malukdas says: "The pain of all is the same, but the fool does not realize it; when even the prick of a thorn hurts, why should men cut the throats of animals for their food?"[5] Paltu says that those who hurt God's creatures are kafirs or heretics: "In all beings life is the same, within all dwells the One, and no other. O Maulvi, it does not behoove you to kill living beings. . . . Why do you deprive them of life, why do you sin? Says Paltu, he is the kafir who is cruel and heartless."[6]

Learning and knowledge of scriptures is of no consequence if the scholar is hard-hearted and cruel. Non-violence, compassion and a merciful heart are of greater value on the path to God-realization than intellectual knowledge and analytical excellence. Kabir adds: "If a person is devoid of mercy and kindness and yet boasts of vast learning, he will go to hell in spite of his knowledge even of Saints' works."[7]

Dharni Das expresses the same idea with Kabir-like acuity: "They who eat meat and at the same time boast of their knowledge are like a naked woman trying to veil her face; seeing them, Dharni feels ashamed."[8]

The religion which propagates killing and meat-eating is deluding its followers. Kabir calls all such religions irreligious, and the piety they propound, impiety:

1. *K.S.S.*, p.161:1.
2. *K.S.S.*, p.162:6.
3. *K.S.S.*, p.162:4.
4. *Satt Kabir ki Shabdavali,* ed. Manilal Tulsidas Mehta, p.356:886.
5. *Malukdasji ki Bani,* p.33:54.
6. *Paltu Sahib,* I, *Kundli* 215.
7. *K.S.S.*, p.141:6:1.
8. *Dharnidasji ki Bani,* p.47:65.

Ritual sacrifices of goats,
　　Of cows, horses and human beings,
Are acts of impiety
　　Which the Vedas and scriptures teach
As noble and pious deeds.
　　Kabir, acts of violence,
Of killing the living,
　　Will pile a heavy load
Of sins on man's head.
　　Not one has ever reached heaven,
Nor ever will
　　Through such heinous deeds—
Even if the scriptures
　　Praise them and preach.[1]

Intoxicants

Another important aspect of the path is abstinence from all
types of alcoholic drinks and other intoxicants. Kabir says:

O wise ones, consider
　　The curse of wine:
You part with money
　　That with effort you earn,
In order to turn from man
　　Into beast.[2]

Intoxicants degrade a man to the level of a beast; they deaden
his sensitivity to noble qualities and cripple his will power.
Besides being a social evil, they are a great hindrance on the
spiritual path.

　　The practice of taking intoxicants unsettles the poise of the
mind, and it starts relishing the false feeling of elevation produced by them. It becomes difficult to divert the mind's attention from these pleasures and turn it inwards. When they become a habit, intoxicants—like all habits—turn the mind into

1. *Satt Kabir*, p.353:886, 883.
2. *K.S.S.*, p.163:4.

147

a slave. Even if they do not become a habit, they draw the mind into physical pleasures and obstruct the devotee's efforts to withdraw it to the eye center. The aim of meditation is to take the mind to the subtle regions of spiritual bliss, whereas intoxicants keep it involved in and tied to the gross world. They land the mind in a world of make-believe, while the devotee's object is to go within and experience Reality.

Saints always warn against the evils of intoxicants. Nevertheless, alcohol is advocated by some religions as a ritual necessity; there used to be, and still are a few types of yogis and sadhus who use and prescribe intoxicants and sex as an aid to meditation. In medieval days such people were called *sakats,* and Saints like Kabir, Guru Nanak, Ravidas and Dadu have strongly denounced them as charlatans who seek to gratify their low desires in the name of spirituality. Kabir says: "O Kabir, a swine is better than a *sakat,* for it keeps the village clean;[1] when the wretched *sakat* dies, no one takes his name."[2]

Guru Amar Das says: "The *sakat,* lured by evil tendencies, knows not the ambrosia of divine love. He dissipates the nectar of spirituality in deluded practices; he is engrossed in the poison of sensuousness."[3] In the words of Guru Arjan Dev: "While living he never awakes, at death he becomes one with dust; O Nanak, he worships and craves the world—such is the *sakat,* ignorant and impure."[4]

Saint Ravidas says that even if wine were to be made out of the holy and pure waters of the Ganga, the men of God would not touch it.[5] Intoxicants are an obstacle in the seeker's efforts to realize God; they can never be an aid. Kabir declares:

> Opium and hemp,
> Tobacco and wine,
> Kabir, discard them all

1. In India pigs are considered to be among the lowest of the animals since they act as scavengers in villages and towns, eating all the filth and refuse from the streets.
2. A.G., *Salok,* Kabirji, p.1372:143.
3. A.G., *Bilawal,* M.3, p.854.
4. A.G., *Gujari Var,* M.5, p.523.
5. A.G., *Malar,* Ravidasji, p.1293.

> If you crave a glimpse
> Of the Lord.[1]

Saints say that wine and intoxicating drugs lead a man to other allied evils. They pull him away from the path to God. According to Dadu, those who eat meat and drink wine, also sink into the evils of sensuousness. They fail to realize Him who pervades every being; they lose kindness and compassion.[2]

The intoxication of divine bliss that the devotee enjoys on going within is the real wine—the wine of the Lord's love, an intoxication that never fades. Absorbed in the joy of the inner worlds, the devotee becomes oblivious of the outer one. The intoxicants of the world only cloud the mind and result in physical and spiritual misery. Guru Amar Das says: "These drinks are made by man and by man are they poured; he who drinks them loses his senses and becomes mad, he loses the discrimination between who is his and who is another's, and he is spurned by the Lord. He drinks and forgets his Master and receives punishment from the Court. Never drink this vicious wine if you long for an abode in the beyond. O Nanak, with God's grace, he who meets a perfect Master drinks the true wine; he stays ever intoxicated in God's love and finds a place in the palace."[3] Kabir echoes the same thought:

> Kabir is intoxicated with Nam,
> Not with wine, nor with drugs;
> He who drinks from Nam's cup
> Is the truly intoxicated one.[4]

Not a path of extremes

A pure life and moral conduct are of prime importance on the path of the Saints. But mystics do not ask their disciples to adopt celibacy, nor to leave family and children. The devotee must do his duty towards his family, look after his children and

---

1. *K.S.S.*, p.163:3.
2. *Dadudayal*, p.148:8.
3. *A.G., Bihagare ki Var*, M.3, p.554.
4. *K.S.S.*, p.163:8.

149

earn his own living by honest means. His involvement in worldly relationships should, however, be limited to the fulfillment of his duties and obligations, and not carried so far as to become an obsession.

Kabir advocates a controlled family life, not renunciation. While leading a householder's life, the disciple should attend to his meditation and keep his mind aloof from the world. Kabir asks the devotee to live as a householder, but at the same time to lead a life of purity; to develop discrimination, contentment and purity of thought and conduct. He calls upon the devotee to follow the directions of the Master, to keep the company of the Saints and to serve them with mind, body and heart.[1]

Kabir describes his path as the middle path. It is neither a path of attachment, nor of renunciation; neither of involvement, nor of segregation; neither of abstinence, nor of indulgence. It is not a path of an ascetic, nor that of a hedonist. The path of the Saints is a path of moderation. Kabir conveys this in his metaphorical style:

> Too much speaking is not good,
> Nor is too much silence;
> Excess rain is no use,
> Nor is excess sunshine.[2]

Saints impress upon the disciple to live in the world, but not belong to it. He should be like the lotus flower, which is born in water, grows in water and lives in water, yet remains dry; or like the waterfowl, which stays in water, eats in water, but flies away with dry wings. Living thus in the world, the devotee will cross the ocean of phenomena through the practice of Shabd. Guru Nanak says: "As the lotus lives in water, untouched by it; as the waterfowl floats in the rivers, but remains dry; so (live and) cross the ocean of the world, by joining your soul to Shabd; such is the glory of Nam, O Nanak."[3]

---

1. *K.S.S.*, p.129:1.
2. *K.S.S.*, p.76.
3. A.G., *Ramkali*, M.1, p.938.

Under the heading, "The Middle Path," Dadu praises Kabir and also recommends his way: " 'In between' was the manner of Kabir, which those attached to the one or to the other cannot adopt. They may try but will land again on the earth, as do the deer after their long leaps. The way of Kabir's life was extremely hard to adopt, yet he crossed the firmaments and gained union with the One, where Kal cannot fling his net.[1] Dadu neither stays at home nor retreats to forests, nor does he mortify his body; within himself he controls his mind, as the Master has taught."[2]

Kabir says that those who adopt the middle path swim across in no time. Those who go to one extreme or the other sink in the ocean of the world.[3] "O Kabir, remain aloof from the two, stick to the one (middle path); things extremely hot and things extremely cold are both injurious, like fire."[4]

Saints enjoin upon the devotee to remain detached in the midst of attachments; for physical renunciation is meaningless as long as the mind is not weaned from worldly attachments and sense pleasures. Speaking of the true devotee, Kabir says: "In his songs there is a note of melancholy and in his sighs there is music; the devotee living in the family is a recluse within, while the minds of those who have renounced the world dwell in the family."[5] That is, while apparently involved in the world, the true devotee constantly feels the pain of separation from the Beloved. In his weeping for the Beloved there is music, because the sorrows of the world do not affect his inner happiness and tranquillity.

This inner detachment comes through spiritual practice. As the mind begins to become still and turn inwards, it starts enjoying the taste of the divine melody. It then automatically becomes detached from worldly possessions, family and friends. It is a natural and simple process, being a gradual transformation effected by the devotee's inner spiritual experiences.

---

1. *Dadudayal,* p.194:16-17.
2. *Dadudayal,* p.195:31.
3. *K.G.,* p.42:1.
4. *K.G.,* p.42:2.
5. *K.G.,* p.46:20.

Detachment, in the path of the Saints, is the sequel of attachment to the Master and the Lord. It is not a form of forced renunciation and escape from worldly responsibilities, nor is it a deliberate denial of the world, its objects and pleasures. Guru Nanak says:

> The *manmukh* gives up his own home in a fit of detachment and starts begging at others' doors. He evades his duties towards his family and, without meeting a Satguru, is trapped in the eddies of delusion. He roams from land to land and tires himself by reading scriptures, but his cravings increase all the more. He forgets that the body is as frail as a ball of clay, and fills his belly like a beast.[1] Having left his own wife, assailed by lust his mind dwells on others'. . . . He is the real detached one who serves and adores the Master and banishes ego from his mind.[2]

As against the ascetic, who achieves only an outer renunciation, the true disciple of a perfect Master stays in his family, fulfills his obligations and attends to his spiritual exercises—thus attaining a state of inner renunciation while living in the world. He gradually succeeds in controlling his mind and attaining his goal. Says Kabir:

> Gradually and easily
> > All left my mind:
> Son and wealth,
> > Wife and lust;
> And Kabir the slave
> > And his beloved Lord
> Fused into one.[3]

---

1. A.G., *Maru*, M.1, p.1012. *Manmukh:* 'one whose face is towards the mind', as against the *gurumukh*, 'whose face is towards the guru'. The *manmukh* acts according to the dictates of his mind and runs after worldliness.
2. A.G., *Maru*, M.1, p.1013.
3. *K.G.*, p.33:21:4.

The devotee vacates his body during meditation and transcends the physical boundaries of body and mind. Enjoying inner bliss, he becomes impervious to the world and its lures. Yet he does not neglect his worldly duties. Kabir says:

> Such is the achievement of the lovers of Nam:
> With their body they do their duty.
> But within they meditate
> In a bodiless state.[1]

Saints' criticism of renunciation, celibacy and austerities does not imply a license to get deeply involved in worldly pursuits or to run wildly after sensual pleasures. Mind has to be controlled. In the words of Kabir, an elephant has to be taught to obey the signals of the goad. If the mind is allowed to continue its wayward trends without any effort to check it, it will never come to the eye center. That is why Saints ask their disciples to adhere strictly to certain principles of diet and codes of moral conduct.

The code of conduct includes earning one's own honest livelihood. The disciple should be truthful and straightforward in his dealings. He should neither steal nor beg, nor deprive others of what rightfully belongs to them. A good disciple is an earnest devotee who supports himself and helps others as much as he can. He is not a parasite; he is a good citizen and a conscientious member of society. Namdev, Kabir, Guru Nanak, Ravidas, Dadu, Paltu, Dariya and all other Saints have insisted that their disciples should live on their own income, earned through clean and honest means. Themselves living according to this high ideal, Saints have always set an example for others to follow.

In family life, they have suggested a controlled sexual relationship, limited strictly to one's own spouse. Kabir says: "He who flirts with others' wives and he who cheats others of their profit might remain verdant for four days, but at the end will

---

1. *K.S.S.*, p.40:57.

be destroyed from the roots.[1] The adultress does not control
her mind and body; says Kabir, without chastity she ruins her
human birth."[2]

Kabir is equally critical of lustfulness: "Those who are engrossed in sensual pleasures are like a grain whose core has
been devoured by weevils; the sprout of knowledge will not
grow in them, however much they may try."[3]

The devotee has to sublimate his lustful tendencies. He has
to turn his mind inwards and taste inner bliss. Giving the example of Sukhdev from Hindu mythology, whose attention was so
deeply turned inwards that he lost all sense of distinction between man and woman, Kabir says that when a person turns
his attention within, he will become immune to the onslaughts
of lust: "Lust can lead to realization provided one knows how
to control it and turn his attention inwards; this not only the
humble Kabir says, even the scriptures give the account of
Sukhdev as evidence."[4]

An essential discipline for the disciple on the path of Sant
Mat is to devote time regularly to the prescribed method of
meditation. Besides the regular fixed hours, all possible spare
time should be devoted to the spiritual practice. All Saints proclaim that the human birth is precious and it is not often that
one is given this opportunity. Kabir says: "Rare is the human
birth, one does not obtain it again and again. Do not lose it in
vain; a leaf on falling from the tree cannot again join the
branch."[5]

Men ignore the importance of this priceless gift and dissipate it in worldly pursuits. Kabir comments: "Nights you have
wasted in sleep, days in pursuit of food and pleasure; the
priceless pearl of human birth you have exchanged for a bunch
of shells!"[6] Laziness and the habit of procrastination are also
great obstacles in the way of spiritual practice. Kabir warns:

1. *K.G.*, p.30:20:3.
2. *K.S.S.*, p.31:10.
3. *K.G.*, p.32:20.
4. *K.G.*, p.40:11.
5. *K.S.S.*, p.71:178.
6. *K.S.S.*, p.56:8.

Today you say, 'I'll meditate tomorrow';
When tomorrow comes you say, 'Not now, next day.
Saying 'tomorrow, tomorrow',
This golden chance will pass away.[1]

False, false is the world

Saints have described the world as false and unreal, an illusion and a dream. Kabir says: "False, false, I declare, false is the world."[2] Guru Nanak describes the entire world and its relationships, kings and commoners, wealth and possessions as false, and says that the false have become enamored of the false and forgotten the Creator.[3]

Certain schools of philosophy, like Vedant, have come to the conclusion that Brahm is the only reality, and the world, being an illusion, does not exist. Some scholars maintain that Saints like Kabir and Guru Nanak essentially belonged to or were influenced by this philosophy.

While calling the world an illusion and a dream, Kabir, Guru Nanak and other Saints do not subscribe to the views of the philosophers. By 'illusion' they mean that which is perishable and is changing from one moment to the next. They do not deny the existence of this world of matter, nor its importance in the scheme of creation. To the soul separated from its source—God—this material world is of supreme importance, for it is only from here that it can go back to the Lord on being born as a human being.

If the Saints have described this world as a dream, and life here as a bubble in the water; as the stars that must fade away with the advent of dawn;[4] as a column of smoke and as a castle of sand,[5] it is because nothing is lasting here. Sense pleasures, wealth and possessions, fame and status, all come to an end. When the soul departs from here, it cannot take with it the objects of pleasure, its belongings and its loved ones; it cannot

---

1. *K.S.S.*, p.57:13.
2. *K.S.S.*, p.65:113.
3. A.G., *Asa*, M.1, p.468. Man, being perishable, is here referred to as "the false."
4. *K.G.*, p.57:14.
5. *K.S.S.*, p.60:50.

155

even take its own body and name. Although all these things do exist, they are false in the sense that they are transitory and come to an end, either during the soul's sojourn here or on its departure.

The deceptive nature of the creation gives the illusion that for the present, one has all the time in the world; and as for the future, he feels and acts as if he is to live here forever. Saints say that if a person looked back, the days, months and years that have passed away would appear as a dream; and the days of the future will also seem like a dream one day. Kabir says: "When a weaver weaves cloth, by and by the end of the yarn does come; in the same way death approaches—escape if you can!"[1]

Saints warn man of the limited time available to him in this world. They remind him that the human birth is an extremely precious and rare gift of the Lord and should be utilized for the purpose for which it was given, namely God-realization.

The human body, which men cherish and preserve, which they adorn with fineries, is made out of matter and ultimately will disintegrate into matter. Kabir says: The body is one day burned and turns into ash; it is buried and becomes food for a host of worms. An unbaked pot is dissolved by drops of rain— such is the glory of your body, O man.[2] The Bible says: "Dust thou art, and unto dust shalt thou return."[3] Christ warns that one can practice devotion only as long as it is the daytime of life, for "I must work the works of him that sent me, while it is day: the night cometh, when no man can work."[4]

Kabir says that nothing in the world is lasting, however vast and mighty it may be. Fire turns forests into heaps of ash, and earthquakes raze mansions to the ground. He adds: Where are the trees that once blossomed there? Where are the rich and the powerful whose presence once adorned the palaces? Where are the monarchs whose courts resounded with music and beat

1. *K.S.S.*, p.70:170.
2. A.G., *Sorath*, Kabirji, p.654.
3. Gen. 3:19. See also Eccles. 12:7, "Then shall the dust return to the earth as it was: and the spirit shall return unto God who gave it."
4. John 9:4.

of drums, and at whose gates stood caparisoned elephants? Did they not depart with empty hands?[1]

Kabir tells the votaries of Sant Mat to take their mind out of this fickle and transient world. This world is like a caravan-serai, which is left by the guest after a night's halt. With the practice of Nam or Shabd, the devotee should leave this inn and take permanent abode in his true home. A guest in an inn never plans to buy rooms there, for he knows that at daybreak he has to leave forever. His thoughts are more towards his own home: "You have to dwell there, why crave and collect things here? Live in the world like a guest, do not get involved in the affairs of others.[2] As long as the breath in your body comes and goes, adore the Lord's Name. You have come to earn the wealth of redemption; do not gamble your life away to earn a few shells. This is your chance to amass the treasure of the true Name; gather as much as you can, for soon death will come and block the nine doors."[3]

Saints say that Shabd or Nam is the only true and permanent thing in the entire creation. In a couplet that sums up the teachings of the Saints, Kabir says:

Treat this half-stanza as the essence
Of a million scriptures: 'Nam is true,
The world is false'; and realize Nam
Through the practice of Surat Shabd, O Kabir.[4]

Realization, not reading

Some scholars have accused Kabir of complete ignorance of 'the depth and intricacies' of the various systems of Hindu philosophy. According to them, Kabir had no comprehension of the analytical excellence of the philosophies, nor did he have a proper background to grasp the significance of idol worship, pilgrimages and fasting; and since he was unlettered, his criticism of these practices was superficial.

1. Various couplets of Kabir from the chapter "Warning" (*Chitavani*) in *K.S.S.*
2. *K.S.S.*, p.70:169.
3. *K.S.S.*, p.57:11.
4. *K.S.S.*, p.103:54.

Kabir always held that mere learning is meaningless without actual realization of the Absolute Truth. His concept of knowledge is not of something acquired through the erudition and mental dissection of the various philosophies. Knowledge, for Kabir, is an experience and realization of the Ultimate Truth—God:

> If you know the One,
>> Then know that you know all;
> If you know not the One,
>> Then all your knowledge
> Is nothing but fraud.[1]

Kabir tells the seeker to devote himself to spiritual practice and give up professing and preaching knowledge gleaned from books, for mere talking of water will not quench a man's thirst.[2] If a person does not know the Lord, what worth is his vast knowledge, asks Kabir. Once he knows God, he knows everything.[3]

Saints have denounced erudition and scholarship, not because they are averse to learning, but because in the context of God-realization it has no pertinence. Book knowledge is an acquisition of the mind, realization is of the soul. Guru Nanak, looking at erudition from this point of view, says that mere reading of books is futile:

> Read and read till you load carts with books,
> Read and read till caravans are packed with them;
> Read and read and with books form a fleet,
> Read and read and fill caverns
> With what you have read;
> Read all through the years you have,
> Read all through your allotted months,
> Read through the entire span of your life,

---

1. *K.G.*, p.15:8.
2. *K.S.S.*, p.78:4.
3. *K.G.*, p.15:9.

158

And read even with each breath you take;
O Nanak, in the court of the Lord
Only one thing will count,
The rest is nothing but empty errands for ego.[1]

Reading treatises and acquiring knowledge of scriptures and theology are of little value on the spiritual path. In this precious human birth, love and devotion, self-realization and union with the Lord are the only things of significance. Kabir says: What is there to read, what to ponder upon? Of what avail is the learning of Vedas and scriptures? And of what use reading and hearing if they lead not to the state of Sahaj?[2] Truth is beyond the scriptures, beyond analysis; it is beyond the reach of intellect and beyond the power of reflection. O Kabir, it is beyond the three worlds, beyond the regions of mind and maya.[3]

Saints have deprecated preaching without realization. The learned man's own heart is afflicted with lust, avarice and ego, and scorched by jealousy and anger; yet he preaches piety to others. According to Kabir, he is like the person whose own house is burning, but who goes about teaching others how to fight fire. Guru Amar Das also says: "The learned one reads and explains philosophy to others, but is unaware of the fire consuming his own house. Without serving the Master, no one can obtain Nam; and peace cannot be gained even if one exhausts oneself with reading."[4]

Knowledge acquired from books is not the knowledge Saints speak of. Wisdom gained from reading, in the absence of realization, is imperfect. Speaking of such wisdom, the Old Testament says: "For in much wisdom is much grief; and he that increaseth knowledge increaseth sorrow."[5]

Kabir, always emphatic and outspoken in his expression, in order to give a jolt to people, at times denounces erudition in a

1. A.G., *Asa*, M.1, p.467.
2. A.G., *Sorath*, Kabirji, p.655.
3. *K.G.*, p.121:220.
4. A.G., *Maru*, M.3, p.1046.
5. Eccles. 1:18.

manner that could hurt any scholar's ego: "Without practice and realization, the inexperienced ones talk and preach day and night. They repeat only hearsay, like a dog repeating the bark of another dog."[1]

In the first stanza of his epic composition *Japji,* Guru Nanak declares that the Truth cannot be realized by thinking, though one may think a hundred thousand times.[2] Kabir also says: "If ten million types of learning were to become personified and sing Thy merits, O Lord, they would not be able to comprehend Thee."[3]

From the most ancient times, the philosophies have been changing, but not the inner path of realization. Philosophies give their own interpretations of the Ultimate Truth, but Truth does not change itself to suit their interpretations. Mystics say that the conclusions of metaphysics and philosophy are based on intellectual analysis, not on actual experience of the Reality. Saints reveal the Truth, philosophy only talks about it.

Some schools of philosophy insist that Brahm—the ultimate power, according to them—is everything; only Brahm exists, the world being an imaginary or unreal transformation of Brahm. Rejecting this monism, termed Advait, some say that Brahm and his power, Maya (or Prakriti, Nature), are two different entities and yet are inseparable.[4] Similarly there are diverse theories propounded by various schools of philosophy: that Brahm is only an inactive spectator and Prakriti (Nature) is the motive force;[5] that the soul is neither different from Brahm nor is it without difference;[6] that the soul and Brahm are two different entities and remain different up to the time the soul becomes one with Brahm;[7] that Brahm is an entity with attributes and has come to the world in the form of ten incarnations;[8] that the mantras of the Vedas are the ultimate

---

1. *K.S.S.*, p.78:5. In villages whenever a dog starts barking, other dogs even at a great distance also start barking; scholars, Kabir implies, without true realization merely repeat what they have read and heard others say.
2. A.G., *Japji*, M.1, p.1:1.
3. *K.G.*, p.152:340.
4. *Vishishtadvait* or conditional monism.
5. *Sankhya.*
6. *Bhedabhed* or dualistic monism.
7. *Dvait* or dualism.
8. Pluralism.

truth, and one should follow the practice of formal worship, *yajna* or ritual oblations and so on, and that the law of karma is the final governing factor of the universe;[1] that Brahm is the instrument or the root cause of the creation, and Prakriti is the material or contributory cause.[2]

Commenting on the various schools of philosophy, Kabir says: "Between earth and sky, duality is all-powerful; it has deluded the six philosophies and the eighty-four *siddhas*."[3] All philosophies, in the absence of true realization, talk from the level of duality or separateness from the Supreme Being; Saints, having become one with the Lord, speak from the level of unity or oneness.

In one of his hymns, Guru Nanak describes the entire creation that comes within the range of mind, matter and maya as diseased and perishable, and all scriptural knowledge as of no avail in realizing God: "Diseased are the six philosophies and they who adopt different religious mantles, as also the ones who undertake austere practices. What help can the Vedas and scriptures be? They know not the Only One."[4]

The Bible says: "The world by wisdom knew not God."[5] Guru Arjan Dev also states that the Lord cannot be found through analysis, and the votaries of the six philosophies who adopt different mantles to distinguish themselves, are in delusion. Through external practices and study of holy books one cannot know the Truth: "Through intellectual skill one cannot reach Him who is unfathomable and beyond calculations. The six philosophies are roaming in delusion and the garbs they adopt do not take them to God. Those who undertake the rigorous *chandrayan* fast[6] are of no worth on the path to God. Even if one read all the Vedas in full, he would not realize the Ultimate Truth."[7]

---

1. *Mimamsa.*
2. *Nyaya.*
3. A.G., *Salok,* Kabirji, p.1375:202.
4. A.G., *Bhairau,* M.1, p.1153.
5. 1 Cor. 1:21.
6. *Chandrayan vrat:* a rigorous type of fast in which the quantity of food is regulated according to the phases of the moon, beginning with one morsel on the day of the new moon and increasing by one morsel per day until the day of the full moon, thereafter decreasing by one morsel per day with the waning of the moon.
7. A.G., *Maru Var,* M.5, pp.1098-1099.

Having realized the Truth, Saints know the limitations of intellectual knowledge. Kabir makes it clear in his poems that the philosophies talk of the Limitless, although they are confined, like all mental pursuits, to the boundaries of the limited. If once they could transcend all limits, enter the region of the Limitless and realize Him, the philosophers would have nothing to say.[1]

Experience is the basis of true knowledge. Merely accumulating theoretical information without practice is meaningless. A thirsty person needs water to drink, not books on the way to dig a well. Reading a book on the culinary art cannot appease a person's hunger; he has to cook the food and eat it in order to be satisfied. Theoretical knowledge becomes real only when one learns through experience. According to Kabir, so long as a person does not know the mystery of what Reality is, his theoretical analysis is of no avail.[2]

In one of his poems Kabir mentions some of the systems of the philosophies and refers to the well-known tale of the four blind men 'seeing' an elephant for the first time and concluding —according to whether they felt its leg, trunk, tusk or tail— that it was like a pillar, a branch of a tree, a sharp but smooth pointed weapon, and a rough rope with a tuft of hair at the end. Since none of them could agree, they began to argue and quarrel, calling one another liars.

Kabir says the knowledge of the philosophers is like the knowledge of the blind.[3] They insist and argue on their own surmises and deductions arrived at through 'groping'. Their conclusions are vague and incomplete and at best 'true' to a very limited extent, for their 'truth' is the truth of the blind man. According to the Saints the paths propounded by various schools of philosophy can lead the devotee only up to a very short distance; and a road that goes a few paces and ends is of no use to the traveler whose view is fixed on the supreme destination—God.

---

1. *K.S.S.*, p.126:6.
2. *K.S.S.*, p.143:1.
3. *K.S.*, I:58-59:6-7.

Saints are not opposed to reading scriptures and studying metaphysical treatises. They are against looking on learning as an end in itself, as the ultimate reality. Kabir says not to call Vedas and holy books false; false are they who do not ponder and practice what the scriptures teach.[1] Without practice, without realization, erudition is only a burden on the mind, and this is what the Saints deprecate. Kabir's expressions on this topic are both candid and strong:

> O learned one, without practice and experience your erudition is like a load of sandalwood on a donkey's back. You do not try to realize the true meaning of God's Name, and despite your learning your face in the end will be smeared with ash. If your knowledge of scriptures is true then you should be able to see the Lord in every being.[2]

Like most Saints, Kabir had to face opposition both from the scholars and the priests. The faith that philosophies and religions seek to generate is based either on intellectual analysis or on ritualism—the former often running into the dryness of logic, the latter into make-believe and superstition. The Saints view all aspects of life, the cosmos, the soul, mind and matter from an understanding available only at a high level of consciousness. Viewing from that spiritual plane, they find that most schools of philosophy are far from the reality, while a few contain a small particle of truth. But in the absence of realization they are all incomplete.

The Infinite cannot be comprehended through the finite means of intellect and logic, nor can He be described in language, which again is limited to the world of mind and matter. Yet the Saints have to resort to language to convey their message. Kabir says: "He cannot be seen by the eyes nor perceived by the senses; He cannot be heard by the ears nor described through words; He is beyond the reach of physical efforts. Yet,

---

1. A.G., *Bibhas Prabhati*, Kabirji, p.1350.
2. K.G., p.78:39.

for the convenience of expression, we call Him the Ultimate Creator of all."[1]

The various interpretations of Truth, the multifarious conclusions arrived at by intellectual explorations, are limited to the world of reason. Kabir explains that the destination of the realized one is different from that of persons who have not realized Him but only talk of Him.[2] Only he who is at the level of the supreme throne can tell what it is like; how can he speak of the interior of the Palace who has not raised the curtain and entered it?[3]

Speaking of the different paths, Dadu explains: "Dadu, if you ask those who have reached Home, their words will be the same. The tenet of all Saints is one and the same, but diverse are the views of those wandering in the way.... All realized ones have said the same thing, for the home of the realized is the same. But, O Dadu, different are the views of those who wander outside."[4]

Scholars, theologians and ritualists take exception to the teachings of the Saints. If Saints say that God is within, they want to be shown where and what 'within' is. When Saints explain that the path to God starts at the eye center, they question the existence of such a point in the body. They do not try to ascertain the truth of Sant Mat by following the method of spiritual practice under a Master's directions, and yet they expect to be convinced. Without taking practical steps to do so, they want to become fully conversant with the Reality which, according to Kabir, is ineffable, a matter of personal experience obtainable only through spiritual practice under a perfect Master's guidance.

Sant Mat is a practical philosophy, an applied science. The hypotheses of the Saints' teachings have to be proved in the laboratory of one's own body. But the intellectuals and ritualists both want to know the spiritual truth at the level of language. Like a man who wants to learn swimming and become

1. *K.G.*, p.183, *Barahpadi Ramaini, Doha* 3.
2. *K.S.S.*, p.145:8.
3. *K.S.S.*, p.18:16.
4. *Dadudayal*, p.168:159, 161.

an expert swimmer but refuses to go near water, they want to know about spirituality, soul and God, on the dry land of reason.

Saint Dariya of Rajasthan, commenting on the approach of the intellectuals and ritualists, says: "The dogmatist knows not the realized one's path; when the sun shines in full brightness, owls treat it as a dark night. The erudite learn from books and give discourses on God; outside they try to spread light, within they are as lightless as a dark night, says Dariya."[1]

Knowledge of books and scriptures, power of analysis and acumen in debates, are irrelevant on the path of the Saints. To go within, one has to get rid of these attainments and tendencies. Saint Dharni Das says that one has to unlearn all that one has acquired by deep study and long scrutiny of books and treatises: "O Dharni, he is not the learned one who has read, ruminated and acquired the means of impressive speech; all praise to that learned one who has unlearned all he has ever read."[2]

On the path of the Saints, realization, not reading; devotion, not dissertation, are of real significance. Kabir says:

> Reading and reading men toil to death,
>> But no one can thus become truly learned;
> He who has read the one word *love*
>> Is the real learned one.[3]

The one word, 'love'
The prime object of all spiritual practice is to develop love for the Lord because, as the Saints say, God is love and love is God. When questioned about God, Dadu replied:

> Love is God's caste,
> Love is God's nature,
> Love is God's form,
> And God's color, O Dadu, is love.[4]

1. *Dariya Sahib Marwarwale ki Bani*, p.21:7, 9.
2. *Dharnidasji ki Bani*, p.46:61.
3. *K.S.S.*, p.167:7.
4. *Dadudayal*, p.41:143.

Kabir, describing the union of the soul with the Lord, says that in the region of Truth resides the true Lord; here the flame merges in the Flame, and the soul becomes one with His form, which is love.[1] Guru Nanak declares: "The Lord is true, his true Name is boundless love."[2]

And St. John says: "He that loveth not knoweth not God; for God is love. . . . God is love; and he that dwelleth in love dwelleth in God, and God in him."[3]

Soul is a particle of God. It is a drop of that Ocean of love and bliss. It can be happy only when it returns to its source and becomes one with it. The aim of all worship and devotion is to attain union with Him. Saints say that the devotee does not have to go running about to meet the Lord; He is within, and the seeker has to go within to meet Him. Kabir says: "Within the heart is the Beloved, He is the inexhaustible cup of love; but only he who knows its worth tries to drink it, only a devotee of the Master tastes it and becomes truly intoxicated."[4]

Intensity of devotion, and desire and longing to become one with the Lord is love. Love is an all-absorbing force. When the devotee loses himself, his will and his identity in the Beloved, he becomes the Beloved. Kabir says: "Day and night I looked for Him, I looked and looked and my eyes turned red. When thus looking for Him I found Him, the seeker and the sought became one.[6] When the drop mingles with the Drop, the drop does not part from the Drop; he who becomes a slave and adores the Lord, the Lord becomes his protector and cherishes him."[6]

Kabir further adds that the devotee should have one-pointed attention towards God, the object of his love: "One should be so absorbed in his love for the Lord that he goes not elsewhere; then he will attain the highest Truth. If he loves God with such unwavering absorption, he will obtain the Lord and merge in his lotus feet."[7]

---

1. *K.S.*, II:108:4.
2. A.G., *Japji*, M.1, p.2:4.
3. 1 John 4:8; 4:16.
4. *K.S.*, III:16:8:2.
5. A.G., *Gauri, Bawan Akhari*, Kabirji, p.341:26
6. Ibid., pp.341-342:29.
7. Ibid., p.342:36.

In order to explain spiritual truths, Saints cite examples from the world. In the world the deepest love is between a bride and her groom or a devoted wife and her husband. Saints have used this relationship of worldly love to present an ideal of divine love. The union of the soul with God has been described by them as the union of a long-separated loving wife with her husband. In many poems of love and longing, Kabir identifies himself with the bride reaching the chamber of the bridegroom, or with a wife pining to meet her husband who has gone away. On a larger scale, Saints regard all souls as brides who are unable to see their Husband because of the curtain of duality. Kabir says:

> My Beloved resides
> In the chamber of every heart,
> No couch is empty of Him;
> All praise to that heart
> In which He has become manifest.[1]

Guru Amar Das expresses the same thought thus: The Husband of all is one; no one is bereft of Him; she alone is blessed with the Husband's love who has merged in the Satguru.[2] And Guru Nanak says that a married woman, wherever she lives, remembers that she belongs to her husband and always has his love in her heart: "Whether she is in the father-in-law's house or the father's, she (remembers that she) belongs to her infinite and boundless Husband; such a wife is truly blessed, for she is loved by the carefree Lord."[3]

The intensity and one-pointedness of divine love, however, has no parallel in the world. The devotee will never be blessed with the Beloved's love if his attention is towards anything other than the Lord. The Husband will not be pleased if the wife is not entirely absorbed in thought of Him. She cannot be called a faithful wife if her fickle mind runs in all directions;

---

1. *K.S.S.*, p.106:5.
2. A.G., *Maru Var*, M.3, p.1088.
3. A.G., *Maru Var*, M.1, p.1088.

how can such a wife win the Husband's love?[1]

> The faithful wife
> Knows only you, dear Lord,
> No one else enters her heart.
> All hours of the day,
> All watches of the night
> In you she is absorbed;
> She is the truly blessed one
> For she will attain union with Him.[2]

Divine love is a sublime spiritual experience, an irresistible attraction between the soul and God. There is no scope for lust in this love; rather love is the complete elimination of all blemishes like lust, avarice, jealousy, attachment, anger, ego and similar maladies of the mind. Maulana Rum says: "The love I talk of is not the physical love common between two persons, which is just an aberration caused by food and drink." Kabir says:

> The beautiful wife steps
> Into the arena of love,
> She sports her Beloved,
> She lights the lamp of realization
> Which consumes lust like oil.[3]

In the path of divine love the Beloved is not lured by physical beauty, nor pleased by fineries and adornments. Here the wife can only please her Husband by bedecking herself with love, faith, purity and one-pointed devotion. Sheikh Farid says that a lover does not mind if his youth and beauty fade, for one day they have to go; the lover's only concern is that his love for the Lord never dwindle.[4] Kabir says that in the eyes of the Beloved, physical beauty and ornaments are of no merit:

---

1. *K.S.S.*, p.28:10.
2. *K.S.S.*, p.28:9.
3. *K.S.S.*, p.28:12.
4. A.G., *Salok*, Sekh Farid, p.1379:34.

Even if the faithful wife
    Be ugly and ungainly,
Before her inner beauty and grace
    A million beauties of the world
Will fade.[1]

Even if the faithful wife
    Be ugly and ungainly,
Even if she be without ornaments,
    Amidst all women she will shine
Like the sun during the day,
    Like the moon at night.[2]

Guru Arjan Dev expresses the same thought: "Without my Husband I will throw all fineries into the fire; even if I am smeared with dust, I will shine in glory if you, beloved Husband, are with me."[3]

The wife and the Husband, the soul and the Lord, are both in the same 'house' of the human body. They are together in the same chamber, but they have never seen each other, for the heavy veil of ego stands between them. Kabir says: "The wife and her Husband are living in the same house and they are even on the same couch, yet union is impossible. All praise to the loving wife who wins her Beloved's heart; O Kabir, such a wife will not be born again."[4]

Guru Amar Das emphasizes that Saints do not refer to physical love when they talk of the love between the soul-bride and the Lord. Nor can divine love be understood on the physical and worldly level because all worldly love has a tinge of selfishness and culminates in lust. He says: "We do not speak of the wife and husband who live together in the world. Though in two bodies, whose flame within is merged into one, them we call wife and Husband."[5]

---

1. *K.S.S.*, p.27:2.
2. *K.S.S.*, p.28:15.
3. A.G., *Salok*, M.5, p.1425.
4. A.G., *Asa*, Kabirji, p.483:30.
5. A.G., *Suhi Var*, M.3, p.788.

Kabir gives hints that divine love is obtained in a higher state of consciousness, when the soul goes within:

> In the pitcher of his soul,
> With the rope of love
> And with mind as the water drawer,
> From the well in the lotus above
> The devotee drinks
> The ambrosia of love again and again.[1]

And again:

> In the forest
> Where the lion dares not enter,
> Where birds cannot come and fly,
> Where night and day do not reach,
> There, absorbed in love, stays Kabir.[2]

In exchange for one's head

Divine love is a treasure not easy to acquire. It is not available in worldly relationships, it cannot be secured through austerities and penances, nor through fasts and ritual prayers. It can neither be obtained by virtue of one's wealth and possessions, nor by renouncing them. Kabir says that love does not grow in flowerbeds and fields, nor is it on sale in some shop. The king or the commoner, the rich or the poor, whoever wants love can readily have it—in exchange for his head.[3]

Hafiz has the same thing to say: "The smallest price that love demands is your head; if you cannot do this much, do not utter the word *love*." And Guru Nanak is equally explicit: "If you are eager to play the game of love, enter my lane with your head (placed) on your palm; if you will step upon this path, give your head, do not hesitate."[4] In the words of Kabir, only he can drink the wine of divine love who offers the price of his

1. *K.G.*, p.14:10:2.
2. *K.G.*, p.14:10:1. *Lion:* Kal or the negative power; *birds:* passions, desires and cravings; *night and day:* misery and happiness.
3. *K.S.S.*, p.43:3.
4. A.G., *Salok*, M.1, p.1412:20.

170

head.[1] Many crowd round the wine merchant's stall, but only he drinks the wine of love to his fill who offers his head; those who cannot are turned away.[2]

The true lover cuts off his head to experience the intoxication of love, that is, he annihilates his 'I'-ness. To win the Beloved's love any price is small and any sacrifice insignificant. The lover is willing to pay the price, for he is anxious to lose his identity in that of the Beloved. Only the Beloved exists for him. His unwavering attention is fixed on Him. He has no desires or cravings—he only craves to see the Beloved, to always be with Him, to become Him.

To pay the price of love with one's head may sound a grim demand to a modern world used only to interpret love on the physical plane. A person is willing to lose everything but his individuality. The thought of annihilating the 'I' frightens him. But in the narrow lane of love two cannot remain: If the lover is there, the Beloved cannot enter; if the lover loses himself, he becomes one with the Beloved, and only the Beloved then exists.[3] There is no other way to taste the elixir of divine love and attain immortality.

Saints always put before their disciples the ideal, and though it may appear impossible to attain, the impossible becomes a reality when the perfect Master is there to guide the devotee on the path to becoming one with the Beloved.

Love the lover of the Lord

"Adore him who adores the Lord,"[4] says Kabir, for "seeing him is seeing the Lord."[5] God is invisible, He is beyond the reach and comprehension of the mind and senses. Saints know that it is impossible to love a person one has not seen, heard or felt. Kabir says that without seeing and coming in actual contact, one cannot love God; and only talking about Him or singing his praises will not help one to become a lover of God.

---

1. *K.S.S.*, p.43:4.
2. *K.G.*, p.13:6:3.
3. *K.S.S.*, p.44:10.
4. *K.S.S.*, p.48:59.
5. *K.S.*, II:18:2:3; cp. *Satt Kabir*, p.345:723.

Mystics, therefore, teach the devotee to love the lover of the Lord, who through his perfect love has attained union with the Beloved. Such a person is a Saint or perfect Master.

Guru Arjan Dev declares that the true devotee of God is like God himself; that one should not look on him as different because of his human form.[1] But, according to Kabir, such lovers of the Lord—the Saints—are not easy to find. If the one who craves for divine love finds such a lover of God, he will be rid of the poison of worldliness and will be saturated with the ambrosia of true love. "I wandered in search of the true lover, but such a lover is hard to find; if the lover meets such a lover, the world of poison will turn into nectar."[2]

Guru Arjan Dev says: "Worship Guru, the Lord; love him with body and mind."[3] Guru Nanak says that without the Guru, love is not born and the stain of ego does not go.[4] And in different words, Dadu says: "The Master fills, and fills to the brim, the cup of love and offers it with his own hands. Dadu surrenders himself to such a Master, he sacrifices his entire being to him again and again."[5]

When the disciple is lost in love for his Master, he becomes oblivious of the world and is lost in spiritual ecstasy. Guru Ram Das says: "Lord, I have been bewitched by my beloved Guru; seeing my Guru, I have lost my senses, I am in ecstasy."[6]

Love for the Master begins with love for his physical form, yet there is nothing physical about it, for it is a deep spiritual experience—a joy felt and experienced by the soul. Describing this love for the Master, Kabir says:

> He who is stricken with love is restless, he is oblivious of his body and self, and his soul drinks the ambrosia of bliss—he is tied to his Master by love.[7]
> I am oblivious of everything; I am aware only of

1. A.G., *Maru*, M.5, p.1076.
2. *K.S.S.*, p.17:12.
3. A.G., *Siri Rag*, M.5, p.52.
4. A.G., *Siri Rag*, M.1, p.60.
5. *Dadudayal*, p.5:43.
6. A.G., *Bilawal*, M.4, p.836.
7. *K.S.S.*, p.35:8.

love, which clings to me. Whom am I to welcome, to
whom to say, "go"?[1] My heart is dyed in my
Master's love.[2]

Love for the Satguru is an invaluable boon. It is the means
to go within and become one with Shabd. The Master engenders love in the devotee's heart, and longing for him sustains it.
Kabir describes the Master as the repository of ambrosia and
says that even if one obtains his love at the cost of one's head,
it is a cheap bargain.

Love for the Master is a gift from him and has to be preserved by complete surrender to him. That is why Kabir describes devotion to the Master as walking on a sword's edge.[3]
It is not a path for the timid to tread, for only he who removes
his head with his own hands can adopt the path of devotion.[4]
Yet love is an important and unavoidable step for one who
longs to attain realization.

Saints tell us that on the physical plane the Master is love
personified. On the spiritual level, in his radiant form, he is the
manifestation of love. But in the ultimate realm of bliss the
Master is one with love; love is the Master. Therefore a true
devotee wants nothing except the Master. Kabir says:

> I beg for neither pleasures
> > Nor possessions;
> I only want love and devotion.
> > Nothing else do I beg for—
> I beg only for you,
> > From you, my lord.[5]

One who accepts and never complains

As love for his Satguru grows in the disciple's heart, he begins
to lose his own will in that of the Master. He surrenders his ego

---

1. The lover is not concerned with trying to develop good qualities nor in discarding
bad tendencies, for through love he has risen above both.
2. *K.S.S.*, p.35:16.
3. *K.S.S.*, p.31:3.
4. *K.S.S.*, p.31:4.
5. *K.S.S.*, p.20:15.

to him and accepts all that comes in life as the Master's will. He submits his self to the Master's higher self and looks upon himself as a slave at the feet of his spiritual guide.

This spirit of surrender, called *sharan* and *bhana* by the Saints, is an important part of love. When only the Beloved exists for the lover, he can have no thought of himself. His mind stays in the Master's service, he acts in the Satguru's will, he does not allow his thoughts to divert from the Master even in his dreams, and he accepts all pain and hardship without ever complaining.[1]

In this state of surrender, says Kabir, the devotee's outlook becomes identical with the Master's outlook, and his mind becomes one with the Master's mind. He has no desires left except to please the Master and to live in his will. But Kabir warns that this cannot be achieved through intellect and cleverness: "The Master and the slave will have the same outlook only if the devotee merges his intellect into that of the Master; he can win the Master's mercy and grace, not through intellect and cleverness, but through love."[2]

Persian mystics have laid great importance on living in the Master's will. Maulana Rum says: "O Master, whatever you want me to see, only that I see; whatever you wish me to know, only that I know; in whatever condition you choose to keep me, in the same way do I live. If you give me happiness, I accept it; if you give me pain, even that I accept as your will."

The highest ideal of love, living in the Master's will, culminates in what the Persian mystics call the state of *fana-fil-sheikh* —losing one's identity in that of the Master and merging one's self in the Master's higher self. Guru Amar Das says: "That alone is repetition, that alone is austerity which is approved by the Satguru; by living in the Satguru's will one attains true glory. O Nanak, such a disciple loses his self and merges in the Master."[3]

The realization of the Master within, that is, merging in his

---

1. *K.S.S.*, p.19:2.
2. *K.S.S.*, p.19:3.
3. A.G., *Gujari ki Var*, M.3, p.509.

radiant form, is possible only when ego is completely eliminated. It is the apex of love and surrender. Kabir says: If the disciple annihilates his ego, he becomes one with the Master; if he clings to his ego, he loses the Master's grace. Such is the ineffable tale of love; even if I could narrate it, no one would believe.[1] When I turned inwards and merged in him, eternal light appeared before me, the Master and the slave became one; now they revel in the bliss of everlasting springtime.[2]

Love for the Master leads the devotee to love for the Lord; surrender to the Master develops into surrender to the Supreme Being. The Master has become one with the Lord, he lives in the Lord's will, he is the manifestation of the supreme will. To live in the Master's will is to live in God's will. The disciple can attain this state through the Master's grace and through meditation done under his guidance.

Saint Namdev says: "Nothing happens of my doing; only that happens which the Lord wills."[3] "If He gives me a throne, the glory is not mine; if He causes me to beg, the loss is not mine."[4] Even if a devotee prays, it is in a spirit of surrender. Guru Ravidas says: "Lord, I have taken your refuge; pray, emancipate me if you deem fit."[5]

Kabir illustrates the ideal of surrender through the example of a dead body. A dead person is neither elated if adorned in fine clothes, nor dejected if covered with rags; he neither asks to be laid in a palanquin, nor objects to being placed on rough ground; in the same way, a true lover of the Lord accepts as his will all that comes in life. He is so much engrossed in love that he does not discriminate between happiness and misery or pleasure and pain.[6]

Guru Nanak attributes everything to God, even suffering, as his blessing: "Countless become prey to misery, hunger and strife; this too is Thy gift, my bountiful Lord."[7] Kabir also ex-

1. *K.S.S.*, p.116:28.
2. *K.S.S.*, p.108:4.
3. A.G., *Bhairau*, Namdevji, p.1165.
4. A.G., *Gujari*, Namdevji, p.525.
5. A.G., *Suhi*, Ravidasji, p.793.
6. *Anurag Sagar*, pp.3-4.
7. A.G., *Japji*, M.1, p.5:25.

presses the same idea: "Whatever happens is Thy will, O Lord; he who realizes this merges into Sahaj. Then, O Kabir, all sins vanish and the mind becomes absorbed in the Life of all life."[1]

In another poem, after describing how God has given thrones, silken robes and elaborate couches to some people, and to others not even a tattered coat and a straw roof, Kabir says: "Do not be envious, do not complain; stick to the righteous path. The Potter who kneaded the clay has made pots of different shapes and has applied different colors; some He has adorned with strings of pearls, over others he has applied coats of misery.... The man of God (the Saint) is truly high, he is the real devotee of the Lord; he lives within the Lord's will and is at peace within. Whatever pleases God, the same he accepts as true and final. He has absorbed God's will in his heart."

Concluding the poem, Kabir sounds a warning to the seeker to bear in mind that all he has in the world belongs to the Giver, it is futile to look upon the world's objects as his own and to cling to them: "Says Kabir, listen, O friends, all your 'mine, mine' is false, for one day the cage will be wrecked, the bird will be seized and taken away, and the battered cage will be all that is left."[2]

Guru Ram Das expresses his feelings of loving surrender with profound emotion and remarkable simplicity: "Lord, if you give me happiness, I will adore only you; in pain too I will contemplate on you alone. If you give me hunger I will be content with it, and sorrow I will accept as joy.... Nanak, the poor one, lies at your door; Lord, if you own me it will only be because of your greatness.... If you keep me close to yourself, only you will I worship; if you drive me away, only you will I think of. If the worldly adulate me, the credit belongs to you; if they despise me, even then I will not leave you. If you are with me, let people say what they will; if you forsake me, I will die. Again and again I sacrifice my entire being to my Master, I fall at his feet to earn his pleasure and grace."[3]

---

1. A.G., *Bibhas Prabhati*, Kabirji, p.1349.
2. A.G., *Asa*, Kabirji, pp.479-480:16. *Cage:* the body; *bird:* the soul.
3. A.G., *Suhi*, M.4, p.757.

According to the Saints, the path of surrender, though hard, is the surest way to be rid of the bonds of karmas and attain union with the Lord. Love and surrender go hand in hand. The very idea of eliminating the ego or giving one's head in order to gain love implies complete surrender to the Beloved. Swamiji asks the devotee to "take the refuge of the Master in order to pay off the tax of karma."[1] "Surrender yourself to the Satguru and be rid of the rounds in the wheel of eighty-four."[2]

In this world of strife and turmoil, of disease and death, the only shelter is the Master. Being one with the Supreme Being, he is the only source of comfort and the only haven in the world's turbulent sea. Kabir says:

> The body is a palace of straw, time a raging fire:
> such is the design laid all around me. To go across
> this ocean of terror, I have taken the refuge of my
> Master.[3]

Longing, the way to union

Just as union is the blessing of the Lord, longing in separation from Him is also his gift, and a sure means to reach Him. Kabir says that the Beloved has sent longing to enliven the heart of the devotee, to look for the souls that are restless for Him and bring them back to Him.[4] Guru Ram Das also says that the Lord himself creates longing in the devotee's heart: "The Lord has himself kindled within me the yearning for his Name; only when I meet my beloved Lord, my loving Friend, will I find solace."[5]

Longing strengthens love. It makes love all-absorbing and intense. The lover's only desire is to see the Beloved, to meet Him and to be always with Him—a desire which consumes all other desires of the world. Taking the imagery of a mendicant who goes from door to door with a begging bowl, Kabir says:

1. *S.B.*, p.82:13:1.
2. *S.B.*, p.156:4:2.
3. A.G., *Gauri*, Kabirji, p.336:59.
4. *K.S.S.*, p.37:11.
5. A.G., *Gauri*, M.4, p.175.

With the begging bowl of longing, my two eyes, like a recluse, beg for the alms of Thy darshan; Beloved, nothing else do they ask for.[1] My eyes have become mad: from moment to moment they look, and look only for you. Neither do they find you, nor do they find solace—such is my agony.[2] My eyes have turned flaming red, people think they suffer some ailment; they know not that pining for the Beloved my eyes have cried and cried and thus turned red.[3]

Almost all Saints have portrayed their anguish in separation from the Lord. Scholars agree that some of the finest songs of emotional richness and poetic beauty have come from the Saints. Their love is the love of the soul and their longing, the longing of the spirit. Though they lean on examples and metaphors from the physical world to express their feelings, their expressions are sublime and the intensity of their longing essentially divine.

Saint Namdev expresses his longing in his concise and simple style:

> I am afflicted with restlessness:
> A cow is in anguish without her calf,
> A fish writhes without water;
> So is poor Nama without the Lord.[4]

Dadu says: "My Beloved's love has settled in the depths of my being, each pore of my body raises the plaintive cry 'Beloved, Beloved'; nothing else does it know."[5]

In spite of all the suffering, the devotee will not give up his love, nor forget the Beloved even for a moment. Hardships and the pain of longing cannot deter him from love's path, and no amount of pleasure and comfort can make him oblivious of the object of his love. He will either be in the Beloved's company or be engrossed in yearning for him. The Beloved may be out of

---

1. *K.S.S.*, p.37:14.
2. *K.S.S.*, p.37:22.
3. *K.G.*, p.7:25.
4. A.G., *Gond*, Namdevji, p.874.
5. *Dadudayal*, p.40:124.

sight for the lover, but he cannot go out of his heart. On the path of devotion, once the true devotee develops love, he is always a lover, for the color of true love is indelible. Saint Paltu says: "Paltu, let your love be deep like the color of *majeeth:* the cloth may be worn and washed and torn to shreds, but the color does not give up the company of the cloth."[1]

Saint Dharni Das identifies himself with a bride separated from her husband: "My heart throbs with pain, my entire being aches like a sore wound, my eyes flow with tears; the Beloved is not on my couch."[2] Even when the Beloved is before the eyes, the longing to see him again and again continues unabated. Dharni Das adds: "My eyelids do not blink, my Beloved's beauty keeps them thus engaged; they drink and drink the supreme nectar of his resplendence, yet they thirst for more and more."[3]

Vakhna, a sixteenth-century devotee, expresses the helplessness of a lover separated from the Beloved: 'Without seeing Him my heart pines for Him with unabated pain; and like a dike broken with the pressure of too much water, my eyes cease not to overflow."[4]

Guru Arjan Dev, during his days of discipleship, had to stay away from his Master, Guru Ram Das. His lyrics, a spontaneous outcome of deep love and intense longing for his Satguru, are regarded as some of the most beautiful poems on longing:

> My heart is yearning for the darshan of my Master,
> Wailing for him like the rainbird for a drop of rain.
> My thirst increases, my heart grows restless
> Without seeing my Saint, my loved one.
> I will sacrifice myself, my entire being,
> For one glimpse of my Master, my Saint, my Beloved.
> Your face is pleasing, your words echo
> The divine melody of Sahaj;

---

1. *Paltu Sahib*, III:70:24. *Majeeth:* a plant from which a dark red color is extracted; the color is indelible.
2. *Dharnidasji*, p.42:12.
3. *Dharnidasji*, p.42:16.
4. *Sant Kavya*, ed. Parashuram Chaturvedi, p.313:5.

Eons after eons have passed since I saw you,
    my beloved lord.
Blessed is that land where you reside,
    my beloved friend, my lord.
I will sacrifice myself, my entire being to you,
    my Master, my friend, my lord.
A moment without you, and the age of darkness
    descends on me;
When will I meet you, my beloved lord, again?
My nights of agony are endless,
Sleep has forsaken me,
Without a glimpse of my Master's court.
I will sacrifice myself, my entire being,
To reach the true court of my Master.[1]

Union is the reward of true longing. There is no failure or frustration in divine love, for the wings of love, despite all obstacles, inevitably carry the lover into the Beloved's fold. This is amplified by the last stanza of the above hymn, written after Guru Ram Das, moved to mercy, blessed his loving disciple Arjan Dev with union:[2]

Great is my good fortune—my Master,
    my Beloved, has met me;
I have found my eternal lord within my own home.
Ever will I serve him, not for a fraction
    of a moment will I part from him;
Says Nanak, I am forever your slave, dear lord.[3]

When the devotee will long only for the Master and want nothing but him, his yearning will be fulfilled and he will attain

1. A.G., *Majh*, M.5, pp.96-97.
2. Guru Ram Das sent his disciple Arjan Dev to Lahore on a mission, telling him to come back only when the Master recalled him. The letters of Arjan Dev expressing his longing were intercepted by some jealous disciples and it was almost three years before one of the letters reached the Master's hands. Guru Ram Das, greatly moved, immediately recalled his devoted disciple. Perhaps Guru Arjan Dev was made to go through the fire of longing because his Master wanted him to be made worthy of the great responsibility of mastership that was to fall upon his shoulders.
3. A.G., *Majh*, M.5, p.97.

union with the Beloved. Kabir says: When he saw me burning in the flames of longing, my Master came running; he sprinkled the cool nectar of love and quelled the blaze.[1] The pain of separation whispered to me: If you hold onto me with all your might, I'll carry you to the bliss of the Beloved's lotus feet.[2]

Thus, longing leads to the ultimate goal of love—union with the Beloved. So long as the lover and the Beloved are two, the pain of separation will naturally continue to afflict the lover. When the two meet, only love remains, for love and the Beloved are essentially the same. Kabir says that the married soul, that is, the soul who has met the Lord, is unable to describe the radiance of her Husband:

> Friends, how am I to recount
> The beauty of my Beloved,
> For in my Beloved's beauty
> I have merged;
> His color I have acquired,
> In his radiance, immersed;
> I am unaware
> Of my body,
> My mind,
> The world.[3]

Dadu, describing the ultimate union effected by the pangs of separation, says:

> God has become one with the longing wife
> And she has become God;
> Dadu, such is the achievement
> Of the much maligned pain of longing.[4]

The two wings

Love is the essence of all spiritual pursuits. All efforts, even the practice of Nam or Shabd, must have at their base a burning

---

1. *K.S.S.*, p.36:3.
2. *K.S.S.*, p.40:53.
3. *K.S.*, I:13:22:3.
4. *Dadudayal*, p.41:138.

181

desire to meet the Lord. Shabd, the all-pervading power of God, is love; and once a soul is connected to Shabd by a perfect Master, the link of love with the Supreme Being is established. The practice of Shabd generates love in the devotee's heart and love draws the soul to higher regions within. Kabir says: "The yogi, the recluse, the silent hermit, the dervish and the fakir—without love, none of them can reach my Master's precious Home."[1]

The love Saints talk of is not the sentiment of attachment on the physical level; the physical love of the worldly is perishable and ends with the end of life. Divine love is love between the soul and the Supreme Soul; it is the attraction of a drop for the Ocean. Love between the disciple and the Satguru has its physical aspect insofar as it is generated by the physical beauty of the Master and creates a longing in the disciple to be always in his Master's company. Yet it is essentially an inner bond between the soul and the Shabd, for the Satguru is the manifest form of Shabd. Love is elevating and ennobling, an experience that transcends all physical bonds and cannot be expressed in words.

Unlike worldly love, which is ephemeral, the love between disciple and Master is everlasting. Death, which severs all bonds, cannot break the link of this divine love. After death, the loving disciple's soul stays with the Master in the inner regions, and his love, an ever-increasing force, enables him to accompany the Master to the higher regions beyond the realms of cause and effect. Kabir therefore says: Love him who maintains your love to the very end; the multicolored love of the world will stain you all the more.[2] Give your body, mind and soul to him who will never, never forsake you.[3]

Love for the Master leads the seeker to love for the Lord, for in the words of Kabir one cannot love Him who cannot be seen, felt or perceived and with whom one cannot talk or communicate.[4] In order to impress on the seeker the exigency of

---

1. *K.S.S.*, p.45:31.
2. *K.S.S.*, p.48:62.
3. *K.S.S.*, p.48:64.
4. *K.S.*, III:45:21.

loving the Master, Kabir advises him: "Do not try to love God; love the man of God. The Lord gives you wealth, prestige and possessions, but the man of God gives you the Lord."[1]

Sant Mat is the path of love. Love is a shortcut to God, for the practice of Nam carried out with love adds speed to the soul's homeward journey. Maulana Rum says: "If you want to reach the home of God, proceed by the path of moisture; all your dry fasts and penances and all your dry prayers, without the tears of love, are futile."

Guru Arjan Dev says: "Chanting, austerity, luxury, pleasure, prestige, honor and pride, O Musan,[2] I sacrifice them all for just one moment of love."[3] A Persian mystic says that even a thousand years of ritual prayers cannot make you a devotee; so long as one is not full of love, God cannot be pleased.

Love is a path of agony, sighs and tears. It is a path of sacrificing one's entire being on the altar of love. Kabir describes the path of love as the road to the true home, but the way is hard; only when one cuts off his head and steps on it, can one drink the nectar of love.[4]

And Paltu echoes the same thought: "Divine love is not easy to gain; the devotee has to cut off his head with his own hands; yes, to become a lover is not child's play; it is not a candy that one readily eats. . . . Paltu, day and night the lover lives on the executioner's pike."[5] Guru Arjan Dev also says: "O my Beloved, if you just ask, I will cut off and offer my head to you. My eyes are athirst—when will I have your darshan?"[6]

Shams-i-Tabriz has described love and longing as the two wings that carry the devotee to the Lord; if he develops these wings, he will not need long and arduous ladders to climb up to Him. Although the path of love is that of pain and shedding tears in separation from the Beloved, the devotee who has tasted divine love prefers its anguish to all the joys and luxuries the world can offer. Guru Gobind Singh, who had to endure at an

1. *K.S.S.*, p.48:59.
2. A devoted disciple of Guru Arjan Dev.
3. A.G., *Chaubole*, M.5, p.1364.
4. *K.S.S.*, p.47:54.
5. *Paltu Sahib*, I, *Kundli* 64.
6. A.G., *Maru*, M.5, p.1094.

early age the agony of separation from his own Master, says:

> Pray, narrate the plight of this disciple
> To my beloved, my friend.
> Without you, gorgeous quilts are a malady,
> And mansions, dens of snakes;
> Flagons are spikes,
> And goblets, deadly daggers.
> Like a beast
> Under the butcher's merciless blade,
> I writhe in agony.
> All hardships and afflictions of the world
> Are welcome like pleasure and joy,
> If the Beloved is with me.
> Fie upon comforts and luxuries:
> Without you—seething cauldrons of pain.[1]

Love songs, in the hands of the Saints, have acquired an epic and soul-stirring depth. The poems of divine love by the mystics continue to be a source of inspiration to modern poets. Deeply moving, the Saints' songs of love and longing are endowed with an ethereal delicacy, a spiritual fervor and an intoxication intense and yet elevating. Saints convey the idea of the soul's union with the Supreme Being as 'light merging into Light'. Kabir says that the soul-bride, having become one with the supreme light, herself reflects his radiance:

> Truly that bride has met
> The Beloved
> Whom the Beloved holds
> In his loving embrace—
> On whose face shines
> The Beloved's radiance,
> Dazzling those
> Who look at her.[2]

---

1. Dassam Granth, *Khial Ramkali*, Patshahi 10, p.711.
2. *K.S.S.*, p.107:1.

Dadu describes the union of the soul-bride with the Lord with an equally spontaneous ecstasy:

> The ground is of Light,
> The House is of Light,
> Of Light alone is my beloved Groom.
> The union is of Light,
> The game is of Light,
> Only Light is, and I dwell in Light.
> I am in love with Light,
> I am drunk with Light,
> I thrive on Light—
> Thy Light, O Lord.[1]

The flame merges into the Flame

The Saints are the true lovers of the Lord. They live in his love, preach his love and radiate his love. On the physical plane they are love personified. Although they have attained such a high state, the Saints are always humble. They have become the Lord, yet they live as his slaves. A loving wife attributes all comforts and possessions provided by her husband as a gift from him. The Saints attribute everything to the Lord, who alone, according to them, is the Giver and the Doer. Kabir says:

> After endless days of separation I have met my Be-
> loved within my own home. My temple[2] is flooded
> with light and in bliss I lie with my Beloved in the
> deep trance of his loving embrace. My efforts were
> of no avail, the glory is to you, dear Lord, that in
> your grace you came and met me within my own
> home. I did nothing, O Kabir, to deserve his grace;
> the Lord himself in his mercy blessed me with the
> bliss of union.[3]

---

1. *Dadudayal*, p.67:203.
2. *Home, temple:* the body.
3. *K.G.*, p.69:2.

Guru Arjan Dev, identifying himself with a devoted wife, says:

> He took into account
> Neither my merits, nor faults;
> Nor my lack of beauty,
> Adornment and grace.
> I was ignorant of love's demeanor,
> Decorum and proper ways;
> Yet, taking me into his arms,
> My Beloved brought me to his bed.[1]

Saints have become one with the Beloved. On the spiritual level they are the Beloved, and their union is a reality. However, on the physical plane they are the lovers, always longing to meet the Beloved. Kabir says: "I have filled the vessel of my body with the ambrosia of pure light; I drink and drink, yet want more and more. Such is the thirst of Kabir."[2]

But when the realized soul, the mystic, is with the Lord within, his joy is boundless. He is the cherished bride of the Supreme Bridegroom. The devotee who attains this state of union deserves all praise. Taking the example of an Indian bride who receives gifts from her husband when she first meets him, Kabir says:

> My dress is designed and made by my Husband
> himself. Only that bride can wear it who is dear to
> her Beloved's heart. My gown is eight cubits long
> with pleats rippling in five hues.[3] My scarf is gar-
> nished with suns and moons; the dazzling beauty of
> my dress radiates all round. Its cloth is not woven
> with warp and weft. Says Kabir the slave: I surren-
> der myself at the feet of my Beloved, who has
> fashioned the dress.[4]

---

1. A.G., *Asa*, M.5, p.372.
2. *K.S.S.*, p.34:3.
3. *Eight:* all the eight inner regions, from Sahansdal Kanwal (the land of the thousand lights) to Anami (the Nameless One); *five:* the five melodies.
4. *K.S.*, I:92:11.

Kabir's poems, woven with words soft as silken threads, radiate the glow of deep emotions. His songs of union, vivified by the exuberance of love's fervor, depict a loving bride's fascination for her beloved bridegroom endowed with ineffable divine beauty. His poems of longing are laden with intense pain and an all-consuming desire to meet the Beloved; each word echoes the sighs of a heart pining for the Loved One.

Kabir-panthi traditions maintain that on the last day of his earthly sojourn, the Saint, while giving darshan to his disciples, asked some of them to sing the song on the divine wedding. After the recitation he retired to his hut, and 'the flame merged into the Flame'. Kabir himself lived in divine love, he taught love and merged into Love. The song portrays the essential unity of soul and God, and the bliss of ultimate union—the aim of all spiritual effort:

> Sing, come sing, O happy brides,
> Wedding songs of joy and bliss;
> My royal Bridegroom
> Has come to my home today.
>> Sing, O brides, songs of joy and bliss...
> My long-awaited Guest has come
> And I am aflame
> With the youth of my devotion...
> The Everlasting One
> Has wed me, O Kabir,
> And He is taking me home with Him.
>> Sing, O brides, sing the songs
>> Of joy and bliss,
>> For today, my Husband,
>> My Beloved Lord
>> I meet.[1]

---

1. *K.G.*, p.68:1.

Selected Poems

KABIR'S PRAYER

This is a devotee's earnest prayer at the Lord's feet. When he looks at his shortcomings and misdeeds, he feels that God, from whom nothing can be kept hidden, will not forgive him. He shrinks at the idea of paying for his evil actions, knowing that the tetribution must be long and heavy. In all humility he surrenders himself at the feet of the Almighty and prays to be forgiven.

Lord, Thou art my father,
Pay heed to my humble prayer.
Many misdeeds have I done,
Deeds I kept concealed from others
But which are no secret to Thee.
Lust and desires corrupted my mind,
And many a wrong have I done;
I look at them and my heart shudders
With fear and shame.
Almighty Lord, I implore Thee
Concede my prayer:
First, grant me Thy pardon,
Then ask me to reckon
For my misdeeds.

Says Kabir: Mighty Lord!
Thou art my father;
I have now taken the refuge
Of Thy lotus feet.
Pray grant me Thy pardon,
Then ask me to reckon
For my sins.

Kabir Granthavali,[1] *p.156:357*
Bāp rām sun binti mori[2]

---

1. Hereafter cited as *K.G.*
2. Hindi poetry is usually identified by its first line. The Hindi first lines are given after the source of each poem.

191

THE WEAVER OF GOD'S NAME

Kabir uses his weaver's profession to convey the merits of the practice of Nam. Worldly people weave the cloth of misery, with desires and expectations as the warp and weft, set upon the frame of mind. In return for their work they get paid with births and rebirths and continue their rounds in the cycle of transmigration. Kabir enjoins upon man to weave the cloth of the Lord's Name and earn the 'profit' of union with Him.

Kabir says that *surat* (the hearing faculty of the soul) and *nirat* (the seeing faculty of the soul) are the two pegs that hold the frame; knowledge is the processed yarn with which the shuttle is loaded; repetition is the dabber with which one cleans and applies starch to the warp; and realization or inner spiritual experience is the beater or wire comb that removes the twists and knots from the yarn.

Through such weaving Kabir has overcome his wayward mind and its wild tendencies and has forever rid himself of the world's misery and delusion. He has realized his true self, earned the wages of the Lord's love and attained the sublime state of truth and bliss.

> Lord, I am the weaver of Thy Name;
> I weave and reap the profit
> Of inner rapport with Thee.
>   I weave the cloth of Thy Name, O Lord.
> I have firmly strung my loom
> With ten hundred threads;
> The sun and moon
> I hold as my witness.[1]
> Endlessly I count Thy Name
> And take it as my wages;
> I gently deposit it
> Within the lotus of my heart.[2]
>   I am the weaver of Thy Name.
> Surat and nirat are the two pegs
> That hold the frame of my loom;

---

1. The 'ten hundred threads' is a reference to the inner spiritual region of the thousand-petaled lotus (Sahansdal Kamal), which is preceded by the sun and moon region; that is, Kabir weaves the Lord's Name in the higher spiritual regions within.
2. In the terminology of the Saints, the 'heart' is behind the eye center.

Thus I weave with care and discernment
The cloth of Thy Name.
 I weave and reap the profit
 Of inner rapport with Thee.
The shuttle I have loaded
With the yarn of divine knowledge;
While engaged in such weaving
I realized my own true self.
Sublime and imperishable
Is the wealth I have earned,
And I have gained
The state of perfect peace.
 Lord, I am the weaver of Thy Name;
 I weave and reap the profit
 Of inner rapport with Thee.
In vain men search for Him
In mountains and dales;
Within my body I found Him,
So close to me.
 I weave the cloth of the Lord's Name.
Repetition I made the dabber
To clean and purify my mind;
Realization I made the comb[1]
To remove the twists and twirls
That entangled my being.
Thus become immaculate,
I remain absorbed in His love.
Without wandering about,
I earned the gift of love
Within my own home.
 I am the weaver of the Lord's Name.
The fruitless toil
Of weaving for the world
Has come to an end;
Evil tendencies have owned defeat;

---

1. A wooden- or wire-toothed beater used by weavers to remove twists from the weft and
to make the lines of yarn smooth and straight.

I have attained
The dazzling state of bliss—
   Free from fear, free from pain.
Kabir, Thy slave, thus weaving
Realized supreme truth;
His doubts are dissolved,
His misery, ended.
   I am the weaver, O Lord, of Thy Name;
   I weave and reap the profit
   Of inner rapport with Thee.

K.G., p.139:288
Terā hari nāmai julāhā

THE PROPITIOUS MOMENT

People in India try to find an auspicious day and time for undertaking new projects. Kabir says that for a true seeker of the Lord, the day, hour and moment when he meets his Master are the most propitious. Trying to recount the numerous blessings of the Master, Kabir says that through the Master's grace the disciple's inner eye is opened, enabling him to see the divine light within; his inner ear is opened, enabling him to hear the divine melody within; he is rid of duality and is freed from the bondage of karmas. In a word, his entire being is purified and transformed, turning him into a true devotee.

> Blessed is that day, that hour,
> That propitious moment
> When the man of God came
> And graced my home.
>
> Such was the effect of his darshan[1]
> That the veil fell from my eyes,
> I heard the divine melody within
> And duality came to an end.
> The gates that blocked my hearing
> Were hard as granite,
> Yet they broke to pieces
> When the man of God came
> And blessed my home.
>
> One touch from my Master remolded
> The ill-shaped pot of my being;
> The chains of karma
> Fell from my body
> When the man of God came
> And graced my home.
>
> Says Kabir: I love, I adore the Saint;
> Through his grace I found the Supreme One,
> The diadem of all, within my own body.

---

1. For explanation of terms, see Glossary.

Blessed indeed is the day, the hour,
The precious moment, when
The man of God, my Master,
Came and graced my home.

K.G., p.165:395
Dhanni so ghari mahuratya dinā

Listening to the melody of Shabd within has been termed by Saints 'singing God's praises'. Kabir urges man to sing the Lord's praises, to listen to the sound of the bagpipe in the highest spiritual region and make his permanent abode there. If the devotee becomes absorbed in the divine melody, if he once drinks the elixir of the Lord's Name, all his thirst for the world's objects and pleasures will disappear.

The world has been created from the region of Omkar—the seat of the negative power—and it continues to exist through the deceit and delusion of mind and maya. Kabir says that realizing the nature of creation, man should accept with equanimity pleasure and pain, prosperity and adversity. All that is happening and all that is going to happen has already been chalked out for man by his previous good and bad karmas; now he is simply playing his allotted part.

Kabir tells man not to run to holy places, nor take up chanting, penances and austerities in order to gain heaven or avoid hell. He says these pursuits are futile—they do not lead to God-realization. The devotee should seek instead the company of Saints and learn from them the practice of Shabd—the way to go to the inner spiritual regions, to develop love for the Lord and to become one with Him.

> Sing the praises of the Lord,
> O brother, and obtain
> The treasure of supreme bliss.

> From Omkar the world came into being;
> Through deception it continues to be.
> Play the unstruck tune of bagpipe,
> Make the highest firmament your home
> And stay there, happy and carefree.

> You have been hoodwinked
> By the world's glittering pageantry:
> Why cling to life's vain hopes and desires?
> Those who drink the elixir of the Lord's Name
> Do not suffer the pangs of thirst again.

> Even a life of half a moment is worthwhile
> If spent in devotion to the Lord;

Wasted is the life of a million eons
Without a trace of love for God.

Be not elated by riches,
Be not shaken by misfortune;
Let joy and sorrow
Be the same to you,
For whatever comes,
Comes by His command.

Crave not the pleasures of paradise,
Fear not the fires of hell,
For whatever is to happen
Has already come to pass;
Torture not your mind
With empty dreams.

What worth is your chanting,
Your arduous penances,
Your rigid austerities?
What worth your pilgrimages,
Your fasts and holy baths,
If you do not know the true way
To love and worship the Lord?

Search in the region of Sunn
For the resplendence of His love
Where exists neither shape nor form,
Where the firmament blossoms
Without any flowers.

Says Kabir: With your heart absorbed
In the company of Saints,
Sing the praises of God;
The slave who serves Him with love,
Only in his heart dwells the Lord.

K.G., p.96:121
Gobyandā guna gāiye re

LIGHT THE LAMP

Saints describe the world as a dark well, an abyss of sorrow where it is impossible to see things in their true perspective and realize the Lord. Kabir says that if man will light the lamp of his heart with the spark of the Master's Word, he will be able to see his way out of this blind well. The Lord is within the body, but He is hidden by the veil of ego. God, the mighty mountain, is obscured by a blade of grass—man's ego and selfish motives. Yet man's delusion is so formidable and the veil of ego so strong that he is unable to pierce them and see the Truth. Kabir says that only by taking the shelter of a Master and getting the spark of divine knowledge from him will a seeker be able to attain God-realization.

> O friend, light your lamp
> With the Master's spark;
> The world is a blind well,
> Dismal and dark.
>
> Maya's tinsel glitter blinds one and all;
> They fail to see the Lord.
> Light your lamp with the Master's spark.
>
> The Primal One lives in your body,
> A mountain behind a blade of grass.
> The scent is within its navel,
> Yet the musk deer wanders around
> Sniffing jungle trees and bark.
> Light your lamp with the Master's spark.
>
> If you listen to Kabir's words,
> My friend, the bars of delusion
> Will fall apart.
> O friend, light your lamp
> With the Master's spark;
> The world is a blind well,
> Dismal and dark.

Kabir Sahib ki Shabdavali,[1] *II:74*
Guru diyanā bāru re

---

1. Hereafter cited as *K.S.*

PIOUS LIARS

This poem denounces the priests and preachers who claim to be evolved souls, who give an impression to others that they have realized God and who talk about Him at length. They relate stories from the scriptures and build their own imaginary dogmas around them; they teach others from the Vedas and holy books but themselves never bother to live according to what the scriptures command. Kabir says that such men live in lies, thrive on lies and propagate lies. They are themselves deluded, and they delude others also, for without spiritual experience their preaching is nothing but perpetation of fraud on others.

> Those who day and night give sermons
> On religion and dogma,
> Each morning begin their day uttering lies.
> Lies they embroider at dawn,
> At dusk they weave the web of lies;[1]
> Lies have found a snug abode in their heart.
>
> They know nothing about God;
> According to their own notions
> They propagate dogmas
> Based on Vedas and Puranas,
> But do not follow
> What the scriptures command.
> They continue to burn
> In the world's blazing furnace,
> Whose fire never abates.
>
> To others they sing about God,
>   The One without attributes;
> But without realizing Him
>   They are themselves lost;
> In the end, earth returns to earth
>   And air into air dissolves.

Bijak, Ramaini 61
Dharam kathā jo kahte

---

1. Dawn and dusk were held in sanctity by medieval Indians, who believed that one should not tell lies or perform any other bad deed at these times of day.

THE SLUMBERING WIFE

The time of youth, when the body is strong, the spirit lively and the will firm, is the time to attend to meditation and realize the Lord. Kabir calls it the nighttime of life, the time for soul—the wife—to meet the Lord, her Husband. But the soul has wasted this time in sleep; she has remained indifferent to the treasure of divine love and spiritual bliss that lies within the human body. The best time of life has been spent in lethargy, neglect and worldly pursuits, and the opportunity of union with the Lord has been lost. Now the daytime of old age has come when body and will have both grown weak. Kabir says that even now one should try to make the best use of whatever period of life is left and devote it to the pursuit of God-realization.

> Awake, dear friend,
> Awake—sleep no more;
> The night has faded away,
> Why in sleep waste also the day?
> Awake, dear friend, sleep no more.

> Those who have awakened
> Have found the rare ruby;[1]
> O foolish woman, while you slept
> You even lost what you had.
>   The night has faded away,
>   Why in sleep waste also the day?
> Your Husband is wise and alert;
> You are foolish, O witless wife—
> You never prepared the bed
> For your Husband to rest.
>   The night has faded away,
>   Why in sleep waste also the day?
> O crazy woman,
> A blunder you've made:
> During the vivacious days
> Of your youth
> Not once did you try

---

1. Kabir here calls spiritual bliss a 'rare ruby' rather than a diamond or a pearl, because the deep red color of the ruby conveys the thought of love and union.

To recognize your Husband,
To make Him your own.
   The night has faded away,
    Why in sleep waste also the day?
Wake up, become aware—
See, your bed is empty,
The Beloved is not there;
He left you while you were
In the embrace of sleep.
   The night has now faded away,
    Why in sleep waste also the day?
Says Kabir: Only that wife awakes
Whose heart is pierced
By the arrow of Shabd.

Kabir, p.263:36
Jāg piyāri ab kyā sovai

THE COLOR OF NAM

Once the soul is absorbed in the Lord's Name it becomes impervious to the attractions of the world. The Name washes away passions and worldly attachments, purifies the mind and saturates the soul in the rich hue of divine love. Kabir says that only this color is lasting; all others fade in time.

> I am dyed in the hue of the Lord's Name,
> In a hue that can never fade;
> There is no color in the world
> That can vie with the color of God!
>   I am dyed in the hue of Nam,
>   A hue that can never fade.
> All other colors are washed away
> By the gorgeous color of Nam.
> The soul once dyed in the Lord's hue
> Will never lose its luster.
>   I am dyed in the hue of Nam,
>   The hue that never fades.
> The Lord himself is the color
> That has suffused me, says Kabir.
> His glow will stay forever;
> All the colors of the world
> Will turn pale and fade away.

K.G., p.120:215
Rām nām rang lāgo kurang na hoi

THE STRENGTH OF CRAVINGS

With the coming of old age, eyes, ears and other sense organs, even the entire physical body, become weak; but the wayward tendencies of the mind, cravings for wealth, fame and power, and attachment to worldly objects and faces show no sign of abating. When the physical capacity to enjoy worldly pleasures becomes feeble, sometimes the longing for them increases all the more. Kabir says that man should realize the importance of human birth and try to gain real knowledge through meditation and spiritual practice. Cravings and desires, called 'thirst' by Kabir, will die out only through Shabd practice. Identifying Shabd with the 'order' or will of God, Kabir says that the disciple who realizes the Order or Shabd gains true detachment and plays the game of life, winning a place in the Lord's home.

Eyes are fatigued from seeing,
Ears are fatigued from hearing,
Even the beautiful body
Is fatigued and toil-worn;
At the beck of old age
All senses grow languid—
Only craving for the world
Stands untired and strong.
You foolish one, you did nothing to gain
The wealth of knowledge and meditation;
You have spent your human birth in vain.

O man, remember the Lord
As long as there is breath in your body;
Such should be your love for Him
That though your body die,
Your love ever remain
And take you to the sanctuary
Of the Lord's lotus feet.
    But true knowledge you did not gain,
    In vain you've spent your human birth.
He within whom the Lord
Implants his Shabd
Is forever rid of thirst;

He realizes the Order
And throws the dice well[1]
To vanquish his mind.
  But true knowledge you did not gain,
  In vain you've spent your human birth.
They who know and adore
The one everlasting Lord
Will not come to grief.
Says Kabir: They will never lose
Who know how to throw the dice.

Adi Granth,[2] Suhi, p.793
Thāke nain sravan sun thāke

---

1. Kabir refers to chaupar, a game played with dice or cowrie shells. The pawn has to circle the four corners of the board—the four types of species—and the player wins the game when it enters the center square, known as 'home'.
2. Hereafter cited as *A.G.*

WITHOUT THE MASTER

Kabir emphasizes here the imperative need of a Master to save man from the miseries of birth and death and to lead him to the Lord. When he meets a perfect Master, all that a devotee has to do is become a *gurumukh*—a disciple who implicitly obeys his Master, overcomes his ego, controls his mind and surrenders himself to the Master. As directed by the Master, the disciple does his spiritual practice, goes within and merges himself into the radiant or Shabd form of the Master.

A temple roof
Cannot stay up without rafters;
So without Nam
How can one cross the ocean?
Without a vessel
Water cannot be kept;
So without a Saint
Man cannot be saved from doom.
Woe to him
Who thinks not of God,
Whose mind and heart
Remain absorbed in plowing
The field of the senses.

Without a plowman
Land cannot be tilled,
Without a thread
Jewels cannot be strung,
Without a knot
The sacred tie cannot be made;[1]
So without a Saint
Man cannot be saved from doom.

A child cannot be born
Without father and mother,

---

1. Refers to the wedding ceremony among Hindus in North India during which the border of the bride's garment (usually a type of sari) is tied to the scarf of the bridegroom.

Clothes cannot be washed
Without water,
There can be no horseman
Without a horse;
So without a Master
None can reach the court of the Lord.

Without music
There can be no wedding;[1]
Rejected by her husband,
A bad woman suffers misery;
So man suffers
Without a Saint.
Says Kabir, My friend,
Only one thing attain:
Become a gurumukh
That you not die again.

A.G., Gond, p.872
Jaise mandir mahi

---

1. Kabir uses the words *pheri lena,* which literally means 'to take rounds' or 'circumambu-late'. In an Indian wedding the bride and bridegroom circumambulate the fire or altar as part of the ceremony. In medieval days this ceremony was never performed without the accompaniment of music. Some scholars have interpreted this line to read, 'Without music there can be no dancing'.

A BRIDE YEARNING

When a daughter is born into an Indian family, the parents bring her up with love and concern, but always remind themselves that their daughter's real home is her husband's house; that she has taken birth in their home only to be reared and looked after till the object of her birth, namely getting married and going to her own home, is achieved. Using this analogy, Kabir says that the soul has taken birth in the human body for the single purpose of attaining union with her true husband, the Lord. The 'marriage' has already taken place, for the soul and God—the bride and Bridegroom—reside within the same body, although the two have never met nor seen each other. The agony felt by the separated soul is depicted by Kabir in this plaintive song of a bride yearning for her husband.

> When will that day dawn, O mother,
> When the One for whom I have taken birth,
> With ardent love will clasp me to his heart?
> I long for the bliss of divine union,
> I long to lose my body, mind and soul
> And become one with my beloved Lord.
>   When will that day come, O mother?
> Beloved, pray fulfill my longing of eons,
> For nothing is beyond you, Almighty Lord.
> In lonely moments laden with sorrow
> I yearn and yearn for you,
> I spend sleepless nights looking for you,
> Looking with unblinking, covetous eyes.
>   When will that day dawn, O mother?
>   When will my Lord clasp me to his heart?
> The vacant couch, like a hungry tigress,
> Devours me whenever I try to rest.
> Heed your pining slave's prayer, O Lord,
> Come and allay the fire of separation
> That consumes my being.
>   When will He clasp me to his heart?
>   When will that day dawn, O mother?
> Says Kabir: If once I meet my Beloved,
> I'll cling firmly to Him

And sing auspicious songs of union—
Jubilant songs of everlasting bliss.
    When will that day dawn, O mother,
    When the One for whom I have taken birth,
    With ardent love will clasp me to his heart?

K.G., p.143:306
Vai din kab āvainge māi

ONLY WHILE LIVING

Most religions, holy books and paths promise salvation after death, after the soul leaves this world of matter. But the Saints neither attach importance to such promises nor give similar assurances to their disciples, for they say that a worldly person will not turn into a holy man after death, nor an illiterate person become a great scholar. They tell their disciples to rely only on what they achieve while living, and while living reach the region of liberation—the region from where they will not be required to return to this world of birth and death. The spiritual heights a man attains while living will be his even after death.

In these two poems Kabir says that the inner regions of bliss that the Saints speak of are to be reached through spiritual practice during one's lifetime. The shackles of karma, which keep man tied to the circle of transmigration, must be broken while living. A person who is born within the bonds of karma, who lives in them, strengthens them through his good and bad actions and also dies in them, will not suddenly become free from them through the agency of death. Kabir says that if a man breaks the bonds during his lifetime, he will while living become free to go to the inner spiritual regions at will and reach the state of liberation. But in order to attain this high state a devotee must give up his delusions, try to realize what is true, seek the association of a perfect Master and undertake the practice of Nam under his directions.

> O friend, rely only on that
> Which you get while living.
>
> Learn while you are living,
> While living realize Him,
> While living attain
> The state of liberation.
>   O friend, rely only on that
>   Which you get while living.
> While living you did not shatter
> The shackles of karmas,
> Yet you expect to gain
> Salvation after death!
>   O friend, rely only on that
>   Which you get while living.

Those who say, 'After death
Your soul will merge in God,'
Only give you false assurances;
Whatever you gain now
Will be with you hereafter,
Or you'll become a citizen
Of Yama's domain.
   O friend, rely only on that
   Which you get while living.
The deluded wander seeking God
In remote and distant places,
But it does not end the agony
Of their visits to the womb;
Only if they adore the Saints
Will the noose of their karmas be cut.
   O friend, rely only on that
   Which you get while living.
Know the truth, hold onto it,
Realize the true Master
And build faith in the true Name.
The Saints, O Kabir,
Are my benefactors—
And I, their slave.

K.S., I:38
Sādho bhāi jeevat hi karo āsā

He alone is liberated
Who gains liberation while living.

Until one attains
Salvation in his lifetime,
He will continue to suffer
Both pleasure and pain.[1]
If while living in the body
Liberation is not attained,

---

1. That is, he will continue to return to this world of pleasure and pain.

How can one after death
Obtain salvation?
  He alone is liberated
  Who gains liberation while living.
By spending one's entire life in holy places
Liberation cannot be had,
Nor by making bare earth one's bed.
While living, if a man fails to cut
The deadly noose of delusion
But looks forward to liberation after death,
He is like the thirsty man
Who thirsty remains
Even after visions
Of water in his dreams.
  He alone is liberated
  Who gains liberation while living.
He who becomes detached,
Who gains freedom from his bonds,
He can, while living, go where he likes.[1]
He who is not detached,
Who is chained to his bonds,
Cannot go beyond his ties.
  He alone is liberated
  Who gains liberation while living.
Through the practice
Of the Everlasting One's Name
He has severed the chain
Of coming and going—
Such is my Master;
He has delivered Kabir
From delusion's deadly noose.
  He alone is liberated
  Who gains liberation while living.

K.S., II:10
Jeewat mukta soi muktā ho

---

1. While living, he can travel unhindered in the inner regions.

212

HOLY BATHS

Kabir rejects the popular belief that baths in 'holy' rivers or ponds remove the dross acquired by bad actions, cleanse the mind and enable one to become fit for realizing the Lord. Baths cleanse the physical body but cannot wash away the layers of dirt gathered through evil deeds and thoughts, through blind indulgence in sense pleasures or through sins committed to fulfill worldly desires and cravings. Kabir clearly states that only the practice of Nam can remove these stains, purify the mind and enable the devotee to attain God.

> What use are your ablutions
> And your dips in holy waters
> If you have not realized
> Your true self within?
>
> What will you ever gain
> From scrubbing and washing your body
> When your inside is covered
> With layers and layers of dirt?
> Without the Lord's Name
> You'll not escape the fires of hell,
> Though a hundred times
> You wash and bathe.
>
> In order to attain the Lord
> Men, like clowns, adopt different garbs;
> They wear ochre robes,
> They smear their body with ash.
> A frog living in the holy river[1]
> Will not attain salvation.
> Without himself realizing the Lord
> Man can never be liberated.
>
> O deluded one, give up your base cravings,
> Repeat the Lord's Name—
> This is my counsel, good friend.

---

1. Bathing in the Ganges is believed to wash off all sins and lead to salvation.

Kabir the weaver submits:
The Lord's Name alone will lead you
To the high state,
Free from fear,
Full of bliss.

K.G., p.154:346
Kyā hwai tere nahāi dhoi

From the day of creation when it was separated from the Lord and sent to this realm of birth and death, the soul has been going from one species to another according to its karmas. Whenever it obtained the human form—the only form privileged to love and realize God—it involved itself in external practices, yogic exercises, asceticism and penances. Sometimes it was born as a king, sometimes as a beggar, but both in prosperity and penury it failed to realize the Lord. It continued therefore to revolve in the wheel of transmigration. Kabir says that the *sakats*—people who crave worldly pleasures and possessions and cling to them—continue to live and die again and again. But the Saints, who devote themselves to the practice of Nam, go within and drink the nectar of Nam and achieve freedom from the chain of birth and death; they become one with the Lord and attain eternal life.

> In the immobile and the mobile,
> Among the worms and the moths,
> Many births I had,
> In many forms I reveled.
>
> Since the day Thou subjected me, Lord,
> To visitations to the womb,
> In many a home have I made my sojourn.[1]
> Sometimes I was a yogi,
> Sometimes an ascetic;
> Sometimes I was a hermit,
> Sometimes a celibate;
> Sometimes I became an emperor,
> Sometimes a beggar on the streets.
> Since the day Thou subjected me, Lord,
> To visitations to the womb,
> In many a home have I made my sojourn.
>
> The sakats die again and again,
> But the Saints forever live,
> For they imbibe the elixir of God.[2]

---

1. Took birth in many species.
2. Prof. Sahib Singh interprets *rām rasayan,* 'the elixir of God', as Nam.

Kabir submits: O Lord, have mercy on me;
Wearied,[1] I have come to Thy feet,
Pray bless me with the state of perfection.

A.G., Gauri, p.325
Asthāvar jangam keet patangā

---

1. Wearied of repeated births and rebirths.

TETHERED TO PREJUDICE

Men try to realize God but their efforts are circumscribed by their own pre-conceived notions, their deeply ingrained prejudices and fanatical belief in formal practices. Kabir says that just as farmers tie two donkeys together to hinder their movement, men tie themselves to their religious prejudices and fail to follow the true path of God-realization. Giving hints of this path, he says that the seeker should develop love and devotion, realize the One Lord and see Him with his inner eye—his soul's eye. Such a seeker, while living in this imperfect world, will become perfect; in other words, he will be free from his prejudices, free from the bonds of mind and maya and the shackles of karma. Having thus become pure, he will merge in the Pure One.

> Biased with one view or another,
> The entire world dwells in delusion.
> He who adores the Lord,
> Without bigotry or bias,
> Is the Saint, the enlightened one;
> Biased with one view or another,
> All the rest dwell in delusion.
>
> As a donkey is tied
> To another donkey,
> So are men tethered
> To their own predilections.
> He who sees with his soul's eye
> Is the truly realized one.
> Biased with one view or another,
> All the rest dwell in delusion.
>
> They who realize the One,
> Realize the Truth.
> They are always engrossed
> In their love for the Lord,
> Never again will they come
> To this valley of pain;
> They become perfect,
> Perfect becomes their vision,

And they see the Perfect One.
Biased with one view or another,
All the rest dwell in delusion.

Unique is the bliss of Realization,
It is inconceivable,
It is beyond words, O Kabir.
But biased with one view or another
The entire world dwells in delusion.

K.G., p.111:181
Pakhā pakhi ke pekhnai

THE BLIND SEE

In this poem of paradox, Kabir points out that the path of the Saints is unusual because it avoids the beaten track of external observances and formal practices that people generally adopt for finding God. Metaphorically speaking, Kabir says that those who take refuge in a ship, follow a smooth highway or seek the shelter of large mansions fail to achieve their destination; that is, those who remain in the world and follow the practice of pilgrimage, almsgiving, worship in temples and holy places, and those who renounce the world, retreat to forests, become recluses and take to penances and austerities, despite their efforts still remain within the snares of mind and maya.

The devotee whose inner being is pierced by the arrow of Shabd attains true happiness. Those who have eyes for the world and its lures remain blind to the inner realms of spiritual bliss; those who have turned their attention inward and have opened their inner eye see the Lord in the entire creation.

> Such is true knowledge, O friend—
> Those who take refuge in a boat
> Sink midstream;
> The shelterless and forlorn
> Reach the opposite shore.
> Those who take the arduous thorny path
> Reach the town;
> Who take the easy highway
> Are robbed midway.
> In one string[1] all are entangled,
> Be they worldly, be they recluse.
> Those who take shelter
> Under the edifice of forms and rituals
> Are rocked and drenched by the storm;
> Who remain in the open
> Are left dry and safe.
> Those wounded by the arrow
> Attain everlasting bliss;
> They suffer pain and misery
> Who remain unhurt.

---

1. The string of illusion or maya.

Those without eyes
See the entire creation;
Who possess eyes
Remain blind.
Says Kabir: When I realized the Truth,
I saw the world's strange character.

K.G., p.110:175
Avadhu aisā gyān bichāram

THE SHIP OF NAM

Name or Word is the means by which one can escape from this region of mind and maya, of birth and death. Kabir calls it a strong ship in which one can cross the turbulent ocean of phenomena and reach the haven of everlasting bliss. The ship of Nam has been made by the Lord himself and after creating it, He has handed over its captaincy to the Master, who alone can guide the ship across. In other words, God has designed the path of Nam and has handed over its secret to the perfect Master. Those who recognize the Master can board the ship and reach the Lord. Those who fail to recognize him, or who continue to have doubts about him, do not obtain the boon of Nam and keep drifting in the ocean of misery and sorrow.

> Lord, Thou Master of all creation,
> Thy Name is the sturdy ship
> To cross the dreadful ocean of existence.
>
> Had the Lord not designed this ship,
> The entire world would have been consumed
> By the raging flames of passion.
> My gracious Lord in his mercy
> Raised the ship of Nam,
> And its command He entrusted
> To the Saints.

> Nam is the destroyer of all pain,
>   The adornment of the entire creation;
> The source of all love and devotion,
>   It is the haven of peace and bliss.
> The Lord himself has made this ship,
>   And it is called the Lord's Name.

> Those who hold onto the ship firmly,
> Cross over to the shore of bliss;
> Those who keep wavering in two minds
> Lose their footing, and no one knows
> Their whereabouts in the stormy sea.

Such people drown or stay moored
To this shore of misery and pain—
They keep burning in the world's deadly fires,
No one comes to their rescue.
They do nothing to save themselves;
They do not recognize him
Who has come to rescue them.
Those who discover the savior
Become pure and whole;
Those who fail to recognize him
Burn in their own blazing passions,
Like moths in the flame.

O man, attach yourself to the Lord's Name;
Wake up, be aware of your true self.
Says Kabir: Only they gain liberation
Who remain absorbed in the Lord's love.

K.G., p.183, Barahpadi Ramaini 5
Sirjanhār nāu dhu terā

INDEED MAD

The pundits, priests and the orthodox mostly look upon Saints and devotees as deluded, lost and even mad. The orthodox claim that God resides in temples, mosques and churches; the Saints say the human body is the real temple of God. The priests propound various forms of rituals and worship to find Him; the Saints only ask their disciples to go within the body and meet Him there. Holy men give assurances of salvation after death; Saints give little value to such promises and ask the seeker to attain the goal while living. Kabir accepts the charge of the orthodox that he is mad, but adds that his 'madness' came to him as a divine gift when his Master destroyed all his delusions. He ends by saying that the object of human birth is in fact to become mad in the Lord's love and if one fails to develop this love, he wastes this glorious opportunity.

> I am not learned,
> I am no adept at debates;
> Listening and dwelling
> Upon God's virtues,
> Yes, I have become mad.

> My friend,
> I am indeed mad,
> The entire world is sane,
> Only I am mad.
> Yes, I am past cure;
> Let others not be ruined
> By my example.

> I am not mad of my own choice—
> It is God who has made me mad,
> And my Master burned
> Whatever traces of delusion I had.

> Yes, I have gone astray,
> But it's my own sanity I have lost;
> Let others not become mad
> By accepting my 'delusions'.

He is mad who knows not
His own true self;
Had he known his self,
He would have known the One.

If now you don't become
Mad in divine love,
You never will, my friend.
Says Kabir: I am dyed
In the glorious hue
Of God's love.

A.G., Bilawal, p.855
Bidiā na parao

SHABD, THE WORD

Calling upon the devotee to adopt the practice of Shabd, Kabir explains what Saints mean by this term. Shabd is the power of the Supreme Being that has created the creator of the three worlds, Kal or the negative power. Even this world of illusion has also come into being from the power of Shabd or the divine Word and is sustained by it. It is the form in which the Lord pervades the entire creation.

Although most scriptures, holy men and schools of philosophy talk about Shabd, they are not aware of its true nature and identity. Its secret is in the hands of the Saints or perfect Masters and it can be experienced, not spoken, expounded upon or analyzed. Kabir distinguishes this divine Word or Shabd from the words that can be spoken, written and read. The written words can point to the real Word, can extol its merits, but cannot take its place.

Men try to obtain Shabd through renunciation, austerities and yogic practices. But Kabir says that these paths and practices can never open the gates of Shabd. True detachment and desirelessness come as a natural result of the practice of Shabd, and when the disciple goes within and contacts Shabd, he develops true love for the Lord.

> Apply yourself, O friend,
> To the practice of Shabd—
> The Shabd from which even
> The creator came into being;
> Imprint that Shabd
> In your heart, O friend.

> The Vedas and scriptures
> Extol the merits of Shabd—
> The Shabd that sustains
> All shabds in the world.[1]
> Men, sages and gods
> Sing its praises
> Yet its mystery they know not.
> Imprint that Shabd
> In your heart, O friend.

---

1. *Shabd* literally means 'word'.

Shabd is the Master,
And listening to Shabd
One becomes a disciple;
But rare are they who know
The true meaning of Shabd.
Shabd is the real Master,
Shabd is the disciple's soul too;
Only he knows this
Who goes within
And realizes the Shabd.
  Imprint that Shabd
  In your heart, O friend.

Between Shabd and shabd
There is a vast difference;
Churn the primal Shabd
And realize the Truth, O friend.
Who does not taste
This true Shabd,
His life, O Kabir,
His achievements,
Are all a waste.

Satt Kabir ki Shabdavali,[1] *p.33:69*
Sādho shabd sādhanā keejai

A rare slave of the Lord
Contemplates on His Shabd.
The secret of Shabd
Is with the Master:
Test it on the touchstone within.

Men hear about Shabd
And varied garbs
They adopt to gain it;
But he who hears Shabd itself
Becomes a true lover.

---

1. Hereafter cited as *Satt Kabir.*

The six philosophies
Elaborate on Shabd,
But he who hears Shabd itself
Becomes truly desireless.

Vedas and scriptures
Sing the praises of Shabd,
All claim to know its merits;
Hermits and ascetics
Expound upon Shabd,
But not one of them
Obtains its secret.

Even this world of delusion
Through Shabd came into being;
All that is,
Is the expansion of Shabd.

But from where
Does Shabd emanate?
On this, Kabir,
Few contemplate.

Satt Kabir, p.132:325
Santo koi jan shabd bichāre

CASTLES OF SAND

Pointing to the transient nature of the world, Kabir tells man to realize the value of human birth and utilize his limited time by following the path of love and devotion. Like all Saints, Kabir has reached the Lord's mansion and urges man to follow his example and reach this abode of supreme bliss.

My mind, kindle within thee
The flame of love for the Lord;
They become free who take refuge
With loving surrender at his feet.

Be not enamored
Of physical beauty—
It is just a drop of dew
On a blade of grass,
A castle of sand
On the changing shores of the sea.

This precious human birth
You will not get again;
Your numbered days
Are slipping by in vain.

Kabir, the slave, has ascended
To the pinnacle of the fort;
From there, to the beat of drum,
He calls all men to victory.

K.S., II:6
Man re kari le sāhib se preet

PLAYTHING

In India men put on ochre, saffron, yellow, blue or white dress, smear ash on their body, apply sandalwood paste to their forehead, wear rosaries of different types around their neck, believing that all these things are an essential part of holiness, necessary for realizing God. They worship idols with flowers and leaves; they serve them by bathing them, waving a fan over them and offering them fruits and sweets. Kabir says that such devotees have taken God to be a plaything. Lost in their own world of make-believe, they have no idea of the path of true devotion. Saints do not bother with such external formalities and shows of holiness. Outwardly they live, dress and behave like ordinary men, but within they have realized God and become one with Him. Worldly people, unaware of their inner attainment, criticize and malign them. Kabir says that in order to attain the inner state of the Saints, a seeker should give up all external formalities and worship and serve a perfect Master.

> People put saffron marks on their forehead,
> Carry rosaries in their hands
> And don religious garb;
> They take God to be a plaything!
> If I am mad, O Lord, I am still Thine;
> What do others know of my inner state?
> I'll not pluck leaves,[1]
> I'll not worship idols,
> For other than devotion to God
> All worship is futile.
>   What do people know
>   Of my inner state?
> I only worship my true Master;
> Ever, ever I try to please him
> —And through such service
> I'll attain bliss in the Lord's court.
>   If I am mad, still I am Thine, O Lord;
>   How can others know my inner state?
> People say Kabir has gone mad,
> But only the Lord knows Kabir's state of bliss.

A.G., Bhairau, p.1158
Māthe tilak hath mālā bānā

---

1. In some forms of idol worship, leaves of a certain number of different trees are offered to the image of the deity.

THE UNTOLD TALE

Divine love defies all attempts to describe it because one has to experience it in order to know what it is. But it can be experienced only when the devotee stills his mind and withdraws his consciousness to the inner spiritual realms. The Master not only teaches the disciple how to go within; he also enables him to actually do so and taste the nectar of love. Then the disciple's doubts and delusions vanish and his mind, a particle of the universal mind, goes back and merges in its source. Kabir says that it is not within the power of the disciple to attain this sublime state of love; it is purely the Master's gift.

> Ineffable is the story of love,
> A tale that can never be told;
> It is the sweet of the dumb man
> Who eats it and silently smiles.
>> Ineffable is the story of love.
> Without earth and without seed
> Grows the tree of divine love, my friend;
> A tree laden with countless radiant fruits
> That my Master enables me to taste.
>> Ineffable is the story of love,
>> A tale that can never be told.
> When I stilled my mind
> And contemplated within,
> The Lord's love like a flame
> Sprang within me;
> All my false beliefs were scattered,
> Chaff blown away by the wind.
>> Ineffable is the story of love,
>> A tale that can never be told.
> Says Kabir: Not through my efforts
> But only through my Master's grace
> Did I learn the lesson of love;
> Now my coming and going has ended
> And my mind has merged in the Mind.
>> Ineffable is the story of love,
>> A tale that can never be told.

K.G., p.104:156
Akath kahāni prem kee

KABIR'S HOMELAND

The inner spiritual region of supreme bliss is the home of Saints, but Kabir says that the material limits of human vocabulary make it impossible to describe that land. It cannot be understood through erudition, analysis or intellectual speculation. The conditions of this world of phenomena do not exist there: Although there is dazzling light, there is no source that produces it, it exists by itself; the melody of Shabd, called 'the divine voice' by Kabir, is not dependent on an instrument or singer; and although Saints have tried to describe the Shabd experienced by a devotee on different levels of consciousness as the melodies of *kingri, sitar* and *been,* it is without rhythm, cadence or tone.

In order to comprehend the beauty and brilliance of that region, a seeker has to go within and see it for himself. But only a devoted disciple who has surrendered his entire self to the Master and lives in his will; who has vanquished his mind, turned his face away from the world and looks only towards his Master; who loves and adores his Master and none else, looking upon him as God in human form—only such a *gurumukh* will reach the land of the Saints. Kabir says that through one-pointed love the devotee reaches that land and shares supreme bliss with the Saints; only he will know about the land where Kabir lives.

> Who shares my secret
> Alone knows, O friend,
> The mystery of my homeland.
>
> Vedas and holy books
> Have no clue to my home;
> Neither speech, nor speculation,
> Nor reason, nor intellect
> Can ever fathom it.
> Who shares my secret
> Alone knows, O friend,
> The mystery of my homeland.
> Where there is neither caste,
> Nor color, nor lineage,
> Where neither ceremonies,
> Nor ritual prayers,
> Nor canonic laws hold sway;
> Such is my homeland, O friend.

Where rain pours down
Drops with a divine taste—
Neither salty nor sweet;
Where in the mansion of Sunn
Endlessly reverberate
The sonorous melodies
Of kingri, sitar and been.
   Who shares my secret
   Alone knows, O friend,
   The mystery of my homeland.
Where lightning flashes without clouds,
Where dazzling light shines without a sun,
Where pearls of radiant sheen form
Without mother-of-pearl,
Where the sweet music
Of the divine voice resounds
Without a speaker, without rhythm or tone;
   Such is my homeland, O friend.
Where all the lights of the world
Put together, fade with shame
Before the light of the region of Brahm.
Beyond that; beyond, in the realm
Of the Inaccessible, the Boundless,
Is the land where lives Kabir—
But only a gurumukh will,
Through love, reach my home;
   Only he who shares my secret
Will know and attain
That homeland of mine, O friend.

K.S., I:59
Mahram hoi so jānai sādho

The following poem also gives hints of the inner spiritual regions. The gateway to the inner world is the eye center, described here as an inverted well with a narrow opening. But, says Kabir, only a 'married soul' can draw water from that well; that is, only a soul initiated by a Master can go within and taste the water of divine bliss. Kabir tells the devotee to leave the courtyard of his body's house, go within and be saturated with the nectar of inner realization.

Come, swan, let us go to that land
Where dwells your Beloved.

That land has an inverted well
With an opening, narrow as a thread,
Through which the married soul draws water,
Without a pitcher, without a rope.
    Come, swan, let us go to that land
    Where dwells your Beloved.
Clouds never gather in that land,
Yet it rains without a stop.
Do not keep sitting in the courtyard,
Go in, and without a body be drenched.
    Come, swan, let us go to that land
    Where dwells your Beloved.
That land is always suffused with moonlight,
And never a trace of darkness comes.
That land is ever flooded with the light
Of not one, but a million suns.
    Come, swan, let us go to that land
    Where dwells your Beloved.
Says Kabir: Listen, O friend,
That land is the land of true freedom;
He who learns of that land
Will reach his original home.

K.S., II:60
Chalu hansā vā des

WHO DWELL IN NAM

Kabir urges the seeker to undertake the practice of Nam and remain absorbed in it day and night. Those who have attained success in their quest for God have done so through their absorption in Nam. Sages, hermits and other holy men who took to practices other than that of Nam failed to gain their objective of God-realization in spite of all their hard labor. Kabir calls Nam the *kalpataru*, the mythological tree which fulfills the wishes made before it, because Nam grants the highest wish of a true seeker—union with the Lord.

They who day and night are awake
Only to the Name of God
Attain fulfillment
Through their absorption in the Name.

Seekers, seers and hermits,
All toil to win Him, but fail;
For it is only the Name
That, like a wish-fulfilling tree,
Grants the boon—liberation.

Those who dwell on the Lord
Do not from Him remain apart,
For they have realized, O Kabir,
The Lord's Name.

A.G., Gauri, p.330
Ahi nisi ek nām jo jāge

THE CREATED GODS

While talking about God, all Saints have the same thing to say: God is one, He is the origin of all, the source of all creation. Himself beyond the limitations of the created world, He pervades each particle of his creation; and yet He is indivisible—aloof from everything. Instead of worshipping Him, men worship idols, images and paintings made with their own hands out of matter. They pray to such handcrafted gods, bring offerings to them and beg for worldly boons from them. They 'divide' the Indivisible One into various gods, goddesses and deities. But God, the Supreme Being, cannot be made to live in an idol, nor can He be confined within the precincts of man-made temples, mosques or churches.

Talking of the ten incarnations, Kabir says that a look at their life stories shows that even they, like ordinary human beings, bore the burden of their own karmas and were made to account for them. In the last stanza Kabir says that the practice of Shabd is the true worship of the Lord; it is the path that enables a soul to get release from the bondage of mind and matter and reach the Supreme Being.

> Who worships Thee,
> My uncreated Lord?
> All rush to worship gods
> From stone and matter carved;
> To them men bow in supplication,
> To them are offerings brought.
> But none, oh none adores Thee,
> My uncreated Lord.

> Men are ignorant of Him—
> My perfect, my indivisible Lord;
> They worship only created gods.
> The ten incarnations are considered
> Free from maya, free from bonds;
> But not one of them is my Lord—
> The object of my adoration.
> They taste the fruits
> Of their own deeds;
> Different from them is my True Lord,
> The Creator of all.

But who worships Thee,
   My uncreated Lord?
Even deities and incarnations
Bear on their heads
The stigma of karmas.
Depend not on them, O man,
For even they could not gain salvation.
   Yet all rush to worship gods
   From stone and matter carved;
   Who worships Thee,
   My uncreated Lord?
The yogi and the recluse,
The ascetic and the hermit
Argue and wrangle,
One with the other.
Says Kabir: Listen brother,
He who realizes Shabd[1]
Crosses the turbulent sea
To the shore of bliss.
   But who worships Thee,
   My uncreated Lord?

K.S., II:17
Ungadhiā devā

In the following poem, Kabir continues the same theme and asks the devotee to adore the One Formless Lord and try to live in his Nam or Shabd, that is, be absorbed in the divine melody within. The learned talk of Shabd and Nam but have no idea of the source of Shabd and how Shabd leads the devotee's soul back to its original home. The *mukti* or liberation that the scriptures speak of is only the second stage on the soul's inner journey; and though this region is full of joy and happiness, it is within the limits of mind and maya. Therefore, even after reaching there, the soul has to return to the world of matter after a period of enjoying its stay. The freedom Saints talk of is a higher state, beyond the bounds of mind and maya. It means merging in Shabd, and along with Shabd into the source of Shabd—the Lord.

---

1. Another version of this line reads: 'He who realizes love'.

He who is imperceptible
Yet who can be perceived,
Who is one, yet dwells in all;
Forgetting such a Lord,
Those who worship gods
Are groping in delusion's dark maze.

Even Shiva says he knows not,
Lord, how to contemplate on you.
But such is your grace, beloved Lord,
That Kabir remembers you,
He abides in your Name.

Tell me, tell me, O man,
From where does Shabd arise,
Where does it merge again?
Ignorant of the secret of Shabd—
Shabd that is beyond all matter, all form—
People wander in doubt and delusion.

What worth is freedom
From the bonds of matter
If one fails to attain
The state of true freedom within?
Hermits and sages sing
Of liberation from the world
But know not the supreme state
Of merging in Shabd.

The Truth that is manifest, yet hidden,
The secret that is hidden, yet manifest,
How can it remain hidden for Kabir?
He ever enjoys the bliss
Of union with that Truth,
But he cannot describe
His ineffable state.

K.G., p.78:36
Achyant chyant e mādhau

237

THE CITY OF THE DEAD

Death is the law in this world, for all that is created must perish, all that is born must die. Kabir describes this world as a city of the dead and goes on to say that the sun, the moon and the earth, in fact the entire physical world is subject to destruction and will cease to exist one day. Further, the law of death covers even the astral and causal regions, including all the gods, goddesses, angels and deities that live there. At the time of dissolution they will all perish. In this city of death the soul takes birth and dies again and again. The Name of the Lord, the divine Word, is the only thing that is eternal and deathless, that is not subject to decay, disease and death. Kabir tells the seeker to realize the Truth through Nam and be freed from this realm of death.

Friends, this is the city of the dead.
Holy preceptors have died here,
Incarnations have died,
So too have died adept yogis.
   This is the city of the dead, my friends.
Mighty rulers have died,
And the ones over whom they ruled;
Great physicians have died,
And the ones they healed.
   This is the city of the dead, my friends.
The moon will die,
So will die the sun;
The earth will die,
So will die the sky.
Even the strong headmen
Of the fourteen forts will die;[1]
Then who can hope to survive?
   This is the city of the dead, my friends.
The nine are dead,[2]
The ten are dead,[3]
So too are dead the eighty-eight thousand;[4]

---

1. According to Hindu mythology the universe is divided into fourteen regions; the gods of the Hindu trinity are believed to be the lords of these fourteen regions.
2. *Nine* refers to the nine main yogis of the Nath school of yoga; some scholars interpret it as the nine goddesses in Hindu mythology.
3. The ten incarnations of Lord Vishnu.
4. 88,000 rishis or sages of ancient India.

The three hundred and thirty-three million are dead,[1]
Such is the infallible noose of death.
 This is the city of the dead, my friends.
The Name of the Nameless One
Lives and will ever live,
But all that is created will die,
 For this is the city of the dead, my friends.
Says Kabir: Realize the Truth, friends,
Do not die again and again in delusion.

Satt Kabir, Shabd 318
Sādho ih murde kā gām

---

1. 333,000,000 gods of Hindu mythology.

THE SHAMELESS QUEEN

The lure of the world, with its riches and possessions and the charm of its transient pleasures, has been called Maya in Hindu mythology and is often depicted as a beautiful woman. Kabir calls her the shameless queen who has beguiled the entire world. 'Shameless' because she is faithful to no one, for the objects of worldly attachment and pleasure are always changing hands; 'queen' because her sway is supreme and no one can resist her lure, for everyone adores and craves wealth, power and position in one form or another.

In an Indian family a daughter, sister or niece is always loved and pampered because she will one day be married and will leave the family; but in the husband's house, as a wife she is expected to abide by the family discipline, be submissive to the husband, and with him bear the ups and downs of life with fortitude. Using this as a metaphor, Kabir says that those who marry Maya—those who overcome her guile and become impervious to her charms—succeed in enslaving her.

Kabir further adds that the soul whose husband is a Saint or perfect Master—in other words, one who is a disciple of a perfect Master—is not troubled by the designs of Maya. He concludes by saying that he has completely vanquished and destroyed Maya, the shameless one, who is dear to all the three worlds—to men, angels, gods and deities. Saints have always regarded her as an enemy and never yield to her lure.

> On one plate is meat and fowl,
> In one vessel, liquor;
> Around these sit five jogis,[1]
> In their midst, the shameless queen.
>
> Vast is the sway
> Of this brazen one's coquetry;
> Only a rare man of wisdom
> Has tamed her.
>
> In all resides the shameless one;
> All she has made her abject prey
> And is ever looking out for fresh quarry.
> All adore and humor her
> As one pampers a sister or niece;

---

1. Derogatory reference for *yogi;* here, the five passions.

But the one who marries her—
She becomes his bondslave.
  Vast is the sway
  Of this brazen one's coquetry;
  Only a rare man of wisdom
  Has tamed her.
Supreme and wise is my husband,
He is the true Saint.
No one ventures to come near me,
For over my head is spread
The shield of his protection and grace.
  Vast is the sway
  Of this brazen one's coquetry;
  Only a rare man of wisdom
  Has tamed her.
I have cut off her nose,
I have sheared her ears,
I have dismembered her,
I've wrecked the edifice of her wiles;
A foe of the Saints, O Kabir,
She is the darling of the three worlds.

A.G., Asa, p.476
Ikat patar bhari urkat kurkat

THE TREASURE MAP

Most religions claim to know who God is and how to reach Him. Kabir points out that they are regarding the negative power or Kal as God since they have no knowledge of the Supreme Being. Brahma, mind, karmas and maya or illusion are all different aspects of this negative power and are all mistaken for the Supreme Being by different religious groups. Kabir goes on to say that people know nothing of their own soul, let alone their origin or the Supreme Being. When someone realizes the Lord, he sees Him present in each particle of the creation; but this realization can come only through Shabd. Kabir here describes the Word as the *bijak,* the treasure map[1] that leads to God, the treasure hidden within the human body.

The first wise is not the Wise One;[2]
The second wise[3] no one knows;
The third wise preys on the wise;[4]
The fourth wise[5] drives the soul
From place to place;
The fifth wise[6] none is aware of;
The sixth wise[7] beguiles one and all.
If you know the seventh Wise
You will see Him in the entire creation;
You will know the One
All Vedas and scriptures
Point towards.
  As the treasure map leads
    To the secret of hidden treasure,
  So does Shabd reveal the Lord;
    But only a rare one knows it.

Bijak, Ramaini 37
Ek sayān sayān na hoi

---

1. A *bijak* could be in the form of a code message, usually in poetry, or a riddle or diagram, which would give a clue to the whereabouts of the hidden treasure.
2. *The first wise:* Kal or the negative power, worshipped by most religions as the Lord; *the Wise One* is God, the Supreme Being.
3. Brahma, the god of creation.
4. *The third wise:* mind; *the wise:* soul.
5. Karmas.
6. The soul.
7. Maya or illusion.

FORGIVE THY CHILD

In this world the love of the mother for her child is an example of unselfish love. She protects and nurtures her child purely out of love. She even overlooks the child's faults and misbehavior. Kabir in this poem prays to the Lord to look upon him as His child and forgive his sins, to give him the support of Nam enabling him to cross the ocean of the world, and to bless him with a pure heart so that he is able to succeed in his devotion and merge into Him.

> The son commits many faults,
> The mother does not take them to heart;
> I am your child, I am your son,
> Lord, will you not pardon my sins?
>
> If a child in anger
> Runs and hits his mother,
> She bears no grudge
> Nor takes offence;
> I am your child, I am your son,
> Lord, will you not pardon my sins?
>
> My mind sinks
> Into a gloom of anxiety:
> How will I reach
> The opposite shore
> Without the power of Nam?
> I am your child, I am your son,
> Lord, will you not pardon my sins?
>
> Dear Lord, bless Kabir
> With a pure heart,
> A clear mind,
> That he easily attain Sahaj
> And become absorbed
> In your virtues.
> I am your child, I am your son,
> Lord, will you not pardon my sins?

A.G., Asa, p.478
Sut aprādh karat hai jete

SLAVES OF MIND

This poem deals with *manmukhs* or men who follow the dictates of their own mind and are deeply engrossed in the affairs of the world. They plan their own methods of devotion or seek the guidance of scholars and intellectuals, who involve them in outward practices and promise heaven after death. But, says Kabir, disillusionment awaits them at the time of their death because the practices they undertake cannot dispel the fear and suffering at death nor what they have to face thereafter. Had they sought the company of Saints and adopted the inner path of spiritual practice under their guidance, they would have saved themselves from the misery of further births and deaths. Kabir declares that without the help of a perfect Master they can never gain liberation.

Those who put their trust
In paths laid down
By their own mind
Go to hell
And make hell their home;
They get no respite
From coming and going,
Morning and evening
They are the prey
Of the ruthless hunter, Kal.[1]

They become proficient
In letters and sciences
But are not aware
Of their own impending death.
For others they draw rosy pictures
Of a happy afterlife;
When themselves faced with death
They shudder
With dread of the unknown.

---

1. In medieval days the morning and evening times were regarded by hunters as most suitable for hunting. Here Kal, the negative power or 'hunter', follows the same practice attacking his prey in the mornings and evenings—with each birth and at death.

They avoided the company of Saints
And took to vain pursuits;
Now on their heads
They carry a heavy load
And march towards hell.
Let all men and women know:
   Averse to the Master,
     Slaves of their own mind,
   They'll revolve in the whirligig
     Till the sun and moon
  Cease to shine.

Bijak, Ramaini 43
Jin jiv keenha

WITHIN THE HOME

In this poem Kabir explains some of the main aspects of Sant Mat. God resides within the human body and the bliss of union with Him can only be attained by going within. Men seek Him outside, but fail to find Him. They renounce the world and seek the seclusion of forests and mountains, but the obstacles of mind, desires and cravings cannot be overcome by turning one's face away from the world. The perfect Master removes the veil of delusion from the devotee's mind, shows him the way to find God in the 'home' of his body and helps him to realize the Lord through the practice of Shabd. When mind and soul withdraw from the nine portals of the body and go beyond the eye center, mind merges back in its origin—Brahm, or the universal mind. The soul becomes free to proceed further in the pure region of spirit, called 'Sunn' by Saints, and on going even higher, realizes the Ultimate Truth—the Lord.

> He who brings the lost traveler back home,
> Him I like and admire, O friend.
>
> Within the home is all joy,
> Within the home is true union;
> Do not give up home
> And run to forests.
> If desires assail your mind
> In the wilderness,
> Where will you run for shelter?
>   Who leads the lost one home,
>   Him I like, I love, O friend.
> Within the home is the way,
> Within the home is salvation,
> But only if the Master reveals
> That unseen Truth within;
> Then with ease you will enter Sunn,
> You will become entranced
> In the realm of Sahaj.
> Your mind will turn inwards
> And realize the Universal Mind,
> The soul will contemplate
> On the Ultimate Truth.

Through the union of surat and nirat
The soul will play the unstruck music.[1]
   Who leads the lost one home,
   Him I like, I love, O friend.
Your home is the place for practice;
In your home lies the hidden treasure,
In the home alone will it be found.
Says Kabir: Listen, my friend,
Reach that Home
From where you once came.

K.S., I:52
Avadhu bhoole ko ghar lāvai

---

1. *Surat* is the soul's faculty of hearing and *nirat,* that of seeing. At a stage on the inner journey, the two faculties merge into one, which is a step toward the soul's merging into the Shabd or melody of the unstruck music.

FROM THE SAME LIGHT

The Lord is one, He has created all beings and He is present in every particle of his creation. The physical form of every human being is made out of the same five elements; in view of this there is no justification for looking on any-one as good or bad, superior or inferior. Kabir says that to call a human being bad amounts to finding fault with the Lord. A devotee who realizes that the world is moving under the order of God and accepts everything as his will, recognizes the Lord's presence everywhere. Kabir says that his Master has given him the nectar of inner realization and now he sees the Lord present in everyone.

> In the beginning God projected Light,
> From that Light came into being all men;
> From the same Light emanated
> The entire universe—
> Whom then shall I call good, whom bad?
> O man, do not be led into delusion:
> He, the Creator, is in his creation
> And the creation is Him—the Creator;
> He fills all,
> He pervades everything.

> The clay is one,
> But the Great Designer has designed it
> In varied shapes, in many forms.
> It does not become us to find fault
> With the vessels of clay,
> Nor with the Potter who shaped them.

> He, the True One, dwells in all;
> Whatever happens, happens by his will.
> Whoever realizes his Order
> Realizes Him—the One;
> And only such a person can be called
> The Lord's devotee, his true slave.

Allah, the Lord, is invisible,
He could not be seen,
But my Master gave me
The nectar of realization;
Its sweet bliss,
Like a dumb person
I taste but fail to express.

Says Kabir: My delusion is destroyed
For now I see the Boundless Lord
Present in all.

A.G., Bibhas Prabhati, p.1349
Aval alah noor upāiā

Man is always engaged in the pursuit of physical pleasures, not realizing that indulgence in them is the cause of the misery of further births and deaths. Saints, knowing this, do not crave for the world or its pleasures. As long as mind runs after sense pleasures, man cannot attain true freedom and reach the Lord.

Kabir says that the seeker must go within his own body and realize what mind is, where it comes from and where it goes in the end. In the past, great devotees like Jaidev and Namdev solved this mystery through their Master's grace and through the path of love and devotion, and one can do so even now. If the delusion of duality is removed, the devotee will realize that, like the soul, the mind can also become free from the chain of birth and death.

By realizing the *hukam* or 'order' of the Lord, that is, by manifesting the Word, Nam or Shabd within, the devotee will know that the mind's origin is Brahm—the lord of the second region in the inner spiritual realms—and merge his mind into its source. Then the soul will be free from all physical bonds and will enjoy bliss in the company of the Lord.

> Man prays for worldly happiness,
> But all happiness comes
> Accompanied by pain;
> I don't like to beg
> For such happiness.
>
> Man craves sense pleasures
> Yet hopes to attain peace;
> How can he find an abode
> At the feet of the Lord,
> The King of all?
>
> Even Shiv and Brahma
> Dread these pleasures,[1]
> But the same pleasures we take
> As lasting and real.

---

1. According to Hindu mythology some of the gods, in their pursuit of pleasure, had to suffer much humiliation.

The sons of Brahma,
Narad the seer,
And the mighty snake,[1]
Even they could not probe
Into the body
And see the mind.

Search into the mind, O brother:
Where goes the mind
After the body dies?

By the Master's blessings,
Through love and devotion
Jaidev and Nama
Solved the mystery of the mind.

He whose delusion is dispelled
Realizes the Truth;
Then his mind has neither to come
Nor to go.[2]

This mind has neither form nor shape;
It has come by His Order,
And by realizing His Order
It will merge into its origin.

He who unravels
The mystery of the mind,
Through the mind merges in Him
Who is the Bestower of bliss.

---

1. The four sons of Brahma, the god of creation; Narad, a great devotee of Lord Vishnu;
and Sheshnāg, the mythical serpent that supports the earth on its thousand hoods: Kabir
says that these holy personalities did not know the path of going within, their devotion
being limited to gods and deities within the world of the three attributes.
2. The mind, along with the soul, takes birth and dies; after realizaton it also is freed from
coming and going.

The soul in essence is one,
Many are the bodies
In which it takes abode.
Kabir has merged his mind
Back into its source,
And his soul
Revels with the Lord.

A.G., Gauri, p.330
Sukh māngat dukh āgai āvai

THE BIRD THAT SINGS WITHIN

Scriptures and holy books speak about the soul but do not enable the seeker to experience its presence, to gain self-realization. Kabir describes the soul as a bird that is hidden behind the coverings of the physical body. Separated from its original source, the Lord, the soul is sustained by the energy of Nam or the divine Word, which is the all-pervading power of God in this world.

Continuing the imagery, Kabir says that although the bird lives in the hollow nooks and gloomy corners of this vast tree of the world, it has over it the imperceptible protecting shade of Nam. The bird flies from branch to branch, that is, the soul moves from birth to birth, from species to species. The ways of the birds that live in the tree of the world are unusual, for they fly away in the evening and return in the morning; the soul leaves the world at the end of its sojourn here and returns to the world the next morning—the beginning of the next birth.

Birds keep pecking at grains and eating a variety of fruits the whole day; but this bird, the soul, comes to the world to taste only two fruits—the fruits or results of its previous good and bad actions. Kabir concludes the poem by pointing out that if the bird returns to its original home, the Lord's abode, it will forever become free of the bondage of birth and rebirth in this vast tree of the world.

No one tells me about the bird
That sings within the body.
Its color is a colorless hue,
Its form a formless form,
It lives under the shade of Nam.
    No one tells me about the bird
    That sings within the body.
In the vast tree dwells a bird,
It hops, it pecks, it eats,
And from branch to branch it flies.
No one knows where it comes from,
No one knows what makes it sing.
    No one tells me about the bird
    That sings within the body.
Numerous vines entwine the tree,[1]

---

1. Worldly relations and attachments.

Throwing shadows dark and dense;
Numerous birds huddle together
To build their nests
In the tree's sunless gloom.[1]
But they fly away in the evening,
Morning they return for the day;
No one understands their strange ways.[2]
    No one tells me about the bird
    That sings within the body.
Only to taste two fruits comes the bird,
Not for ten, not for twenty,
Nor for countless, nor for many.[3]
But vast and inaccessible,
Boundless and eternal
Is the bird's true home;
If the bird will only return
To its original home,
It will not be forced
To come and go again.
    But no one tells me about this bird
    That sings within the body.
Says Kabir: Yes, my friends,
The story I tell you
Is hard to comprehend;
But where, O Pundits,
Where, O learned ones,
Is the Home of that bird
That no one is able to see,
That sings within each body?

Satt Kabir, Shabd 358
So panchhi mohi koi na batāvai

---

1. Sunless and gloomy because the light of divine knowledge does not penetrate.
2. *Evening and morning:* death and rebirth. Normally birds settle in trees for the night and fly away in the morning, hence Kabir's reference to the strange ways of these birds.
3. The soul, apparently engaged in countless pursuits in the world, is moved by only two factors—the good and bad actions of previous lives.

FEAR OF GOD

Man is always afflicted with fear in this world—fear of the unknown, fear of ill health and physical calamities, fear of others and of their opinions, fear of losing wealth, prestige and possessions, and above all the fear of death. Numerous anxieties, both imaginary and real, intimidate man. Kabir says that the root cause of all fears that loom over man, birth after birth, is ego. The devotee can overcome this fear by eliminating his ego and inculcating fear of God in his heart.

In Sant Mat, fear is an important part of love, and the two go hand in hand on the path. It is not fear in the ordinary sense, but the anxiety of the devotee not to do anything consciously or unwittingly that will offend or displease the Beloved. When a devotee develops true love for the Lord, his ego is eliminated and all his worldly fears come to an end; they dissolve in divine fear, the essential companion of divine love.

Why need I fear any more?
All my fears dissolved
Before my fear of the Lord,
The moment I recognized
My true self and the Self of God.

As long as I was involved
In 'mine' and 'thine',
Life after life the misery
And fear of birth and death
Trailed me tenaciously.

Those who realize the One
Both within and without,
Their mind is always
Absorbed inside.
Men who look upon others
As high or low
Are no better than beasts;
They keep wandering
In varied forms of delusion.

Says Kabir: Since I discarded
'I' and 'mine',
Nothing but the Lord exists.
Why need I fear any more?
All my fears have dissolved
Before my fear of the Lord.

K.G., p.84:66
Ab kā daraon dar darhi samānā

THE STATE OF SAHAJ

In this poem Kabir describes what Saints mean by the term *sahaj*. Sahaj is that natural state of the soul from which it originally came. It is beyond all the physical limitations and changes that govern the world of matter. It is also beyond the causal factors of time and space, creation and destruction. It is changeless, uniform and everlasting. Beyond the spiritual region of Sunn—a realm above the domains of mind, maya and the negative power—it is not to be confused with the state of *samadhi,* the trance of the yogis. Kabir, describing it as inaccessible, indestructible and everlasting, makes it clear that Sahaj is the supreme region where the Lord abides. Concluding the poem, he says that Sahaj is the region where the Master, inwardly, always stays and the devotee too can attain it—through the Master's grace.

Where there is neither sea nor rains,
Nor sun nor shade;
Where there is neither creation
Nor dissolution;
Where prevails neither life nor death,
Nor pain nor pleasure;
Beyond the states of Sunn and trance;
Beyond words, O friend,
Is that unique state of Sahaj.
It can be neither weighed
Nor exhausted,
Is neither heavy nor light;
It has no upper regions
Nor lower ones;
It knows not the dawn of day
Nor the gloom of night;
Where there is neither wind
Nor water nor fire,
There abides the perfect Master.
It is inaccessible,
It is incomprehensible,
It is, and it will ever be;
Attain it through the Master's grace.

Sayeth Kabir: I surrender myself
At the feet of my Master,
I remain absorbed
In his true company.

A.G., Gauri, p.333
Tah pāwas sindh dhoop nahi chhahiā

THE WEAVER OF BANARAS

This poem is in answer to a pundit of Banaras who derided Kabir for his ' low' profession, lack of learning and sacrilegious way of disregarding all orthodox practices. Kabir says that if wearing a thread around the neck is a sign of holiness, then his own house is holy, being full of thread which is put to the good purpose of making cloth. What is the use of merely reading the Vedas and chanting holy mantras if there is no realization of God? A true devotee's mind, heart and soul are constantly absorbed in the Lord.

Kabir says that after wasting his human birth in external pursuits and show of piety, the ritualist has to face the messengers of death. All his pious and formal practices will fail to help in that hour of crisis, and repeating names of the Lord at the last moment will be of no help, for during his life-time he did nothing to realize the true Name within himself.

The Brahmins are looked upon as teachers and guides on the temporal and religious paths, and as the guardians of man's spiritual future. Kabir says, on a note of sarcasm, that for ages the Brahmins have been driving men like a herd of cows from one ritual to another, from one form of worship to another, but they have never taken them to the opposite shore of the river where the grass is always green—beyond the physical bonds and the limits of mind to the inner regions of bliss. They guide men only for the sake of money, food and gifts; they flatter the rich and mighty and stand as beggars at their doors. But a true devotee is a beggar only at the door of the Lord and begs for nothing except union with Him.

Around your neck is a sacred thread,
But there is no dearth of thread in my house—
I daily weave it into cloth.
You study Vedas and chant gayatri,[1]
While the Lord himself
Resides in my heart.

On my tongue dwells the Lord,
In my eyes dwells the Lord,
And the Lord alone dwells in my heart.
O deluded one,

---

1. A Vedic mantra, considered sacred by orthodox Hindus, and repeated morning and evening by Brahmins; it is taught to Hindu children as an essential part of their religious upbringing.

When you are questioned
At the door of death,
What avail will be
Your taking God's Name?

O pious Brahmin,
We are like cows, you the cowherd;
You are man's guardian at every birth,
But you never take us across
To graze on the banks of bliss;
What sort of guardian are you?

You are a holy Brahmin
And I, a poor weaver of Kasi[1]—
Why ask what my knowledge is?
You are engaged in begging
From monarchs and kings,
And I, merely in the devotion
Of my Lord.

A.G., Asa, p.482
Ham ghar sut

---

1. Kāsi or Kāshi is the ancient name for Banaras.

260

ONLY THROUGH FEAR

Kabir, addressing this poem to a *bairagi* or recluse, says that the Lord who is free from all fears cannot be attained without divine fear in the devotee's heart. Divine fear has two aspects. The first is that the devotee might fail to achieve his object of union with God before the rare and brief opportunity of human birth comes to an end. This fear urges him on to utilize his time in devotion and spiritual practice, to walk firmly on the path and not be led astray by worldly attachments and cravings.

The second aspect is the fear that the devotee might do something by action or thought that offends or displeases his beloved Lord. This fear is an important aspect of divine love; it strengthens the devotee's love and keeps the flame of longing constantly burning in his heart. Kabir says that the devotee who has this true fear in him realizes God's Order.

The term *hukam* or 'order' has been used by the Saints to denote God's will, his plan, the wave of his grace or *mauj*, his power in action—the Shabd or Word. It is through Shabd that the Lord pervades the entire creation, through Shabd He sustains it, through Shabd He regulates it and through Shabd He showers his love and grace; thus Shabd is his power, his will, his order, his love.

One who realizes God's Shabd or Order is rid of all fears for he becomes one with Him who is free from all fear. In the end Kabir says that one can attain the state of true detachment or freedom only through a perfect Master, and one can meet the Master only by the grace and mercy of the Lord.

> No one has seen the Fearless One,
> For the Fearless One cannot
> Without fear be obtained—
>   So reckon I, Bairagi. [1]
> If one sees the King
> Ever present within,
> Then does he gain true fear;
> When one realizes his Order,
> He becomes free from fear—
>   So reckon I, Bairagi.

---

1. This poem is in a tune and style typical of the folksongs of Uttar Pradesh. The refrains, *bairāgi'* and *'vanā hambai'*, come alternately at the end of each stanza. *Vanā hambai* is from one of the dialects of U.P. and is supposed to convey 'indeed, so it is, so be it, even so, is it not so, so think I'. *Bairāgi* is a type of recluse or anchorite who leaves his family and the world, puts on saffron clothes, does not touch money, eats through begging and lives on others' charity.

Do not practice hypocrisy
To please the Lord,
For in hypocrisy the world
Is already involved—
   So reckon I, Bairagi.
The noose of craving
Ever tautens
And attachments consume
Your being—
   So reckon I, Bairagi.
But he burns all worries,
He conquers his body[1]
Who makes his mind dead—
   So reckon I, Bairagi.
Without the Master
There can be no detachment,
Though men keep striving
And longing for it—
   So reckon I, Bairagi.
Only through the Lord's grace
One meets the true Master;
Only then will he attain
The state of real detachment—
   So reckon I, Bairagi.
This is the one prayer
Of Kabir at Thy feet:
Beloved Lord, ferry me
Across the dreadful sea—
   So reckon I, Bairagi.

A.G., Maru, p.1104
Anbhao kinai na dekhiā

---

1. Physical desires.

THE OILMAN'S BULLOCK

Kabir compares a worldly man to the oilman's bullock, which is made to trot in a circle in order to move the oil-extracting gears of the oil press. Its eyes are covered with thick blinders and it is forced to run the press from morning till night with hardly a break. Without devotion for the Lord and without a Master, man is blindly toiling to gain worldly possessions and selfish ends. He has taken upon himself a heavy load of karmas and has to circle the wheel of birth and rebirth to atone for them.

Kabir says that in order to gain happiness man eats the leavings of ghosts —that is, he worships past sages, prophets and holy men who are no more in the physical body. Man also worships stone images and deities and involves himself in a variety of external practices in the hope of attaining salvation. But Kabir says that these are like attempting to cross the turbulent ocean of trans-migration by holding onto a dog's tail.

Without the Husband
You have become an oilman's bullock;
You do not sit in the company of Saints,
You pass your entire life in harness.
  Without the Husband
  You are an oilman's bullock.
You sweat and toil
After your own selfish ends;
You will be swept away by death
Again and again, and suffer
Much pain under Yama's rod.
For love of wealth, wife and son,
For prestige in the state,
You have laid a heavy burden
On your head.
  Without the Husband
  You are an oilman's bullock.
You have forsaken the Husband,
You have become infatuated
With pleasures of the world;
You are sowing the seeds of sin
In the vain hope of salvation.

Longing for happiness and health,
You eat the leavings[1] of evil spirits.
    Without the Husband
        You are an oilman's bullock.
You will keep tossing
In the turbulent sea
Of countless species.
Calls Kabir: Listen, O friends,
All your efforts will fail
If you try to go across
Holding onto a dog's tail.

Bijak, Shabd 107
Khasam bin teli ko bail bhayo

---

1. It is regarded as harmful and offensive to eat food left over on another's plate; 'leavings of ghosts' are presumably even more obnoxious than normal leavings.

THE STORM

Sometimes, during the summer or early rains, dust storms hit the countryside in India. The strong winds often blow away the ordinary thatched huts of village farmers. The gale is usually followed by rain, and later, when the clouds are swept away by the wind, the sun appears in a clear blue sky. In this poem the storm is spiritual knowledge, the hut is the false pageant created and held in position by Maya, and the roof is the state of delusion under which the seeker has till then lived; the rain after the storm is that of divine love, and Realization is the bright sun which dispels the darkness of ignorance, delusion and misery.

> The storm of knowledge has come;
> Its blast has swept away
> My thatched roof of delusion.
> My hut, built by Maya,
> Can no longer hold its own:
> The two posts of duality
> Have come crashing to the ground,
> The rafters of attachment
> Have been torn apart,
> The eaves of avarice
> Have collapsed,
> And the pitcher of evil tendencies
> Is shattered into fragments.
>
> With concentration and technique
> The Saints have rebuilt the roof,
> A roof strong and stable,
> Free from leaks and drips.
>
> When falsehood and duplicity
> Fled from my body's house,
> I realized the Lord
> In all his glory.

Rain came in torrents
After the storm,
Torrents of divine love
That drenched this slave,
Heart and soul.
Then, O Kabir, emerged the sun,
The glorious sun of Realization,
And darkness faded away.

K.G., p.73:16
Santo bhāi āee gyān ki āndhi

266

THE DEPRAVED PRIESTS

Kabir is strongly against killing, whether for sacrifices or for food. The hard-hearted and merciless, who advocate killing animals, invite their own misery at the hands of the lord of divine justice.

The first poem Kabir addresses to Muslim high priests and secular leaders. He says the qazis and mullahs talk much about God, but have no idea what He is or what pleases Him. They do all sorts of cruel acts in the name of God, but such acts can never please Him for they are neither approved nor ordained by Him. The priests who advocate killing beasts, birds and other living beings are themselves deluded and delude others also.

> Tell me, O Dervish, about that Home:
> What is the attire of the King of kings?
> When does He march,
> Where does he halt?
> To what form do you make salutations?
> Is He robed in red or in brown,
> Or in multicolored garments?
>
> O Qazi, what cruel deeds you do!
> In every house you ordain
> The slaughter of buffaloes.
> Who has empowered you
> To slaughter goats and fowls?
> By whose permission
> Do you wield the blade?
>
> Though devoid of mercy
> And blind to others' suffering,
> You claim to be a high soul.
> You read and recite scriptures
> And mislead the world.
>
> Says Kabir: Some claim a divine descent,
> But, themselves deluded,
> Delude also the world.

During the day they fast,
  At night they slaughter a cow;
Here they kill, there they worship—
How can they ever please the Lord?

Bijak, Ramaini 49
Dar ki bāt kaho durvesā

The following poem deals with Hindu priests and *pandas,* who preside over similar sacrificial rights and slaughter beasts, and it denounces them in equally strong terms. According to Kabir, these priests become prey to the lord of death, who sends them to hell or into the lower species for their heinous deeds. They denounce Muslim priests for killing cows, but Kabir says they are no better, for they also are guilty of the crime of killing God's beings.

O friend, pandas are adroit butchers—
They slaughter a goat, they rush upon a sheep;
They feel no remorse, they have no pity.
They bathe and apply tilak to their forehead,
They make men worship gods and goddesses
With varied rites and ceremonies;
Without remorse they immolate the living
And cause streams and streams of blood to flow.

Most holy and highborn are they deemed,
They demand reverence and homage from all;
Men beg to be initiated by such priests—
This makes me laugh, O brother.
They narrate stories from holy books
Which once listened to, they claim,
Will grant the remission of sins;
But they oblige men to do heinous deeds.

They and their followers will drown together,
And Yama with glee will take hold of their souls.
Those who slaughter cows are called Turks,
But are Pandas any better than they?
Says Kabir, listen, O friends,
These priests of the Iron Age
Are thoroughly depraved.

Kabir, p.319:151
Santo pānde nipun kasāi

THE PROMISED DAY

Most religions and schools of spiritual practice promise union with the Lord after death. Saints do not give value either to these paths or to the promises they make, for no one knows whether these hopes are ever fulfilled. Saints attach value only to liberation while living, realization while still in the body.

Kabir illustrates the meaninglessness of these promises with the imagery of an Indian wife who waits in her parents' home to be sent for by her husband. The promised day, when she is seemingly called back by her Husband, is the day of death, and death is the palanquin apparently sent by her Husband to take her back to him. But after leaving the house of her body, the soul-bride realizes that, instead of the promised land, the palanquin bearers—the messengers of death—have brought her to a strange place: neither is the Husband there, nor anyone known to her. She wants to turn back, but cannot; she begs the bearers to delay her departure so that she can say farewell to her near and dear ones, but they are unmoved. In other words, rituals, worship, austerities, renunciation of the world and all such efforts that man makes to attain detachment from the world prove to be of little avail at the time of death. The attachments remain suppressed in the mind and are projected prominently at the time of death.

Concluding this unusual poem, Kabir says that this world is the only place where the soul can pay off the debt of its karmas, finish its dealings with others and become free to attain its goal of union with the Lord. It is while living in the world that the soul can acquire the rare article of realization, for there is no other place where one can 'purchase' it.

The day of union
With my Husband has come,
The palanquin has arrived,
Thoughts of meeting Him
Fill my heart with joy.
The day of union has come!

But the bearers have brought the palanquin
To an unknown wilderness
Where no one is my own.
O bearers, I bow at your feet,
I beg, I entreat:
Pray wait, for a moment wait,

Put down the palanquin
Just for a while
That I turn back and meet
My friends, my confidantes,
My much-loved kinsmen.

Kabir, the slave, sounds a warning
From beyond the attributes:
Think well, O friends,
Complete all your trading,
All buying and selling,
For in the land where you go
There is neither a shop
Nor a market.

Kabir, p.278:73
Āyou din gaune ke ho

THE FIND

Saints describe Shabd or Nam as *vastu,* a very rare 'thing'. Kabir says that he has found it, and it is priceless, indivisible and indestructible. Shabd—variously called the Word, the Name of God, Nam, the sound current, the divine melody or nectar—pervades the entire creation. It is beyond the reach of scholarship and intellect, yet dwells within every human being. Kabir says that those who know Shabd, those who go within and realize it, become free from the chain of birth and death. The Saints come from Shabd, they remain merged in Shabd, they are Shabd. They attain true love for the Lord and themselves become an ocean of supreme love.

> I have found something,
> Something rare have I found;
> Its value none can assess.
>
> It has no color, it is one,
> Indivisible and everlasting—
> Untouched by the waves of change,
> It fills each and every vessel.
>
> It has no weight, it has no price;
> Beyond the bounds of measurement,
> It cannot be counted,
> And through erudition
> It cannot be known.
> It is neither heavy nor light,
> No touchstone can assay its worth.
>
> I dwell in it, it dwells in me,
> We are one, like water
> Mixed with water.
> He who knows it,
> Will never die;
> He who knows it not,
> Dies again and again.

Kabir, the Lord's slave, has discovered
An ocean filled with the nectar of love;
But I find no one disposed to taste it.
When men do not believe my words,
Words from my own experience,[1]
What else can I say to convince them?

K.G., p.108:169
Lādhā hai kachchu lādhā hai

---

1. The lines are also interpreted to mean:
When Brahma cannot conceive of what I say,
What proof can I offer to convince men?

272

WHEN REALIZATION COMES

In this poem Kabir describes the devotee's state of bliss on attaining God-realization. His rounds of transmigration finally come to an end, the dark shadows of doubt and delusion melt away and he is freed from all miseries. His mind, initially an obstacle on the spiritual path, becomes an ally when it starts relishing the spiritual joy within. Purified, it becomes still; from tinsel it emerges as a jewel. Realizing the supreme authority of the Lord, the devotee accepts all that comes in his life as the Lord's will, and thereby merges into the state of Sahaj.

> My dread of death and birth came to an end
> When the Lord in his glorious hue
> Revealed himself to me.
> His light shone within me
> And darkness disappeared.
> When I contemplated within I obtained
> The rare gem of the Lord's Name;
> In the wake of my bliss
> All miseries fled away.
> The jewel of my mind became absorbed
> In the Lord's love within;
> Whatever now happens, O Lord.
> I accept as Thy will.
> One who lives in Thy will
> Merges in Sahaj.
> Says Kabir: My sins have become ineffective,
> And my soul is suffused by the One
> Who is the life of the entire creation.

A.G., Bibhas Prabhati, p.1349
Maran jeewan kee sankā nāsi

A LOVER'S THIRST

This poem conveys the devotee's intense longing to meet the Lord. Like the *chatrik*, the rainbird, which drinks only drops of rain, the devotee thirsts for a glimpse of his Beloved.

When will my Beloved come home?
Only on seeing Him
Will my lovelorn heart
Find repose.

The agony of separation
Has set my body aflame;
Without his soothing vision
How will the fire within my being
Ever be quenched?
Oh, when will my Lord,
My Beloved, come home?

From morning to evening,
From night to day,
In my heart I'm cheerless and sad.
I thirst only for a sight of Him,
Like a chatrik athirst for rain.

Kabir is restless, he longs for Thee;
Dear Lord, pray hasten to meet me.
Only on seeing Thee, O Beloved,
Will my lovelorn heart find repose.

K.G., p.122:225
So mere rām kabai ghari āvai

274

SIMRAN

This poem from the Adi Granth extols the virtues of simran, or repetition of the Lord's Name, and urges the seeker to do it at all times without even a moment's break. The simran of the Saints is not an oral repetition of certain names or mantras; it is a process to be performed by the mind, and its technique can only be obtained from a spiritual adept or perfect Master.

Kabir says that this simran opens the disciple's inner eye or the 'gateway' to the inner spiritual worlds, enables him to come into contact with the divine melody or Shabd and leads him to self-realization and realization of the Lord. Kabir emphasizes that on the soul's inner journey, simran wards off whatever obstacles the negative power may put in the way, for no magic, charms, incantations or negative forces can prevail over the power of simran.

The simran that unfolds
The gateway of liberation;
That carries you
Not to this world of turbulence
But to the divine realms within;
That enables you to play
The music of drum[1]
In the home of the Fearless One;
That takes you to the region
Where rings the unstruck melody
In its all-pervading glory—
Do that simran within your mind,
For without such simran
You'll not find true freedom.

The simran before which
The negative forces
Cannot put obstacles in your path;
That will give you salvation
And rid you of your heavy load—
Cherish that simran in your heart

---

1. *Toor,* derived from Sanskrit *toorya,* a type of drum (*mridang*); also rendered 'clarion', 'trumpet'. 'Playing the *toor*' is a phrase in Hindi which implies enjoying complete freedom of thought and action. Here it is suggestive of listening to the inner music.

So you do not come again
To this world of pain.
Do that simran within your mind;
Without it you'll not find freedom.

The simran that enables you
To revel in bliss;
That kindles within you
A lamp without oil,
A lamp with an immortal flame
Whose light dispels the poisonous gloom
Of lust and anger from within you—
Do that simran within your mind,
Without it you'll not find freedom.

The simran that emancipates you,
Keep that simran wreathed in your heart,
Wear that simran like a precious necklace:
Never, never take it off;
Then will you earn the Master's grace
And you will be ferried across—
Do that simran within your mind,
Without it you'll not find freedom.

The simran that puts an end
To your indigence;[1]
That enables you to sleep
Within your temple
In undisturbed calm;[2]
That helps your soul to bloom
On the couch of bliss—
Drink, day after day,
The nectar of that simran;
Do that simran within your mind,
Without it you'll not find freedom.

---

1. Kabir uses the word metaphorically to convey the poverty and want that are the outcome of cravings and from which even a wealthy person may suffer.
2. Kabir uses a phrase in Hindi which translates literally as 'sleeping with a sheet pulled over oneself', meaning a state free from all worries and care, conducive to peace and calm.

The simran that dissolves
All calamities;
The simran that allows not
The snares of maya to entrap you—
Do that simran:
Repeat, repeat the Lord's Name,
Sing his Name within your heart.
The method of this simran
Only from the Master will you obtain—
Do that simran within your mind,
Without it you'll not find freedom.

Day and night, over and again,
Repeat, repeat his Name.
Repeat while you walk or sit,
Repeat with each morsel you eat,
Repeat with each breath you take,
While sleeping or awake, relish,
Relish the ambrosia of simran.
Only through good fortune will you gain
The simran of the Lord's Name;[1]
Do that simran within your mind,
Without it you'll not find freedom.

The simran that puts no load upon you,
Let that simran of God's Name
Be your succor and support.
Says Kabir: Boundless indeed
Is the power of simran,
Before which neither sorcery
Nor incantations can stand.
Do that simran within your mind;
Without it you'll not find freedom.

A.G., Ramkali, p.971
Jih simran hoi mukat duār

---

1. These lines could also be interpreted: 'Through simran will you have union with God'.

LOST IN THE WILDERNESS

Kabir uses the allegory of a wife who, separated from her husband, tries to reach him with the help of a guide who claims to know the way through the thick forests that lie in between. Evening has fallen, dark clouds have gathered, and the guide has himself lost his way in the dense forest. The folded blanket the wife was asked to carry as protection against the cold is getting wet in the rain and becomes heavier every moment.

The soul is the wife, separated from the Lord, her Husband. Scholars, ritualists and priests, who claim to be guides, have lost their way in the forest of dialectics, rituals and ceremonies. The dark clouds of ignorance and delusion have gathered, and the daytime of human birth is turning into the evening of age and infirmity. The fourfold blanket of chanting (*jap*), penances (*tap*), worship (*puja*) and reading holy books (*path*), instead of being a help, entails an increasing load of karmas, and the more one indulges in these practices the heavier the burden becomes. The soul, in its pure state, cannot bear the slightest weight of karma, not even as light as a flower's; she now suffers in agony because the prescribed acts of piety only add to the ever-increasing load of her karmas.

Dark clouds have gathered,
The evening shadows have spread;
In the maze of the dense forest
The guide himself has lost his way.
The wife is here, the Husband elsewhere,
And she carries on her head
A fourfold blanket.

The delicate wife,
Who could not even
Bear a flower's weight,
Complains to her friends,
Her eyes filled with tears:
As my blanket becomes
Every moment wetter and wetter,
Heavier and heavier,
So too, alas, does my burden.

Bijak, Ramaini 15
Unhi badariyā

FROM ONE COLOR

All men, irrespective of their caste, color or creed, originate from the One Lord. The true devotee realizes this and disregards the distinctions that men practice on social, religious and political grounds. Kabir is critical of those who hold onto such prejudices, looking on men as high or low, good or bad, according to their caste and color, and completely forgetting the Lord who lives within each one. He says that holy books, containing the teachings of past Saints, do not advocate discrimination against other human beings. People who approach the teachings of holy men with eyes already blinded by prejudice of caste, color and religion fail to realize the Truth and die in their ignorance.

> Those who know
> That from one color, from one form,
> Came into being
> Varied colors and varied forms,
> Give no recognition
> To the four castes.
>
> They perish
> Who do not recognize the Lord;
> They perish
> Who give their heart to others;
> They perish
> Who eulogize the Vedas,
> Which they read and read
> But never realize
> What the Vedas say.
>
> They apply collyrium[1]
> To their eyes blinded by prejudice;
> They cannot see the truth,
> They shroud themselves
> With their own ignorance.

---

1. The word *bimlakh* is interpreted by various scholars as 'void', 'the clear sky' and 'without seeing'. The editors of *Satt Kabir*, however, maintain that *bimlakh* is from a dialect of N. India and means "that which purifies the eyes, that is, collyrium" (*Introduction, p.36*).

They dance like rope-dancers,
They perform acrobatics,
And they make others dance
To different tunes in different ways.
O Sheikh Taki, realize
The Eternal Lord resides
In every pot.

Bijak, Ramaini 63
Nānā roop baran

THE ONLY SUCCOR

The world is transitory and one day everyone has to leave it. Worldly achievements, power, prestige, riches and all possessions will be left behind. Kabir says that man wastes his valuable time in vain pursuits at the dictates of his mind and fails to realize that only the practice of Nam will save him from the clutches of the negative power.

As if in reply to a seeker's question why Kal or the negative power was created, Kabir says that both Kal and Akal are created by the Supreme Being in order to continue this creation of duality. Akal is the positive power or the power of the Lord himself. While Kal is conducting the entire working of the physical, astral and causal worlds, the Lord's positive power is permeating each particle of the creation and sustaining it. Thus the two are necessary components for the continuation of the creation.

> Even Ravan, who raised forts and ramparts
> Made of gold, had to depart—
> Empty-handed.[1]
>
> O man, why act
> On the dictates of your mind?
> When Death comes
> And catches you by the hair,
> Your only rescuer
> Will be God's Name.
>
> Kal and Akal[2]
> Are both created by the Lord
> To continue this complex game.
> Says Kabir: In the end
> He will be saved whose heart
> Is filled with the elixir
> Of God's Name.

A.G., Maru, p.1104
Jin gadh kot keeye

---

1. The mythical king of Lanka (not today's Sri Lanka) who amassed fabulous riches and built his capital and its fort out of gold.
2. *Akal,* literally 'non-Kal', means that which is beyond the reach of time and space, change and death; it is not conditioned or subject to any rules or limitations.

PARTICLE OF GOD

People adopt various religious garbs and follow different paths of practice but fail to realize the true identity of the soul. Kabir says that castes and sects, garbs and titles like *jogi, jati, avdhoot, sheikh* and so on, are all limited to the physical body; they are not the attributes of the soul. Likewise father, mother, husband, wife and other relations are also limited to the physical level. Men mourn the death of a friend or relative but do not realize that the physical covering of the body dies, not the soul, which is only a temporary inhabitant of the body.

Kabir says that a perfect Master puts a devotee on the spiritual path and enables him to attain knowledge of the self, to experience the purity and immortality of the soul, and realize that soul is a part of the Supreme Being. His rounds of birth and death end, and his soul—the drop—merges into the Lord —the Ocean.

It is not a man nor a demigod.
Not a jati nor a shaivite,
Not a yogi nor an avdhoot;[1]
It has no mother
Nor is it anyone's son;
No one unravels the mystery
Of what dwells within this temple.[2]

It is not a householder nor a recluse,
Not a monarch nor a beggar door to door;
It has no body nor a drop of blood;
It is not a Brahmin nor a Khatri.[3]
No one unravels the mystery
Of what dwells within this temple.
It is not known as a monk
Nor as a sheikh;[4]
It does not live

---

1. *Jati:* a type of anchorite who practices severe austerities; *shaivite:* a worshipper of Shiva; *avdhoot:* a type of mendicant.
2. The human body.
3. The first two castes among the Hindus.
4. A Muslim holy man.

Nor has anyone seen it die;
He who cries at its 'death'
Invites sorrow and loses face.
  No one unravels the mystery
  Of what dwells within this temple.
With my Master's blessings
I have found my path;
Through his grace
My birth and death
Are both effaced.

Says Kabir: It is a particle of God;
Like the indelible mark of ink on paper,
It cannot be erased.[1]

A.G., Gond, p.871
Na ih mānas na ih deo

---

1. This is Kabir's way of expressing the immortality of the soul. This expression may have come out of the well-established tradition in medieval India that something once written in a formal letter or document could not be scratched out or wiped away. If anything was to be erased it was circled with dots or a solid line.

Saints come to the world to give the path of Shabd or Nam to seekers. But the Name that the Saints talk of cannot be spoken, written or read; it is ineffable. Even incarnations of gods did not know the path of Shabd and remained deluded in rituals and other forms of worship. Kabir counsels man to follow the path of Shabd—the only way to escape from the clutches of Yama, the negative power. However, men fail to listen to the Saints. Doubt is entrenched in their heart and leads them to take up different types of external observances and worship. Like gamblers they put their spiritual future at stake, throw the dice of their precious time and leave the world as spiritual paupers.

My path is unique,
It is beyond description.
Even incarnations are deluded;
Deluded is the entire world.
    Ineffable, unique is my path.
Awake, O friend,
Awake if you will,
Or Yama will seize your soul
And carry it away.
You put no faith
In the path of Shabd,
Yet try to impart
True knowledge to others;
Yama is pleased—he has reserved
A place for you in his mansion.
    My path is unique,
    It is beyond description.
Doubt, the ruthless hunter,
Lurks within your body;
His arrow has pierced
The flawless diamond of your soul.
    Ineffable, unique is my path.
Doubt resides within you,
It makes you throw the dice
Till you lose all your wealth;

It blindly attacks
Like a wounded beast,
Destroying one and all.
   My path is unique,
   It is beyond description.

Bijak, Ramaini 18
Adbhut panth barani nahi jāi

PURE AS GOLD

Kabir describes the devotee's bliss on realizing the Lord. He has found God within his own body. As a goldsmith tests the purity of gold on the touchstone, the devotee, who has purified his entire being through meditation, is tested by the Lord and made whole. The devotee now realizes that all the time he spent searching for God through external observances, rites and rituals was a waste of his precious human birth. When he conquers his mind and, through meditation and concentration, crosses the regions of mind and maya—the third stage in his spiritual journey—only then does he realize the Lord within his own body.

The Lord has revealed himself
To me within my body;
My entire being, cleansed,
Now shines like pure gold.
Just as the goldsmith essays
Gold on the touchstone,
I have been put to the test
And made whole.

One after another,
Many births I took;
Many paths I followed
To escape this relentless cycle.
Only when I made my mind still
Did I attain the state
Of lasting repose.

I searched and searched for Him
In external pursuits,
But wasted the precious days
Of my human life.
When I became absorbed
In the realm beyond mind and maya,
Within my own body
I found the Lord.

Without knowing Him
I was base metal;
On realizing Him
Kabir became gold,
Precious and pure.

K.G., p.73:17
Ab ghati pragat bhaye rāmrāi

THE LIMITS OF INTELLECT

The object of devotion and love is to become one with the Lord. The main obstacles in attaining this union are intellect, ego and the mind. Kabir says that if I-ness is eliminated, only the Lord will remain. As long as the devotee depends on the strength of his analytical faculties and approaches the path of devotion with intellect as his guide, he cannot obtain the spiritual strength of realization. The mind, asserting its individuality, cannot comprehend what the lover's ideal of becoming one with the Lord is. But once the devotee eradicates his ego and attains inner rapport with the object of his love, the mind accepts the idea of the individual merging in the Lord—the drop merging in the Ocean.

> Lord, you are my Emperor,
> Free from all fear;
> O mighty King, you are
> The boat to ferry me across.
>
> When I existed, you did not;
> Now I am not, you alone are.
> You and I have become one,
> And seeing this oneness
> My mind accepts our unity.
>
> As long as I had intellect
> How could I gain strength?
> Now the power of intellect
> Cannot prevail over me.
> Says Kabir: The Lord
> Has deprived me of my intellect,
> He has transformed it
> Into realization.

A.G., Gauri, p.339
Rājā rām tu aisā

288

THE ONE IN THE MANY

The Lord, described by scriptures and holy books as invisible and inaccessible, becomes manifest to the disciple through his meditation, when done according to the instructions of a perfect Master. The gateway to the Lord's mansion is the eye center, for at this point the disciple's soul enters the inner spiritual regions and, after crossing the different stages, arrives at the Lord's abode.

It is commonly said that the Lord exists in each and every particle of his creation. But Kabir says that when a disciple attains access to the highest spiritual realm and sees the Lord within, only then does he perceive Him everywhere in the outer world as well. Such a disciple can vouch from his own experience that the Formless One is present within every form; others only repeat it on the basis of the hearsay evidence of books and scriptures.

The second of these two poems illustrates that once the Lord is realized, the mind, which is an obstacle on the path because of its cravings and outward tendencies, becomes a friend. The realized devotee does not feel the necessity of curbing his mind, for wherever it goes, it sees only God. When duality is destroyed, none else exists except the Lord.

> Almighty Lord!
> Thou art eternal and peerless;
> Who realizes Thee is liberated.
> O Thou life and essence of all,
> If Thou be merciful to me,
> No more will I dwell in delusion.
>
> The Lord was unattainable,
> Impervious and imperceptible;
> Through his own knowledge
> My Master revealed Him to me.
> The One in whose quest
> I kept wandering in all directions,
> Him I see, through my Master's grace,
> Present all over the world.
>
> My Master opened the stubborn door within;
> The eternal flame became visible
> And the yawning gates
> Of misery and death were sealed.

The Supreme One revealed himself;
I found Him through my meditation—
The same Lord I once looked for
In temples, trees and worship.
Now the One assumes manifold shapes,
I see the Formless in many a form.

Says Kabir: O merciful Lord,
Varied paths I followed in quest of Thee;
Now through Thy Name all my obstacles,
All my blemishes have dissolved,
And I've attained the state of supreme bliss.

K G., p.133:267
Rāmrāi tu aisā anbhoot anupam

O mind, I give you freedom to roam
Wherever you feel inclined to go.
To curb your movements now
I'll not put a goad on your head,
For wheresoever I cast my eyes
There I see none else but the Lord.
Having recognized the Lord within,
My thoughts rest only in Him.

As long as I was tied to the body,
Duality existed for me;
Since Realization came,
Here, there, everywhere,
The One alone do I see.
I am merged in Him,
My 'I' exists no more.
Says Kabir: I am completely absorbed
In the Ocean of bliss.

K.G., p.102:149
Re man jāhu jahān tohi bhāvai

EMPTY WITHIN

Kabir rejects external forms of worship, sacred baths and holy dress, saying that an untamed, restive animal will not give up its habit of waywardness even if the owner ties a wooden clog around its neck to restrain it. Similarly, the mind cannot be made to give up its devious ways by the various external means people adopt to control it. Holy baths can cleanse the body, not the mind; and white and glittering attire may attract attention, but is not a sign of inner attainment.

> What use the tilak on your forehead,
> What use the rosary around your neck
> When you know not the way to meet the Lord?
> A restive beast, though bound with a clog,
> Will not give up its truculent ways.
>
> Your attire is shining white,
> Your mind within is dark as night;
> What worth your holy garb,
> What use your rosary and beads
> When you know not the way to meet the Lord?
>
> Without true love and longing
> What worth are your tears for Him?
> Your mind within is covered
> With layer upon layer of dirt;
> How can you become clean and pure
> By washing and rinsing the body?
> What use your tilak, what use your rosary
> When you know not the way to meet the Lord?
>
> You are only after worldly tastes,
> You know not the flavor of true devotion.
> Says Kabir: You glitter like tinsel
> And are empty within;
> You know not the way to meet the Lord.

K.G., p.100:136
Kahā bhayao tilak garai japmālā

291

WHO DIES WHILE LIVING

During the process of death the soul withdraws from the nine portals of the body and comes to the eye center, from where it proceeds further, leaving the body dead. Those initiated by a Saint into the mysteries of Shabd go through the same process of death during their spiritual practice. Consciously withdrawing their soul to the eye center, they leave the body and enter the inner spiritual regions; but they return to the body after the period of meditation is over. Saints have called this practice 'dying while living'. The devotee who thus dies while living conquers the fear of death, subdues his ego and becomes impervious to the lures of the world. He is freed from the chains of cause and effect; he rises above the law of karma. Kabir says that one who has died while living finds death sweet, but one can only experience such a death through the guidance and grace of a Master.

If one dies while living,
For him death is sweet;
Death is sweet for him
Who has experienced it
Through the Master's grace.

Cause has died for him,
So too has died effect;
The coquette has also died
With all her alluring ways.[1]
    If one dies while living,
    For him death is sweet.
His rank and honor are dead,
So too is dead his I-ness;
His pride is dead, with it
All his deceptive desires.
    If one dies while living,
    For him death is sweet.
Those who while living die
By merging into the Lord

---

1. Maya or the lures of the world is represented as an attractive woman who trifles with man's affections.

Become immortal, O Kabir.
  If one dies while living,
  For him death is sweet;
  Death is sweet for him
  Who has experienced it
  Through the Master's grace.

K.G., p.80:46
Je ko marai maran hai meethā

DELUDED PUNDITS

The pundits, despite their study of scriptures, Vedas and Puranas, know nothing of their true self. Without spiritual practice and realization, all their acts of piety and worship, all their orthodox rituals and ceremonies are futile. Kabir maintains that by merely reading scriptures, chanting mantras and undertaking formal practices, no one has ever attained God-realization and no one ever will. The path to realization lies in searching for the Lord in the place where He resides, and that place is the human body. Referring to the pundits' haughty attitude of regarding themselves as so holy that if others touch them they feel they have been made unclean, Kabir says such pride will never lead them to the Lord, for He loves humility and showers his grace on the humble.

> The pundits are deluded
> Through reading and studying the Vedas;
> They know not the secret
> Of their own self.
>
> Evening prayers, chanting
> And the six deeds of piety[1]
> They perform and preach,
> And consider them the essence
> Of true religion.
>
> During each of the four ages,[2]
> O Pundit, men kept chanting
> The prescribed holy mantras;
> Go and ask them, who
> Has earned liberation this way?
>
> If touched by others
> You rush to wash your body,
> But tell me, pray,
> Who is lower than you?

---

1. Giving and receiving alms; learning and teaching scriptures; performing and having the *yagya* sacrifice performed.
2. Golden, Silver, Copper and Iron Ages.

Of your holy and pious acts
You are vain and boastful;
But pride opens the doors to doom.
The One who loves the humble,
How will He tolerate your pride, O Pundit?

Those who give up pride of status and lineage
    And search for the abode of the Pure One,
They destroy the shoot, even the seed,[1]
    And while yet in the body, transcend its bounds.

Bijak, Ramaini 35
Pandit bhoole padhi guni beda

---

1. The seeds of *sanchit* karmas and the shoots of karmas sown in the present life (*kriyaman*).

THE SWAN

In Indian folklore the swan is a symbol of purity, with sublime traits and a unique quality of discernment. It lives on the shores of Mansarovar, a lake with crystal clear water situated at a high altitude in the Himalayas. The swan is spotlessly clean, it only associates with birds of its own kind, it eats pearls and has the power of separating milk from water.

The Saints have called the realized soul a swan. In this hymn Kabir describes the qualities of the Saints by calling them swans who, though moving about and acting in the world, always remain in their spiritual state of unalloyed purity. Mansarovar, according to the Saints, is the lake of bliss situated in the inner realms of pure spirit, beyond the bounds of matter, mind and maya. The Saints, though present in the world, are spiritually always beyond these regions and thrive on the pearls of divine love. Like swans separating milk from water, they separate their soul from matter and mind—with which it is blended in this world—and they merge in the Lord.

> The man of God moves about in the world,
> Yet stays pure like the swan.
> From him flows the nectar
> Of the immaculate Name,
> And he always sings
> The praises of the Lord.
> Within he dwells
> On the celestial shores
> Of the lake, Mansarovar;
> His heart, detached from all else,
> Remains absorbed
> In the Lord's lotus feet.
> He never opens his beak
> For anything but the pearls
> Of divine love and grace;
> He stays silent, or he speaks
> In praise of the Lord.
> The crows of depravity
> Cannot come near him;
> Such a swan, O friend,
> Has realized his true self.

He alone, O Kabir,
Is the man of God;
He alone is dear to Him,
Who separates milk from water.

K.G., p.153:344
Harijan hans dasā liye dolai

HOUSE OF CLAY

The human body, being subject to disease, decay and death, is described by Kabir as a house of clay. Although this hut is tottering, although its walls are full of holes and it shakes during the storms of passions and cravings, there is no way for the soul to obtain release because the tenth door or eye center, which is the gate to the inner spiritual regions, is firmly locked. Intellect, reasoning, discernment and intuition, each stands as a sentinel on the four sides of the house. With the aid of these sentinels—the qualities of the mind— man should protect himself from the 'thieves'—the passions and cravings.

But even when the sentinels are awake, the thieves easily rob the house; in other words, the mind, in spite of all its higher qualities, is unable to resist the onslaught of passions and desires. Kabir says that only through devotion can one overcome these thieves, reach the eye center and leave the miserable mud hut of the physical body to attain a permanent dwelling in the Lord's mansion.

I will no longer live
In this thatched house of clay;
I'll go and dwell with the Lord,
I will become one with Him.
  I'll not stay in this house of clay.
Its thatch is tattered,
Its walls are full of holes;
At each roar of thunder
It shakes ominously
And my heart shudders with fear.
  No more will I stay in this mud house,
  I'll dwell with the Lord and be one with Him.
My destination is far
And it is hard to proceed,
For the tenth door is firmly locked.
On the four sides of my hut
A sentinel stands on guard;
Even when the sentinels are awake
Thieves enter and steal my wealth.
  I will not stay any more
  In this house of clay.

Says Kabir: Listen, my friends,
He gave me my life;
He alone can deprive me of it,
He alone is my protector.
I'll dwell with that Lord and be one with Him,
No more will I stay in this house of clay.

K.G., p.135:273
Ib na rahoan māti ke ghar men

HOUSE AT WAR

Kabir describes the human body as a house in which the owner finds no peace because the inmates are always at daggers drawn with each other. The inmates are his five sons (the five senses), and his wife (the evil tendencies and cravings of the mind). Each sense pulls the soul in a different direction, seeking different forms of gratification; and the wife, the wild desires of the mind, pulls the soul towards various objects in the world. Kabir says that the person who controls the five senses and overcomes his mind brings peace in the home of the body and attains true realization—the object of human birth.

Within the house, O friend,
There is a great conflict.
Five sons and one woman,
Ever at variance with each other,
Quarrel night and day.
Each demands food of a different kind;
Each one, more than the other,
Craves savory dishes.
Not one listens to the others,
Each is intent on gratifying
His own vile desires.
One who bridles the willful lady
Of evil inclinations,
Who disciplines the five wayward sons,
Who settles the dispute
And brings peace in his home,
Such a one, O Kabir,
Is dear to my heart.

Bijak, Shabd 3
Santo ghar men jhagrā bhāri

ALL LIFE INVIOLABLE

Kabir strongly denounces non-vegetarian food. He is against killing any living being, whether for sacrifice or for food. In his time, people believed that eating the meat of one kind of animal was sinful, but eating that of others was acceptable because it was sanctioned by religion. Kabir rejects this belief and says all life is inviolable; there is no difference between the flesh of one being and that of another. In those days it was also believed that most animals do not eat human flesh. Kabir says that though the flesh and blood of all living beings is the same, man has so much degraded himself eating the meat of all types of animals that even jackals will not touch his polluted flesh.

All flesh is the same,
Be it a man's
Or that of a beast;
All blood is the same color too.
Man eats the flesh of beasts;
Man's flesh not even jackals like to eat.

Brahma the potter molded the earth
Into the varied pots
In which many dwell,
Soon to depart.
Do you know where they come from
And where they go?
Yet you devour them
As if they were sown
In your own fields.

You fashion gods and goddesses
Out of earth and stone;
Mercilessly you cut
The throats of living beings
To appease them.
If your deity indeed craves flesh,
Why does she not eat it
While it is grazing in the pastures?

Says Kabir: Listen, my friends,
Keep yourself always engaged
In repetition of the Name.
Whatever deeds you do
To gratify your palate,
In return you'll have to pay
A heavy penalty.

Bijak, Shabd 70
Jas māsu pasu kee tas māsu nar kee

Enumerating some of the different ways people adopt to gain salvation, Kabir points out that these practices do not lead to contact with Nam, essential for attaining freedom from the cycle of birth and death. Rejecting all external observances and ritualistic practices, Kabir stresses the importance of the Master, through whose grace the seeker can acquire Nam—the essence of all knowledge—and merge in the Lord.

Seeing the ways of the world,
O Lord, my mind is puzzled.
Hence I keep myself absorbed
Day and night in thought of Thee.

Some read and ponder holy books,
Some wander about indifferent to everything;
Some stay naked even in rain and storm,
Some make themselves feeble and thin
Through intricate yogic practices;
Such people will never merge
Into the Lord's Name.
　Seeing their ways, O Lord,
　My mind is puzzled.
Some give up all and become mendicants,
Some dole out alms to earn merit;
Some become kalapis[1] and take drugs,
Some take to mantras, some to medicines;
Some control the breath and gain miraculous powers,
Some visit all the pilgrimage places;
Some undertake fasts and austerities
And gain control over their body;
Such people will never develop
True love for the Lord's Name.
　Seeing their ways, O Lord,
　My mind is puzzled.

---

1. A type of ascetic who moves in a group and takes intoxicants.

Some sit with fires around them
And become dark in the smoke;
None, oh none of them will gain salvation,
Unless they take to the practice of Nam.

My Master gave me true knowledge;
Through his grace I seized the essence
And within myself experienced the truth;
The cycle of old age and death has ended,
And the Lord is pleased with Kabir.

K.G.,p.163:386
Aisau dekhi charit man mohiyo mor

Averse to the Lord,
They are forlorn
Like orphans;
They stray into forests
Dense and dark
And find no way out.

They set their faith
On Vedas and scriptures
Which do not contain
The Truth itself
But dissertate
Upon Reality;
Those who know Truth
Do not bother
With holy books.

They look upon him as God
Who is performing feats
Like an adroit rope-dancer;[1]
But He who plays
Within each body,
Alone is the Lord:
None other counts.

---

1. Kal or the negative power.

Good or bad, whatever
Be your fate in life,
Try your best, O man,
To attain the Perfect One.

Whose heart is pierced
　　By the shaft
Of the Master's Word
　　Knows its pain;
If he not flinch when struck,
　　The ocean of bliss,
O Kabir, he will attain.

Bijak, Ramaini 68
Tehi viyog te bhae

LOADED WITH STONES

Powerful kings, incarnations, gods, men and hermits have all been ruined by the malady of ego. When death comes, they all go empty-handed. They do not realize God nor do they separate their soul from mind—milk mixed with unclean water. The intricate paths of breath control, intellectual analysis, asceticism and penances that they follow cannot take them to their destination. Kabir says such paths are long and arduous and only inflate the ego. Man's allotted life span ends before he can gain any success through these practices. The village of the body is ruined in all ten directions, that is, the ten senses become enfeebled through these rigorous practices and perish along with the body.

Men, deluded by ego, believe they have come to the threshold of emancipation, but fail to see that they have fallen for the bait of worldliness and that the paths they took to gain liberation were like boats made of iron, loaded with stones. When death comes and destroys their physical bodies, their soul sinks into the sea of birth and rebirth.

> Harnakus, Ravan and Kans are gone,[1]
> Krishna has gone, and so have
> All gods, men and hermits gone,
> Along with their kin,
> Along with their progeny;
> Even Brahma has gone
> Without realizing
> The secret of God.
> All those great ones are gone
> Who claimed to be wise;
> Not one understood
> The mystery that the Lord is—
> Not one could separate pure milk
> From unclean water.
> While the path still remained untrod,
> Their breaths abandoned them, fatigued,
> And their hamlet was ruined
> In all ten directions.

---

1. Three tyrannical kings of Hindu mythology who enjoyed great power and prosperity.

The world became for them
Like a net to the fish,
Like a rowboat made of iron
Loaded with stones.
All try to row, and all claim
To know the way to row;
They have sunk midstream
But insist they've reached
The shore of safety.

As an earthworm in the mouth of a fish,
 As a lizard between the teeth of a mouse,
As a shrew in the fangs of a snake,
 So are all between the jaws of Kal.[1]

Bijak, Ramaini 45
Harnākus rāvan gau kansā

---

1. Another translation of the last line would be, 'Thus ends everybody's life'. The images used in the first three lines of this stanza are all open to an alternative interpretation also, since the fish, mouse and snake may well be the victims of their apparently harmless prey. The fish, for instance, is the victim of the earthworm because it is caught and killed by the hook hidden inside it. Similarly, the mouse is killed if it eats the poisonous chameleon; if it lets it go, it is attacked and killed by this fierce lizard. According to folklore, if a snake eats a shrew, the snake goes blind; if it lets it go, it becomes leprous from contact with the shrew. Kabir suggests that this is man's dilemma—if he swallows or suppresses the mind through a variety of rigorous disciplines, he will die to be born again into this world of pain and sorrow, since he has failed to free himself of ego; on the other hand, if he lets the mind go and indulges his desires and cravings, the mind will lead him to actions that bring about lifetimes of suffering and agony. The only solution is to separate soul from mind so that soul dominates and directs mind rather than being its victim. By following Kabir's path of separating milk from water, the ego is conquered, the mind is purified and tamed, and the soul is finally freed to return to its original state of purity and bliss.

307

THE SECRET OF NAM

People talk endlessly about the Lord's Name without really knowing what the Lord's Name is. Kabir says that outward talk about the Name is of no value. Name can neither be conveyed through spoken words, nor can it be seen with the physical eyes; it has to be experienced within. Only he who has experienced the Name within himself can reveal its secret to others.

Is there anyone
Who can tell me of the Lord's Name?
Anyone who can bring to my view
That[1] which is invisible?
All talk endlessly about His Name;
No one knows its profound secret.
Outward talk and show
Are meaningless;
He alone can give me joy and peace
Who himself sees, experiences,
And then reveals the Name.
The true Name, O Kabir,
Cannot be conveyed
Through spoken words.
Without himself realizing the Name,
Who can ever know its secret?

K.G., p.120:218
Hai koi rām nām batāvai

---

1. Saints in India have called the Lord's Name *vastu*, which means 'thing' or 'article'.

BLIND MAN'S MIRROR

Without putting the teachings of holy books into practice and experiencing the spiritual truths they mention, merely reading and reciting them is of no use. A learned man, with book knowledge but no practice or personal experience, is like a blind man with a mirror, for he cannot see what the mirror reflects. Without experience the scholar is like the spoon that stirs delicious food but is ignorant of its taste. Kabir points out that a man may read all the scriptures and explore even the skies in his quest for the ultimate truth, but he will not be able to obtain it. It is through spiritual practice that he can acquire Shabd, which alone will give him spiritual experience and true knowledge and rid him of ego, the barrier between himself and the Lord.

> Without true knowledge
> What worth are holy books?
> They are the mirror of the blind.
> Howsoever delicious the food,
> What does the spoon know of its taste?
> The donkey may be laden
> With the finest sandalwood,
> But the ignorant beast knows nothing
> Of the sweet fragrance of its load.
> Says Kabir: O man,
> You have explored even the skies,
> But you could not obtain That
> Which alone can rid you
> Of the affliction of your ego.

Bijak, Ramaini 32
Andh so darpan bed purānā

THE ENLIGHTENED

In this poem Kabir denounces all external forms of worship, rites and rituals. He disapproves of metaphysical dialectics and is critical of those who say "I am He" without true realization. These 'holy' or 'enlightened' ones are bound by ego; they crave reverence and deceive themselves as well as others. Kabir, in his outspoken manner, declares that the worldly are much better than these so-called enlightened ones.

O Lord, it is a great irony—
The worldly are much better
Than the 'enlightened'.
Some take to austerities,
Some rush to holy sites to bathe,
Some crave honor and reverence,
Some remain bound by 'me' and 'mine,'
Some claim 'I am He' and rejoice,
Some indulge in theoretical talk
And further spread delusion.
None is able to obtain
The rare boon of realization.
O Lord, what an irony:
The worldly are much better
Than these enlightened ones.
Alas, O Kabir, they know not the way.
Apply to your eyes, O man,
That collyrium[1] which reveals the Lord.

K.G., p.136:276
Rāmrāi bhai biguchani bhāri

---

1. There was a belief that certain collyriums gave one the sight to find hidden treasure; here refers to adopting the practice that leads to God-realization.

THE AVID CAT

In medieval India people used to keep parrots as pets and teach them to repeat one of the many names of God. This was looked upon as a pious act. Kabir, using the parrot as an analogy, tells man to repeat ceaselessly the Lord's name because no one knows when and where death will strike, putting an end to the rare opportunity of human birth. Along with the technique of simran or repetition, the Master also gives the 'essence of truth', the divine sound, to the disciple. He urges the disciple to give up his pride, ego and base inclinations, and devote himself to the practice of Shabd, the sound current. Only Shabd will break the bonds of transmigration and make liberation of the soul possible. But man cannot achieve this through his own efforts; the grace, guidance and company of a perfect Master are essential.

> Repeat, O parrot,
> Constantly repeat the Lord's name,
> For the cat, with gaze fixed on you,
> Is purring avidly.
>
> Don't garnish your body
> And go flaunting about;
> Give up your ego and base tendencies,
> For your Master has given you
> The Essence of Truth.
>   Constantly repeat the Lord's name;
>   The cat of death has its eyes on you.
> Always be in the company of Saints
> And enjoy with them the bliss
> Of everlasting springtime.
> Without their grace
> You will never be free
> From the unyielding chains
> Of birth and death,
> Even though you may struggle
> Eon after eon.
>   Repeat constantly the Lord's name,
>   For the cat has its gaze fixed on you.

Says Kabir: My mind overflows with bliss,
For I have met the Master
Of boundless glory.
Repeat, O parrot, the Lord's name;
The purring cat has its gaze
Avidly fixed on you.

K.G., p.162:381
Hari boli soovā bār bār

THE BRIDE'S AGONY

All scriptures and sages say that the soul is a particle of God, the bride of the Lord. Kabir, in this poem of longing, identifies himself with the lonely bride and prays to the Lord to come and end the agony of separation. If the soul is truly the Lord's bride, she can only be convinced of this when the Lord, the Bridegroom, grants her the bliss of union. The soul's yearning for the Lord is conveyed by Kabir in a simple but impassioned manner.

Beloved Lord, pray come to my home;
Without Thee my entire being
Aches in the agony of separation.
All say that I am Thy bride
But I am not convinced,
For until I attain union with Thee
On the couch of divine bliss,
How can I be certain,
O Lord, of Thy love?
  Pray come to my home, dear Lord;
  Without Thee my entire being
  Aches in the agony of separation.
I have become averse to food,
Sleep has deserted my aching eyes;
In company or alone, my restless heart
Finds not a moment of peace.
  Without Thee my entire being
  Aches in the agony of separation.
As the lustful long
For the object of their lust,
As the thirsty crave water,
So do I yearn for Thee, dear Lord.
  Come to my home, O Beloved,
  Without Thee my entire being
  Aches in the agony of separation.
Will no one take pity on me
And narrate the tale
Of my sorrow to the Lord?

Such has become the plight of Kabir
That without seeing Thee, dear Lord,
The lamp of his life is dwindling.
Beloved Lord, pray come to my home,
Without Thee my entire being
Aches in the agony of separation.

K.G., p.144:307
Bālhā āve hamāre greh re

THE RUTHLESS AUTOCRAT

In Indian mythology and literature, Maya is represented as a woman endowed with alluring beauty and lethal guile. On the material plane she represents wealth and possessions, power and prestige, and all the objects of luxury and pleasure that men long for. On the mental level she represents the lures and attractions of the world, the desires and cravings, and all those emotional bonds and attachments that keep men tied to the world. Saints say that she is the design of the negative power—the creator of the physical and astral worlds —and she acts as his accomplice in keeping souls strongly attached to this world of matter and deeply involved in its affairs.

The following poems depict the power that Maya has over all mankind. In the first poem Kabir presents her as a domineering wife, and her biddable husband is man, her abject slave. He toils day and night at various tasks, that is, he engages himself in a variety of rites and rituals in order to gain her favor— wealth and worldly possessions. Early in the morning he sweeps the courtyard —he undertakes ritual baths and ablutions every morning; he gathers cowdung[1] and heaps it on the backyard mound—he gathers the dross of karmas, which are stored and then reaped in a later life; he eats rice left over from the previous day—in the present life he is experiencing happiness and misery according to the results of his actions in previous births. Maya says that she has such a strong hold on her 'husband' that she can take him from market to market—from one birth to another—selling him to the world and worldliness.

Kabir feels sorry for the 'husband' because he neither realizes his own state of slavery nor feels ashamed of wasting his entire life toiling to please Maya, toiling day and night to gain worldly objects, wealth, prestige and power.

> O mother, my husband is compliant:
> He toils at his chores morning till midnight;
> He rises before the break of day
> And sweeps the courtyard spick and span;
> Before the first sun ray touches the ground
> He's gathering cowdung in baskets
> And heaping it on the backyard mound.
> > Mother, my husband is compliant,
> > He toils at his chores day and night.
> With relish he eats stale rice
> Left over from the previous day;

---

1. The scene of the poem is a farmer's house in rural India where milk cattle are kept in the courtyard of the house; the cowdung is used for fuel and manure.

Then he picks up a large pail
And draws water from the well.
 Mother, my husband is compliant,
 He toils at his chores day and night.
I have made my husband my thrall,
I have tied him to my apron strings;
If I wish I can take him
From market to market
And put him on sale.
Says Kabir: This is all
The creator's game
That this woman's spouse
Has become her slave,
And in his slavery
Feels no shame.

Bijak, Basant 6
Māi mor mānusā

The second poem represents Maya as an adroit and ruthless huntress who
has indiscriminately slain men, sages, hermits, anchorites and yogis. She has
not spared the priests, pundits and scholars either. The hidden lure of Maya is
so powerful and subtle that one cannot escape it through learning and ritual
practices, yoga or worship. Men who give up everything, even their own dress,
cannot escape her; nor can those escape who hide themselves in jungles and
monasteries, keep themselves engaged in worship and meditation, study of
Vedas and holy scriptures. They all become a prey to the formidable lure and
captivating guile of Maya.

Kabir says that although Maya rules over the entire world and has en-
slaved everyone, she is ineffective at the door of the true lovers of the Lord—
the Saints.

This crazy Maya,
A friend of the creator,
Has set out on a chase,
Keen on the scent of her prey.
One by one she picks out
The clever and the wise
And the men-about-town;
She slays them all,
She spares not one.

Maya, the huntress, is out on a chase,
Keen on the scent of her prey.
She slays the maunis, she slays the brave;
She even slays those who make
The earth and sky their dress.[1]
She slays the yogis
Even while they're in meditation,
She slays the jungams
Who have made the jungles their home;
No one can subjugate Maya.
Maya, the huntress, is out on a chase,
Keen on the scent of her prey.
She slays the erudite
Who delve into the pages
Of Vedas and holy books;
She slays the priest
While he performs his worship;
She slays the pundit
While he expounds the scriptures.
She has tamed one and all;
She keeps them under bit and reins.
Maya, the huntress, is out on a chase,
Keen on the scent of her prey.
In the home of the sakat
She wields the scepter,
But at the doorstep
Of true devotees
She stands an abject slave.
Says Kabir: Listen, O friends,
The moment she approached me
I drove her away.

Bijak, Kahra 12
Ee māyā raghunāth kee

---

1. The *digambar*, a group of ascetics who do not put on any dress; *mauni:* a type of hermit who takes a vow of silence.

THE BOAT OF NAM

This poem in praise of Nam, the Lord's Name, describes it as a priceless diamond of rare beauty and luster that is the panacea for the sufferings of the world. In the second part of the poem Kabir says that the world is a turbulent ocean that has to be crossed by boarding the boat of Nam, steered by the perfect oarsman—the Master.

Embed the Lord's Name
Deep within your heart.
It's a rare diamond,
Priceless, pure and bright.
Its luster will give you
Glory in the three worlds[1]
And allay the agony
Of the threefold fever.[2]

In the world's deadly ocean
Surge waves of desire and avarice,
The billows of lust and anger
Make the waters turbulent.
The sharks of ego and envy
Lie in wait to prey on you;
Joy and sorrow, pleasure and pain
Are its ever changing shores.
The whirlpools of women and wealth
Have drowned many a valiant one.
Kabir, the Lord's slave, declares:
The Lord's Name is the boat,
The Master its adept oarsman.

K.G., p.147:321
Rām nām hirdai dhari

---

1. Physical, astral and causal.
2. Physical, mental and spiritual suffering.

318

THE MALADY OF EGO

Men undertake various forms of external practice in order to gain self-realization: They read scriptures, suppress their senses and give up all worldly possessions; they perform ritual fasts, acts of penance and all the prescribed deeds of piety. But, says Kabir, ego still remains entrenched in their minds. The bane of ego is not only the cause of all worldly strife and suffering, it is also the greatest obstacle on the path of God-realization. To realize the Truth and reach his original home, a devotee must exterminate ego from his mind and surrender himself completely to the divine power within.

Only he will cross the ocean, O friend,
Who banishes ego from his mind.

Some say they are learned, O brother,
Some say they have renounced everything,
Some say they have subdued their senses;
But the malady of ego afflicts them all.
Only he will cross the ocean, O friend,
Who banishes ego from his mind.
Some say they are jogis, O brother,
Some say they enjoy inner bliss;
But 'me' and 'mine', 'thou' end 'thine'
They have not expelled from their mind.
What chance have they to survive
When afflicted with such a malady?
Only he will cross the ocean, O friend,
Who banishes ego from his mind.
Some say they generously give alms,
Some say they vigorously do penances;
But they do not know the Truth,
They are not aware of Nam—
They will all be consumed by Maya.
Only he will cross the ocean, O friend,
Who banishes ego from his mind.
Some say they are adepts in many methods,
Some say they are living a life of purity.

But they are all ignorant of their soul,
Of their own true self;
All their claims are empty.
  Only he will cross the ocean, O friend,
  Who banishes ego from his mind.
Some say they have practiced all forms of piety,
Some say they have done all the ritual fasts;[1]
But the knot of their ego is not untied,
They have only heaped
More debts on their head.
  Only he will cross the ocean, O friend,
  Who banishes ego from his mind.
Drive out your pride,
Exterminate your ego,
Be not vain about your efforts.
Says Kabir: He who becomes
A slave of the Lord
Reaches his true home.

K.S., I:89
Sādho so jan utare pārā

---

1. The many varieties of ritual fasts, simple and complex, prescribed in the scriptures.

THE FINAL ACCOMPLISHMENT

Kabir says that the practice of Nam is the highest spiritual pursuit. The devotee of Nam need not indulge in rites, rituals, austerities, penances or the practice of breath control, for they are of no value on the path of God-realization. But Nam can only be had from a perfect Master, and only through his grace can one conquer the obstacles of the mind, the senses and the five passions, and attain everlasting union with the Lord.

> O mind, the day you started
> The repetition of the Lord's Name,
> Nothing else remained to be done.
> What worth yoga and oblations,
> What value penance and austerities,
> What use almsgiving
> If one has not realized
> The Lord's Name.
>
> Lust and anger were tenacious foes,
> I destroyed them through my Master's grace.
> Says Kabir: I have annihilated
> All doubts and delusions,
> And attained union
> With my almighty and everlasting Lord.

K.G., p.133:265
Man re jab tain rām kahiyau

321

THE DEBT

Kabir compares man to a trader who has been given a loan to undertake business and make good earnings with which to repay his debt. Man, with the capital of the human body given to him on loan, instead of engaging in the wholesome trade of the Lord's Name, indulges in external forms of worship, austerities, penances, holy baths and reading of scriptures, and tries to find God in temples, mosques, forests, mountains and holy places. Although his coffers are full of what he considers true silver, in the eyes of Dharam Rai[1] they are counterfeit coins and are not accepted as repayment of the debt. Through these practices man further increases his debt or load of karmas, and as a result he loses the rare privilege of human birth and is thrown into the dreadful prisonhouse of the 'eighty-four'. Kabir calls upon man to seize the opportunity of human birth and seek the company of a perfect Master, who will stand as a surety, give him the precious jewel of the Lord's Name and enable him to climb Home on the ladder of the Lord's love and grace.

O mind, redeem your bill of debt.
What value is your thriving trade
That grew through shady deals?
What worth are your coffers
Full of jingling coins of silver
When you have cheated the Great Merchant
Of the precious capital He lent you?
And in requital of your debt
You proffer counterfeit coins!
Your debt now amounts
To eighty-four hundred thousand,
And you will pay the penalty
With forfeiture of human birth.
 O mind, pray redeem,
 Redeem your bill of debt.
If this time you fail to clear it,
You will face the wrath of Dharam Rai:
He will impound all your wealth,
He will hurl you into the dungeon of sorrow

---

1. Kal or the negative power, who sits in judgment on all actions performed in the material world.

322

Where all your pleas for mercy
Will be of no avail.
   O mind, pray redeem,
   Redeem now your debt.
My Master, the true and realized one,
Readily stood as my surety;
He gave me the priceless jewel of simran
With which to discharge my obligations.
He raised for me the mighty ladder of Nam,
And Kabir, though feeble as a worm,
Ascended to his Home with joy and ease.

K.G., p.94:108
Man re kāgad keer parāyā

THE DIAMOND

Shabd or Nam has been described by Saints as a rare jewel, a priceless diamond. It is within every human being, but man, ignorant of the treasure within him, is deeply engrossed in worldly pursuits. He has gathered the tinsel of worldly possessions and accumulated the mud of greed, lust and attachment; as a result the diamond is encrusted with dross, and he can neither see its luster nor know its worth. The jewel of Nam is lost for him. Kabir's poems on the diamond have as their theme the loss of Nam and the way to find it.

> The diamond is lost in the mud.
> Some run to the east to find it,
> Some rush to the west; in search of it
> Some plunge themselves in holy waters,
> Some bow their heads to stone idols.
> Gods, men and ascetics,
> Sages and the learned are deluded,
> And stay deluded in the pride
> Of rituals and ceremonies.
> Kabir, the slave, has appraised
> The value of this rare jewel;
> With tender care he has wrapped it
> Safe in the folds of his heart.
>
> *K.S., II:38*
> *Tor hirā hirāilbā*

> God is the diamond,
> Men of God the jewelers;
> They have put the jewel
> In the market for sale.
> When the one who knows its worth
> Approaches the jeweler's stall,
> Only then will the deal be made.
>
> *K.G., p.62:49:3*

The diamond fell in the street,
There it lay covered with dust.
Many fools went by ignoring it;
When he who knew its worth came,
He picked it up, he placed it
Next to his heart.

Bijak, Sakhi 171

The true diamond is the Lord's Name,
Seek it, find it within your heart;[1]
Outside, it is present everywhere;
Within, it fills every pot—
Yet it has ever been
Unwritten and unseen.

K.S.S., p.83:3

Kabir has acquired the diamond
Through barter, at a very high cost.
Though his body became lean
And his bones began to crumble,
Yet the jewel he could not gain;
But when he offered his head
The deal was made.

K.G., p.55:28

---

1. The eye center is often called 'the heart' by the Saints.

THE TRUE BENEFACTOR

Kabir calls the Master a benefactor because he brings the seeker, deluded by unfruitful outward practices, to the path of inner spiritual practice. Kabir also praises the disciple who, once put on the path, continues his spiritual practice with determination and patience. Calling the Master a son of God, he says that the way to worship the Lord is through the Master, for a perfect Master is the devotee's only savior in this world of misery and pain.

Only that benefactor
Is dear to me, O friend,
Who brings to the right path
Those who have gone astray.

He is the man of wisdom
Who stays firmly on the path,
Who is never weary
In his search for the Lord.

He is false
Who renounces the Son;
He is true
Who worships the Lord
Through the Master's grace.

But men are dazzled
By the world's glitter;
Seeing their riches and sons,
They are puffed with pride.

Who goes within his own body
  And lights the lamp within,
His temple is flooded with light;
  All die and remain dead,
Only they are saved
  Who the savior's shelter take.

Bijak, Ramaini 66
Soi hit bhandhu mohi bhāvai

BETWEEN THE EYES

The spiritual path of the Saints starts from the eye center, a point between and behind the two eyes. Kabir calls it a star, a petal and the door for going within, and says that the Master is also within the disciple's eye center. When the disciple withdraws his consciousness from the body and enters the eye center, he takes the first step in his inner spiritual journey.

On going further, he meets his Master in his radiant or Shabd form. This form is not physical, it is the Master's spiritual form, which he projects from the Shabd. In his Shabd form the Master is always present within the disciple. This is what Kabir means when he says that the Master is "between the eyes." From here onwards the Master accompanies the disciple on his inner journey to the higher spiritual regions. He is the disciple's true friend and well-wisher because he neither leaves the disciple at the time of death nor even afterwards. He is always with him in his Shabd form and leads him to the home of Shabd —the abode of the Lord.

Between the two eyes is the Master,
The messenger of the Lord.
Between the black and the white moles
Is the shining star,
And within the star dwells
That unknown and unseen Lord.
  Between the eyes is the Master,
  The messenger of God.
Between the eyes shines
A tiny petal,[1]
And within the petal
Is the hidden door;
On that door adjust
Your telescope,
Thus with ease go across
The world's deadly sea.
  Between the eyes is the Master,
  The messenger of God.

---

1. Scholars have interpreted the word *pānkhi* as 'bird', but it seems rather to be a poetic form of *pānkhuri*, which means 'flower petal'.

In the city of Sunn
I reside, O friend,
Where resounds the melody
In its all-pervading force.
Now the Master and Kabir
Are eternal companions,
And he leads Kabir within
To the mansion of Shabd.
  Between the eyes is the Master,
  The messenger of God.

K.S.S., I:64
Mursid nainon beech nabi hai

THE HUNT

This verse, in the form of a dialogue between a tribal hunter and his wife, is one of the paradox-poems of Kabir. The hunter, before setting out on his hunting trip, asks his wife what type of meat she wants for their evening meal. The wife, in this poem the realized soul, through an apparently absurd demand indicates that a man's real quarry is his mind, which has no body or shape but still has energy—"flesh and blood"—to run about in the wild forests of the world. Man can only return to his home in the inner spiritual regions if he slays this "animal," which has no beak, hoof or body; only when he stills his mind can he go within.

The hunter's wife induces her husband to hunt this animal by pointing out the achievements of a rival hunter who has shot his quarry with a bow that has no string and has slain a deer yet kept it alive, thus bringing home a quarry which is not alive and at the same time not dead. The devotee has to 'slay' his mind not through any material weapons but by the arrow of simran shot with the stringless bow of meditation. The mind thus slain becomes dead to the external world but alive to the inner realms of spiritual bliss.

Kabir says that it is from the Master that the disciple learns the method of this 'hunting' and the skill to keep his mind alive even in its state of death; it is with his grace that he succeeds in his expedition.

> Kill not the living,
> Bring not the dead;
> But without meat, dear husband,
> Pray do not come home.
> Hunt a creature that is
> Without hoof, without beak,
> Without even a body;
> But kill not that beast, O husband,
> Which has neither flesh nor blood.
>   Kill not the living,
>   Bring not the dead;
>   But, dear husband, I entreat,
>   Come not home without meat.
>
> Look! The hunter across the river
> Wields a bow which has no string.

See! The deer has pounced
Upon the delicate creeper,
A deer without a head.[1]
The hunter has slain the deer
But keeps it alive too—
Such is the skill he has attained
Through the grace of the Master.
    Kill not the living,
    Bring not the dead;
    But, dear husband, I entreat,
    Return not home without meat.

Says Kabir: Beloved Lord,
I am a creeper,
I'll entwine Thee—
Though I am a creeper
Without a tendril,
Without even a leaf.

K.G., p.119:212
Jeewat jini mārai

---

1. The headless deer is the mind, which is trying to devour the creeper of the devotee's love for the Lord and his spiritual efforts to meet Him.

THE LOVELESS WIFE

This poem is a tête-à-tête between two married women, one of whom enjoys the love and favor of her husband, while the other has done nothing to win the love of her spouse. The second woman represents the soul who has not tried to inculcate the Lord's love within her heart and has not attended to the task of dwelling constantly on the love and virtues of her Husband, the Lord. Instead, she has played about with worldly friends and companions, indulged in the pursuit of material pleasures and clung to worldly possessions. Now she finds it hard to ascend to the Beloved's palace and win his love.

Her friend, the realized soul, in response asks her to remove her veil of ego and attachment and, discarding concern for all else, adore the Husband, contemplate on Him, think only of Him and thus win his love. Concluding the poem, Kabir hints that just as an unloved wife's adornments are futile if she has neither love nor longing for her husband, external worship and show of piety are meaningless without tree devotion for the Lord.

> Day and night I kept playing
> With my friends and companions,
> Now I am afraid
> To face my Husband.
> High is the tower of my Lord's palace,
> My heart trembles at every step.
>> Day and night I kept playing with friends,
>> Now I'm afraid to face my Husband.
> If you long for the bliss of his love,
> Then break the fetters of your reserve
> And through intense love become his own.
>> But day and night I played with my friends,
>> Now I'm afraid to face my Husband.
> Remove your veil;
> With vibrant abandon
> Efface your self
> In his loving embrace;
> Adore Him, entice Him
> With your love-hungry eyes.
>> But day and night I played with my friends,
>> Now I'm afraid to face my Husband.

Says Kabir: Listen, my cherished friend,
Only she who has such love
Will enjoy the bliss of union.
But she who is devoid
Of longing for her Beloved,
Vain are her adornments,
Vain the collyrium she applies
To enliven her eyes.

Kabir, p.243:11
Nis din khelat rahi

SHAM DEVOTEES

People put on saffron, yellow, blue or white robes, necklaces of beads, and pose as holy men. With hardly any devotion, they are full of pride about their love for God. Kabir says that in the Lord's court these sham devotees are given no merit and cannot gain admittance. Far from realizing the Lord, they have not even recognized their own true self. Kabir points out that the true devotee vanquishes his ego or I-ness, and through love and devotion loses his identity in that of the Lord, becoming one with Him.

Of what use are they to the Lord,
Who do not try to realize their true self?
With hardly a drop of devotion in them,
They are swollen with self-esteem;
Such devotees are legion,
But of what value are they to the Lord?

Those who have no love for the Lord,
Who do not long to see Him,
Who merely wear a rosary around their neck
Like the necklace of buckets
Round the axle of a persian wheel,
What worth are they to the Lord?

One who annihilates his ego
Is the true and loving devotee;
He, O Kabir, is the same
As the Lord.

K.G., p.100:137
Te hari ke āvahi kihi kāmā

SON BEGETS THE FATHER

When a devotee attains self-realization, all his intellectual pursuits and analytical inquiries come to an end. When he goes to the Master with the humility and earnestness of a beggar, he receives from the compassionate Master the wealth of Nam. He is then rid of his miseries and spiritual poverty and is no more required to go begging from door to door—seeking spiritual knowledge through various external practices. This divine gift becomes his very life; it destroys all his worldly desires and cravings.

Through the practice of Nam he withdraws his consciousness from the body and brings it to the eye center, a process called by the Saints 'dying while living'. The invisible Lord now becomes visible—visible not to the two physical eyes but to the inner eye, which opens when the devotee learns and perfects the art of dying while living. Kabir says that when the devotee realizes God, he attains that state of unity with Him in which all duality ends; the individuality of the devotee is lost in that of the Beloved and the son realizes the Father, merges in Him and becomes Him.

Why need I ponder now?
Why need I analyze?
I have realized my true self
And risen above such formalities.

This beggar has met
The munificent giver,[1]
The wealth he has bestowed
I cannot exhaust through use;
None can rob me even of a grain
Of this bounty.
Now I have ceased to go
Begging from door to door.

If deprived of this gift
I cannot stay alive.
This treasure, once obtained,
Consumes all worldliness;

---

1. The Master.

Only his life is fruitful
Who has earned this boon.
But without dying while living
This life is no life.

When I destroyed the sandalwood grove,
When I ravaged the wilderness,[1]
Without eyes I perceived
My Beloved's beauteous form.
The son begot the Father,[2]
And without foundation, without ground,
He raised a gorgeous town.[3]

One who knows the art
Of dying while living
Ever enjoys the bliss
Of the five peaks within.[4]
Says Kabir: Having obtained the treasure,
I met my beloved Lord;
I met Him
And was rid of my I-ness.

K.G., p.137:282
Ib kyā keejai gyān bichārā

---

1. The five passions; *sandalwood grove*: worldly lures, attractions and desires.
2. The seeker, the 'son', has realized the Father and become the Father.
3. The devotee has reached the inner spiritual regions.
4. The five spiritual regions.

335

EVEN GODS CRAVE

Human birth is a priceless gift from the Lord. After endless lives in the lower species and long sojourns in heavens and hells, one is blessed with this opportunity to go back to the Lord and become one with Him. Kabir says that only the human life of one who goes to a Master and worships the Lord under his guidance is worthwhile. Even gods, goddesses and angels cannot realize God until they come to the world in human form—the gateway to the Lord's mansion. Kabir also says that God is within the human body and the seeker must contemplate and realize Him within his own body. When the seeker meets the Master, his inner eye—the door to the inner spiritual regions—is opened and his rounds of birth and death end.

If you earn devotion
Through service to the Master,
Only then consider yourself
A human being.

Even gods crave a human form;
You've obtained this precious body,
Now keep yourself engaged
In devotion for the Lord.
Worship Him, forget Him not,
For realization of God
Is the profit to be reaped
From this human form.

Before age and disease pounce upon you,
Before death's shadow eclipses your body,
Before senility muffles your speech,
Worship the Lord, O man,
Worship Him.

If you do not adore Him now, brother,
When will you adore Him?
When the end hangs over your head
You'll not be able to worship the Lord.

Whatever you must do,
Do it now; do it now
Or you'll repent
When you're adrift in the ocean.

He is a true devotee
Who is absorbed
In devotion for the Lord;
He alone will obtain
The Immaculate One.
He who meets the Master,
His inner door is flung open;
He will never return
By way of the womb.

This is your opportunity,
This your only chance
To contemplate and realize God
Within your own body.
Kabir proclaims over and again:
It's now up to you,
Win or lose the game.

A.G., Bhairau, p.1159
Gur sewā te bhagati kamāi

You neglect to repeat the Lord's Name;
O man, have you become blind?
Without His Name
Yama will entrap you
In his deadly noose.

Wife and son, upon whom
You were always doting,
For whom you toiled
—And toiled all your life—
At the time of your death,
Like robbers they will deprive you
Of all your wealth, worldly and spiritual.

Avidly you gather
Hoards and hoards of wealth,
But not even a dented pan
Will go with you
When it is time for you
To quit the world.

With arms raised Kabir calls:
Repeat,
Repeat the Lord's Name
Each day, with each breath,
For Nam alone will be your savior
At the perilous hour of death.

K.G., p.98:128
Rām na japahu kahā bhayou andhā

338

THE PALANQUIN

In this poem Kabir takes the imagery of a medieval Indian household where the wife, after a few years' stay with her husband, is sent by him to her parents' house to spend some time with them. The well-to-do man prepares a comfortable palanquin for his wife, carried by four or five bearers and fitted with a canopy for shade against the strong tropical sun.

The soul, longing to meet the Lord, mourns like the wife who has been sent away to her father's house and is not called back by her husband. The palanquin she rides in is the human body, which is made of tattered rags and suspended from its poles by flimsy threads; that is, the body has nine openings, is subject to disease, and life hangs by a thin thread, for death can come at any moment. The five senses are the bearers who pull the soul in different directions in order to fulfill their cravings. There is no protection against the blazing sun of worldly suffering.

Kabir urges the soul to return to the Lord on the path of love and devotion, a path generally described by Saints as a sword's edge. It might appear difficult to follow because it is not easy to withdraw the mind from worldly pleasures and because it requires one-pointed devotion and complete elimination of one's ego; yet this is the only way for the soul to return to the Lord and attain everlasting union.

My Husband prepared a palanquin
And sent me to my father's house.

The palanquin laughs,
And is laughed at;
It speaks the language of 'I',
Of 'me', 'mine' and 'thine'.

The litter is made of tattered rags,
It is slung with flimsy threads,
And in the gale of cravings
It sways wildly to and fro.

The moods of the five bearers
I fail to comprehend;
They do not listen to one another,
They pull the litter different ways.

339

The blazing sun is raining fire,
The palanquin is without a shade;
O Beloved! I have suffered,
Suffered much misery
On the way to my father's house.

Says Kabir: Even greater hardship,
Even greater pain, O bride,
You may have to undergo.
Do not lose heart, adore your Lord;
Love Him, love Him, to go back
And be with Him forever.

K.G., p.90:90
Sāin mere sāj dai ek doli

AN INVERTED WELL

In the process of his spiritual practice the disciple has to withdraw his consciousness from the body and bring it to the eye center in order to taste the divine water of the Lord's grace. Looking at the eye center from below, the Saints have called it an inverted well. The "village girl" is the soul in the physical body; the rope of her attention is going downwards, and instead of drawing the water she is enlisting the help of five bearers to do so. In other words, man's attention is running outwards and he remains under the domination of the five passions, while spiritual bliss lies within his own body at the eye center. Kabir points out that it is only by following the directions of a perfect Master that one can go within, draw the "water" with ease and enjoy true bliss.

Drawing water from the well
Is an arduous task,
Yet your intense thirst will not be quenched
Without the water of the Lord's grace.

The water is above,
Far below lies the rope;
How can the poor village girl
Fill her pitcher?

The well is inverted,
Its edge hard to reach;
The five bearers
Return empty-handed.

Through my Master's directions
And through his grace, says Kabir,
I draw the water with ease
And drink it to my fill
With joy and ecstasy.

K.G., p.101:140
Doobhar paniyā bharyā na jāi

DWELL IN THE LORD

This poem is addressed to those who pretend to be devotees but lack depth and sincerity. Through examples from nature and folklore, Kabir brings out the importance of one-pointed attention, self-effacing endeavor and ardent love on the path of devotion.

To what purpose is your sham devotion?
Immerse your mind in the Lord's love:
The deer, enamored of music,[1]
Is captured and cut to pieces,
Yet his attention
Wavers not from the melody
That is dear to his heart.

    Immerse your mind in the Lord's love.
Love Him as the fish loves water;
Separated, she dies longing,
Longing for what is dear to her heart.

    Let such be your love for the Lord.
The worm keeps its attention
Unwavering on the mason wasp;
It dwells on the object of its love
And through its loving attention
Itself becomes the wasp.[2]

    Let your heart thus dwell on the Lord.
The Lord's Name, the true nectar,
Is the essence of all love;
But you are averse to the elixir,
O witless one! You clamp your mouth
With the muzzle of ignorance
And keep dying again and again.

---

1. In Indian folklore it is said that the deer is enamored of the music of the *mridang*, a kind of drum or tambourine. The hunters play on the mridang in the forests and the deer, drawn by love of its music, comes and places its head on the instrument and is thus captured and killed.
2. It is a belief in Indian folklore that the mason wasp catches a worm and keeps hovering and humming over it. In course of time the worm, in the company of the mason wasp, itself turns into a mason wasp. Indian mystics have adopted this lore to explain the transformation that the satsang or company of a Saint brings about.

To what purpose is your sham devotion?
   Immerse your mind in the Lord's love.
Says Kabir: Beloved Lord,
I am the slave even of Thy slaves—
I'll never forsake
The loving shelter of Thy lotus feet,
And my heart will ever dwell
In Thy love.

K.G., p.165:393
Aisai man lāi lai rām sanā

TALE OF TORMENT

This poem depicts the agony of the devotee separated from the Master or the Lord. He cherishes the heartache of separation and will not disclose it to anyone except the one who is the cause of his suffering. The gift of love and longing, Kabir points out, comes only through contact with Shabd or the divine melody that the Master gives. The devotee who has merged into the Shabd longs only to become one with the source of Shabd—the Lord.

> To whom can I narrate
> The tale of my woe,
> Except to you, beloved Lord?
> My heart is wounded—
> The pain I suffer, O Lord,
> Is beyond measure.
>
> The sharp spear of longing
> Has pierced my very being;
> It smarts constantly,
> Smarts day and night
> Deep within my heart.
>   To whom can I narrate
>   The tale of my woe,
>   Except to you, beloved Lord?
> Who else will understand
> The torment I undergo?
> My Master's Shabd
> Like a pointed arrow
> Has penetrated my heart,
> And the pain has spread
> Throughout my body and soul.
>   To whom can I narrate
>   The tale of my woe,
>   Except to you, beloved Lord?
> There is no patient
> Mortally ill like me,
> And no physician
> With your healing touch.

Are you unaware
That I cannot, for long,
Bear this pain of separation;
That one parted from you
Cannot bear to stay alive?
   To whom can I narrate
   The tale of my woe,
   Except to you, beloved Lord?
My nights and days pass
With thoughts fixed on you,
With my anxious eyes
Craving for your darshan.
Still, dear Lord,
You are not moved
To come and meet the one
Who, pining for you,
Is on the verge of death?

Kabir's agony is beyond measure.
Without seeing you, beloved Lord,
How can life endure within him?
To whom can I narrate
The tale of my woe,
But to you,
Beloved?

K.G., p.138:287
Tumha bin rām kavan saun kahiye

TO MEET THE MOST HIGH

Kabir says that a true devotee does not bother with the distinctions of caste, color and lineage, nor with the canons laid down in scriptures and holy books, nor with the decrees that the priests of different religions pronounce while interpreting their respective religious texts. The devotee turns his attention inwards, withdraws his mind to the eye center and, entering the spiritual regions, weaves the cloth of God-realization with the yarn of his soul. He goes into the region of Sunn and, even beyond that, into Sahaj, the highest region, the soul's original home. The devotee weaves the cloth of realization, of bliss, of divine love in these regions and then himself wears it—that is, he himself enjoys the bliss. Kabir asks the seeker to search for the Lord within his own body, for only through this search will he meet the Lord.

> I have inverted my mind,
> I disregard the distinctions
> Of caste and lineage;
> Now I weave in the regions
> Of Sunn and Sahaj.
>
> I am above doctrinal disputes;
> Pundits and mullahs, both I disregard.
>
> I weave; I myself weave,
> Myself wear what I weave.
> In the region where 'I' am not,
> I sing the praises of my Lord.
>
> What pundits and mullahs decree
> I accept not, I have left it behind.
>
> Through a pure and loving heart
> See the Supreme Lord;
> Search for Him within:
> Only through such a search
> Will you meet Kabir—the Most High.[1]

A.G., Bhairau, p.1158
Ulat jāt kul dou bisāri

---

1. Literally, *kabir* means 'the Great One', 'the Most High'.

BEHIND THE MOLE

Men who are spiritually ignorant, who have no direct knowledge of the spiritual wealth that lies within their own body, usually talk about the inner worlds and try to prove themselves on the scale of others' judgment. But the devotee, who goes within and enjoys spiritual bliss, has little inclination to speak about his experiences. Kabir enjoins upon such a devotee to treasure his wealth of realization, keep it securely deposited in the vaults of his heart and make no attempt to impress others or to gain their esteem.

One who has tasted the ambrosia of inner bliss, who is intoxicated with the wine of divine love, does not go after the insipid taste of worldly pleasures and possessions, any more than a swan, or soul who has reached the divine region of Mansarovar, would be pulled down by worldly attachments. Concluding the poem, Kabir says that the Lord resides within the human body, but one cannot see Him with the physical eyes. He is hidden behind the third eye, called by Saints 'the mole'. The seeker has to withdraw his consciousness to this point and open his inner eye in order to see Him.

> When the mind is filled with ecstasy
> It has no inclination to speak.
>
> When you have obtained
> The rare diamond,
> When you have embedded it
> In your heart,
> Why display it
> Again and again?
> When you were light and empty
> The scale of adulation
> Raised you high;
> Now that you are whole and filled,
> Why mount the balance?
>
> The soul has become intoxicated,
> It has drunk the wine of divine love
> Beyond limit, beyond measure.
> When the swan has regained
> The crystal shores of Mansarovar,
> Why would it go to ponds and pools?

Within your own body
Resides your Lord,
Why open the outer eyes
To look for Him?
Says Kabir: Listen, O friends,
I found the Lord
Behind the mole.

K.S., 1:7
Man mast huā

HE IS NOT FAR

Kabir says that God is one; He is almighty and supreme. But man, craving worldly boons, worships deities, gods and goddesses, and pays homage to stone idols. Failing to realize that God is within everyone, he tries to find Him in mountains and rivers, in temples, mosques and churches. Kabir enjoins upon man to worship only the One Lord, and that too within his own body.

O unabashed fool, are you not ashamed?
Leaving the Lord, you go to others;
Why, to what purpose?
He whose Lord is the Mighty One,
It behooves him not
To run to others' houses.

The Lord pervades all:
He is ever with you,
He is not far.

At whose door
Even the goddess of plenty[1]
Serves as a maid,
Tell me, O friend,
What boon can be scarce
In His court?

Whose glory one and all sing,
That mighty and powerful One
Is my Lord, my Husband—
The giver of all boons.

O Kabir, in this world
He alone is perfect
Who enshrines in his heart
None other than the Lord.

A.G., Gauri, p.330
Re jeea nilaj

---

1. Lakshmi, the consort of Lord Vishnu, is the goddess of wealth in Hindu mythology.

Every action bears fruit and becomes the cause of further action or karmas. The circle of cause and effect, karmas and their result, is endless. Kabir, speaking in paradoxes, says he has seen action destroying cause—meaning that devotion to the Lord destroys the chain of action and reaction. The River Ganges, he says, has reversed its direction and is returning to its source—the current of mind and soul, which flows in a downward and outward direction away from its center, has now reversed its flow and is going back towards its source in the eye center, the point between the two eyes. The earth has become one with the sky—that is, the attention of the mind has withdrawn from the physical body, 'the earth', and turning inwards has reached the spiritual regions within. The demon Rahu who, according to Indian mythology, causes a lunar eclipse by swallowing the moon, has now been swallowed himself—by the moon. Kabir means that mind, the demon which was swallowing the soul or moon, has been vanquished and become subordinate to the soul; it is now the soul that dominates or swallows the mind.

> Wonder of wonders, O Kabir:
> Through action cause came to an end.
> Action has destroyed karmas—the cause;
> In the raging fire of passions
> The flower of devotion blossomed.
> From the flower shot flames of knowledge
> Which consumed the delusion
> Of both sin and virtue.
> The fragrance of devotion
> Filled the air,
> The stink of desire faded away.
> Knowledge of my original descent dawned;
> All thoughts of lineage were lost.[1]
> Concern for the true home developed,
> Concern for all else departed,
> And the illusions of the world vanished.
> Ganga reversed its flow and sped upwards
> To meet its source—the Mount of Meru;[2]

---

1. Pride in ancient lineage and noble descent, which plays an important part in Indian social life.
2. In Hindu mythology the River Ganges originates from the Mount of Meru. According to the Saints, Meru is in the second spiritual region, the source of the 'river' of mind.

Earth turned and became one with the sky.
Kabir, the Lord's humble slave,
Tells the truth: The moon
Turned back and swallowed Rahu.
   A wondrous thing has happened:
   Through action cause came to an end.

K.G., p.150:329
Ek achambhā aisā bhayā

WATER MIXED WITH WATER

The disciple who achieves inner rapport with his Master feels that whatever is happening to him in this world is happening according to the Master's will, and all his actions are dictated and directed by the Master. He develops a spirit of surrender to his spiritual guide. Kabir, expressing the feelings of such a disciple, concludes the poem by saying that the Master is one with the Lord and the disciple has lost his identity by merging in the Master.

You are supreme, my Master;
Please look at my state
And come to my aid.

With gourd, stalk and strings[1]
Has been fashioned the instrument
Of this human body.
Truth or falsehood, good or bad
I know not; I give out tunes
According to how you strum the strings.

The thieves are yours,
It is with your leave that they plunder
This hamlet that belongs to you—
The hamlet of my body.
For their sins, why apprehend me?
Please tell me, how am I at fault?

Master, you are the Lord;
I have become one with you,
I have lost the distinction between
What is yours and what is mine.
Water once immersed in water
Can never be separated again;
So has Kabir merged in you, O Master.

K.G., p.140:292
Param gur dekho ridai bichāree

---

1. The body—skull, bones and sinews—is described as a musical instrument common in Kabir's time, made from a hollow gourd attached to a bamboo stick and strung with wires.

SLANDERER, WELL-WISHER

Devotees and lovers of the Lord are usually criticized and slandered by worldly people. Kabir says that he is not bothered by what people say, for like the devoted wife who decorates herself only to please her husband, he has adorned himself with the way of life that pleases the Lord. The person who slanders others takes on himself the burden of the bad karmas of the slandered one; thus while the slanderer sinks under the load of his karmas, he lightens the burden of the devotee.

> Slander me, slander me, O men,
> Slander me to your heart's content.
> My mind, body and soul are engrossed
> In the love of my beloved Lord.
>
> Yes, I'm mad, but my husband
> Is the Lord; to please Him
> I adorn myself with meticulous care.
> Slander me, O men, to your heart's content.
>
> As the washerman rids cloth
> Of all its dirt and stains,
> The slanderer removes layers of dirt
> Gathered through the ages;
> Like a mother and a father
> The slanderer is my well-wisher:
> He rids me of the sins
> Acquired from birth to birth.
>
> The slanderer is dear to me,
> Dear as my own life;
> Without any wages, he carries my load.
> Says Kabir: All praise
> To the slanderer,
> For he sinks himself
> But helps devotees
> To be ferried across.

K.G., p.153:342
Bhalai nindou bhalai nindou

353

THE TREE OF KARMAS

Pride, ego and a false sense of honor are some of the major obstacles on the spiritual path. Kabir asks the devotee to get rid of them so that the willful mind acquires humility and comes under his control. Kabir also disapproves of begging and living on the charity of others, for whatever man takes or obtains without due payment adds to his already heavy debt of karmas. The devotee must support himself with his own earnings. Men do many dubious deeds to acquire wealth and gain status and fame, but they only increase their load of karmas and have to come back to the world to settle the account. Saints urge seekers to give up all false pursuits, realize that the world is false and try to gain release from it.

Renounce honor,
Renounce false pride,
Then will your haughty mind bend.

Those who steal and eat,
Those who beg
And live on charity
Only help the tree of karmas
To thrive and bear more fruit.

Those who run after wealth,
After status and fame,
Only nurture that tree;
They encourage it
To grow and expand,
Then come back to the world
To eat its fruits.

Give up all vain pursuits,
Know them to be false.
This world is an illusion—
That is why I urge:
Give up all that is false,
Escape from this maze of lies.

Bijak, Ramaini 60
Chhādahu pati chhādahu labrāi

354

THE WANDERING BRIDE

God resides within the human body, but men try to find Him outside in hills and forests, temples and churches. They try to reach Him through pilgrimages, fasting, chanting and austerities; but despite their best efforts He is not to be found. Kabir, describing the soul as the wife and the Lord as her Husband, says that the two are in the same chamber of the human body, but the wife has never met the Husband, for instead of going within the chamber she is roaming around outside in search of Him. How can the soul enjoy the bliss of the Lord's love when her face is turned away from Him?

> None comprehend the lofty state of the Lord.
> Lord, the chintamani,
> The bestower of all boons,
> Is not far—He is close by;
> Yet men overlook this
> And in search of Him
> They wander and wander
> Till they lose their balance
> And their vision.
>
> Through pilgrimage and fasting,
> Through chanting and austerity,
> Through varied practices
> They try to find the Lord;
> But tell me, how can the bride
> Win her Husband's love
> If she keeps running away from Him?
>
> The wife and her Husband live together,
> Yet day after day they pass
> In the gloom of silence.
> She does not forsake her ego
> And makes no effort
> To meet the Beloved within;
> Instead she wanders about
> From forest to forest, vale to vale
> In search of Him.

Says Kabir: Ineffable
Is the tale of my Lord's love;
Only a rare one knows it.
His love has pierced my heart,
It permeates my entire being;
How can I adequately describe
The inner state of my bliss—
And who will believe me
Even if I could?

K.G., p.146:316
Rām gati pār na pāvai koi

THE GARDEN

The devotee who develops true love for the Lord cannot live without Him. Kabir compares such a devotee to an alert gardener who channels the water of attention in the right direction and looks after the flowerbeds day and night. From the divine well of love, the devotee draws cool and pure water; his garden never fades because the Lord himself acts as its protector.

Kabir also compares the devotee's inner being to a field where the Master has planted the seed of love and carefully tends it by removing the weeds, the obstacles of the devotee's wayward mind. Only the true lover brings in the produce and reaches his Home carrying the rich harvest of love; others, posing as devotees but making no effort to obtain spiritual wealth, only pick up a few spilled grains and gain nothing spiritually.

> The lake of love within me,
> O Kabir, overflows its banks
> And I can no longer live
> Without my beloved Lord.
>
> Strengthen the water channel,
> Irrigate the seedbeds
> So the plant of divine love
> Can thrive and grow.
>   The lake of love within overflows;
>   Without the Lord, Kabir can live no more.
> Within the garden of the body
> The alert gardener day and night
> Tends the beds.
> Ever vigilant, he never sleeps.
> He controls the channels[1]
> That lead the water astray.
>   The lake of love within overflows;
>   Without the Lord, Kabir can live no more.
> The well within is brimming
> With water cool and pure;

---

1. The nine portals of the body *or* the five passions, through which the attention spreads outside around the world; the devotee controls these outward tendencies in order to channelize his attention inwards.

There the world's evil winds
Never blow.
   Thus the lake of love overflows;
   Without the Lord, Kabir can live no more.
I am, indeed, fortunate,
For the Lord, in his grace,
Himself looks after my garden;
And the garden does not have to face
The dreary decline of autumn.
   Kabir, the lake of love overflows;
   Without the Lord I can live no more.
My Master planted
The seed of divine love,
He husbanded the farm well,
He helped me remove the weeds
Of my wayward mind.
   Now the lake of love overflows,
   And without the Lord I can live no more.
Only the true devotee
Reaps a perfect harvest;
The rest try to pick up spilled grains
But fail to earn true benefit.
Those who reach Home
Enjoy the harvest of bliss,
Their efforts crowned with glory.
   Their lake of love, O Kabir, overflows,
   And without the Lord they can live no more.
Says Kabir: Listen, friends,
The praise of such divine lovers
I can never adequately sing.

K.G., p.120:216
Kabīrā prem kool dharai

MASTER SHOWS THE WAY

A seeker's delusions only end when he comes in contact with a perfect Master and learns from him the way of spiritual practice. Then he realizes that God cannot be met through fasts, pilgrimages, chanting, asceticism, austerities and other external observances. With the grace of the Master he gives up all the rites, rituals and forms of worship to which he was deeply attached; he inculcates noble qualities, overcomes his pride and receives the blessing of Nam.

When I was deluded, O brother,
My perfect Master showed me the way.

I gave up all acts of piety,
All rituals and ceremonies,
And I gave up baths in holy waters.
The world is indeed wise and sane,
It is only I who am mad.
    When I was going astray, O brother,
    My perfect Master showed me the way.
Now I don't care for the complex ways
Of serving and worshipping gods;
I do not ring the temple bells,
I do not install idols on thrones,
Nor offer flowers in obeisance.
    I was going astray, O brother,
    But my perfect Master showed me the way.
The Lord is not pleased
With chanting and austerities,
Nor with self-mortification.
The Lord is not pleased
With discarding clothes,
Nor with suppressing the senses.
    I was going astray, O brother,
    But my Master showed me the way.
He who is kind and loving,
Truthful and righteous;
Who lives in the world
But lives unconcerned;

Who looks upon all creatures
As he looks on himself;
He meets the Everlasting One, my friend.
  When I was deluded, O brother,
  My perfect Master showed me the way.
He who bears slander and harsh words
With grace and patience;
Who discards disputes and arguments
And gives up ego and pride;
Such a one, O Kabir,
Obtains the blessing
Of the Lord's true Name.

Kabir, p.274:65
Jab main bhoolā re bhāi

THE TRUE DEVOTEE

This poem describes the state of a true devotee. Devotion has purified his entire being, his eyes elicit the Lord's love and radiate it. Through various methods men have tried in vain to meet the Lord, the world being full of such devotees; but Kabir says the true devotee is the one who has attained union with the Lord within. That darshan of a Saint is worthwhile which inspires saintly qualities in the devotee. Such darshan comes out of deep love and devotion. In conclusion, Kabir says that the true lover of the Lord ultimately merges into Him.

> The devotee alone knows the Lord,
> Others know Him not.
>
> Many apply collyrium
> To add charm to their eyes,
> But rare are the eyes that elicit love.
> The eyes that enchant the Beloved's heart
> Are eyes of beauty and worth.
>
> Many a devotee there is in the world,
> With varied methods and varied emotions,
> But rare is the devotee
> Who within his own heart
> Attains union with the Lord;
> And rare are the ones
> Who know the inner state of such a devotee.
>
> Of what worth is that darshan
> Which kindles not the merits
> Of the observed one
> Within the observer's heart?
>
> Kabir has merged in the Beloved
> As salt dissolves in the sea;
> Crystal, though pure and clean,
> Will not lose its identity.

K.G., p.76:28
Dās rāmhi jānihai re

In medieval northern India, the bride would keep her face veiled during the wedding ceremony. After the wedding she would accompany her husband to her in-laws' house where the bride and groom would see each other for the first time. Using this as an analogy, Kabir says that the soul has come to the world with her Husband, the Lord, and resides with Him in the same house of the human body; but she has never met Him, for the dark curtain of mind and maya keeps them apart. The days of youth—that is, the precious opportunity of human life—are fleeting, and the soul, though married, suffers the life of a forlorn single woman.

Elaborating on the analogy, Kabir says that the wedding canopy of the human body was fashioned by five craftsmen, the five elements; the time of the wedding was fixed by three wise men, the three attributes or *gunas;* the friends that sing the wedding songs are the five senses; and karma, the soul's confidante, has decorated her for the wedding ceremony. The age-old traditions or *sanskaras* in which man grows up are represented as the father, who ties the bride's scarf to the groom's robes as a token of giving away the bride; and mind, which Kabir calls the brother because it comes to the world along with the soul, has built the wedding altar.

But the five elements, the three attributes, the *sanskaras* and karmas, and above all the mind, who have been instrumental in bringing about the marriage, are themselves obstacles on the path to Union. They keep the soul imprisoned within the nine gates of the human body and prevent her from going within to the eye center—the wedding chamber—and meeting the Lord. The bride's longing to meet her Husband thus remains unfulfilled.

At the end of the poem Kabir describes the way union with the Lord is attained. Aflame with love and longing, the soul must die while living and through Shabd Yoga, the practice of the sound current, reach the Lord.

> I came to my in-laws' house
> In the company of my Husband,
> But my longing to meet my Spouse
> Remained unfulfilled.
> The vibrant days of my youth
> Faded away like a vain dream.
>
> Five craftsmen built the wedding canopy,
> Three wise men chose the auspicious hour;
> My friends sang the nuptial songs,

My confidante applied on my forehead
The turmeric paste of sorrow and joy;[1]
Yet my longing to meet my Spouse
Remained unfulfilled.

With colorful ceremonies
The wedding was solemnized.
My father tied my scarf
To the Bridegroom's robes
At the altar that my brother built.
The longing to meet my Consort,
Alas, still remained unfulfilled,
And the vibrant days of my youth
Passed away like a vague dream.

From the very hour of my wedding
I remained single and forlorn—
Aloof from my own Husband!
I never met Him;
Even a glimpse of his face
I never had.
I deluded myself; I thought
I was a married woman.
The vibrant days of my youth
Waned like a distant dream,
And the longing to meet Him
Alas, remained unfulfilled.

Says Kabir: I'll raise a pyre of love
And I'll die while living;
To the sound of drum[2]
I'll cross the ocean
To attain everlasting union
With my beloved Husband.

K.G., p.122:226
Main sāsri piya gauhin āiye

---

1. In a Hindu marriage, the bride's forehead is decorated with turmeric paste.
2. The Sound in the second stage within; after the wedding when the bride accompanies the groom, a drummer leads the procession.

HOME WITHIN THE HOME

One of the prerequisites for the soul to go within the eye center is that the mind be stilled. In order to overcome the wayward and wandering tendencies of the mind, people go so far as to renounce their families and retreat to the forests, but fail to make the mind stationary. Kabir says that the mind has ruined many homes; that is, whenever the soul is given a human body, the mind leads it off the true inner path of God-realization and keeps it involved in worldly pleasures and pursuits, thus wasting the rare chance of human birth. Kabir points out that the true home, the Lord's abode, can be found only within the home of the human body. Guru Nanak expresses the same idea when he says that the true Master is the one who shows us that Home within this home.

> My mind does not stay still
> Within my own house.
> This mind has ruined
> Many a home, O Lord.
>
> It renounced the family
> In its search for peace,
> It made forests its abode;
> But whether at the hearth
> Or in the wilderness,
> In its quest it met
> With despair and failure.
>   Yet the mind does not stay still,
>   O Lord, within its own home.
> Wherever I go, I find
> Nothing but grief and woe;
> All are afflicted with the misery
> Of old age and death.
>   Yet the mind does not stay still,
>   O Lord, within its own home.
> Beloved Lord, at Thy lotus feet
> Kabir, Thy slave, bows and prays:
> Within this home of mine
> Show me that Home of bliss.

K.G., p.88:79
Man thir rahai na ghar hwai merā

THE SCREEN

This poem is the prayer of a devotee who longs to see the Lord, but who has not been able to pierce the veil of duality. Weary of repeated failures in his efforts to cross the eye center and go within, the devotee prays helplessly to the Lord either to call him into his presence or to come and meet him.

Between me and Thee, O Lord,
The screen still exists;
How can I get a glimpse of Thee?
And without seeing Thee, dear Lord,
How can my aching heart find solace?

Is it I that am a worthless slave,
Or Thou that art callous to my suffering?
Of the two of us, my Lord,
Pray tell me who is at fault?
  Without seeing Thee, dear Lord,
  How can my aching heart find solace?
Thou art called the Lord of all,
Thou art the bestower of all boons
Thy devotees beg and long for.
  Yet between me and Thee, O Lord,
  The screen still exists.
  How can I get a sight of Thee?
Kabir begs for a glimpse of Thee;
Pray summon him to Thy feet
Or hasten to meet him, dear Lord,
For without seeing Thee, Beloved,
How can my aching heart find solace?

K.G., p.156:358
Ajahun beech kaise darsan torā

PURE AND SUPREME

Kabir refers to the different modes of worship adopted by Hindus and Muslims in India and says that they have both failed to reach anywhere near God because they do not know the true way to worship Him. The Muslims undertake day-long fasts during the month of Ramazan, they worship God through the ritual form of obeisance called *namaz*, and they journey to the holy Ka'aba. The Hindus fast on their pious days of the month, worship idols in temples, and travel to the sixty-eight holy places in India. A true devotee, says Kabir, keeps himself engaged in the repetition of the Name; he knows that God resides in the human body, therefore he goes within and bows at His feet in his own heart—the eye center; and having realized Him within, he has no need to go to the various holy places in the outside world. Men address Him with many names, but the Lord of Kabir is nameless, He is pure and supreme.

Pure and supreme is my Allah;
Hindus and Turks have both failed
Even to reach his vicinity.
Pure and supreme is my Lord.

I undertake no fasts, nor observe
The canons of the Ramazan month;[1]
I only repeat the Name of the One
Who is the Ultimate.
I will not indulge in worship
Nor engage myself in namaz,
For I bow to the Formless One
Within my own heart.
   Pure and supreme is my Lord.
I will not journey to the holy Ka'aba
Nor will I visit pilgrim places;
I have recognized the One
Within my own self—
Why need I run after others?
   Pure and supreme is my Lord.
Says Kabir: All my delusion

---

1. The ninth month of the Muslim calendar; in this month all pious Muslims fast from sunrise to sunset.

366

Has vanished; I am absorbed
In the One, pure and supreme.
   Hindus have failed,
   And so have the Turks,
   Even to reach his vicinity;
   Pure and supreme is my Allah.

K.G., p.152:338
Ek niranjan alah merā

Why don't you stay absorbed
Day and night in Allah's Name?
Why don't you repeat
Without a break the Name of Ram?

With the Master's Word as your kalma,[1]
With the Master's knowledge as your knife,
Within your own body
Engage in the holy slaughter of the five foes.[2]
Day and night, without a break,
Repeat only the Lord's Name.

No one goes to pray in the true mosque
Within his own body.
No one tries to discover the Lord
Through the five enlightened ones.[3]

Says Kabir: I sing the praises
Only of the Supreme Father
And I give the same message
Both to the Hindus and to the Turks.

K.G., p.130:256
Alah lyo lāye kāhe na rahiye

1. Every Muslim must recite the *kalma*, a short eulogy of God, "who is One and whose Prophet is Mohammed." Kabir, like the Persian mystics, calls Shabd or Word the *kalma*, which is obtained only from a perfect Master.
2. It is a practice among orthodox Muslims to recite the *kalma* when sacrificing an animal. Kabir says that the true Muslim, with the 'knife' or technique of meditation given by the Master and with the *kalma* of the Word, should annihilate the five passions instead of killing an innocent animal.
3. The five *pirs* or prophets, also interpreted as the five religious figures of Prophet Mohammed's time. Kabir, according to the context of the poem, seems to refer here to the five sounds of the divine melody. Some scholars have interpreted the line to mean: 'The five holy ones also speak of the same Lord'.

367

THE WEALTH OF NAM

Saints realize Nam or Shabd and become one with the Lord. They earn the wealth of Nam, which they share with true seekers without accepting anything in return. Kabir says that Saints do not acquire worldly assets and amass riches; they do not lean on friends and relatives; they do not involve themselves in the affairs of the world. Nam is their property and possession, Nam is their friend and companion; absorbed in Nam, they live in the world, but live completely detached from it. Kabir, identifying himself with a devotee, says that he will surrender himself to such a Saint and become his slave.

> The Lord's Name is my wealth;
> I neither hoard it for myself
> Nor sell it for a living.
> Nam is my farm, Nam my orchard;
> Thy slave worships Thy Name
> And seeks Thy shelter.
>
> Nam is my asset, Nam my capital.
> Other than Thee, O Lord,
> I know of no riches.
> I neither hoard Thy Name
> Nor sell it for a living.
>
> Nam is my kinsman, nam my brother;
> Nam is my companion
> Who will be my succor
> At the hour of death.
> I neither hoard it
> Nor sell it for a living.
>
> Whom the Lord keeps in the world
> Yet keeps detached from it,
> Of such a one Kabir is a slave.
> My wealth is the Lord's Name;
> I hoard it not for myself,
> I sell it not for a living.

A.G., Bhairau, p.1157
Eh dhan mere hari ko nāu

Saints identify Nam with God, and so does Kabir in this poem. Describing God as the protector and sustainer of all, he says that those who have realized God in their heart do not become a prey to the negative power, and Yama or the messenger of the negative power cannot put his chains around them. In other words, the Name of God—Nam, Shabd or Word—protects the disciple at the time of his death. It is the real wealth of a devotee, his true friend, the only treasure in this world that goes with him at death.

What fire cannot consume,
What air cannot evaporate,
What thieves cannot approach,
Amass that wealth of God's Name,
A wealth that will last forever.

My wealth is the Supreme Lord—
The protector of the forlorn,
The sustainer of the entire world;
He indeed is my real wealth.
The joy of serving my beloved Lord
Cannot be found even on the throne of kings.

Shiva and Brahma's four sons
Labored and searched for this wealth,
But failure dampened their spirits.
He in whose heart is God,
On whose tongue is God,
Will never fall into the noose of Yama.

He who receives from the Master
His wealth of devotion
And divine knowledge,
His mind becomes pure
And turns towards the Lord.
This wealth is water
For those burning with cravings;
This wealth is a pillar
That holds steady the wavering mind;
This wealth unties the knot of delusion
And drives away all fear.

Says Kabir: O man
Intoxicated with wealth,
Reflect within your own heart:
In your mansions are millions
Of horses and elephants,
In mine is only my Lord.

A.G., Gauri, p.336
Agan na dahai

TO LOVE THE MASTER

Love for the Master is of vital importance on the path of the Saints. But it is not easy to love the Master because it requires complete annihilation of ego on the part of the disciple. He has to merge his will in the will of his Master and his identity in the personality of the Master. Kabir gives the examples of the rainbird, the deer, the *sati* and the warrior to illustrate the quality of love that is essential on this path and says that without developing this one-pointed, self-effacing love for his Master, a disciple will not gain his objective of God-realization.

> It is hard to love the Master;
> But without loving him, brother,
> You will not gain your end.
> Without love your soul will suffer
> Misery and pain, over and again.
>
> As the rainbird loves the drop of rain
> —'My love, my love' she fervently calls,
> Day and night parched with thirst,
> Yet craves no water save that of rain—
> So love your Master, O friend,
> Or else your object you will not gain.
>
> As the deer loves music
> —He forgets himself and rushes
> Towards the source of his love;
> Listening enrapt he loses his life,
> Yet never shrinks from the hunter's knife—
> So love your Master, O friend,
> Or else your object you will not gain.
>
> As the sati loves her husband
> —Unruffled by the blazing fire,
> She follows the path of death
> That her husband has trod,
> And without a trace of fear
> She gladly enters the flames—

So love your Master, O friend,
Or else your object you will not gain.

As a warrior treasures valor
—Dauntless, he takes to the field,
Boldly he faces the attack;
He is cut to pieces,
Yet to the enemy
He never shows his back—
So love your Master, O friend,
Or else your object you will not gain.

Give up all concern for safety,
All hope for physical well-being,
And fearlessly sing the glory of his love.
It is hard to love the Master;
But without loving him, brother,
Your object you will not gain.

Listen, says Kabir, listen, my friend,
Without such love for the Master
The gift of human birth
Will be lost,
Lost in vain.

K.S., I:50
Guru se lagan kathin hai bhāi

A LAMP IN EVERY HOME

The lamp of true knowledge, of realization, is within every human being, but men do not turn their attention inwards and therefore remain blind to it. If they learn the way to go within and make proper efforts to do so, they will attain self-realization and become free from the bondage of coming to this world. But, says Kabir, men involve themselves in intellectual analysis, ritual observances, yogic practices, chanting, penances and piety. The Lord is within, but they try to find Him outside through such external pursuits. Men go to ignorant guides, priests and pundits, who initiate them into outward forms of worship. Kabir says that this is not the way to find the Lord, nor to earn his pleasure and grace.

> In every home burns a lamp,
> But you do not see it, you are blind.
> Keep trying to see;
> By and by you will behold it
> And be free of Yama's noose.
>
> In every home burns a lamp.
> It is not a matter of eloquence,
> Nor of listening, nor of ritual acts;
> In order to behold it
> You have to die while living,
> And then you'll never die again.
>
> In every home burns a lamp.
> The yogis suffer separation,
> For they imagine the Lord lives
> Far off, in some remote land;
> The Lord is close by, O yogi,
> Yet you climb a date palm
> In search of Him.[1]
>
> In every home burns a lamp.
> The priests roam from door to door
> Initiating men into their faith;

---

1. Reference to a folk tale where a simpleton loses a piece of jewelry on his travels and climbs a date palm, thinking to spy it from the top. He is wounded by the spikes of the tree but fails to find the jewel, which is in his pocket all the time.

The panacea is within
But they teach men to nurture stones.[1]
   In every home burns a lamp.
Neither yoga, nor chanting,
Neither piety, nor vice
Is the way to win his heart;
Says Kabir the slave, such
Is my winsome Lord.

K.S., II:8
Ghar ghar deepak barai

---

1. Pundits go to their *jajman* (priest's clients), initiate their children by whispering a mantra (holy words) into their ear and teach them the rituals of idol worship. In return they receive money, gifts and food. Kabir uses the idea of nurturing stones because the stone idol is bathed, clothed, offered milk and sweets, put in a swing and rocked, and sometimes even 'put to bed' and 'woken up' in the morning.

THE GREAT WEAVER

This poem is believed to be a reply to the high-caste and orthodox people of Banaras who looked down upon Kabir as a low-caste man and ridiculed him for his 'undignified' profession of weaving. Kabir says that the pundits earn their living by reading and reciting scriptures to others and accepting money and gifts in return. Without themselves understanding the real message of holy books, they 'guide' others and mislead them. The weaver, on the other hand, supports himself by hard and honest labor done with his own hands. The time that the pundits spend reading scriptures, Kabir the weaver utilizes weaving the cloth of divine love.

The Lord himself, like a weaver, has made the world on the warp and weft of duality, the duality of good and bad, pleasure and pain, life and death. Kabir takes the image of the entire universe as a weaving loom made out of the earth and sky, or place and time, with the sun and moon—day and night—as its shuttles. Kabir, through his 'weaving' or meditation has realized the play of the Great Weaver. His mind has now become still and he has recognized that the human body is the true home of the Lord. He has broken the loom of duality, of birth and death, and his soul has merged in the Lord.

No one has understood
The mystery of the Great Weaver,
Who has made the entire world
The frame, and spread his warp.
While you were engaged, O Pundit,
With your Vedas and Puranas,
I spread my warp
And wove some cloth.

The earth and the firmament,
The Weaver has made his loom;
He runs it with the shuttles
Of the sun and the moon.

When I applied starch to the warp
And made it strong and straight,
This poor weaver's mind
Became calm and still.

Kabir, the weaver,
Has recognized his true home;
Within this vessel of his
He has realized the Lord.

Kabir has broken the loom—
This weaver has joined
His piece of thread
With the thread of the Lord.

A.G., Asa, p.484
Kori ko kāhu maram na jānā

THE INDIFFERENT WIFE

Kabir compares the indifferent disciple to a wife who is negligent towards her husband: she sleeps while her husband is awake and does not realize her husband's love for her. God is ever with the disciple, but the disciple does not open his inner vision and see Him; instead he is engrossed in the pleasures of the five senses, keeps the company of the five passions and is awake only to worldliness. He neither has any idea of the depth of divine love, nor does he know the bliss of meeting the Lord.

In order to emphasize another shortcoming of the disciple, Kabir shifts the analogy to a bashful Indian bride of medieval days who has to climb to the upper floor of the house to enter her husband's bedroom. She is shy and wants to go to him unnoticed by the other members of the family. She is unable to do so, for her mother-in-law and sisters-in-law are alert and notice all her movements. Thus hesitation and shyness prevent her from meeting her husband. Likewise, sometimes the disciple is shy of public opinion and feels greatly concerned with what others say. He therefore hesitates to live in the company of Saints, accept a Master who may be socially lower than him or give up orthodox ceremonies and accepted forms of worship. Shy to follow the path of divine love, like the bashful bride he fails to experience the bliss of union with the Husband.

> My Beloved is awake
> But I am lost in sleep.
> I am engrossed in the love
> Of my five confidantes,
> My childhood friends;
> Never have I basked
> In the glow of my Husband's love.
> For He is awake
> And I am lost in sleep.
> My mother-in-law is clever,
> So are my sisters-in-law;
> Afraid of being discovered by them,
> I never steal to my Husband's chamber,
> I never experience the depth,
> The bliss of his love.
> My Beloved is awake,
> But I—I'm lost in sleep.

His couch is laid
Beyond the twelve;[1]
Stricken with bashfulness
I cannot climb up
And reach my Beloved's bed.
    He is awake
    But I am lost in sleep.
Within my heart, day and night
Rings his beckoning call,[2]
But I do not heed it;
I keep flirting with others,
I've never realized the joy
Of my Husband's love.
    He, my Beloved, is awake
    And I, alas, am lost in sleep.
Says Kabir, Listen, dear friend,
Listen to what I say:
No one has gained
And no one ever will gain
Union with the Beloved,
Without a perfect Master.

Kabir, p.337:198
Piyā merā jāge

---

1. The ten senses (five of action and five of perception), the mind and the intellect; Kabir implies that the Lord is beyond the regions of matter and mind. Some scholars have interpreted *twelve* as the six philosophies and the six acts of piety.
2. Shabd or the divine melody, which is always ringing within every human being.

SHAKE OFF YOUR SLUMBER

Kabir calls upon man to wake up from his sleep of eons and obtain the real wish-fulfilling jewel—God-realization. Although physically awake, man has remained spiritually asleep since the day of creation. Kabir says the real indication of a person's spiritual awakening is that the formal practices advocated by the scriptures appear to him as poison.

Wake up, O man,
Shake off your slumber;
Be alert within, obtain chintamani,
The rare wish-fulfilling jewel.
You have slept, slept on and on;
Countless days you have lost in lethargy.
Get up now
So the plundering thieves[1]
Depart empty-handed
From your house.

This is the sign, O friend,
That you are now awake:
The Vedas and Puranas
Appear to you like poison.

Says Kabir: I'll sleep no more,
For God, the precious jewel,
I have found within my own body.

K.G., p.155:352
Jāgiyā re nar neend nasāi

---

1. The five passions, which deprive man of his spiritual wealth.

THE YARN OF LOVE

The soul, separated from the Lord, is represented here as a bride longing to meet her husband. Day and night she is engaged in spinning a fine and delicate yarn to prepare her wedding dress—without which the wedding cannot take place and she cannot meet her groom.

The practice of contemplation on the Lord and the repetition of the Name is the process of spinning; love is the yarn, the outcome of this practice. The wedding will take place in one of the inner spiritual regions within the body, a region described by Kabir as the "palace of light" for its resplendent beauty. The soul will meet the Lord on the throne of realization, which is decorated with the jewels of Knowledge. The wedding dress is woven out of the yarn of longing, for longing leads to the fulfillment of love—union with God. Identifying himself with the yearning bride, Kabir says that the only offering his soul has for the Beloved is tears of love and longing.

The longing soul,
The separated bride,
Sits at the spinning wheel,
Spinning the yarn of love,
Day and night.

In the gorgeous city
Of the human body
Stands a palace of light;
There in the resplendent sky
The yearning soul
Will wed her Beloved
Seated on a throne
Bejeweled with knowledge.
  The longing soul spins
  The yarn of love,
  Day and night.
With longing the bride spins
Yarn subtle and fine
To prepare the wedding dress
Of love and devotion.

The separated bride
Sits at the spinning wheel
Spinning the yarn of love.
Says Kabir: Listen, O friends,
I weave the garland of day and night;[1]
When my Beloved comes,
When He takes his first step
Into my palace within,
To his lotus feet I'll bring
My tears as an offering.

Kabir, p.287:92
Charkhā chalai surat birhin kā

---

1. During the wedding ceremony, when the bride comes before the bridegroom, she places a garland (*varmala*) around his neck as a token of love. Weaving the garland of day and night suggests the same idea as spinning—keeping oneself constantly engaged in simran and contemplation.

TAX-FREE WEALTH

The soul has been suffering births and rebirths in the world since the day of creation. Bound by the law of karma, the soul has to account for its good and bad deeds, and according to them is sent back into the world in lower or higher species. The negative power, called Yama in this poem, demands that all actions be accounted for and dispenses justice accordingly. Kabir uses the analogy of a merchant who goes to a foreign land, earns money, and on his return has to pay duty to the officer at the border. Kabir says that those who meet a Master, learn the technique of spiritual practice from him and realize Nam or the Word within themselves are not required to render account to the negative power; they earn the tax-free wealth of Nam and freely return Home.

O Yama, I am not a merchant
Who is obliged to pay your tariff.
Discarding all worldly pursuits
I undertook my own primal trade
And amassed the wealth of the Lord's Name.
I have filled my panniers with his Name
And I follow the Lord's own caravan.[1]
The wealth before which even you must bow,
On which, O Yama, you can charge no duty,
That tax-free wealth I have earned.
Kabir, the Lord's slave, declares:
Over me, O Yama, you have now
No jurisdiction.

K.G., p.130:254
Re jam nāhin vai byopāri

---

1. In medieval times small merchants returning from their trips abroad used to join the caravan of some powerful merchant or chief in order to gain protection against bands of highwaymen. Kabir, the merchant in the poem, seeking protection against the robbers—the five passions, the desires, cravings and evil tendencies of the mind, and the lures of the world—has come to the company of Saints, the leaders of the Lord's own caravan.

THE THUGS OF BANARAS

This poem from the Adi Granth depicts the condition of the priests and religious leaders who dominated the social and religious life of Banaras during Kabir's time. Kabir exposes their hypocrisy and rejects their claims to holiness, condemning their insistence on the so-called purity of their food which has to be cooked on a fire of washed wood and is not allowed to be touched by others. Their assumed piety and superiority is just a way of beguiling and cheating simple people to earn wealth and respect. Kabir calls them the thugs of Banaras.

Concluding the poem, Kabir hints that such priests and religious leaders will continue to come to this world of pain and suffering again and again. Those who seek the shelter of a Master and follow his directions will never return to the world and will gain release from the cycle of birth and death.

> They put on loincloths
> Of three and a half yards
> And sacred threads of threefold strings,[1]
> They display rosaries around their necks
> And in their hands, glittering brass jugs;
> Call them not the saints of God,
> They are the Banaras thugs.
>
> I like not such 'saints'
> Who devour basketfuls of pedas.[2]
> They scour their pots
> Before they put them on the stove,
> They wash their wood before lighting it.
> They dig up the earth
> And make two fireplaces,[3]
> But hesitate not to swallow a man whole.
> They are sinners, guilty of devious deeds,
> Yet call themselves pious and pure.

---

1. *Janeo,* the sacred thread put around the neck and arm by Brahmins and the high caste, is usually made of three strands of string.
2. A sweet made with milk and sugar, usually offered by devotees to priests and sadhus.
3. Some orthodox Brahmins cook food on two separate fireplaces to avoid cooking bread on the same fire as vegetables.

They go strutting about with a haughty mien;
Their deeds are the ruin of even their kin.
They hasten where their minds direct them,
According to its dictates they act.

Says Kabir: He who meets the Master
Never returns to this world of misery.

A.G., Asa, p.475
Gaj sādhe tai tai dhotiā

THE THIRSTY SWAN

Even after attaining human birth the soul is unable to realize the Lord because she has not learned the method of spiritual practice from an adept. Kabir says the soul is like a swan who has reached the vicinity of a lake, but is unable to fly to the water's edge because its wings have become too heavy. Having obtained the human form, the soul has reached the threshold of liberation, but is weighed down by her load of karmas, worldly longings and cravings, and does not know how to get rid of this burden. She is like the village girl who has gone all the way to the well, but cannot draw water because she has no rope. Kabir says that his Master gave him the method for realizing the Lord, and by following it he has met Him with ease.

> Although close to the lake's shore,
> The sawn is still thirsty.
> The water of divine bliss she cannot drink,
> For she knows not the method.
>
> If she wishes to quench her thirst
> She must reach the water's brink;
> But her two wings[1] have become heavy
> And she is unable to fly.
>   Close to the lake's shore,
>   Yet the swan is thirsty;
>   The water of divine bliss
>   She knows not the way to drink.
> With an empty pitcher in her hand,
> Helplessly stands a village girl
> By the parapet of the well.
> How can she draw water,
> How can the pitcher be filled,
> When she does not have the rope with her?
>   The water of divine bliss she cannot drink,
>   For she knows not the method.
> Kabir's Master showed him the way;
> Effortlessly he attained the Lord.

K.G., p.141:298
Sarvar tati hansini tisāi

---

1. The two wings of good and bad karmas.

385

THE FORTRESS

A devotee has to go within his own body, overcome the forces of the passions, the guiles of Maya and the tricks of his mind, and develop divine love in order to attain God. Kabir explains this through the imagery of a strong fortress that is protected by the double ramparts of duality, the triple moat of the three attributes[1] and by a garrison of the five elements and the twenty-five tendencies,[2] who are inspired by Maya, the lure of the world. Lust, avarice and attachment are the sharpshooters, who aim their arrows from hidden embrasures. Pleasure and pain are the gatemen that keep the soul involved in the world; virtue and sin are the gates that keep the soul confined here. Anger is the commandant and mind is the king of this fort of the human body. The troops, arrayed in the armor of sense pleasures and the helmet of ego, attack the soul with the shafts of low tendencies, desires and cravings.

Nevertheless, for the one who knows the way to storm it, the fortress is not invincible. The passions are to be overcome by the weapons or noble qualities of purity, forgiveness, tolerance, contentment, detachment and humility; the obstacles of the five elements, three attributes and twenty-five tendencies, which keep the soul bound to the world of matter, are to be removed through meditation, inner experience and divine love; the doors of the duality of virtue and sin, of good and bad karmas, are to be shattered through association with Saints; and mind, the formidable foe, is to be vanquished and made captive through the Master's grace. He who enters the fortress of his own body, in the words of Kabir, drives away the enemies that possess it, captures or stills his mind and wins the everlasting empire of God-realization.

> Brother, how am I to seize
> The formidable fortress
> Protected by dual ramparts
> And a triple moat?
> The five and the twenty-five,[2]
> Pride, attachment and envy,
> Inspired by Maya the powerful,
> Are arrayed for battle.
> Thy wretched slave
> Is powerless to seize
> The fortress by storm;
> Lord, what am I to do?

---

1. Three *gunas* or attributes: harmony, action and inertia.
2. Five elements: earth, water, fire, air, ether; the twenty-five *prakritis* or tendencies.

Lust is its embrasure,
Pleasure and pain its sentries,
Virtue and sin its gates;
Anger is the belligerent chieftain,
And the willful mind holds sway as the king.

The troops wear the armor of sense pleasures
And the helmets of I-ness;
They raise the bow of evil tendencies
And aim the arrows of cravings
—Cravings that are stored
In the quiver of the heart.
I am unable, my Lord,
To storm and seize this fortress.

When I made love the fuse,
Meditation the cannon,
Loaded it with the shell of knowledge,
With Sahaj[1] lit the torch of the divine flame,
In one shot, the fortress fell.

With truth and contentment
As my sure weapons, I gave battle
And battered down the two doors.
Through the company of Saints
And through the grace of my Master,
I took captive the king of the fort.

Through fear of God,[2]
Through the power of simran,
I have cut the dreadful noose of Kal;
Kabir, the Lord's slave, mounted
To the top of the fortress
And won an everlasting empire.

A.G., Bhairau, p.1161
Kiu leejai gadh bankā bhāi

---

1. Sahaj is another name for Surat Shabd Yoga, the path of the Saints.
2. 'Fear' in Sant Mat is an essential part of divine love; not fear of punishment but fear of offending the Beloved. This fear strengthens love.

THE UNLOVED ONE

The sun, the moon, men and even gods and angels are within the perimeter of time and space, and therefore subject to change and death. They all revolve in the whirlpool of birth and rebirth and suffer pain. Man does not know the real cause of his suffering, and the attempts he makes to know it only lead him into delusion. The Lord is within the human body but instead of going within, people try to find Him outside through external practices. Kabir says that the true devotees of God, the Saints, alone know Him. Without meeting the Saints man fails to conquer death and to obtain any reprieve from the penalty he has to pay to Yama, the negative power, for his good and bad deeds. Without the Saints he finds no one to stand ransom for his debt of karmas. In the end his soul departs from the world sad and unhappy, like the beautiful woman who stays in the house but remains unnoticed, uncared for and unloved.

> In the vast expanse of water,
>
> In the depth of the sea,
>
> Toss the sun, the moon,
>
> All men and deities;
>
> In its vicious whirlpool
>
> They revolve and revolve.
>
> They crave happiness,
>
> But fail to gain release
>
> From the embrace of pain.
>
> No one discerns
>
> The real cause of sorrow;
>
> Searching for its cause
>
> They become lost
>
> In endless forms of delusion.
>
> In their search for the Lord
>
> Some become frenzied,
>
> In their search for Him
>
> Some become clever and wise;[1]
>
> Yet they fail to know the true Lord
>
> Who dwells within every heart:

---

1. Through study of scriptures and theological treatises, they gain intellectual knowledge but not true realization; *frenzied* because they arrive at certain conclusions and hold onto them with fanatic zeal.

He is the true Lord,
He is the true Deity,
And his devotees are his true slaves.
But deluded man
Neither conquers Yama
Nor finds the one
Who will stand ransom;
His soul, alas, has to depart
Frustrated and downcast,
Like a woman unloved.

Bijak, Ramaini 41
Ambuk rāsi samudra ke khāi

THE DIVINE HUE

The colors of worldly pleasures and possessions, affections and attachments are dull and easily fade; no worldly joy or happiness lasts forever. The devotee who goes within and tastes the bliss of the inner spiritual regions is dyed in the indelible color of love and devotion. Intoxicated with bliss he becomes disinterested in worldly pursuits. Kabir says that worldly people, ignorant of the devotee's inner state, look upon him as an abnormal person; but the devotee, unconcerned with what others think or say, remains deeply absorbed in divine love, in a joy which is everlasting.

> I absorbed my attention within
> And realized my true self;
> The color with which I'm dyed,
> That I know is fast, is true.
> My mind and soul are imbued
> With that brilliant color,
> I am dizzy with joy;
> But people say Kabir has gone mad.
> These fools know not the divine hue
> That pervades all living beings.
>
> In a color that is constant,
> In a hue that will never fade,
> In that glorious flush of divine love
> Kabir stays forever immersed.

K.G., p.75:26
Apnai men rangi apanpo jānu

DISTILLING BLISS

In this poem Kabir employs the imagery of a distillery to illustrate the joy of divine bliss. The human body is the vat in which the distilling has to be done and Shabd is the molasses from which the 'wine' is extracted.[1] In other words, one can only taste the wine of divine bliss within the human body and through the practice of Shabd as given by a true Master. Kabir says that if he comes across a Saint, the vintner of divine bliss, he will give up all external forms of worship, religious routines, pilgrimages and austerities, and surrender himself to the Master in order to obtain a drop of that intoxicating drink. He implies that rejection of all external observances and complete surrender to the Master are essential prerequisites for attaining that inner bliss. The cup of the soul is what holds the wine—that is, the elixir can be enjoyed only by the soul, and once it tastes it, all pleasures of the world become insipid.

In the vat of my body I'll mix the leaven,[2]
And the Master's Shabd will be the molasses.
I'll mince up craving, lust, anger and jealousy
And add them to spice up the brew.

O Lord, tell me, is there a Saint
Absorbed in the bliss of Sahaj,
To whom I can offer all worship and austerities
As brokerage for a sip of this wine?[3]
I'll surrender my body and mind to the vintner
In exchange for the merest drop of this liquor.

I have made the fourteen worlds[4] the furnace,
I have lit it with the flame
Of divine knowledge within.

---

1. Indian way of making alcoholic drink; cp., use of honey in making mead.
2. The practice of Shabd.
3. In medieval India the broker was an important figure, bringing the customer and the merchant in contact with each other and effecting a deal. Brokers would always be there to procure good quality wine for the wealthy customer who could not himself mix with the common drunkards surrounding the wineshop.
4. According to both Hindu and Muslim mythology, the universe is divided into fourteen regions.

With the melody of Sahaj
I have sealed the pot,
And in the Sukhman
I've put the cooling pad.[1]

Pilgrimage, fasting and religious routines,
Ablutions and austerities
And the practice of breath control—
I will pawn them all
For that intoxicating drink!
I will fill the cup of my soul
With the ambrosial wine
And joyfully drink
This juice of eternal bliss.

From the still drips ceaselessly
The immaculate nectar;
Tasting it, my mind is in ecstasy.
Says Kabir: All other wines
Are bitter and false,
This elixir alone
Is sweet and true.

A.G., Ramkali, p.896
Kāyā kalālani lāhani melau

---

1. To distill the alcohol, a cold compress or cooling pad is wrapped round the tube to condense the vapor and turn the steam into liquid. Sukhman is the central path on the spiritual journey, beginning at the eye center, where the soul begins to enjoy the inner spiritual 'intoxication'.

THE HOUR OF TRYST

In Indian literature poets regard nightfall as the meeting time of lovers. For the devotee, too, the quiet period of the evening when he has finished the day's work is the time for meditation, for going within and bathing in the light of divine love. Instead of wine, the devotee drinks the nectar of the divine melody and becomes intoxicated with bliss. Kabir says that the devoted wife, the soul, can attain union with her Beloved only by going within the body and entering the inner spiritual regions resplendent with the light and sound of Shabd.

> The evening shadows are gathering,
> Nestling in from all sides;
> The hour of tryst has come:
> The nimbus of love envelops
> My body, mind and soul.
>
> Open the window to the west,[1]
> Dive into love's firmament within
> And eagerly drink nectar
> From the cup of lotus petals;
> Let love's intoxication
> Surge through your entire being
> In waves of joy.
>
> Conch, gong and trumpet resound
> In the divine palace,
> Which scintillates with bliss.
> Says Kabir: Listen, O friend,
> Meet your everlasting Husband
> In the vessel of your body.

Kabir, p.256:23
Tiwir sānjh kā

---

1. Whatever is in front of the body or outside the body has sometimes been described by Saints as the 'east'; thus 'west' in this context means 'within the body'. The window in the west here implies the eye center, the gateway to the journey through the inner spiritual regions.

THIRST FOR THE LORD

A seeker's hopes of God-realization cannot be fufilled until he comes in contact with a perfect Master. There is no dearth of sages and spiritual leaders in
the world who profess to guide others but have not realized God themselves.
The true seeker, who wants nothing but the Lord, remains thirsty in their
company. The rainbird stays thirsty even on the shores of a lake, since it is not
ordinary water but drops of rain that it yearns for; likewise the true seeker is
not satisfied with empty promises of realization after death, intellectual surmises or practices that merely lead to the lower spiritual regions. Kabir says
that it is only through the Lord's own grace that a man comes across an adept
who has himself realized the Lord.

My hopes of meeting the Lord
Remained unfulfilled;
Other than the Lord, who can sever
The deadly noose of my karmas?

The lake is brimming with water,
Yet the rainbird is sad.
Such is the brunt of my karmas
That I'm parched; I am thirsty
For one glimpse of my Lord.

I came across many a sage,
Yet obtained not an inkling of God;
Only the Lord can lead me
To the one who has met Him.
When you meet the true, the valiant Saint,[1]
All sufferings and miseries end.

A fish in shallow waters
Suffers in anguished thirst;[2]
So Kabir tosses in agony,
Longing for Thee, beloved Lord.

K.G., p.96:119
Ās nahi pooriyā re

1. The Saints are described as intrepid warriors because they have conquered mind and the
forces of the negative power and have won a place in the Lord's region.
2. In shallow water a fish cannot get sufficient oxygen and is restless; the movement of its
gills is commonly interpreted in folklore as the fish drinking water. The analogy is used
here to illustrate the unsatiated state and anguish of the seeker's soul.

THE THIEF

The intricate practices of *pranayam* or breath control do not lead to God-realization. In trying to gain perfect control of the breath, yogis permanently damage their body—the earthen vessel, as Kabir calls it. They believe that they have overcome their passions and desires and subdued their mind; but it is their mind that continues to rob them of their spiritual wealth, and they remain unaware both of the thief and of his tricks. They look at the creation through the lower *chakras*—the centers below the eye center—and fail to realize that the one whom they take to be the Supreme Being is none other than the lord of the three worlds, the universal mind. Kabir says that in the end the practitioners of breath control realize that the mind whom they took to be a friend is indeed an enemy who leads the soul into the circle of birth and death.

By constantly stuffing and emptying,
The yogis have broken
The earthen vessel of their body,
But they know not
Who robs them of their wealth.
One thief robs the entire world,
But few know
Who that thief is.
The deluded yogis take the thief
To be the guardian
Of the earth, the heavens
And the underworlds;
They look upon him as the Lord.
They all become dead
Like stones;
Their efforts go to waste
Like attempts to draw
A picture in the air;
And the one whose friendship
All their life
They tried to win,
Proves in the end
To be their foe.

Bijak, Ramaini 59
Chadhat chadhāvat bhandhar phori

MAD NEIGHBOR

Cravings, expectations and lures of the world are a hindrance in the devotee's progress on the path. Even an advanced devotee has to guard himself against giving in to the lures of the world, because by submitting to them he is likely to lose his spiritual gains. In this unusual poem, Kabir likens Maya or worldly attractions to the proverbial troublesome neighbor who is always asking for things on loan, but never returns them. Here she is asking for the devotee's husband, the Lord himself. The devotee is willing to share the gifts of her husband with her neighbor, provided she agrees to look after the devotee's son, the wayward mind. The devotee knows her neighbor will not agree to this proposal, since it is Maya herself who is responsible for the mind's restive tendencies. Kabir concludes by saying that only a rare devotee develops such one-pointed love for the Lord that he disregards all other attractions.

My neighbor makes a strange demand:
She asks for my Husband on loan!
Neighbor, O neighbor, you must be mad,
How my Husband on loan can you have?

If you beg for an ounce,
I'll not part with a grain;
If I lose his love,
Who in this world
Will make good my loss?
If you agree to look after
My wayward son, O neighbor,
Of my Husband's gifts
I'll give you half as your share.
   But neighbor, neighbor, you must be mad,
   How my Husband on loan can you have?
When He parts from me,
Eyes athirst with longing
I look for Him, I look
From grove to grove,
From vale to vale.
If I find Him not, I sigh and suffer
And my heart cries in agony.

396

Neighbor, O neighbor, are you mad?
How my Husband on loan can you have?
Says Kabir: Through Sahaj[1]
The Beloved has become mine.
A rare wedded one
Alone loves her Husband
With all her heart,
With all her being.
Neighbor, O neighbor, you must be mad,
How my Husband on loan can you have?
You ask for an ounce,
Not a grain will I give;
If I lose my love
It'll break my heart.

K.G., p.159:371
Parosani māngai kant hamārā

---

1. The path of Surat Shabd Yoga or sound current has also been called the path of Sahaj by the Saints.

A DEVOTEE'S YEARNING

This poem conveys the devotee's love and longing for the Lord. He has been blessed with divine love, his desires and passions have been subdued and he wants nothing except union with God; yet there is no response from Him. Kabir takes examples from nature to express the devotee's yearning to meet the Lord. After the summer months of scorching heat the monsoon showers cool the atmosphere and everything becomes green. Even lovers, at the coming of the rains try to be together, and wives are blessed by the return of their husbands from afar. But the pining soul, the devotee, is the only wife who has not met her Husband. Similarly, the approach of spring brings new life to nature, and plants affected by frost recover and bloom; but the heart of the loving devotee remains withered from the severe winter of separation.

After describing the depth of the devotee's agony, Kabir ends the poem on a note of happiness: A devotee's intense love and longing for the Lord can never go unfulfilled; it is always rewarded with the bliss of union. Kabir also points out that this union is only achieved by attaining the state of Sahaj through the divine melody of Shabd.

> The Lord has become merciful to me,
> The deadly viper of the passions has perished,
> My soul has awoken from its long slumber
> And within me love has emerged
> In a surging wave.
> There is joy all around me:
> Joy for them who have met the Lord,
> Whose long-cherished desire is fulfilled.
>
> When the month of Ashad[1]
> Scorches the earth
> With sizzling heat,
> Cool showers come
> To quench the earth's anguish.
> In the refreshing rains
> The earth comes back to life:
> Raindrops fall like nectar from the skies;
> Soft blades of grass sprout,
> Shining with verdant smile.

---

1. A month in the Indian calendar: the hottest month, just before the coming of the rains.

So springs joy once again
In the hearts of separated wives,
For they're all united with their husbands;
All, except me.
My heart, beloved Lord,
Is burning to meet you.

What is it I have done
That you ignore me?
This creation is your play
But what is play to you
Has become for me
An endless agony of death,
For I have had to take
Round after round
In this whirligig of eighty-four.[1]

I am your slave,
I am your child.
Despite my faults
I belong to you;
My reputation and my disgrace
Are yours too.

Beloved Lord, how am I to tell
The woeful tale of my countless misdeeds?
I am unfortunate that never once
Did you deign to grant me
One look of loving concern.

Dear Husband, separated from you
I have suffered, suffered much pain;
You know all, yet how is it
That your heart melts not,
That you remain unmoved?

---

1. *Chaurasi* ('eighty-four'), the cycle of transmigration.

If the clouds do not rain,
If heartlessly they race away,
The thirsty rainbird will not turn
Its face towards oceans of water,
Nor be drawn by lakes of nectar;
It will die, but not open its beak
To anything but the raindrop.

Thus I long for you, beloved Lord;
I am parched with thirst,
Pray quench it
With the nectar of union.
Without you I am averse
To all the pleasures of the world;
Lord, I yearn only to be with you.

This miserable beggar
Treasures only your love;
When she came across
The jewel of your Name,
Love and longing
Flared up within her.

Water is the life
Of the lotus flower;
A moment's separation
And it is scorched
By the sun's fiery rays.

So does my soul burn
In endless agony
Parted from you, my beloved Lord.
Even the mind, burning with desires,
Is trying to consume my soul.

The lotus flower,
Mercilessly hit
By the onslaught of winter and frost,

Is restored to life
By the tender touch of spring;
Once again the love-intoxicated
Bumblebee hovers
Over the lotus bloom;
Valleys and dales resound
To koel's jubilant strains.[1]

Springtime brings joy to all;
To all but me, dear Lord.
Pining for you
My tearful nights,
Heavy and long,
Linger on like an age.
Without meeting you, Beloved,
Eon after eon has passed.

But when my soul awoke,
When to me your play
Appeared false,
I obtained the precious jewel
Of your love, my Lord.
You are moved to mercy;
Within my soul resounds
The divine melody of love.
Through Sahaj,[2] O King of kings,
You have become mine;
You have occupied
The throne of my heart.

After endlessly burning in separation's flame,
I have reached the cool ocean of love and bliss;
Says Kabir: Through the Master's mercy and grace
Misery has ended, the bane of delusion has gone.

K.G., Dupadi Ramaini 1, p.177
Bhayā dayāl bikh-har jari jāga

---

1. *Koel*, Indian cuckoo.
2. *Sahaj*, 'with ease' or 'through the path of Sahaj', i.e., the spiritual path that leads the disciple to the highest region, beyond matter, mind and maya.

THE BESTOWER OF BLISS

In this poem Kabir describes the manifold blessings of coming in contact with a living Master. The Master, himself the possessor of supreme knowledge, initiates the seeker into the practice of Nam (the Word), engenders divine love within his heart and tells him about the mysteries of the inner spiritual regions. Spiritually, the Master confers true knowledge and inner bliss on the disciple, enables him to attain inner poise and carries him across the ocean of phenomena to the shore of eternal peace. Kabir points out that physical contact with the Master, whether through a glance or a touch, removes the disciple's fears, doubts and evil tendencies, allays the fire of cravings that rage within his mind and generates true devotion within him.

With the Lord's grace
I have met the Satguru;
Possessor of divine talent,
Bestower of supreme bliss,
He is the conferer of true knowledge.

I was burning in the flames of desire,
He poured the elixir of devotion
And quenched the fire;
I became placid and cool.

A glimpse of him,
A touch from him,
And my evil tendencies vanished.
He gave me the technique
Of repetition
And I developed divine love.

He shattered the doors
Of pretense and delusion
That blocked my way;
He told the tale of my true home
And all my fears faded away.

402

Deep and dreadful is the world's ocean;
Who could have dared take me across?
In the boat of Nam
Kabir's Master, the adept oarsman,
Ferried him to the eternal shore.

K.G., p.113:189
Rām mohi satgur milai

THE NET

Man, represented as a fish in this poem, rejoices at the vast variety of pleasures and worldly possessions available to him in the waters of the world. But he fails to realize that all these are a part of the scheme laid down by the negative power to keep him enmeshed in the web of the world. Man plunges into the shallow waters—the insipid pleasures of the world—and like the fish, is caught in the fisherman's net and 'sold' in the market of birth and death.

> The fish rejoices at the sight
> Of vast expanses of water,
> Unaware of the net that Kal has laid.
> Vain and buoyant,
> It frolics in shallow waters,
> It gambols along rugged shores.
> Soon it is parted from water,
> To be put in the market
> For sale.
> Intoxicated, it noticed not
> The mesh laid around it.
> Alas, says Kabir, the world,
> Craving for sense pleasures,
> Is entangled in the net of Kal.

K.G., p.89:86
Ranjasi meen dekhi bahu pāni

FREE FROM FEAR

As long as man is engaged in external forms of worship and rituals and runs after worldly pleasures, his face is towards the negative power. When he takes to the path of true devotion he turns towards God: his worldly sorrows give place to inner peace and happiness; his mind and senses, previously 'foes' on the spiritual path, now cooperate in his devotion and become his friends; and the evil tendencies of his mind give way to noble qualities. When he realizes the Lord, he attains lasting peace. Having realized Him within, he sees the One Lord present everywhere and begins to live in his will. The devotee, through the process of dying while living—that is, withdrawing his consciousness from the physical body to the eye center—purifies his mind, which then returns to its own original state of purity. Kabir says that such a devotee merges himself in Sahaj, the state of supreme bliss, becomes free from the fear of birth and death and does not inspire fear in others—in other words, he helps others also to be rid of the fear of birth and death.

> I have veered from Yama to the Lord.
> My woes have vanished,
> Happiness abides within me.
> Those who were foes
> Have turned into friends,
> The evil have become gentle and pious.
> Everything that happens
> I now accept as a blessing;
> I attained peace
> When I realized the Lord.
>
> A million afflictions infested my body;
> Through my absorption in Sahaj
> They have given way to bliss.
> He who realizes his true self
> Sees the Lord
> And only the Lord
> In everything;
> Nor disease, nor three fevers[1]
> Afflict him now.

---

1. Physical, mental and spiritual suffering.

My mind has returned
To its own primal state;
I realized the Lord
When I died while living.
Says Kabir: I am merged
In the bliss of Sahaj;
I no longer know fear,
Nor inspire it in others.

A.G., Gauri, p.326
Jam te ulat bhae hai rām

406

THE WORLD'S LURES

Kabir makes this prayer on behalf of the struggling devotees who try to transcend the world and its lures, but feel they are unable to do so. A bird's enjoy-
ment of flying in the skies is cut short by the bird itself because of its own
attachment to its nest on earth. The elephant, lured by the dummy of a she-
elephant, falls into the pit prepared to trap it. The musk deer has the musk in
its own navel, but overcome by the fragrance runs about in the forest searching for it. Similarly, the five passions and sense pleasures keep man trapped
and entangled in the outside world. Man has to face death again and again,
and after each death he has to suffer according to his actions at the hands of
the *yamdoots* or messengers of death. Kabir points out that detaching oneself
from mundane attractions and taking refuge in the Lord is the only way out
of this dilemma.

> Beloved Lord, such has become my plight,
> I cannot overcome the world's lures.
>
> I am like the bird that soars high in the skies
> But whose longings force it back to earth;
> Its hopes and desires do not end,
> The bonds that imprison it do not break:
> How can its attempts to fly free succeed?
>
> All the efforts I make to gain bliss
> Only add to my misery.
> My plight, my suffering,
> I have no words to convey;
> I cannot overcome, O Lord,
> The world's manifold lures.
>
> Like the elephant,
> Through my own folly I land in the trap;
> Like the musk deer,
> Through my own infatuations I go astray.
> I cannot overcome, O Lord,
> The world's manifold lures.

Says Kabir: I am helpless,
I have no strength to resist
The spate of earthy desires.
Almighty Lord, pray heed my suffering:
Here I dread this world,
And I shudder in terror
At the thought of the messengers of death.
Lord, I have taken Thy refuge,
For of myself I cannot be free
From this world's endless misery.

K.G., p.133:266
Rāmrāi so gati bhai hamāri

NOT THE WAY

Men adopt various methods to attain salvation: Some chant hymns and sing songs, some jump and dance till they fall into a self-hypnotized trance, some keep standing for years, some hold one arm raised for decades, some contort their bodies with intricate postures and some go about in colorful ritualistic dress; yet others, devoid of devotion themselves, try to impress by initiating devotees. Saints firmly reject all such practices, for they only inflate ego, cause frustration and lead the practitioner away from God. Sometimes the sham devotee feels resentful towards Saints for their forthright repudiation of such deluded practices and candid enunciation of truth. Out of malice and ego, he starts slandering the Saints. Although Saints are unaffected by the slanderer's efforts to malign them, the slanderer is not spared by the law of karma and is sent into lower species to suffer and atone for his deeds.

> To jump and jiggle,
> To rock and sway
> Is not the way of devotion.
> Men ape devotees:
> They go flaunting about
> In ritualistic garbs,
> But there is no genuineness
> In a loud show of piety.
> Such men do not appeal to me,
> For to rock and sway
> Is not the way of devotion.
>
> They have one thing on their tongue,
> The opposite in their heart;
> Even in their dreams
> They'll not know me,
> Nor my path.
> In this world, sorrow
> Will always be their lot,
> For to rock and sway
> Is not the way of devotion.

If they wake up,
If they become aware
Of their delusion,
Then there is a chance
Of their salvation.
But to rock and sway
Is not the way of devotion.

Those whose heart is averse
To the Master,
Those who speak ill of him
Will be born as swine and dogs.
To rock and sway
Is not the way of devotion.

In the vicious circle of lower species
    They'll rotate and rotate, suffering misery;
Only those who realize the Lord
    Are dear to my heart, O Kabir.

Bijak, Ramaini 67
Deh hilāye bhakti na hoi

THE LORD'S SHERIFF

The human body has been described by Saints as a house, a fort and sometimes as a town. Here Kabir says that the soul is given the job of sheriff in this town. While performing its duties the soul should respect and adore the good and noble, that is, the Saints, and reprimand and keep a vigilant eye on the evil—the base tendencies of the mind. To this imagery Kabir adds the analogies of a slave and a dog to illustrate a disciple's love and devotion for the Master: The disciple has the devotion and obedience of a slave and the faith, humility and loyalty of a pet dog; he feels that birth after birth he has been lying at the Master's door and cannot be turned away.

Referring to his inner experiences, Kabir says the divine melody that emanates from the highest region, Sahaj, is branded on his forehead. It is at the eye center in the forehead that the Sound is heard. Those who hear it at this point gain the strength and courage to fight and win the battle against mind, maya and the negative power, and become worthy of entry into the Lord's treasury. The rest, who are not tuned in to the melody, cannot face the onslaughts of the enemy and desert the battlefield; they are found wanting on the touchstone of the Lord's treasury and are rejected like counterfeit coins.

Kabir compares the eye center to a cell within the larger house of the human body. The devotee has to take his seat in this cell and then contemplate on the supreme chamber, the Lord's mansion within. When soul, the separated wife, goes within and enjoys the bliss of the divine melody, she attains everlasting union with her Husband.

> I adore the Saints,
> I reprimand the evil,
> Thus do I perform my duties
> As the Lord's sheriff.[1]

> Day and night I massage Thy feet
> And I softly wave my hair
> Like a whisk over Thee.[2]

> I am a docile dog in Thy court;
> With my face turned towards Thee,
> I gently bark in supplication.

---

1. *Kotwāl*, the keeper of justice in medieval times, used to enjoy administrative and judicial powers in maintaining law and dispensing justice.
2. In medieval days slaves or low-caste people were entrusted with the duty of waving a fan or fly whisk over kings and high officials.

In my past lives, too, I was Thy slave,
I'll not be turned away from Thy gate.
The sound of Sahaj
That rings at Thy door
Has been branded on my forehead.[1]

Those who are thus branded
Plunge boldly into the battle;
Those not branded take to flight.
He who is a Saint knows how to serve God,
And God admits him into His treasury.

Within the house is a cell;
Therein contemplate on the supreme chamber.
The Master has blessed Kabir
With the real Thing,[2]
And he cherishes it
With love and care.

Kabir offers it to the world,
But only he receives it
Whose forehead bears the stamp
Of divine good fortune.

The soul that receives this elixir
Enjoys the bliss of ever-abiding love
In the company of her Spouse.

A.G., Ramkali, p.969
Santān mānau dootān dānau

---

1. Sometimes slaves were branded by their owners. Here the Lord's slave is branded on his forehead by the Shabd or sound; in other words, the third eye has opened and the devotee constantly hears the sound coming at this point.
2. *Vastu*, 'the Thing', 'the Article', is an expression used by Saints for Shabd and Nam.

THE KNOT

Men try to attain the Lord through means devised by their own mind. With all the sincerity and courage of their efforts, they cannot achieve their object of God-realization. Under the dictates of mind, men have adopted many rites, rituals and forms of worship that involve both good and bad acts. Kabir says that by spending long years in external observances and formal practices in order to earn the wealth of God-realization, men have wasted and even lost the capital of their precious human birth. Pious deeds of charity, pilgrimage and fasting, though good deeds, are still a chain that keeps one tied to the physical world. A shackle, whether of gold or iron, is still a means of bondage.

> Many a courageous attempt,
> O mind, you made on your own;
> Yet union with the Lord
> Remained a far-off dream.
> You did not discern
> Between good and evil,
> Genuine and counterfeit.
> In your efforts to make a profit
> Even your capital you lost.
> Misguided, you strengthened your bonds;
> You failed to realize that a knot,
> Whether big or small,
> Is still a tether to keep you bound.
> Says Kabir: Whom will you blame
> When you depart from here
> With all your hopes shattered?

Bijak, Ramaini 80
Bahutak sāhas kar jeea apnā

413

THE RARE WEALTH

The human body is a rare chance to realize the Lord, a chance that may not be given again and again. Man should utilize his human birth by going to a Saint and following the path of God-realization under his guidance. But, says Kabir, man wastes this opportunity in vain pursuits, and fritters away the precious wealth given to him by the Lord. Instead of seeking the company of Saints, he dissipates his life in the company of worldly people and involves himself in worldly pursuits.

You never kept the company of Saints;
You have frittered away
The wealth of human birth
That was in your hands.
   You never sought the company of Saints.
You will not gain this rare chance
Of dwelling in the human body again;
You did not realize the value
Of the company of Saints.
   You have frittered away
   The fortune that lay in your hands.
Now hell will be your home,
For day and night you relished
The company of the vile and the false.
   Seeing everyone rushing to his doom,
      Kabir loudly calls: Wake up,
   Wake up, O men! In broad daylight
      You are being robbed.

Bijak, Ramaini 44
Kabhun na bhavau sang

414

THE FLAME OF LONGING

The soul yearning to meet the Lord is represented in this poem as the wife intently awaiting the return of her husband who has gone to some distant land. In Indian folklore the crow, believed to be flying to far-off places, is the messenger of the separated wife. The forlorn wife, who has no means to convey to her beloved the agony of separation she feels, in desperation turns to the crow as a messenger who can fly to her husband with her pleas for an early reunion. Kabir uses this motif to emphasize the deep longing of the separated soul. At the end he extols divine love as a ladder to union and eternal bliss.

The separated wife
Stares and stares at the path,
With heaving sighs and tear-filled eyes;
But tears fail to drench
The flame of longing in her heart.
Her feet are firmly set,
Untired by the endless wait;
She lives on one hope:
A glimpse of the Beloved.

'Fly, fly, black crow,
Fly with speed,
That swiftly my loved one
I meet.'

Says Kabir: Love the Lord
To gain eternal life;
Let your only refuge be
The Lord's Name—
Repeat it and become
One with Him.

A.G., Gauri, p.337
Panth nihārai kāmni

415

SAD LOTUS

This poem, addressed to the lotus flower, is a figurative reference to the condition of man in this world. He is miserable and restless, always searching for peace and happiness. Kabir says, just as the lotus flower germinates, grows and lives in water, man's origin is the Lord and the Lord is ever with him. The soul is a particle of God; He is the source from which it has come. At the source there is no pain or misery, and even in the world there should be no cause of anguish for the soul, for the Lord is always with it. But, like the lotus flower that withers in spite of being in water, man suffers misery although the Lord is within him. Man has turned away from the Lord and has attached himself to the passions and transient pleasures of the world, like the lotus flower which, having forgotten its source of life and existence, has attached itself to the blazing sun. If he were to become cool and calm like his source, if he were to merge in Him, he would escape from the miseries of the world, from the cycle of birth and death.

> Why are you withered,
> Why sad, O lotus,
> When the lake of fresh water,
> The source of your life,
> Is ever with you?
>
> Born in water,
> In water you thrived,
> And water itself is your home.
> Why are you sad, O lotus?
>
> There is no fire at your roots,
> No blaze at your head;
> Tell me to whom, O lotus,
> Have you given your heart
> That you are burning with agony?
>
> Those who, like water,
> Become cool and tranquil,
> Who merge themselves in water,
> They, O Kabir, never wither or die.

K.G., p.84:64
Kāhe re nalini tu kumilāni

THE ONE I LONGED FOR

This poem expresses the devotee's joy at attaining union with the Lord. Scriptures and holy books sing the praises of the Lord, but He is not to be found there. He cannot be met through fasts, pilgrimages and austerities. Acts of merit are just as much the cause of bondage as sinful ones, for one has to return to the world of matter to enjoy their reward. Kabir says that only through devotion, longing and love for the Lord can one experience the truth and merge in God—the ocean of love.

Now I have met my Beloved,
My Lord, the Emperor of all,
Without whom my heart ached
With pangs of longing,
Songs of whose praise and glory
The Vedas and scriptures sing—
Him I have met, my beloved King!

Pilgrimage and austerities
Can never cut Yama's deadly noose.
Sins and acts of merit
That cradled my births and rebirths,
Both seem illusive and empty to me—
Through the Lord's devotion.
Without whom ached my heart,
Him I have met, my King,
My beloved Lord.

Says Kabir: I have kindled
The flame of knowledge,
I have plunged and become one
With love's infinite ocean.
Without whom ached my heart,
Him I have met, my King,
My beloved Lord.

K.G., p.137:283
Ab main pāyā rājā rām sanehi

417

THE BUMBLEBEE

The soul that vacates the physical body and enters the inner spiritual regions is symbolized in this poem by the bumblebee. Like the bumblebee that goes from flower to flower collecting nectar, the soul soars within and collects the ambrosia of bliss from the lotus in the inner regions. Kabir also refers to the practice in medieval times, when sailors' wives would light a lamp in front of their house and keep an all-night vigil for their husbands' return. The wife or soul who has realized the Lord's love within her heart keeps a vigil within herself and does not look for Him outside the body. Kabir says that this state of inner love and realization is the gift of the Master; it is only with his grace that the disciple overcomes the passions, stills his mind, goes within and tastes the ambrosia of divine love.

The bumblebee has tasted
The ambrosia within.

Why need that longing wife light the lamp,
Whose heart is lit with love's flame?
If she ceases to go elsewhere,
If she seeks Him within her own body,
She will gain union with her Husband.
The bumblebee will taste
The ambrosia within.

In an instant
I vanquished the robbers
Through the power of my Master.
Says Kabir: Listen, O friends,
While living I won the battle
When I conquered my body and mind.
And the bumblebee tastes
The ambrosia within.

K.S., III:14
Ami ras bhanwarā chakhi liyā

418

ONE CARDINAL TRUTH

Kabir points out that all external observances, yogic practices, oblations, austerities, intellectual pursuits and even striving for miraculous powers are of no help on the path of God-realization. Love or devotion is the highest truth and this alone can lead the seeker to the Lord.

Why should I strive
For supernatural powers?
They are empty and vain.
I ever cherish within me
The nectar of the Lord's Name

Intellect and knowledge,
Mental deliberations,
Yoga and austerities—
Fallow and futile,
They lead only to maladies.

What use your becoming a recluse
And making forests your home
When your mind is still bound
By the subtle chains of desire?

All practices are hollow,
Except devotion to the Lord—
The one cardinal truth.
Says Kabir: Discard all outward pursuits,
Love the Lord with all your heart.

K.G., p.99:130
Kā sidhi sādhi karaun

WEB OF LEARNING

Kabir says that intellectual and dialectical books are the web woven by the deft fingers of *vidya*[1] or book knowledge, whom he represents as a clever woman. She is bare of true experience and shamelessly displays volumes of well-knit words. All run after her, trying to become proficient in learning. She adores the lifeless—letters and words devoid of living experience—and plays on the lyre of the human mind as she pleases: to some she promises liberation through reading, others she threatens with doom if they ignore her. Kabir says that the Saints and devotees of the Lord are indifferent to her, for their knowledge is the outcome of their spiritual experience, not of reading books and scriptures. The Saints depend on what they know, others on what they read.

> With her nimble fingers
> This woman weaves a web;
> If you are truly learned
> Then realize the truth:
> She wears no dress,
> She goes unveiled;
> This beloved of all
> Adores only the lifeless;
> At random she plucks
> The strings of the lyre;
> To some she forebodes doom,
> To some she promises liberation;
> To some she brings remorse,
> To some she gives joy;
> With her nimble fingers
> She weaves a web,
> But becomes a slave, O Kabir,
> Of the slaves of the Lord.

Kabir, p.308:124
Kar pallav ke bal khelai nāri

---

1. Some scholars have interpreted the woman as Maya; H.P. Dwivedi's interpretation as *vidya* or book knowledge seems to fit the context of the poem better.

THE DAY THAT COUNTS

In the court of the Lord only the practice of Nam counts and only time spent in meditation is fruitful. Kabir says that men, gods and deities are all infatuated with the wiles of Maya. Only the devotee of Nam overcomes the obstacles of mind and maya, attains true detachment and peace within himself, and crosses the ocean of phenomena to his true home.

Only the day spent
In repetition of the Lord's Name
Is reckoned fruitful
In the court of the Lord.
He who is absorbed in the Name,
The Lord is always with him
As his companion.
   The day spent in repetition
   Alone counts in the Lord's court.
Ceaselessly burns the lamp of Maya,
And men and gods, like moths,
Rush blindly into its flames.

Having attained the state
Of poise and detachment,
Kabir, the Lord's slave,
Has swum across the ocean
And reached the haven.

K.G., p.112:185
Hari nāmai din jāe re jāko

THIS PRECIOUS CHANCE

For eons the soul has been taking birth in the world, wearing the different dresses of different bodies by taking birth in various high and low species. Now God has given the rare gift of the human body, a chance to escape from the cycle of births and rebirths. But man wastes this chance toiling to support a family and earning wealth, status and fame. Kabir says that all the hard work a man does to gain worldly objectives is unremunerative labor because it is of no avail on the spiritual path and keeps him bound in the shackles of transmigration. Kabir urges man to understand the importance of the human birth, seek a 'perfect man', the perfect Master, learn from him the way to realize God and thus put an end to his long chain of suffering.

> This precious chance
> You will not get again:
> The chance to seek a perfect man
> And through him, meet the Lord.
> Many times you have come,
> Many times you have departed.
> Like a serf you toiled;
> You toiled, yet received no wages.
> Although one, you donned manifold garbs;
> Like a clown you assumed myriad forms.[1]
>   Now is your chance to find a perfect man
>   And through him, attain the Lord.
> Dear Lord, only one boon I beg of Thee:
> Pray end the long trail of Kabir's misery.
>
> _K.G., p.94:110_
> _Aisā ausar bahuri na āvai_

---

1. The same soul assumes different forms in its different births in various species.

A LOVER'S STRATAGEM

In this poem Kabir uses the imagery of a loving wife whose husband has come home after many years' absence. She is grateful that he has come of his own accord, but is anxious that they should not be separated again. Now she will cling to his feet and entreat him with all humility not to leave her again; she will even try to entice him with a woman's artifice.

The devotee has met the radiant form of the Master within the temple of his heart, the eye center, and like the anxious wife longs to be always with him. Like her, he will try to hold his Master within through humble entreaties and will use the stratagems of surrender, devotion and love to keep the Beloved from going away. Identifying himself with the loving wife, Kabir asks the Beloved, with a tinge of irony, not to be lured elsewhere but to remain always with him.

My beloved lord,
Now I'll not let thee go.
Whatever pleases thee I will do;
Pray become mine, remain with me.

After endless days of separation,
Beloved lord, I have at last met thee.
I am fortunate indeed
For thou hast come within my home
Of thine own accord.[1]
   My beloved lord,
   I'll not let thee go.
I will cling to thy feet
And insist upon thy staying;
With all the stratagems
At my love's command
I will hold thee ensnared.
Pray rest with joy
In the temple of my heart.

---

1. The devotee, on realizing the radiant form of the Master within, feels that it is not through his own efforts that he has met the Master, but through the grace of the Master alone.

Lord, my beloved lord,
I will not let thee go.
Kabir, O Lord, begs of Thee:
Do not be enticed elsewhere,
Become mine, remain with me.

K.G., p.69:3
Ab tohi jān na daihun

THE ERUDITE

Intellectuals, on the basis of their erudition, claim to know the Lord. But, says Kabir, they do not know the Lord nor do they know anything about Kal, the negative power, who is the cause of the creation and of the changes that continually take place in it. The learned have only book knowledge; they lack the true knowledge that is the outcome of spiritual experience and attainment. Their talk about God and spiritual matters, about heaven and hell, is theoretical, based only on intellectual speculation and imagination. It is like the make-believe of children, arranging marriages for their dolls. The learned pundits and priests also act as spiritual guides and initiate by shaving heads or having people perform certain ceremonies. Kabir says that since they do not even know where their disciples' souls will go after death, they can hardly guide them on the spiritual path.

The erudite, the clever, the intellectual,
Claim to know the Wise One,[1]
But in truth know Him not.
They know not the mystery
Of the second wise one[2]
Who is the cause of creation
And of destruction,
Of the advent of night
And the dawn of day.

They have all adopted the trade
Of rites and rituals,
Of piety and ceremonies,
Of worship of many gods.
Ignorant of the One, the Lord of all,
They talk of heaven and salvation
Like children at play
Arranging marriages for their dolls.

---

1. The Lord.
2. Kal, the negative power, the creator of the three worlds.

Tell me, O learned ones,
Where do they go after death
Whom you tonsure
To make your disciples?
Realize
That the Lord's Name alone
Is the real treasure
And give up all counterfeit.

Bijak, Ramaini 36
Gyāni chatur bichakhan loi

THE LORD'S SLAVE

The devotee who follows the path of surrender lays his entire being at the Lord's feet. Having crushed his mind, he has no desires left. He has become the Lord's slave and is happy in his will. He has no objection even if the Lord wants to sell him in the marketplace of the world; in other words, if the Lord wants the devotee to continue taking births in the world, he will be content to do so. Kabir has attained such a state of surrender and has become a salve of the Lord. He is happy in his Master's will. Like a good slave he asks for nothing from the Lord, not even freedom.

> I am thy slave;
> Sell me, O Lord,
> Sell me, if such be thy will.
>
> My body, mind and soul
> I have laid at his feet.
> The Lord brought Kabir to the market
> And put him up for sale.
> He himself is the vendor,
> He himself the buyer, too.
>   I am thy slave; sell me,
>   Sell me if such be thy will.
> When the Lord wishes to sell,
> Who can save you?
> If it be his wish to save you,
> Who can sell?
>   Sell me, O Lord,
>   Sell me if such be thy will.
> Sayeth Kabir: My body[1] and mind
> I have reduced to dust;
> Never for a moment
> Do I forget my beloved Lord.
>   I am thy slave; sell me,
>   Sell me if such be thy will.

K.G., p.95:113
Main gulām mohi bech gosāin

---

1. Physical desires and cravings.

THE EMPTY GAME

The Muslim divines and the Hindu holy men lay down numerous laws and dogmas to find the Lord, and prescribe various ritualistic practices for seekers. Kabir asks how they can guide others to salvation when they themselves are deluded and bound by the chains of birth and rebirth. The Lord is within the human body and the seeker has to go within to find Him, which is made possible by learning the technique of devotion from a spiritual adept. Kabir points out that the inner sound current or Shabd, being pure, true and everlasting, alone can lead us to the true and everlasting state of bliss.

Seek the Lord within your own body;
O man, boast not about your devotion,
For without learning the technique
Who can become a true devotee?

Some call themselves mullahs, some qazis,
But without realizing the Lord
All their zeal is an empty game.
The pundit and the Brahmin
Talk of scriptures, planets and stars,
But they too have failed to sunder
The dreadful noose of Yama.[1]
 Seek the Lord within your body;
 O man, without learning the way
 Who can become a true devotee?
False and transient is the human body;
Shabd and the Lord's Name alone
Are true and everlasting, O Kabir.

K.G., p.101:142
Tan khojo nar nā karao badāi

---

1. The god of death, also known as Kal, the negative power.

428

A RARE DEVOTEE

In this poem Kabir urges the seeker to give up rites, rituals, false beliefs and external observances, and take to the practice of Nam. Describing the state of those who waste their human birth in such vain pursuits, Kabir says that they continue to rotate in the wheel of eighty-four, facing death again and again. On the other hand, those who take to the practice of Nam under the direction of a perfect Master, in whom the Formless has taken form, are dyed in the indelible hue of divine love and themselves become the Lord.

All remain deluded in false practices;
Only a rare devotee, O Lord,
Repeats Thy Name.

If men were to seek the herb,[1]
Pulverize and ingest it,
They would be freed of their ailment;
But without the Master
They wander deluded,
Involved in vain observances.
    Only a rare devotee, O Lord.
    Repeats Thy Name.
He, the Almighty One,
Is ever present;
But without faith and love
How can you invoke his grace?
Look upon sorrow and joy as one
And firmly hold your mind still.
Turn the ten and the one[2] towards the Lord
And remain ever absorbed in Him.
But he who remains involved in the twelve,[3]
Whirls in the vortex of eighty-four;
Again and again he dwells in the womb,
Again and again he is doomed to die.

---

1. Nam or the Word.
2. Ten senses (five of action and five of perception) and the mind.
3. The six schools of Indian philosophy and the six pious acts.

Only a rare devotee, O Lord,
   Repeats Thy Name.
He who discards 'me', 'mine' and 'thine',
Who gives up rites and rituals,
Who rises above caste distinctions,
Who tries to attain the Formless
Through the one with form,
Such a one will never sink;
He will swim across the ocean
To the shore of divine bliss.
   But only a rare devotee,
   O Lord, repeats Thy Name.
He who is absorbed in the Lord,
Who is dyed in the Lord's own hue,
Whose coming and going has ended,
Who is freed from misery,
Who remains always content,
Who is unaffected by joy and sorrow,
Who looks on pleasure and pain as the same,
Such a one, O Kabir,
Becomes the Lord himself.
   But only a rare devotee,
   O Lord, repeats Thy Name.

K.G., p.112:183
Sab bhoole ho pākhand rahe

PAIN OF SEPARATION

The pain of separation from the Lord is too intense to be expressed in words. Only the devotee who suffers this pain knows its intensity; others are unable either to understand his suffering or share it with him. Kabir prays to the Lord to come and meet him and thus put an end to the anguish he is undergoing in separation from Him.

One who has suffered the misery
Of separation from Thee, O Lord,
Alone will know the ache of my heart.
The uninjured can never know the pain
The wounded have to endure.

To him who has no eyes,
Morning is the same as evening;
A barren woman cannot know
The throes of childbirth.
Only the one parted from Thee, O Lord,
Will know the pain of my heart.

I feel the agony,
Although the wound
Somewhere deep within
I cannot see.
Beloved Lord, pray come,
Be my healer, make me whole.
Only the one parted from Thee, O Lord,
Will know the pain of my heart.

With whom shall I speak of my anguish?
Who can share it with me, O Kabir?
I hold my tears within my heart,
In silence I bear my agony,
For the one parted from Thee
Alone knows the pain of my heart.

K.G., p.138:285
Jā tan bedan jānaigā jan soi

NO TERROR

Fear of death afflicts the entire world, but not the devotees who have been connected with Shabd or Word by a perfect Master. By the practice of Shabd they vacate their physical body and withdraw their mind and consciousness to the eye center in the same way that one leaves the body at the time of death. Death is neither an unknown terror for them nor a mystery, because they experience it during their daily spiritual practice and know exactly what it is. Kabir says that such devotees die in Sahaj—that is, they merge themselves in Sahaj, the highest spiritual region, the home of supreme bliss. The devotee who merges in Sahaj becomes immortal, for he is not required to return to this world of births and deaths.

Death terrifies the entire world;
That death has been unmasked for me
    by the Master's Word.

How can I die, for I have experienced
    death within myself?
Only they die again and again
    who know not the Lord.

'Death is certain', 'Death will come',
    says everyone;
But one who dies in Sahaj becomes immortal.

Says Kabir: I am immersed in ecstasy,
Delusion has dissolved and supreme bliss
    abides within me.

How can I die now, for I have known
    death within myself?
They die again and again
    who know not the Lord.

A.G., Gauri, p.327
Jih marnai sabh jagat tarāsiyā

432

THE LORD'S REFLECTION

This poem enumerates some of the qualities of the Satguru or perfect Master. The Master initiates the disciple into the practice of true Name or Shabd, enables him to open his inner eye, go within and come in contact with the divine melody of Shabd and attain the supreme state of fearlessness. He does not advocate observance of rituals and ceremonies or outward forms of worship; his path is that of going within the body. Such a Master has himself gone beyond the regions of mind and maya and become one with the Lord; as Kabir puts it, seeing him is the same as seeing the Lord.

That Master I cherish, O friend,
Who fills the cup of true Name,
Who himself drinks it
And enables me to drink with joy.

That Master is dear to me, O friend,
Who is not fond of pageantry,
Who does not pose as a high priest,
Who performs no external worship,
Who accepts no gifts for himself.

That Master I cherish, O friend,
Who enables me to hear
The unstruck melody,
Who removes the veil from my eyes
And reveals his own form within,
Seeing whom is seeing the Lord.

That Master I cherish, O friend,
Who knows that the pleasures of maya
Are the source of misery and pain;
Who does not involve his disciples
In the chimera of false beliefs;
Who keeps me absorbed day and night
In the bliss of his elevating company;
Who merges my soul in Shabd;
That Master is dear to me, O friend.

Says Kabir: Who knows no fear
And enables me to attain
That divine state of fearlessnes,
He alone is my Master,
Him I love and cherish, O friend.

K.S., II:18
Sādho so satguru mohi bhāvai

WORSHIP THE TRUE WORSHIPPER

The world tries to worship the Lord by adoring idols, paintings and symbols; by chanting hymns, telling beads or reading scriptures; and by indulging in various rituals in temples, churches, mosques and other holy places. Kabir says that such worship is not acceptable to the Lord. To love the Lord is the best way to worship Him and is the worship He approves of. Only the true lover of the Lord, who has become one with Him, is the true worshipper; he is the Saint or Master. Kabir calls upon the seeker to love and worship such a true worshipper.

> Beloved Lord,
> Either I have lost my senses
> Or this world of Thine is insane.
>
> The worship that the Lord approves not,
> In that worship the world is entangled;
> The worship that is dear to his heart,
> These worshippers know nothing of.
>
> To love Him, love Him and none else,
> Is the worship that pleases Him.
> To adore the Lord through love
> The soul was parted from Him.
>
> Why be involved in vain formalities?
> Worship the true worshipper of the Lord.
> Kabir sings the glory of His love,
> He sings of what he has himself seen.
> Who attains the rank of a lover
> Is the true worshipper of the Lord.

K.G., p.136:275
Rāmrāi bhai bikal mati mori

435

THE WINE OF LOVE

Saints have often described love as a strong wine, and love's ecstasy as a state of deep intoxication. Kabir says that in the 'vat' above his eyes he has fermented his own wine. The Lord's grace is the precious molasses, devotion is the rare leavening, and the finished product is the highly intoxicating wine of the Lord's love. Only through the Lord's grace and blessing can the devotee imbibe the wine of love, and experience the joy of this intoxication; in other words, it is not within the power of the devotee to become a lover of the Lord, for his love is a divine gift not an acquired treasure. Kabir, therefore, seeks the Lord's blessing that he may drink more and more of the wine of his love.

Dwelling on the Lord
And drinking the wine of his love,
My entire being is fervid
With intoxication.

Paying a high price I obtained
The rare molasses of his grace;
With the leavening of devotion
I fermented it and made it strong:
In the vat within my body
I refined the priceless wine
Of the Lord's love.
   Drunk with the wine of his love,
   I am fervid with intoxication.
I beg, I implore my Beloved,
Pray enable Thy poor slave
To drink more and more
Of Thy love's vinous nectar.
   Dwelling on the Beloved,
   Drinking the wine of his love,
   I am fervid with intoxication.
Says Kabir: My drunken insanity adorns me
With a ceaseless glow of joy.
I drink and drink the wine of his love
And I am lost in the blissful trance of intoxication.

K.G., p.86:73
Chhāki paryo ātam matiwārā

436

THE LAND OF NO RETURN

Describing the inner regions, Kabir says that the path of Truth is a path of realization, not of analysis or explanation. If the seeker meets a perfect Master and is initiated into the practice of Shabd, if he stills the mind at the eye center and contemplates on the divine power according to the Master's directions, then he will attain his object of God-realization. He will not be required to face death again, that is, he will be free from the chain of birth and death. He will reach his original home, the Lord's abode, from where there is no return to the world of matter.

> When the body dies,
> To what home goes the soul?
> How does the soul merge
> Into the primal Unstruck Shabd?
> Only he who has realized the Lord
> Knows the truth;
> He revels in his knowledge
> Yet remains speechless
> Like a dumb man who has eaten sugar.
>
> The Lord himself
> Has expounded this knowledge:
> Hold your fleeting mind firmly
> At the point of Sukhman;[1]
> Adopt such a Master
> That a Master again
> You do not need to seek;
> Dwell in such a state
> That a dwelling again
> You do not have to make;
> Undertake such a contemplation
> That contemplation again
> You do not have to undertake;
> So die that you do not need again to die.

---

1. The central path starting from the eye center and leading upwards to the higher spiritual regions, located and traversed by means of the spiritual practice taught by a perfect Master.

Reverse the flow of Ganga and Jamuna
And merge them into one;[1]
With no water, bathe within
At the confluence of the three rivers.
Worldly pursuits are like the torments of hell;[2]
If you realize the Truth,
What else remains to be realized?

As water, fire, air, earth and ether
Stay mixed in man,
So should you stay merged in the Lord.
Says Kabir: Meditate on the Lord
Free from all stain;
Go to that home
From which there is no return.

A.G., Gauri, p.327
Pind mue jio kih ghar jātā

---

1. The current of the soul and mind are flowing downwards from the eye center. The seeker should reverse their direction inwards and bring them back to the eye center; in other words, soul and mind have to be withdrawn from the nine portals of the body and concentrated at the point behind the two eyes. Thus the soul reaches Triveni, the confluence of the three rivers, in the second region of the inner journey.

2. Most scholars have interpreted the word *lochā* to mean 'to see' or 'to look at'. Dr. R.K. Varma has pointed out that the word *lochā* is used as a noun and not as a verb; according to him it refers to Locharak, one of the hells in Hindu mythology.

TRUANTS FROM DEVOTION

While expressing his longing for the Lord and praying for his mercy, Kabir criticizes the different religious leaders who preach piety, claim to be highly evolved souls and seek to guide others. According to Kabir, they are devoid of true devotion, spiritual attainment and even the quality of mercy, for they kill animals, eat their flesh and tell their followers to do the same. Kabir ends the poem with a prayer to the Lord to accept him and take him under his shelter.

You are pure, my Lord,
You, the ocean of supreme bliss!
Even sages and prophets
Crave your refuge;
What chance have I,
A poor beggar at your door?

You are the river, beloved Lord,
That flows deep within every heart;
You are an ocean of mercy and bliss,
Yet never have you blessed me
With even one loving look:
Alas, how unfortunate I am!

They devise ways to guide others,
But have no qualms at killing beasts—
And they claim to be highly evolved souls!
They play truant from devotion,
From the service of the Lord,
Yet keep begging
And craving for reward;
Vile at heart, they defy God,
Invoking blessings on some,
Wielding a knife on others.

Seeing them, this beggar
Feels sad and helpless.
Beloved Lord,
Kabir is your bondslave,
He craves your refuge;
Accept him,
You who are the support
Of all beings,
Accept him.

K.G., p.148:323
Tu pāk parmānande

440

KEY TO ECSTASY

When the disciple is initiated by the Master into the practice of Nam or Shabd and when he learns to open the door of the inner eye with the key of Nam, the melody of Shabd always stays with him. Describing the body as a palanquin and the eye center as the litter, Kabir says that now the disciple stays peacefully at this point and the five palanquin bearers—the five passions that keep moving and driving the body in various directions—have become weak or ineffective. The soul, steeped in divine love, goes to the eye center and enters the inner spiritual regions whenever she wants and there revels in bliss. Free now from the chain of birth and death, she is not required to return to the city of this world any more.

> I have found the true Name,
> It is always with me
> Like a string of pearls
> Around my neck.
> I now repose
> In the narrow litter
> Of the palanquin
> Whose five bearers
> Have become feeble.
> My Master has given me
> The key to the unyielding lock;
> Whenever I like I open the door:
> Dressed in the dancing costume of love,
> I enter the town[1] whenever I please
> And I dance, and dance in ecstasy.
> Says Kabir: Listen, friends,
> I'll not come to this city again.

K.S., II:74
Pāyau satnām gare kai harvā

---

1. Inner regions.

THE HAZE OF CONFUSION

In order to gain salvation people worship idols, undertake arduous journeys to holy places, take to wearing various garbs, grow long tufts of matted hair, undergo penances and austerities, and inflict pain on their own body by fasting, plucking out hair or going about naked. Such people, says Kabir, far from realizing God, live and die in a state of confusion or delusion and become an easy prey to the lord of death who casts them into heaven, hell or the lower species, according to their karmas. Neither do monarchs, rulers and the wealthy attain salvation by virtue of their position, power and wealth, nor do pundits and scholars meet the Lord through their erudition. Those who learn the way of true devotion and the method of spiritual practice give up all such external pursuits and search for God within their own body. They will surely attain their object of God-realization.

> Without devotion to the Lord
> The entire world remains overcast
> With the haze of confusion;
> Yama hovers over their head
> Ready to hurl his deadly net.
>
> Hindus kill themselves worshipping idols;
> Turks,[1] undertaking holy journeys;
> Jogis die raising and combing
> Tufts of matted hair all their lives.[2]
> None, oh none of them
> Ever finds the Lord.
>
> Poets pass away weaving mythology in verse;
> Kapris, threading their way to Kedarnath;[3]
> Fasting ascetics waste their lives
> Plucking out their hair.[4]
> None, oh none of them
> Ever finds the Lord.

---

1. 'Turks' in Kabir's time referred to Muslims.
2. Many sadhus in India keep long matted hair (*jatā*) which they dress in a variety of styles and look on this practice as an important part of asceticism.
3. *Kapris* are wandering sadhus who make it a point to visit all the holy places in India, including Kedarnath in the high Himalayan ranges beyond Rishikesh.
4. Jain and Buddhist monks who undertake fasts and pluck out their hair.

Kings die usurping wealth;
The rich, amassing gold;
Pundits die reading scriptures;
Women, gazing at their own beauty.
None, oh none of them
Ever finds the Lord.

But they who know the way
Of practice and devotion
Search for the Lord
Within their own body;
Says Kabir the weaver,
They will surely attain salvation,
They will without doubt
Meet the Lord.

K.G., p.146:317
Rām binā sansār dhundh kuherā

THE JEWEL OF LOVE

Only when the devotee realizes the Lord within his own body does he develop true love and devotion for Him. Then alone is he blessed with firm faith in God, a faith which remains unshaken in the face of any adversity. But, Kabir says, the jewel of divine love cannot be had for nothing; one has to surrender one's entire being in order to obtain it.

> The Lord has made me his own
> And I am drenched in his love.
>
> Even were my body put to flames,
> I would not flinch for a moment;
> Even were I to lose my life,
> I would not break the bond of his love.
>
> How can the jewel of love
> Be obtained for nothing?
> In exchange for my very being
> I bought Him, the Priceless One.
>
> The Lord for whom Brahma searched in vain[1]
> I have found within my own body.
> Says Kabir: I have become free
> From the ties of hopes and desires;
> I have met the Lord and am blessed
> With unshakable faith in Him.
>
> The Lord has made me his own
> And I am drenched in his love.

K.G., p.151:334
Ab hari hun apnau kari leeno

---

1. The reference is to an anecdote according to which Brahma, the god of creation in the Hindu trinity, tries to learn about the Supreme Being, but in spite of his efforts, fails to meet the Lord.

EVERLASTING COMPANION

There are many who adopt the life of a recluse and believe that they have become detached from the world, but Kabir points out that true detachment comes only through attachment to the Lord. The devotee who remains absorbed in the Lord's love naturally becomes detached from the world and its pleasures. Referring to a myth, Kabir says that even Brahma, the creator of the world, wandered about in search of the Lord but failed to find Him because he had no knowledge of the path leading to Him. Similarly, man keeps wandering in the outside world of delusion without trying to go within and taste the ambrosial fruit of the tree of bliss. Kabir urges man to take instructions from a Master and by following them become absorbed in the Shabd within, which will be his companion in this world as well as after death.

Rare is the detached one
Who adores you, O Lord;
Who remains lost in your love
And averse to mundane pleasures.

Brahma, who created the world,
Who has earned the name, 'the great potter'
—And many a motley pot he has fashioned—
Even he toiled yet failed to know the Lord.

There is a tree that bears luscious fruits;
A tree that has neither roots,
Nor trunk, nor branches.
Lured into the sea of delusion,
O man, you have kept drifting endlessly;
Never did you try to taste
The fruit of that sublime tree.

Says Kabir: Cherish the Master's directions;
Remember, the entire world is false and perishable.
Your body of dust must one day return to dust.
Only the Word given by the Master
Will go with you as your everlasting companion.

K.G., p.134:268
Rāmrāi ko aisā bairāgi

445

DANCED ENOUGH

Although the soul is a particle of the Supreme Being, it is suffering the disgrace of birth and death in the various lower species. According to its actions, the Creator gives the soul different bodies and it keeps dancing around from one body to another, all the time gathering the dross of karma. Kabir prays to the Lord to have mercy and meet him, and thus put an end to the varied roles he has been playing in the world for eons.

This is my humble prayer to Thee:
Keep not aloof from me, O Lord.
Save me, dear Lord, pray save me
From further disgrace and shame.

To the beat of Thy tabor
I danced and danced
And suffered great misery.
Rid me of the taint
I have acquired through the ages.
This is my humble prayer to Thee:
Keep not aloof from me, O Lord.

Do not further make me repeat
The protean roles I have played
For so long.
Says Kabir: End my rounds of dancing;
Grant me, beloved Lord,
A glimpse of Thy lotus feet.
It is my earnest prayer to Thee,
Keep not aloof from me now, O Lord.

K.G., p.88:78
Beenti ek rām suni thori

446

NO MORE WEAVING

Kabir has set this poem against the background of his profession as a weaver. Addressing Maya, who personifies the lures and expectations of the world, Kabir says that he will no longer weave to her bidding. Under the sway of Maya, man for eons has been weaving intricate designs on the loom of his mind. The warp, stretched on the frame of human life, is the hopes and expectations (*asa*) under which man lives and toils in the world; his cravings (*mansa*) are the weft; and the finished design becomes the basis of his future births.

Kabir says that he is now intoxicated with the wine of divine love and has no need to follow the dictates of Maya. He has given up 'weaving' and has steeped the frame of the human body and the warp and weft of expectations and cravings in the ambrosia of love. All his hopes and desires have turned Godwards, and even the loom of his mind is intoxicated with the bliss of divine ecstasy. Kabir suggests that man can become free from the lures of the world, servitude to Maya and the domination of mind only through deep love for the Lord.

Who will weave now,
For I'm stricken with love;
O Maya, who will weave at your bidding?
I am drunk with the elixir
Of the Lord's Name.
O Maya, who will weave now at your bidding?

You have laden my weaver's frame
With pile after pile of yarn,
But I have sold it all for a farthing.
O Maya, who will weave now?
   I'm drunk with the wine of the Lord's love,
   Who will weave now at your bidding?
The moment you strung
The warp on the frame,
I steeped it in the ambrosia
Of divine love.
O Maya, who will weave now?
   I'm drunk with the wine of the Lord's love,
   Who will now weave at your bidding?

The warp dances in ecstasy,
The weft in frenzy;
Even the old loom dances
In transports of joy.
Who will weave now, O Maya?
  I am intoxicated, O Maya,
  With the wine of the Lord's love;
  Why need I weave now
  At your bidding?

K.G., p.74:19
Ko beenai prem lāgo ree māi ko beenai

THE TRUE WORSHIP

Aarti, translated in this poem as 'worship', is a ritualistic form of offering made to an idol in a spirit of invocation, devotion and self-effacement. Usually leaves from five different plants, flowers or fruits of five different trees, and a brass or earthenware lamp are placed in a salver which the devotee circles in front of the idol, ringing a bell all the while. Kabir, rejecting such formal *aarti,* calls upon the devotee to undertake that *aarti* which not only can emancipate him but also liberate all the three worlds, physical, astral and causal. Kabir tells the devotee to make simran or repetition of the five words the five leaves, and the five melodies of the Shabd within, the five flowers; divine knowledge, the lamp, and the sound of Shabd, the bell that the devotee rings. As a final offering in the *aarti,* instead of bowing his head before the idol, Kabir tells the devotee to lay down his body, mind and ego at the feet of the Lord.

> Perform that worship which has the power
> To redeem all the three worlds.
> Take your self and put it as an offering
> For the One who is the storehouse,
> The source and the essence of Light.
> With the five leaves of simran,
> With the five flowers of Shabd,
> Worship Him who has not a whit of maya,
> Who is without an equal,
> Who is One, without a second.
> Lay your body and mind,
> Lay even your head at his feet,
> That his Light may appear within;
> That your soul, with love,
> May merge into his Light.
> Hold the lamp of divine knowledge,
> Ring the bell of the Sound within
> And see the Being who is supreme,
> Whose command all gods and deities obey.
> Through such worship, the primal Light
> Has flooded my entire being,
> And Kabir, O beloved Lord,
> Has forever become thy slave.

> *K.G., p.168:403*
> *Aisi ārati tribhuvan tārai*

449

THE MUSIC OF NAM

Nam, the Lord's Name, is beyond the material, astral and causal worlds. It is beyond the reach of scriptures, intellect and reasoning, since it transcends the limited sphere of the mind. Kabir identifies the Name with the Word, Shabd or sound current, and points out that the Name of the Lord, which is invisible, intangible and ineffable, is present within everyone in the form of divine music.

Endlessly resounds
The music of the Lord's Name.
None has understood
His Name's real mystery;
Free of hunger, free of thirst,[1]
Free of all attributes,
It is present in every vessel.[2]
  Endlessly resounds the Lord's Name.
Inaccessible to the scriptures,
Beyond the reach of reasoning,
It is free from piety and sin.
  It resounds in every vessel.
Beyond intellect, beyond reflection,
It is beyond the limits
Of the tangible and the void.
  It resounds in every vessel.
Unattainable through holy robes,
Unobtainable through begging,
Free of all forms and shapes,
It is beyond the reach of pretense and piety;
Far beyond the precincts of the three worlds,
Invisible and ineffable
Is that unique Truth, O Kabir,
Present within every vessel.
  Endlessly resounding
  Is the music of the Lord's Name.

K.G., p.121:220
Rām ke nāi neesān bāgā

---

1. Hunger and thirst denote worldly desires and cravings.
2. The human body.

THE BELOVED COMES HOME

This love song portrays the soul's union with the Lord, through the imagery of a wife's joy at the arrival of her beloved husband after long separation. Her mind is absorbed in singing songs of loving welcome, her heart relishes the nectar of the fulfillment of her love, and the room where she slept in the dark shadows of loneliness is flooded with the light of ecstasy at her meeting her husband. The Lord has blessed the devotee with union and the devotee's joy knows no bounds. He did not meet the Lord anywhere outside; he met Him within the temple of his own body. Kabir concludes the song on a note of gratitude, saying that it was not through any of the devotee's efforts that the Lord was realized, but through the Lord's own mercy and grace.

> After untold days of separation
> I have met my Beloved.
> Boundless, indeed, is my good fortune,
> For He has himself come to me
> Within my own home.
>
> I keep my mind engaged
> In blissful songs of welcome,[1]
> And I taste within my being
> The elixir of his Name.
> > After endless days of separation
> > I have met my Beloved
> > Within my own home.
> My temple is flooded with light,
> And in bliss I lie with my Beloved
> In the deep trance of his loving embrace.
> > He himself has come to me
> > Within my own home.
> I was in despair, I had lost
> All hope of meeting Him;
> It is He who has blessed me
> With the rare wealth of union.
> > He himself has come to me
> > Within my own home.

---

1. The mind remains engrossed in the inner melody of Shabd.

451

My efforts were of no avail;
The glory is to you, dear Lord,
That in your grace you came
And met me, within my own home.
  Boundless is my joy,
  Boundless, indeed, my good fortune.
I did nothing, O Kabir,
To deserve his grace;
The Lord himself, in his mercy,
Blessed me, O friend,
With the bliss of union.
  After endless days of separation,
  I have met my Beloved today;
  He himself has come to me
  Within my own home
  And boundless is the bliss
  Of our union.

K.G., p.69:3
Bahut dinen thein preetam pāye

I AM THINE

This is the prayer of a loving devotee who, conscious of his shortcomings and limitations, begs the Lord to take him under his shelter and release him from the chains of cravings and delusions. Kabir also suggests that God cannot be attained through renunciation and outward practices. The true path of God-realization is the practice of Nam, which should be undertaken with love and humility.

Dear Lord, Thy slave has been erring,
Yet with all his faults he is Thine.

So long as I indulged
In 'mine' and 'thine',
The miseries of the world
Tormented me.
   I have sinned, I have erred, dear Lord,
   Yet bad as I am, I am Thine.
The yogis, the sages, the seers,
All claim they have attained the goal;
But without the Lord's Name
They have lost even what they had.
The recluse and the ascetic
Renounce the world and seek solitude,
Yet cravings and hopes still linger;
The lure of the world
Has not left their heart.
Says Kabir: Lord, I'm Thy slave,
Demolish the edifice
Of lures and enticements.
Though numerous my faults,
Still, dear Lord, I am Thine.

K.G., p.102:146
Hai hari jan thain chook pari

453

LORD, END THIS MISERY

In strong terms Kabir warns man of the transient nature of the world and the inevitability of death. After every death the soul is given a new birth—a new body—which again has to meet its end in death. Devotion to God is the only way to escape this misery. Kabir prays to the Lord to rid him of this suffering, but at the same time, in a spirit of surrender, says that even if the Lord desires that he be handed over to the lord of death and thus his coming and going be continued, still he will submit to the Lord's will—with only the prayer that he be granted the Lord's darshan before he is handed over to the angels of death.

> The mouth that relished
> The five delicacies,[1]
> Within a moment on that mouth
> A flaming torch is placed.[2]
> My beloved Lord,
> Thou Emperor of all,
> Rid me of the affliction
> Of burning in the fire
> And dwelling in the womb.
> The body is subject to waste
> In many ways;
> Some consign it to flames,
> Some to the vigil of earth.
>
> Prays Kabir: Beloved Lord,
> Deign to give me at least
> One glimpse of thy lotus feet;
> After that Thou mayst
> Even send Yama to take me,
> If such be thy pleasure.

A.G., Gauri, p.329
Jih mukh pāchau amrit khāe

---

1. According to some scholars the five delicacies are milk, yogurt, butter, sugar and honey; here the idea is of a variety of tasty foods.
2. In India at the time of cremation the torch is placed at the end of the pyre where the head of the deceased lies.

DIVINE WATER

The entire world is burning in the fire of desires and cravings, of attachments and hate, of ego and strife. Kabir says that the practice of Nam is the only means to eliminate mind's negative tendencies, which are the cause of all misery and turmoil. So long as this fire is not extinguished, man cannot obtain real peace of mind. Once the water of Name puts out the fire, man will attain a happiness and peace within himself that cannot be shaken by any external circumstances. In fact, he will become at peace with the world, he will radiate peace and will live in a state of inner and outward happiness and peace.

> I was burning, I was aflame,
> I found the water of God's Name.[1]
> The water of the Lord's grace
> Removed all trace of fire
> From my heart that was burning.
>
> To vanquish their mind
> Men run to forests,
> They cannot find that water
> Without the Lord's compassion.
>   I was burning, I was aflame,
>   I found the water of God's Name.
> The fire that consumes
> Gods, deities, men and all,
> From that fire the water
> Of God's Name saved this slave.
>   I was burning, I was aflame,
>   I found the water of God's Name.
> The dreadful sea of the world
> Has become the sea of peace;
> I drink the water of his Name,
> I drink, but it does not decrease.
>   I was burning, I was aflame,
>   I found the water of God's Name.

---

1. Kabir has used the word 'God-water' or the water of God; Prof. Sahib Singh interprets it as the 'water of God's Name' (*Satik Bhagat-Bani*, IV:86).

Says Kabir: Adore the Lord,
The water of whose Name
Has extinguished the flame
That was scorching my heart.

A.G., Gauri, p.323
Ab mohi jalat rām jal pāiā

WHERE, O PUNDIT?

Pundits, following their holy books, promise the four boons of piety, wealth, fulfillment of desires, and salvation; they vividly describe heaven and hell and persuade men to undertake fasts, almsgiving, pilgrimages and oblations. Kabir says that they promise the four boons but do not know what they really are; they talk of heaven and hell with no personal knowledge of either; they preach about acts of merit and sins, but have no idea whether the various rituals they ask people to perform are really acts of merit or not.

Kabir says that the result of good and bad actions—heaven and hell—are for those who have not realized the Lord. One who realizes the Lord goes neither to heaven nor to hell but merges in the Lord. The fear of death and of the unknown hangs over the head of all, but it holds no terror for the true devotee because he knows where he will go after death.

> O Pundit, think well before you tell me
> The way to end this coming and going.
> O brother, in which direction dwell
> The promised boons of wealth and piety,
> Of fulfillment and salvation?
> In the north, in the south,
> In the east, in the west?
> In the heavens above,
> In the realms below?
> Why are you rushing towards hell
> With your deluded ways?
> Remember, there is no refuge other than God.
> Heaven and hell are for those
> Who do not know the Lord;
> Those who know Him
> Do not bother with either.
> The fear that afflicts all men
> Holds no terror for me;
> I have no delusions about good and evil,
> Neither will I go to heaven nor to hell.
> Says Kabir: Listen, O friends,
> From where I once came,
> There I'm going to merge.

Bijak, Shabd 42
Pundit sodhi kaho samujhāi

THE DAYS OF THE WEEK

Saints in India have composed lyrics on the months of the year, dates of the lunar calendar, and days of the week. This poem of Kabir on the days of the week, though composed in a simple, nursery-rhyme style, is not wanting in the spiritual depth characteristic of his other poems. Many orthodox religions prescribe certain rituals and ways of behavior for each day of the week. Kabir, however, tells the disciple to "sing the Lord's praises," that is, listen to the divine melody of Shabd, and thereby attain the kingdom of God in the inner region of pure and unalloyed spiritual bliss. His code of conduct for the week is not external observances, but keeping in mind the ultimate goal of union with the Lord, doing spiritual practice and, with the help of the Master, reaching the Lord's abode.

Each day of the week
The Lord's praises sing;
Through the Master's grace
God's kingdom win.

Sunday start your devotion:
In the temple of your body
Let your mind like a pillar be still;
Day and night without a break
Hold your attention within;
Then in the state of equipoise
Will the sound of bagpipe unfold.[1]

Each day of the week
The Lord's praises sing;
Through the Master's grace
God's kingdom win.

Monday the moon showers nectar;[2]
Taste it and at once be rid
Of the world's blazing fever.
Let your mind, held by the Word,

---

1. Sound of the highest spiritual region, heard in the state of Sahaj.
2. A reference to the devotee's experience during his inner spiritual journey.

458

Be ever inside at the door;
Then it will taste that nectar
And be drunk with ecstasy.

Each day of the week
The Lord's praises sing;
Through the Master's grace
God's kingdom win.

Tuesday tune yourself to the Truth within:
Boldly give up the ways
Of the five evil ones;[1]
Do not leave your home's treasure[2]
And go out, or you will earn
The displeasure of the King.

Each day of the week
The Lord's praises sing;
Through the Master's grace
God's kingdom win.

Wednesday let the wisdom dawn
That the Lord ever resides
In the lotus of your heart;[3]
Meet the Master and realize
That he and the Lord are one,
And turn the inverted lotus[4]
Upwards once again.

Each day of the week
The Lord's praises sing;
Through the Master's grace
God's kingdom win.

---

1. The five passions.
2. The spiritual wealth of Nam.
3. In the terminology of the Saints, 'heart' is the eye center; here 'lotus of the heart' refers to a stage in the spiritual journey within, where the disciple meets the radiant form of his Master.
4. At this point, the attention of the mind and soul, which had been turned downwards, reverses and turns inwards and upwards.

Thursday throw away your evil passions;
Discard the three[1] and attach
Yourself only to the One.
In Trikuti within,
Where the three rivers meet,[2]
Bathe and wash away your sins.

Each day of the week
The Lord's praises sing;
With the Master's grace
God's kingdom win.

Friday feast on ambrosia,
Let this be your firm resolve.[3]
Within yourself, day and night,
Battle with your lower self;
Boldly enslave the five.[4]
A look at other than the One
Let not your eyes ever crave.

Each day of the week
The Lord's praises sing;
With the Master's grace
God's kingdom win.

Saturday stay still,
Be within your body.
Light the inner lamp
That your within and without
May sparkle with radiance divine;
In its brilliance let the shadow
Of your karmas fade.

---

1. The three attributes.
2. Trikuti is the second stage in the soul's inner journey; here, there is a confluence of three currents, called Tribeni by Saints. A bath in the currents of the inner light in this region purifies the soul of all its sins.
3. On Friday some orthodox people in India observe a fast. Early in the morning on the day of the fast, they take a vow or make a 'pious resolve' that they will not take any food on Fridays, or will take only water or milk, etc. Kabir suggests that the true resolve is the determination to subdue the low tendencies of the mind, and the real fast is to abstain from indulgence in passions and enjoy inner bliss.
4. The five senses.

Each day of the week
The Lord's praises sing;
With the Master's grace
God's kingdom win.

If even a trace of love
For others lurks in your heart
You will not gain entry
Into the mansion of your Lord.
He who is dyed through devotion
In the hue of divine love,
His entire being, O Kabir,
Becomes pure and true.

Each day of the week
The Lord's praises sing;
With the Master's grace
God's kingdom win.

K.G., p.157:362
Bār bār hari kā gun gāvai

THE STEED OF MIND

Saints have described a worldly person's mind as an unbroken horse, a wayward camel without reins, or a wild elephant without the mahout's goad. The devotee, however, has to ride his mind on the spiritual journey; in other words he has to control the mind and win its cooperation in order to travel on the inner path. In this poem Kabir addresses mind as his horse and indirectly tells the devotee to put mind under the bit and bridle of meditation, detach it from all else and race it towards the higher regions within. The devotee should control mind's desires with the power of discernment or realization and urge it onwards by the inspiring power of divine love.

I'll put the bit and bridle
On you, O steed of my mind;
Discarding all else
I'll gallop you towards Gagan.[1]

Self-realization is my saddle;
In the stirrup of Sahaj
I place my foot and ride,
Astride the steed of my mind.

Come, my steed, I'll take you
On a trip to heaven;
If you balk
I'll urge you on
With the whip of divine love.

Says Kabir: The adept riders
Remain aloof from both
The Vedas and the Koran.

A.G., Gauri, p.329
Dei muhār lagām pahrāo

---

1. The firmament of the second region in the inner spiritual journey of the soul.

A SAINT'S INNER STATE

Perfect Masters or Saints are fully realized souls who have crossed the regions of mind, maya and the three attributes and transcended the limits of time and space. They have reached the highest spiritual realm—the mansion of the Lord—and become one with Him. Sometimes, in a spirit of ecstasy they proclaim their oneness with the Lord. Such rapturous declarations are rare. They are not the outcome of pride, nor are they contrary to their natural humility. This poem of Kabir is a spontaneous outburst of his joy and ecstasy at union with the Lord.

> I am in all,
> All that is, is I.
> The different forms in existence
> Are my myriad manifestations,
> Yet I am apart from all.
> Call me Kabir,
> Call me Ramrai,[1]
> It is one and the same.
> I am not a child,
> I am not old,
> And the glow of youth
> Never can touch me.
> I go not at anyone's bidding
> Nor come at anyone's command.
> In my state of Sahaj
> I am ever in the verdure of bliss.
> > Call me Kabir,
> > Call me Ramrai,
> > It is one and the same.
> My covering is a single sheet
> And people sneer at me:
> My weaver's calling inspires no respect;
> My dress is tattered,
> Patched at ten places—

---

1. One of the names for God, literally 'God the Emperor'.

Yet beyond the three attributes,
Beyond the region of the 'fruit'[1]
I dwell in the realm of bliss;
Thus have I acquired the name Ramrai.
I see the entire world,
The world cannot see me;
Such is the unique state
That Kabir has attained.
  Call me Kabir,
  Call me Ramrai,
  It is one and the same.

K.G., p.81:50
Main sabani men

---

1. The law of karma, the fruit of one's good and bad actions, holds sway throughout the physical, astral and causal worlds.

THE SOUL'S HOMECOMING

In this poem the devotee's inner experiences are described with unusual metaphors. Through spiritual practice the devotee's soul goes into the inner regions, where it enjoys bliss without the aid of physical perception. In the higher regions the devotee obtains the pearl of love which dangles on a shining string—love sustained by divine grace. This love is not a physical instinct, nor is it experienced on a physical level.

In order to stress the purity and spiritual quality of this love, Kabir says that it is purified by the breeze of longing in the inner spiritual regions. The earth rains and the sky becomes wet; that is, mind and soul, which before were absorbed in earthly pleasures, have now reversed their attention, turned inwards and are attending to the melody and beauty of the inner regions. The sun and the moon are *surat* and *nirat*—the faculties of the soul to hear and see. At a stage on the inner journey these two faculties become one, even as the sound that the soul hears and the light it sees are two aspects of the same power—Shabd. When *surat* and *nirat* become one, only then the soul merges into Shabd.

The river or current of the soul goes through the tree of Brahm, and going further it enters into Shabd, the vessel of gold. Giving a general description of the inner regions, Kabir says that the soul comes into contact with the five melodies of Shabd, the five parrots; withered by the agony of long separation, the soul now blossoms. Originally parted from this region of supreme bliss, the soul has now regained its primal home.

> Kindle within your heart
> The flame of love for the Lord:
> Dance without feet,[1]
> Without tongué, his praises sing,
> Ever remain engrossed in Him.
>
> Where pearls of rare beauty are formed
> Without the raindrop,
> Without mother-of-pearl,
> Without even the sea;
> Pearls that dangle
> On the string of light;[2]

1. This line has been translated by some scholars, 'Dance at (the Lord's) lotus feet'. Here the expression 'dance without feet' conveys the idea of a heart full of happiness and bliss.
2. Literally, the string of water; in India the luster and purity of a pearl is described as the pearl's 'water'.

Pearls washed by the luminous breeze
In the vault of the firmament,
Made pure and bright;
Where the ground rains
And the sky is drenched;
Where the sun and the moon
Join and become one;
Where the two[1] unite
To fuse into one
In the glory of union;
Where immaculate swans[2]
Play with delight
In the billows of eternal bliss;
Where the river flows into the tree[3]
And flows further to fill
The radiant vessel of gold;[4]
Where five parrots alight
And perch with joy,
And the wilderness blossoms
Into dazzling blooms of light.

From there I was once severed,
And there have I been attached again;
I've made the sky of supreme bliss
My everlasting abode.
Kabir, Thy slave, O Lord,
Was a wandering wayfarer;
With love and joy
He has trod the path
Back to Thee.

K.G., p.137:280
Ihi bidhi rām su lyo lāi

---

1. Soul and Shabd.
2. Souls.
3. The 'tree' or region of Brahm, the second stage on the soul's spiritual journey.
4. In medieval days anything precious was usually kept in a chest or vessel made of gold; here, the Shabd.

466

HEAVEN

Scriptures, priests and the orthodox promise heaven after death, and men are deluded by them into believing that they will go to heaven through pious acts, worship and austerities. Kabir says that such men are ignorant, for they have not gone within and realized their own self, their true identity in the creation; neverthless they talk at length of heaven.

True devotees do not bother about heaven, where it is and what it is like. They only want the Lord and know that craving for heaven and even salvation is an obstacle to union with the Beloved. Saints clearly point out in their writings that heavens and all astral worlds are within the limits of the three attributes and therefore subject to destruction; the Lord's abode is immutable and everlasting. Kabir says that for a true seeker if there is any heaven it is only the company of the Saints, which is a source of peace and bliss and a means to achieve God-realization.

> One and all say they will go to heaven;
> Their heaven's whereabouts, I know not.
>
> They are ignorant
> Of the mystery of their own self,
> Yet spin endless yarns
> To describe their heaven.
> So long as a man's mind longs for heaven
> He'll not find abode at His lotus feet.
>
> I know not where heaven's fortress stands,
> Where its moat, its rampart, its precincts,
> Nor do I know where its gateway is.
> O Kabir, whom can I tell?
> True heaven is only
> The company of Saints.
> Men say to heaven they'll go;
> Where their heaven is, I know not.

A.G., Bhairau, p.1161
Sabh koi chalan kahat hai ūhān

THE SPINNING WHEEL

Until the introduction of modern industry, spinning yarn on a spinning wheel was a common practice among poor and middle-class families. It was mostly the womenfolk who spun the yarn during their free time. In this poem, Kabir identifies the devotee with a daughter-in-law in the family who is encouraged by devotion, her mother-in-law, to spin the yarn of meditation. Just as spinning provides a means of subsistence for the family, meditation sustains the devotee's love and yields the profit of spiritual bliss.

> My mind is the spinning wheel,
> My tongue its spindle.[1]
> My mother-in-law urges me
> To repeat the Lord's Name:
> Repeat, my good daughter-in-law,
> And keep spinning at the wheel.
>
> With four pegs[2] I hold the wheel's base,
> With two washers[3] I protect the spindle,
> And I turn the spinning wheel
> With the belt of Sahaj.
>
> My mother-in-law urges,
> Spin, dear daughter-in-law, spin
> With great care and diligence,
> For without your spinning
> How will we make a living?
>
> Deftly did Kabir the spinning wheel ply,
> Keen and strong is the yarn he spun;
> For him it is not a spinning wheel,
> But the provider of supreme bliss.

K.G., p.123:228
Man mero rahatā

---

1. Not the physical tongue but the tongue of the mind, that is, the faculty of the mind that thinks; it is with this faculty of the mind that the devotee has to do simran or repetition.
2. Humility, love, longing and devotion; also interpreted as the four types of service to the Master and his disciples, namely: service with wealth, body, mind and soul. (Service with soul is doing meditation according to the Master's directions.) Some scholars have interpreted the four pegs as mind, intellect, the faculty of understanding or reasoning, and ego.
3. Pure living and regularity in spiritual practice.

468

WORSHIP ONLY THE SUPREME

Like all Saints, Kabir also pleads with the seeker to worship the One Supreme Being who is free from birth and death, rise and decline. Beyond attributes, beyond mind and maya, and beyond the bounds of karma, He is far above and beyond the reach of the various gods, goddesses and incarnations men commonly worship. If the seeker adopts the practice of Nam with love and devotion, his soul will merge into its own primal, formless state—the Lord himself.

Kabir discourages the seeker from the worship of idols, deities and incarnations because they are all within the limits of the physical, astral and causal worlds. An individual's soul will go to the place and object of its attachment. The devotee who worships gods that are within the limits of the attributes will not go beyond the attributes; similarly, if he loves a spiritual guide who has not transcended the boundaries of the three worlds, he too will remain within the limits of the three worlds, for a guide cannot take a disciple to a state beyond his own reach. Kabir says that the worship of the one all-pervading Lord is the true worship, and the way of this worship is the practice of Nam with one-pointed devotion and love.

> Take the shelter, my mind,
> Of the all-powerful One.
> Serve and adore Him—
> He who has no origin,
> No zenith, no decline,
> Whom none can fathom.
> If once you embed his Name within,
> Like the devoted wife who cherishes
> Her husband's love deep in her heart,
> Then all your tasks,
> Though a million they be,
> Will be accomplished,
> And all attributes of the body
> Will be destroyed,
>   If once you embed his Name within,
>   Like the devoted wife who treasures
>   Her husband's love deep in her heart.

Taking shelter with one who has form
Will not free you from the bondage
Of physical forms,
Even if you take the shelter
Of Shiva, Brahma or Vishnu.
You will only reach in the end
The one you serve and adore,
For no one can go beyond
The object of his worship.
    Embed the Lord's Name within,
    Like the wife who treasures
    Her husband's love in her heart.
Through the worship of images,
Through the worship of gods with attributes,
The soul earned again and again
Different garments to wear,[1]
But she never attained repose
In her own lofty, formless state.
Worship of idols and forms,
Though performed for ages,
Will not take the devotee
Beyond the limits of attributes.
    Embed the Lord's Name within,
    Like the wife who treasures
    Her husband's love in her heart.
By skillfully kneading
The five elements
And the three attributes,
The human body is made;
Without these eight the physical body
And karmas cannot come into being.
Through the body and the karmas,
The seeds of actions good and bad
Germinate and sprout and wither
To form seeds again and again;
And all take birth and die in delusion.

---

1. Different bodies; the soul has been caught in the cycle of transmigration, taking on the garment of different bodies in various species.

470

Embed the Lord's Name within,
Like the wife who treasures
Her husband's love in her heart.
That which is artificial
Is worshipped by men
As the Supreme Being;
How can they reach the true home
Through love of the handcrafted?
The entire world has fallen
Into the mire of delusion.
Says Kabir: That rare one
Who worships the all-pervading Lord,
With ease crosses over
To the opposite shore of bliss.
Embed the Lord's Name within
Like the wife who treasures
Her husband's love in her heart.

K.G., p.116:199
Sei man samajhi samrath saranāgatā

471

In this devotional poem Kabir depicts the love and spirit of surrender of the devotee. He accepts the Lord's will without hesitation or reservation. Whatever comes from Him—whether it is love or anger—the devotee accepts as his will. A true lover becomes one with the Lord, loses his own identity in Him, and is so much engrossed in love that he is unable to distinguish between pleasure and pain or between love and anger, since both come from Him. All that comes from the Beloved is accepted as a gift and a blessing by the lover.

Thy command is over my head.
I do not question it, my Lord.
Thou art the river,
Thou the Boatman,
Only through Thee can I go across.

Embrace devotion
For the Lord, my friend,
Whether He be angry,
Whether He love you.

Thy Name, dear Lord,
Is my only support;
It sustains me
As water sustains the lotus bloom.
Kabir is Thy bondslave:
Give him life or give him death—
Whatever, Lord, be Thy pleasure.

A.G., Gauri, p.338
Pharmān terā sirai ūpar

THE ROPE BROKEN

Kabir says people mourn the death of their near and dear ones as if they themselves were going to live in this world forever. Those who meet a perfect Master and learn from him the method of attaining eternal life do not face death again; they are freed from the chains of birth and death. Those who are engrossed in passions and sense pleasures, who do not meet the Master and follow his directions, continue to die again and again. Kabir calls the human body a well from which five water bearers—the five senses—draw the water of sense pleasures. But now the devotee's mind, which once enjoyed the pleasures through the five senses, has turned inwards—the rope or the means to draw the water is broken. Now even if the lower tendencies try to distract his attention they will fail to do so. Kabir says that when the attention of the mind is turned inwards, the well and water carriers do not exist, that is, the limitations of the physical body and the downward tendencies of the senses become ineffective.

> When others die,
> Why need you mourn?
> Mourn, if you were to live forever.
> The world dies, but I'll not die,
> For I have met the giver
> Of everlasting life.
>
> This body emits
> The perfume of passions;
> In its luring fragrance
> Man has forgotten
> The source of supreme bliss.
>
> There is one well, five damsels
> Draw water from it;
> Even though the rope is broken,
> These foolish ones
> Try to fill their vessels.
>
> Says Kabir, I have realized the truth:
> There is no well, nor water carriers.

A.G., Gauri, p.325
Avar mooe kiā sog kareeje

473

MERGING IN HIS ORDER

This poem describes the devotee who, through the practice of Nam, merges himself into Nam. Now he is no longer required to come back to the world of matter since he has merged in the Lord as water merges in the sea. Kabir says that coming and going, death and birth, are according to the Lord's Order or *hukam*. The word *hukam* or 'order' has been used for Shabd by many Saints, and Kabir uses it here in that sense. He says that the devotee will realize the Order and merge into it. In the following stanza he uses the word Shabd in the same way, saying that if the Lord is merciful, the devotee will merge into the Master's Shabd. Concluding the poem Kabir says that one who dies while living will not be required to take further births.

Like water in the waters of the sea,
Like a ripple in the river
I will merge in Thee.
I will look upon all as alike,
And attaining Sunn, I will merge in Sunn;
Free of bonds and unhindered,
Like air I will be.
Why will I then come to the world again?
Coming and going is under his Order;
I will realize the Order and merge in it.

When I transcend this creation of five elements,
I will bring my wandering to an end.
Forsaking all philosophies,
I will become impartial,[1]
I will dwell only on his Name.

Where He likes to keep me,
There will I stay,
There will I act as I am directed.
If the Lord is merciful to me,
I will merge in my Master's Shabd.

---

1. The six schools of Indian philosophy; becoming impartial or unconcerned with them.

He who dies while living
And lives again after dying
Will not be born again.
Says Kabir: He who merges in the Name,
His attention remains absorbed
In the pure state of Sunn.

A.G., Maru, p.1103
Udak samand salal ki sākhiā

TO ATTAIN TRUTH

This poem enunciates Kabir's path of practice. The devotee, realizing the significance of his human birth, must give up his craving for worldly gains, purify his mind, accept life and death as they come, and learn the way of dying while living—the method of withdrawing the soul from the nine doors of the body and bringing it to the eye center. If he merges in the Master's words, that is, if he completely molds his life according to the Master's directions, he will be attached to the Lord's Name within and will be rid of all delusions. The practice of Shabd will then lead the disciple step by step to the highest spiritual realm, the court of the Lord. At the end of the poem, Kabir refers to the disciple's spiritual union with the Master in one of the inner spiritual regions and says that only after this union the disciple realizes what Truth really is.

> You may not get the human body again;
> Keep remembering the Lord with ardor and joy.
>
> If your mind discards not its vile ways,
> How will you cross the dreadful ocean?
> If mind will give up its wayward trend
> The Lord himself will come and meet you.
>
> Since you were born, you will one day die;
> Be not dejected on this account.
> But one who willingly dies while living
> Will never have to face death again.
>
> When one merges in the Master's words
> He will be attached to the Lord's Name;
> When he is attached to the Lord's Name
> His delusions depart, his fears end.
>
> When the moon becomes one with the sun[1]
> The unstruck melody resounds within;
> When the melody of the bagpipe resounds[2]
> The soul shares the throne with the Lord.

1. This is a reference to a spiritual experience within; it has also been interpreted as a metaphor for the mind's downward trend turning inwards and upwards.
2. *Been:* the melody of the highest region has been compared by Saints to the music of the Indian snake charmer's pipe, the *been,* somewhat similar to the sound of a bagpipe or oboe.

Keep constantly the company of Saints,
Then your mind will be dyed in the Lord's hue;
Have firm faith in the Saints' lotus feet[1]
And you will take abode where there is no fear.[2]

It is not a game for the unripe[3] to play,
The rare valiant one alone plays it well;
When he plays the game with audacity,
The firmament within he makes his home.

Hold your restless mind, keep it still
And taste the elixir of his love;
When you drink this elixir within,
Death dies and you begin truly to live.

Thus singing, Kabir the Lord's slave,
Through mind controls
His wayward mind;[4]
When he stilled his mind within
He became one with his Master,
He realized the Truth.

K.G., p.109:173
Nar dehi bahuri na pāiye

With six articles this cell[5] is built,
Within it is kept a unique thing;
Under lock and key the soul is held,
The Architect did not take long
To fashion the cell.

---

1. An Indian way to express love and reverence towards a Saint; here it implies that one should have unshaken faith in the Saint or Master.
2. The state of ultimate bliss, which is free from all fear of birth and death, pleasure and pain, action and its retribution.
3. The timid; also those who have not yet become 'ripe' or strong through meditation.
4. By 'singing' Kabir implies listening to the melody and enjoying the spiritual experiences referred to in the poem. The higher mind or purer mind is normally under the domination of the lower or base mind, which runs toward vices and sense pleasures. Through meditation the higher mind gains control over the lower mind and enables the soul and mind to go within.
5. The human body; *six articles:* the five elements and the mind.

O my mind, keep awake now,
Through indolence you have
Wasted away your human life;
Burglars[1] have crept into your house,
They are robbing you of your wealth.

Five watchmen guard the doors
But they cannot be trusted;[2]
If you will become alert,
You will be illumined
By divine light within.

The wife who remains enamored
Of the body with nine portals
Will not attain the priceless treasure;[3]
Says Kabir: When the nine doors
Are vanquished, one enters the tenth
And realizes the Truth.[4]

A.G., Gauri, p.339
Khat nem kar kothari bāndhi

---

1. The five passions.
2. The five senses of perception, which cannot be trusted because they ally themselves with the passions.
3. Nam.
4. This line has also been interpreted as follows:
   Thieves plunder the house of nine doors,
   But beyond them Truth abides in the tenth.

UNDER THE SWAY OF NAM

The soul has been wandering from species to species in the cycle of eighty-four, assuming various forms. Even after obtaining a human birth, the soul dances to the tune of the mind and, under the influence of cravings and passions, again goes into the circle of birth and death. Kabir says the soul that comes under the shelter of Nam overcomes the domination of mind, becomes free from delusion, and through the practice of Nam realizes the Lord.

> Though I have assumed
> Myriad forms in the past,
> No more forms will I take on now;
> The wires, the strings and even
> The instrument is frayed,[1]
> And I am under the sway
> Of the Lord's Name.
> Now I will not dance
> To the beat of the drum—
> The drum my mind played so long,
> But plays no more.
> Lust, anger and the world's lure
> I have reduced to ashes,
> The pitcher of avarice is shattered,
> The gown of cravings has become old
> And I am freed from the chains of delusion.
> I recognize the One within all beings,
> All polemics are at an end for me.[2]
> Says Kabir: Through his own grace
> I have found Him, the Perfect One.

A.G., Asa, p.483
Jau main roop kiye bahutere

---

1. *Wires:* desires, cravings; *strings:* hopes, expectations; *instrument:* mind.
2. In medieval days, Indian philosophers, scholars and religious heads used to gather to hold discussions and debates (*shashtrartha*) about the nature of God and his creation, some favoring monotheism, some pantheism and some the cause of one or other of the various schools of philosophy. Kabir, like Guru Nanak and other Saints, says that such arguments cannot lead to God-realization and they become redundant once a devotee realizes God within himself.

479

FISH CLIMBS TO THE PEAKS

The change that takes place in the devotee's mind and soul on attaining inner spiritual realization is depicted by Kabir through paradoxes. Mind, the rabbit which roamed in the wild forests of the world and its attachments, now rests in the ocean of bliss; soul, the fish living in the sea of the world, now stays on the high peaks of the inner spiritual regions. Mind, which was debased by its own low tendencies, has drunk the wine of inner joy, but it is the soul that enjoys the intoxication of that spiritual experience. The fruit of true knowledge—spiritual knowledge—grows without a tree, that is, realization does not come out of the 'trees' of scriptures and learning; independent of all else, it is complete in itself.

The senses were the weaver, sitting at the loom of mind and weaving the cloth of physical pleasures. Now the mind dominates the senses and directs them to weave the cloth of virtuous living. The mind was tied to the 'earth' or physical world with the gross pegs of attachments and outward bonds; now the sublime pegs of spiritual inclinations hold the 'earth'—mind's inward inclination has completely overcome its earlier outward attachments and downward tendencies. Cravings and hopes (*mansa* and *asa*) have given way to love and surrender, which are the warp and weft that control the mind, and now mind itself urges the disciple to weave the cloth of spiritual practice with devotion and concentration.

Concluding the poem, Kabir says that all this has been achieved with the Master's grace; and mind, which swollen with ego was as huge as an elephant, has now become humble and small and easily goes and comes back through the needle's eye—the eye center—on its journey to the inner spiritual regions.

> The wave of knowledge surges, O friend,
> Producing strains of sweet melody;
> I merged in the boundless Shabd
> And thus wiped out the stain
> Of desires and cravings.
>
> The vagrant rabbit of the wild woods
> Has made the ocean its abode;
> The lively fish of the seas
> Has made the mountain peaks its home.
> The base one has devoured liquor,
> But the noble one has become intoxicated.
> Without an orchard, without a tree
> Grows a fruit of rare delicacy.

The loom's paddle sits on the weaver
And weaves the cloth;
The ground is fastened
To the loom's pegs;
The warp and weft hold the frame,
And the yarn itself urges:
'Weave me, weave me well, O friend.'

Says Kabir: Hearken, O sages,
On the path of supreme knowledge,
By my Master's grace
The elephant comes and goes
Through the needle's eye.

K.G., p.72:10
Avadhu gyān lahari dhuni māndi re

FUTILE PURSUITS

Saints value the path of spiritual practice and experience, not that of talking, listening and professing. Kabir says that mere talking about the path of spirituality and the inner worlds will not lead the devotee to God-realization. He has to practice, he has actually to tread upon the inner path and experience the bliss of divine love. In the following two poems, Kabir rejects external observances, rituals and ceremonies, calling them vain and misguided practices. The mind is infested with passions and cravings, which will only be overcome if the devotee goes within, enjoys inner bliss and develops true love for the Lord.

All talk, all assertion,
Is confusion, a trap;
The Lord and love for Him
Are unique, beyond words.

Men talk, they profess, they hear,
But nothing is achieved by talking;
Practice alone bears fruit.
Through evil actions,
Through false and misguided practices,
Never can the Lord be met.
He who is steadfast in truth,
Who adopts the right practice,
To Him the Lord reveals His true form.
  All talk, all assertion,
  Is confusion, a trap;
  The Lord and love for Him
  Are unique, beyond words.
Your body's home is afire
With cravings and passions,
But within the home also exists
The reservoir of love and grace;
Become aware of it
And quench the raging flames,
Says Kabir, the Lord's slave.

All talk, all assertion,
Is confusion, a trap;
The Lord and love for Him
Are unique, beyond words.

K.G., p.117:201
Kathni badni sab janjāl

Without devotion to the Lord
All your practices are an illusion;
Although with zeal you indulge in them,
It's all in vain, you ignorant fool.

Vain are your penances,
Vain your austerities,
Vain what you deem
Your vast knowledge;
Without the Lord's Name,
Vain are your meditations;
Your contemplations, vain.

Vain your rites and rituals,
Vain your adorations,
Vain your do's and dont's;
They plunge you into the depths
Of the sea of delusion,
They will never let you reach
The shores of bliss and peace.

Men crave sense pleasures,
They always rush to satisfy
The palate of their mind;
But where truth is taught they raise doubts
And indulge in endless arguments.

Kabir the slave is absorbed
In the love of his Lord;
He has dispelled all delusions,
He has given up all vain pursuits.

*K.G., p.129:252
Hari bin jhoote sab byohār*

483

THE DISCIPLE'S YEARNING

This poem depicts the disciple's love for the Master. The Master's real form is the Name or Shabd, and this unity of the two has been brought out by Kabir when he identifies the disciple's love for the Name with his love for the Master.

I am smitten with the love of your Name;
Not for a moment can I forget it.

Bless me with one kind look of love;
Beloved Master, pray meet me.
  I am smitten, my Master,
  With the love of your Name.
Separation ceaselessly torments me,
My heart aches in agony;
I yearn for just one glimpse of you,
Dear lord, hasten to meet me.
  I am smitten, my Master,
  With the love of your Name.
My eyes thirst for your darshan,
Not for a moment do they rest.
Afflicted with longing for you,
I am without sleep, day and night.
  I am smitten, my Master,
  With the love of your Name.
This time if the Beloved comes,
Not for a moment will I let him part;
Kabir has met his Master,
The beloved of his heart.
  I am smitten, O Master,
  With the love of your Name.

K.S., II:64:6
Preet lagi tum nām ki

WHY ADORNMENTS?

In this poem Kabir takes the example of a wife who adorns herself with ornaments and tries to beautify herself with collyrium, rouge and rich clothes in order to draw the admiring attention of her neighbors; but devoid of the inner qualities of love, faithfulness and purity, she fails to win her own husband's love. The wife here is the devotee, the neighbor is the world and the husband, the Lord. The devotee who gives importance to the world and worldly opinions puts on the mask of piety and benevolence, undertakes external forms of worship and wins the admiration of the world. Kabir says that such a devotee, even if he earns the esteem of the entire world, will not gain the boon of the Beloved's love, for outward show, external practices and semblance of holiness do not please the Lord. He is pleased only with the qualities of the heart—faithfulness, one-pointed devotion, humility and love.

What if you fascinate your neighbor,
When you fail to entrance your own Beloved?

Why parade bangles and anklets
Inlaid with gold and jewels,
Why prance with toe rings that tinkle and shine,
If you fail to win your Husband's heart?

Why beautify your eyes with collyrium,
Why display the mark of vermilion,
Why use the sixteen adornments,[1]
If you fail to enchant your Beloved?

Why apply rouge and mascara,
Why wear rich garments and flaunt your beauty
To impress and beguile others,
If through love you fail to win
Your Husband's one look of approval?

---

1. The sixteen *shringār*. In ancient India, woman used various methods for beautifying themselves, such as applying collyrium to the eyes, a vermilion dot on the forehead, wearing beautiful clothes, jewelry, perfume, etc. These have traditionally been classified as 'the sixteen adornments'.

Why all these feminine wiles
To attract others, O senseless woman?
You may fascinate your neighbor,
But what use, if you please not your Husband?

If the wife is devoted to her Husband,
If she adores Him with all her heart,
Be she bejeweled, be she plain,
She is dear to her beloved Lord.

The wife who loves Him,
Loves Him with body, mind and soul.
Who surrenders her entire being
At the Beloved's feet,
Such a wife, O Kabir,
Is the truly fortunate one,
For she enjoys everlasting union
With her Husband, her Lord.

K.G., p.100:139
Jau pai piyā ke mani nahi bhāye

486

MULTIPLICITY

Soul in essence is the same as God, all souls being drops of the same Ocean. But when the souls originally came into the world, each one was given a different body. Thus the diversity of form, shape and color came into being. Kabir says that all souls are still the same, and tells the seeker to give up his illusion of diversity and realize that the One God pervades all.

> The Lord and the swan
> Are in essence the same;
> The physical covering
> Makes a swan differ
> From other swans.
>
> From the same clay
> The potter produces
> A multiplicity,
> In many colors,
> In many forms.
>
> Milk ten cows
> Of five different colors
> And their milk
> Will be the same.
>
> Says Kabir: O man,
> Set aside thy delusion;
> Know that the One,
> The Lord of all,
> Fills every vessel.
>
> The physical covering
> Makes a swan differ
> From other swans;
> But the Lord and the swan
> Are in essence the same.

K.G., p.82:53
Soham hansā ek samān

487

LONELY NIGHTS

The soul pining for the Lord is mostly represented by Saints as a loving wife longing to meet her absent husband. The spiritual longing and pain of the soul is also reflected on the physical level—in the form of agony, sleepless nights, restless days, aching eyes and a burning heart. In this poem Kabir depicts the soul's yearning in separation and prays to the Lord to end it by granting union with Him.

When will my yearning eyes
Behold you, beloved Lord?
Without seeing you
My entire being ails
With the agony of separation.
    When will my yearning eyes
    Behold you, beloved Lord?
I gaze and gaze at the path
For you to come;
Lord, are you not aware
Of my heart's innermost sighs?
And yet you are not moved to come.
    When, oh when, beloved Lord,
    Will my yearning eyes see you?
As a fish tosses in anguish
When parted from water,
So writhes my heart
Without you, dear Lord.
    When, oh when, beloved Lord,
    Will my yearning eyes see you?
Without you,
Neither the dreary hours of the day
Nor the lonely watches of the night
Allow sleep to soothe my aching eyes.
How can the pining wife
Who thirsts only for your darshan
Find solace elsewhere?

When, oh when, beloved Lord,
    Will my yearning eyes see you?
Prays Kabir: Delay not,
Delay not, my Lord;
Remember, I belong only to you,
And bless me with union.
    Let my yearning eyes
    Behold you, beloved Lord!

K.G., p.122:224
Kab dekhon mere rām sanehi

REMOVE THE VEIL

This is a realized soul's advice to a soul who is still struggling on the path, torn between the desire to meet the Lord and pride in wealth, youth and beauty; between her love for the Beloved and hesitation before others' opinions. Kabir, in the words of the attained soul, asks the devotee to give up the obstacles of ego and worldliness, remove the veil at the eye center which is keeping him away from the inner spiritual realms of bliss, light the lamp of love within and see the Beloved face to face. But as long as the disciple keeps his face turned towards the world, towards the nine portals of the body and away from the eye center, he is like the bride who, in the presence of her husband, hides her face behind a veil—and so cannot see him.

Remove your veil, O bashful bride,
That your Beloved you meet;
Do not hide your face from your love,
Remove your veil, O bashful bride.

Utter not harsh words,
For in each heart God resides;
Be not proud of wealth and youth,
False is your garment of five hues.[1]
Remove the veil, O bashful bride,
That your Beloved you meet.

In the nuptial chamber of Sunn[2]
Light the lamp of love with joy;
Let nothing ever sway you
From the resolve to meet Him, O bride.
Do not hide your face from your love,
Remove the veil, O bashful bride.

Through love and concentration
My precious Lord I have met
In the chamber of bliss inside;

---

1. The human body, made out of five elements.
2. Here Kabir refers to the region beyond mind and maya.

Do not hide your face from your love,
Remove the veil, O bashful bride.

Kabir floats in waves of bliss,
To the divine melody's sweet strains;
Your veil before the Lord is vain,
Hide not your face from your love.
Remove the veil, O bashful bride,
That your Beloved you meet.

K.S., II:73
Ghunghat kā pat khol re

BLISS OF SAHAJ

Self-realization is an essential step towards God-realization. Kabir says that when the devotee goes to the eye center and enters the inner spiritual planes he gains self-knowledge, and the dark night of delusion and ignorance vanishes in the presence of the sun of realization. The devotee enters the inner regions, his soul is filled with the nectar of bliss and his mind becomes pure. The soul, soaring to great spiritual heights, merges in the Lord. Kabir says that this state of Sahaj is attained through the mercy and grace of the Master. Now the soul has reached the state of everlasting repose and its coming and going into the world has ended.

> Now I have attained, O friend,
> I have attained supreme knowledge;
> I am absorbed in the bliss of Sahaj,
> I have earned eternal repose.
>
> When my compassionate Master
> Took mercy on me,
> The lotus of my heart blossomed;[1]
> The darkness of delusion vanished
> And in the dazzling light within,
> All directions stand revealed to me.[2]
>> Absorbed in the bliss of Sahaj,
>> I live in eternal repose.
>
> The hunted victim has risen
> With bow and arrows in hand
> And Kal, the ruthless huntsman,
> Has fled in fear.
>
> When I arose
> From my slumber of eons,
> The sun appeared at its zenith,
> Night fled and hid under the horizon.

---

1. The Saints describe the eye center as the heart; here Kabir says that with the Master's grace his inner eye opened and he reached the eye center.
2. All barriers to knowledge removed, the devotee knows the mystery of the entire creation. These lines could also be translated: 'And in all directions I see His supreme light'.

The Unfathomable,
The Indivisible,
The Peerless One,
I saw.
I try to describe Him
But I am silent
Like the dumb man
Who tries to describe
With empty gestures
The taste of a sweet;
He fails, yet he enjoys
The sweetness in his heart.
    Absorbed in the bliss of Sahaj
    I live in eternal repose.

Without flowers the tree
Bursts into bloom;
Without hands the drum
Is being played;
Without a village girl the pitcher
Is filled to the brim;[1]
That state of Sahaj
I have attained.

In moments my entire being
From raw nugget
Turned into pure gold,
And without pleading or persuasion
My mind became calm and still.

The bird[2] has soared to such heights
That its whereabouts no one knows;
It has merged in Him
As a drop merges in water.

---

1. A reference to the inner regions where the disciple hears the melody of Shabd and also sees its light sparkling like flowers; the sound comes from the highest region and is not produced by any instrument or musician, the light also has no physical source. Here the pitcher of the soul is filled with the nectar of divine bliss.
2. The soul.

Many deities I worshipped,
Never again will I bow to them;
Numerous baths I took in holy rivers,
Never will I go for such baths again.
Through devotion to the One
My delusion has faded away;
Countless trips to the world
I had to take,
Now I will not come again.
   Absorbed in the bliss of Sahaj
   I live in eternal repose.

When I sought within my body
I realized my true self;
By contemplating within
I realized the Lord's true identity.
By knowing my self, I became lost
In the bliss of divine love,
And then of its own accord
My self merged into Him.

Who contemplates within
Will know his own self;
No longer, O Kabir,
Will he come and go.

K.G., p.71:6
Ab main pāibo re

494

A WARNING

Kabir, like all other Saints, warns man of the transient nature of the world and its relationships. The human body is subject to disease and death. Man lavishes it with care, feels proud of it and does everything possible to preserve it, but cannot avoid its inevitable fate.

> Why be proud of your body—
> A body that is fickle and false;
> When death overtakes it,
> It is not allowed to remain
> In its own home a moment longer.[1]

> With milk and sugar,
> With butter and cheese,
> You nurture the body with care;
> When life departs, that same body
> Is cast out from the house
> And consigned to flames.

> The body, once cosseted
> With creams and perfumes,
> Will one day
> Burn on the pyre
> In the company of logs of wood.

> Thus does Kabir the slave ruminate:
> One day this will also be my fate.

K.G., p.91:93
Jhoote tan ko kahā garbaiye

> Deem not your mansion[2] beautiful.
> You may adorn the palace
> With gold and jewels,

---

1. In India the body of the deceased is not kept in the home for long; it is usually cremated within a few hours of death.
2. The human body.

But without repitition
Of the Lord's Name
It is a heap of dust.
   Deem not your mansion beautiful.
Its tawdry glitter has lured
The minds of one and all;
No one can gain
Peace and joy in it.
Mighty kings and emperors,
Great chiefs and rulers,
All in the end turned to dust.
   Deem not your mansion beautiful.
Pure and sublime
Is the company of Saints,
Where flock true devotees of the Lord.[1]
Free from all worldliness
They sing His praises
And remain content
Even with a piece of dry bread.
In the Saints' company adore Him,
Adore Him who is the essence of all,
And thus sever your ties with Yama.
   Deem not your mansion beautiful.
Only a rare valiant one, O Kabir,
Takes to the path of divine love.

K.G., p.89:85
Grihi jini jānau roorau re

In the same warning tone, Kabir says in this third poem that since the body does not remain with us after death, how can the objects of the world, which become ours through the body, continue to belong to us? All friends and relations gather round us for their own selfish ends; they come in contact with us to fulfill previous karmic obligations, and when the obligations are over, either they leave us or we leave them. Kabir calls this world a daily market that winds up in the evening, where we undertake the transactions of giving and taking according to our karmas. We should realize the real nature of things and adopt that path which will enable us to become free from physical bonds forever.

---

1. Some scholars have interpreted this line: 'It is the ferry that carries the true devotees across'.

'Mine, oh mine,' says everyone;
They all try to own the world,
But only involve themselves
In attachment and jealousy
And come into a body again and again.
Monks and monarchs of old
And men of might would say,
'Mine, oh mine'—and pass away.

What is mum, what is dad,
What is son, what is spouse?
The world is a daily market;
Only a devotee of God
Knows this reality.
    Monks and men of might would say,
    'Mine, oh mine'—and pass away.

I am an alien, who can I call on,
Who is mine in this foreign land?
I have explored the entire world;
Other than you, O Lord, there is no one
Whose help I can depend upon.
    Monks and men of might would say,
    'Mine, oh mine'—and pass away.

Those who eat meat sanctioned
By the decree of scripture,
And deem it a virtue
To avoid meat that is forbidden,[1]
How can they gain a place in heaven?
They know not the secret
Of the five elements,[2]

---

1. In certain religious communities, eating the meat of certain animals is forbidden, while that of other animals is permitted.
2. A reference to the five *tattwa* or elements present in every living being, and the karmic load incurred by killing. Vegetables have one active element (water), insects have two (air and fire), birds have three (water, air and fire), higher animals have four (earth, water, air and fire), and man has five (earth, air, water, fire and ether). The larger the number of active elements a living entity has, the higher it is in the scale of evolution and the greater is the onus involved in killing it. The Saints say that one should try to incur the least possible karmic load and therefore enjoin a completely vegetarian diet on their disciples.

They'll be cast into the dungeons of hell.
   Monks and men of might would say,
   'Mine, oh mine'—and pass away.

For the sake of your kith and kin
You perform devious deeds, you sin;
You think they belong to you,
And say, 'They are mine, they are mine.'
For their own selfish ends
They crowd around you;
No one is yours, O friend.
   Monks and men of might would say,
   'Mine, oh mine'—and pass away.

Follow the course
That will take you across
The dreadful ocean;
Live in the world
But do not harm anyone
Because, says Kabir,
For all that you do
You will have to answer
To the Lord, your Husband.
   Monks and men of might would say,
   'Mine, oh mine'—and pass away.

K.G., p.92:102
Meri meri duniyā karte

INFLUENCE OF COMPANY

The main pursuits of man in this world are health, wealth and possessions. Deeply involved in them, he has neither the time nor the inclination to strive for spiritual wealth and inner peace. He pays no heed to the advice and warnings of the Saints and wastes the chance of his human birth. Kabir says that the disciple who lives according to the directions of a Saint or Master gains true devotion and love for the Lord and becomes worthy of admittance to His treasury. Those who want to succeed on the touchstone of the world are living in delusion and will continue to do so, for winning the esteem of worldly people does not entitle one to entry into the Lord's court.

Men take great pains to preserve
Their health, possessions and wealth;
In multifarious ways their mind
Remains involved in them.
Even if I exhort them a hundred times,
They do not give up their ways.

He who abides within the words
Of the Lord's slave[1]
Gains all powers, all boons
That men strive for.[2]
Devotion takes abode in his heart;
He puts himself on the Lord's touchstone:
He is tested and made whole.
But he who goes elsewhere to be tested
Is a fool, he continues to revel
In his own foolishness.
    The deadly noose of Kal
        Tautens around your neck;
    It is time you thought of release.

---

1. The Saint.
2. The reference is to the nine *nidhi* or treasures of Kuber, the lord of wealth, and the eight *siddhi* or psychic powers. All these powers, which yogis and ascetics strive to gain, automatically come to the true devotee. The disciples of the Saints, however, neither use these powers nor are they conscious of their presence.

In the company of Saints
Men become divine like the Saints,
But in the company of the vile
Men become vile and mean.

Bijak, Ramaini 64
Kāyā kanchan yatan karāyā

Rare are the friends of Kabir, O brother;
To whom can he reveal the Truth?

Live cheerfully as and how the Lord
In his wisdom deigns to keep you,
For he has the power to create,
To destroy and to sustain one and all.
I thoroughly scanned the entire world;
I realized: Without knowledge of God
All knowledge is ignorance.
The six philosophies,
The ninety-six rituals[1]
Know not the One—
The One who has no lineage.

Engaging themselves in chanting,
In austerities and penance,
In worship and obeisance,
In the appeasement of stars,[2]
People have added
To their own bewilderment.
They scrawl roll after roll of paper;
Juggling with words,
They delude the world,
But never does their mind go within
To merge in the universal mind.

---

1. The ninety-six rituals detailed in the scriptures.
2. Kabir uses the word *jotig*, 'astrology', but the reference seems to be to the various rituals and worship performed under the direction of pundits to counteract unfavorable aspects in one's horoscope.

Says Kabir: The yogis, the jangams,[1]
All toil in the vain hope of salvation.
Repeat the Name blessed by the Master;
Repeat with the ardor of the rainbird
Wailing in thirst for the rain;
Then will your devotion be fruitful,
Then the everlasting abode you will gain.

K.G., p.77:34
Bhāi re birle dost kabir ke

---

1. A school of Indian ascetics.

WHAT IS TRUTH?

This poem, in the form of a dialogue between mind and soul, explains what are wisdom and folly, happiness and misery, friend and foe, truth and falsehood, and similar questions that may at times confront a seeker. Through the answers, Kabir gives the Saints' point of view on these questions and urges the seeker to judge these things from the higher objective of his ultimate spiritual goal.

Listen, my mind, you are
The storehouse of intelligence,
Ponder on what I ask you
And let me have your answer.

Who is wise, who is insane?
What actions lead to misery,
What actions bring misery to an end?
What is the source of happiness,
What is the cause of pain?
What is of benefit, what entails harm?
What is fruitful, what is vain?
Who is foe, who is friend?
What is truth, what is falsehood?
What is bitter, what is sweet?
Who burns in agony, who basks in joy?
Who is free from bondage,
Who has the noose around his neck?
  Tell me, my mind,
    Tell me the truth,
  For doubts like thorns
    Are hurting me, says Kabir.

O swan, think carefully on what I tell you.
The three worlds, the myriad species,
All dwell and suffer in darkness.
He is wise who values

The rare chance of human birth
And tries to realize the Lord;
He surely is insane
Who heedlessly wastes
The gift of the human form
And repents when it is dawn.[1]

Devotion is the source of happiness,
Without devotion all is pain;
The Lord's love is the only nectar,
All else is a heap of poison.

To be absorbed in God
Alone is beneficial,
All other pursuits
Lead to sorrow and harm.

Company of the realized
Is fruitful,
Company of others
Is futile and vain.
The entire world is an enemy,
Only he who loves the Lord
Is your friend.

Truth is that
Which is immutable and permanent;
What comes and goes,
What changes and perishes,
Is false.

Sweet is that which is gained
Through Sahaj,
Bitter is that which comes
Through suppression and strain.[2]

---

1. Kabir compares life in the world to a night's stay in an inn, which is left at daybreak.
2. Kabir seems to be referring here to the paths of hatha yoga, *pranayam*, austerities, penances, etc., which are arduous and fraught with danger. The path of Shabd Yoga is also known as the path of Sahaj.

He does not burn in agony
Who gives up 'me' and 'mine',
But basks in bliss,
Trusting in the Lord,
Seeking only his pleasure.

He, indeed, is free
Who realizes his true self
And knows what is alien;
What do they know of liberation
Who still revolve in delusion?

The Lord is the support
Of the entire world,
He is dearer to me
Than my own life;
Love for Him I cherish
As the rarest of all treasures;
To live for sons and wealth,
For belongings and health,
O Kabir, is to be like the bird
Which during one night's stay
Starts loving the tree.

K.G., p.176:6,7
Re re man budhiwant bhandārā

THE TALONS OF DELUSION

The human mind always runs after sense pleasures, justifying its pursuits by calling them 'small' or 'innocent' pleasures. But Saints warn the devotee to be wary of them, for one indulgence leads to another, the small pleasures become an obsession and thus the cause of the further misery of births and deaths. Kabir urges the devotee to give up his attachment to the objects and pleasures of the world which, being transient, only lead to sorrow and frustration. The world, caught in the delusion of maya, fails to realize that all relationships, all pleasures and possessions, are perishable, a fraud practiced by the negative power to keep man bound by the chain of transmigration.

> Small pleasures in the beginning
> Turn into pain in the end,
> Yet mind revels in them
> Like a rogue elephant.
> Indifferent to true happiness,
> How can man attain salvation?
> He forsakes the truth
> And runs after the false.
> The raging fire of desire
> Consumes one and all;
> To gratify the hunger of its eyes
> The moth rushes into the flame.
> Ponder and act with wisdom
> That all your troubles may end:
> Give up your infatuation
> For what is fleeting and false.
> Swayed by cravings, you are wasting
> This precious chance of human birth;
> Old age and death are coming,
> Each moment drawing closer.
> Caught in the talons of delusion
> The world continues to come and go;
> You are blessed with the human birth,
> O man, why deceive yourself?

> *Bijak, Ramaini 23*
> *Alp sukh dukh ādi o antā*

505

Look, look at the folly of men:
They neglect the roots
And water the stem.
The One who is free from all bonds,
Who himself resides in the body,
They pay no heed to Him
And go to worship stones.
　　Look at the folly of men!
　　They neglect the roots
　　And water the stem.
They wash stone idols
And drink that water
As a blessing from their gods—
Gods which were 'born' from stone
And which will in the end
Become a heap of rubble.
　　Look at the folly of men:
　　They neglect the roots
　　And water the stem.
He whose head is beyond
All the firmaments,
Whose feet go past
The farthest underworlds,
How can that Mighty Lord
Ever be contained
In your caskets of gold?[1]
He who is invisible,
Who has not a trace
Of maya and attachment,
How can you expect Him to live
On the delicacies you offer?[2]
　　Look at the folly of men:
　　They neglect the roots
　　And water the stem!

---

1. Some people make small idols of their deities and carry them in caskets made of gold or silver.
2. A variety of sweets and fruits are offered to the idols; some worshippers believe that if they forget to offer the sweets, their deity will remain hungry.

Again and again I call,
But men pay no attention
To my message of Shabd;
They only argue,
They resent what I say.
  Look at the folly of men:
  They neglect the roots
  And water the stem.
Says Kabir: Men do not try
To search for Truth;
They wander and die
Like a meandering doe.[1]

Satt Kabir, Basant 3
Dekho dekho re yā nar ki bhool

---

1. The reference is to a large type of deer called *roz* or *neelgāi* which keeps constant company with its mate. Sometimes, in a moment of stress or fear they are parted, and it is believed that the doe runs about in confusion looking for the stag.

THE LAMP OF NAM

Kabir tells the seeker to light the lamp of Nam in order to perceive the Lord within himself. Once the seeker attains God-realization, the 'lamp' of Nam will merge along with the soul into the Lord. At this stage the soul, Nam, and God, which are in essence the same, become one. The dirt of ego, karmas, and past impressions or *sanskaras* have blurred the mirror of the soul. The seeker has to clean the mirror through spiritual practice and realize the Lord. Kabir says that whatever he has learned and realized is not through reading and intellectual analysis but through the path of Surat Shabd Yoga, the path of Sahaj.

> Why not repeat the Lord's Name,
> O fatuous one,
> Why keep dwelling on worldly things?
>
> Five thieves hide within your fort,
> Day and night they pilfer the vaults;
> If the fort's chief is alert and firm,
> Who dare rob him of his wealth?
>
> In the dismal darkness of ignorance
> One needs the lamp
> To find the imperceptible jewel;
> Once the Imperceptible is found,
> The lamp merges and stays merged in it.
>
> If you long to see the Lord within,
> Scour the mirror, keep it clean;
> If the mirror is covered with dirt
> You'll not have one glimpse of the Lord.
>
> What is there to read,
> What is there to ponder on?
> Why listen to recitals from holy books?
> What men seek through reading and pondering,
> I have attained through the path of Sahaj.

Says Kabir: I have realized the Truth;
I have realized, and my mind is at rest.
What can one do with such obstinate fools
Who trust not the evidence
Of the realized ones?

K.G., p.132:262
Hari kā nāu na lehi gawārā

THE OCEAN, A HOOFPRINT

Kabir says that the company of the Saints and the practice of Nam is the only way out of the miseries of existence in this transient world of matter. The practice of Nam helps the devotee to overcome his passions and desires and enables him to go through the hardships of life with patience and fortitude. It also serves as the means to attain self-realization and God-realization and makes the devotee one with the Lord.

Do only that, my friend,
Which will end your misery.
Give up your flirtation
With sense pleasures.
The world is burning in the blaze
Of cravings and attachments;
What will you gain
By plunging into the flames
To be consumed like the rest?
Protect yourself from the blaze,
Let your soul cry in agony:
'Mercy, mercy, dear Lord, mercy!'
Go to the company of the Saints
And contemplate with them
On the truth.

Friends, my friends,
There is no respite
In this world of anguish;
The Lord's Name is the only
Destroyer of all pain,
The Lord's Name is the only
Succor that will sustain
You in this vale of misery,
The Lord's Name is the only
Ship that will take you across
The world's turbulent sea.

Man hears and recites the scriptures,
    But these pursuits are a waste;
Earrings and ornaments
    Do not make a woman beautiful
If she is devoid of charm and grace.[1]

Firmly grasp the Lord's Name,
Supreme and everlasting.
If you forsake the Lord
Where else will you go?
Go where you will,
You will be consumed like a moth
In the flame of passions.
Sense pleasures are poison;
Realize it, my friend,
Don't be burned by them.

He who adorns himself
With the jewel
Of God's immaculate Name
Is never again separated
From the Lord;
He becomes the Lord
As the worm becomes a wasp
Under the spell of the mason wasp.

Shoreless, unfathomable, vast
Is the dreadful ocean of this world;
Take measures to be ferried
To the banks of bliss.
The labyrinthine currents
Of cravings and passions
Captivate and confuse the mind;
Through their swirling tides
One finds no way
To steer homewards.

---

1. External practices, like ornaments on a woman, do not give real beauty; it is the charm and grace of inner spiritual attainment that is of value.

The ocean of existence
  Is dark and abysmal;
Man's only succor
  Is the boat of God's Name.
Says Kabir: When I took
  The shelter of my Lord,
The ocean became
A hoofprint in the mud,
Filled with rain.[1]

K.G., p.173:6,7
Soi upāv kari yahu dukh jāi

---

1. In rural India hoofprints are a common sight. During the monsoon the cows' hoofs make hollow prints in the mud and when it rains, water fills them. Indian Saints often use this image to convey that through devotion and the Lord's grace, the vast ocean of phenomena becomes insignificant and the devotee crosses it as simply as one steps across the print of a cow's hoof.

WHICH IS GREATER?

Through a series of questions, Kabir conveys that the Lord, the One Supreme Being, is greater than Kal, the negative power, who created the physical, astral and causal worlds, because Kal was created by the Lord and is subordinate to Him. The source of all knowledge, God, is greater than all the knowledge that one can acquire in this world. Further, the devotee who goes within, crosses the regions of mind and maya and learns the truth about Kal is greater than Kal because such a devotee goes beyond the three worlds, overcomes the obstacles laid down by the negative power and enters the divine regions of pure spirit. In the end, Kabir says that the true lovers of the Lord—the Saints—are greater than all the places of pilgrimage because their company is truly elevating and purifying.

O Lord, if you feel concern
For this slave of yours,
Pray solve this problem for me:
Is the creator of the world greater
Or the One who created him?
Is knowledge greater, O Lord,
Or the source of all knowledge?
Is this mind greater
Or the place where mind
Finds lasting rest?
Is the lord of the three worlds greater,
Or the one who knows him?[1]

Kabir is perplexed!
Are holy places greater,
Or Thy slaves and lovers, O Lord?

K.G., p.76:27
Jhagrā ek nabero rām

---

1. The Saint or God-realized soul, having gone beyond Kal and his realm of the three worlds, is "the one who knows him."

SOOTHING COMPANY OF SAINTS

The devotee, longing to meet the Lord, turns from one school of philosophy to another, from one form of worship to another, but fails to attain his goal. Like the loving wife parted from her husband, the devotee suffers the pangs of separation from the Beloved, but finds no one who can end his misery by leading him to the Lord. Applying sandalwood paste and trying other methods to alleviate the fever of longing prove futile; in other words, different forms of worship fail to end his agony of separation. But Kabir, concluding the poem, suggests the way: the company of the Saint will give the devotee solace through the practice of Shabd Yoga, also known as the path of Sahaj; by undertaking this method of true worship, he will attain his objective of union with Him.

With my heart plunged in gloom
From place to place I roam,
For I fear my store of breaths
Might drain away
Without my meeting the Lord;
Day after day my hopes dwindle
And my heart remains plunged in gloom.

Wherever I go in quest of Him,
Whatever means I adopt,
They lead me not to the Lord.
Tell me, O friends,
How can I stay alive?
My body burns
With the fever of longing,
I find no one
Who can quell the flame;
Nights emerge burning hot
From the furnace of separation,
Sleep has become a distant dream,
And my heart sinks into gloom.

I make sandalwood paste,
I anoint my body
Repeatedly with the salve,
But without seeing my Beloved
I suffer unbearable pain
And my heart plunges into gloom.

Absorbing himself
In the company of Saints,
Kabir finds solace and relief;
He learns the way of Sahaj,
He worships the Lord.

K.G., p.95:115
Jiyarā merā phirai re udās

THE MASTER'S GIFT

When the Master bestows the gift of Nam on a disciple, all barriers to God-realization are removed. The Lord, described as imperceptible and unknowable, becomes perceptible and knowable for the disciple. Following the path of spiritual practice under the Master's directions, he goes within, travels through the inner regions and enjoys divine bliss. Kabir explains that this state is not attained through hands or feet, nor are the inner visions experienced through eyes or ears; the disciple enters these regions in his spiritual body and not in the physical one, sees with his spiritual eye and hears the Melody with his spiritual ear. Thus blessed by the Master, the disciple is indeed fortunate, for he is freed from the bondage of matter and attains the state of everlasting bliss.

> My Master in his mercy
> Gave me the rare gift
> Through which the Unknowable
> I have come to know.
>
> Without feet I walk,
> Without wings I fly,
> Without beak I peck
> The pearls of divine bliss;[1]
> Without eyes I see,
> Without ears I hear.
>   My Master in his mercy
>   Gave me such a rare gift
>   That the Unknowable
>   I have come to know.
> Where there is neither sun nor moon,
> Where there is neither day nor night,
> In that land now dwells my soul.
> Without food I eat,
> I feast on nectar divine;
> Without water my thirst is allayed.

---

1. *See* "The Swan."

My Master in his mercy
Gave me such a rare gift
That the Unknowable
I have come to know.
Here I now live in contentment,
There my joy is perfect and supreme;
To whom and how can I narrate
The state of my everlasting bliss?
My Master in his mercy
Gave me such a gift
That the Unknowable
I have come to know.
Says Kabir: My entire being
I sacrifice at my Master's feet;
And I marvel again and again
At this disciple's good fortune.

K.S., II:21
Satguru soi dayā kari dinhā

517

THE NECKLACE

When an Indian bride first steps into the house of her in-laws, her mother-in-law asks the bridegroom to present her with a necklace as a token of love and welcome. In this poem, the bride is the devotee who, through spiritual practice, has gone within and met the radiant form of the Master. Devotion is the mother-in-law, through whose suggestion the Master gives the soul-bride the precious necklace of love and surrender. In other words, only on going within, entering the gateway of the inner mansion and meeting the radiant form of the Master does the disciple obtain the blessing of true love and surrender.

Kabir stresses the importance of preserving this rare gift of love through the example of the bride who is deprived of the necklace. The bride in a moment of weakness is swayed by five friends—the five senses—and sinks to the pleasures connected with the three attributes. As a result, the newly acquired gift is lost. The bride bathes in the currents of the three *gunas,* and when looking in the mirror to apply the auspicious mark of vermilion to her forehead, she discovers that the necklace has been stolen by one of her friends. The devotee succumbs to the pleasures of the senses, and when he tries to concentrate at the eye center he realizes that he has lost the gift of love that is essential for going within.

Kabir also brings out two important aspects of Sant Mat. First, the mother-in-law, devotion, is strict—implying that the path of devotion has to be followed with firmness and that no compromises are permissible. Second, the soul-bride loves her husband but at the same time fears him. Fear is an important, even essential part of divine love and cannot be separated from it. It is not fear of punishment, but fear of offending the one whom the devotee loves.

Concluding the poem, Kabir prays to the Lord to have mercy, forgive the erring soul and enable her to regain her lost treasure.

I have lost my necklace, O friend,
I am sad, I feel ashamed;
My mother-in-law is strict,
And I love yet fear my husband.
I have lost my necklace, O friend.

The string of the Lord's Name
Threaded and held my necklace;
It was studded with rubies
Rich with roseate tints—

Rubies of love and submission;
It was interspersed with jewels—
Jewels that scintillated
With the warmth of devotion.
Between the jewels were pearls
Pure and sparkling as snow—
Pearls aglow with true knowledge.
  I have lost that necklace, O friend,
  I am sad, I feel ashamed;
  My mother-in-law is strict,
  And I love yet fear my husband.
My five friends prevailed upon me
To accompany them for a bath
At the confluence of the three streams.[1]
There we bathed and played,
And as I put the vermilion mark
On my forehead
I was stunned:
My necklace was gone!
I felt forlorn and ashamed.
I wondered who could have taken
My precious wealth.
  I have lost my necklace, O friend,
  I am sad, I feel ashamed,
  For my mother-in-law is strict
  And I fear my beloved husband.
I have lost my necklace,
I am helpless, I am sad;
Deep is my despair.
I suspect my neighbor is the one
Who stole my necklace so cleverly.
  My treasure is lost, I feel ashamed;
  My mother-in-law is strict
  And I fear my beloved husband.
  I have lost my necklace, O friend.

---

1. All worldly pleasures are within the confines of the three attributes and the devotee has to transcend them in order to proceed inwards. The devotee who indulges in pleasures remains confined within the precincts of the three attributes.

O Kabir's Lord, you who are aware
Of the agony of the three worlds,
You who are the diadem of all—
Have mercy, allay my pain,
Let me my necklace regain!
    I have lost my necklace, O friend,
    I am sad, I feel ashamed;
    My mother-in-law is strict
    And I love yet fear my husband.
    I have lost my necklace, O friend.

K.G., p.161:378
Mero hār hirānou main lajāon

WITHOUT SEEING

It is a traditional belief of most of the religions that by verbal repetition of one of the many names of God one will gain salvation, or by merely reading and reciting scriptures and sacred hymns one can attain God-realization. Kabir says that hunger or thirst cannot be allayed by uttering the words 'food' or 'water'; a person has to actually eat food or drink water to satisfy his hunger and thirst. Similarly, a seeker has to learn the secret of the practice of Nam, undertake meditation and experience the spiritual truth within himself; mere reading or talking about these experiences will be of no avail.

Kabir also explains that a man cannot adore a prophet or holy man of the past, whom he has not seen or met or with whom he has not come in physical contact, because while man is in the physical world the object of his love and devotion has to be someone he can perceive with the physical senses. Thus Kabir points out the importance of a living Master who, though inwardly on the level of God, is accessible to the seeker on the physical level in the form of a man and can respond to his love and guide him on the path.

> O Pundit, all your sermons are lies.
> If by merely uttering 'Ram'
> The world could be emancipated,
> Then by repeating 'sugar'
> The mouth should be sweetened,
> By saying 'fire'
> One's feet should burn,
> By saying 'water'
> One's thirst should be quenched;
> If by repeating 'food'
> One's hunger were allayed,
> Then surely by saying 'Ram'
> The world would be emancipated.
>
> Trained by men, a parrot cries 'Hari, Hari',[1]
> But it knows nothing of Hari's lofty state;
> If it should ever escape to the forest
> It would no more remember Hari.

---

1. Hari is one of the names of God.

What purpose will be served
By merely uttering the name,
Without seeing, without feeling, without touching?
If by saying 'wealth' one could become rich,
Then no one would remain poor.

O Pundit, your real love
Is for worldly pleasures and riches,
And you ridicule the true devotees of the Lord.
Says Kabir: Without devotion to the One God
You will be bound and taken
To the city of Yama.[1]

Bijak, Shabd 40
Pandit bād badai so jhootā

---

1. Yama, the lord of death.

HOW LONG, O LORD?

This is a prayer of the restless devotee who, tired of the endless rounds of birth and death, longs to reach the Lord. Helpless over his own inadequacy either to please the Beloved or to make proper efforts to reach Him, the devotee prays to the Lord for mercy and help.

> Tell me, Lord, tell me
> How many days more
> Will I have to endure
> Before my soul
> Becomes one with Thee?
>
> Countless lives have I spent
> Tossing in this ocean of gloom;
> Not once did I get
> A glimpse of Thee, beloved Lord.
> Through my own doing,
> Through my own delusion,
> I drift in this dismal sea.
> I am helpless. O Thou Lord of all,
> I am too feeble to swim across.
> Prays Kabir: Lord, Thou art
> The destroyer of misery,
> The eradicator of sins,
> Have mercy, meet me, beloved Lord.
> Tell me, Lord, pray tell me,
> How much more must I endure
> Until I become one with Thee?

K.G., p.95:116
Rām kaho na ajahun kete dinā

523

NO CREDIT TO KASI

When Kabir decided to leave Banaras (Kasi) for the 'unholy' town of Magahar in order to spend his last days there, some disciples and many well-wishers tried to dissuade him from going. This poem, addressed to the Lord, is actually Kabir's reply to some of his orthodox well-wishers. The so-called holy men live in Banaras not for any spiritual ends, but only because of the reverence they receive from others and the material gains in the form of alms or gifts that they derive from their show of piety; or because of their superstition that those who daily bathe in the Ganges or who live and die in Banaras will gain salvation. Kabir, having realized the Lord and having attained the state of salvation while living, has scant regard for such beliefs.

Why should they leave Kasi, dear Lord,
Who have become thieves
Serving and worshipping you?

Yogis and anchorites,
Hermits and ascetics,
Sit in temples and monasteries
And profit from their stay in Kasi.
   Why should they leave Kasi, dear Lord?
Three times a day in Ganga they bathe
But are unaware of the dirt
That lies within their body.
From temple to temple they rove
But never dwell on the Lord's Name.
   Why should they leave Kasi, dear Lord?
What I have earned
At Thy lotus feet,
I'll not let Kasi
Be given its credit.
Thus, beloved Lord,
Will Kabir firmly declare;
For this, be he thrown
Into hell, he does not care.

K.G., p.139:290
Vai kyun kāsi tajai murāri

524

NO PLACE IS UNHOLY

Striking at the roots of the age-old belief in the sanctity of baths in holy waters and pilgrimages to holy places, Kabir says that people may be impressed by such outward practices of piety, but God, the all-knowing One, cannot be deceived by them. The worship of the One Supreme Being is the highest form of worship, and service of the Master is the true 'bath' that purifies the mind. Kabir says if a dip in a holy river entitles one to salvation, the frogs that live there should also be emancipated; but despite all holy baths, men continue to take birth in the world again and again.

It is a common belief among the orthodox Hindus that if one dies in the holy city of Banaras he will go straight to heaven, while the one who dies in the town of Magahar will either go to hell or be born as a donkey. Kabir points out that a cruel and hard-hearted man devoid of devotion may die in Banaras, yet he will not escape the fires of hell; on the other hand, a devotee of the Lord, a Saint, even if he dies in the 'unholy' town of Magahar, emancipates himself as well as the entire fold of his disciples.

When his end approached, Kabir deliberately left Banaras and went to Magahar. The following poems are Kabir's reply to some well-wishers who tried to dissuade him from his decision to leave Banaras.

If a man is unclean within,
By bathing at pilgrim places
He will not become pure and reach heaven.
Nothing will be gained by impressing people,
For the Lord is not ignorant or naive.
Adore the Lord, the only God,
And know: Service to the Master
Is the true holy bath.

If bathing and dipping in water
Could lead one to salvation,
What about the frogs
That bathe day after day?
Like frogs men bathe,
Like them they'll be cast
Into the womb again and again.

A hardened sinner
Will not escape the fires of hell
Even if he dies in Banaras;
But a Saint of God,
Even if he dies in Hadamba,[1]
Emancipates the entire fold
Of his disciples.

Where there is neither day nor night,
Neither Vedas nor scriptures,
There dwells the Formless Lord.
Says Kabir: O man,
Adore only that One,
Do not run after
This crazy world.

A.G., Asa, p.484
Antar mail je tirath nāvai

Brothers, you are simple and credulous:
If in Kasi, Kabir leaves the body,
Then what credit to his Lord's grace?

What I was once,
I am not now.
I have reaped the benefit
Of my precious human birth;
As water once mixed in water
Can never be taken apart,
So has this weaver flowed
And merged into the Lord.

One who is always absorbed
In God's love and devotion,
What is there to wonder at
When he attains this high state?

---

1. A name given out of derision to Magahar, a town in the Basti district of Uttar Pradesh, about 175 miles from Banaras.

Through the blessings of his Master,
Through the company of the Saints,
This weaver marches onwards,
He has conquered Kal's domains.

Says Kabir: Listen, friends,
Let no doubts remain—
He who has true faith in the Lord,
For him holy Kasi
And barren Magahar
Are the same.

K.G., p.167:402
Lokā mati ke bhorā re

I WILL NOT DIE

The devotee who meets a perfect Master—described in this poem as the giver of everlasting life—realizes the Lord and is no more required to come to the world and face death. Kabir says that such a devotee, through the guidance of the Master, becomes one with the Lord and, like the Lord, is free from the chains of birth and death. The *sakat,* or the man who hankers after worldly pleasures, who is cruel of heart and who is an abject slave of his own mind, dies again and again. The Saint, who has merged with the Ocean of bliss, is immortal.

The world dies, but I'll not die,
For I have met the giver
Of everlasting life.

I will not die any more,
For I've learned the secret of death.
Only those keep dying
Who have not realized the Lord.
The sakats die;
The Saints forever live,
For the elixir of the Lord's love
They drink, and drink to their fill.
   I'll not die, for I have met
   The giver of everlasting life.

If the Lord dies,
Then I will die too;
If the Lord knows no death,
Then how can I die?
O Kabir, I have merged my self
In the Lord's Supreme Self;
I have plunged into the Ocean of bliss,
I have become immortal.
   The world dies; I'll not die,
   For I have met the bestower
   Of everlasting life.

K.G., p.80:43
Ham na marain marihai sansārā

528

I AM NOT

Ego is the greatest obstacle in the way of God-realization. When the devotee eliminates I-ness and realizes the Lord, he becomes one with Him and then only the Lord exists for him. Erudition, ritualistic worship and external formalities, instead of leading the seeker to God-realization, only ensure further rounds in the cycle of birth and death. Kabir, concluding the poem with a paradox, says that having attained the state of 'dying while living', he is no more among the living because he is dead to the world and its attachments; and he is not among the dead because he is now fully alive to the spiritual life within himself.

> Now you alone exist, O Lord;
> You alone exist,
> I am not, I am not.
>
> The scholars in their quest for God
> Read books and scriptures;
> But through their pride of learning
> They journey towards perdition.
>
> So long as 'I', 'I', 'I',
> I kept saying,
> I could not recognize the Lord.
> But now, O Lord, you alone exist;
> I am not, I am not.
>
> Says Kabir: O the crown of all men,[1]
> Pray listen to my submission—
> I am no more amongst the living,
> Nor am I amongst the dead.
>
> Now the Lord alone is,
> I am not, I am not.

K.G., p.84:65
Ib tu hasi prabhu

---

1. Kabir here addresses the Master as the highest among men.

THE WEDDING

Saints have described God-realization as the soul's wedding, the happiest event in the soul's journey from species to species in the cycle of eighty-four. Kabir describes the joy of the soul's union with the divine bridegroom. The five virtues are the wedding party, and in the crystal lake of Mansarovar the wedding altar is erected; Brahma, the lord of creation, chants the Vedic hymns. The wedding is depicted by Kabir against a vast canvas; it has to be so, for the bridegroom is none other than Kabir's beloved Lord, the Supreme Being.

Sing, come sing, O happy brides,[1]
Wedding songs of joy and bliss.
My royal Bridegroom, the Lord himself,
Has come to my home today.
Sing, O brides, songs of joy and bliss!

I'll dye my body,
I'll steep my mind
In the color of his love.
The five virtues[2] will be
The wedding party.
The Lord has arrived
—My long awaited Guest—
And I am aflame
With the youth of my devotion.
   Sing, O brides, songs of joy and bliss;
   To my home has come my royal Bridegroom.
In the lake within my body
I'll set up the wedding altar;[3]

---

1. *Brides* here refers to married women, i.e., souls who have already attained the state of God-realization. Formerly, it was only the newly married women who sang the wedding songs at an Indian marriage; here the implication is that the realized souls are best qualified to sing the songs celebrating divine union.
2. Kabir uses the expression *panch tat,* which can also mean 'the five elements'; commenting on the Adi Granth version of this poem, some Sikh scholars—Professor Sahib Singh, Bhai Jodh Singh, M.A. Macauliffe—in view of the context of the poem, have appropriately interpreted it as 'the five virtues', namely truth, contentment, compassion, righteousness and discernment (*sat, santosh, daya, dharam, vivek*).
3. A well-decorated canopy or altar is essential in an orthodox Indian wedding. The lake is Mansarovar, in the inner spiritual region beyond the realm of Brahm, mind and maya.

Brahma himself will chant
Nuptial hymns from the Vedas.
I'll circle the altar
With my beloved Lord,[1]
And all the sages, gods and deities
Will look on in wonder.
I am indeed fortunate;
Unbounded is my joy.
   Sing, come sing, O happy brides,
   Wedding songs of joy and bliss.
The Everlasting One
Has wed me, O Kabir;
And He is taking me Home with Him.
   Sing, O brides, sing the songs
   Of joy and bliss,
   For today, my Husband,
   My beloved Lord,
   I meet!

K.G., p.69:1
Dulahani gāvahu mangalāchār

---

1. The wedding is considered complete only when the bridegroom and bride walk together around the wedding altar.

Selected
Couplets

The *doha, sakhi* or *salok*, termed here 'couplet',
is a two-line verse form popular with the
medieval Saints of India. The *doha* is a complete
poem in itself, each line divided into two parts,
separated by a short pause. Thus, the *doha* is a
quatrain in couplet form. In rendering these
'couplets' no rigid form has been adopted here
and the number of lines varies according to the
spirit and tone of the original.

PRAYER

With folded hands
    I pray to Thee,
Merciful Lord,
    Grant me the bliss
Of the Saints' company
    And the gift
Of a kind, loving heart.
K.S.S., p.96:1

If this time
    My Master I meet,
With tearful eyes
    My long tale of woe
To him I'll submit;
    With my head
Bowed at his feet
    I will try to convey
What my heart
    Ever longed to say.
K.S.S., p.96:2

Have mercy on my plight,
    O Master, I am tossing
In the turbulent sea;
    I will be swept away
By its stormy waves
    If you don't hold my arm
And rescue me.
K.S.S., p.96:4

With what face can I pray
    To you, O Lord?
My head hangs in shame,
    O All-knowing One—

In your very presence
    Again and again I sin;
How can I win
    Your mercy and grace?
                K.S.S., p.97:5

I have been a sinner
    From the day I was born,
My body's every pore
    Harbors wickedness;
Only you can cure me
    Of my evil ways,
Of my misery and pain;
    Redeem this sinner,
Dear Lord, I pray.
                K.S.S., p.97:7

My countless faults,
    O Father, forgive;
Though this son of yours
    Is an unworthy one,
Yet it is the father
    Who has to face
Disgrace for the deeds
    Of his wayward son.
                K.S.S., p.97:8

When it came to sinning,
    I committed countless sins,
Never did I tire
    Of doing misdeeds.
Now I am at your mercy, Lord—
    Chastise or forgive,
Do with me
    Whatever you please.
                K.S.S., p.97:9

I've lost the rare chance,
    Time is flying,
Body is becoming frail,
    And far, in some foreign land,
Lives my Beloved.
    Lord, remove
This stigma of separation;
    The shackles of delusion,
Break.

K.S.S., p.97:13

My beloved Lord,
    You who know every thought
Of my restless heart,
    You are the only
Succor and support
    Of my yearning soul;
If you forsake me,
    Who else can take me
To the shore beyond?

K.S.S., p.97:15

This ocean of dread
    Is deep and vast,
Unfathomable and dark;
    Kind Lord, only through your grace
Can I fathom its mystery and depth.

K.S.S., p.97:16

Only you, O Master,
    Are my merciful lord;
Only to you
    Can I run:
The crow on the ship
    In the deep seas
Has no place to rest
    Except the ship.

K.S.S., p.97:17

If you forsake me,
    O Master, not mine
But yours will be the loss:
    Your reputation
As the emancipator
    Will be at stake;
Your fame will be put to shame
    If you reject the one
Who came to take
    Refuge at your feet.

K.S.S., p.98:18

My mind is devoid of faith,
    The nectar of love
It does not taste,
    Nor does it know
How to behave
    In the Master's presence;
Lord, how will I imbibe
    My beloved Master's hue?
How will I obtain
    His love, his grace?

K.S.S., p.98:22

Give me the gift
    Of devotion and love,
You who are, O Master,
    The God of all gods;
Nothing else do I ask
    But to love you,
To serve and obey.

K.S.S., p.98:29

HE FILLS EVERY VESSEL

A large section of mankind and most of the religions and scriptures maintain that God can be found in holy retreats in forests, caves and mountains, in temples, mosques and churches or in pilgrimage places, holy rivers and waters. But Saints clearly point out that the human body is the real temple of God and it is here that one can find Him. In these short poems Kabir says that God is present in every 'pot', within the vessel of the human body, and the seeker who goes within his own body and realizes Him earns the true benefit of the gift of human birth. This, however, can only be achieved by meeting a perfect Master and by learning from him the way to go within.

> Kabir, musk abides in its navel,
>> But in search of its fragrance
> From forest to forest
>> Wanders the musk deer;
> Thus dwells the Lord
>> In every vessel,
> But the world
>> Perceives Him not.
>
> *K.G., p.64:1*

> The Lord dwells within your body;
>> Unaware, you roam in delusion
> Like the musk deer that roves about
>> Sniffing every blade of grass.[1]
>
> *K.G., p.64:3*

> My Beloved resides
>> In the chamber of every heart,
> No couch is empty of Him;
>> All praise to that heart
> In which He has become manifest.
>
> *K.S.S., p.106:5*

---

1. Kabir uses the imagery of a musk deer in both these couplets: in the first couplet, however, he points to man's search for God in mountains, forests, pilgrimages and outer practices; in the second couplet, with the image of the deer sniffing each blade of grass, he indicates man's search for God through reading religious books, scriptures and treatises.

The One for whom you search
    In all corners of the world
Is within your own body;
    The veil of illusion
Covers your eye:
    You see Him not.
                                    K.S.S., p.106:3

He is neither less here
    Nor more there;
To the brim He fills each pot.
    Who realize Him as near,
Near indeed is He to them;
    Who say He is remote,
For them no doubt He is far.
                                    K.G., p 64:5

I believed God to be far away
    But He is within one and all;
Who does not realize his own self,
    Though near, for him the Lord is far.
                                    K.G., p.64:6

Like the iris within the eye
    Is the Lord within the body;
The ignorant ones know it not—
    They search for Him far and wide.
                                    K.G., p.64:9

Like oil in a sesame seed,
    Like spark in a flint stone,
Your Lord resides within you;
    Wake up, if you will,
And realize Him.
                                    K.S.S., p.106:8

Hidden behind a blade of grass
    Is the Lord,
On the peak of some mountain
    Is He, I thought;
When I met the Master
    I realized the truth
And within my own body
    I found Him.

K.G., p.64:7

When I met the Master
    I became cool within,
The raging fever of avarice
    And desires was allayed;
Night and day I float with joy
    In the ocean of bliss
And within my own body,
    O Kabir, God
Has revealed himself.

K.S.S., p.109:21

HE IS WHAT HE IS

If I call Him heavy,
    I fear I am wrong;
If I call Him light,
    It may be a lie.
How can I say I know God,
    For who has seen Him
With the physical eyes?

K.G., p.13:1

If I have seen Him,
    How to describe?
If I try to describe Him,
    Who will believe?
The Lord is like
    What He himself is;
Adore Him,
    Sing his praises with joy.

K.G., p.14:2

Keep the Wonder[1]
    That you have seen
Concealed within your heart,
    For it is beyond the reach
Of Vedas and Koran,
    And no one will believe you
If you try to speak.

K.G., p.14:3

The Lord's abode
    Is hard to reach,
Yet proceed
    At your own speed;

---

1. God.

542

Softly but firmly
  Take each step,
You'll surely attain
  Your home of bliss.

K.G., p.14:4

If I say He is one,
  It is not so;
If I say He is two,
  It is slander;
From his own knowledge
  Proclaims Kabir:
He, the Lord, is
  What He is.

Bijak, Sakhi 120

The bundle of nectar
  I've brought down
From my head,
  But when I say
He is one,
  Men recoil and claim
He is two, He is four.[1]

Bijak, Sakhi 122

Kabir, when you arrive,
  When you reach and become
Truly immortal,
  Only then may you speak;
Your boat is still
  In the turbulent sea—
Who knows what
  The next wave may bring.

K.G., p.14:5

---

1. In medieval days tradesmen used to carry their goods tied up in a cloth bundle on their head. Kabir suggests that the Saints come to the world as travelers, with the bundle of Nam on their head. He echoes the door-to-door tradesmen, whose customers haggle and try to purchase two or four articles for the price of one: When he says, "He is one," they argue "He is two, He is four"; that is, people insist that God has many forms—incarnations, deities, etc.

I have realized the Perfect One,
 Pleasure and pain
Are left behind;
 The account with Kal is closed;
I have met my Lord,
 Whom I find
Ever with me.

K.S.S., p.110:40

I merged in the One,
 Through the One I became
One with all;
 Now all are mine,
I am in all—
 Other than the One
There is none.

K.S.S., p.113:69

From water was snow formed,
 Into water it has
Melted away;
 What it once was
It has become again—
 Nothing more
Is left to say.

K.G., p.10:17

WHERE DWELLS THE LORD

With nine and seven adornments[1]
    The wife decorates her body,
But if she fails to win
    Her Beloved's heart,
Futile is all her toil,
    Her pains to look trim.

                    K.G., p.37:23

So long as the wife
    Does not realize
Her Husband's love and grace,
    She is still a woman
Lone and loveless;
    With fervor and eagerness
The wedding oaths she takes,
    But fails to recognize
Her beloved Husband
    And stays unloved, disgraced.

                    K.G., p.37:24

Kabir, deep is the ardor
    Of devotion in your heart,
But the vile chieftain
    In your fort holds sway;
You slave to please his valets,
    Yet claim to love the Lord![2]

                    K.G., p.37:25

I have crushed the chieftain
    And his vile valets effaced,

---

1. The Indian woman would decorate herself with sixteen traditional adornments.
2. *Chieftain:* mind; *fort:* body; *valets:* senses.

545

I have established the reign
    Of my Beloved;
Now my entire fortress
    Is filled with his love and grace.
                              K.G., p.37:26

Whom the Lord dyes
    In his own love's hue,
Her radiance never fades;
    Day after day
Her beauty and glow
    In multicolored splendor grow.
                              K.S.S., p.98:23

If I sleep,
    I meet Him in my dreams;
When awake,
    I see Him in my heart;
My inner eye opened
    At such a happy hour
That my beloved Lord
    Is never out of my sight.
                              K.S.S., p.168:3

If sense pleasures
    Are dearer to you
Than love for the Lord,
    Never will the Beloved
Enter your heart.
    When the Beloved
Takes abode in you,
    All sense pleasures
Will fade and depart.
                              K.G., p.40:13

Kabir, that heart
      The Lord will not grace
Where delusion dwells;
      Between the lover and himself
The Beloved does not tolerate
      Even a blade of grass.
                              K.G., p.40:14

The heart in which
      The Lord takes abode,
How can that heart
      Be kept concealed?
Though all efforts be made
      To keep it veiled,
Yet the light finds ways
      To penetrate.
                              K.G., p.40:16

THE SUBTLE PATH

From beyond no one returns
    To whom I could run
And learn of the path to God;
    From here all depart
With load after load[1]
    Of the weight they amassed.

From beyond comes my Master
    With knowledge
Profound and pure;
    He pilots the battered
Boat of seekers
    And ferries them
To the opposite shore.

K.S.S., p.53:1,2

That door is atop
    Your physical frame,[2]
Like the tiny pot
    The water girls place
Over the larger vessels.
    On the gibbet
The Beloved has laid his bed[3]—
    There he beckons your soul
To reach and merge
    In his loving embrace.

K.S.S., p.53:3

---

1. The load of karmas.
2. The reference is to the eye center.
3. One has to die while living—completely withdraw the consciousness from the physical body—in order to reach the eye center and meet the Divine Being.

What attachment brings one here,
    What attachment takes one back?
What attachment leads
    To the state of permanence?
Beloved Master, pray explain.

Attachment to passions
    Brings one to this world;
Attachment to Shabd
    Takes one back;
Attachment within,
    Which leads to realization,
Takes one to the state
    Of permanent bliss;
But the method
    Of that attachment
The true Master alone gives.

K.S.S., p.53:4,5

I go to the city
    Of eternity,
Without baggage,
    In tattered clothes;
Join me, if you're keen to come—
    But remember, my path
Through the scaffold runs.

K.S.S., p.53:9

How can Kal harm him
    Who has made his home
Atop the scaffold,
    Who poison as nectar takes,
And throughout the watches eight
    Is alert and awake.

K.S.S., p.54:10

549

My Husband calls me
  With great love and grace,
But I'm unable to go—
  For when the wife is impure,
The Husband immaculate,
  How can she reach
And embrace his lotus feet?

K.S.S., p.54:11

Men even know not
  The name of the Town;
Without knowing
  How can they go?
For ages and eons
  They have been walking,
But have failed to arrive
  At the Town,
Less than quarter
  Of a mile away.[1]

Kind and merciful
  Is my perfect Master;
He came and blessed me
  With his grace—
The path that was
  A million lives long,
I covered in the twinkling
  Of an eye.

K.S.S., p.54:12,13

Kabir's Home is on a peak,
  The path is slippery and hard;
Where even an ant's foot
  Finds no hold,
Scholars want to reach
  With bullock carts of books.

K.S.S., p.54:18

---

1. An expression to convey the idea of closeness; the Lord and his realms—'the Town'—are within the body.

Where even an ant
    Cannot climb,
Even a mustard seed
    Cannot stay,
There Kabir has placed
    His attention,
There he has reached
    With effortless ease.
        K.S.S., p.54:19

Hard and tortuous
    Is the path, O Kabir;
Where ascetics and hermits
    Toiled and toiled
But failed,
    Kabir climbed
With the Master's
    Strength and grace.
        K.S.S., p.54:20

This is a path
    Which needs no feet to tread;
This is a country
    With neither house
Nor lane;
    The Lord here
Has neither body nor shape.
    Realize it, says Kabir.
        K.S.S., p.55:25

Kabir, narrow is the door
    Of salvation—
A tenth of a mustard seed;
    My mind has grown huge
Like an elephant,
    How can it ever
Pass through the door?

If a true Master
    I meet, O Kabir,
Who in his mercy
    Is pleased with me,
Salvation's gate
    Will become large and wide,
And I will come
    And go with ease.

A.G., p.1367:58,59

THE FIRE OF LONGING

These six couplets depict the loving disciple's state of longing and are given under the heading "Longing Arising out of Realization" in most selections of Kabir's poems. The devotee who attains self-realization also realizes that his soul is a particle of the Supreme Being. A desire to merge back into the source —the Lord—is awakened in him. His love and devotion gain strength and he develops an intense longing to meet the Lord. In the presence of this longing all worldly desires and cravings are destroyed, sensual pleasures become insipid and mind gives up its wayward tendencies.

With paradoxes and unusual images, Kabir conveys that this longing is the Master's gift to the disciple, for it is the Master who sets fire to the sea of worldliness, to the restless waters of the disciple's mind; it is he who sets the forest of sense pleasures and desires ablaze and drives away the wild stags of the passions. In the Master's company the soul soars to the higher regions of bliss.

The lake has caught fire,
    Even its mire and moss
Have been burned by the flames;
    The scholars of the north,
The scholars of the south
    Pondered and pondered
But failed to know its cause.[1]

K.G., p.9:5

The Master is scorched,
    The disciple is burned,
Such is longing's raging blaze;
    The petty bit of grass
Soared to its salvation
    In the perfect one's embrace.[2]

K.G., p.9:7

---

1. *The lake:* worldliness; *mire and moss:* deep-rooted cravings and desires; *fire:* the fire of longing for the Lord; *the scholars of north and south:* the scholars of the various schools of Indian philosophy.
2. *The perfect one:* the perfect Master.

The ruthless hunter has
    Set fire to the forest,
The flock of deer cry with pain:
    'The welcoming woods
Where once we reveled
    Are charred by the flames.'[1]

K.G., p.9:8

The fire has spread,
    The sea is ablaze,
But tiny birds have found
    Shelter amidst the flames;
The one thus burned to ashes
    Will not thrive again,
For it is the Master
    Who has lit the blaze.[2]

K.G., p.9:6

Water is burning
    In flames rising high,
The restless river
    Has ceased its quest;
The fish that once flourished
    Have now deserted
Their watery nest.[3]

K.G., p.9:9

---

1. *Hunter:* the Master; *forest:* the forest of sensual pleasures; *flock of deer:* the senses and base tendencies; *flames:* the flames of love and longing.
2. *The sea:* the sea of the world and its desires; *tiny birds:* the birds of love and devotion who find a place of shelter in the flame of longing—that is, love and devotion thrive in longing for the Lord; *not thriving again:* worldliness, desires and cravings destroyed in the flame of longing will not afflict the devotee again.
3. *Water is burning:* the mind of the disciple, which was cold and unresponsive to spiritual suggestions, is aflame with longing for the Lord; *restless river:* the attention of the disciple, which was always running outside in quest of pleasures; *the fish:* the low tendencies and cravings of the mind, which lived in the river of the devotee's mind, find it impossible to survive in the atmosphere of love and devotion.

The ocean is burning,
    The rivers are reduced
To cinders; says Kabir:
    Awake and see,
The fish have climbed
    To the top of the tree.[1]

K.G., p.9:10

---

1. *The ocean:* the mind of the disciple; *the rivers:* the lures of the world, cravings and sensuous inclinations; *cinders:* such lures and inclinations have not only dried up but also been completely burned; *the fish climbing the tree:* the mind and soul have risen to the eye center and have ascended to the spiritual regions within.

IMPORTANCE OF THE MASTER

A perfect Master is a primary necessity on the spiritual path. Without his guidance a seeker can never realize God nor, without his grace, can he escape from the clutches of the negative power. The Master initiates the seeker into the way of spiritual practice, connects his soul with the Word or Shabd and helps him to develop the inner faculties of hearing and seeing—*surat* and *nirat*. The physical faculties of hearing and seeing are essential in daily life on the physical plane; even more so are *surat* and *nirat* needed on the soul's spiritual journey towards its original home.

Speaking of the greatness of the perfect Master, Kabir says that the Master's power and might cannot be conveyed in words; even an entire lifetime devoted to enumerating the aspects of his greatness would not be sufficient.

> Whose color is colorless,
>   Formless whose form,
> How can He be seen?
>   You will see Him within
> When your surat and nirat awake
>   Through the Master's grace.
>
> *K.S.S., p.4:41*

> Pundits read and ponder
>   In order to find God;
> They toil to exhaustion,
>   But without the Master
> Knowledge[1] cannot be gained,
>   And without knowledge
> There's no release.
>   The true Word of the Master
> Is the only way.
>
> *K.S.S., p.4:42*

---

1. Knowledge or *gyān* here refers to realization of the Ultimate.

At the door of death
  The minions of Yama
Would have plagued me,
  There could have been no escape;
I would have been engulfed
  By the whirlpool of birth and death.
K.S.S., p.6:71

In the wheel of species
  I would have revolved,
Never could I have found release;
  But all the misery
Of my wandering ended
  When I met the Master
And he blessed me
  With his love and grace.
K.S.S., p.6:72

The deadly ocean of the world
  Is made tumultuous
By the tempest of desires;
  Mind finds neither rest nor relief.
But I met the Master,
  Powerful and loving—
He took Kabir across the sea.
K.S.S., p.10:117

Without the Master
  No one can be saved,
You will sink again and again
  In the dreadful sea;
From the torment
  Of its battering waves
Only the Master
  Can hold you by the arm,
Only he can save.
K.S.S., p.10:120

He who ascends not
      The ladder that the Master is
And who remains without Shabd,
      No one can save him
From being dragged by Kal
      Into his dark domains.

K.S.S., p.3:35

The Thing lies somewhere,
      Elsewhere you go in its quest;
How can you obtain
      The precious jewel?
Says Kabir: Only when you seek
      In the company of the one
Who is conversant with its secret,
      This treasure will you gain.

K.S.S., p.5:59

When I took with me
      The master of the secret,
He revealed the jewel;
      The path that was
A million lives long,
      In a twinkling
I covered it and reached
      My destination.

K.S.S., p.5:60

This body is a creeper
      That bears poisonous fruits,
The Master is a reservoir of Nectar;
      Even in exchange for your head
If the Master you gain, Kabir,
      It is a cheap bargain.

K.S.S., p.6:62

558

Many read, ruminate
    And analyze,
Many toil to death
    In yoga, yagya
And austerities;
    But without a true Master
They never attain God,
    Though a million techniques
They try.

                    K.S.S., p.11:124

If one lights sixty-four lamps
    And brings fourteen moons[1]
Within his house,
    Yet how can there be light
In the home
    Where the Master is not?

                    K.S.S., p.16:9

To dispel the darkness of night,
    Even if a million moons[2]
Simultaneously rise,
    The man without a Master
Will still be a man without sight.

                    K.S.S., p.16:10

In the depths of the firmament
    Reigns His dazzling radiance,
Which a man without the Master
    Will never attain;
But he who has a Master
    Will gain a lasting abode
In the mansion of the Lord.

                    K.S.S., p.16:11

---

1. Fourteen moons, the fourteen *vidyā:* attaining proficiency in the fourteen branches of scriptural learning. Sixty-four lamps, the sixty-four *kalā:* gaining perfection in the sixty-four types of fine arts and crafts; i.e., with all the knowledge and accomplishments in the world, one would still be without true enlightenment.
2. Kabir has used the word *84 lakh* (8,400,000), interpreted by scholars as 'countless' or 'millions'.

If the whole earth were my paper,
　　All the trees my pen
And the seven seas my ink,
　　They would not suffice
To write the glory
　　Of my Master.

K.S.S., p.2:14

Puppets carved out of stone
  Men worship as the Lord;
Those who put their trust in them
  Drown in the dark currents
Of the dreadful sea.

K.G., p.34:1

The pundits have made
  A cell out of soot,
And from the ink of rituals,
  Its dismal doors;
They have planted stones
  In the earth
And lie in ambush
  To rob the world.[1]

K.G., p.34:2

Why adore stone idols?
  If worshipped all our life
They will never give an answer
  To our prayers;
Blind men hunger for worldly gains
  And lose their luster in vain.[2]

K.G., p.34:3

I too would have adored stones
  And like an antelope
Wandered in the wild woods;[3]

---

1. In olden days, ink was made out of soot; here refers to books, the 'doors' being the written words that propagate ritual practices. Like robbers, who used to put boulders on the road to obstruct carts and rob the passengers, they block people's spiritual progress and rob them of the wealth of the human birth.
2. Inborn spiritual inclinations.
3. External worship; temples and holy places.

But my Master blessed me
With his love and grace,
    And I threw the burden
Off my head.
            K.G., p.34:4

Empty are all chanting,
    Penance and austerity,
Empty are fasts,
    Empty, pilgrimages—
Putting faith in them is vain;
    As the deluded parrot
Pecks at the semal bloom,[1]
    So goes the world
With empty hands.
            K.G., p.35:8

The vicious creeper
    Of fasting and pilgrimage
Has spread its tentacles
    Over the entire world;
But its very roots
    Kabir has destroyed,
Why need he its poison eat?
            K.G., p.35:9

Men have made it a business
    To sell idols of stone,
Calling them the Lord of all;
    You spend money and buy one,
But find it dead and dumb,
    For indeed it is counterfeit.
            K.S.S., p.165:6

---

1. The parrot is attracted from far off by the cotton tree fruit, but when it pecks at the fruits they break open and the cotton blows away, leaving the parrot with nothing.

Men worship water and stone;
    All their service goes to waste.
Kabir, serve and adore the Saints
    And keep repeating
The Lord's true Name.
K.S.S., p.165:8

Men gather stones
    And raise big temples
Where large idols
    They enshrine.
But idols can break;
    Themselves helpless
And dependent on others,
    How can they ferry one
Across the stormy sea?
K.S.S., p.165:9

Kabir, men rush to temples
    And in devotion bow their head;
But within your heart
    Lives the Lord—
Adore Him within,
    Within stay absorbed.
K.G., p.35:11

Gathering stone and mortar,
    Men raise a high mosque;
Climbing to the top
    The mullah shouts his prayer—
But tell me, O mullah,
    Is the Lord deaf?
K.S.S., p.165:13

O Mullah, you climb
   And shout your prayers;
Remember He is not deaf,
   The Invisible One ever hears.
The One for whom
   You yell and shout,
Go within and see Him,
   See Him within your heart.
                         K.S.S., p.165:14

Your mind is Mathura,
   Dwarka is your heart,
Your body is Kasi;
   The true temple
Is at the tenth door,
   Therein realize
The Light of God.
                         K.G., p.35:10

The Turks to the mosques,
   The Hindus to their temples
With blind fervor run;
   Within the body
Dwells the Invisible One,
   But they do not try to find
The door of his mansion.
                         K.S.S., p.165:15

Running to holy places,
   Undertaking fasts,
Bathing in icy waters,
   Men have toiled
And toiled to death;

But without knowing
The true Name
    They became morsels for Kal
Eon after eon,
    Again and again.

                    K.S.S., p.166:3

What avail your holy baths
    If the mind is not rid of its dirt?
Fish always remain in water,
    But even with washing
Their stench does not fade.

                    K.S.S., p.166:5

Who give alms in profusion,
    Craving for much in return,
They'll be born as elephants
    In the stables of the rich
And get mounds of food to eat.

                    K.S.S., p.166:11

Kabir, a hundred times
    I warn the world, but in vain;
Men hold onto a sheep's tail
    And wish to cross the ocean!

                    K.S.S., p.166:17

A million pilgrimages
    A man might undertake,
And a million journeys
    To the four holy spots;
Until he takes the refuge
    Of a Saint,
All his efforts
    Are false and vain.

                    K.S.S., p.166:7

Worship, service, holy fasts,
    And conduct that conforms
To canonical law
    Are like a girl's play
With her dolls;
    To give up this make-believe
Will be hard,
    Till the soul-bride goes in
And face to face
    Meets her Lord.

K.S.S., p.166:16

THE LEARNED

Reading volume after volume,
    Men tire themselves to exhaustion,
But not one becomes
    A real scholar;
Who learns the one word *love*
    Is the truly learned one.

K.S.S., p.167:7

Reading and reading,
    Men have become
Dead like stones;
    Writing and writing,
They have become
    Dumb like bricks;
Kabir, not even a spark
    Of love has entered
Their heart.

K.S.S., p.167:8

Through reading and ruminating,
    Through studying and listening,
Delusion's deadly thorn
    Can never be removed;
Few listen to Kabir when he says
    Learning is the cause of all pain.

K.S.S., p.167:11

Learning and intellect
  And an astute mind
Are simple and easy to gain;
  To vanquish desire and lust,
To control the wayward mind,
  To reach the sky within,
Are trying tasks indeed.

K.S.S., p.167:13

The pundit and his books
  Are like the knowledge
Of the trained partridge;
  To others their future it shows,
But never knows its own bondage.[1]

K.S.S., p.167:10

The learned and the torchbearer
  Are both unable to see;
To others they show light,
  Themselves in darkness stay.

K.S.S., p.168:14

Kabir tells the pundits:
  What you keep reading
Does not enter your heart;
  Others you seek to guide,
But yourself sink
  In your pride of learning.

K.G., p.29:13

---

1. There is a type of Indian fortuneteller who uses a trained partridge to pick out cards from a pack on which different predictions are written, claiming that the partridge has divine vision and will pick out the fortune of the particular client.

They give sermons
      On the four Vedas,
But love for the Lord
      They do not earn;
Kabir has sifted
      And picked out
All the grain,
      The pundits
Are rummaging the husks
      In vain.

K.G., p.28:9

Even a parrot learns to speak
      The words of holy books;
A captive of the cage,
      It repeats wise words to others,
Unaware of its own sorry state.

K.G., p.29:14

The priest is the guide of the world;
      By deluding others
With rites and rituals
      He earns his living.
He entangles himself
      In Vedas and scriptures
And wastes his human birth.

K.S.S., p.168:18

Sink your scriptures, O Pundit,
      Discard your books, O Qazi;
Tell me the date
      When there was neither the sky,
Nor was there the earth.

K.S.S., p.168:17

Put aside your scriptures, O Kabir.
　　All the world reads,
But reads in vain;
　　If love's divine pain
Has not sprung in your heart,
　　Futile are your efforts
To meet the Lord
　　Through reading and reciting.

K.G., p.30:3

Reading and reading,
　　Men toil to death,
But no one can thus
　　Become truly learned;
He who reads
　　The one word *Beloved*
Is the truly
　　Enlightened one.

K.G., p.30:4

Wrap up your holy books, O Pundit,
　　Make them your pillow
And sleep with ease;
　　That one word *love*
Is not in your books,
　　Discard them happily
—Or with tears in your eyes—
　　For they are futile.

K.S.S., p.167:9

THE GYANI

As against a pundit or learned man, a *gyani* has carried out a deep study of philosophy, theology and scriptures, and is capable of elaborating on them at length. Kabir calls such highly learned intellectuals *vachak gyani* or 'verbalists' who excel in the field of the spoken and written word.

Real knowledge, according to the Saints, is the inner knowledge obtained through actual spiritual experience. All knowledge of the physical and mental planes, in the absence of inner realization, is meaningless on the spiritual path. Kabir rejects all such external knowledge, for to 'know' is better than to profess, to speak from experience of the reality is far more significant than mere repetition from books.

Like the blind men's knowledge
    Of the elephant
Is the book knowledge
    Of the learned ones;
Each commends his own views,
    And the seeker wonders
What is false, what is true.

K.S.S., p.77:1

Their knowledge is like
    The blind men's elephant—
Within limits, what they say
    Might be right;
But their deductions
    They derive
From guessing and groping,
    For with their own eyes
They neither can see
    Nor the Truth realize.

K.S.S., p.77:2

What can one say to the gyani?
  Kabir feels ashamed
To explain to them,
  For it is futile
To dance before the blind—
  A waste of one's art,
A waste of one's time.

K.S.S., p.77:3

The gyanis are lost
  In lecturing
On their studies about God;
  But God is near
Their own self—
  They toil to find Him
Everywhere else,
  While hidden within them
Lies that rare wealth.

K.S.S., p.77:6

They do not pierce
  The veil within,
Outside they lecture
  And make many a claim;
If they go in and see Him
  They will know:
Within and without,
  The Truth is the same.

K.S.S., p.77:7

The gyani loses all
    When he claims 'I am God';[1]
Much better are the worldly
    Who always live in awe
Of the Almighty Lord.

                    K.S.S., p.77:5

Truth has to be realized,
    It is not a topic of mere talks;
Every gyani that you see
    Lives in the webs of delusion.

                    K.S.S., p.78:8

When I realized
    My true self,
I rose above
    Pleasure and pain;
My heart like a lamp
    Emits divine light,
All debating
    For me is vain.

                    K.S.S., p.77:5, Anubhav Gyan

They who fill papers,
    Who tracts and volumes indite,
Are learned men
    Or men worldly-wise.
Where and how
    Can the realized man write,
For wherever he looks,
    The Beloved alone he sees.

                    K.S.S., p.77:6, Anubhav Gyan

---

1. Some students of certain schools of Indian philosophy intellectually arrive at the conclusion that the soul and God are one, and without attaining actual union with God start saying, "I am God." Saints say that without realization this assertion is merely a mental stance.

573

TRUE BEAUTY

The devotee who loves the Lord, who longs not for worldly objects but only for union with Him, who overcomes his desires and cravings, conquers his ego and stills his mind, has been described by Kabir as a beautiful wife who is always loved and admired by her husband. The beauty of the devotee is not physical; it is the beauty of a pure and loving heart. Such a devotee attains God-realization, which destroys his lust, anger, ego and other base tendencies. He goes within, crosses the ocean of mind and maya and enjoys spiritual rapport with the Beloved.

Kabir, thus entreats the beautiful wife:
My kind Husband, beloved Lord,
Come fleeting like the wind to meet me—
Without Thee I can no longer live.
K.G., p.63:52:1

Kabir, if the beautiful wife
Will look at others
With adulterous eyes,
Never will her Beloved, her Husband,
Accept and honor her love.
K.G., p.63:52:2

If the beautiful wife
Adores only her Lord
And not a glance at others casts,
Never will the Husband ignore her,
Not for a moment will He part.
K.G., p.63:52:3

If she will grind her mind
    Into flour even and fine,
If she'll pulverize it to dust,
    Then will the beautiful wife
Enjoy the bliss of union,
    Then on her forehead will shine
The glow of love divine.

K.G., p.64:52:4

The beautiful wife steps
    Into the arena of love,
She sports with her Beloved,
    She lights the lamp of realization
Which consumes lust like oil.

K.S.S., p.28:12

The beloved Husband
    Has set up a swing
Across the turbulent sea;
    That wife is wise and loving
Who daily crosses the ocean
    To swing in bliss
With her Husband.

K.G., p.64:52:5

THE FAITHFUL WIFE

A disciple who has once accepted the path from a perfect Master does not seek or accept spiritual guidance from anyone else. Once he has taken to the path of divine love, he does not entertain thoughts of others in his heart. Kabir compares the one-pointed devotion of the disciple with the unflinching love of a faithful wife who never even thinks of another man. Like the faithful wife, the disciple looks upon the Lord as the husband, loves Him, longs only for Him and has no desire other than union with Him. Only the Beloved dwells in the disciple's heart, mind and soul; there is no room for anyone or anything else. In the end Kabir says that the loving and faithful disciple attains union with the Lord by merging in Nam.

The faithful wife is always happy,
    Her only love is her Husband, her Lord;
Filthy is the mind of the adulteress,
    Who ignores the One and loves many.

K.S.S., p.27:1

Even if the faithful wife
    Be ugly and ungainly,
Before her inner beauty and grace
    A million beauties of the world
Will fade.

K.S.S., p.27:2

The faithful wife adores
    Only her Husband,
She is never inclined
    To look at others;
The lion cub will starve
    But never eat grass.

K.S.S., p.27:3

The shell in the sea
    Cries out in thirst,
Yet refuses the ocean,
    A worthless straw;
It's only the raindrop
    It longs for.[1]

                    K.G., p.15:5

Kabir, in my eyes reddened by love
    How can collyrium be applied?[2]
Within them dwells my Beloved,
    Where is the place for anything else?

                    K.G., p.14:4

Throughout the eight watches
    And the sixty-four beats,[3]
I think of you and you alone;
    You alone dwell in my eyes,
There is no room for sleep to come.

                    K.S.S., p.29:26

I am the slave of the Mighty One,
    No harm can ever come to me;
If the faithful wife went naked,
    Her husband would be put to shame.[4]

                    K.G., p.15:17

---

1. According to folklore, the oyster shell loves the raindrop, and like the rainbird it will not accept any other water.
2. *Kājal,* a type of lamp soot that is applied to the eyes by Indian women for cosmetic and medicinal purposes. When the eyes are inflamed or red, its use is given up until they become normal.
3. One 'beat' or *ghari* consists of a little less than twenty-four minutes; hence, 'throughout the twenty-four hours of the day'.
4. In India the husband is supposed to look after and protect his wife and provide her with clothes, food and all the necessities of life. If the wife is not properly provided for, she is not blamed; but the husband is looked down on by society for not fulfilling his part of the family obligation.

Enter my eyes, O love,
 And instantly I'll close them,
That I do not see others
 Nor let you see anyone else.
       K.G., p.14:2

The hell of separation I accepted,
 Hell now holds no terror for me;
The pleasures of heaven I don't want,
 Beloved, without Thee.
       K.G., p.15:7

Her soul has merged into Nam,
 Nam's light illumines her heart;
The faithful wife has met her Husband,
 Not for the wink of an eye[1] will they part.
       K.S.S., p.29:19

---

1. A favorite expression of Indian poets to convey the idea of 'an instant'.

ABSORPTION IN LOVE

The wine of love
    I have drunk
With avid thirst;
    I am intoxicated
With the experience
    Of my Master's love;
He has sounded
    The marching beat
On the drum of Shabd
    And I am ready to enter
Love's battlefield.

K.S.S., p.43:5

One moment it comes,
    Next moment it goes,
That is not love;
    What permeates the entire being
Like an inexhaustible stream
    Alone can be called love.

K.S.S., p.43:6

'Love, love' say all,
    Few realize what love is;
Whose heart is absorbed
    In love
All day, all night,
    He alone
A true lover
    Can be called.

K.S.S., p.44:8

When I was,
    The Master was not;
Now only the Master is—
    'I' am no more.
Narrow indeed
    Is love's lane, O friend,
Where two cannot be.

K.S.S., p.44:10

I fell in love with Him,
    His love like sugar dissolved
To fill my soul, my heart;
    My body's every pore
Cries 'Beloved, Beloved'—
    Mouth is required no more.

K.S.S., p.45:22

Where there is love,
    There is no law;
Love knows neither ritual
    Nor reason;
When the mind stays
    Absorbed in love,
Who will keep count
    Of dates and days?

K.S.S., p.45:27

Kabir took the cup of love
    And poured it into his soul;
Throughout his being,
    In every pore
It has diffused;
    For other intoxicants
He has no use.

K.S.S., p.46:34

He has truly drunk
  The wine of the Beloved's love
Whose tide of drunkenness
  Ebbs not for a moment;
Who, like one insane,
  Is lost in the Beloved's Name;
Who drinks nectar within
  And always remains
With love intoxicated.

K.S.S., p.46:39

Within the chamber
  Of my eyes
I made the pupil
  The nuptial couch;
To hide my Love
  I softly did slide
My eyelids' curtain[1]—
  My Beloved's heart
Thus I won.

K.S.S., p.47:50

A letter to the Beloved
  I would write
If He were far away
  In some distant land;
Who dwells within my body,
  My mind, my eye,
To Him what message
  Can I send?

K.S.S., p.49:70

---

1. When the soul withdraws behind the two eyes and enters the eye center, called here 'the pupil', it meets the Lord. To maintain this contact, the devotee draws a curtain on the outer world by keeping his attention absorbed within.

People are too involved
    With people in this world
To try to see the Unseen One.
    Without meeting God,
The embers of their misery
    Burst into flames;
They try to quench it
    In a million ways,
Yet unabated it burns.

K.S.S., p.42:82

When my soul involved itself
    Only with the Beloved,
The Beloved took me
    In his embrace;
The written merged
    Into the Unwritten—
Nothing is left to say.

K.S.S., p.42:83

I have banished my I-ness,
    In the Beloved now I dwell;
Ineffable is love's tale,
    And who would believe
Even if I were to tell?

K.S.S., p.140:7

DEPTH OF LOVE

A body empty of love
    Is like a cemetery—dead;
It is like the bellows
    Of the blacksmith,
Which breathe
    But have no life.
                K.S.S., p.44:11

He who does not undertake
    The barter of love,
Who does not tread
    The lane of Nam,
Is a bullock
    That strolls about
Wearing the hide of a man.
                K.S.S., p.45:26

Put on the sandal of love,
    Apply the collyrium
Of patience to your eyes;
    Let chastity and faithfulness
Be the lucky marks on your face[1]—
    Then will you enjoy the bliss
Of the Beloved's embrace.
                K.S.S., p.45:28

Kabir, love him[2]
    Whose only lord is God;
Pundits, kings and nobles—
    What worth are they!
                A.G., p.1365:24

---

1. Vermilion marks on the forehead and in the parting of the hair, applied by married women in India.
2. The *gurumukh* or Saint.

Kabir, love only the One
        That your duality may depart;
Then whether you wear long hair
        Or shave your head clean
Will make no difference.

                              A.G., p.1365:25

The jogi, the roving recluse,
        The ascetic, the silent hermit,
The dervish and the fakir,
        Without love, O Kabir,
Not one of them will reach
        My Master's precious Home.

                              K.S.S., p.45:31

The love that the devotee has
        For his family,
With the same intensity
        If the Master he loves,
Kabir, no one can hold him back
        By the sleeve.

                              K.S.S., p.47:49

THE INTOXICATION OF LOVE

Divine love can only be obtained when the devotee pays the price with his head; that is, only when he completely crushes his ego and becomes oblivious of the world, its lures and attachments can he taste the wine of love. Love is the merging of the individual's identity in that of the Beloved. In these couplets Kabir says that love is the wine that intoxicates the soul and keeps it in a perpetual state of bliss; it is the nectar that makes one immortal, the alchemic potion that transforms man into God.

Avidly did Kabir drink
    The nectar of God's love:
He is transformed and made whole;
    The well-baked vessel
Cannot be placed
    On the potter's wheel again.[1]

The wine of the Lord's love
    Becomes more delicious
The more you drink it;
    But it is hard to obtain,
For the wine merchant, O Kabir,
    Demands your head in exchange.

Kabir, many crowd around
    The wine merchant's stall;
Only he drinks to his fill
    Who offers his head,
Others are turned away
    Empty and dry.

---

1. The wheel of transmigration on which the soul is placed after every death unless it becomes perfect.

He is truly drunk
       With the wine of God's love
Whose intoxication
       Never wanes,
Who roams
       Like a mad elephant—
Oblivious of himself.

The intoxicated elephant
       Will not eat grass,[1]
For the arrow of love
       Rankles within his heart;
He's tied to the door of love,
       He throws dust on his own head.[2]

The intoxicated one
       Is absorbed in the Unknown,
He has conquered desires
       And become free of cares;
Under the spell of love's wine,
       While living he goes beyond
The stage of salvation.[3]

The lake[4] in which once
       Not even a jug could be sunk,
The love-intoxicated elephant
       Now bathes in it with bliss;
The temple has submerged
       Along with its spire,
Yet thirsty go the birds.[5]

---

1. Grasses are the staple food of elephants; here it means sensual pleasures.
2. The elephant tied in its stall has the habit of picking up dust with its trunk and throwing it on its head. Here the love-intoxicated devotee throws dust on his ego, eliminates his I-ness.
3. When the soul crosses the region of Brahm, the second stage in the inner journey, it is liberated from all bonds. The Saints' ideal, however, is much higher, for they go to the fifth stage—the realm of everlasting bliss—and attain union with the Lord.
4. The lake of the disciple's love, which was originally so shallow or devoid of divine love that not even a jug could be filled from it—that is, it gave no spiritual joy or inspiration to the disciple.
5. The birds of the senses remain thirsty because they do not get their drink of pleasures; *elephant:* soul; *temple and spire:* mind and ego.

Kabir, I tried
    Many alchemic recipes
But found not one
    Like the Lord's love;
If even one drop
    Enters the body,
Your entire being
    Turns into gold.

K.G., p.13:1-8

FAITH

Faith in the Master and the Lord is an essential part of devotion. Doubt and devotion, love and hesitation, do not go together. In these couplets Kabir emphasizes the importance of faith in its three aspects. First, the devotee must have faith that the Lord, who has created all beings, has arranged also for their sustenance and is looking after them, providing for all their needs. Man needs clothes to cover his body, a roof over his head, and food to maintain him. Kabir says that the Lord provides these facilities even to beasts, birds and insects, so why should He forget man? The devotee should not allow these worries to enter his mind.

Second, whatever man has to undergo during his life in the world has already been ordained. His *prarabdh karma* or the fate with which he is born is changeless. No efforts, pleading or planning can change even a comma in what is written in his destiny. He should have faith in the immutability of his destiny and accept it with a composed and carefree mind.

Third, the devotee should have faith that the practice of Nam will never go to waste, nothing can stop it from bearing fruit in the course of time. He should also know that a devotee of Nam has nothing to do with the negative power and cannot be sent to hell, for Nam will always keep him linked with the Supreme Being and never let him go into lower regions or lower species. Kabir says that firm faith in the Master and the Lord is the outcome of the practice of Nam, but this faith also helps to strengthen the devotee's love for the Lord and enables him to attend to his devotion with greater earnestness.

> Kabir, why need I worry,
> What can my worrying achieve?
> My Lord feels concern for me,
> I have no worries of my own.
>
> *K.S.S., p.73:1*

> Do not be anxious,
> Cast away your cares,
> The Beloved is all-powerful;
> Do beasts, birds and insects
> Have money in their pockets?
>
> *K.G., p.45:9*

The wish-fulfilling Jewel[1]
    Is ever present in your heart;
Dwell upon Him, realize Him.
    Even if you do not worship Him,
He constantly looks after you—
    For such is his wont.

K.G., p.45:5

Why do you keep crying
    'I'm hungry, I'm hungry'?
Why clamor about it to the world?
    He who has fashioned the jar
And given it a mouth,
    Is also able to fill it.

K.G., p·45:2

Even for the dead He provides
    Dress, sheet and fire;[2]
If a man, alive, worries—
    That's his bad luck!

Satt Kabir, p.338:697

Your fate the Lord has written,
    No alterations can now be made;
Not a dot can be added,
    Not a point removed,
Though a million efforts
    You make.

K.G., p.45:7

---

1. *Chintāmani,* a mythical jewel that fulfills all the wishes of the one who possesses it; here, the Lord.
2. Even when the body is dead, it is given the basic necessities of life—clothes, a sheet (shroud), and 'food' in the form of fire, for in India when a pyre is lit, the fire is first placed right at the head.

Whatever God has determined,
    That alone will be your lot;
Not by a mustard seed
    Will it decrease,
Nor increase
    Even by a sesame,
However much you toil.

K.G., p.45:8

Plow your field[1] with the Lord's Name,
    Sow the seed of devotion;
Even if there is a drought
    Till the end of the world,
The seed will not fail to sprout
    Nor fail to yield a rich crop.

K.G., p.45:4

My heart is absorbed in the Lord's Name,
    My dealings with Yama are broken;
I have firm faith in my Lord,
    I know his slave cannot
Ever be sent to hell.

K.G., p.46:11

What are you afraid of, O Kabir?
    The protecting hand of the Lord
Is always over your head;
    When you are given a seat on an elephant,
Do not be perturbed by the dogs
    That bark.

K.G., p.46:12

My body is a flowering shrub
    Filled with the fragrance of desires,
My mind hovers like a bumblebee;

---

1. The field of the body.

When I watered the plant
With the ambrosia of Nam,
    It bore the fruit of divine faith.

K.G., p.46:16

Kabir, when 'me' and 'mine' dissolved
    I became free of all bonds
And gained true faith in my Lord;
    Now none else exists for me:
I long, Beloved, only for Thee.

K.G., p.46:17

You sing His praises
    In melodious tunes,
But without true devotion
    The chains of doubt will not break;
Without faith in the Lord
    All efforts are like
Gathering chaff.

K.G., p.46:19

The Master is always with him
    Whose heart is filled with faith;
A million ways Kal may adopt,
    He'll not waver from the path.

K.S.S., p.74:9

He who adores the Master
    With faith deep and unshaken,
From iron he turns into gold;
    He is enabled to practice Nam
With love and devotion,
    He becomes free
From sorrow and joy.

K.S.S., p.74:16

IN PRAISE OF FEAR

Divine love is a path of complete surrender to the Beloved. The lover's only concern is the Beloved, his only object is to please Him. Unlike the worldly lover, the divine lover demands nothing, his thoughts are constantly on the Lord and all his actions are aimed at meeting His approval. He is always careful not to offend or displease the Beloved. Though completely free from fear in the world, the devotee always fears the Lord.

In a hymn included in the Adi Granth, Kabir says: "In fear is love; one who understands such love obtains the elixir of union with the Lord" (A.G., *Kedara*, p.1123). This is not a fear of punishment; it is the fear of offending the Beloved, of incurring his displeasure. According to the Saints, the true adornments of the soul-bride are fear and love. She who is adorned with these two qualities gains admittance to the Beloved's chamber.

> Without fear
> > Love cannot be born,
> Without fear
> > Love will not endure;
> The moment fear departs
> > From the devotee's heart,
> The decorum and depth
> > Of love is lost.
> > > *K.S.S. p.63:91*

> Be devoted to the Lord,
> > But have fear in your heart—
> With fear and love, adore Him.
> > Fear is the magic stone
> For the lover's heart;
> > Let no devotee
> Be free from this fear.
> > > *K.S.S., p.63:92*

Fear is the true act of worship,
　　Fear, the devotee's perfect guide;
Fear is the magic stone,
　　Fear, the essence of love.
Whose heart is filled
　　With fear of the Lord,
Ultimate freedom he will gain;
　　The careless and unfearing
Always remain in this world
　　Of woe and pain.

K.S.S., p.63:93

MERGED INTO THE ONE

The devotee, the true lover, should keep only the Beloved in his heart, enjoy inner rapport with Him and keep his eyes closed towards all other objects in the world. But, says Kabir, if the lover has attained that inner spiritual state in which he realizes the Lord and becomes one with Him, he need not try to avoid others for he sees the One Lord present in every being and in each particle of the creation. In the last stanza Kabir describes that lofty state of love in which the lover and the Beloved become one.

Keep your eyes downcast,
　　Hold the Beloved
Captive in your heart;
　　Revel with Him in all bliss,
But let no one see
　　Your ecstasy.

Eight watches, sixty-four beats[1]
　　My entire being looks only at Thee;
Why need I lower my eyes
　　When in every vessel
My beloved alone I see.

Listen, friend, I dwell in my Beloved
　　And my Beloved dwells in me;
I cannot distinguish between
　　My Beloved and myself:
I know not whether
　　The soul dwells in me
Or dwells my Beloved.

A.G., p.1377:234-236

---

1. All the twenty-four hours.

PRIDE

In these couplets from the Adi Granth, Kabir warns man against ego and pride, for in this world of matter nothing is permanent. The ultimate reality behind youth, beauty and health is disease and death. Death is the final leveler, reducing young and old, beautiful and ugly, rich and poor, to the same state.

Kabir, be not proud of your body—
    A sheet of skin stuffed with bones;
They who rode stately horses
    Under canopies of gold
Now lie wrapped in earth.

Kabir, be not proud
    Of your lofty mansions:
Today or tomorrow
    The earth will be your bed
And grass will cover your head.

Kabir, be not proud
    Nor sneer at the forlorn;
Your canoe is still in the sea,
    Who knows what its fate will be?

Kabir, be not proud
    Of your beauty and youth;
This day or the next
    You will have to leave it,
Like a serpent its slough.

A.G., p.1366:37-40

HUMILITY

These couplets depict the humility that the devotee should try to inculcate within himself. He should feel as insignificant as a pebble on the street; but unlike pebbles, which sometimes hurt the traveler, the devotee should never hurt anyone by his words, thoughts or actions. He should feel as low and trivial as dust, but avoid the characteristic of dust of flying up and falling on people—that is, he should never talk ill of others in their presence or otherwise, nor try to expose their faults. He should also be like water, which has no I-ness insofar as it adopts the shape of the vessel that contains it; but he should never lose his coolness and composure, nor his love and devotion. In the end Kabir says that the devotee, though living in the world and dealing with others, should be completely absorbed in God; thus he will reflect the divine qualities of the Lord himself.

Kabir, become a pebble of the path,
    Banish all pride from your heart;
He who becomes such a slave
    Meets the Lord.

Kabir, what if one does become a pebble—
    It could hurt the traveler's feet;
The Lord's slave should rather be
    Like dust on the earth.

Kabir, what if one does become dust—
    Dust rises and clings to people;
The devotee should rather be like water
    Which takes the shape of the pot it fills.

Kabir, what if one does become water—
    Water becomes hot, water becomes cold;
The Lord's lover should rather be
    As the Lord himself is.

A.G., p.1372:146-149

Kabir, do not follow
　　The dictates of your mind,
Give up this habit
　　Which is ages old;
Just as the yarn
　　Spun on the spindle,
On the spindle is wound again,[1]
　　So bring your mind back
To the center from where it came.

K.G., p.21:1

Do not follow
　　The trends of your mind,
There is no end
　　To its tricky ways;
One who tames his mind,
　　Kabir, is a rare sage.

K.S.S., p.146:1

The lane leading to the Home
　　Is narrow, O Kabir,
But like a thief
　　The restless mind
To others' houses runs;
　　Even when the devotee
Believes he is absorbed
　　In the Lord's worship,
His mind is engaged
　　In thoughts other than God.

K.G., p.22:4

---

1. The reference is to the notched metal stick that is used for spinning cotton into yarn by hand: after a short length of cotton is spun, it is wound onto the spindle itself.

Mind knows well
        What is good, what is bad,
But knowingly
        Adopts evil ways;
What happiness
        Can a man obtain
When he falls into a well
        With a lamp in his hand?
                                                K.G., p.22:7

Kabir, you made no efforts
        To curb your restive mind,
Nor the onslaught of the five
        Did you try to repulse,
Nor purity, truth and faith
        Did you inculcate;
Shamelessly your senses run
        To pleasures one should shun.
                                                K.G., p.22:15

Kabir, your mind has sunk
        Into desire's dungeon,
Through blind pursuit of pleasures
        It has brought about its own fall;
Though forewarned,
        It swallowed the bait—
How can it now escape
        Its dreadful fate?
                                                K.G., p.23:16

Your mind has become
        Heedless and indolent,
It does not attend
        To simran;
Much will be the torment
        It will have to endure
When hauled into Kal's court.
                                                K.G., p.23:17

598

In a twinkling the mind
    Does a thousand deeds
Under the sway
    Of craving for pleasures;
It heeds not the Master's words
    And wastes
This precious human birth.

K.G., p.23:18

Kabir, where has that mind gone
    Which yesterday was
Towards God inclined?
    Like the rain that falls
On the top of a hill,
    Mind went gushing down,
Desire's dirty ponds to fill.

K.G., p.23:22

Kabir, I'll not trust my mind
    Though it become docile and dead;
Even a dead mind I dread
    Lest with the gale of passions
It should come to life again.

K.G., p.23:23

Body is a temple
    And mind its flag[1]
Fluttering in the wind
    Of desire and craving;
If the temple sways
    With the fluttering of mind,
The entire edifice
    Will become debris one day.

K.G., p.23:28

---

1. Indian temples usually have a flag on the steeple.

Kabir, do not trust your mind
    Even if you find it dead,
Even if you have crushed
    And made it sublime;
A true devotee
    Is wary of his mind
As long as the birds of breath
    Come and go
In his body's cage.
                                K.G., p.23:28, fn.

Kabir, mind is only one,
    Engage it in the direction
That you choose—
    In the Master's devotion
Or in the pursuit of desire.
                                K.S.S., p.147:8

Throughout the three worlds
    The thief steals
With cunning and stealth
    And deprives all
Of their true wealth.
    No one can see
And catch the thief,
    For he goes about
Without a head.
                                K.S.S., p.147:10

Far less are the waves in the sea
    Than the waves of mind;
Many surge and submerge
    Helpless souls,
Many spring
    And ebb with the tide.
                                K.S.S., p.147:14

Mind is the ocean,
  Desires, the wild waves;
Many have been sunk,
  Many swept away—
Only they escape
  Whose heart stays
Absorbed in Truth.

K.S.S., p.151:60

In the very presence
  Of the soul,
Mind sways and runs
  In devious ways.
Mind rules over
  The three worlds;
Mind is worshipped
  By one and all
In every spot,
  At every place.

K.S.S., p.151:61

CONTROLLING THE MIND

I'll make my mind dead,
    That the Invisible
In full view I perceive;
    But if I try
To preserve my 'I'
    May the fires of hell
Rain over my head.
                 K.G., p.22:6

The mirror is within the heart,
    Still you cannot see
The face of the Lord.
    His face you will perceive
When your mind is free
    From duality.
                 K.G., p.22:8

Such a one my friend
    I have made
Who has donned a robe
    Of everlasting red.
If all the washermen
    In the world
Were to try to wash
    That color away,
With all their scrubbing
    Its hue would not fade.
                 K.G., p.22:11

Thinner than water,
    Finer than
A screen of smoke,
    More lively and lithe
Than the restless wind;

Such a one
Kabir has made his friend.

K.G., p.22:12

When my mind
Became thin and fine,
It made its home
In the sky;
It saw its origin
And attained peace;
It will not part
From its source again.[1]

K.G., p.22:14

Out of paper
The body's boat is made,
The river is in spate
With desire's violent waves;
How can I cast anchor
On the opposite shore,
With the oar, O Kabir,
In the charge
Of the five knaves?[2]

K.G., p.23:21

Bound with the five
One dons body's dress
Again and again;
Who enslaves the five[3]
Will easily arrive
At the opposite shore.

K.S.S., p.149:34

---

1. The source of mind is Brahm or the universal mind.
2. The five passions.
3. That is, rises above the domain of the five elements that constitute the human body.

Mind, like a restless bird,
 Will keep flying
In the wilderness
 Of desires
And on the tree of passions
 Will continue to perch—
So long as the hawk of love
 Does not pounce from above.

K.S.S., p.149:36

This stag without a head
 Roams in all directions
And goes to graze
 In wild forests;[1]
Bind it with the knowledge
 That your Master gave,
Hold it in the courtyard
 Enclosed by the fence
Of love and truth.

K.S.S., p. 151:67

Kill your mind,
 Its desires destroy.
Grind it, make it thin;
 Then will the bride enjoy
The bliss of union divine,
 Then will the love
Of her Beloved
 Like a radiant lotus
On her forehead shine.

K.S.S., p.150:50

---

1. *Stag without head:* the mind, which has no form of its own; *wild forests:* desires, passions, sense pleasures.

THE ROSARY OF THE MIND

Man feels happy
 And gratified
By telling beads,
 But no spiritual gain is made;
If he repeats the names
 On the rosary of his mind,
His entire being
 Will be flooded with light.

K.S.S., p.88:15

For ages have men kept rolling
 The beads of rosaries,
But their rolling minds
 Could find no rest.
Friend, cast away the beads
 From your fingers;
Roll the rosary
 Of your mind.

K.S.S., p.88:16

Your hands are busy
 Rolling the beads,
But your heart resounds
 With passions' thundering beat;
You are like the man
 Who tries to run
With frostbitten feet.

K.G., p.35:1

Hands hold the rosary,
>   Fingers turn the beads,
But mind wanders
>   In all the four directions.
By turning the one[1]
>   The Lord could be met,
But that one has become hard
>   Like the beads.

>   *K.G., p.35:2*

He, the Supreme Lord,
>   Has in each body kept
An unrepeated repetition;[2]
>   In that simran Kabir's mind
Stays ever engrossed.

>   *K.S.S., p.88:17*

Why flaunt piety?
>   Repeat the Name within.
Why seek to impress the world?
>   Your concern is
Only with Him
>   Who is the Lord of all.

>   *K.S.S., p.89:23*

Kabir, the true rosary
>   Is the rosary of the mind;
The rest is a ruse
>   The hypocrites choose
To beguile others.
>   If by turning the beads
God could be met,
>   Then the persian wheel
Is well set to meet Him.

>   *K.S.S., p.89:18*

---

1. The mind.
2. In an advanced stage of simran or repetition, the mind becomes so much engrossed in the simran that the repetition of the words goes on automatically without any conscious effort at repetition.

What if you do
    Ceaselessly count the beads;
The mind's knots
    Are not untied.
If you become absorbed
    In the Master's lotus feet
You'll have a glimpse
    Of your eternal home.

K.S.S., p.89:22

On its own the melody
    Resounds in each vessel,
Constantly, without a break;
    The soul and Shabd
Have become one,
    The mouth is not needed
To repeat the words.

K.S.S., p.89:24

The rosary rolls in the hand,
    The tongue rolls in the mouth,
And the mind runs
    In the ten directions;
Says Kabir, friends,
    This is not simran.

K.S.S., p.89:25

Some ramble on
    About doctrinal intricacies;
Some gabble and prattle
    Till their throats are hoarse;
Some resort to various
    Arduous practices;
But to me my Master said:
    Be absorbed in simran
To attain your goal.

K.S.S., p.90:40

Till the soil of mind
　　With the plow of simran
And sow the seed of Nam;
　　If all the three worlds
Are parched with drought,
　　Even then the seed of Nam
Will not fail to sprout.

K.S.S., p.92:60

By repeating the Name
　　I became calm and still,
Dwelling on true knowledge
　　I became absorbed within;
My soul and Shabd
　　Have become one:
The fish has turned
　　Into sea.

K.S.S., p.92:62

ABSORPTION IN SIMRAN

Keep your mind in simran
    As the water girl
Keeps her attention
    In the pitchers;
She walks, she talks,
    But her attention,
O Kabir, stays in the pitchers
    On her head.[1]

K.S.S., p.88:7

Keep your mind in simran
    As the cow's thoughts
Are fixed on her calf;
    All day she grazes
Out in the meadows
    But never forgets
The calf in the cowshed
    Who awaits her return.

K.S.S., p.88:8

Keep your mind in simran
    As the lustful
Lives in thoughts of lust;
    Not for a moment
Does he forget—
    Night and day,
All through the eight watches,
    On the object of his lust
He dwells.

K.S.S., p.88:6

---

1. In India the village women bring water from wells or ponds which may be at some distance from their home. They carry two or more full pitchers on their head, one on top of the other, without using their hands to support them.

Keep your mind in simran
    As the miser broods
Over his wealth;
    Every moment his thoughts
Hover over his hoard.
K.S.S., p.88:9

Be engrossed in simran
    Like the deer absorbed
In the sound of the drum;
    The hunters' darts
It gladly bears, O Kabir,
    But leaves not the company
Of what is dear to its heart.
K.S.S., p.88:10

Live always in simran
    As the fish in water—
A moment's separation
    And it gives up its life, O Kabir.
K.S.S., p.88:13

Be attuned to simran
    As the worm
To the mason wasp's call;
    It acquires the hue
Of the mason wasp
    And loses its self.
K.S.S., p.88:12

Keep your attention in simran,
    Let your mouth and tongue
Their silence hold;
    Close the outer portals,
Open the inner door.
K.S.S., p.88:14

The Lord's Name is his own essence,
It is the tilak,[1] the diadem
Of the three worlds.
When Kabir the slave
Put it on his forehead,
He acquired
Boundless beauty and grace.

K.G., p.4:3

Kabir, simran is the essence
Of all paths,
All else is nothing
But a fruitless task;
I have scanned
The origin and the end
Of all practices,
And found them all
Within the bounds of Kal.

K.G., p.4:5

If he has any concern,
This slave has concern only
For the Lord's Name;
About other matters
He worries not.
All thoughts
Save that of God
Only tighten
The noose of Kal.

K.G., p.4:6

---

1. An auspicious mark of distinction put on the forehead.

Kabir's heart shudders
>Seeing the world aflame;[1]
Pick up the pail
>Of the Lord's simran,
Lose no time,
>Extinguish the blaze.
>>*K.G., p.6:32*

Simran leads to happiness,
>Through simran pain departs;[2]
Says Kabir, do simran
>And you will merge in the Lord.
>>*K.S.S., p.87:1*

Of the monarch and the mendicant,
>Of the affluent and the pauper,
He alone is noble and high
>Who repeats the Name;
But, Kabir, the highest of the high
>Is the one who repeats
With no expectation of reward.
>>*K.S.S., p.87:2*

Men and women
>Will suffer misery
As long as desire
>Guides their efforts;
Kabir, he is dear to the Lord
>Who does simran
But desires no reward.
>>*K.S.S., p.87:3*

All do simran
>During the gloom of adversity;
In days of sunshine
>Few repeat the Name.

---

1. In the fire of desires and passions.
2. The pain and misery of births and deaths.

If man does simran
In happiness,
He will not suffer
Adversity's pain.

K.S.S., p.87:4

The five confidantes will call
'Beloved, Beloved'
If the sixth will repeat the Name;[1]
Through simran
Kabir blossomed
And obtained his Beloved—
The priceless gem.

K.G., p.4:7

My mind does simran
Of the Lord's Name,
In Him it stays absorbed;
To whom shall I bow my head
When through simran
I have become one
With the Lord?

K.G., p.4:8

'You, you' I repeated,
And you I became;
No trace of 'I'
Is left in me.
Through this barter
I have lost my 'I'—
Wherever I look
Only you I see.

K.G., p.4:9

---

1. *The five confidantes:* the five senses of perception; through simran they will also lovingly turn Godwards. *The sixth:* the mind.

The fruits of chanting and piety,
  Of penance and austerity,
Can all through simran be gained;
  Kabir, the true devotees know:
No other practice
  Can reach the heights of simran.

K.S.S., p.91:45

Simran of the true Name
  Is always fruitful,
Whether done with fervor
  Or with frown;
The seed in the field sprouts
  Whether it falls with its face
Upward or down.

K.S.S., p.91:53

DYING WHILE LIVING

The process of withdrawing mind and soul from the body and bringing them to the eye center has been called 'dying while living' by the Saints. This is the first step in the soul's inner spiritual journey, for only after vacating the body or leaving the physical world can the soul enter the inner spiritual worlds. When the mind, soul and consciousness are withdrawn, all awareness of the physical body and surroundings is temporarily lost. The body becomes dead to everything, although the physical functions of the body, such as breathing, blood circulation and so on, continue undisturbed.

In these short poems Kabir praises dying while living as a factor essential in gaining the treasure of spiritual knowledge—the diamond of Shabd or Nam, the rare jewel of God-realization. Those who vacate the body and go to the inner regions during the period of their spiritual practice—that is, those who die while living—conquer death and become free from the chain of birth and death.

> To die is better than to live
>   If one only knew how to die;
> He who dies before death's approach,
>   Ageless and deathless he becomes
> In Kaliyug, this age of darkness.
>
> *K.G., p.50:8*

> Infallible is the Lord's touchstone,
>   The counterfeit cannot pass by;
> He alone will stand the test
>   Who while living knows how to die.
>
> *K.G., p.51:9*

> Kabir, rare are they
>   Who while living die;
> Free from all fear they merge
>   In the Lord's qualities
> And wherever they look
>   Only Him they see.[1]
>
> *A.G., p.1364:5*

---

1. Merging in the Lord's qualities implies merging in the Lord or becoming one with Him; it is only then that one sees Him everywhere.

Death after death the world dies,
　　But no one knows how to die;
Who knows how to die, O Kabir,
　　Never faces death again.

A.G., p.1366:29

Kabir, a vast ocean is this body,
　　Hard to fathom its depth;
One who dies while living
　　And plunges within
Earns the rarest of jewels.

K.S.S., p.114:2

Like the diver of the deep seas,[1]
　　Dying while living, I dived
Into the ocean within;
　　A handful of knowledge I brought back
Which contained a vast treasure.

K.S.S., p.114:3

I dived into the ocean
　　And emerged from the sky—
The firmament I made my home;
　　This slave thus obtained
A priceless diamond.

K.S.S., p.114:4

How can you find God, the diamond,
　　While you long to remain alive?
The disciple, while living, who dies
　　Fetches the jewel
From Master, the ocean.

K.S.S., p.114:5

---

1. The deep sea divers were a group of professionals in medieval India who were adepts in diving and could hold their breath for several minutes while they stayed under water. They were therefore called *marjeeva*—'who die and live again'. Here Kabir uses the metaphor of a diver to describe the devotee who dies while living.

Kabir, tall is the tree
　　With fruits high in the skies;
Only he tastes the fruit
　　Who while living dies.

K.S.S., p.115:11

He who burns the house
　　Emancipates it;
He who preserves it
　　Will lose it.[1]
A great wonder I saw:
　　Who died while living
Killed death itself.[2]

K.S.S., p.116:29

---

1. Through this paradox Kabir says that the devotee who 'destroys' the house of his body attains liberation; that is, if he withdraws from his body during his spiritual practice, leaving the body as 'dead,' he gains liberation from the chain of birth and death. However, if he 'preserves' his body, that is, if he remains engrossed in physical pursuits and is afraid to die while living, he loses the gift of human birth, which was given to him to attain God-realization.

2. Symbolically the devotee destroys death because he conquers the fear of death and once for all ends the torture of taking birth and dying again and again.

THE CREEPER

The path of the Saints is not that of renunciation, of practicing austerities and harsh self-discipline in the seclusion of caves and forests. It is the path of love and devotion, of going within and experiencing spiritual bliss. When the devotee goes within and develops true love and longing for the Lord, his mind —previously dominating the soul—becomes a slave, and worldly desires and cravings fade away. Enjoying the taste of inner spiritual bliss, mind becomes averse to worldly pleasures.

The ascetics, hatha yogis, hermits and recluses make their bodies emaciated through rigorous practices—fasting, penances and austerities—but when faced with the world, the withered creeper of their passions and cravings again sprouts and starts bearing bitter fruits. The fire of austerities appears to have destroyed the forest of attachments, but when the fire dies down, the forest takes no time to become green again.

Kabir says that the tree of life bears fruit only when its roots are cut, that is, when the soul separates itself from the physical body and goes into the inner spiritual regions. If one tries to cut the creeper of the passions, it spreads and blossoms—the more one suppresses the passions and desires, the greater the force with which they rebound—but if it is given the water of devotion, it dries up naturally.

In the path of the Saints, the sublimation of desires and passions is not a deliberate or forced process; it is the natural result of the diversion of the mind and soul currents from the outside world to the inner regions of ineffable bliss. Kabir, through paradox, amplifies this essential aspect of Sant Mat.

Kabir, the creeper withered,
    Neither its fruit
Nor its form was left;
    I brought it home
To use as fuel,
    But it turned green
And tendrils began
    To sprout again.

The fire runs through the forest
    Consuming everything in its path;
But greenery trails the fire,
    The woods regain their verdant sheen.

Kabir, all praise to the tree
                   That bears fruit
Only when its roots are cut.

Kabir, if I cut it,
                   It flourishes all the more;
If I water it,
                   It wilts and dies.
Strange are the ways
                   Of this wondrous creeper
Which I have no words
                   To describe.

Kabir, in the courtyard is the creeper,
                   Its fruit is in the sky;
It is like a heifer's milk,
                   Like an arrow
Made from a rabbit's horn,
                   Like the antics
Of a barren woman's son.[1]

Kabir, bitter is the creeper,
                   Bitter the fruit it bears;
Only when the fruit
                   Gives up the creeper's company
Is it called the property
                   Of the holy ones.[2]

---

1. The cravings, desires and fantasies of man are endless and can never be satiated because the chain of desires has no limits. The creeper of man's desires bears fruits in the sky, that is, while living in the world he dreams of things impossible to attain. A heifer or calfless cow cannot give milk, an arrow cannot be made out of a rabbit's horns because rabbits do not have horns, and a barren woman has no son; in the same way the endless cravings, hopes, desires and dreams of man have no basis in reality.
2. After removing the kernel and carving the top into a handle, ascetics carry around the bitter gourd—one of their few possessions. Kabir says that the bitter fruit gains this elevated position only after it is cut off from the creeper; man can stay in the company of Saints only after he parts from the company of the creeper of worldly desires and longings.

Kabir, what if it reaches
The hands of an ascetic,
Still its bitter smell
Spreads all around,
And its seeds yet
Hidden in the shell
Can sprout again.[1]

K.G., p.67:58:1-6

---

1. The bitter gourd retains its smell for some time even after the kernel is removed, and often a few seeds remain embedded in the shell. Kabir says that even if one reaches the company of the Saints, one should not be complacent, for the seed of desires and passions might still be lying in the mind and is liable to sprout at any time.

ON SLANDER

Devotees who are engrossed in the practice of Nam and have attained self-realization do not bother about anything else. They become truly humble and fail to see anything bad in others. But among the worldly, says Kabir, there are few who do not indulge in talking ill of others. A devotee should have affection and regard even for the slanderer, for according to the Saints, critics are a devotee's best friends. They make him aware of his faults and through their own malice lighten the burden of his karmas and thus make him clean.[1]

The couplets selected here praise the slanderer for his cleansing role, but at the same time warn a devotee never to indulge in maligning others. If he is inclined to find fault, he should try to realize his own shortcomings and re-form himself. Like the bumblebee that looks only at the nectar in flowers and not at their shape, size, color or fragrance, the devotee should see the One Lord present in everyone.

Kabir, those miserable ones
  Indulge in slander
Who have not attained knowledge;
  But those intoxicated
By the Lord's Name
  Relish nothing else.

K.G., p.65:1

Men laugh and make fun
  Of others' shortcomings
But never look at their own,
  Which are countless, not few.

K.G., p.65:2

Keep the slanderer near,
  Give him a hut in your yard,
For without water, without soap,
  He will wash you and make you clean.

K.G., p.65:3

---

1. See the poem, "Slanderer, Well-wisher."

Do not drive away the slanderer,
    Give him respect and regard;
He will cleanse your heart and mind
    When he decries and maligns you
With unscrupulous zeal.

K.G., p.65:4

May my slanderer never die,
    May he for ages live;
Kabir realized his Master
    Through the slanderer's kind words.

K.S.S., p.160:3

I have scanned the seven seas
    And the vast Jambu Deep;[1]
Hardly a person could I find
    Who does not love to malign.

K.S.S., p.161:7

Kabir, never malign
    Even the bit of straw
That lies under your feet;
    Some day it may fly up
And land in your eyes—
    The pain will remind you
That nothing is worthless
    In this world.[2]

K.G., p.65:6

---

1. According to the Hindu Puranas, *Jambu Deep* is one of the seven continents of the world; India forms a small part of it.
2. Kabir means that even someone who looks trifling and ordinary has his own importance in that he also is playing the role, good or bad, assigned to him by his fate karmas.

622

He who speaks ill of a Saint
 Will fall into calamity;
In hell he will be born,
 In hell he will die,
And never will he attain
 Salvation.
K.G., p.65:5

Praise not your own self
 Nor speak ill of others;
There is still a long way to go—
 Who knows what may happen tomorrow.
K.G., p.65:7 fn

Praise not your own self
 Nor call others bad;
Who knows under which desolate tree
 Your carcass will rot
And turn into a heap of bones.
K.G., p.65:7

Kabir, I set out
 To find an evil person
But could not find
 A single one;
When my own heart I searched
 I found out
There is none worse than me.
K.S.S., p.141:11

I am the worst of all,
 All are better than me;
One who realizes this
 Is a friend of Kabir.
K.S.S., p.141:12

Kabir, look not at others' faults,
    Pick out only their merits;
Like the bumblebee
    That hungers only for honey,
See the Lord in the flower
    Of every heart.

K.G., p.43:3

INTOXICANTS

In Kaliyug, Kal has sent
   Tobacco, opium and wine
As his agents, to make man
   Lose his head, forget devotion
And stay in Kal's confines.

K.S.S., p.163:2

Opium and hemp,
   Tobacco and wine,
Kabir, discard them all
   If you crave a glimpse
Of the Lord.

K.S.S., p.163:3

O wise ones, consider
   The curse of wine;
You part with money
   That with effort you earn,
In order to turn from man
   Into beast.

K.S.S., p.163:4

The drug-addicted
   Will never, never
Gain the opposite shore;
   Kabir firmly says:
O men, understand
   And from such habits refrain.

K.S.S., p.163:5

Kabir, men who take
　　Fish, hemp and drink,
Despite fasts and pilgrimages
　　And many a pious deed,
They'll suffer endless agony
　　In hell's bottomless pit.
　　　　　　A.G., p.1377:233

Many are the intoxicants
　　That afflict the world;
Few are aware of them.
　　Intoxication of wealth,
Of a keen mind,
　　Of physical beauty,
Of high caste
　　And a noble name,
Assails one and all.
　　　　　　K.S.S., p.163:6

Intoxication of learning,
　　Of merits and virtues,
And that of power and position—
　　Only when one gives up
Such intoxications, can one enjoy
　　The intoxication
Of the divine Word.
　　　　　　K.S.S., p.163:7

Kabir is intoxicated
　　With Nam—
Not with wine,
　　Nor with drugs;
He who drinks
　　From Nam's cup
Is the truly
　　Intoxicated one.
　　　　　　K.S.S., p.163:8

WHO EAT MEAT

The man who eats meat
    Is a demon in human form,
Keep away from him—
    His company
Will ruin your meditation.
                    K.S.S., p.161:1

Who eat meat and fish,
    Who relish drugs and wine,
Their very roots as human beings
    Will be wiped out,
Like radishes uprooted
    By the farmer.
                    K.S.S., p.161:2

All flesh is the same,
    Be it of cow, deer or hen;
Men who fondly eat their meat
    Will find a berth
In the fires of hell.
                    K.S.S., p.162:3

Flesh is a dog's food,
    Not his who is blessed
With a human form;
    If a man allows meat
To enter his mouth,
    He will one day enter
The gates of hell.
                    K.S.S., p.162:4

They who kill
    Will in turn be killed,
Whether they kill
    For eating or for sport;
They will be dragged by the hair
    And taken to task
By the ruthless minions
    Of Kal.

K.S.S., p.162:6

If one eats even a grain of fish,
    And then gives
A million cows in charity,
    Or submits
To the holy saw at Kasi,[1]
    Still the inevitable result
Will be a seat
    In the flames of hell.

K.S.S., p.162:7

The poor goat which eats
    Only grass and leaves
Suffers the fate of being flayed;
    What will be the fate
Of those who eat the goat?

K.S.S., p.162:8

The suffering of all beings
    Is the same,
But foolish man
    Is blind to others' pain;
Why not cut your own throat[2]
    So that the bliss
Of liberation you attain?

K.S.S., p.162:9

---

1. In medieval times there was a large saw kept in the city of Kasi (Banaras). It was believed that those who sacrificed their life on this saw were assured of salvation after death.
2. Destroy your own ego.

To the mullah says the hen:
    Ruthlessly you cut my neck,
But one day the Lord will demand
    An account for your deeds—
Then you will have no answer,
    Then you will suffer
Endless agony and pain.
K.S.S., p.162:10

Blacken the face
    Of your ritual laws,
Banish duality
    From your heart;
All souls belong
    To the One Lord—
O fatuous Mullah,
    Forbear from killing
Any being of God.
K.S.S., p.162:11

Who eats grain is a man,
    Who eats meat, a dog;
Who renders a living being dead
    Is a demon incarnate.
Satt Kabir, p.356:886

Cut the throat of your wrath,
    Your urge to cruelty destroy;
He who ruthlessly kills the five[1]
    Will surely meet the Lord.
K.S.S., p.162:12

---

1. The five passions.

You violently slaughter
     Innocent animals
And claim it to be in keeping
     With the canons of your creed;
But when God places before you
     The record of your cruel deeds,
What will your fate be?
                    A.G., p.1375:199

Kabir, eat porridge to your fill
     With the seasoning of salt;
Who would eat meat
     And get his own throat cut?
                    A.G., p.1374:188

The qazi and the priest
     Both embraced delusion
And took to the ways
     Of the world—
God and religion
     They forgot
The moment they took
     A knife in their hands.
                    K.G., p.33:7

The evil ones,
     Even sitting in worship
Eat meat and drink wine;
     They will never gain salvation,
In the fires of hell
     They will sink a million times.
                    K.G., p.33:13

Hindus have no kindness,
    Turks no mercy
In their hearts;
    Says Kabir,
Both will be dragged down
    By the currents
Of the eighty-four.

K.S.S., p.163:16

I tell you, O men,
    Again and again I warn,
Remember what I say:
    Whose throat today you cut
Will cut yours one day.

K.S.S., p.163:15

O man, such indeed
    Is your utility
That your meat
    Can be put to no use:
Nor from your bones
    Can ornaments be made,
Nor can your skin
    Be mounted on a drum.

Bijak, Sakhi 199

Cherish kindness and mercy
    Within your heart;
Man, why should you become
    Merciless and harsh
When from the tiny ant
    To the mighty elephant
All beings belong to God?

Satt Kabir, p.356:940

631

COMPANY OF THE EVIL

The company that a person keeps makes a deep impression on his mind. Association with cheats, drunkards and the immoral will pull one's mind down to their level. It is an accepted fact that most bad habits are acquired through the company of those who indulge in them. Saints, fully aware of the working of the human mind, know that evil company has a subtle degrading influence, inevitably marring a man's mind just as a rotten fruit spoils the fruits next to it. Kabir warns man of the pitfalls of bad company and through examples from folklore and nature says that those who wish to tread the path of devotion should avoid bad company.

> The raindrop, pure in the sky,
>> Becomes dirty
> In contact with earth:
>> Without good company
> Man loses his essence,
>> His mettle;
> He turns into slag
>> And ruins his worth.
>
> *K.G., p.37:1*

> Seek not the company
>> Of the evil—
> An iron bar will not float
>> Nor take you across the sea;
> The drop of rain falls
>> On the roots of a plantain,
> Into an oyster's shell
>> Or the mouth of a snake:
> The results accord
>> With the company it keeps.[1]
>
> *K.G., p.37:2*

---

1. According to folklore, the rainfall under the constellation *swāti* produces different results depending on where it falls. The drops that fall in the roots of the plantain tree turn into camphor, those that fall into an oyster shell become pearls, and those that fall into the mouth of a snake become poison.

Those who oppose the men of God
       And adore the worldly
Will never thrive,
       Like seeds that fall
On barren ground.

K.G., p.37:3

I'm wounded by the thorns
       Of bad company,
Like the plantain tree
       Near the jujube:
Each time the jujube
       Moves its branches
The plantain is torn
       By its thorns—
Lord rescue me from the company
       Of those averse to Thee.

K.G., p.37:4

'Me and mine' is the sign of death,
       The company of the evil
Is the company of Kal;
       Says Kabir: My friend,
Listen to the words
       Of the God-intoxicated ones.

K.G., p.37:5

The fly is caught in treacle,
       Her wings are stuck;
She wrings her hands,
       She beats her head,
But cannot free herself
       From the treacle
That causes her ruin.

K.G., p.37:6

633

What if you are highborn,
       If your actions are not high;
Though a flask be made
       Of pure gold
It will not find favor
       With the Saints
If it is filled with wine.

K.G., p.37:7

Who willfully turns
       His face away from truth,
Who adores all that is false,
       Spare me his company, Lord,
Even in my dreams.

K.G., p.39:9

In these couplets Kabir tries to impress upon the seeker's mind the importance of good company. The word used for good company is *satsang*, 'association of the true' or 'company of those who have realized Truth'. Kabir calls such realized persons 'men of God' or 'Saints' and says that the Lord can only be attained through their company. The time spent with them never goes to waste, for their elevating and inspiring presence and the atmosphere around them, surcharged with spirituality, leaves a deep impression on the seeker's mind and soul. A seeker becomes worthy of the gift of Nam only through his association with men of God and it is from them that he receives the blessing of Nam. Kabir says that the devotee should not expect worldly benefits and material comforts in the Saints' company, but should accept whatever hardships or discomforts he may have to face. Association with them is truly purifying—infinitely more than pilgrimages to holy places—and a short while spent in their company destroys numerous sins and removes many doubts from the seeker's mind.

Kabir, from forest
    To forest I roamed
In search of the Lord;
    Only when I found
The man of God
    Did I attain my object.

K.G., p.39:5

Time spent in a Saint's company
    Is never in vain;
Neem in the vicinity
    Of the sandalwood tree
Itself becomes fragrant—
    No longer is it known
By the bitter tree's name.[1]

K.G., p.38:1

---

1. The neem or margosa tree is extremely bitter; its leaves, branches, bark, fruit— even its smell is bitter. But according to folklore, if it grows near a sandalwood tree, it loses its bitterness, acquires the fragrance of sandalwood and is even called sandalwood.

Keep the company of Saints,
    Whose mind is always
Perfect and pure;
    Beyond measure they give
The rare wealth of Nam.
                      K.S.S., p.49:2

Stay in the company of Saints
    Though you may only get
Oat chaff to eat;
    Never go to the company
Of the evil
    Even if you are offered
Milk, sweets and delicacies.
                      K.S.S., p.49:4

Kabir, the company of the Saint
    Is like the perfumer's shop:
Even if the perfumer
    Gives you nothing,
Still the fragrance
    Will fill your heart.
                      K.S.S., p.49:5

Miraculous powers,
    Wealth and prosperity
I do not ask for;
    Only for one boon I pray—
Lord, grant to Kabir
    The Saints' darshan
Night and day.
                      K.S.S., p.49:6

Go to Mathura,
Go to Dwarika,
Go to Jagannath, if you so please;
But without a Saint's company
And without meditation
Nothing will you ever achieve.

K.S.S., p.49:9

The city may be thriving,
Full of beauty and glow,
At every turn celebrations and joy;
But if it is devoid
Of a true devotee of God,
In the eyes of Kabir
It is a city
Barren and bleak.

K.G., p.41:2

The house in which
The Saint is not adored,
The house which is empty
Of devotion for the Lord,
Kabir, that house
Is like a graveyard,
And there dwell
Only goblins and ghosts.

K.G., p.41:3

For one hour, for a half hour,
Even for a half of a half,
Kabir, the company of Saints
A million sins destroys.

K.S.S., p.50:23

637

THE HAWK OF DEATH

Men look upon the false
   Pleasures of the world
As lasting and blissful,
   They cherish them
With fervor and joy;
   But all beings
Are food for Kal: some
   Are between his jaws,
Some in hand, and some
   Await their turn
In the plate.

K.G., p.56:1

Kabir, this day or the next,
   Or in the dark of night,
During work or walk,
   All of a sudden,
At a moment unthought,
   Kal will attack—
As the ruthless hawk pounces
   On the bird of prey.

K.G., p.56:2

Kal stands by your bed,
   Gazing at you with glee;
Awake, says Kabir,
   Dear friend, awake!
Neglecting the Lord's devotion
   How can you afford
Thus to sleep carefree?

K.G., p.56:3

Soundly sleeps the world,
   But not the Lord's devotee;
He knows that Kal is waiting
   Like the eager groom
At the bride's door.
                              K.G., p.56:4

Turn by turn depart
   Your dear ones;
Each day, my friend,
   Your turn comes nearer.
                              K.G., p.57:9

What has risen
   Must one day set,
What has bloomed
   Must wither away,
What has been made
   Must crumble;
So also must go
   The one who has come.
                              K.G., p.57:11

Like a bubble in water
   Is our fate;
One day we will vanish
   Like the stars
That with the coming of dawn
   Fade.
                              K.G., p.57:14

What is this world, O Kabir—
   One moment sour,
Next moment sweet;
   Those who yesterday
In palaces sat,
   Today in cemeteries sleep.
                              K.G., p.57:15

639

Towering mansions
    Shining and high,
With painted gates
    Aglow with color,
Without the Lord's Name
    Will be turned by Yama
Into mansions of woe.

K.G., p.58:18

What are you vain of,
    Proud man?
Kal already holds you
    By the hair,
Who knows when he'll wield
    The final blow—
At home or in some
    Distant land.

K.G., p.58:19

Kabir, love the Lord,
    Do not be attached
To the world,
    Filthy and false;
How can one foretell
    The age of the goat
Tied at the butcher's door?

K.G., p.59:27

The mourners have died,
    So too have died
Those who lit the pyre;
    They have passed away
Who wept and cried
    And pined for the dead;
There's none in the world
    Towards whom one can turn
To be saved.

K.G., p.60:31

Kabir, real happiness
    Lies in the love of God;
All else is a fountain
    Of misery and pain—
For men and sages,
    Demons and gods
Are all firmly held
    By the noose of Kal.

K.G., p.59:29

THE HERB OF IMMORTALITY

Where death and birth
    Do not prevail,
Where no one has
    Even heard of death,
Come, Kabir,
    To that land of bliss
Where the Lord
    Is the healer
Of all your ills.

K.G., p.60:1

Live in the world's ocean
    Of turmoil and dread
As a lotus lives in the lake
    But is never wet;
Take your soul
    To that land, Kabir,
Where Kal and his agents
    An entry cannot find.

K.S.S., p.114:2

Kabir proceeds
    To his Beloved's feet,
Having unfettered himself
    Of cravings and maya's lure;
High in the sky
    He has made his dwelling—
Kal in frustration
    Curses his fate.

K.G., p.60:3

Subdue the mind,
      Fell it to the ground,
Wipe out the evil ego;
      Thus vanquished, your mind
Will cry, 'Beloved, Beloved';
      Then Kal will not dare
To touch even a hair
      On your head.

K.G., p.60:4

Who makes his home
      The top of a scaffold,
Who gladly poison eats,
      How can Kal touch him,
For he is alert
      Throughout the eight beats.[1]

K.S.S., p.116:25

Kabir has made his self
      Sharp and thin
By whetting it
      On love and longing's hone.
My heart thus made fine
      Has merged with each petal
Of my Beloved's lotus feet;
      Kal is in retreat,
For I am beyond his reach.

K.G., p.60:5

---

1. One who has attained the state of dying while living and whose attention is most of the time at the eye center ("scaffold"), who desires nothing and accepts all hardships ("poison") that come in life as the Lord's will, who is always on his guard against the lures and pitfalls of mind and maya, for such a devotee the negative power holds no terror; having died while living, he has no fear of death or of Kal, the lord of death.

MEETING THE MASTER

In the absence of guidance from a spiritual adept, man pursues the path of external observances, reading scriptures and visiting holy places; but true knowledge, which is an internal experience, eludes him. In these couplets, Kabir describes the Master as the torch-bearer of divine knowledge, an adept who has himself merged in the Lord and enables the seeker to do the same. He dispels the darkness of delusions, removes all worldly fears, protects the disciple from becoming a prey to worldly cravings and lures, gives him the spiritual strength to travel on the path, opens his inner eye to see the Lord, and teaches him the way to play the game of life in this world and win the prize of union with God. The devotee who merges in the Master loses all prejudices of caste, color, religion and lineage and obtains real love for the Lord.

Kabir, I was trailing
    The shadows of rituals,
Of customs and holy books;
    But my Master came
And placed a lamp in my hand.
                    K.G., p.2:11

A lamp brimming
    With the oil of love he gave,
With a wick that will never run short;
    In its light
I have finished all transactions,
    I will never again visit
This marketplace.
                    K.G., p.2:12

When Kabir met the Master
    The light of knowledge
Illuminated his heart;
    Let me never forget him!
In him I found a savior—
    Through the grace of the Lord.
                    K.G., p.2:13

644

When I found my Master,
    Perfect and powerful,
I merged in him
    Like salt into flour;
Kabir has lost his caste,
    His creed, his self—
For which trait now
    Will you give him a name?[1]
            K.G., p.2:14

It is a great blessing
    That I found the Master;
Without him I would have
    Led myself to ruin,
As the moth flies into the flame
    The moment it sees the lamp.
            K.G., p.2:19

From the throne of realization
    My Master gave me
Solace and strength;
    Without any fear,
Without a shade of doubt,
    Worship the Absolute, says Kabir.
            K.G., p.2:23

I gained poise, I attained
    The state of Truth
When my Master gave me
    Wisdom and strength;
Kabir now trades in divine diamonds
    On the banks of the Crystal Lake.
            K.G., p.3:29

---

1. A person is identified by his name, which is often based on his caste, creed or country. The devotee who merges into the inner Master rises above all such distinguishing traits.

Kabir, infinite is my Master's glory,
    Infinite is the bounty he gave;
He opened my eye to see the Infinite,
    The Infinite he revealed to me.

                                    K.G., p.1:3

When the perfect Master I met
    All my worries were driven away;
He made my soul immaculate—
    Now he is ever at my side.

                                    K.G., p.4:35

The chaupar is laid
    At the crossroads
In the market between
    The high and the low;[1]
Says Kabir, the Lord's slave:
    With the Master's guidance
Play the game well.

                                    K.G., p.3:31

I took the dice of love,
    I made my body the pawn;
As taught by my Master
    I threw the dice—
Thus played Kabir
    And won the game.

                                    K.G., p.3:32

---

1. *Chaupar:* a game played on a board with dice and pawns. "The high and the low":
aradh and *uradh*. *Aradh* literally means 'halfway' or 'midway', but Kabir, as also some
other Saints, uses it for the 'low' or 'lower point' in the inner journey of the soul, thus
implying the eye center. *Uradh* is the 'high' or 'higher point' and refers to the higher region
of pure spirit which is beyond Brahm. Thus "between *aradh* and *uradh*" means the region
between the eye center and the highest region, hence Trikuti, the second stage in the soul's
spiritual journey.

The Master became pleased with me,
He whispered one word of grace;
The cloud of love poured forth
And drenched my entire being.

K.G., p.3:33

Kabir, clouds laden with love
In abundance poured down on me;
Within, my soul was drenched,
And around me
Even the desert turned green.

K.G., p.3:34

GURU IS GOD

Saints, sages and holy books have described the Master as God. The Master is that person who either comes directly from the region of the Supreme Being or who has reached that region and merged into the Lord. Though he lives in the world like any other human being, he is always in communion with the Lord within. Kabir, while praising the Master, repeatedly calls him God or greater than God. For man the Master is greater than God because it is through the Master that the Lord manifests himself to man; and the manifest form of the Lord is more important for the seeker than the unmanifested, which cannot be contacted, perceived or comprehended on his present physical level of consciousness.

> Know that the Master is the Lord,
> > Be engrossed in the Shabd he gives;
> Bow to the Master, adore him,
> > Contemplate on him without a break.
>
> *K.S.S., p.1:8*

> The Master and God are one,
> > All else is a reflection;
> Vanquish the 'I',
> > Adore the Master,
> Only then will you find the Lord.
>
> *K.S.S., p.3:29*

> Those who look upon the Master
> > As a man, O Kabir, are blind;
> In this world they suffer misery,
> > In the next, Yama's noose.
>
> *K.S.S., p.3:31*

> O Kabir, those men are indeed blind
> > Who think the Master is other than God.
> If the Lord is angry
> > The Master is your asylum;

648

If the Master is displeased
　　There is no refuge
In the entire creation.
                          K.S.S., p.3:33

Kabir, if God is annoyed
　　Take the refuge of the Master's feet;
But, asserts Kabir, if you earn
　　The Master's displeasure,
Not even God will come to your aid.
                          K.S.S., p.4:46

In the three worlds, nine continents,
　　Greater than the Master there is none:
Even God cannot act
　　Against the Master's will;
What the Master wills,
　　That alone will happen.
                          K.S.S., p.4:45

Master and God both stand
　　Face to face with me—
To whom should I pay my respects?
　　Hail to thee, my Master,
Who revealed the Lord to me!
                          K.S.S., p.2:10

I sacrifice myself
　　At your feet, my Master,
A million times, again and again;
　　From man you made me divine—
And in doing so, took no time.
                          K.S.S., p.2:11

Master is greater than the Lord,

    Reflect and realize in your heart;

They who worship the Lord

    Remain bound to this shore,[1]

Who adore the Master

    Cross over to the shores of bliss.

K.S.S., p.3:34

---

1. That is, they who worship God without initiation and guidance from a perfect Master. On the physical plane, man has not seen God, and his attempt to worship Him is only the worship of a mental concept and not of the reality. It is a natural instinct in everybody to worship the Lord; but ignorant both of the object of their devotion and of the way to worship Him, people worship in their own way—according to the dictates of their own mind. This kind of worship does not take them beyond the realms of mind to the 'shore' of liberation.

MASTER, THE PERFECT CRAFTSMAN

Saints have described the Master with similes from nature and daily life in order to bring out his various qualities and the spiritual benefits he bestows on the disciple. Here Kabir says the Master is a grinder who removes the rust of ingrained habits and superstitions; he puts the disciple on the hone of Nam and purifies his mind. Like a washerman, he cleanses the disciple's mind of all worldly attachments, and like a potter, he molds the disciple's mind and soul into a vessel fit to contain the elixir of spiritual bliss. Like a blacksmith, he heats the iron of the disciple's mind to remove its impurities and shape it into an instrument of spiritual utility. The Master is a beacon of spirituality and the disciple coming in contact with him is spiritually illumined. Like the philosophers' stone he completely transforms the disciple, and like the banker he judges the worth of the disciple and admits him into the Lord's treasury.

In the end Kabir identifies the Master with Shabd or the Word when he calls him the ship of Shabd. He further says that the Master and God are one, therefore all attempts to describe him are incomplete because one cannot say that the Master is a man and not God, nor that he is God and not a man, for he is both God and man at the same time.

> Submit yourself to the Master
> —The adept grinder—
> Let him burnish your mind;
> He'll remove all layers of rust,
> Like a mirror it will shine.
>
> *K.S.S., p.3:24*

> Disciple is the sword,
> Master, the grindstone;
> He'll put the disciple
> On the hone of Nam[1]—
> If he bears the scouring by Shabd
> And still stays firm
> At the Master's feet,
> He will emerge a disciple
> Pure and bright.
>
> *K.S.S., p.3:25*

---

1. A rusted blade is first put on the grindstone to remove the rust and give a preliminary sharpening; then it is put on the hone to polish it and to even the cutting edge.

Master is the washerman,
  Disciple, the soiled cloth,
And soap is the Lord's Name.
  On the rock of meditation[1]
The Master washes the cloth
  Luminous and clean.

K.S.S., p.3:26

Master is the potter,
  Disciple, the pot;
The Master puts him on the wheel
  And removes his rough corners—
He raps the pot on the outside
  But inside keeps
His hand of support.

K.S.S., p.3:27

I met the true Master
  As hot iron meets the blacksmith:
He put me under the hammer
  And brought out my essence;
He made me pure gold.

K.G., p.3:28

Master is the magic stone,[2]
  Approach him
With humility and care;
  He is the burning candle
To which neighbors come
  To light their candles
From its flame.[3]

K.S.S., p.10:113

---

1. In medieval India—and even today—the washerman would wash clothes on large rocks or boulders near a river or pond, rubbing the cloth or beating it against the stone.
2. *Pāras* or the philosophers' stone, which turns iron into pure gold.
3. In medieval times when there were no matches, a well-to-do household in the village or town would always keep a lamp burning throughout the day. In the evening, housewives from the neighborhood would come with their lamps to light them.

The Master is an adept banker[1]
    Who picks out the true
From the counterfeit;
    He rescues suffering souls
From the world's dreadful sea,
    He provides them
With a haven
    At his lotus feet.
K.S.S., p.10:116

The Master is the ship of Shabd,
    Only few know of his state;
When the drop and the Ocean are one,
    How can I say, he is this, not That?
K.S.S., p.10:118

---

1. In early days the banker used to be an independent businessman who combined the functions of giving loans, accepting deposits and judging good coins from counterfeit.

MASTER, THE TRUE WARRIOR

Kabir describes the Master as a warrior who shoots the disciple with the arrow of Shabd or Word, with unfailing aim. When the disciple's soul is connected to the Shabd, he develops a longing for the Lord or, in Kabir's words, his heart is wounded by the arrow of Shabd. He falls to the earth, his ego is destroyed; his deep-rooted dogmas and beliefs in outward practices, his cravings, desires and attachment to the world and its objects are all 'killed' by the shaft of Shabd. Now the Word or Nam alone lives in the devotee's mind and soul. This Shabd is a gift of love and grace from the Master and, though accompanied by the pain of longing, it is sweet and enraptures the disciple.

The process of withdrawing the soul current from the nine portals of the body and vacating it, called by the Saints, dying while living, begins only after the disciple is connected with the Shabd. The devotee who thus dies while living begins his journey to higher spiritual realms, merges into the Shabd and reaches the Lord. He becomes free from the chain of birth and death. In the last stanza Kabir says that one who is blessed by the Master with Shabd or who is 'shot' with the arrow of Shabd, will not 'live' again; that is, a person once connected to Shabd will be pulled up by Shabd to the inner, higher regions and will be free from the cycle of birth and death forever.

My Master, the true warrior,
　　Shot only one arrow of Shabd;
Pierced to the core,
　　I fell flat on the earth.
　　　　　　K.G., p.1:7

My Master, the adept warrior,
　　Shot and wounded me
From my feet to my head.
　　From outside I appear whole;
Within, I am torn to shreds.
　　　　　　K.S.S., p.7:76

My Master pulled the bow
　　Loaded with arrows sharp;

One he shot with such love
      And grace
That it entered my heart—
      And there it is still.

K.G., p.1:6

My Master shot an arrow
      At the center of my heart
With his ruthless aim;
      Only Nam lives in me,
I am dead to all else.

K.S.S., p.7:80

Deftly he balanced the arrow,
      He pulled the string with skill,
It hit the mark in my heart:
      All who lived in me are dead
And I, though living,
      Am alive no more.

K.S.S., p.7:81

The shaft pierced my heart,
      I am enthralled with joy—
I am not dead, nor alive;
      Kabir, they become immortal
Who thus while living die.

K.S.S., p.8:87

The restless one[1] is killed,
      It neither laughs nor talks—
Within itself it is absorbed;
      For to its depths, O Kabir,
It has been wounded
      By the Master's shot.

K.G., p.1:9

---

1. The mind.

Dumb and witless I became—
    My ears could no longer hear,
My feet could no longer walk—
    When my Master shot me
With the arrow of Name.

K.G., p.2:10

My Master shot me
    With a savage aim,
It destroyed all
    That I held dear:
My ego, my practices,
    My rosary, my books.

K.S.S., p.8:90

The Master shot me
    With a perfect aim,
An arrow dipped
    In Shabd's radiant flame;
He declared: Let all know,
    If one shot by me lives anew
I'll not again pick up the bow!

K.S.S., p.7:84

THE SHABD OF THE SAINTS

With love as the mortar,
    A magnificent palace
My Master has raised;
    For the darshan of the Lord
The peephole of Shabd
    He has kept.

K.S.S., p.3:28

The one Shabd
    Of my perfect Master
Many try to know
    Through musing and thinking;
But even the pundits
    And the erudite,
The hermits and ascetics,
    The Vedas and scriptures,
Fail to grasp the Shabd
    That the true Master gives.

K.S.S., p.93:14

Shabd is mine,
    I am of Shabd;
Realize that Shabd
    If you crave salvation—
Don't let this chance slip by.

K.S.S., p.93:12

Shabd is mine,
    I am of Shabd;
Shabd is the support
    Of the entire universe.
If you long to see the Lord,
    Realize the form of Shabd.

K.S.S., p.93:13

The dark shadows of night vanish
    With the rising of the sun;
The contact of Shabd
    Dissolves the gloom of delusion.
                                K.S.S., p.95:37

All mantras, all practices
    Are futile and false,
Let no one fall in their trap;
    Without realization
Of the true Shabd
    A crow cannot
Turn into a swan.
                        K.S.S., p.95:38

Who know the Shabd
    As the essence of Truth,
Who realize it
    And develop faith,
Discard their crow-ness
    And become swans—
Immaculate;
    The turbulent waves
Of this woeful sea
    They conquer,
And reach the shore
    Of bliss.
                    K.S.S., p.95:39

There is no wealth
    Like the wealth of Shabd;
Few know its value.
    Diamonds have a price,
But no one can bid
    A price for Shabd
Nor assess its worth.
                    K.S.S., p.94:20

He who obtains Shabd,
　　Who keeps his soul
In Shabd absorbed,
　　Reaches the royal
Audience Hall;
　　Kabir, there he will see
The Supreme One—
　　My Beloved Lord.
　　　　　　　K.S.S., p.94:22

Men have taken many medicines,
　　Not one their illness cures;
The one panacea my Master gave,
　　And now in Shabd I forever dwell.
　　　　　　　K.S.S., p.94:23

It is not that pearl
　　Which is strung on a thread,
It is the pearl of Shabd
　　That threads one and all.
　　　　　　　K.S.S., p.95:34

The world is caught
　　In the noose of rituals,
Of worship and chanting,
　　Of austerities and penance;
No one tries to realize Shabd—
　　The key to salvation.
　　　　　　　K.S.S., p.95:42

Without Shabd the soul is blind,
　　It knows not where to go;
It wanders in the world
　　Over and again,
For the door of Shabd
　　It fails to find.
　　　　　　　K.S.S., p.93:15

Such is the blow of Shabd,
    It kills, yet the killed
Appears not dead;
    Kabir, he gains liberation
Who lives in the body
    But without his head.

K.S.S., p.94:19

The unhurt cry for the Lord,
    But different is the cry
Of the one who is wounded;
    Kabir, stabbed by Shabd,
Is dumb and lifeless.

K.G., p.50:40:8

So deep is the love
    Of the magnet for iron
That it draws it
    To its own self;
Such is the Shabd of Kabir—
    It pulls the soul
Away from Kal.

Bijak, Sakhi 318

In all the three worlds
    I see Him;
Why do you say
    He is invisible, unseen?
You have failed to know
    The true Shabd,
For you have donned
    The dress of delusion.

Bijak, Sakhi 352

Remember, O learned ones,
　　From the Satguru alone
The true Shabd you can obtain;
　　That Shabd is your essence,
All else is vain.

K.S.S., p.96:48

Catch the Shabd,
　　Your origin and essence;
The ocean will then
　　Merge in the drop,
The part will contain the whole,
　　Like the seed that holds
Within it a mighty tree.

K.S.S., p.96:50

THE ONE WORD

One Word is the source of bliss,
  The other word, of misery and pain;
One Word shatters all chains,
  The other is a noose
Around your neck.
         K.S.S., p.93:6

Between Shabd and shabd
  The difference is vast;
In the primal Shabd
  Be forever absorbed.
The Shabd through which
  The Lord is met,
The practice of that Shabd adopt.
        K.S.S., p.92:4

'Word, Word,' say all,
  But that Word
Has nor form nor shape,
  It is beyond
The reach of speech;
  See it, realize it
Within your own body.
       K.S.S., p.92:5

'Word, Word,' say all,
  But that true Word
Has neither hands nor feet.
  One Word is the panacea
For all maladies;
  Other words, the cause
Of suffering and pain.
       K.S.S., p.93:7

The Shabd I speak of
 Is the primal Shabd;
Each moment stay absorbed
 In that Shabd.
In the end the inner tree
 Will thrive and bear fruit,
The outer roots will wither
 And become dry.[1]

     K.S.S., p.93:9

Such is the nature of Shabd,
 Like a magnet it pulls the soul.
Though a million means
 One may adopt,
There is no salvation
 Without Shabd.

     K.S.S., p.93:16

Read the book that contains
 Neither letters nor ink,
Neither digits nor form;
 Play cymbals without hands,
And without feet dance.

See that inaccessible home
 Suffused with light
But without a lamp.[2]
 Let the floodgates
Of Shabd open that you merge
 In the Being
Who is supreme.

     K.S. II:91:6-7

---

1. The spiritual practice of the disciple will take him within and will bear the fruit of spiritual bliss; outward tendencies and bonds of attachment to the physical world will become ineffective.
2. That is, there is no physical source for the inner light.

THE FRUITS OF NAM

The moment I placed
    Nam within my heart
All my sins were destroyed,
    Like a small spark
Burning a huge haystack.

K.S.S., p.84:11

Let your soul stay
    Absorbed in Nam,
Be indifferent to the world;
    Have unshaken faith, Kabir,
In the Master's lotus feet.

K.S.S., p.85:22

A golden chance like this
    You'll not obtain again;
Catch hold of Nam,
    The true savior of all:
In the twinkling of an eye
    You will swim across
The world's dismal sea.

K.S.S., p.85:23

Fix your hope only on Nam,
    All other hopes discard;
Even if you succeed
    In building your house in water,
You will die in a state
    Of unfulfilled thirst.[1]

K.S.S., p.85:24

---

1. Man's worldly desires can never be satisfied since the innate tendency of the mind is to create new desires and expectations no sooner then the earlier ones are fulfilled.

If your practice of Nam
      Be as little as a grain
And the load of your sins
      A thousand pounds,
Even if half a grain of Nam
      Penetrates your being,
All your sins
      Will burn to ashes.

K.S.S., p.85:26

The bonds of a million karmas
      Will in a moment be annulled
If once Nam comes within;
      Deeds of merit
Done for eons
      Are futile
Without the practice of Nam.

K.S.S., p.85:27

How can man become free
      From Kal's noose
When with manifold shackles
      He is held?
The merciful Lord
      Has provided Nam
To sever once for all
      The noose of Kal.

K.S.S., p.87:48

Sever the noose of Kal,
      The noose that throttles
The entire world;
      The Master has given
The saber of Nam—
      Slash the chain
To gain freedom
      From misery and pain.

K.S.S., p.87:49

THE ONE ABSORBED IN NAM

The primordial Name
    Is your essence,
He who realizes it
    Becomes a swan;[1]
Who merges in Nam
    Joins the family
Of the immortal ones.

K.S.S., p.83:3

He who takes Nam
    Knows the secret
Of all Vedas and scriptures;
    But devoid of Nam
He will burn in the fires of hell,
    Although a savant
Of the four Vedas
    He may be.

K.S.S., p.86:36

Woe to the days of plenty
    If Nam from the heart departs;
Blessed be the days of adversity
    If each moment
The heart turns to Nam.

K.S.S., p.86:39

The way your mind
    Stays engrossed in maya,
Remain thus absorbed in Nam;

---

1. A realized or pure soul.

Then you will pierce the region
Of the starlit firmament
And proceed to the city
Of eternity.

K.S.S., p.86:42

Numerous sinners
Have been redeemed
By the practice
Of the true Name;
O Kabir, never forsake
The shelter of that Nam.

K.S.S., p.90:33

All praise to the pauper
Who is absorbed in Nam,
Under his thatched roof
Full of holes;
Where devotion to the Master[1]
Is not known,
A disgrace are such mansions
Of gold.

K.S.S., p.90:35

All praise to the leper
In Nam absorbed,
Although his body
Ulcerates and wastes away;
What worth is that body
Perfect as gold
But devoid of Nam?

K.S.S., p.86:35

---

1. Here Kabir identifies practice of Nam with devotion for the Master.

667

THE GLORY OF NAM

The primordial Name
    Is the magic stone,
Mind is iron
    Covered with dross;
One touch and it turns
    Into flawless gold,
And the shackles
    Of attachment
Fall into fragments.

K.S.S., p.83:1

The primordial Name
    Is the root, the essence;
Other names
    Are mere twigs.
Kabir, without the true Name
    The world is sinking
Into the sea of misery.

K.S.S., p.83:4

There are a million names
    In the world,
But not one to freedom leads;
    The mystic primordial Name
Few know how to repeat.

K.S.S., p.84:5

'Ram, Ram,' all repeat,
    But none knows
What the true Name is,
    For the secret of true Name
Only a Master reveals.

K.S.S., p.84:6

668

The Lord's Name
    Pervades each particle
Of the three worlds;
    Kabir, let that intellect
Be reduced to ashes
    Which drives man to wander
In its search from place to place.

K.G., p.64:8

Many remedies I tried,
    No panacea like Nam
Could I find;
    Even if a minim
Enters within,
    The entire body
Becomes pure as gold.

K.S.S., p.84:10

None have escaped
    The noose of Kal,
He devours all
    Who are without Nam;
But at the sight of those
    Absorbed in Nam,
He trembles with awe.

K.S.S., p.84:12

My treasure is the wealth of Nam,
    It keeps me happy and fulfilled;
With the power of his Mighty Lord
    Roars Kabir: Not even a mote
From my treasure-trove, O Kal,
    Dare you steal.

K.S.S., p.84:13

Light the lamp of knowledge
    In your mansion within;
There repeat
    The true Name of God
And in the bliss of Sahaj
    Be absorbed.
                                    K.S.S., p.84:16

He who'll realize the only Name
    And discard the others,
Without pilgrimage and fasting,
    Without chanting and austerities,
Will merge in the Master's lotus feet.
                                    K.S.S., p.85:18

The hissing snake
    Meekly folds its hood
At the sound of a mantra;
    So with Nam's magic herb[1]
Kal bows his head.
                                    K.S.S., p.85:19

The true medicine of Nam
    The Satguru has prescribed;
He who sticks to the diet
    And follows the regimen
Is fully cured
    Of his illness of eons.
                                    K.S.S., p.85:29

---

1. It is a folk belief that a vicious snake can be tamed by chanting certain words or mantras; eating certain herbs is believed to counteract the poison of a snakebite, and possessing the herbs will keep the snake away.

Plunder and amass,
     If you can, O friend,
Plunder the booty
     Of the true Name,
Or else you will
     Rue and repent
When your soul discards
     This physical frame.
               K.S.S., p.87:46

671

Devotion to the Master
    Is arduous;
It is to walk
    On a sword's edge.
Without truth and fervor
    One cannot succeed,
For intricate are the ways
    Of devotion.
              K.S.S., p.31:3

The path of devotion
    Is trying and hard,
Acute as a sword's edge;
    Those who waver
Fall to pieces,
    The steady go across.
              K.G., p.55:25

Devotion to the Master
    Is trying and hard,
Not for the timid to adopt;
    Who with his own hands
Removes his head,
    Alone is fit to tread
The path of true Nam.
              K.S.S., p.31:4

Devotion to the Lord
    Is trying and hard,
Like a path of blazing fire;
    Who plunge into the flames
Go safely across,
    Who waver and wait
Are scorched.
              K.G., p.55:26

Devotion is the ladder
That leads to salvation,
Which Saints promptly ascend
And reach Home with ease;
Those who become a prey
To mind's lazy ways,
Birth after birth repent.

K.S.S., p.32:8

So long as men relish
The bonds of worldly pleasures,
They will not progress
On devotion's path;
Him I call a true devotee
Who, detached from all,
Adores only the Lord.

K.S.S., p.32:10

The field is ruined by weeds,
The group of the noble
By the presence of the wicked;
Devotion is ruined
By avarice and greed,
As saffron
When mixed with sand.

K.S.S., p.33:23

Darkness departs
At the sight of the sun;
Evil tendencies,
With the knowledge
That the Master grants.
Wisdom vanishes
In the presence of greed;
Devotion,
When pride comes.

K.S.S., p.33:24

673

The lustful, the wrathful
    And the greedy
Can never adopt
    The path of devotion;
Only the valiant
    Can adore the Lord—
All pride of caste,
    Race and rank they discard.

K.S.S., p.33:26

Without devotion
    To the Master, O Kabir,
Of no worth is your birth
    In this world;
It's like a tower of smoke
    Which in moments dissolves.

K.S.S., p.33:28

All devotion done with desire
    Is devotion that is lost;
How can you thus meet
    Kabir's desireless Lord?

K.S.S., p.34:34

Kabir, through devotion
    To my Master
I have washed away
    The dirt of delusion;
The days that have passed
    Without devotion
Rankle in my heart
    Like an arrow's broken shaft.

K.S.S., p.34:33

THE SEED OF DEVOTION

Kabir, adore the Master,
    Give up pleasure's insipid tastes;
You'll not obtain again and again
    The chance of a human birth.

K.S.S., p.31:1

The seed of devotion
    Can never go to waste
In whatever frame it falls;[1]
    Gold does not lose its worth
Even if it drops
    On a heap of dirt.

K.S.S., p.31:2

No one will gain freedom[2]
    Without devotion,
Though a myriad other means
    He were to adopt;
Who merges in Shabd,
    That devotee alone
Will reach his Home.

K.S.S., p.32:9

In the path of devotion
    There are no garbs of pretence,
Nor the bias
    Of caste and creed,
Of high and low;
    Who adores Nam
Is the highest of all
    And a rare soul.

K.S.S., p.32:13

---

1. The external status of a man—rich or poor, black or white, high caste or low caste—is immaterial on the path of devotion.
2. Freedom or liberation from the chain of birth and death.

The rare jewel of devotion
> Only then can you obtain
When the Master in his grace
> Comes to your aid;
If great good fortune is yours,
> You will be blessed
By the Master
> With devotion and love.

K.S.S., p.32:15

To all I firmly say,
> Whether he be a pundit
Or a sheikh:
> With unswerving devotion
Practice Shabd,
> Another garb ·
You'll not be asked to put on.[1]

K.S.S., p.32:16

Never will sham devotion
> Color a man's soul
In love's radiant hue;
> In the face of adversity
Such devotion will leave him
> Like a snake's dead skin.

K.S.S., p.32:17

That is true devotion
> In which mind and heart
Stay still and absorbed.
> With purity and truth
Play devotion's game
> And discard
Both 'I' and 'you'.

K.S.S., p.34:30

---

1. That is, a devotee who adopts the practice of Shabd will not have to take birth again.

As water is dear to the fish,
    Wealth to the greedy,
A child to the mother,
    So is Nam dear
To the devotee's heart.

K.S.S., p.34:32

Devotion to Nam
    Is dear to me,
As fire is to the housewife;
    Even if the entire town
Is burned to ashes,
    She does not refrain
From begging for fire
    From her neighbor again.[1]

K.S.S., p.34:35

---

1. In medieval days the poor used to bring fire from one of their wealthier neighbors every morning. At times, due to carelessness, the entire colony of their thatched huts would be consumed by fire, yet the housewife would not hesitate to beg for fire from her neighbor for cooking and other daily needs. Using this imagery, Kabir conveys that although devotion inflames the fire of longing in the devotee's heart and he suffers constant agony, his need for devotion is as urgent as the housewife's need for fire.

677

Kabir, no doubts about
    My triumph do I hold,
For my Lord's love
    Has made me bold.
Against lust and rage,
    Against passion's lure
An open war I now wage.

K.G., p.54:7

The valiant one
    In his hand holds
The weapon of Truth;
    His body with the armor
Of Sahaj he adorns;
    This is his chance
To ride upon
    The elephant of knowledge,[1]
And for final victory
    Through the battlefield advance.

K.G., p.54:8

Kabir, the true warrior
    Never flees from the field;
With vigor he battles
    The forces of the two;
He fights but desires
    Neither life nor death.[2]

K.G., p.54:10

---

1. In the middle ages, chief warriors used to fight, riding on an elephant.
2. He fights as a matter of duty and to please his Master and has no desire for the reward of either victory or death; *the two:* mind and maya.

By remaining a coward,
    Freedom you will never gain;
Your body with valor adorn,
    Pull out the darts of delusion,
Hold simran's lance in your hand.

K.G., p.53:1

By hiding in a corner
    You will not be saved.
Says Kabir: O foolish one,
    Plunge into the field,
Battle against the senses
    With valor and faith.

K.G., p.53:2

Kabir, he is the brave one
    Who with all his might
Battles with his mind,
    Fells mind's five troopers,
And before whose onslaught
    Delusion takes to flight.

K.G., p.53:3

High is the tree with fruits
    Far away in the sky;
Many birds try
    But in vain,
Many clever ones toil
    But do not succeed,
For the fruit,
    Pure and divine,
Is beyond their reach.

What if the fruit is far—
    If your head you stake,
It will be as close to you
    As your own breath;
But so long as your head
    You do not offer,
You will not attain your object.
K.G., p.54:17,18

When the warrior brave
    Made the offering of his head,
When his desire to live
    Became dead,
The Beloved with radiant smile
    Came forward to greet
His loving slave.
K.G., p.55:23

Kabir, if my enemies
    Be as many
As the stars
    On a moonless night,
My trunk be impaled
    On a spike,
My head be dangled
    From the fort's turret,
Yet I'll not forget
    Thee, my Beloved.
K.G., p.55:29

Kabir, the awakened warrior
    Mounted the steed of love;
With the sword of knowledge
    He inflicted heavy blows
On Kal's head.
K.G., p.55:27

If I lose the battle,
    Kabir, I become
My Beloved's slave,
    And if I win,
Mine becomes the Lord;
    In the worship of God
If you lose your head,
    Let it be lost.
                    K.G., p.55:30

With the awakened mind
    As their horse,
With absorption in the Lord
    As their bridle,
With the Master's Shabd
    As the whip,
The valiant Saints march
    And reach the kingdom of God.
                    K.S.S., p.22:12

With the whip in your hand,
    You too, Kabir,
Gallop the horse;
    Reach the Beloved
While it is day,
    For all will be dark
When comes the night.
                    K.S.S., p.22:13

Try to protect the head,
    And your head will go;
If your head you cut,
    Your head will glow:
The lamp emits more light
    When one trims its wick.
                    K.S.S., p.22:20

For nothing
　　You will not get the Lord,
Nor will you attain Him
　　Through mere talk;
Without offering your head,
　　Kabir, the deal of Nam
Cannot be made.

K.S.S., p.23:28

To bear blazing flames
　　Is easy,
Easy to endure
　　The sword's blade;
To maintain
　　One-pointed love for God
Is hard indeed.

K.S.S., p.24:37

Maintain your love
　　At all costs,
If to victory you aspire;
　　By shirking and shrinking
Nothing will you gain—
　　Give your body,
Give your mind,
　　Give even your head,
But never an iota
　　Of love let go.

K.S.S., p.24:38

Ego's mighty citadel
　　Kabir took by storm,
And he collared
　　The five ferocious dogs;[1]

---

1. The five passions. In medieval days the chief of a fortress would often keep watchdogs to warn and guard against a sudden invasion of the enemy at night.

With the axe
 Of realization,
The dense wilderness
 Of karmas he destroyed
And turned it into a plain.
K.S.S., p.24:45

The fortress of ego
 Kabir conquered,
He felled the five foes,
 A fierce battle he won;
Thus did he reach
 His Beloved,
And bowed his head
 At His feet.
K.S.S., p.25:46

Who fights with bows and arrows
 Is not the true valiant one;
Who banishes from his mind
 All cravings, lures and greed
Is a warrior indeed.
K.S.S., p.25:52

When he conquers
 The five firmaments,[1]
Only then deem him
 To have fought well;
Who gave his head
 Did save his head
And with love greeted
 His Beloved.
K.S.S., p.26:64

---

1. The five inner regions.

Without feet
    The path has to be trod;
In the center of the town
    Is the starting place;[1]
The way is rough and intricate
    With ravines and forests;
Only a valiant Saint
    Attains the goal.

K.S.S., p.26:63

---

1. The eye center; *town:* the human body.

The Five Passions

Under the influence of mind, man is assailed by lust, anger, hatred, enmity, avarice, envy, attachment to the world's objects and faces, dishonesty, pride, haughtiness, ego and various other evils. Saints have named the five main passions, which include all these negative tendencies that cause man to act in devious ways.

After elaborating on the five passions, Kabir enumerates the five opposite virtues that act as an antidote to the poison of the five evils. Instead of trying to suppress the passions, Saints suggest the positive method of dwelling upon and inculcating the corresponding virtues. The devotee should try to replace lust with purity and chastity of mind and body, anger with forgiveness, attachment with a spirit of detachment, avarice with contentment, and ego with humility.

The selections that follow include Kabir's views on the five passions, the last few couplets in each section dealing with the opposite virtues.

THE POISON OF LUST

The master of the amorous
    Is the object of their lust,
The master of the greedy
    Is money and wealth;
The Master of Kabir
    Is the perfect Saint,
The Master of the Saints
    Is the Name.
K.S.S., p.130:1

The lustful ruin their devotion
    By indulging in sense pleasures,
The rare diamond of divine love
    They let slip from their hand
And ruin the precious chance
    Of the human birth.
K.S.S., p.130:5

Lust, the ruthless horseman,
    Gallops in all directions,
He makes everyone his prey;
    That rare devotee escapes
Who takes the shelter of Nam.
K.S.S., p.131:17

The lustful will not relish Nectar,
    The poison of pleasures he craves;
Over him sensualness prevails—
    He does not listen,
Though warned again and again.
K.S.S., p.131:14

Kabir, doubt and delusion
    Never leave a lustful man;
He always remains
    Away from the Lord,
And the fire of lust
    Constantly burns his heart.

K.S.S., p.131:13

As long as the body's storehouse
    Abounds with the hoard
Of lust and anger,
    Of ego and greed,
The learned and the lout
    Are no doubt the same.

K.S.S., p.131:19

Lust, like the wick of a lamp,
    Drains the oil
Of the house
    In which it dwells;
Kabir, the Saint is the diamond
    That shines in the brilliance
Of its own inner light.[1]

K.S.S., p.130:2

As long as the devotee
    Loves sense pleasures
He is not a gurmukh;
    When the Satguru
Dwells in his heart,
    For him such pleasures
Will lose their charm.

K.S.S., p.138:5

---

[1]. It was believed in medieval times that certain gems of extraordinary quality emitted brilliant light.

Many are the learned,
　　Many the recluse;
Many are the benevolent,
　　Many the brave;
Many are the ascetics,
　　Many too the celibates;
But rare is the one
　　In whose heart
Chastity dwells.
K.S.S., p.137:3

When chastity and purity
　　Spring in the heart,
The eye that sees the Unseen opens;
　　Without purity
No one can attain the goal,
　　Although men may make
A million claims.
K.S.S., p.137:1

Where lust is,
　　Nam is not;
Where Nam resides,
　　Lust has no place;
Sun and darkness both
　　Cannot be together
At the same spot.
K.S.S., p.139:9

THE FIRE OF ANGER

In every hearth
    Burns the fire of anger—
The entire world
    Is scorched by its flames;
Only at the feet
    Of the Lord's humble
And loving devotee
    Can one find refuge
From anger's blaze.

K.S.S., p.131:2

A million karmas come
    In the wake of anger;
All spiritual gain is lost
    The moment anger and ego
Enter the heart.

K.S.S., p.131:3

From all the ten directions
    Comes billowing
The wildfire of anger;
    Run to the cool, soothing
Company of the Saints
    From this raging fire to escape.

K.S.S., p.132:5

Abuse is the ember,
    Anger the raging flames,
Slander the suffocating smoke;
    One who keeps away from all three
Is a true devotee of God.

K.S.S., p.132:6

Harsh words is the worst evil,
They hurt and scorch
The listener's entire being;
Cool as water,
A stream of nectar,
Are the words of a Saint.

K.S.S., p.132:8

The spirit of forgiveness
Dissolves anger;
The devotee who is tolerant
And forgiving, O Kabir,
Cannot be assailed
By the forces of Kal.

K.S.S., p.138:1

Piety resides
In a kind heart,
Sin resides
In the company of greed;
Where lives anger
Also lives Kal,
Where dwells forgiveness
Dwells the Lord.

K.S.S., p.138:4

Sharp as arrows
Are the harsh words
Of the evil ones,
But the Saints
Are not affected by them:
The ocean is never hurt
By bolts of lightning.

K.S.S., p.138:6

THE WITCH OF AVARICE

Greed is a harlot,
>   Don't lend her your heart—
She will dog your every step
>   And urge you to sin.

K.G., p.26:14

The flame of greed
>   Cannot be put out
By sprinkling it
>   With the water of fulfillment;
Day after day
>   More and more it will grow.
Shower it with the water
>   Of love and devotion
And it will die out
>   Like the jawasa
Withering in the rain.[1]

K.G., p.26:15

How am I to narrate
>   The merits of avarice?
Even when the body
>   Becomes feeble
And the senses effete,
>   Avarice continues
To stay young and strong.

K.S.S., p.137:2

Avarice is a wicked witch,
>   The doom of all beings;
'More, more,' it cries day and night,
>   Spelling misery and gloom.

K.S.S., p.137:3

---

1. The jawasa shrub withers and sheds its leaves during heavy showers.

Avarice, greed and cravings
　　Are a violent fire
That never abates;
　　Men, gods, sages,
And even paupers are consumed
　　By its blaze.

K.S.S., p.137:4

When desires die,
　　All worries vanish—
The mind becomes happy
　　And carefree;
He who desires nothing
　　Is the king of kings.

K.S.S., p.139:2

Cows and elephants,
　　Palaces and jewels—
All the wealth of the world
　　Becomes like dust
The moment the wealth
　　Of contentment
Enters the heart.

K.S.S., p.139:6

THE BONDS OF ATTACHMENT

Kabir, the dark night
    Of maya and attachment
Blankets the entire world;
    Their house is pilfered
Who submit to sleep,
    And they mourn and repent
After losing their wealth.

K.G., p.27:24

Like a creeper that spreads
    Over a thorny hedge,
The world has entangled itself
    With attachment and desires;
The creeper will break
    But not release its hold,
Like a man bound
    By an irrevocable vow.[1]

K.G., p.27:26

Kabir, attachment's bow
    Cannot be broken
Without a Master;
    Men, gods and sages
Try their utmost to break it,
    But it becomes
Heavier and stronger
    With their touch.[2]

K.S.S., p.174:73

---

1. In the Middle Ages a vow once taken was considered sacred and inviolable; a man would die rather than break his vow.
2. Reference to the bow of Shiva that only Ram, at the bidding of his Guru, was able to lift and break; the others who tried to lift it, found it became heavier at their touch.

693

The entire world
    Is a field of action,
Men plow it
    To raise a good crop;
But the wild deer
    Of attachment
Ruin the harvest,
    And men return
Empty-handed to the barn.
K.S.S., p.133:5

Men do not know the way
    To protect their harvest;
They are devoid
    Of devotion,
Of humility,
    Of love for the Saint.
K.S.S., p.133:6

When the vessel is brimming
    With attachment,
It is dense and dark within;
    Only a keen devotee
Realizes the truth,
    Becomes detached
And reaches the other shore.
K.S.S., p.133:7

Many mighty men,
    Scholars and thinkers too,
Have been swept away
    By the strong currents
Of attachment;
    But the purified soul
Like a tiny fish
    Swims against the current
And climbs to its goal.
K.S.S., p.134:10

694

THE MALADY OF I

The two strings of mine and thine—
    Entwined into a firm rope—
Hold the world captive;
    But how can Kabir,
The Lord's slave, be bound
    When Nam is his support,
His hope.

K.S.S., p.60:56

'I, I' is a great malady,
    Run away from it
Before it's too late;
    Friend, how long
Can you preserve the cotton roll
    That holds an ember
In its folds?

K.G., p.21:60

Do not say 'I, me and mine',
    For 'I' leads to perdition;
'I' is a fetter on your feet,
    A noose around your neck.

K.G., p.21:61

It is easy to give up wealth,
    Easy to give up love for a woman;
But ego, pride and jealousy
    Are hard indeed to discard.

K.S.S., p.134:1

The world's honor and praise
    Is superficial,
For the world's ways
    Are like a dog's ways:
Make friends with it,
    It licks your mouth;
Antagonize it,
    It growls and bites.
K.S.S., p.134:6

All worship power,
    Few worship the Powerful One;
Says Kabir, if you worship
    The Powerful One,
All powers become your slaves.
K.S.S., p.135:13

He in whose heart burns
    The fire of ego,
Who craves respect
    From his Master,
Receives an invitation
    From Yama:
'Pray come, be my guest.'
K.S.S., p.135:15

What if you have become
    Eminent and high,
High as the date palm—
    It provides no shade
To the wayfarer
    And bears fruits
That are out of reach.
K.S.S., p.134:10

Kabir, wipe out from your heart
     The craving for prestige and praise;
For their sake do not lose
     Your original wealth.

                         K.S.S., p.134:11

Lightning suddenly strikes
     A pot of bronze,
But from my Master
     I have heard
That free from peril
     Is the humble potsherd.[1]

                         K.S.S., p.170:19

Humility, gentleness, devotion,
     And regard for one and all:
Says Kabir, he is truly high
     In whose heart
These qualities reside.

                         K.S.S., p.140:4

All bow to themselves,
     Few to others bow;
Kabir, the pan of the balance
     That bows
Is the weightier of the two.

                         K.S.S., p.140:6

Water will not stay at the heights,
     Only in low land will it lie;
One who bends[2]
     Drinks to his fill,
He goes thirsty
     Who remains high.

                         K.S.S., p.140:8

---

1. In folklore it is said that something made of bronze is prone to be struck by lightning, whereas earthenware is not.
2. In medieval times, travelers would quench their thirst with the water of lakes, ponds or rivers, bending down to fill their bowls or their cupped hands with water.

Blacken the face of pride,
　　Throw prestige to the flames;
Give up pride and I-ness—
　　Become absorbed
In the Lord's Name.
K.S.S., p.134:3

He who is humble and meek,
　　Who meditates with love,
Who surrenders to the Saints,
　　In him the Lord dwells
As in water dwells the fish.
K.S.S., p.140:1

THE SATGURU'S TORCH OF GRACE

The five passions are a dominant factor in the world. They cannot be coerced into submission nor driven away by force, nor can the noble qualities be deliberately acquired through discipline and external observances. Suppressed passions, like embers, easily flame up in the strong winds of desires. Outer show of humility, detachment and chastity are meaningless if they have not made the devotee's heart their home; physical renunciation is futile if the mind clings to worldly attachments; vows of continence are of little help if the mind hovers over objects of lust; verbal forgiveness has no value if the heart harbors feelings of anger and hatred. The remedy for darkness is to light a lamp.

Kabir, like all Saints, says that the practice of Shabd and the taste of inner bliss generate noble qualities, which are the antidote to the five passions. When the devotee drinks the nectar of spiritual joy, all worldly pleasures and attractions become tasteless for him. Inner contact with Nam generates detachment, and the devotee, though living in the world, automatically becomes detached from it. Shabd and the Master's grace are the light that dispels the dark shadows of the passions.

In the last couplet, Kabir suggests that the devotee can rise above the passions through the blessing, grace and, in fact, instrumentality of the Satguru. The perfect Master has burned the 'house' of his own desires, passions and cravings, and with the flame of Shabd and divine love is also ready to burn the 'house' of those who will follow him on the path of God-realization.

> Lures and passions
>   Are a burning lamp,
> Men the heedless moths—
>   They come circling[1]
> And plunge into the flame;
>   Those rare ones escape, O Kabir,
> Who receive from the Master
>   The precious boon of Nam.
>
>   K.G., p.2:20

---

1. Taking rounds in the circle of repeated births and deaths, implying that in each birth the soul is burned in the fire of the passions.

I, too, was sinking
    In the sea of sense pleasures,
But came my Master
    The refulgent wave:
I realized my frail boat[1]
    Was rotting,
I jumped off
    And the wave bore me
To the Shore.

K.G., p.3:25

Through laughter and revelry
    If one could meet the Lord,
Who would submit
    To the scouring
On love's whetstone?
    He who forsakes
Lust, anger and cravings
    Will find the way to God.

K.G., p.8:30

I had come to the world
    To see its beauty and charm,
But, says Kabir,
    I forgot all
When I saw
    My Master's peerless form.

K.G., p.11:24

What can attachment do to me?
    To me love has opened its gates,
My merciful Beloved I have met,
    The world's sharp thorns
Have turned into a quilt of bliss.

K.G., p.12:48

---

1. The boat of passions and desires, which cause men to sink in the ocean of misery.

700

Kabir, the lotus blossoms,
　　The immaculate sun
In its splendor shines,
　　The darkness of night fades
When the Anhad Shabd resounds.

K.G., p.12:43

I have burned my house;
　　Now I stand
With a flaming torch[1]
　　In my hand:
His house, too, I'll burn,
　　Who joins me
On my homeward march.

K.G., p.53:13

---

1. Kabir uses the Rajasthani term *murādā* for 'torch', *murādā* being an improvised torch made from reeds and straw, used for lighting a funeral pyre. This image conveys that when the Master destroys worldly passions and attachments, he does so in totality. The same sort of finality has been brought out by Jesus Christ when he says that he has not come to bring peace on earth, but has come with a sword to sever all attachments (Matt. 10:34-36; Luke 13:51-53).

701

KARMAS

Move freely in the world,
    Who can put you in bonds?
If you have no burden
    Of baggage on your head,
What demands can the tax collector
    At the port make?

K.S.S., p.1, 1:29

Dharam Rai, the customs officer,
    Frisks each entrant at the port;
He throws them
    Into the dungeons of hell
Who come without
    The permit of Nam.

K.S.S., p.171:30

Kabir, my mother was a stranger,
    My father was a stranger,
And I am a stranger too;
    Like canoes in the sea,
We were brought together
    By the waves of fate.

K.G., p.21:56

Kabir, this is an alien land,
    Our own home is beyond;
We come to trade
    In this market—
We dispose of the grocery
    Of our karmas,
Wind up and take
    Different roads.[1]

K.G., p.21:57

---

1. Traders from different villages come to the weekly market in town to sell their goods, returning home in the evening when the market closes,

When you had the power to act
　　Why did you indulge
In evil deeds?
　　Having done them,
What use repenting now?
　　Having sown the seed
Of the wild acacia,[1]
　　How can you obtain
Mangoes to eat?

K.G., p.23:27

One deed is sowing:
　　Scores of seeds are raised;
Another deed is roasting:
　　The seeds cannot germinate.

K.S.S., p.174:69

The heyday of youth
　　Has slipped away,
You did not adore
　　And serve the Master;
It is futile
　　To rue and lament
After the birds
　　Have ravaged the crop
And the field lies
　　A barren waste.

K.S.S., p.171:39

In the seven islands,
　　The nine continents,
The three worlds,
　　In the entire creation,
Kabir, all have to pay the price
　　Of adopting a body.

K.S.S., p.171:33

---

1. Babool, Indian acacia, is a wild thorny tree with insignificant flowers and inedible fruits.

The penalty
   Of donning a body
One and all have to pay;
   The realized endure
With understanding,
   The blind suffer
With tears and cries.
                    K.S.S., p. 171:34

There is fire on the left,
   Fire on the right,
In fire all move and act;
   Behind and in front
Deadly fires burn—
   One's only refuge
Is the Almighty One.
                    K.G., p.48:7

Kabir describes longing as a sultan or emperor, because longing is the royal road to the Lord's home. The path to the Beloved is paved with sighs and tears. No one can keep indulging in worldly pleasures, clinging to material possessions and desires, and still hope to meet the Lord. The path to God-realization is a path of one-pointed love, and if there is such a love in the devotee's heart he will continue to suffer the pangs of separation till union is attained. In these couplets Kabir praises *virah* or longing, which is the precursor of the Beloved's grace and the steppingstone to ultimate union with Him.

Do not blame love's agony,
    It is the sultan of all paths;
The heart not stirred with longing
    Is a heart forever dead—
A burial ground.

K.G., p.7:21

Kabir, shun worldly rejoicings,
    Let your heart pine for Him and weep;
Without weeping how can you obtain
    Union with your Love,
Your beloved Friend?

K.G., p.7:27

Through laughing and rejoicing
    You will not find
Your long-lost Husband—
    Whoever found Him,
Found Him through tears and sighs;
    If through merry-making
The Lord could be met,
    Then who would remain
A luckless, lonely wife?

K.S.S., p.37:19

You crave for union
    With the Beloved,
And also covet
    Comforts and joys;
Without the pain of labor
    How can the wife
Ever experience
    The transport
Of holding in her arms
    A son?
                    K.S.S., p.38:29

The pain of separation
    Whispered to me:
Hold onto me with all your might
    And I'll carry you to the bliss
Of the Beloved's lotus feet.
                    K.S.S., p.40:53

The Father's beloved son
    Tried to run and be with Him;
He put the sweets of greed
    Into the son's hands—
The Father faded from his mind
    As he became absorbed
In the sweets.

When he hurled the sweets away
    He developed the deep pain
Of longing in his heart;
    With tears, sobs and cries
He followed the Father's trail—
    The son attained bliss
In the beloved Father's lap.
                    K.G., p.8:31,32

706

If your longing were true
How could you stay alive
And for the Beloved not die?
Cease, O foolish one,
Cease to complain of your pain,
Do not put love to shame.[1]

K.G., p.8:36

The sky is on fire,
Raining embers live:
Kabir is burned
And turned into gold,[2]
But as dead as lead
Remains the world.

K.S.S., p.43:84

---

1. A true lover tries to keep his longing to himself and tries to meet the Beloved through the practice of dying while living; he never complains about the pain of longing but treasures it as a gift from the Beloved.
2. When the disciple goes into the inner spiritual regions, an intense longing to meet the Lord burns in his heart. It destroys all worldly desires and attachments and purifies the soul.

Cheerless are my days,
    Sleepless my nights,
Even in dreams, no respite;
    Kabir, parted
From his Beloved, finds rest
    Neither in sunshine
Nor in shade.
K.G., p.6:4

The yearning wife
    Stands at the roadside,
She runs to stop
    Each passerby:
Give me news of my Beloved—
    When will He come
And bless me with union?
K.G., p.6:5

For days I have kept gazing
    At the path, beloved Lord;
My heart is restless
    And for union cries my soul.
K.G., p.6:6

Kabir, your sad bride rises
    At the footsteps of each passerby;
Dejected, she falls back again.
    If you grant her darshan
When she is dead,
    What use such darshan, dear Lord?
K.G., p.6:7

Begs Kabir: Beloved Lord,
    Come before my soul
Leaves this body;
    When rust has turned
Iron into dust,[1]
    What use will be
The mystic stone's touch?

K.G., p.6:8

My misery will not be ended
    By a mere message
Of consolation;
    It will only end
If my Lord comes to me—
    Or if I
Win my way to Him.

K.G., p.6:9

I have no strength
    To reach you, dear Lord,
Nor the power
    To induce you to come;
It seems you wish
    To take my life
By slowly roasting me thus,
    In separation's flame.

K.G., p.6:10

Kabir's yearning is intense,
    Not for a moment
Does it leave him;
    The one pain
Of the Beloved's love
    Has made my heart
Its home.

K.G., p.7:13

---

1. The rust of separation; *iron:* the body.

My eyes have become dim, gazing—
    Gazing at your path;
My tongue has become parched, calling—
    Calling for you, O Lord.
K.G., p.7:22

My tears are streaming
    Like a forest fountain;
Day and night, without respite
    Turns the persian wheel.[1]
Like the rainbird,
    'Beloved, Beloved' I cry;
When will you meet me, my Lord?
K.G., p.7:24

The serpent of separation
    Has wounded my inmost being;
The yearning wife does not turn away:
    'Bite me as it please thee,' says she.
K.S.S., p.37:10

In the world's dreadful sea
    I have found a raft,
Bound with the snakes of separation.
    If I let go, I sink;
If I hold on, I am bitten to death.
K.G., p.8:43

If I weep in separation,
    I become weak;
If I laugh,
    My Beloved I displease.
In the depths of my being
    I sob and cry in silence;
Within, my heart is worn out
    Like a worm-eaten beam of wood.
K.G., p.7:28

---

1. The water falls in a continuous stream from the buckets of the turning wheel.

Kabir, heavy clouds
    Gathered in the sky;
They rained and filled
    Lakes that before were dry;
But who will consider the plight
    Of those who, like the rainbird,
Endure the agony of thirst
    And long only for Thee.
A.G., p.1371:124

All night weeps the lonely wife,
    Like the crane
Parted from her mate;
    Her heart is lit up
With leaping flames,
    Her body burns
In separation's agony.
K.G., p.6:1

I'll make a lamp of this body
    And my yearning soul, its wick;
For oil I'll fill the lamp
    With my tears of blood,
And in its light I will see
    The face of my Beloved.
K.G., p.7:23

I will burn my body
    To cinders,
That the smoke may rise
    To His home;
Perchance my Love,
    Moved to mercy,
Might rain
    And quench the flames.
K.G., p.6:11

Day and night burns the wife
   In longing's inner flame;
Says Kabir the slave:
   How can that fire recede
Which the Master
   With his love has lit?
                    K.S.S., p.41:59

The wildfire of longing
   Secretly rages within my heart;
Not even the smoke escapes.
   Only one who burns like me
Knows—and the one
   Who has set me ablaze.
                    K.S.S., p.40:48

Pray, grant your yearning wife,
   Grant relief through death—
Or come, my enchanting Lord,
   And her ailment cure;.
Burning day and night
   With every breath,
No more, O Beloved,
   Can I endure.
                    K.G., p.8:35

When, O Lord, will that day dawn,
   When my merciful Master
Will hold me in his arms,
   When he will accept me
And make me his own,
   When he will grant me
The shelter of his lotus feet.
                    K.S.S., p.41:65

The agony of longing has been personified by Kabir as a hunter—ruthless, but at the same time dear to the devotee's heart. The pain of separation from the Beloved is unbearable, but also sweet. The lover would like to be always in the presence of the Beloved, failing which he would like his thoughts to be fixed on Him without a break. Longing keeps the Beloved's memory alive in the lover's heart, and despite the anguish that accompanies it, its constant pain keeps the Beloved almost present with him. Kabir, while presenting *virah* or the agony of separation as a remorseless tormentor, also admires it as the necessary means for the devotee to realize the depth of divine love.

> Don't resent the pain of longing,
> O my mind, sensible and wise;
> Let it consume
> Your flesh, your bones,
> And make you, while living,
> Like a graveyard: dead.
>
> *K.S.S., p.38:24*

> Severe is the blow of separation,
> It has lacerated
> My body and soul;
> Only he will know my agony
> Who has dealt the blow—
> Or who like me bears the wound.
>
> *K.G., p.7:14*

> The Beloved took the arrow
> And balanced it on the bow;
> The fatal shaft entered my heart—
> Who knows if I'll survive
> The agony
> . . .or die.
>
> *K.G., p.7:15*

With my arteries as the strings,
My body as his lyre,
Separation day and night
Plays plaintive tunes.
Only my Beloved hears—
Or my lonely heart;
None else can hear
The wistful strain.

K.G., p.7:20

The moment my Beloved
Shot me with his ruthless aim,
I realized the depth of his love;
I received a mortal wound
When his love pierced
My heart, my soul.

K.G., p.7:16

The axe of longing
Has cut into my heart,
There is not a sign
That the wound will heal;
My doubts and delusion,
Avarice and attachment,
Have all dissolved—
Death seems to be certain.[1]

K.S.S., p.43:86

Longing, with forces arrayed,
Has advanced and besieged me;
He neither kills me
Nor lets me live—
I endure the anguish
Of a slow death.

K.S.S., p.40:55

---

1. When the organs of a severely wounded person stop functioning properly, it is clear that death is approaching him. The devotee, absorbed in love and overwhelmed with longing, loses all worldly preoccupations and attachments, and for all practical purposes is 'dead' to the world.

Kabir, the arrow with which
    You wounded me yesterday
Has bewitched my heart;
    With the same arrow today
Hit me again, O Beloved,
    For without it I am
Restless and downcast.

K.G., p.7:17

715

THE PRICE OF LOVE

The path of divine love is that of complete surrender to the Beloved, of eliminating the ego and all desires except the desire to become one with Him. Kabir says that true love can only be obtained by offering one's head as the price, that is, by completely annihilating I-ness. It might appear to be a grim precondition for love, a price hard to pay; but no sacrifice is too great and no price too high for the invaluable treasure of love.

This is the abode of love,
    Not the house of your auntie;[1]
Remove your head,
    Put it on the ground,
Then alone dare step
    Into love's home.

K.S.S., p.43:1

Remove your head,[2]
    Place it on the ground,
Step upon it
    With a firm resolve;
Says Kabir the slave:
    If you do this,
Welcome to love's home.

K.S.S., p.43:2

Love grows not in your flowerbeds,
    It is not on sale in some stall;
The king or the commoner,
    Whoever wants love,
Can gladly have it—
    In exchange for his head.

K.S.S., p.43:3

---

1. In India in the maternal aunt's home, nephews and nieces are received with great affection and warmth—they are offered sweets and special dishes to eat and are generally pampered by the family, who try to fulfill all their desires.
2. Ego.

You long to taste
    The elixir of love,
But at the same time
    Cling to your self-esteem;
Whoever has heard of two swords
    In one scabbard?

K.S.S., p.46:32

So long as you are afraid to die
    Don't call yourself a lover;
For the one like you,
    Far—beyond reach—
Is the mansion of love.

K.S.S., p.47:51

He drinks the wine of love
    Who offers his head;
The selfish cannot
    Pay the price,
Yet talk of love—
    To no effect.

K.S.S., p.43:4

I've heard love is on sale
    In the market square
And the price demanded
    Is only your head.
Don't waste time bargaining,
    Cut off your head
And confirm the deal
    Before it's too late.

K.S.S., p.44:13

Saints repeatedly remind man that the world is transitory, time is fleeting and death is sure to come. Human life is precious and should be utilized to attain spiritual awakening before death overtakes one. But man wastes the precious gift of human birth, spending over one-third of his allotted time in sleep; and even during the rest of it he is in a hypnotic slumber produced by desires, cravings and attachments, unaware of the spiritual wealth that lies within.

In these couplets Kabir tells man to wake up from his sleep of ages, become aware of the Lord's Name and attend to spiritual practice under the guidance of a perfect Master. The practice of Nam is the only remedy for man's endless slumber, his spiritual inertia.

Kabir, without fear
    Adore the Lord
As long as the wick
    Burns within the lamp;
When the oil runs dry
    And the light dissolves,
You will sleep—
    Day and night.
            K.G., p.4:10

Kabir, it's no time to sleep—
    Wake up, repeat the Lord's Name!
A day will come
    When you'll sleep undisturbed
With legs outstretched.
            K.G., p.4:11

Kabir, it's no time to sleep,
    Wake up, realize
You have been severed
    From your origin.
Return and rejoin the source
    From where you came.
            K.S.S., p.4:12

Kabir, it's no time to sleep,
    Get up and narrate
The tale of your sorrow
    To the Lord.
How can he sleep carefree
    Whose abode is the grave?
               K.G., p.4:13

Kabir, it's no time to sleep,
    Sing the praises of the Lord;
Yama hovers over your head
    Watching you
Waste your capital.[1]
               K.G., p.5:14

Kabir, it's no time to sleep,
    Sleep leads to disaster;
Even Brahma's throne shakes
    At the thunderous call
Of Death.[2]
               K.G., p.5:15

Death has arisen
    From its slumber;
Beware, Kabir, be alert—
    Give up all alchemies,
Take the panacea of Nam.
               K.S.S., p.160:7

Let 'Beloved, O Beloved'
    Be your constant cry,
Get up from your slumber
    Of eons;

---

1. The capital of human life, which is given to man to invest in devotion to God.
2. Brahma, the god of creation, dies at the time of dissolution. It is believed that each time a new creation takes place after dissolution, a new Brahma is appointed.

Your day- and night-long
>   Cries for Him
Might some day
>   Earn a response.
>>   *K.S.S., p.160:9*

His life goes fruitless
>   Who remains lost in sleep;
Who keeps awake
>   Gathers the fruit.
The Lord never withholds
>   From his children their dues—
He gladly gives
>   To whoever begs
At his door.
>>   *K.S.S., p.160:8*

In the following two couplets, Kabir reverses the metaphor, saying sleep is better than keeping awake. As long as the attention is running out in the world towards worldly desires and attachments, man is awake to the outer world but asleep to the inner spiritual regions. When he withdraws the attention inwards, enters the inner regions and becomes absorbed in spiritual bliss, he is unaware or 'asleep' to the world but fully conscious or 'awake' within.

To sleep is better
>   Than to keep awake,
If one knows how to sleep;
>   The attention is absorbed within
And simran continues
>   On its own.
>>   *K.S.S., p.160:11*

Who while awake, sleeps
>   And while sleeping
Is absorbed within,
>   The string of his soul
Stays tied to its source;
>   Not for a moment
Does he break the link.
>>   *K.S.S., p.160:12*

720

KABIR'S LORD

Men worship idols, paintings or symbolic representations of their deity, looking upon them as the Supreme Being. Kabir rejects such forms of worship and says that the Almighty One, the Beloved, pervades every particle of the creation and at the same time is aloof from all. Men have been misled into worshipping various deities, incarnations and symbols as God. Like the wife who has not seen her husband and mistakes other men for her spouse, these devotees prove unfaithful to their Husband, the Lord. Kabir says that only when a seeker meets the perfect Master does he come to know what God is and where and how He can be found.

What is contained by a casket,[1]
O Kabir, cannot be the Lord;
The One who pervades the entire creation,
He indeed is the Lord of all.

K.G., p.47:36:1

Who remains apart from the creation
Yet enfolds the creation within himself,
Him alone does Kabir worship—
Other than Him, he knows no God.

K.G., p.47:36:2

Mistaking them for her Spouse,
Many men did the wife adore,
Proving unfaithful to Him;
When the perfect Master she met,
He gave her the secret:
She realized her real Husband.

K.G., p.47:36:3

---

1. People sometimes carry with them an idol of their deity in a small gold, silver or copper box.

Who has neither face nor forehead,
  Who is neither handsome nor ugly,
Whose reality is finer
  Than the fragrance of flowers—
Such is He, the Unique One.

K.G., p.47:36:4

Through worship of the three[1]
  The entire world is drifting
In delusion's dark sea;
  Says Kabir:
Without the true Name
  How can they be ferried
To the shore of bliss?

K.S.S., p.104:3

He is within the body,
  Yet bodiless is He;
In his Spirit form
  He pervades countless realms,
Yet He has no color,
  No shape.

K.S.S., p.105:11

It blossoms, it also withers,
  Such is the world of three gunas;
Remember only the One
  Who has laid out this vast expanse.

K.S.S., p.105:4

Within the soul in Shabd form
  Resides the Unalloyed,
The Invisible One;

---

1. The three *gunas* or attributes. The various gods, goddesses and incarnations are within the region of the three attributes. These attributes do not go beyond the region of Brahm, the second stage on the soul's inner journey, and are subject to destruction at the time of dissolution. The region of pure spirit, of true enlightenment, is beyond the reach of the attributes.

722

Only that seeker sees Him
Who has received from the Master
The gift of Nam.[1]

K.S.S., p.105:5

In all the three worlds I see Him,
Why do you call Him Imperceptible?
You know not the essence of Shabd
But don holy garbs to deceive others.

K.S.S., p.105:6

I am weak, He is strong,
So I call Him the Mighty One,
The One Lord of all;
He who dies and takes birth,[2]
To him Kabir will not bow his head.

K.S.S., p.105:14

The One beyond birth and death
Is the Lord of Kabir;
All glory to that Beloved
Who has fashioned us all.

K.S.S., p.105:15

Kabir asks his Beloved:
Mighty Lord of worlds big and small!
You have created everything,
And in each particle you dwell;
Lord, tell me the secret
Of how you still remain
Apart from it all.

K.G., p.67:1

---

1. Kabir uses the word *guru-gyān*, 'the Master's knowledge', which according to the Saints is initiation into the practice of Nam.
2. Here Kabir refers to the various incarnations who are within the region of Brahm and therefore subject to birth, death, action and retribution.

A SAINT'S TRUE HOME

Saints have attained their original home, the Lord's abode, and become one with Him. Though they are physically present in the world, within they are always in rapport with the Lord. Kabir says that Saints are citizens of the ultimate realm; from there they come to this mortal world, but in their Shabd form still live in their original home. He adds that the seeker can also reach there, but only in his Shabd form and not in the physical body.

I am a denizen of that land
    Where in his full splendor
The True One reigns,
    Where there is not a shade of pain
Nor a flicker of pleasure,
    Where all days are filled
With undiminished bliss.

K.S.S., p.108:6

I am a denizen of that land
    Where every day
Is a day of celebration,
    Where flows the nectar of love,
And in the reservoir of light
    The lotus of the lover's heart
Blooms with boundless joy.

K.S.S., p.108:7

I am a denizen of that land
    Where revels the Lord
In supreme bliss;
    Where without oil, without wick,
Brightly burns the lamp
    Of the Inaccessible One.

Kabir, p.217

Where there are awnings
    Of radiant pearls,
Where shine lamps
    Of divine diamonds,
Where the sun and the moon
    Have no access,
In that land this slave beholds
    His beloved Lord.

K.S.S., p.111:48

I am a denizen of that land
    Where there is no caste,
Color or clan;
    Where union is attained,
Not in the body,
    But in the Shabd form.

K.S.S., p.112:65

Where there is neither
    Air nor water,
Nor earth nor sky,
    There, O Kabir,
The Saints are the valets
    Of the Lord.

K.S.S., p.109:23

THE DROP AND THE OCEAN

In order to realize the Lord, mind and soul have to turn inwards, go within the body and enter the inner spiritual worlds. Kabir says that when the soul, crossing the regions of mind and maya, becomes perfect like the Lord, it will merge in Him—the Perfect One. Mind, a particle of universal mind or Brahm, can become pure by getting rid of the dross of desires and passions, but cannot become perfect because the state of true perfection is beyond the reach of mind. On meeting the Lord, the soul becomes one with Him. Conveying the state of complete unity of the soul and the Lord, Kabir says that the soul, the drop, has merged in God, the Ocean, and God has merged into the soul.

I've filled the vessel of my body
    With water luminous and pure;
With my body, mind
    And the vigor of youth
I drink it; I drink it,
    Yet thirst for more.

My mind turned inwards,
    It plunged into the sea
Of love and bliss
    And it bathes with joy;
It tries to fathom Thee:
    It tries
But does not succeed
    For Thou art perfect,
My merciful Lord,
    While mind is not.

Searching for Him, O friend,
    Kabir lost himself;
When the drop has merged
    Into the Ocean,
How can the drop be found?

Searching
    And searching
For Him, O friend,
    Kabir lost himself;
The Ocean has merged
    Into the drop,
Now how can the Ocean
    Be found?

K.G., p.13:1-4

727

THE COLOR OF LOVE

When turmeric is mixed with lime it loses its yellow color and lime its whiteness; both turn red—the color of love. This image is used in these two couplets to convey the merging of the lover and the Beloved into one. The lover is dyed in the Lord's love and the Lord, pure and colorless, manifests himself in the loving disciple in the form of love. In this state of union only one color remains—the color of love; only one exists—the Lord. Men have divided themselves into groups and factions on the basis of countries, castes, colors, lineage, race and religions. These external traits or 'colors' are lost when one comes to the company of Saints and acquires a new color—the color of love.

> Kabir, turmeric is yellow,
>   Lime is milky white;
> When the lover and the Lord meet
>   Both colors are lost
> In the hue of love.
>
> Turmeric sheds its yellowness,
>   Vanishes the whiteness of lime;
> Blessed, O Kabir, is that love
>   Which dissolves all the shades
> Of caste, color and clime.
> *A.G., p.1367:56-57*

The aim of divine love is union with the Beloved. These poems, though independent of one another, depict the fulfillment of the lover's efforts to meet the Lord. Kabir describes it as the reunion of a long-parted wife with her husband, the reawakening of an age-old love. The devotee is rid of all his delusions in the presence of the "Lamp"—the Beloved. He loses his ego and merges his identity in that of the Lord. He reaches the Beloved's radiant presence, himself becomes radiant, and reflects that radiance. He now dwells in love, he becomes the embodiment of love, and the beauty and sweetness of the Lord's love reflect in all his words and deeds.

> Kabir, such is the radiance
>   Of the Eternal One
> As if I am in the presence
>   Of a row of suns;
> The beautiful wife who keeps awake
>   With her husband[1]
> Sees this glorious sight.
> *K.G., p.9:5:1*

> My body is flooded
>   With the light of love;
> My love, eons old,
>   Has awoken now;
> Delusions dispelled,
>   I am united again
> With my beloved Husband.
> *K.G., p.10:13*

> My body is flooded
>   With the light of love,
> My soul radiates with bliss;

---

1. Keeping awake with the husband implies going into the inner spiritual regions in the company of the radiant form of the Master, called 'husband' by Kabir, and proceeding to the higher regions and the home of God. The soul can travel on the inner path only in the company of a perfect Master.

Love's fragrance
Fills my mouth,[1]
Its aroma spreads
With each word I speak.

K.G., p.10:14

The bird flew high in the sky,
Its body remained
In this foreign land;
Without beak
It drank divine water
And became oblivious
Of this domain.[2]

K.G., p.11:20

Surat merged into nirat
And nirat lost its base;
When I experienced
The union of the two,
The doors of the lion gate[3]
Swung apart.

K.G., p.11:22

Whoever has obtained the Nectar
Cherishes it with boundless joy:
They drink it, they become addicts;
They have acquired a rare jewel
And know the futility
Of groping in the world.

K.G., p.12:33

---

1. Kabir here uses the expression 'the fragrance of musk'. In the Middle Ages the very rich used to put a minute particle of musk in the betel leaves they chewed, the strong aroma of musk—a rare and costly thing even in those days—perfuming their breath for several hours.
2. *Domain, foreign land:* the world.
3. At a certain stage on the inner journey, *surat* (the hearing faculty of the soul) and *nirat* (the seeing faculty) merge into one; when this happens, the soul merges into Shabd and the "lion gate," the royal gateway to the regions of pure spirit, opens.

When I was, God was not;
    Now that God is,
I am no more.
    The dark shadows
Of I-ness vanished
    When I came
Face to face with the Lamp.

K.G., p.12:35

Truly that bride has met
    The Beloved
Whom the Beloved holds
    In his loving embrace,
On whose face shines
    The Beloved's radiance
And dazzles those
    Who look at her.

K.S.S., p.107:1

Such is the radiance
    Of my Beloved
That wherever I look
    His radiance alone I see;
To fathom His radiance
    I went,
But I myself became
    Radiant.

K.S.S., p.107:2

Whatever could be said
    I have tried to say,
Beyond this nothing
    Have I to convey:
Only the One remains,
    The other has vanished—
The wave has merged in the Sea.

K.S.S., p.108:13

APPENDIX

Kabir's Dates

SCHOLARS DIFFER about Kabir's dates. According to sectarian writings, he was born on Monday, the full moon day of the Indian month Jyesht in Vikram Samvat 1455, which corresponds to June–July, 1398 A.D. This date is based on a couplet attributed to Dharam Das, one of the prominent disciples of Kabir.

All scholars have not accepted 1398, the traditional date of Kabir's birth. The difference of opinion ranges from 1300 to 1440 A.D.

Similarly, there is a great diversity of views regarding the year of Kabir's death. Scholars cite four couplets from the oral tradition that give four different years—1448, 1492, 1512 and 1518. Out of these dates, most scholars have favored 1518, that couplet being the oldest of the four. Although no historical evidence is available in support of any date, Hindi, Punjabi and English scholars have arrived at different dates, ranging from 1420 to 1518 A.D.

A statement in the *Archaeological Survey of India*[1] has led some scholars to conclude that Kabir died in 1450 or a few years earlier. The Survey report says that Nawab Bijli Khan erected a mausoleum of Kabir in 1450 in the town of Magahar, district Basti, on the east bank of the river Ami, and that this structure was repaired and renovated by Nawab Fidai Khan in 1567. But most scholars have rejected these dates as hearsay and unsubstantiated.

Dr. S. S. Dwivedi, for example, says that on making inquiries at Magahar, it was discovered that there is no basis for claiming that this monument at Magahar was erected in 1450. Dr. R. K. Varma, Dr. G. Trigunayat, Dr. R. C. Tiwari and many modern scholars feel that the dates given in the Survey are incorrect, the author of the report, Dr. Fuhrer, failing to give even a hint as to the source from which he obtained the dates.

In his treatises on the Saints of North India (*Uttari Bharat ki Sant Parampara*) and Kabir's literature (*Kabir Sahitya ki Parakh*), Parashuram Chaturvedi, one of the most eminent and keen scholars of Hindi Sant literature, has examined the various dates of Kabir and pointed out the flaws inherent in each one of them. He has tried to give new dates based on his own deductions —1368 to 1448, which according to most scholars are based only on surmises; nevertheless, his analysis of all other dates carries great weight.

In the fourth volume of his detailed history of Hindi literature (*Hindi Sahitya ka Brahat Itihas*), Chaturvedi favors the traditional dates of Kabir (1398–1518) when he says: "Although there is no historical evidence available in support of these dates, there are, at the same time, no facts to disprove them. The day, date, month and year of birth have been found to be correct

---

1. *The Archaeological Survey of India,* New Series, North Western Provinces, II:224.

through astrological calculations."[1]

Scholars have found it easier to question and reject the dates of Kabir than to establish them. Although one is inclined to accept the dates of Kabir as 1398–1518, as most scholars have done, adopting an impartial view one has to admit that it is almost impossible to establish the dates of Kabir's birth and death on irrefutable grounds. It should, however, not be wrong to say that Kabir was born in the last few years of the fourteenth century or the first decade of the fifteenth century and lived all through the fifteenth century, perhaps up to the first decade of the sixteenth.

A Note on Ramanand

As discussed in the text of this monograph, there is strong traditional and written evidence suggesting a deep spiritual link between Kabir and Ramanand. Some scholars, who do not agree with this, maintain that according to the dates of Ramanand, either Kabir was not his contemporary or he was very young at the time of Ramanand's death. But there is as great a diversity of views regarding Ramanand's dates as about Kabir's.

Scholars like Dr. R. G. Bhandarkar and Dr. Grierson, basing their views on *Agastya Sanhita,* a Sanskrit composition, maintain that Ramanand was born in 1299, and if he lived for 118 years, as is traditionally accepted, he died in 1417. Scholars who accept these dates deny that Ramanand and Kabir had any association with each other.

F. E. Keay and J. N. Farquhar hold that Ramanand "most probably" lived from 1400 to 1470; R. C. Shukla gives Ramanand's period as 1418 to 1518; S. A. A. Rizvi gives 1350 to 1470; and Parashuram Chaturvedi says that Ramanand was born about 1343 and died in 1448. Dr. Tarachand, unable to arrive at definite dates, says that the last quarter of the fourteenth and the first half of the fifteenth centuries was the period of Ramanand's career. Acharya Baldev Upadhyaya, an eminent Sanskrit scholar and Indologist, says that Ramanand was born in 1410 A.D., and Dr. B. N. Mishra endorses his views.

An old manuscript, "Prasang Parijat," by Chetandas,[2] composed in 1460, gives the date of Ramanand's death as 1448. The poet says that he personally attended the first death anniversary of Ramanand in 1449. Dr. Trigunayat accepts the date given by Chetandas, saying that there is no reason to doubt the evidence of this poet that Ramanand died in 1448.

Ramanandis or votaries of the Ramanand sect, who held that the sage was born in 1299, yielding to the opinion of modern scholars, have accepted that Ramanand died in 1448.[3] Nabhadas, Priyadas, Hariram Vyas and other

---

1. Parashuram Chaturvedi, *Hindi Sahitya ka Brahat Itihas,* IV:126-127.
2. Referred to by Dr. R. K. Varma in *Sant Kabir* and by Dr. Shrikrishna Lal in *Ramanand ki Hindi Rachnae.*
3. Shrikrishna Lal, *Ramanand ki Hindi Rachnae,* p.37.

medieval poets have clearly stated that Kabir had accepted Ramanand as his Guru. In view of the oral and written traditions and the consensus of modern scholars, there is little reason to doubt that Kabir and Ramanand were contemporaries for over forty years.

Ramanand's two Sanskrit works, *Ramarchan Paddhati* and *Vaishnava Matabja Bhaskar,* provide some details of his way of worship. The former work deals entirely with the various types of rituals, external observances and forms of worship taught by Ramanand. The latter treatise deals with his philosophy which, according to some scholars, is akin to one of the schools of the Six Philosophies, Vishishtadvait or conditioned monism. Ramanand also favored idol worship and was a firm believer in the caste system.

This picture of Ramanand suddenly changes when one reads his Hindi poems. The one poem in the Adi Granth, given in the Life section of this book, was for long the only generally known Hindi composition of Ramanand. Some early scholars doubted the authenticity of this poem, while others conceded that Ramanand preached the worship of incarnations, fasting and pilgrimages simultaneously with the rejection of external observances and the adoration of the One Formless God.

Almost all Hindi, Punjabi and English scholars confirm the authenticity of the hymns of the Adi Granth. Not even a letter has been changed since the day this great treasury of spiritual and devotional literature was compiled by Guru Arjan Dev in 1604. There can be little justification for raising doubts about Ramanand's poem only because it presents a portrait of the sage that does not fit in the traditionally accepted framework. To suggest that two contrary forms of devotion were practiced and preached by Ramanand simultaneously and that he edified and rejected idol worship and formalism in the same breath would be doing an injustice to Ramanand and casting aspersions on his integrity both as a devotee and as a teacher.

In this connection, Parashuram Chaturvedi's comment on this poem is significant. He says: "This poem also suggests that although in the beginning Ramanand was engaged in external worship, he later became a devotee of the Nirgun (the Formless One)."[1]

Ramanand's hymn in the Adi Granth is not the only Hindi poem of the sage.[2] Rajjab, the Saint from Rajasthan, has included two songs of Ramanand in *Sarbangi,* his collection of Saints' works. The first poem is in praise of simran, meditation and Saints' association as the means of cleansing the mind, removing the miseries of birth and death and attaining the Lord. The second poem expresses the bliss of spiritual nectar and union with God.

In the late thirties, Dr. P. D. Badthwal (1901–1944) came across a few Hindi poems of Ramanand. They could not be published during his lifetime and

1. Parashuram Chaturvedi, *Hindi Sahitya ka Brahat Itihas,* IV:125.
2. The poem included in the Adi Granth has also been found, with minor differences, in an old manuscript dated 1660 and preserved in the Kashi Nagari Pracharini Sabha.

were brought out in 1955, almost a decade after his death.[1] Some of the poems conform to the teachings of Kabir and other Saints. The following extracts from two of the poems should illustrate the point:

> The Lord revels in the eye center, but no one knows
> this mystery. One who meets the Satguru gains com-
> plete knowledge of the secret.... The adept, like a
> perfect rope-dancer, plays this game with his eyes
> closed. He sees the everlasting flame that burns
> without wick, without oil. The adept realizes Shabd;
> he plays the game with his *surat* and *nirat*.[2]

> Shabd is the key,
> > Shabd is the lock too;
> Shabd reveals the light of Shabd.
> > He who unravels Shabd's mystery
> Becomes the Creator,
> > Becomes the Lord.[3]

The Hindi poems of Ramanand confirm that the one hymn included in the Adi Granth is not an isolated example nor something written in a casual vein, but reflects strong views that identify his teachings with those of Kabir, Guru Nanak and other Saints.

Both the poem in the Adi Granth and the Hindi poems depict the striking change that came about in Ramanand. From a traditionalist he became a rebel against narrow formalism. The diversion from orthodox thinking to what one may describe as a Kabirean outlook is clear and unambiguous. Like Jaidev, Namdev, Tukaram, Mira and some other devotees who in the beginning were worshippers of incarnations and later followed the teachings of the Saints, Ramanand also adopted the Sant Mat path during his later life.

This dynamic change in Ramanand was the result of his association with some perfect Saint. From all accounts, Kabir was the Saint who revolution-ized the personality of Ramanand. Ramanand, who would not look at the face of any low-caste person,[4] adopted such a man—Kabir—as his friend and guide. And the popular and oft-quoted lines, attributed to Ramanand as his reply to the orthodox people of Banaras, reveal his great transformation:

---

1. A short note on Ramanand suggests that Badthwal wanted to write more about the poems and their content. He could not properly edit them nor examine their authenticity and present them as he must have wanted to.
2. *Ramanand ki Hindi Rachnae*, p.10:19, 22.
3. Ibid., p.13:10.
4. According to Priyadas.

Do not ask
  The devotee's creed,
Nor his caste;
  Who adores the Lord
Becomes the Lord's.

A Bibliographical Note

The various collections of Kabir's works available today owe their origin to oral traditions, for there is no record to prove that Kabir wrote or dictated them. One cannot, therefore, vouch for their absolute authenticity. This is also true in the case of many other Saints, like Ravidas, Dadu, Bhikha and Dariya of Rajasthan. Scholars have accepted those compositions as reliable that are proved to be old and that can be corroborated from different sources. From this point of view, the *Kabir Granthavali,* the Adi Granth and the *Bijak* appear to be the most reliable sources of Kabir's poems and have been accepted as authentic by most modern scholars.

Kabir Granthavali

This collection of 403 poems, 810 couplets and 7 *ramainis,* edited by Dr. Shyam Sundar Das Dwivedi in 1928, is based on an old manuscript preserved in the archives of the Nagari Pracharini Sabha, Varanasi, and discovered there by scholars in 1922. The colophon at the end of the manuscript dates it as v.s. 1561, i.e., 1504 A.D., which makes it the earliest known collection of Kabir's poems. It is generally accepted that Kabir died in 1518; thus this collection was made during the Saint's lifetime, fourteen years before his death.

Another manuscript, discovered at the same time, is dated v.s. 1881 (1824 A.D.). There is very little difference between the two texts, except that the second manuscript contains an additional 5 poems and 131 couplets, which have also been included in the *Kabir Granthavali.* The thought, language and style of these additional compositions are the same as those of the 1504 recension and, as noted below, these poems were also known to Saints like Dadu and Rajjab in the sixteenth century.

The collections of Kabir's poems that form a part of *Panch Bani* and *Sarbangi,* preserved by the devotees of Saint Dadu at Daduwara, Naraina, Rajasthan, were compiled in the later sixteenth and early seventeenth centuries.[1] There is practically no difference between the Rajasthan recensions and the 1504 manuscript; the Rajasthan collections include all the poems and couplets of the 1504 and 1824 manuscripts with no significant differences even in the arrangement of poems.

---

1. *Panch Bani* and *Sarbangi* are collections of the writings of various Saints and were started by Rajjab and other devotees of Dadu during his lifetime.

The 1504 manuscript appears to be genuinely dated; even if the type of paper and the script are found to be of a later date, there is no reason to doubt that this manuscript, if not the original 1504 manuscript, is a genuine copy of the original 1504 version. Examining the manuscript itself, P.D. Badthwal says:

> There is nothing in it which may go against the m.s. being as old as the colophon claims it to be. The same may perhaps be said of the colophon itself. . . . The colophon of the present m.s. may, indeed, be in the hand of the copyist himself, though written with a different or too much used pen and somewhat hastily.[1]

The Adi Granth

The Adi Granth, a collection of hymns by Guru Nanak and his successors, also includes devotional compositions by Jaidev, Namdev, Ramanand, Kabir, Ravidas and many other devotees. Compiled in 1604 by Guru Arjan Dev, the fifth Guru in the line of Guru Nanak, this unique treasure of spiritual literature has not been subjected to any alterations and thus has been preserved in its original form.

The Adi Granth includes 228 poems and 243 *saloks* (couplets) of Kabir. Prof. Sahib Singh in his *Bhagat-Bani Satik* has tried to prove that most, if not all of the Adi Granth compositions of Kabir were collected by Guru Nanak (1469–1538), who was a contemporary of Kabir for over forty years. It would therefore be right to presume that out of the poems of Kabir included in the Adi Granth, a large portion were collected during the first quarter of the sixteenth century.

Scholars regard the Adi Granth as a "most authoritative collection"[2] of the compositions of Saints. Dr. Ram Kumar Varma says: "The 1604 recension of Kabir's poems, as included in the Shri Adi Granth, is very authentic."[3] The hymns of the Adi Granth have not been tampered with by any successor in the line of Guru Nanak, their devotees or later scholars. Appreciating this point, P. D. Badthwal says: "Though Sikhism is at present [1940] as much a sect as any, yet the *Adi Granth* is absolutely free from sectarianism."[4]

Despite the variations in words and lines, the spiritual import and tone of the two recensions is the same. A large number of poems in the Adi Granth that are not found in either the *Kabir Granthavali* or the *Bijak* are nearer to the old Hindi of Kabir's times and have been accepted by most Hindi scholars as

1. P. D. Badthwal, *Indian Mysticism*, pp.276-277.
2. Ibid., p.282.
3. R. K. Varma, *Sant Kabir*, Introduction p.25.
4. Badthwal, *Indian Mysticism*, p.282.

authentic. Thus, the poems of Kabir, as available in the Adi Granth, form a significant and reliable contribution to Kabir's literature.

Bijak

The *Bijak* is a collection of Kabir's poems of different types in traditional poetic forms—*ramaini, shabd, sakhi, kahra, basant, hindol*. It has been preserved by various Kabir-panthi branches and is held in great esteem by them. It is generally accepted by scholars that the *Bijak* was compiled many decades after Kabir's death, perhaps not earlier than the first quarter or middle of the seventeenth century. Puranic influence over later disciples has been responsible for the inclusion of references to Puranic mythology not otherwise found in Kabir's other collections, like the *Kabir Granthavali* and the Adi Granth. Some poems of the *Bijak* do not reveal Kabir's usual depth, poetic beauty and characteristic imagery. In view of this, some scholars have raised doubts about the authenticity of the *Bijak* as a whole.

Dr. Shukdev Singh, in his *Kabir Bijak* (1972) has forcefully pleaded the cause of the *Bijak*. And although few will agree with his thesis that the *Bijak* is the only authentic collection of Kabir's work, Dr. Singh's *Bijak* is a noteworthy and remarkable presentation.

An impartial study of the *Bijak* reveals that it is a later collection than the *Kabir Granthavali,* the Adi Granth and the Rajasthan recensions of Kabir's poems, and there are some poems that have been edited by later adherents of Kabir. Nevertheless, a very large number of *ramainis, shabds* and *sakhis* do bear the stamp of Kabir's spiritual insight and poetic genius and can safely be accepted as genuine works of Kabir.

Other Collections

Many collections based on oral traditions and different recensions of Kabir's works have been printed during this century. The most remarkable of these are *Kabir Sahib ki Shabdavali* and *Kabir Sakhi-Sangrah,* originally published in the first years of the twentieth century. Printed by the Belvedere Press, Allahabad, *Shabdavali* consists of poems and *Sakhi-Sangrah* of couplets (*sakhi*) of Kabir.

Around the year 1902, the owners of the Belvedere Press undertook the task of collecting the works of various Saints of North India, Kabir being one of them. They visited many Kabir-panthi centers, met adherents of the sect and made copies from the old manuscripts available there. They also recorded a few poems from oral traditions. The result of their painstaking efforts is the *Shabdavali* and *Sakhi-Sangrah.*

Unfortunately, the editors of these collections have not given the original sources for the poems and couplets. Scholars have doubted their reliability because there is no way to verify their authenticity; moreover, in some instances the language, and more so the spellings, are nearer to modern Hindi than to the language of Kabir's time. The language in some of the poems may have undergone minor changes, either at the Kabir-panthi centers or while noting down the poems. The editors state that they have taken the poems from many old manuscripts and have included them in their publications after careful scrutiny and comparison of the various manuscripts at the Kabir-panthi centers.

Some scholars feel that the entire Belvedere collection of Kabir's works is unreliable and that most of the compositions are by his successors. However, none of Kabir's successors, Dharam Das included, possessed either the poetic genius of Kabir or the facility and force of expression that one finds in the Belvedere collection. The literature available in the names of Dharam Das, Kamal and other devotees of Kabir proves this point.

The Belvedere Press collection—*Shabdavali* and *Sakhi-Sangrah*—are important contributions to the Kabir literature and are significant insofar as they were published much before the *Kabir Granthavali* (1504 and 1824) manuscripts were discovered; nor had Kabir's poems in the Adi Granth come to the notice of Hindi scholars at that time. Despite the occasional change in language, by and large the Belvedere collection bears the mark of Kabir and conveys his message and teachings in a forthright and authentic manner.

The poems collected by Hazari Prasad Dwivedi in his thesis, *Kabir* (1953), contains 100 poems from Kshitimohan Sen's 1910 edition of Kabir's poems and 156 poems from Belvedere, *Bijak* and other sources. K. M. Sen's collection, according to Evelyn Underhill, has been gathered from books and manuscripts and "sometimes from the lips of wandering ascetics and minstrels."[1] Many of these poems are also found in the Belvedere edition.

Kabir's influence in Gujarat has been deep-rooted, there being "not a single village in Gujarat where one does not find a temple of Kabir or a follower of Kabir-panth."[2] Two important publications from Gujarat are *Satguru Kabir Saheb ka Sakhi-Sangrah* and *Satt Kabir ki Shabdavali*. Both are based on old manuscripts, preserved by Kabir-panthis in Gujarat. Although scholars have not examined the original sources of these books, they contain many poems of Kabir found in the *Kabir Granthavali,* Adi Granth, *Bijak* and Belvedere publications. From the point of view of thought, poetic rhythm and directness of expression, a fairly large number of them can easily be accepted as genuine Kabir compositions.

The Basis for the Present Selection

The present selection is primarily based on the *Kabir Granthavali,* the Adi Granth, the *Bijak* and the Belvedere Press publications. A few poems have also been taken from H. P. Dwivedi's *Kabir* and from *Satt Kabir ki Shabdavali*. While selecting the poems and couplets, the main concern has been to

---

1. *One Hundred Poems of Kabir,* Introduction.
2. *Hindi Sahitya ko Gujarat ke Sant Kaviyon ki Den,* p.61.

present Kabir's teaching in all its aspects. The authenticity of the sources, discussed above, has been taken into consideration and an attempt has been made to select from those poems that represent Kabir's teachings—as corroborated by those of earlier and later Saints—and those that conform to Kabir's profound, meaningful and penetrating manner.

Kabir has chosen to use words in his own style. His verb forms and adjectives, strikingly meaningful, reflect amazing vigor and freshness. He uses words of Sanskrit, Prakrit, Arabic and Persian with the same facility and freedom as those of Hindi, Rajasthani, Punjabi, Gujarati and Marathi. Language in his hands becomes ductile and, like an adept potter, he molds it into unusual shapes, varied and diverse.

His language is the language of the masses, his imagery comes from daily life; unsophisticated yet refined, he is a poet of the soil whose compositions present a subtle and intimate picture of the contemporary social and cultural life of the people. At the same time his vision, deep insight into the human mind, the vast canvas of his similes, occasional hints of his own spiritual experiences and his intense love for the Lord act as a constant reminder that this extraordinary poet is above all a great Saint.

The authenticity of Kabir's poems should therefore not be judged only according to style, language and other extrinsic factors, but rather with reference to their intrinsic spiritual meaning.

GLOSSARY

ACROSTIC.   Many Indian Saints have written acrostics, *bawan akhari,* poem cycles beginning with each letter of the alphabet, a traditional limerick form originally devised for memorizing the letters of the alphabet. Kabir, Guru Nanak and other Saints used this form to convey their teachings, a new thought often being introduced with each letter of the alphabet.

AGES, THE FOUR.   See KALIYUG.

AMAR DAS, GURU (1479-1574).   Third Guru in the line of Guru Nanak.

ANAHAD SHABD.   'The unlimited sound'. The divine melody of Shabd that emanates from the limitless regions of pure spirit. See also SHABD.

ANGAD, GURU (1504-1552).   Second Guru in the line of Guru Nanak.

ARJAN DEV, GURU (1563-1606).   The fifth Guru in the line of Guru Nanak.

ATTRIBUTES.   See GUNAS.

AKAL.   'Timeless'; epithet for God.

BEEN.   Musical instrument whose sound resembles that of an oboe or bagpipe. When the Saints speak of the sweet music of the *been,* they are referring to the Sound of the fifth region.

BANARAS.   Also called Kasi, Kashi, and Varanasi.

BANI.   See SHABD.

BENI.   Not much is known about his identity. Three of his poems are included in the Adi Granth.

BHIKHA.   An eighteenth-century Saint, born in District Azamgarh in Uttar Pradesh. Saint Bhikhan, one of whose hymns is included in the Adi Granth, is different from Bhikha.

BOONS.   The four *padarth: dharma* (piety), *arth* (wealth), *kam* (fulfillment of desires) and *moksha* (salvation), the four boons that all Hindus are enjoined on to strive to attain.

BRAHMA.   God of creation in the Hindu trinity of creator-preserver-destroyer (Brahma, Vishnu, Shiva).

BRAHMIN.   The highest caste in the Hindu four-caste system. They are the priestly caste, whose function is the acquisition of knowledge.

CHAKRA.   'Wheel'; six energy centers in the human body.

CHATRIK.   In Indian folklore the chatrik or rainbird is always longing for the drops of rain that fall during the constellation *swanti;* it will die of thirst rather than drink any other water.

CHAUPAR or CHAUSAR.   A game played with dice or cowrie shells. The four pawns have to circle the four corners of the board—the four types of species—and the player wins the game when all his pawns enter the center square, known as 'home'.

CHAURASI. 'Eighty-four'; hence, the wheel of eighty-four, the wheel of trans-migration. The name indicates the eight million four hundred thousand species into which the soul may have to incarnate, referred to as the eighty-four lakh species.

CHINTAMANI. A mythical jewel that fulfills all the wishes of the one who possesses it.

CHISHTI, MUINUDDIN (1141-1236). Born in Sistan and brought up in Khurasan. He spent the last thirty years of his life in Ajmer (Rajasthan).

CRYSTAL LAKE. See MANSAROVAR.

DADU (1544-1603). Of the many Indian Saints, Dadu's works have been comparatively well preserved, by his main disciple and successor, Rajjab. Like Kabir, his expression is precise and powerful, and Dadu, at places, admits his indebtedness to Kabir for this.

DARIYA OF BIHAR (1596-1702). Born in a Muslim family, tailors by profession, Saint Dariya spent most of his life in Bihar, in northeast India. Though a contemporary of Dariya of Marwar, there is no record that the two knew each other.

DARIYA OF MARWAR (1676-1758). Born in Rajasthan in a family of Muslim carders; unlike Dariya of Bihar, very few compositions of Dariya of Marwar are extant.

DARSHAN. Implies looking intently at the Master with a deep feeling of respect and devotion and with one-pointed attention.

DASWAN DWAR. The tenth aperture; appellation of the third spiritual region.

DHARAM DAS. One of the prominent disciples of Kabir and also one of his successors. Dharam Das has written many poems, some of them in the name of Kabir.

DHARAM RAI. 'Lord of justice'. See KAL.

DHARNI DAS. A Shabd-margi Saint who was born in Bihar in 1656.

DHYAN. Inner contemplation. In Sant Mat, a special technique taught by the Saints in which the devotee contemplates on the form of his Master within.

DWARKA. An ancient city of Saurashtra, situated on the coast of Western India, and regarded by Hindus as one of the holiest of their pilgrim places.

FAKIR. Muslim term for a holy man, ascetic or religious mendicant.

FARID, SHEIKH (1173-1265). Also known as Farid-ud-Din Ganj-i-Shaker, he was the disciple of Khwaja Qutab Bakhtiyar Kaki of Delhi.

GAGAN. 'Sky'; the firmament of the second region in the spiritual journey of the soul.

GANGES or GANGA. For the Hindus, the holiest of all the rivers in India.

744

GAYATRI MANTRA. A Vedic mantra, considered sacred by orthodox Hindus.

GHARI. Twenty-four minutes. See also WATCHES.

GOBIND SINGH, GURU (1666-1708). The tenth Guru in the line of Guru Nanak.

GUNAS. The three attributes or qualities of *prakriti,* the primordial matter out of which the creation proceeds: *sattva* (harmony, serenity), *rajas* (action or activity) and *tamas* (inertia, darkness). The three *gunas* have their source in Trikuti and do not go higher than this region. The soul that crosses Trikuti on its spiritual journey transcends the limitations of the three *gunas* and enters the regions of pure spirit, which are free from the influence of the three *gunas.*

GURUMUKH or GURMUKH. 'One whose face is turned towards the Guru'. One who has completely surrendered to the Guru; a highly advanced soul; sometimes used for the Saint or perfect Master.

HAFIZ (1325-1390). Well-known Persian Saint; was born and died in Shiraz (Iran). Famous for his beautiful poetry, Hafiz wrote his compositions in what is known as *lisan-ul-ghaib,* 'the language of mystery'.

HANSA. 'Swan'. In the Indian spiritual tradition, the highly evolved souls in the regions beyond Brahm are called swans or *hansa.* Kabir has sometimes used the term to denote soul in general.

HARI. One of the Hindu names for God; the word is also used for Vishnu, the preserver in the Hindu trinity of creator-preserver-destroyer.

HEART. The eye center has also been called *hridai* or 'heart' by the Saints, for it is from this center that the consciousness permeates the body and acts, the eye center being the spiritual energy center of the body, as the heart is on the physical level.

HUKAM. Literally, 'order, command'. The Saints refer to *hukam* on the physical level as the order or directions of the Master; however, they mostly refer to the term *hukam* in the context of the Lord's will or command and have often identified it with Shabd or Nam.

ID, BAKAR-ID. Id, 'happy day', is a festival among the Muslims. *Bakar-id* is another Muslim festival, in which an animal is sacrificed in the name of God.

JAIDEV. A Sanskrit poet who flourished between the twelfth and thirteenth centuries. Originally a devotee of Lord Krishna, he seems to have adopted Sant Mat in later life.

JOGI. Yogi, one who practices yoga; *jogi* is sometimes used in a slightly pejorative sense.

KA'ABA. A sacred Muslim shrine in Mecca.

KABIR-PANTH. Traditional followers of the line of Kabir.

KAFIR. 'Infidel'; non-Muslim, a non-believer in Islam. See MOMIN.

KAL. 'Time, death'. The negative power, the universal mind, the ruler of the three perishable worlds (physical, astral, causal); also called Dharam Rai, the Lord of Judgment, Yama, the lord of death. Kal's headquarters are in the second spiritual region, Trikuti, of which he is the ruler.

KALIYUGA. The fourth cycle of time, known as the Dark Age or Iron Age.

KALMA. Arabic for 'word'. Every Muslim must recite the *kalma,* a short eulogy of God, "who is One and whose Prophet is Mohammed." Kabir, like the Persian mystics, calls Shabd or Word the *kalma.*

KALPATARU. The mythical wish-fulfilling tree that grants any wish made before it.

KARMA. 'Action'; the law of action and reaction; the debts and credits resulting from our deeds.

KORAN or QURAN. The holy book of the Muslims.

LAKH. One hundred thousand.

LOTUS FEET. The lotus flower is associated with purity, delicacy, beauty; although it grows in mud and water, it remains untouched by them. Out of reverence, the feet of the Master, of a holy man or of a deity are referred to as lotus feet.

M. Abbreviated form of *Mohilla,* used in the Adi Granth to indicate the authorship of compositions by the Gurus. *M.1* means Guru Nanak; *M.2,* Guru Angad; *M.3,* Guru Amar Das, and so forth. The compositions in the Adi Granth are arranged according to the musical scales or modes of Indian classical music, called *rag; Malar, Asa, Bilawal,* etc., are names of different *rags.*

MAGAHAR. A town in Uttar Pradesh, situated on the banks of the river Ami, about 175 miles from Banaras. In medieval times it was supposed to bear a curse: anyone dying there would be reborn as a donkey.

MALUKDAS (1574-1686). Indian Saint, born in North India. His compositions are simple but full of spiritual depth.

MANMUKH. 'One whose face is turned towards the mind'; someone who obeys the dictates of the mind; a devotee of the mind and the ways of the world; a worldly person.

MANSAROVAR. A sacred lake and place of pilgrimage in the Himalayas situated near Mt. Kailash. The Saints refer, however, to a lake in Daswan Dwar or the third stage in the soul's inner spiritual journey. It is also called the lake of nectar (*amrit-sar* or *ab-i-hayat*). When the soul bathes in this lake, it loses all distinctions of name or sex and emerges as pure soul.

MANTRAS. Group of letters or words repeated in a formal manner to please or appease some deity; a formula to obtain supernatural powers; also the name given to a portion of the Vedas.

MASON WASP. The mason wasp encloses a small worm or maggot in a mud dome where its eggs are laid; the eggs hatch, eat the worm and pierce the thinnest part of the dome, emerging as mature mason wasps. In folklore, it is held that the mason wasp turns the worm into a mason wasp by the sound of its humming. Indian mystics have adopted this lore to explain the transformation that the satsang or company of a Saint brings about.

MATHURA. Holy city situated in Uttar Pradesh (North India) on the banks of the River Jamuna.

MAULVI. A learned Muslim or theologian; also a Muslim high priest.

MAYA. 'Illusion, delusion, deception, unreality'; the phenomenal universe. All that is known through the senses is *maya;* it appears, but is not; it conceals the vision of God, Reality, from our sight. Usually represented as a beautiful but faithless woman who lures mankind and keeps the soul tied to the three worlds.

MOMIN. 'The faithful'; used of a believer in Prophet Mohammed and in Islam. See KAFIR.

MUKTI. 'Liberation, salvation'. Most religions look upon attaining the region of Brahm as salvation; but according to the Saints, true *mukti* or salvation is when the soul goes beyond Brahm and ultimately attains union with its source, God.

MULLAH. Muslim priest, teacher or religious leader.

MYSTIC STONE. See PARAS.

NABHADAS. Author of the well-known poetic composition, *Bhaktamal* ('garland of devotees'), he flourished during the latter half of the sixteenth and the first quarter of the seventeenth centuries.

NAM. 'Name'. The unspoken name or Shabd, the Word; the Immortal Creator.

NAMAZ. Formal prayers recited by devout Muslims at fixed times of the day.

NAMDEV (1270-1350). A Saint born in Maharashtra; originally a devotee of Lord Vitthal, he took to Shabd practice after initiation from Visoba Khechar. He spent the last eighteen years of his life in the village of Ghuman, District Gurdaspur.

NANAK, GURU (1469-1538). Well-known Saint, born in Punjab, who traveled widely, spreading the message of Nam. His compositions were preserved by his successors and form the basis of the Adi Granth.

NAWAB. Governor of a province or state in India under the Muslim rulers; sometimes they became independent rulers and still continued to hold the title of nawab.

NEGATIVE POWER. See KAL.

NINETY-SIX (RITUALS). The Hindu scriptures enumerate ninety-six *pakhand* or rituals as follows: 24 amongst the Brahmins; 12 each amongst Sannyasis, Vairagis and Yogis; 18 each amongst Sauras and Jangams.

NIRAT. The seeing faculty of the soul. See also SURAT.

NIRGUN. 'Without any attributes'. Saints have been described as the devotees of the Nirgun.

PAHAR. See WATCHES.

PALTU (1710-1780). Born near Ayodhya in District Faizabad, Uttar Pradesh, Saint Paltu was a disciple in the line of Saint Bhikha.

PANDA. A Brahmin priest who conducts ceremonies in places of pilgrimage, holy rivers or big temples.

PANTHI. 'One who follows a path, *panth*'; Kabir-panthi, 'one who follows the path of Kabir'. *Panth* is the name given to any of various sects, which distinguish themselves from others on the basis of outer signs.

PARAS. 'Philosophers' stone', 'mystic stone'; a mythical stone that turns iron into pure gold when the iron is brought in contact with it.

PASSIONS. The five passions are lust (*kam*), anger (*krodh*), greed (*lobh*), attachment (*moh*), and ego or pride (*ahankar*); also called the 'five demons', 'five thieves', 'five robbers', etc.

PHILOSOPHERS' STONE. See PARAS.

PHILOSOPHIES, the six. *Shat darshan;* the six main schools of Indian philosophy, which intellectually analyze the existence of God, soul, maya, the creation, sentient and inert forms of creation, karmas, the cause of bondage, and the basis for emancipation.

PILGRIMAGE PLACES. There are sixty-eight places of Hindu pilgrimage in India, situated on mountaintops, seashores and the banks of rivers. They have all become centers of ritualism and commercial pursuits, in the name of religion, and are dominated by the priestly hierarchy.

PIPA. Fifteenth-century Saint from Rajasthan, the king of Gagron Fort, near Kota in modern Rajasthan. Saint Pipa was a contemporary of Kabir. One of his compositions is included in the Adi Granth.

PRAKRITIS. The essential nature of mind and matter, which projects itself in various forms of emotions and actions, and which also influences the various parts of the body. They are twenty-five in number and consist of five principal manifestations of the five elements or *tattwas*.

PRANAYAM. Yogic practice of breath control, consisting of inhaling, holding the breath, and exhaling, in certain prescribed ways.

PUNDIT. 'Learned man'; a Hindu priest, especially learned in theology, religion and Hindu mythology.

PURANAS. 'Old ones'; the Hindu scripture of religio-historical stories describing the lives and deeds of gods, heroes and great kings; there are eighteen different Puranas.

QAZI. Expounder of Muslim law; during the Muslim rule in India, the qazi enjoyed certain judicial powers.

RAINBIRD. See CHATRIK.

RAJJAB (1567-1693). A Saint from Rajasthan, born in Sanganer, near Jaipur (Rajasthan), in a Muslim family. Became a disciple of Saint Dadu at the age of nineteen. He wrote a large number of couplets and poems. He also collected the works of various Saints, in one large volume known as *Sarbangi*.

RAM. One of the Hindu names for God; Ram is also used to identify Ram, the incarnation of Vishnu. Saints have used the term Ram to denote the Supreme Lord who is present within every particle of the creation. Kabir has clearly pointed out that his Ram is God and not any incarnation or deity.

RAMAZAN. The ninth month of the Muslim calendar; in this month all pious Muslims fast from sunrise to sunset.

RAM CHANDRA. One of the incarnations of Vishnu, the god of preservation in the Hindu trinity, he was the son of King Dashrath of Ayodhya and the hero of the *Ramayana*.

RAM DAS, GURU (1534-1581). Fourth Guru in the line of Guru Nanak.

RAVAN. The king of Lanka (not the modern Sri Lanka), believed to be one of the most learned men of his time and fabulously wealthy; falling a victim to low desires, he abducted Sita, the consort of Rama, had to fight a battle with Rama in which he lost his life, and his capital made out of gold was ruined.

RAVIDAS or RAIDAS. Well-known Saint of Uttar Pradesh of the fifteenth and early sixteenth centuries; he was a contemporary of Kabir and, according to some traditions, also his disciple.

RUMI or MAULANA RUM (13th century). Well-known Persian Saint, disciple of Shams-i-Tabriz and author of the *Masnavi*.

SADI, SHEIKH (1184-1291). A Sufi Saint of Persia, born in Shiraz; author of *Gulistan* and *Bostan*.

SAGUN. 'One with attributes'. Devotion to the Sagun God implies worship of one of the incarnations or deities representing certain qualities, such as protection, destruction, learning, wealth, prosperity, success, death, destruction of evil. In India, they are usually represented by idols, paintings and symbols.

SAHAJ. 'Easy, natural'; the natural state of the soul; that level of spiritual consciousness in which the soul, having realized its own true nature or identity, gravitates easily and naturally towards complete merging in God. This state begins in Par Brahm and reaches its culmination in Sach Khand.

SAKAT. Originally the name given to a group of worshippers of certain deities; they combined drugs, sex and animal sacrifices in their form of worship. Saints like Kabir and Guru Nanak have used the term *sakat* for persons who are completely subservient to the lower tendencies of mind, who are wicked and inhuman, and who are generally given over to drugs, drink and depraved behavior.

SAMADHI. A state of concentration in which all consciousness of the outer world is transcended; a state of deep meditation.

SANSKARAS. Impressions or tendencies from previous births, early upbringing, traditions and social influences, which shape the basic outlook and pattern of behavior of a human being.

SANT. 'Saint'; a highly evolved soul who has attained God-realization.

SANT MAT. The spiritual 'path of the Saints'; has also been called SURAT SHABD YOGA ('union of soul with Shabd or Word').

SATGURU. 'Perfect Master, true Master'.

SATSANG. 'Association of the true'; company or association with a Master or perfect Saint; congregation when attended by a Master is also called satsang.

SHABD. 'Word' or 'sound'. Creative power; source of all creation, the one reality behind all appearances. Manifests as sound and light in the spiritual regions. Referred to by many names: *Nam* (name), *Anahad Shabd* (unstruck melody or sound), *Bani* (voice), *Dhun* (sound), *Hukam* (command), *Nad* (heavenly sound), *Sat Nam* (true name), *Kalma* (word), *Logos* (word), etc. Hymns from a scripture are also called *shabd;* collectively they are known as *bani*. See also NAM.

SHABD-MARG. 'The path of the Word' (*shabd*); the practice of the Sound Current, Nam or Word has also been called SURAT SHABD YOGA and SANT MAT.

SHABD YOGA. See SURAT SHABD YOGA.

SHAMS-I-TABRIZ. Well-known Persian Saint of the twelfth and thirteenth centuries, the Master of Maulana Rum; assassinated by religious fanatics.

SHEIKH. 'Chief'. Muslim holy man; Muslim courtesy title for any venerable, elderly man.

SHIVA. God of destruction in the Hindu trinity of creator-preserver-destroyer (Brahma, Vishnu, Shiva); also called Mahesh and Mahadeo.

SIDDHAS. 'Perfected ones'; old yogic traditions claim that there have been eighty-four accomplished yogis or *siddhas* who attained 'perfect success' (*siddhi*) or 'realization' through their yogic practices.

SIMRAN or SUMIRAN. 'Repetition'; repetition of the five holy names according to the instructions of a perfect Master.

SUKHMAN or SUSHUMNA or SUKHMANA. The central path starting from the eye center and leading upwards to the higher spiritual regions, located and traversed by means of the spiritual practice taught by a perfect Master. This is not to be confused with *sushumna* of the yogis, which is the central canal along the spine, the current on the left being called *ida* and the one on the right, *pingla*.

750

SUNN. Derived from Sanskrit, *shunya* has usually been translated as void, emptiness, vacuum; but Saints have not used this term with this meaning. According to them it is an inner spiritual region which is devoid of matter in any form. On entering this region the soul becomes free from the bondage of matter, mind and the three attributes.

SURAT. The hearing faculty of the soul; NIRAT is the seeing faculty. When the soul goes within, it hears the melody of Shabd through *surat* and sees the light of Shabd through *nirat*. At a certain stage the two faculties merge into one, and the soul merges into the Shabd, the gateway to the regions of pure spirit thus opening. The term *surat* has also been used for soul or consciousness.

SURAT SHABD YOGA. The practice of joining the soul (*surat*) with the Word (*shabd*) and merging (*yoga*) with it; once the soul merges into the Shabd, it is carried by the Shabd to its source, the Lord. Also called Sahaj Yoga, Shabd Marg, Sant Mat.

SWAMIJI (1818-1878). Seth Shiv Dayal Singh of Agra, known as Swamiji Maharaj; made Sant Mat popular through simple exposition in conversational Hindi.

SWAN. See HANSA.

TATTWA. The five elements present in every living being; vegetables have one active element (water), insects have two (air and fire), birds have three (air, fire and earth), higher animals have four (earth, air, water, and fire), and man has five (earth, air, water, fire and ether).

TEGH BAHADUR, GURU (1622-1675). The ninth Guru in the line of Guru Nanak.

TILAK. A mark made on the forehead, mostly out of vermilion, saffron or sandalwood paste. Various sects, religions, sadhus and devotees have their own different tilaks which represent the sect or group they follow.

TRIKUTI. 'Three prominences'; appellation of the second spiritual region; also called Musallasi by the Persian Saints, meaning 'three-cornered'. Gagan is the sky of Trikuti, and the region itself is often referred to as Gagan.

TRILOKI. Literally, the three worlds; denotes the physical, astral and causal worlds, which are all within the domain of the negative power.

TRIVENI or TRIBENI. 'The confluence of the three currents'. The name given to a place in Allahabad where the three rivers, Ganges, Jamuna and Saraswati, join; Saints use the term to refer to a portion of the inner region of Trikuti from where the currents of the three attributes (*gunas*) emanate. In the soul's journey through the inner regions, the three attributes appear to conjoin into one current in Trikuti.

TULSI SAHIB (1764-1845). Well-known Saint from Maharashtra, connected with the ruling family of Peshwas; left home at an early age, came to

Uttar Pradesh and settled at Hathras, near Agra. *Ghat Ramayan* and *Ratan Sagar* are two of his main compositions, besides many other smaller poems.

TURK. During Kabir's times the Muslims in North India were commonly called 'Turks' because some of the early Muslim conquerors were of Turkish origin.

UNIVERSAL MIND. See KAL.

UPANISHADS. The philosophical and mystical part of the Vedas, which describes the inner or esoteric teachings.

VAISHNAVITE. Devotee of Lord Vishnu, the god of preservation. The term has generally been used for a sect of Hindus who were originally devotees of Lord Vishnu but gradually changed over to worship of other incarnations and deities. The various schools of thought, like Ramanandis, Ramanujis, Vallabhacharis and devotees of certain Vedas, have all been generally termed Vaishnavites. Gradually they have come to be divided into rigid sects, following their own separate forms of worship, dress, symbols and deities.

VAJID (also called Vajind in Rajasthan). Seventeenth-century Saint, born in a Muslim family; one of the prominent disciples of Dadu.

VAKHNA or BAKHNA. Seventeenth-century Saint of Rajasthan and disciple of Dadu.

VISHNU. God of preservation in the Hindu trinity of creator-preserver-destroyer (Brahma, Vishnu, Shiva).

VEDAS. 'Knowledge'; 'revealed knowledge', as embodied in the four sacred books of the Hindus, the Rig Veda, Sama Veda, Yajur Veda and Atharva Veda.

WATCHES. In the medieval Indian system of counting time, the day was divided into eight *pahar,* 'watches', or 64 *ghari,* each *ghari* or 'beat' equivalent to $22\frac{1}{2}$ minutes.

THREE WORLDS. See TRILOKI.

YAJNA or YAGNYA. 'Sacrifice'; a ritual or religious ceremony of the Hindus, which in ancient India included the sacrifice of some animal.

YAMA. The lord of death, who takes charge of the soul at the time of death. The *yamdoots* are the agents or minions of Yama. Yama is sometimes identified with Kal, the ruler of the three worlds; strictly speaking, Yama is subservient to Kal or Dharam Rai, the lord of justice.

YOGA. 'Union'; a system of exercises or spiritual practice that leads to or aims at the union of the soul with God.

SELECTED BIBLIOGRAPHY

Kabir and His Works (English)

Abu'l-Fazl Allami. *Ain-e-Akbari*. Vol. II and III translated by H.S. Jarrett. Reprint. New Delhi: Oriental Reprint Corporation, 1978.

P.D. Barthwal. *Traditions of Indian Mysticism Based upon Nirguna School of Hindi Poetry.* Reprint. New Delhi: Heritage Publishers, 1978.

R.G. Bhandarkar. *Vaishnavism, Shaivism and Minor Religious Systems*. 1913. Reprint. Varanasi: Indological Book House, 1965.

Briggs. *The Rise of Mohammedean Power in India.*

Richard Burns. Article on Kabir in the Encyclopaedia of Religion and Ethics, edited by James Hastings. Edinburgh: 1918.

J.N. Farquhar. *An Outline of the Religious Literature of India.* 1920. Reprint. Delhi: Motilal Banarsidass, 1967.

F.E. Keay. *A History of Hindi Literature.* Reprint. New Delhi: Award Publishing House, 1980.

—————. *Kabir and His Followers.* Calcutta: Associated Press, 1931.

Max Arthur Macauliffe. *The Sikh Religion.* Reprint (6 vols. in 3). New Delhi: S. Chand, 1963.

R.D. Ranade. *Pathway to God in Hindi Literature.* Sangli: Adhyatma Vidya Mandir, 1954.

Saiyid Athar Abbas Rizvi. *A History of Sufism in India.* 2 vols. New Delhi: Munshiram Manoharlal, 1978.

Kshitimohan Sen. *Medieval Mysticism of India.* Reprint. New Delhi: Munshiram Manoharlal, 1974.

Ahmad Shah. *The Bijak of Kabir*. 1911. Reprint. New Delhi: Asian Publication Services, 1977.

Sri Guru Granth Sahib. 4 vols. Translated by Gopal Singh. Chandigarh: World Sikh University Press, 1978.

Tarachand. *Influence of Islam on Indian Culture.* 2nd ed. Allahabad: Indian Press, 1963.

Ch. Vaudeville. *Kabir.* London: Oxford University Press, 1974.

G.H. Westcott. *Kabir and the Kabir Panth.* 1907. Reprint. Calcutta: Susil Gupta, 1953.

H.H. Wilson. *Religious Sects of the Hindus.* London: 1861. Reprint in 2 vols. Calcutta: Susil Gupta, 1958.

Editions of Kabir's Works (Hindi)

The Kabir Granthavali

Kabir Granthavali. Edited by Shyam Sundar Das Dwivedi. 14th ed. Kashi: Nagaripracharini Sabha, 1977 (2034 v.s.).

Kabir Granthavali. Edited by Mataprasad Gupta. Agra: Pramanik Prakashan, 1969.

Kabir Granthavali. Edited by Parasnath Tiwari. Allahabad: Hindi Parishad, 1961.

Kabir Granthavali. Edited by Dr. Bhagwat Swarup Mishra. 3rd ed. Agra: Vinod Pustak Mandir, 1977.

Kabir Granthavali Satik. Edited by Pushppal Singh. Delhi: Ashok Prakashan, 1962.

Kabir Granthavali. Edited by L.B. Anant. Delhi: 1968.

The Adi Granth

Sri Guru Granth Sahab.* Amritsar: Shiromani Gurdwara Parbandhak Committee, 1952.

Sri Guru Granth Sahib. 4 vols. Translated by Dr. Manmohan Sehgal. (Original text in devanagari, with Hindi translation.) Lucknow: Bhuvan Vani Trust, 1978-82.

Shabdarath Sri Guru Granth Sahab.* 4 vols. Amritsar: S.G.P.C., 1979.

Jodh Singh. *Bani Bhagta Satik*.* Meerut: 1913.

Prof. Sahib Singh. *Bhagat-Bani Satik*.* Vols. 4, 5. 2nd ed. Amritsar: Singh Bros., 1974-75.

——————. *Salok Kabir Ji Satik*.* 3rd ed. Amritsar: Singh Bros., 1974.

Ram Kumar Varma. *Sant Kabir*. 5th ed. Allahabad: Sahitya Bhawan, 1966.

The Bijak

Bijak. Edited by Vichardas Shastri. 4th ed. Allahabad: Ramnarayanlal Benimadhav, 1965.

Bijak Guru Kabir Saheb ka. Lucknow: Naval Kishore Press, 1915.

Bijak-Mul (Kabir Bijak). Edited by Maharaj Raghavdasji. Banaras: 1947.

Kabir Bijak. Edited by Dr. Shukhdev Singh. Allahabad: Neelabh Prakashan, 1972.

Kabir Sahib ka Bijak. Allahabad: Belvedere Press, 1926.

Kabir Sahib ka Bijak. Edited by Hansdas Shastri and Mahabir Prasad. Barabanki: Kabir Granth Prakashan, 1950.

Mul Bijak Satik. Edited by Jairamdevji Maharaj. 2nd ed. Mathura: Hindi Pustakalay, 1971.

Sant Kabir ka Bijak.† 3 vols. Edited by Shivbrat Lal. Gopiganj: 1914.

Other Collections

Kabir Akhravati. Allahabad: Belvedere Press.

Kabir Sahib ka Anurag Sagar. Allahabad: Belvedere Press.

Kabir Sahib ki Gyan Gudri Rekhte aur Jhulne. Allahabad: Belvedere Press.

Kabir Sahib ki Shabdavali. 4 vols. Allahabad: Belvedere Press.

Kabir Sakhi-Sangrah. Allahabad: Belvedere Press.

Satguru Kabir Saheb ke Sakhi-Sangrah. 4 vols. Edited by Vichardas Shastri. Baroda: 1950.

Satt Kabir ki Shabdavali. Edited by Manilal Tulsidas Mehta. Ahmadabad (Gujarat): Ramanlal Vilaldas Patel, 1957 (2014 v.s.).

Sant-Sudha-Sar. Edited by Viyogi Hari. Delhi: Sasta Sahitya Mandal Prakashan, 1953.

Kabir-Padavali. Edited by Ram Kumar Varma. Allahabad: 1954.

Anuragsagar. Edited by Swami Yugalanandvihari. Reprint. Bombay: Shri Venkateshwar Press Prakashan, 1962.

---

*Punjabi; gurmukhi script.
†Urdu.

Bodh-Sagar. Edited by Swami Yugalanand. Reprint. Bombay: Venkateshwar Steam Press, 1950.

Kabir Dohavali. Edited by Swami Shri Yugalanand. Lahore: General Book Depot, 1940.

Kabir Sagar. Edited by Swami Shri Yugalanand. 11 vols. Reprint. Bombay: Shri Venkateshwar Steam Press, 1953.

Satya Kabir Sahib ki Sakhi. Edited by Swami Yugalanand. Bombay: Shri Venkateshwar Steam Press, 1908.

Kabir Vachanavali. Edited by Ayodhya Singh Upadhyaya 'Hariaudh'. Manoranjan Pustakmala. Kashi: Kashi Nagaripracharini Sabha, 1916.

On Kabir and His Works (Hindi)

Pandit Chandrakant Bali. *Panjab-Prantiya Hindi-Sahitya ka Itihas,* vol. 1. Delhi: National Publishing House, 1962.

Dr. Kanti Kumar C. Bhatt. *Sant Kabir aur Kabir Sampraday*. Mathura: Book Centre, 1980.

Acharya Parashuram Chaturvedi, ed. *Hindi Sahitya ka Brihat Itihas,* vol. 4. Varanasi: Nagaripracharini Sabha, 1968 (2025 v.s.).

—————. *Kabir-Sahitya ki Parakh*. Allahabad: Bharat Bhandar, 1972.

—————. *Sant-Kavya*. Allahabad: Kitab Mahal, 1952.

—————. *Uttari Bharat ki Sant-Parampara*. Allahabad: Bharati Bhandar Leader Press, 1964 (2021 v.s.).

————— and Dr. Mahendra, eds. *Kabir-Kosh*. Allahabad: Samriti Prakashan, 1973.

Triloki Narayan Dikshit. *Parichayi Sahitya*. Lucknow: Vishvavidyalay Hindi-Prakashan, 1957.

Hazari Prasad Dwivedi. *Kabir*. Delhi: Rajkamal Prakashan, 1980 (1st ed., 1971).

Grierson. *Hindi Sahitya ka Pratham Itihas*. (Translated from original English.)

Swami Dr. Bhuvaneshwarnath Mishra 'Madhav'. *Vaishnav Sadhana aur Siddhant: Hindi Sahitya par Uska Prabhav*. Patna: Bihar Hindi Granth Akadami, 1973.

Nabhadas. *Bhaktamal*. Lucknow: Naval Kishore Press, 1926.

Priyadas. *Rasbodhini Tika*. Lucknow: Naval Kishore Press, 1926.

Raghodas. *Bhaktamal Raghodas Krit*. Edited by Agarchand Nahta. Jodhpur: Rajasthan Oriental Research Institute, 1965.

Dr. Sarnam Singh Sharma. *Kabir: Ek Vivechan*. Delhi: Hindi Sahitya Sansar, 1960.

Purushottamlal Shrivastav. *Kabir Sahitya ka Adhyayan*. Banaras: Sahitya-Ratna-Mala Karyalay, 1950.

R.C. Shukla. *Hindi Sahitya ka Itihas*.

Shri Babu Lehna Singh and Babu Nihal Singh, eds. *Kabirkasauti*. Bombay: Gangavishnu Shri Krishnadas, 1956 (2013 v.s.).

Garcin de Tassy. *Hindi Sahitya ka Itihas*. (Translated from original French, *Histoire de la litterature hindoustanie*. Paris: 1939).

Dr. Ramchandra Tiwari. *Kabir Mimamsa*. Allahabad: Lokbharati Prakashan, 1976.

Dr. Govind Trigunayat. *Kabir ki Vichardhara*. Kanpur: Sahitya-Niketan, 1942 (2009 v.s.).

Dr. Ram Kumar Varma. *Kabir ka Rahasyavad*. Allahabad: Sahitya Bhawan, 1972 (1st ed., 1929).

Comparative Teachings

English

Isaac A. Ezekiel. *Saint Paltu*. Beas: Radha Soami Satsang Beas, 1977.
The Holy Bible. Authorized King James Version. London: Oxford University Press, n.d.
The New American Bible. Cleveland and New York: The Catholic Press, 1970.
J.R. Puri and V.K. Sethi. *Saint Namdev*. Beas: Radha Soami Satsang Beas, 1977.
Swamiji Maharaj. *Sar Bachan (Prose)*. Beas: Radha Soami Satsang Beas, 1978.
K.N. Upadhyaya. *Dadu, the Compassionate Mystic*. Beas: Radha Soami Satsang Beas, 1980.
———. *Guru Ravidas: Life and Teachings*. Beas: Radha Soami Satsang Beas, 1982.

Hindi

Bhikha. *Bhikha Sahib ki Bani*. Allahabad: Belvedere Press.
Dadu. *Dadudayal*. Edited by Parashuram Chaturvedi. Varanasi: Nagaripracharini Sabha, 1966 (2023 v.s.).
Dariya. *Dariya Granthavali*. 2 vols. Edited by Dharmendra Brahmchari. Patna: Rashtra Bhasha Parishad Bihar.
Dariya. *Dariya Sahib Marwarwale ki Bani*. Allahabad: Belvedere Press.
Sri Dasham Granth Sahibji.* Amritsar: Bhai Jawahar Singh Kripal Singh, 1979 (2036 v.s.).
Dharnidas. *Dharnidasji ki Bani*. Allahabad: Belvedere Press.
Malukdas. *Malukdasji ki Bani*. Allahabad: Belvedere Press.
Namdev. *Sri Namdev Gatha*.† Bombay: Maharashtra Govt., 1970.
Paltu. *Paltu Sahib ki Bani*. 3 vols. Allahabad: Belvedere Press.
Panchamrit. Edited by Swami Mangaldas. Jaipur: Lakshmiram Trust, 1948.
Ramanand. *Ramanand ki Hindi Rachnae*. Edited by Dr. Pitambardatt Badathwal and Dr. Shri Krishnalal. Kashi: Nagaripracharini Sabha, 1955 (1st ed.).
Ravidas. *Raidasji ki Bani*. Allahabad: Belvedere Press.
———. *Ravidas Darshan*. Edited by Prithvi Singh Azad. Chandigarh: Guru Ravidas Sansthan.
———. *Sant Ravidas Vani*. Edited by B.P. Sharma. Chandigarh: Guru Ravidas Sansthan, 1978.
Maharaj Sawan Singh. *Gurumat Siddhant*. 2 vols. Beas: Radha Soami Satsang Beas, 1960-61.
Swamiji Maharaj. *Sar Bachan Radhaswami (Chhand Band)*. Beas: Radha Soami Satsang Beas, 1963.
Tulsi Sahib. *Ghat Ramayan*. 2 vols. Allahabad: Belvedere Press.
———. *Tulsi Sahib ki Shabdavali*. 2 vols. Allahabad: Belvedere Press.
Vakhna. *Bakhnaji ki Bani*. Edited by Swami Mangaldas. Jaipur: Lakshmiram Trust, 1937.

---

*Punjabi; gurmukhi script.
†Marathi.

INFORMATION AND BOOKS
ARE AVAILABLE FROM:

The Secretary
Radha Soami Satsang Beas
P.O. Dera Baba Jaimal Singh 143204
District Amritsar, Punjab, India

CANADA
Dr. J. Khanna, 5550 McMaster Road, Vancouver V6T 1J8, B.C.

Mr. Reginald S. Davis, R.R. 1 Crapaud, Prince Edward Island, COA 1JO

U.S.A.
Mr. Roland G. deVries, 10901 Mill Spring Drive, Nevada City,
    California 95959

Col. E.R. Berg, U.S. Air Force (Ret'd), 4001 Mavelle Drive,
    Minneapolis, Minn. 55435

Mr. Roy E. Ricks, 651 Davis Street, Melrose Park, Ill. 60160   *708 345 6691*

Mr. Henry F. Weekley, 2121 No. Ocean Blvd., Apt. 1108E,
    Boca Raton, Fla. 33431

MEXICO
Mr. Jorge Angel Santana, Cameta 2821, Jardines Del Bosque,
    Guadalajara, Jalisco

SOUTH AMERICA
Dr. Gonzalo Vargas N., P.O. Box 2666, Quito, Ecuador

Mr. Leopoldo Luks, Ave. Maracay, Urb. Las Palmas,
    Qta Luksenburg, Caracas, Venezuela

Mrs. Rajni B. Manglani, c/o Bhagwan's Store, 18 Water St.,
    Georgetown, Guyana

WEST INDIES
Mr. Thakurdas Chatlani, 2A Gittins Avenue, Maraval, Trinidad

Mr. Sean Finnegan, P.O. Box 2314, Port-au-Prince, Haiti

Mr. Bhagwandas Kessaram, c/o Kiddies Corner, Swant Street,
    Bridgetown, Barbados

ENGLAND
Mrs. F.E. Wood, Willow Cottage, Worple Road, Leatherhead, Surrey

SWEDEN
Mr. T. Gunther, Skakeltorp 6018, 441 00 Alingsas

DENMARK
Ms. Inge Gregersen, Askevenget–15, 2830 Virum

HOLLAND
Mr. Jacob Hofstra, Geulwijk 6, 3831 LM Leusden

WEST GERMANY
Mr. Rudolf Walberg, Falkenstr. 18, D–6232 Bad Soden/Taunus

AUSTRIA
Mr. Handsjorg Hammerer, Sezenweingasse 10, A–5020, Salzburg

SWITZERLAND
Mr. Olivier de Coulon, Route de Lully, 1111 Tolochenaz

FRANCE
Count Pierre de Proyart, 7 Quai Voltaire, 75007 Paris

SPAIN
Mr. H.W. Balani, Balani's International, P.O. Box 486, Malaga

PORTUGAL
Mr. Alberto C. Ferreira, R. Machado dos Santos 20, 2775 Parede

GIBRALTAR
Mr. Arjan M. Thadani, Radha Soami Satsang Beas, PO. Box 283

ITALY
Mr. Ted Goodman, Via Garigliano 27, Rome 00198

GREECE
Dr. Constantine Siopoulos, Thrakis 7, 145 61 Kifissia

CYPRUS
Mr. Hercules Achilleos, Kyriakou Matsi 18, Pallouriotissa—T.K. 9077, Nicosia

WEST AFRICA
Mr. Krishin Vaswani, Vaan-Ahn Enterprise Ltd., P.O. Box 507, Monrovia, Liberia

Mr. Nanik N. Balani, Kewalram (Nig.) Ltd., P.O. Box No. 320, Lagos, Nigeria

EAST AFRICA
Mr. Sylvester Kakooza, P.O. Box 31381, Kampala, Uganda

Mr. Sohan Singh Bharj, P.O. Box 47036, Nairobi, Kenya

Mr. D.N. Pandit, United Timber Traders Ltd., P.O. Box No. 1963, Dar-es-Salaam, Tanzania

Mr. David Bowskill, P.O. Box 11012, Chingola, Zambia

Mr. Vernon Lowrie, P.O. Box 690, Harare City, Zimbabwe

SOUTH AFRICA
Mr. Sam Busa, P.O. Box 41355, Craighall, Transvaal 2024

Mr. R. Attwell, P.O. Box 5702, Durban 4000

MASCARENE ISLANDS
Mr. D.S. Sumboo, Harbour View I, Flat Cardinal No. 15, Justice Street, Port Louis, Mauritius

ISRAEL
Mrs. H. Mandelbaum, P.O. Box 2815, Tel Aviv–61000

U.A.E.
Mr. Jiwatram Lakhiani, P.O. Box 1449, Dubai

KUWAIT
Mr. & Mrs. Ghassan Alghanem, P.O. Box No. 25549, Safat, Kuwait

AFGHANISTAN
Mr. Manak Singh, c/o Manaco, P.O. Box 3163, Kabul

SRI LANKA
Mr. D.H. Jiwat, Geekay Ltd., 33 Bankshall Street, Colombo–11

NEW ZEALAND
Mr. Tony Waddicor, P.O. Box 5331, Wellesley St P.O., Auckland 1

AUSTRALIA
Dr. John Potter, Long Wood Road, Heathfield, South Australia 5153

INDONESIA
Mr. G.L. Nanwani, Yayasan, Radhasoami Satsang Beas, JL. Kelinci Raya No. 32A, Jakarta Pusat

Mr. Odharmal Chotrani, 51 Djl. Bubutan, P.O. Box 144, Surabaya

759

SINGAPORE
Mr. Bhagwan Asnani, 1806 King's Mansion, Singapore–1543

MALAYSIA
Mr. N. Pal, c/o Muhibbah Travels Agency, Sdn. Bhd.,
46 Jalan Tanku Abdul Rahman, Kuala Lumpur 01–07

THAILAND
Mr. Harmohinder Singh Sethi, Sawan Textiles, 154 Serm Sin Kha,
Sampheng Street, Bangkok–2

HONG KONG
Mrs. Cami Moss, Hongkong Hilton, G.P.O. Box No. 42

Mr. Gobind Sabnani, G.P.O. Box 3906

PHILIPPINES
Mr. Kay Sham, P.O. Box 2346 MCC, Makati, Metro Manila

JAPAN
Mr. L.H. Parwani, Radha Soami Satsang Beas, 2–18 Nakajimadori
1–Chome, Aotani, Fukiai-ku, Kobe–651

*   *   *   *   *   *   *   *   *   *   *   *

FOR OTHER FOREIGN ORDERS
WRITE TO:
Mr. Krishin Babani, Buona Casa Bldg., 2nd Floor, Sir P.M. Road,
Fort Bombay–400 001, India

Addresses changed since the book was printed:

BOOKS ON THIS SCIENCE

Swami Ji Maharaj
1. *Sar Bachan*

Baba Jaimal Singh
2. *Spiritual Letters* (to Huzur Maharaj Sawan Singh: 1896–1903)

Huzur Maharaj Sawan Singh
3. *Discourses on Sant Mat*
4. *Philosophy of the Masters* (*Gurmat Sidhant*), 5 vols. (an encyclopedia on the teachings of the Saints)
5. *My Submission* (introduction to *Philosophy of the Masters*)
6. *Philosophy of the Masters* (abridged)
7. *Tales of the Mystic East* (as narrated in satsangs)
8. *Spiritual Gems* (letters: 1919–1948)
9. *The Dawn of Light* (letters: 1911–1934)

Sardar Bahadur Jagat Singh Maharaj
10. *The Science of the Soul* (discourses and letters: 1948–1951)

Maharaj Charan Singh
11. *Die to Live* (answers to questions on meditation)
12. *Divine Light* (discourses and letters: 1959–64)
13. *The Path* (first part of *Divine Light*)
14. *Light on Saint Matthew*
15. *Light on Sant Mat* (discourses and letters: 1952-1958)
16. *Quest for Light* (letters: 1965–1971)
17. *Light on Saint John*
18. *Spiritual Discourses*
19. *Spiritual Heritage* (from tape-recorded talks)
20. *The Master Answers* (to audiences in America: 1964)
21. *Thus Saith the Master* (to audiences in America: 1970)
22. *Truth Eternal* (a discourse)

Books about these Masters
1. *Call of the Great Master*—Diwan Daryai Lal Kapur
2. *The Living Master*—Katherine Wason
3. *With a Great Master in India*—Dr. Julian P. Johnson
4. *With the Three Masters*, 3 vols.—from the diary of Rai Sahib Munshi Ram

Books on Sant Mat in General
1. *A Soul's Safari*—Netta Pfeifer
2. *In Search of the Way*—Flora E. Wood
3. *Kabir, the Great Mystic*—Isaac A. Ezekiel
4. *Liberation of the Soul*—J. Stanley White, Ph.D.
5. *Message Divine*—Shanti Sethi
6. *Mystic Bible*—Dr. Randolph Stone
7. *Mysticism, the Spiritual Path*, 2 vols.—Prof. Lekh Raj Puri
8. *Radha Soami Teachings*—Prof. Lekh Raj Puri
9. *Ringing Radiance*—Sir Colin Garbett
10. *Sant Mat and the Bible*—Narain Das
11. *Sarmad, Jewish Saint of India*—Isaac A. Ezekiel
12. *Teachings of the Gurus*—Prof. Lekh Raj Puri
13. *The Inner Voice*—Colonel C.W. Sanders
14. *The Mystic Philosophy of Sant Mat*—Peter Fripp
15. *The Path of the Masters*—Dr. Julian P. Johnson
16. *Yoga and the Bible*—Joseph Leeming

Mystics of the East Series
1. *Saint Paltu*—Isaac A. Ezekiel
2. *Saint Namdev, His Life and Teachings*—J.R. Puri and V.K. Sethi
3. *Tulsi Sahib, Saint of Hathras*—J.R. Puri and V.K. Sethi
4. *Tukaram, Saint of Maharashtra*—C. Rajwade
5. *Dadu, the Compassionate Mystic*—K.N. Upadhyaya, Ph.D.
6. *Mira, the Divine Lover*—V.K. Sethi
7. *Guru Ravidas, Life and Teachings*—K.N. Upadhyaya, Ph.D.
8. *Guru Nanak, His Mystic Teachings*—J.R. Puri
9. *Kabir, the Weaver of God's Name*—V.K. Sethi